REMNANTS OF DAYS PAST

JAPAN LIBRARY

REMNANTS
OF
DAYS PAST
A Journey through Old Japan

Watanabe Kyoji

Translated by Joseph Litsch

Japan Publishing Industry Foundation for Culture

TRANSLATOR'S NOTE
The Hepburn system of romanization is utilized for Japanese words, and macrons are used to indicate long vowels, except for the most common place names and names on the cover and copyright page. People's names are given in Japanese order, surname preceding given name. Original sources were used whenever possible. In the case that original sources could not be accessed due to availability or a similar issue, the Japanese source was used and translated into English.

Remnants of Days Past: A Journey through Old Japan
Watanabe Kyoji. Translated by Joseph Litsch.

Published by
Japan Publishing Industry Foundation for Culture (JPIC)
2-2-30 Kanda-Jinbocho, Chiyoda-ku, Tokyo 101-0051, Japan

First English edition: March 2020

© 2005 Watanabe Kyoji
English translation © 2020 Japan Publishing Industry Foundation for Culture
All rights reserved

This book is a translation of *Yukishi yo no omokage* which was originally published by Ashishobo in 1998 and republished in paperback format by Heibonsha Limited, Publishers in 2005.

English publishing rights arranged with Heibonsha Limited, Publishers, Tokyo.

Book design: Miki Kazuhiko, Ampersand Works

Printed in Japan
ISBN 978-4-86658-140-8
https://japanlibrary.jpic.or.jp/

Contents

Chapter 1

Illusions of a Civilization

Here we stand at the beginning of a long story, one in which the modern history of Japan plays the main character. Our tale begins with the collapse of a civilization.

I will try to bear repeating the cliché that modern Japan was built on the drastic liquidation, so to speak, and disappearance of old Japanese systems and things. This is common knowledge. What many of us may not fully be aware of, however, is that this liquidation caused an entirely unique civilization to disappear. We also do not fully understand what this implies.

I am probably exaggerating a bit here, however, as we do know about the Japanese civilization that existed before modern times. The problem is that many of us simply believe this civilization has never changed and continues to this day under the guise of a new era. In other words, we have come to this point in the present day, blissfully believing in the illusion that Japanese culture is enduring and unbroken and has gone through nothing more than a simple transformation.

In reality, however, a one-time civilization with its own organic individuality completely vanished. This was what historians today popularly call the Edo period or Tokugawa era, centered on an old Japanese way of life that took shape in the early eighteenth century and lasted through the nineteenth century. A renowned intellectual focusing on Japan from the Meiji period, Basil Hall Chamberlain (1850–1935), admired this unique civilization by stating, "What a quaint, picturesque society it was, that of the time, say, between 1750 and 1850- the 'Old Japan.'"[1]

Culture does not disappear and neither do the characteristics of a given ethnic group. These qualities simply change over time. A civilization, meanwhile, embodies the historical characteristics of the lifestyle of a people as a whole. In other words, there is a unique cosmology and value system that supports the civilization, as well as individual social structures, customs, and lifestyles, and these aspects stretch into how people relate to nature and other living things and lead to the production of unique instruments, ranging from dishes and other utensils to accessories and toys. If we view all of these aspects of people's lives together as civilization, then it makes sense to label the old Japanese way of life from the early eighteenth century until the nineteenth century as such. It is this civilization that has collapsed and vanished. But the question is: When, exactly, did this happen?

We certainly cannot determine this by looking at the passage of time, but then again, we do not really need to concern ourselves with this issue. However, even though we can still see lingering images of this civilization to a minute degree in the early Shōwa period (i.e., the mid-1920s to the 1930s), it is fairly certain that it ceased to exist during the end of the Meiji period (i.e., the late nineteenth to early twentieth centuries). We know this because travel logs and other accounts written by foreign observers tell us so. No matter how we narrate the drama of modern Japanese history, we should remember that it only started once the civilization that preceded it

Basil Hall Chamberlain

had been strangled to death and laid to rest. It was considered by all that such death was inevitable and that substantial progress has taken place since then. However, what disappeared, or, rather, what was made to disappear, is lost forever. It remains hidden, and we cannot even question the meaning of the drama or the reality.

Visitors to Japan from this time period accepted the truth that modern Japan was built on the collapse of the previous civilization. Chamberlain, for example, came to Japan in 1873 and left for the final time in 1911,[2] and he had this to say in the introductory chapter of the fifth edition of his 1905 book *Things Japanese*: "We repeat it, Old Japan is dead and gone, and Young Japan reigns in its stead."[3] He did not mean the times or Japan had simply changed. He was saying that one separate and unique civilization had died. This is why he called his book *Things Japanese* an "epitaph" for Old Japan and stated that "Old Japan is dead, and the only decent thing to do with the corpse is to bury it…This unpretentious book is intended to be, as it were, the epitaph recording the many and extraordinary virtues of the deceased-his virtues, but also his frailties."[4]

Walter Weston (1861–1940), a pioneer in modern mountain climbing in Japan, also wrote the following in his book *A Wayfarer in Unfamiliar Japan*, which was published in 1925:[5]

> In the realm of external, material progress and change, Japan of To-morrow will, it is true, be a far wealthier, and in some respects perhaps a better, country than the Japan of To-day, but she will most assuredly never again be simple and picturesque to the same extent as so much of her has been in the Japan of Yesterday.

With the statement "simple and picturesque," it is likely that Weston was also referring to scenes of Japan's natural beauty. As a matter of fact, Weston was someone who introduced the beauty of the Japanese Alps and echoed the sentiment Arthur H. Crow (1840–1915) expressed when he climbed

Mount Ontake (located in present-day Kiso Town, Nagano Prefecture) in 1881 and called it "…A spot so full of dreamy beauty, undisturbed by the hand of man, I never before saw."[6] Crow also lamented that railroads slated to bring tourists to the area and the construction of large hotels would change the landscape and disrupt the beauty sometime in the future. Actually, he was probably already seeing the loss of "picturesque" views rather than making predictions. It is also certain, meanwhile, that Weston not only grieved for the loss of these scenic spots, but also the loss of the livelihoods of people living in these areas. More than anything, Weston thought "picturesque" included the pattern of lifestyles woven into these landscapes. This pattern had vanished forever.

In Crow's case, he saw scenes in the mountains of Kiso during his visit to Japan in 1881 that he would never forget. When he visited the village of Suhara, for instance, it was already dusk, and he saw "inhabitants, who are now, with their children, gossiping in the single street, enjoying a rest in the cool of twilight after their hot day's work." He also mentioned the small, gurgling riverlet that formed in the center of the street and that the "girls are constantly running with wood buckets wherewith to supply the evening tub." Children, including small girls who were carrying other children the same size as they were on their backs, were absorbed in a game of tag. Crow was moved by all of this, noting that "the apparent sociability and happiness of this little community is quite a pleasure to see."[7] Weston first set foot in Japan as a missionary in 1888, so he was most likely still able to see scenes similar to those that Crow witnessed in Suhara.

Needless to say, Chamberlain and Weston wrote their accounts at a point when they were fairly certain that old Japan was dying. However, visitors to Japan who came at the end of the Edo period when Japan was just opening its doors to the rest of the world actually foretold the death of old Japan much earlier. For example, Townsend Harris (1804–1878) wrote a question in his diary that read "Grim reflections- ominous of change- undoubted beginning of the end. Query,—if for the real good of Japan?" He wrote this passage while stationed at the U.S. consulate at Shimoda Gyokusenji temple, the "first Consular Flag 'ever seen' in this Empire," on September 4, 1856, so this is one of the earliest examples that makes predictions about the future of old Japan.[8]

Harris had only been in Japan for two weeks when he made this inquiry, but he could tell that fundamental changes were occurring. He just did not know what would be lost. Two years later, however, Harris met Sherard Osborn (1822–1875), the commander of the ship that took the Earl of Elgin to Japan. Osborn noted that Harris had "warm and sincere eulogisms of the Japanese people" and went on to say:[9]

He expressed a kindly and natural anxiety about the long course of misery and revolution that will most probably ensue, when the introduction of European civilization and a different creed shall break down, and will not, at any rate at first, supply the place of an existing system, which, so far as the material wants of the people are concerned, looks so perfect.

The U.S. consulate at Shimoda Gyokusenji temple (illustration by Henry Heusken)

Harris relied on his attendant Henry Heusken (1832–1861) for his superior interpreting skills. Heusken accompanied Harris almost everywhere, including to the trade agreement negotiations that Harris engaged in with Tokugawa shogunate officials in Edo. He mentioned the following in his December 7, 1857 diary entry:[10]

> Now that I have such affection for your country, I wonder whether these first steps you take into the modern world are really for the benefit of your civilization. I, who have admired the artlessness of your inhabitants as well as their simple customs, who has seen the abundance of your fertile fields, who has heard everywhere the happy laughter of your children, and has never been able to discern misery, I fear, Oh, my God, that this scene of happiness is indeed coming to an end and will be overrun when Western people will bring here their vices.

Heusken had already spent a year and two months in Japan when he recorded this entry, so he had considerable time to observe his surroundings and was by no means expressing the cheapened sentiment of a simple traveler.

In a similar fashion, Willem Huyssen van Kattendijke (1816–1866), head instructor of the Nagasaki Naval Training Center, had already spent over two years in Japan and had gathered a great deal of knowledge about life there. He recorded the following just before his return to the Netherlands in 1859:[11]

> I have always secretly desired in my heart to return and experience this beautiful country again. At the same time, however, I am overcome with fear and I feel sadness in my heart when I think about how Japan, which has truly been blessed with happiness for so long, will face so many difficult issues in the future.

Kattendijke was convinced that the civilization he was bringing to Japan, namely, Western civilization, was more advanced than the one that existed in old Japan. However, he was not sure whether this would actually give the Japanese a greater sense of happiness.[12]

Pompe van Meerdervoort (1829–1908), a physician attached to the same naval training center headed by Kattendijke, echoed this notion. He viewed Western demands for Japan to open its doors to the rest of the world as a disruptive act that would upset the symbiotic relationship between a contented populace that lived in harmony under the rule of the shogunate. Pompe even went so far as to refer to it as a singular act that would collapse the mutual relations between society and the state.[13] Pompe van Meerdervoort remained in Nagasaki until 1862, long after the naval training unit was closed in 1860, so he personally experienced and lamented the fall of old Japan after the country opened its doors to the world.

The collapse of this civilization was also foreseen by Friedrich August Lühdorf (1834–1891), a supercargo on a Prussian merchant ship that arrived in Shimoda in 1855. He wrote:[14]

> The Japanese have taken their first fateful step forward into the new era. However, just like removing one of the foundation stones to your home, soon the rest will follow suit and the walls will surely tumble and fall. And the Japanese will probably be buried under the rubble.

Visitors to Japan foresaw and eventually witnessed and reported the death of old Japan, but this went beyond the disappearance of individual systems, instruments, and scenes such as those mentioned earlier. The entire civilization had ceased to exist as an organic whole. In other words, a separate, unique civilization had ceased to be. This is the absolute truth that I wish to reiterate.

Things Japanese, Chamberlain's treatise that he labeled an "epitaph" for old Japan, is a work that takes the style of what could be called a small encyclopedia on Japan, and it lists topics alphabetically. In the introductory chapter of the sixth edition published in 1934, he states that "the number of items in which interest has disappeared were removed," almost as if the passage of time had destroyed and removed a number of "things Japanese" that disappeared from the public eye in the forty years since the first edition appeared in 1890. We can still see many of the original listings in the contents of the first edition, however, so it is clear that the problem is not with individual phenomenon, but rather the overall meaning of such phenomena. The holistic framework of the old civilization is gone.

Even if Inari, the god of harvests, continues to be enshrined on the roof of a skyscraper, or even if the head of a tea ceremony or ikebana family proudly continues to practice the rituals of his or her tradition, these phenomena have simply been absorbed by what Chamberlain called "New Japan." In other words, they simply exist as a part of a mosaic that relates to modern Japanese civilization. Culture and aspects of culture survive, but the civilization dies. The *hanetsuki*, or shuttlecock, game that existed long ago is quite different from the one played in Japan today during the New Year's holidays, and the kites that used to soar in the skies above Edo look different than those that appear over Tokyo today. The meaning behind these things has completely changed because the entire pattern that appears in the newly erected woodwork of modern Japanese civilization is completely different. It is nothing more than an illusion to say that any remaining fragments of old Japan have been reincorporated into this new pattern.

We can say the same about the characteristics of the people. Chamberlain noted this in the following passage:[15]

> Nevertheless, as Madcap Hal, when once seated on the throne, showed plainly, despite all individual difference, that the blood of prudent Henry IV ran in his veins, so it is abundantly clear to those who have dived beneath the surface of the modern Japanese upheaval that more of the past has been retained than has been let go. It is not merely that the revolution itself was an extremely slow growth, a gradual movement taking a century and a half to mature. It is that the national character persists intact, manifesting no change in essentials.

Chamberlain gives the obedient intellectual training of the Japanese people, loyalty to the state and lord, the group habit of always going along with the crowd, and "the ingrained tendency of the national mind towards the imitation of foreign models" as examples to support this notion. Even without Chamberlain's observations, however, it is stunning to see just how long-lasting and resistant to change the nature of a people can be when we see Europeans who visited Japan at the end of the Edo period (late nineteenth century) repeating almost verbatim the characteristics of the Japanese recorded by Portuguese and Spanish explorers who observed Japan hundreds of years earlier (from the latter half of the sixteenth century to the beginning of the seventeenth century).

Therefore, the problem does not lie in the ethnic character of the Japanese. It certainly shows no sign of disappearing for the time being, much to the delight of observers who greatly praise it and to the dismay of those who harshly deride it. If this is the case, however, why did Chamberlain say, "more of the past has been retained than has been let go" on the one hand

and then claim that "Old Japan is dead" and seek to erect his book *Things Japanese* as an epitaph over its corpse? This is because he realized that the character of a people and the mentality of a civilization are two essentially different things despite appearing to be inseparable at first glance. The civilization dies as does the mentality it cultivated. The character of the people may then take the guise of a new civilization and reappear, but once the mentality behind something dies, it can never come back. For example, the smile that adorned the faces of the Japanese people of long ago has disappeared forever along with the old mentality that gave birth to it.

Speaking of this smile of old, Lafcadio Hearn (1850–1904) wrote an article defending this aspect of the Japanese, but let us set aside the words of someone as famous as Hearn for the time being and look at statements made by French painter Félix Régamey (1844–1907). According to Régamey, every aspect of Japanese courtesy was built on this smile. He also noted that the Japanese were almost always smiling no matter how excruciatingly miserable their lives may have been. It almost seemed necessary to their existence. The Japanese also smiled and showed courtesy to people without expecting anything in return.

This smile was very different from the inscrutable one Westerners criticized in later years for hiding the true intentions of the Japanese. Even Westerners could immediately recognize the generous nature of this old smile. Sadly, however, it was beginning to show signs of fading among a new class in Japan in 1899, the second time Régamey had visited the country. At least this is how he viewed it.[16]

We have to rely on the testimony of visitors to Japan such as Régamey to remember what the old Japanese civilization used to look like. This is because the ancestors of the Japanese were not consciously aware of these qualities and viewed them as natural, everyday things. Therefore, in-depth analyses and descriptions were deemed unnecessary. This is not surprising

Portrait of Félix Régamey, 1876
(illustration by Kawanabe Kyosai)

if we follow the standards of cultural anthropology. One of the tenets of this field states that people who belong to a given civilization are not consciously aware of the unique code that makes up this civilization. Therefore, it is extremely difficult for them to ponder and write about it. In this case, culture and what I call "civilization" have the same definition.

Westerners who came to Japan between the end of the Edo period and the early Meiji period were surprised by and could not help but write about what they saw, as Japanese civilization at the time was so completely different from their own. In addition, they also used another standard of cultural anthropology in which their discovery of a foreign culture made them more aware of the characteristics of the one they belonged to. This, in turn, allowed them to reflect on the code of their own civilization through cultural relativism.

Of course, the sense of pride they held for their own culture led to rampant and intense Eurocentrism. With the exception of a few examples, most Westerners strongly believed that everything about their own civilization was superior to that of the Japanese. Therefore, it is fascinating to see how they lavished Japanese civilization at the time with praise and even willingly criticized and reconsidered elements of Western civilization despite having these strong prejudicial feelings of superiority.

Bias is certainly an issue we have to contend with, but there are other issues we have to address before we can use travel records made by Westerners visiting Japan between the end of the Edo period and the early Meiji period as materials to help us recreate old Japan. One of these issues is that intellectuals focusing on Japan tend to dismiss such records as nothing more than glorified illusions based on the argument that impulses and strong emotions move and determine recorded history. It is also true that we cannot even take one step forward without examining the Japanese quality of self-denial.

According to Chamberlain, "Old Japan was to us [Westerners] a delicate little wonder-world of sylphs and fairies."[17] Words such as these are enough to invite almost instant derision and anger among contemporary intellectuals focusing on Japan, who view such expressions as untrue, reactionary, and as false praise for old Japan. Chamberlain himself knew about this Japanese way of thinking quite well, writing:[18]

> Don't expatiate, in the presence of Japanese of the new school, on those old, quaint, and beautiful things Japanese which rouse your most genuine admiration...speaking generally, the educated Japanese have done with their past. They want to be somebody else and something else than what they have been and still partially are.

Chamberlain cited a speech by British poet Edwin Arnold (1832–1904) as an excellent example of this claim. Arnold arrived in Japan in 1889 and gave a talk at his welcome party in which he praised Japan as "the nearest earthly approach to Paradise or to Lotus-land."[19] He also stated the following, as quoted by Chamberlain:

> So fairy-like...is its scenery, so exquisite its art, so much more lovely still that almost divine sweetness of disposition, that charm of demeanour, that politeness humble without servility and elaborate without affection, which place Japan high above all other countries in nearly all those things that make life worth living.

Indeed, these are words of the highest praise, but editorials in the leading Japanese newspapers slammed Arnold the next morning. They claimed that he did not even touch on Japan's commercial, political, or military advancements and were infuriated that he only had good things to say about its art, scenic views, friendly people and courtesy, and other aspects. They viewed it as an insulting disregard for Japan.

Chamberlain accepted the reason behind this reaction and even approved of it, saying the following:[20]

> The great and instructive case of the West versus China...The Japanese would be blind indeed, did they not see that their best security for continued safety and success lies in the determination to be strong, and in the endeavor not to be too different from the rest of mankind.

For this reason, Chamberlain recognizes that the Japanese people followed their own path. Nevertheless, his interest remains centered on picturesque old Japan. Lamenting its loss is what led him to write the harrowing words of Japan's epitaph.

We have to be careful, though, as Chamberlain made this argument in 1905. In other words, the mindset that opposes praise for old Japan is by no means something that developed after World War II. However, the path that intellectuals focusing on Japan were following at the time in terms of progress and building a stronger country is not something their descendants are ashamed of today. This is because the mindset behind rejecting the glorification of Japan, as such, has evolved over time.

Today's intellectuals focusing on Japan do not reject Arnold's view of "a delicate little wonder-world of sylphs and fairies" based on the same value standards centering on progress that their counterparts used in 1897 to counter Arnold's beliefs. In fact, these standards do not even exist anymore. Rather, intellectuals focusing on Japan feel a deep sense of hatred and contempt for these fairy-like images, especially those disseminated by Hearn and Portuguese writer Wenceslau de Moraes (1854–1929), as they believe that such views promote false claims made by Japanese traditionalists and nationalists about the Japanese ego and ethnic sense of belonging. This created a system of thought, or what I call an ideology, known as "Orientalism" (or "Japanism") that flowered in Western Europe at the time, and according to intellectuals focusing on Japan, the Western Europeans used this ideology as a set of rose-tinted glasses through which they viewed the illusion of Japan's beauty. This system of thought not only failed to relay actual images of Japan, but it was also no more than a backlash from their own Eurocentric worldview and racial prejudice.

The originator of today's meaning of the word "Orientalism" is Edward W. Said (1935–2003).[21] According to Said, Orientalism in no way connotes "an Oriental's human or even social reality," or, in other words, a person's "nationalism, class struggle, the individualizing experiences of love, anger, or human work." Furthermore, Said believes that the concept is not congruent with reality and has an unshakably Eurocentric "western style for dominating, restructuring, and having authority over the Orient." Thus, Said sees it as a high-level political system that Westerners use to repeatedly explain the backwardness of the Orient. Orientalism is a system in which "the Oriental is depicted as something one judges (as in a court of law),… something one disciplines (as in a school or prison), or something one illustrates (as in a zoological manual)."

We need to keep in mind that Said limits the meaning of the word "oriental" to Arabs and Islam and that he, himself, is an oriental born in Palestine, educated in Egypt and the United States, and "a representative pro-PLO intellect in the United States."[22] Yet, we cannot help but feel the logic of Said's argument when we look back with him at the historical use of this word. Said vehemently argues that orientalist records consist of malicious, subtle, and grossly untrue virtual images of the Orient that the West uses to build itself into the ruling power. He adds that orientalists use incredibly racist and damaging terminology to depict Arabs and Muslims as illogical, inferior, infantile, and abnormal people who lack energy and free will, exhibit subordination, and are backstabbing liars.

Not surprisingly, intellectuals focusing on Japan responded to Said's brand of orientalism with zest, and such orientalism became a bit of an ideological fad in Japan for a time. These intellectuals felt and have continued to feel that Said's brand of orientalism is a convenient tool that provides them with a way to negate and nullify the Western images of Japan from the time the country opened its borders to the rest of the world until the Meiji period. Indeed, when Said says "The Orient was almost a European invention, and had been since antiquity a place of romance, exotic beings, haunting memories and landscapes, [and] remarkable experiences," we cannot deny that the same is true concerning Western images of Japan. Furthermore, we can ascribe the features of orientalism, such as the backlash against excessive praise of old Japan, the dependence on images in past texts, and the resultant regret that the modern Orient looked nothing like it did in textbooks, to Westerners' remarks about Japan in the nineteenth century.

However, Said's orientalism also entails huge problems that we cannot easily apply to Japan if we view his idea from one theoretical context, and intellectuals focused on Japan and other proponents of this theory either do not realize or are feigning ignorance of these issues. Said's criticism of orientalism thoroughly discredits the falsehood that Western European standards can understand and criticize the Orient. Said believes that the true nature of orientalism is to objectify, alienate, and, ultimately, separate the West from the Orient in order to obtain a universal Western European identity. On top of this, European criticism of the Orient has absolutely nothing to do with reality or the people who actually live in the Orient. Eurocentric universality is a false idea brought about by dividing the human reality into baseless abstractions of race, culture, and ways of thinking and then building epistemological differences that do not actually exist between the East and West. This is why Said is led "to the extreme position of entirely refusing the designations 'Orient' and 'Occident.'"[23]

Based on Said's ideas, therefore, orientalists must reject European descriptions of nineteenth-century Japan because, regardless of whether such accounts praise or deliver derisive criticism of the country, it is clear that the authors of these records are basing their claims on the universality and centrality of their own culture. There were a few Westerners who may not have been Eurocentric per se, but even they based their ideas on the separation between the East and West, and, from Said's point of view, their descriptions are just as false.

The problem is that people engaged in this debate today negate praise for Japan as orientalist illusions while at the same time triumphantly accept the critical accounts. In other words, they reject positive views of Japan while complacently agreeing with the negative. In short, they do not follow Said's extreme idea of completely rejecting every view of the Orient, be it good or bad, that was built on the Western European identity. Said gives an example of malicious orientalism in a speech given by British Conservative Party leader Arthur James Balfour (1848–1930) in the House of Commons in 1910. In his speech, Balfour stated that, in the Orient, "You never find traces of self-government. All their great centuries…have been passed under despotisms, under absolute government."

However, intellectuals focusing on Japan have never objected to and even share the same kind of feelings about Japan. The same can be said for their reaction to the similarly negative ideas that British Consul-General Rutherford Alcock (1809–1897) repeatedly expressed in his book *The Capital of the Tycoon*. Such intellectuals accept this "oriental despotism" because it resonated with them and was based on the authority of Karl Marx and Max Weber. Here, there is a decisive conflict between Islamologists like Said, who completely reject historical, but most especially modern, Western views that fiercely attack oriental countries and view them as colonies or dependent states, and the Japanese intellectuals who have constantly used a Western value system as a frame of reference within the modern Japanese context of a nation that has succeeded in becoming one of the world powers. They are almost like children who hate their parents when they accept the Western experience as a central and universal entity.

If we strictly follow Said's orientalist criticism, then we have to reject the extensive transformation that Japan went through under American occupation after World War II as explicit orientalism in this regard. A few intellectuals focusing on Japan agree with Said on this issue, but those who do find that rejecting this notion leads to the stigma of being labeled a right-wing nationalist. In other words, we cannot completely reject Western universalism and the way it has organized the world to include the East. Accepting what Said has to say in today's critical circles lacks the basic sensitivity to such a contradiction and can degenerate into just another irresponsible intellectual fad.

In order to overcome orientalism, Said abolishes the divisions that the West created between the East and West and advocates a multifaceted, decentralized, and unsystematic approach. His view states that we should dismiss divisions between ethnicity, culture, and religion, as well as the discriminatory mindset that these aspects are based on, and aim for an understanding based on the human realities of individuals rather than the construct of a world image. His words conform a great deal with deconstructivism, a movement that reached prominence in the 1980s, and even empathize with women and minorities who are empowered and possess the ability to express themselves.

It was also hardly surprising that critical circles in Japan welcomed this view with open arms. However, it remains questionable whether such deconstructivism became the true antithesis to a world order centered on the West. Thus, the movement was just another reaction to Western modernism and concealed its own modernist tendencies. In the end, it lacked the strength to truly open and surmount the modern age.

It can be said, therefore, that Said was primarily angry and frustrated with orientalism because it viewed rational and progressive ideas positively from the standpoint of modern Western values while also remaining steadfast in its claim that Arabs and Islam were unreasonable and stagnant entities incapable of change. When he says the Orient was denied the ability to change and develop due to orientalism, however, he seems to forget that change and development are actually modern Western value standards and frames of reference that do not have any kind of universality. The "reality" of the Orient he wrote about in opposing the orientalists has to do with nationalism, class warfare, politics, and economic issues if we comb through the abstract language he employs to describe the joys and suffering of individual beings. However, assuming these aspects to be "reality" is the intellectual product of Western modernism. This creates a paradox because Said is rejecting the universalism that creates the separation between the East and West while also accepting modern Western wisdom and products as being universal.

Reality is the sum of economic and political relations. Thus, some argue that human suffering and in-fighting result from modern Western attempts to reorganize the world into a single economic and political set of relationships. However, our existential lives and the realities of living do not see economics and politics as central players despite the controls they force on people. We achieve reality by interacting with others in the cosmos we all live in. This includes society, and culture, including religion, is what regulates this cosmos.

While Victorian Britons such as Arnold described nineteenth-century Japan as an "elf-land," Japanese leaders at the time viewed such examples with anger and rejected these descriptions—actions which would later support Said's position. In other words, they believed that the reality of Japan as depicted by the British was nothing more than a way for them to get the Japanese to instigate political and economic reforms in order to survive any cross-national fighting that could have occurred. Even setting this point aside, the Japanese felt that British praise for Japanese courtesy and the beauty of Japanese artwork and scenery are elements of an orientalism that completely ignore reality and try to cast Japan in the light of an entirely fixed set of cultural ideas. However, in today's society in which everyone can see that the modern age has ended, we can re-evaluate orientalist remarks made by Westerners from a new perspective.

Nevertheless, Westerners described the primitive nature of Japan from the standpoint of their own advancement and universality, or in one word, their civilization. It goes without saying that prejudices based on the dichotomy between the East and West played a part in these descriptions. However, prejudice is always about someone or something. Factual errors aside, someone or something certainly existed in Japan that Westerners were wary of. They deciphered this based on the unique context and code of their own culture, and we have to realize that this can elicit misunderstandings and twists in judgments. Despite these mistakes and distortions, however, Westerners saw what they saw and could not erase the reality that gave testimony to the existence of the Japanese people and Japanese things. Furthermore, we do not need to worry about labeling this someone or something as backwards or feudal from the standpoint of our modern standards. This is because we know how to view such characteristics in a completely different light today.

Westerners discovered a number of curious and charming customs from nineteenth century Japan and displayed an undying interest in them. For example, the twenty-one-year-old Ludovic, marquis de Beauvoir (1846–1929) accompanied Pierre, the Duke of Penthièvre and grandson to Louis Philippe I, on his voyage around the world, and they visited Japan in 1867. Beauvoir summarized the details of their thirty-five-day stay in the following account in which he described Japan as a fairy-like lily pad:[24]

> Each house is built of pine wood, without an atom of painting, a real gem, a toy, a little Lilliputian Swiss Chalet, of exquisite taste and delicacy, and beautifully clean and neat. At night, when everything is shut up, and the variegated lanterns spread a soft light within this entirely white kiosk, it looks like a magic lantern.

He also noted the following about a "Lord" he saw walking the streets. He stated that "From this gentleman's waist hangs a most curious apparatus; it is the complicated material for a pipe, of which the bowl is about half the size of a little girl's thimble, a tobacco-box of paper, closed by a lovely little bronze tinder-box, matches, case, etc." He also commented on the Umeyashiki, a place Westerners almost always visited at the time, and could only say that it was the world's most curious garden and fairy-like, as if viewing it from a high place through a telescope in reverse. He thought the small magenta and green trees looked like dwarves stretching their limbs to the surface of a carp-filled pond, the small brook had a bridge big enough for one mouse to pass over, and the final tunnel and the green arches were the right size for rabbits to make their nests in.

Beauvoir came to Japan in 1867, the year French Envoy Léon Roches (1809–1901) eagerly pledged his loyalty to Tokugawa Yoshinobu, the fifteenth and final Tokugawa shogun, and provided him with military support. It was also the time when the twenty-one-year-old Beauvoir was consumed with patriotism and unknowingly went too far in his political talks. Discoveries in Japan gave him pause, however, and eventually he stated, "I see that today I have been too much carried away by politics," and reversed his steps by saying "I hasten to leave these grave topics to turn to the articles of lacquer-work, glass boxes, bronze brooches, pictures, and other charming little odds and ends…[and] trifles." These detailed ornaments were the "Japan" he had discovered, and they had "affected our heads" as he put it. He found the lacquer-work especially appealing, even claiming he had been "attacked with a positive fear."

It is possible to read this innocent description as explicit orientalism. Said would likely be angered and question the reality of Beauvoir's description as well as what exactly the tobacco box and the detailed ornaments were. That being said, Beauvoir was just writing down the reality of the Japan he saw, and I greatly admire him for his sensitivity to this point. Matters related to politics and economics are certainly necessary principles for human beings to live by. Of equal or possibly even greater importance, however, is that tobacco boxes, lanterns, and detailed ornaments are all aspects of a reality that develop through the personal experiences of one individual.

Edwin Arnold also had a number of experiences in Japan. Japanese intellectuals in his day frowned upon his praise for Japan, but he noticed that the Japanese people made their lives happy, built their daily lives on courtesy, and found comfort in the detailed ornaments they kept, and he also commented on Japan's glorious scenery. The exotic turns the eye to the detailed aspects of life that people are not used to seeing, and, consequently, this can recreate the feel of a certain civilization. I find it remarkable that stereotypical images of Japan, even the derisive nature of "Fuji-yama," "sakura," and "geisha," attest to the true nature of a civilization that has now disappeared. Ridiculing such images is nothing more than the victors of modernization hurtling insults at a dead civilization.

An excellent example of a work that criticizes Western views of nineteenth century Japan as stereotypes that are out of touch with reality is Yokoyama Toshio's book *Japan in the Victorian Mind: A Study of Stereotyped Images of a Nation, 1850-80*. This work, which was published by Palgrave Macmillan UK in 1987, is literally a painstaking work that carefully examines British periodicals from long ago and conducts a thorough investigation of the process through which views of Japan came into being, developed, and became stereotypes amongst the nineteenth-century British. Yokoyama not only deals with the same issues as Said in regard to negating the idea of a so-called national character, but also states a similar opinion to Said's criticism of orientalism in regard to how Victorians accumulated and depended on older textbooks for their knowledge and understanding of Japan, saw little interest in changing or developing Japan, and, consequently, firmly established a set of images about the country that strayed from reality. In addition, Yokoyama makes the point that the British saw the image of themselves as a reflection in the mirror of Japan. Yokoyama's awareness of the issues is illustrated well in the following passage:[25]

> The idea that Japan was a "strange and singular country"—which implied uniqueness or bizarre qualities—was to persist in British magazine and review articles not only in the 1850s, but throughout most of the following thirty years. This, of course, does not mean that these writers relied on the same unchanged information about Japan during that period. On the contrary, Japan underwent rapid social changes and British knowledge and understanding of Japanese history and culture also developed. But the general view of Japan not only survived but even reinforced itself on many occasions. Why did this persistence of the image occur? To what extent was the phenomenon the result of random historical factors? Or is it possible to conclude that this image world was naturally self-perpetuating and broadly independent of reality?

Naturally, Yokoyama's argument is that these images are self-realizing and separate from reality. As to why such stereotypes persisted, he gives such examples as the spell that previous texts written by such authors as Engelbert Kaempfer, Philipp Franz von Siebold, and Vasily Mikhailovich Golovnin held over people, along with editors who were trying to play on the curiosity of their readers and the insecurity many writers held about conditions in Britain at the time. The mechanism that helped perpetuate these stereotypes does not concern us here. The issue is whether or not Yokoyama is correct in saying that observers from Victorian Britain truly held stereotypical views of Japan that had nothing to do with reality. If this were the case, Japanese news articles that entered British hands cannot be used as a testament to the civilization of old Japan.

The target of Yokoyama's analysis covers periodicals stretching from the 1850s until the 1880s. An overwhelmingly large number of these authors had never even visited Japan, and Yokoyama gives high marks to Rutherford Alcock, Algernon Freeman-Mitford, Isabella Bird, and other authors who had experience visiting or staying in the country for longer periods of time. However, Yokoyama claims that even though these authors conveyed the truth about Japan, images of a curious and strange country remained entrenched. This is because, in many cases, the world of journalism has nothing to do with the truth, and writers and editors ultimately have the final say on what gets printed. Yokoyama states with great distaste that, with the exception of the articles written by the three individuals mentioned above, most written accounts viewed Japan within a framework of preconceived stereotypical images and do nothing but reinforce those stereotypes.

Yokoyama gave the works of Sherard Osborn and Laurence Oliphant (1829–1888) as good examples of this. Both individuals were members of Lord Elgin's mission to Japan, a party that sought to conclude the Anglo-Japanese Treaty of Amity and Commerce (1858). Osborn was the captain of the *Furious*, the frigate used by Lord Elgin, and Oliphant was Elgin's personal secretary. According to Yokoyama, Osborn's diary about his visit to Japan[26] originally ran in *Blackwood's Magazine*, a monthly British periodical that ran from 1817 to 1980, and became a book in 1859. The 1,575 copies of the first edition sold out in a matter of months, and an additional 1,050 copies were printed in the same year as the second edition. Oliphant's book[27] was also published by Blackwood a little after Osborn's book came out. A total of 3,150 copies were printed in the first edition, and 2,117 copies were printed in the second edition the following year. According to Yokoyama, both men "in their short stays in Japan, saw and described what they knew already from their reading, with much assistance from the Japanese authorities eager to show the country to the best advantage."[28] Thus, the favorable, yet mysterious images of Japan that they circulated were no different from examples described in previous accounts. This hindered the efforts of readers to understand Japan and ended up blocking the flow of information that would disagree with such images.

Before examining the "rosy views of Japan" that these two individuals talked about, we should first consider Yokoyama's argument that Osborn was being deceived by Tokugawa shogunate officials. Indeed, Osborn did not see one beggar along the road to Saiōji temple where the party would stay after landing in Edo.[29] Furthermore, the party embarked on the long thirty-two-mile excursion to Kawasaki with a shogunate official as their guide, and Osborn stated that they only saw two beggars the whole time.[30] Yokoyama claims that the local magistrate told people living along the road that the British party would be coming by and gave them orders to keep the road clean and prevent it from looking unsightly, and obviously this also meant that beggars wandering around would not be tolerated. Yokoyama also states:[31]

In the case of the mission's excursions to the countryside and Asakusa, the East end of Edo, the special decrees issued beforehand were

Laurence Oliphant

stricter than the general one. In particular, some blocks near Asakusa were specifically ordered to close the street gates if necessary, in order to prevent people from rushing to see the excursion party. Therefore, the British Mission of 1858 observed only one face of Japan. Osborn was well deceived.

Indeed, we should accept the fact that Tokugawa officials controlled the people who lived along the road so that the British party could not observe anything that would make Japan look shameful. The question is just how well did their plans succeed? Setting aside the issue of beggars, there were quite a few things members of the British mission noticed despite the efforts of the shogunate officials. Osborn recounts one of the things he saw the day he landed in Edo in the following passage:[32]

Our police-officer is looking out most keenly for any pictures that might be exposed in the shops offensive to our sense of propriety, and they disappear like magic at his approach; still he sees not all, and we are startled by figures and models of the vilest description, swinging about unnoticed amongst men, women, and children, who seemed unconscious of, or indifferent to, the shameless exhibition.

Osborn also saw people in the suburbs taking baths while they were on the long road back from Kawasaki:[33]

In the suburbs, at 5 p.m., every one was bathing and "cleanliness first, modesty afterwards!" seemed to be their motto. In some cases, the tubs were outside the doorways...Others had their tubs in the room on their grounds [the author points out this was an earthen floor], but the front of the house was perfectly open, and the manner in which the fair Eves stepped out of their baths, and ran to stare at us, holding perhaps a steaming and squalling babe before them, was a little startling.

Osborn's party actually saw this scene of bathing men and women rushing outside naked to see the visitors to Japan the day they landed. Oliphant also wrote the following about the mob he saw the day the mission landed:[34]

As for the crowd, it was wild with excitement; the inhabitants of every cross street and lane poured out to see us pass...There were mothers with small babies hanging over their shoulders, reckless of their progeny, hastening to swell the crowd; children dodging under old people's legs, and old people tottering after children and bathers of both sexes, regardless of the fact that they had nothing on but soap, or the Japanese substitute for it, crowding the doorways...Not that the people were the least disorderly, they laughed and stared and ran parallel with us, till stopped by a barrier.

Yokoyama notes the significance that gates were closed when the mission passed by in order to prevent the mob from seeing the procession, but this does not mean that the number of people watching the procession decreased by any degree. The British party even seemed to understand that the system did little to hide the realities of Japan from them and was really no more than a simple means to prevent disorder. Yokoyama is likely saying that shogunate regulations were obviously strict and this limited the information that reached the mission. Nevertheless, it is quite difficult to confirm whether Osborn and Oliphant truly failed to glimpse the reality of Japan and simply reinforced the stereotypical images of Japan that they read in books. This view is based on the assumption that either the Japanese people were submissive and lethargic to a fault and, therefore, easy to control, or that the observers were overly naive and only saw what the shogunate officials wanted them to see. This is doubly suspicious.

We can easily see the reality in Osborn and Oliphant's accounts that the people living in the suburbs of Edo were so curious to see the foreign procession that even efforts by the officials to control them were not enough. When the ship Osborn was on approached the Japanese shore, for example, boys and girls dashed from their houses and ran down to the beach to see them. Osborn noted that "The police officer is in an awful state; he urges them back, waves his fan, expostulates with them; but it is all equally useless: so long as our boat remains on the mud, so long does young Japan remain staring into her and at us."[35]

When the procession arrived in Shinagawa during their long journey to Kawasaki, a throng of people gathered at a tea house in the hopes of seeing the foreign ships in the bay and gazed at them through a large Japanese style telescope furnished there while drinking sake and tea.[36] The mission's destination was Kawasaki Daishi (Heikenji temple),[37] and when they arrived there, they were "followed by a vast throng of wonder-stricken Japanese."[38] The procession was pressed for time and after briefly viewing the temple and leaving the main hall, Osborn noted the following:[39]

The corridors of the temple, the galleries in the cloisters, the walls and roofs which overlook the yard, were black or brown with men, women and children. It was a wonderful sight. They shouted, not violently, but shouted with astonishment and delight at the spectacle the half-dozen Europeans afforded them. The prospect of having to fight a way through such a sea of human beings was not cheering, but three or four policemen quietly cleared the way, and a path opened before us to the gate. There the policemen checkmated the crowd, who were on the point of rushing after us into the street, by securing the gates instantaneously, amidst a roar of indignation from the thousands who found themselves thus shut up within the limits of the temple. Then came cries, and laughter, and a rush; and as we rounded another portion of the temple enclosure, the prodigious crowd had collected for a last gaze at us, where a broad intervening ditch, however, prevented them from incommoding the strangers.

The appearance of a Japanese mob described in this way provides us with valuable information. It is incredibly unfair to only pick out that which agrees with the stereotype of Japan being strange yet desirable, a view that had already formed by the first half of the 1850s, from Osborn and Oliphant's descriptions even if we read into the text with a certain degree of bias. If we look closely at their descriptions, we can find a great deal of concrete experience and information that do not fit the mold of these stereotypes. For example, we should take notice of Osborn's experience at the temple in Kawasaki and his description of not only the angry mob within the temple grounds, but also the sounds of their laughter. In other words, they were a people who could laugh about a situation that made them angry. There are actually many records of the Japanese laughing at themselves after considering the situation they were in. These accounts stretch from the time Japan opened its borders to the world until the beginning of the Meiji period, and they allow us to recall the unique sense of humor that people had at the time. Osborn himself wrote down another instance of this laughter concerning an incident that occurred on the mission's journey to Kawasaki. When the procession entered the wide road on the southern border of Edo, the British suddenly urged their horses into a gallop. Osborn noted:[40]

> The senior police functionary was got up for a walk, not for galloping! He tried all sorts of means to stop us, but failing, dropped astern in a dignified manner, in the society of our horse-boys, who also duly expostulated us upon our unseemly conduct, and then burst out laughing at our ridiculous behavior, and fell behind.

This officer was not laughing at the behavior of the British. He was distraught and laughing at his own foolishness for failing to stop them.

Observations made by visitors to Japan are interesting because they provide details of the reality they witnessed and do not lump together generalized conclusions. Osborn's observations at the lodgings at Saiōji temple during the mission's negotiations with the Japanese are particularly fascinating. It is here that the monks and male and female servants at the temple, as well as observers who filled the temple courtyard in the daytime, focused their attention on the kitchen the British were using. Osborn wrote:[41]

> There were cracks in the wooden walls of the kitchen, which rendered it a perfect peep-show, and there, with eyes fixed firmly to the chinks, a curious individual, after a tough battle for the position, would remain until, in the height of his astonishment, he inadvertently turned round to utter some exclamation, or communicate his information to the bystanders; in a moment he was borne away, and another successful sight seer, won his envied peep-hole. The quantity of animal food consumed in the Embassy was a great source of wonderment.

The British responded to this with their own undying interest in officers that appeared in the guardhouse, but there is no time to introduce this episode here. However, the mission and the Japanese had actual contact that went beyond what the local government office expected, and group members recorded details of their encounters, even going so far as to mention the Japanese girls who wanted to see if the British were truly white to the skin by peeking at them through holes in the sliding doors while they were washing their faces and changing clothes.[42]

The mission only stayed in Edo for about fourteen days. Even though they were certainly influenced by their prejudices and bound by controls imposed by shogunate officials, the Edo they saw was no Potemkin village, the illusion that Grigory Potemkin made to curry favor with Catherine the Great on her journey to Crimea. Even though the Japanese did a lot to make Edo look attractive to the visitors, the mission could still see the reality of the city.

It might be a good idea at this point to question what, exactly, the reality is that Yokoyama is talking about. Osborn and Oliphant saw the reality of external, yet possibly superficial, customs, and these were likely caused by politics, society, and economics.

The key to the problem is that they depict Japan positively. For example, Osborn described his impression of Nagasaki, their first landing site, by saying that "the most striking thing in this city (and it was generally observed by all of us in Japan) was that every man, woman, and child looked happy and contented."[43] Oliphant echoed this by saying "It is a singular fact, that in Japan, where the individual is sacrificed to the community, he should seem perfectly happy and contented."[44]

In Oliphant's case, the excitement had already begun in Nagasaki. The whole experience was like an amazing show that continued to go on and on, something he had never expected when he had set sail from Shanghai. He described it in the following manner:[45]

I find it difficult, in attempting to convey our first impressions of Japan, to avoid presenting a too highly-colored picture to the mind of the reader. The contrast with China was so striking, the evidences of a high state of civilization so unexpected, the circumstances of our visit were so full of novelty and interest, that we abandoned ourselves to the excitement and enthusiasm they produced. There exists not a single disagreeable association to cloud our reminiscences of that delightful country. Each day gave us fresh proofs of the amiable and generous character of the people among whom we were. Each moment of the day furnished us with some new fact worthy of notice. Our powers of observation were kept constantly on the stretch, but one felt they were overtaxed; the time was too short; sights and impressions crowded on each other with a painful rapidity and variety. It was like being compelled to eat a whole *paté de fois gras* at a sitting.

Although his description fell a bit short on specifics, the twenty-nine-year-old Oliphant, who had previously written about his travels to and rich knowledge of several foreign countries such as Ceylon (Sri Lanka), Egypt, Nepal, Russia, and China, did an excellent job in communicating the pleasant surprise he felt when he encountered Japan. He was not simply reinforcing the expectations he had about the country. On the contrary, his experiences in Japan were quite unexpected. In a letter to his mother that he wrote after his visit to Japan, Oliphant was so enamored with the country that he stated that the Japanese people were the most-courteous people he had ever met on his travels and that Japan was the only country in which neither poverty nor beggars could be seen. He also mentioned that he never wanted to revisit China, whatever his position would be, but that he would gladly leave again for Japan.[46]

Oliphant was not the only person to gain a favorable opinion of Japan. According to Osborn, everyone on the mission wanted to revisit Japan someday. Osborn, himself, felt his "love for Japan was hourly increasing."[47]

I stated earlier that Yokoyama considered these "rosy images" of Japan to be mechanical stereotypes that have absolutely nothing to do with the truth. However, when an observer depicts a culture as rosy, it is either because the culture truly is appealing or the observer is just wearing rose-tinted glasses and everything looks perfect even though the reality is far from ideal. A good way to determine this is to draw contrasts with reality. If the resulting image does not agree with reality, then the observer is employing the rose-tinted glasses.

This may seem easy, but the experiment of drawing contrasts with reality includes a problem that is extremely difficult to solve. This is the fact that asking what the reality or truth is presents us with a rather difficult question. Yokoyama never mentions this at all in his investigation. Quite the contrary, you could say he bases a lot of what he says on preconceptions, especially his belief in the reality that Japan from the end of the Edo period to the beginning of the Meiji period was not as happy and bright as Osborn and Oliphant portrayed it to be.

This is not just Yokoyama's own personal view, either, as academia and Japanese intellectuals at the time shared the same knowledge that he shares today. They believe that if we view the reality of unhappy and dreary Japan as actually being happy and bright, then some sort of trick has to be involved. This trick, they claim, is the mechanism though which stereotypical images that have nothing to do with reality repeat themselves. Yokoyama sets up his logical framework this way, so if we can overturn the assumption that Victorian British images of Japan have nothing to do with reality, this can be a keystone that we can use to topple his entire investigation.

Unfortunately, however, Yokoyama does not need to prove his presumption that Victorian British images of Japan are completely false. He simply treats this as common knowledge, and, consequently, there is actually not that much proof at all. Take, for example, the statements made by members of the Elgin mission that mention there were hardly any beggars to be seen. Yokoyama claims these are false because members of the mission could not see what was really going on due to the strict restrictions that the shogunate officials placed on the townspeople. We have already considered whether this is a reasonable explanation.

In any case, we still do not have the proof that can tell us if there were beggars or not. There are also huge differences in observations made by Westerners concerning the time and place of their accounts. This is a point that I shall revisit in a later chapter, but I would like to introduce an assertion made by John Reddie Black (1826–1880), the author of *Young Japan*, in which he indifferently says, "I fancy that one of the most pleasing features that must strike travelers who arrive in Japan after visiting other countries, is the absence of beggars."[48] Black was most likely writing about Edo and Yokohama, cities he knew well enough to include as the subtitle to his book. *Young Japan* features entries made in chronological order, and Black seems to have written this passage at the end of the Edo period. However, Black first came to Japan in 1860 and had been living there for fifteen years by the time his book came out. For this reason, it is absurd to think that the shogunate officials could deceive someone who had been living there for so long.

Let us move on to Yokoyama's second example in which he says that Osborn compares Japan with China and stated that the Japanese sense of color was a spray of refinement. Osborn said the following:[49]

> Many of the favourable conclusions which British diplomats and naval officers drew about Japan were, however, based on misreadings of the phenomena they saw. For example, the prevalence of subdued colours in Japanese clothing was less the result of refined characteristics than of the elaborate sumptuary laws and decrees repeatedly issued by the authorities for almost two centuries.

Yokoyama explains that the Edo government levied controls on everything from the color, pattern, shape, and material used in clothing to eating habits and architecture. He pays particular attention to the strict prohibitions created by the Tempo Reforms (1842–1844), which had lasting effects in this time period. He stated:[50]

> The quiet but refined taste of many Japanese people's lives, shown in the streets and in villages which attracted the eye of the visitors was, therefore, the result of the interactions between the people's desire for luxury and the authorities' admonitions which had been repeated for generations. Thus, this feature of Japanese life, which British writers appreciated as close to their own taste, might have been a testimony to the Shogun's successful rule, but could not be attributed to the nature of the Japanese.

I am honestly not quite sure how to respond to this theory. The British writers simply wrote about the Japanese sense of color they actually saw in the lives of the Japanese and do not ask about the conditions that gave birth to this reality. Osborn, himself, clearly wrote that "Everything in Japan, even to dress, is regulated by law, and the sumptuary laws have been very strict until lately, when contact with Europeans appears to be bringing about a slight relaxation."[51] Osborn clearly witnessed this happening, so how, exactly is he wrong? Yokoyama does acknowledge that Osborn knew about the existence of the sumptuary laws, but then he states, "But it is natural that he [Osborn] was not able to judge how strict the regulations were and to what extent the colours worn by people were the expression of their own taste."[52] Yokoyama claims Osborn's accounts were incorrect because he failed to see the fact that the color of Japanese clothing did not reflect their natural tastes.

But again, what exactly are the tastes of the Japanese people? Yokoyama is likely rejecting the notion of a unique sense of color among the Japanese as a sweeping theory of the Japanese national character. Japanese tastes, in fact, are simply part of a national character theory that rejects itself, but let us move away from this point for the time being and confirm what Osborn said. In his work, he gives examples of the Japanese sense of color in the following two sections:[53]

> The Japanese officials and gentry were very well dressed, and in their attire displayed considerable dandyism, according to their own fashion. But in their dress, as well as in their houses, in Japan, we noticed the prevalence of somber colours, and the absence of that vulgar colouring and tinsel-work so common in China. Here the out-door dress of the ladies, and that of the poor girls at the tea-gardens, and the wives of the tradespeople, was quiet in colour, however fine the texture might be; and amongst the official dresses of the officers, black, dark blue, and black and white patterns, were the most general. Their houses and temples are likewise painted less gaudily than elsewhere in the East, and there was far less gilding about them. This peculiarity in Japanese taste was one of the first impressions received on our visiting Japan, and, like many first impressions, proved to be correct.

The description above regards Nagasaki. The section below continues from Osborn's reference to the sumptuary laws mentioned earlier:

> The colour worn by all classes of men in their usual dress is black, or dark blue, of varied patterns; but the women very properly are allowed, and of course avail themselves of the privilege, to wear brighter dresses. Yet their taste was so good that noisy colours were generally eschewed.

Thus, Osborn says the Japanese taste in colors was stylish. He also saw that the shogunate officials and wealthy townspeople were passionate about dressing up and that the women's kimonos were made from materials of the highest quality. It is clear that the dressy clothes and the high-quality materials were luxuries for the people.

Osborn also wrote about several Japanese houses and temples he observed. Compared to the ones in China and Southeast Asia, for example, he noted that Japanese houses and temples consisted of subdued colors and did not use as much gold as their mainland Asian counterparts. So where exactly does he get it wrong? No one can say for sure whether the sumptuary laws prevented Japanese buildings from being painted in the primary colors of yellow, red, and blue, as they were in China.

This is because it sounds strange to exaggerate the effect of prohibitions originally aimed at the adult entertainment and amusement trades in the Edo period. There was indeed a vicious cycle in which the shogunate frequently announced such prohibitions over the course of roughly two centuries, but even these did not have as strong an effect as we are led to believe. If we take erotic books from the Edo period, for example, foreign visitors to Japan in the 1850s could see such books everywhere even though the Tempo Reforms were supposed to have especially cracked down on the publication of such. In cases such as Commodore Matthew Calbraith Perry's (1794–1858) visit to Japan, some individuals even gave pornographic books to the sailors just for kicks, throwing them onto the boat to the point where Perry had to object.[54]

Meanwhile, the sumptuary laws were also supposed to have limited the number of dishes people could eat at a meal, but it is quite clear that these prohibitions were no longer in effect near the end of the Edo period. This can be seen in records detailing the delegation of the English admiral receiving an invitation from a Satsuma domain (located in present-day Kagoshima Prefecture) representative to dine together in Nagasaki in 1866, at a banquet that featured over forty courses. Three hours and eighteen courses into the affair, the British delegates cried "No more." Then, thinking the dinner was over, they were shocked to see more dishes lining up one after the other and the party would continue for another two hours.[55] Clearly, the Satsuma hosts completely ignored the sumptuary laws on this occasion.

Therefore, we can say the reality is that every foreign observer who visited Japan between the time Japan opened its doors to the world and the Meiji period recognized that the Japanese favored clothes with subdued colors and that none of them thought this was the result of frugality or the sumptuary laws. Like Osborn, they presumed it was due to refined tastes.

Another good example that backs this claim was given by Ivan Alexandrovitch Goncharov (1812–1891), a member of Russian Admiral Yevfimiy Putyatin's diplomatic mission, which arrived in Nagasaki in 1853. He saw the clothes of the officers who welcomed his party and was quite taken by what he saw. He stated:[56]

What I also liked in this gathering of silken gowns, jackets, and shawls was the absence of bold and sharp colors. Not one of the basic colors, red, yellow, or green could be seen; all was a mixture of tones of one or the other…I imagined myself in the Far West; the colors of the toilette were like those of European women, I noticed no more than five dam-ask jackets, and those were of indistinct colors, among the old men.

Goncharov went on to mention other colors he saw and finished his descrip-tion of the scene by remarking that "In short all the fantasy colors of the latest and newest fashions were found here." He clearly felt as if he were in Western Europe.

The issue is clear. Osborn and others spoke of black and dark blue, and touched on the existence of the sumptuary laws. This is what led to Yokoya-ma's argument. The reality of the plain colors that Osborn described shows a diversity and richness that agreed with the standards of Western women concerning the latest fashionable colors, and he was not the only foreign visitor who saw this.

Erwin von Bälz (1849–1913), a German physician who came to Japan in 1867 and helped build the foundation of the Tokyo Imperial University (University of Tokyo) Medical School, had a Japanese wife named Hana. She had a black *haori* coat with an opulent twill damask lining that was almost hidden from view. When Bälz asked her why such a beautiful fabric was used in a place that no one could see it, she answered "One doesn't show one's most precious treasures to everybody. It's such bad taste to cheapen things by making a parade of them."[57] This is, of course, an anecdote given by a Meiji-period Japanese woman describing her sense of beauty and has nothing to do with any prohibitions. However, using a luxurious pattern on the lining of a coat is a custom that probably began in association with prohibitions imposed during the time of the Tokugawa shoguns, and this may have turned into a chic sense of beauty in later years. If we recall the fashion sense of the Azuchi-Momoyama (Shokuho) period (the late 1500s) with its focus on gorgeous and brilliant color tones (although this period was also by no means overly extravagant), it is not unreasonable to think that the sumptuary laws of the Tokugawa era created this belief that plain and simple tastes in clothing were of the utmost elegance.

This is an issue that requires serious research and investigation, but even if we accept this association for the time being, can we follow Yokoyama's belief that the success of the shogun's rule and other aspects created the pro-hibitions and that this is actually what created the elegant tastes that foreign visitors saw in the lives of the Japanese? Furthermore, even if we take it that the shogunate succeeded in making the people wear the clothes that they demanded, we also have to consider that the officials who made these demands were also Japanese and, therefore, quite knowledgeable in the tastes of the people. It is incredibly biased, and I would even say strange, to divide the rulers and the ruled into two groups and then claim that it was the rulers who were instrumental in defining the Japanese character. I think it is safe to say that we have already moved beyond this viewpoint.

It seems that the overall arc of Yokoyama's book summarizes Victorian British images of Japan with the word "singular," and then takes a position that stands in the way of recognizing and understanding the reality of these images. "Singular" is, of course, a word that includes meanings such as uncommon, dissimilar, exceptional, and eccentric. However, mid-nineteenth-century Japan probably looked this way in the eyes of the British and other foreign observers. What, exactly, is the problem with this notion? Yokoyama states that these images make it impossible to accept and understand the reality in question.

Yokoyama admires the works of Algernon Mitford (1837–1916), a diplomat who served at the British Legation from 1866 to 1870, because he held a "belief in human homogeneity" and, therefore, avoided using the word "singular" when describing Japanese manners and customs.[58] This clear and simple schema agrees with those who advocate the universal homogeneity of mankind and opposes the position that presumes the nature of a given people takes precedence, and this is exactly the same position developed by Ota Yuzo in his book, *Lafcadio Hearn*.[59] This is also the contemporary view.

Ota's work is a masterpiece that tries to demolish the deep-rooted myth of Hearn, the man traditionally viewed as the foreigner who best understood Japanese culture. Ota claims that Hearn was actually a staunch racist and by no means a pure and innocent Japanophile. He makes a strong argument for this in his book, but I am not really concerned with his new interpretation. My issue is that he dismisses Hearn as being racially biased and, therefore, inclined to emphasize the notion that Japanese culture was alien and impossible for Westerners to understand. Ota sees this as something that can bring about complete distortions when viewing different cultures. He also states that unlike Hearn, Edward Sylvester Morse (1838–1925), an American who viewed Japan quite favorably, offered much more objective images of Japan due to his strong inclination to treat the Japanese as fellow human beings and their culture as one created and defined by fellow human beings.

With this argument, Ota presumes that emphasizing the individualism and unique characteristics of a culture that is not easily understood by others is a dangerously racist attitude that can lead to blind nationalism. He also maintains that a solid internationalist posture is necessary to help find commonality and develop mutual understanding between cultures. However, if we look at how far cultural anthropology has advanced in the present day, we can shine a light on his verdict from a completely different angle.

According to current cultural anthropological views, we have to operate under the premise of being surprised by a cultural code completely different from our own whenever we interact with other cultures. An observer cannot even begin to understand another culture without realizing what makes it unique and different, and he or she has to completely shed his or her own cultural code in order to reach this understanding. This can sometimes drive observers to despair, however, if they believe that it is impossible to cast off their own cultural code. In other words, they may feel bound by it to the point where they cannot inherently understand the culture they are studying.

Aoki Tamotsu's *Bunka no Honyaku* [Cultural Translation][60] details the experiences and thoughts of one cultural anthropologist who directly faced this problem. It is an eye-opening read, even going so far as to make us deplore the fact that we have to consider things so much. Naturally, Aoki does not dismiss understanding. However, he explains that a multitude of unique cultures exist in the world, with uniquely individual reasons for their existence, and which claim uniquely individual values. Therefore, he claims that the first step that we have to take in order to intrinsically and respectfully understand the heart of the matter is to thoroughly analyze and identify the differences between us and them that go beyond a simple understanding.

I think Hearn was just simply stating the fact that realizing there are differences is the first step to a true understanding. We should not reproach him for seeing these differences even though they fundamentally appealed to the concept of race—the ideology of the time. If we were to sharply accuse Hearn, a man of the nineteenth century, of preaching racism based on views of the present day, what exactly could we accuse him of? After all, Hearn was not aware of the modern anthropological meaning of the word "culture," and if he was, I believe he would have used this term instead of the word "race." However, he was speculating that his own Western culture was binding him and preventing him from understanding Japan when he said that the country and its people were impossible for Westerners to understand. As a matter of fact, the opening of Hearn's final work, *Japan: An Attempt at Interpretation*,[61] states the trouble with perceiving and understanding what lies beneath the surface of the lives of the inscrutable Japanese.

This work focuses on the particularly difficult topic of Japanese religious awareness. Aoki says that, for anthropologists grappling with cultures different than their own, understanding religious ideas is particularly troublesome, and he claims that the reason for this is that anthropologists end up "reading into" different languages and ideas with their mother tongue and that the reality is that they have already modified these factors to fit into their own culture.[62] Aoki is saying that it is by no means easy to understand other cultures even if we believe that all races are equal. After giving a number of examples, he states that understanding different cultures and especially religious awareness, which can be so difficult that researchers go mad trying to interpret it, comes about through a great deal of fieldwork experience. In addition, he also sharply criticizes the traditionally scientific posture of anthropologists that maintains that understanding can only be grasped through objective methods. According to Aoki, realizing that it is impossible to interpret everything in this way is the precursor to understanding the heart of another culture. If this is truly the case, there is no reason to critique or ridicule Hearn for his attempt to interpret Japanese religious awareness. Rather, we should praise the depth of his realization when he reminisces that "After having discovered that I cannot understand the Japanese at all, I feel better qualified to attempt this essay."[63]

However, Ota says that, aside from the fact that Hearn wrote a realistic book that focuses on things the eye can see and the hand can touch, much like Edward Morse's *Japan Day by Day*, it is strange that he should attempt something so reckless as trying to depict the inner lives of the Japanese after claiming he could never understand them.[64] Of course, Ota is trying to ridicule Hearn here, but his argument is rather simplistic. If Hearn was simply trying to record things that the eye can see, much like Morse was doing, then he would have had no need to realize and lament the crevasse opening up between Japanese and Westerners such as himself. This realization was necessary for him to depict the "inner lives of the Japanese."

"Singular" and "strange" are words that can sound as if one is confessing to abandonment or prejudice against something deemed impossible or unnecessary to understand. However, if we take the surprise of interacting with something different from ourselves as a starting point, this can play a huge role in opening the path to realizing our own cultural binds and directly facing and understanding other cultures. Let us say for the sake of argument that Victorian Britons interacting with Japan before and after the country opened itself to the world were surprised and confused by the huge differences with their own culture. Thus, when they use the word "unusual" to describe Japan, they are simply reacting with surprise at what they saw. Based on what we can glean from their experiences in Japan, words such as this were spontaneous utterances rather than conclusions drawn from an intensive study of Japanese characteristics. Richard Mounteney Jephson (1842–1906) and Edward Pennell Elmhirst (1845–1916), who were officers in the Ninth Regiment stationed in Yokohama in 1866, back up this claim with the following passage that appears in their co-authored book:[65]

Novelty is ever charming as a rule, though it wears off in a very short time after arriving in a new place; but with us, Japan and its inhabitants never ceased to be a novelty. There was always something new to observe and wonder at. They are a people so totally different from any other in the world, that in a year's residence amongst them you get a less insight into their manners and customs than could be gained in six weeks into the habits of any other nation.

The issue is now apparent. Observers who came from different countries were probably wearing the glasses of orientalism. Therefore, the Japan they saw likely seemed strange and distorted. However, they did not see things that were unreal. Old Japan provided all the evidence they needed to see through the glasses of orientalism and observe the reality despite the distortions. In addition, they did not just feel affinity and praise for old Japan— they also held true feelings of confusion and disgust.

The issue is that they had discovered a different or, if I dare say, strange culture that they had never seen before and reacted to it by writing down their observations and opinions, regardless of whether this entailed praise or distaste for what they saw. Actually, it might be easier to call their discoveries "illusions." However, even illusions are about something. The existence of this something is the issue we face now. We can see that the observers were definitely aware of the existence of some kind of difference between Japanese civilization and their own, even if their resultant praise was way off target and an illusion completely divorced from reality. Illusions are possible because some kind of evidence is there to give birth to them. We have to focus our thoughts on this evidence.

If we take it that foreign observers viewed old Japan as a mysterious land of dreams and fairy tales, this means that the reality of old Japan possessed the structure and characteristics to give birth to such illusions. Whether the reality was worthy of praise or if it was just something to be criticized does not shape the core of what we are dealing with here. This is because we no longer live in the situation that these foreign observers did, in which their experiences fluctuated between hope and despair. In any case, the point is that Western observers saw enough differences between their civilization and that of Japan.

We should do away with any frivolous opposition to, and think more deeply about, the meaning behind Westerners in the Meiji period labeling Japan as a small, precious, dream-like, and fairy-like country. Fresh surprise is what led Westerners to write the descriptions that would later degenerate into clichés, and the Western standards of civilization at the time triggered this surprise. In other words, there was an extreme gap between the standards of civilization. As I mentioned earlier, Westerners embraced the unshakable certainty of the absolute superiority of their society, but when they encountered a civilization on an island in the Far East in which standards completely differed from their own, they could not help but suffer a kind of shock, despite their self-confidence. The fact that this "small, precious, and dream-like" civilization even existed was a revelation to them. This is because it was the complete opposite of the advanced modern industrial civilization they were a part of.

Take Laurence Oliphant, for example. He cites a number of good examples that show differences between civilizations, such as the elegance of Japanese clothing and ornaments, the refined gentlemanliness of the shogunate officers, the penchant for the Japanese to buy up beautiful things, items never being stolen even if placed in an unlocked room, the strangeness of never hearing a woman's abusive voice, and never seeing a child being abused. However, his descriptions possess the same vitality as other accounts and do not really play up the unique charm of Japan. Where exactly is the *fois gras* he ate in one sitting? In other words, these snippets do not express any positive impressions he might have gained during his brief stay in Nagasaki.

Oliphant felt like he was indulging himself on *fois gras* when he encountered Japan's unique civilization because it was so completely different from his own. He was someone who could critique Westerners who rarely tolerated moral standards or customs and thought patterns that differed from those with which they were accustomed to. In other words, Oliphant had an open mind to move away from his prejudices and accept different cultural codes. He had a free and fresh sense of surprise and happiness when he saw that Japanese civilization shared very few common ideas with the social morality of his country. It was a rare treat for him to interact with Japan, and this is why he compared his experiences to eating *fois gras* in one sitting.

If this were the case, this means that Oliphant should have viewed Ceylon (Sri Lanka), Russia, and China in a better light if they had offered him the same rare treat as the "*fois gras*" of Japan. There would also have to be evidence that Oliphant felt that Japan was like a fine delicacy in his travel log, a record he used to detail his party's experiences in a number of foreign countries during their voyages overseas. The key to understanding his special feelings for Japan lies in the description of his first encounter with this country. It might be best to outline what happened below.

Oliphant's party entered Nagasaki Harbor on a hot August afternoon. There was one guard boat at the entrance to the harbor, and one samurai was sitting on top of the roof of the ship, reading a book and slowly waving his fan. When he noticed the British ship approaching, he raised his head and signaled with his fan to go back. However, when he saw that the British ship had continued moving forward, "he fell to reading again, apparently satisfied that he had discharged his duty and was henceforward relieved from all further responsibility on our account."[66] This samurai had probably grown accustomed to dealing with foreign ships that were entering and leaving Nagasaki, as four years had already passed since the country was opened by Commodore Perry, and he was probably also used to the fact that the foreign visitors occasionally disobeyed the authority of his superiors and the shogunate. In addition, he was probably reading a pulp love story by Shunsui rather than elegant Chinese poetry and other poetic tales. Even so, the scene is peaceful and like something out of a dream.

The scene gives us a good view of life in Japan at the time, but it shows us something else as well. For example, Oliphant expresses in his log that "This man's conduct furnished us with a key in all our future intercourse with Japanese officials." In other words, he realized that if his party pressed the shogunate officers with a resolute attitude, they would eventually give in and let the party do as they pleased. Oliphant's role as a minor diplomat helped him realize this, but he likely noticed other things as well. The focus of this scene is obviously on the official's fan and book, small utensils that seem unsuitable for executing the duty of monitoring foreign ships. This is the scene that creates a quaint and ethereal landscape, a "fairyland" as it were. I wonder if Oliphant viewed it this way. I am not saying that Japan was truly a fairyland during this time period, but scenes such as this helped formulate Western images of Japanese civilization and the Japanese way of life. Oliphant's "*fois gras*" obviously comprised the details of this civilization and lifestyle.

Other good examples also exist. For example, Émile Guimet (1836–1918), founder of the Guimet Museum in Paris, which is known as one of the foremost oriental art museums in the world, came to Japan in 1876 and deliberately wrote down both subjective and poetic impressions of his three-month stay there—a method that differed from other accounts.[67] Immediately after landing in Japan, Guimet met a European who had been living in the country for fifteen years at a hotel in Yokohama. The man reproached him for the insane idea of trying to write a book about Japan after only being in the country for a few months. Guimet began to converse with the man in the following manner:

> There are two ways to describe a country. There is the statistical method which provides accurate information about such things as the people, products, commerce, and laws, and an artistic method in which the observer writes down his impressions even if he has only been in the country for a short time. And please believe me when I say that first impressions are the most vivid.

The man responded by saying "You are quite right, and due to this method, there are a great many works about Japan that are filled with mistakes. If you only knew how much they make us laugh." Then, the man told Guimet to keep his notepad in his pocket until he went home and accept the fact that he should write about France, a country he knew much more about than Japan. Guimet's retort was priceless. "No," he said. "If I wanted to learn something about my homeland, I would be more apt to read a travel diary of a Japanese visitor to France."[68]

Again, this goes back to the cultural anthropological method I mentioned earlier. Guimet is simply stating that we can only understand the characteristics of a civilization by experiencing it as a foreign culture. On top of this, he realizes that writing down one's first impressions is the best method because differences between cultures disappear over time. Illusions and mistakes also appear in these first impressions, and this can help facilitate understanding as well. All in all, first impressions are the best way to make sense of the differences.

Even so, Guimet, who felt that he differed from the vast majority of Europeans who looked for their own culture whenever they went, thought little of the people they interacted with, never laid their eyes on the people, places, and things around them, refused to look for the little idiosyncrasies of local areas, and dismissed anyone different from them as a fool, was overjoyed when he arrived in Japan. He felt the charm of everyone and everything that he interacted with and even believed he could write an entire volume about the first street he came to. He did not hold back in his praise, noting features of the Japanese that resembled the ancient Greeks, "lovely white girls" that gathered around wells to gossip while they fetched water, and Japanese homes and other buildings that he could see all the way through. He also looked upon the delicate and simple tastes of the Japanese quite favorably, describing everything he saw as something in a painting, and he remarked on the beautiful sight of the rice paddies glittering in the sun.

However, Guimet went on to say that the sounds were even more impressive than the sights. He was enraptured by everything from the calls of oarsmen getting into a rhythm to steer their boats onward to the melodic grunts uttered by cart runners whenever they were pulling a heavy load, along with the sharp continuous cries of fishermen every time they paddled, the laughter and cheerful noisy banter of ladies

At the inn in Katase (illustrated by Régamey, from Guimet, *Promenades Japonaises*)

who walked along the street with wide *obi*, or kimono sashes, and their hair tied up into intricate knots, and the falsetto of ladies crying "Bye-bye" while seeing their guests off from an inn. For Guimet, Japan was first and foremost a world filled with sensual sounds.

After viewing the Tsurugaoka Hachimangū shrine and the Great Buddha in Kamakura, Guimet stopped to stay the night at an inn in Katase. He could not get to sleep, however, because of the continual bombardment of unfamiliar sounds he heard after turning the lights out. First, he could hear the sound of waves undulating on the ocean, their rhythmical call enveloping the entire inn. Then, he heard a sinister groan that seemed to be jumping from tree to tree in the sacred forest of Japanese cedar trees behind the inn. When he got out of bed and opened the window to see what was making such a frightening noise, he discovered that it was the wind stirring up the trees and causing the mountain to bellow out a tremendous growl. Guimet called it a duet in which the mountain beckoned and sang in harmony with the sea under the starry night sky.[69] Japan is certainly not the only place where one can hear the wind roaring in the mountains or waves lapping on the shore, but we cannot question the fact that Guimet gained a deep sense of Japan from these night sounds. Perhaps he even thought he was hearing spirits and fairies breathing in the night, as ancient sounds that the Japanese people could embrace and fall asleep to. He was impressed by this because night spirits such as these had long since died in his hometown of Lyon in France.

Another example centers on French artist Félix Régamey. The image of Japan that struck Régamey, who accompanied Guimet on his 1876 visit to Japan and who provided illustrations for his book, was an old wooden bridge that he observed the night his party had arrived in Yokohama. He could see the beautiful curve of the bridge and its remarkable metal fittings from the window of his room in the Grand Hotel. It was like something out of a dream to him. When he came to Japan again in 1899, this valley bridge had already been replaced by a steel structure, and the dream-like scene had vanished, but he reminisced about the vision he saw in the twilight on his first day in Japan and remembered the sights as if experiencing them just yesterday.[70] He recalled naked boatmen paddling their boats under the bridge and the silver reflection of the moonlight bouncing off bubbles left behind by bathers splashing in the water. He also remembered a beautiful young woman on the bridge who was dressed like a queen and carrying a sleeping baby on her back. Régamey even likened the reverberating monosyllabic sounds of her gentle lullaby to a singing voice he had heard during his travels in Naples. He does not give an actual opinion about the bridge itself or elaborate on the nature of its engineering, but the dreamlike scene he paints shows just how much of an impression Japan left on him.

In a similar fashion to Guimet, Régamey fails to use any objective reality in his descriptions. He does little more than use his first impressions to sketch out scenes and gives absolutely no accurate information about the people, products, commerce, laws, and other realities of the daily life that he encountered in Japan. If we wanted to, we could question what meaning fans and books bound in the Japanese style, the falsetto of the servant girls, the duet between the sea and mountains, the lullaby on the wooden bridge, and other such images of Japan have for Régamey beyond exoticism. However, we would have to be blind and ignorant in our view and comprehension of modern Japanese history to simply see his impressions as illusions born out of the tastes of a visitor visiting a foreign country.

The examples above and other phenomena that Westerners saw when they visited Japan for the first time are fragments that hint at the nature and peculiarities of a preindustrial society that had advanced to a unique point in its development through the creation of a sophisticated and rich agricultural system and controls over contact with foreign countries. On this point Alcock even states that "Notwithstanding all our advantages of funded knowledge and civilization of a higher order—our steam and river machinery, and the marvelous perfection to which all mechanical appliances have been brought; I believe the Japanese would hold their own."[71] In addition, Western sensitivity to Japan's position lived in the heart of their industrial society. In other words, they were people living in the nineteenth century and could not help embracing both a sense of pride, while at the same time skepticism and reflection, about the current state of their society. What Western observers experienced when they came across Japanese culture was the universal aspect of human life before modern times. You could say, therefore, that more than a different culture, Westerners had actually entered a different time period. John Reddie Black, the newspaper publisher who came to Japan near the end of the Edo period, wrote the following:[72]

> The life of the nation twenty one years ago was so different to anything known to Europe in modern times, and yet possessed so much of what we know obtained in Europe in bygone days (the days of romance— that days we characterize as the "good old times")—there was novelty, there was real enjoyment, in studying it.

Skepticism and criticism of modern industrial society certainly developed at the end of the twentieth century when everyone could see how stagnant the paradigm had become, but this was by no means the first time this occurred. On the contrary, such criticism has constantly appeared like waves in the currents of modern thought ever since the beginning of the nineteenth century when modern industrial society came to be. This criticism of modern times, however, has been held in contempt as a reactionary movement of nostalgia that has tried in vain to beautify illusions of the past and rewind the cogs of history at the height of industrial society. We have also needed a great deal of time up to the present day to confirm the prophetic meaning of their problem.

We can start with Alcock's work[73] to see how nineteenth century Westerners who believed in science, technology, and enlightened reason had the chance to view a different time, specifically the premodern era that they saw in Japanese culture, and then reflecting on the fundamental nature of modern Western civilization. For Alcock, it was self-evident that modern Western civilization was far more sophisticated than, and superior to, all of the Asian cultures. However, he wondered why there were "antagonistic forces at work in the far East, from Cochin China to Japan" against a sophisticated civilization that, in theory, should have been welcomed with open arms. Alcock said the cause of this was that "She [Asia] has often sought her inspiration in things above, while we have been groveling in earthly and material aims." In other words, the antagonism is a "persistent and silent protest against the materialistic...tendencies of all the European race." In other words, whereas "Asia finds the best elements of its life in rest and contemplation, and its highest happiness in a dreamy repose—enemy to all change and progress," Europe "hastens and presses onward." Due to interacting with progressive Western civilization, Asians "shrink from all contact, as bringing into his existence discord and confusion—forcing upon him the cares of the world, and a struggle for the right to live as he deems best, abhorrent to his nature, and all his habits of thought and being."

After making this argument, Alcock delivers a statement that almost serves as an epilogue to his book:

> Asia, as the counterpoise in the world's activities to the fly-wheel of European progress, and a mute and solemn protest against the all-absorbing pursuits of a more thoroughly mundane and rationalizing existence, may supply, in the dispensations of this lower world, the corrective needed to check and rebuke the exaggerations of a more exclusively practical and unimaginative spirit in nations which, compared with those of the Asiatic stock, are yet in their infancy as to age and experience, whatever they may be in progress and attainments.

Naturally, we can make this rather bulky argument. For Said, it is this contrastive composition between the Occident and the Orient that is the pitfall of orientalism, an arrogant attitude of superiority that feigns reflection. However, Alcock also criticized the point of growth supremacy, which has even become a trend in Japan in the present day. Westerners were already feeling the fatigue of being in the middle of a utilitarian Western industrial society that "hastens and presses onward" at that time.

Others echoed Alcock. Edwin Arnold, for example, said the following to a Japanese crowd in 1889:[74]

> I should say that yours is a civilization which has grown up in the placid atmosphere of secluded Asiatic life, developing fair features that to us, dwellers amid the clash and turmoil of competing nations, present an aspect of refreshing restfulness and content.

He also stated:[75]

> By many a pool of water-lilies in temple grounds and in fairy-like gardens, amid the beautiful rural scenery of Kama-kura or Nikko; under long avenues of majestic cryptomeria; in weird and dreamy Shinto shrines; on the white matting of the tea-houses; in the bright bazaars; by your sleeping lakes, and under your stately mountains, I have felt farther removed than ever before from the flurry and vulgarity of our European life.

Intellectuals in Japan do not even sympathize with the deep futility expressed by Westerners in these statements and tend to set it aside as the carefree, irresponsible exoticism of travelers. However, Lin Yutang (1895–1976), the author of *The Little Critic*, takes the opposite approach and shines a light on problems with Western industrial civilization by saying the following:[76]

> With all your brilliant progress and your intellectual "smartness" and your devilish wars and war-machines, you often seem to us fundamentally childish…[What is important in life is not knowing how to advance, but to work hard], endure nobly and live happily, for this is the alpha and omega of Chinese learning. For life, after all the vain struggle for money and glory, boils down to a few things, which are mainly physical, like good food, a good home, and a peaceful heart without worry and a good bowl of hot congee on a cold morning. All the rest is vanity of vanities.

We should pay even more attention to his following remarks:[77]

> You separate your spiritual and material values, while we blend the spiritual and material in one. You cannot be spiritual and material at

the same moment, but we can, and we see no necessary conflict in it. Your spiritual home is in Heaven, while our spiritual home is on earth.

Lin seems to hit Alcock's blind spot, namely that splitting up the spiritual and the material, or, namely, Heaven and Earth, is what makes modern Western civilization. Alcock separated the spiritual and peaceful soul of Asia from the earthly, material progress of Europe and reflected on his own culture, namely modern Western civilization. However, Asian civilization, which included Japan, was actually still slumbering in a stage that did not yet separate material comforts from the soul while, of course, preserving their mutual differences. The Edo civilization that Alcock and other Western observers encountered in the middle part of the nineteenth century was this kind of civilization.

While praising the advancement of Japan's civilization from a material standpoint, Alcock concluded that "Their intellectual and moral predilections, on the other hand, compared with what has been achieved in the more civilized nations of the West during the last three centuries, must be placed very low."[78] At first glance this appears to contradict the previous argument that separates the material superiority of the West and Asian, and therefore Japanese, spiritual values. However, Alcock's "intellectual and moral achievements" indicate the achievement of a worldly and rational mindset, and the Asian affinity for the spiritual is something completely different. Modern Western civilization separates the soul from the physical world, and this has advanced both material and mental aspects to a high level. This is clearly the case if we think of things in terms of modern Western European liberal arts. However, this can cause us to over-exaggerate the material and lose something from a mental standpoint.

In previous ages of Western civilization, the soul that goes to Heaven was not separated from the mind that seeks pleasure on Earth. Literature and art from the height of the Western European Middle Ages show this aspect in vivid detail. Alcock claimed that Japan at the end of the Edo period shared much in common with twelfth-century Western Europe. He saw that Edo Japan melded mental relaxation and material pleasures into one complete way of life, much the same as it was in Western Europe from the height of the Middle Ages until the beginning of the modern age. Not only Arnold and other admirers of Japan, but also critical observers like Alcock were moved by the characteristics of Japanese civilization that they saw and that no longer exist today.

Charles Wirgman (1832–1891), an English painter who accompanied Alcock on his travels in Japan, wrote about how happy the Japanese people in the middle part of the nineteenth century looked. Ivan Goncharov also

Ōmura Village in Hizen Province (located in present-day Nagasaki Prefecture) (illustration by Charles Wirgman, *Illustrated London News*, 1861)

wrote that many of the attendants to the officers in Nagasaki "mostly gaze vacantly, tiredly…it appears that they just eat and sleep and do nothing,"[79] so we could say that the happy people that Wirgman saw looked foolish in a way. However, Willem Kattendijke could not help but find a soft spot for the men and women taking a bath with facial expressions akin to appearing like the most innocent people in the world.[80]

It is neither my intent to cherish or pine for the "good old days" of Japan with this book. I simply want to relive the aspects of a civilization that has vanished. It is also important to remember that written descriptions made by visitors to Japan, who may have created distortions based on illusions and their emotions, have brought the mysterious nature of old Japanese civilization up to the surface for all of us to view in detail. In addition, I also want to say that we will never be able to truly explain the meaning of our modern age without understanding the realities of this old civilization and its demise.

Notes:

1 Basil Hall Chamberlain, *Things Japanese* (London: John Murray, 1905), 53.

2 Based on Chamberlain's own records, he left Japan for the last time and returned to Great Britain in 1905, and this is the date that historians have traditionally accepted. Proof that the actual date was 1911 is given in Ota Yuzo's book *B. H. Chamberlain* (Libro Port, 1990).

3 Chamberlain, *Things Japanese*, 6.

4 Chamberlain, *Things Japanese*, 6.

5 Walter Weston, *A Wayfarer in Unfamiliar Japan* (London: Houghton Mifflin, 1925), 62.

6 Arthur H. Crow, *Highways and Byeways in Japan* (London: Sampson Low, Marston, Searle, and Rivington, 1883), 119.

7 Crow, *Highways and Byeways*, 111–2.

8 Townsend Harris, *The Complete Journal of Townsend Harris*, ed. M. E. Cosenza (New York: Doubleday, Doran and Co., 1930), 225.

9 Sherard Osborn, *A Cruise in Japanese Waters* (Edinburgh and London: William Blackwood and Sons, 1859), 115–6.

10 Henry Heusken, *Japan Journal 1855-1861*, trans. Jeannette C. van Corput and Robert Arden Wilson (Rutgers University Press, 1964), 151–2. This passage is taken from the Japanese translation. See Hyūsuken [Heusken], *Nihon nikki* [Japan Journal] (Iwanami Bunko, 1989), 221.

11 Huyssen van Kattendijke, *Uittreksel uit het dagboek van W.J.C. Ridder Huyssen van Kattendijke: Gedurende zijn verblijf in Japan in 1857, 1858 en 1859* (Van Stockum, 1860). No English translation of Kattendijke's work exists, so passages that appear in this book have been translated from the Japanese version. See Kattendīke [Kattendijke], *Nagasaki Kaigun Denshūsho no hibi* [Daily Life at the Nagasaki Naval Training Center] (Heibonsha Toyo Bunko, 1964), 208. Subsequent citations will appear as Kattendijke, *Uittreksel*, and will list page numbers from the Japanese text.

12 Kattendijke, *Uittreksel*, 204.

13 Johannes L.C. Pompe van Meerdervoort, *Vijf Jaren in Japan, 2dls, Leiden, 1867-1868* (Firma Van Den Heuvell and Van Santen, 1868). No English translation of Pompe's work exists, so passages that appear in this book have been translated from the Japanese version. See Ponpe [Pompe], *Nihon taizai kenbunki* [Records of My Stay in Japan] (Yushodo Shuppan, 1968), 44–5. Subsequent citations will appear as Pompe, *Vijf Jaren*, and will list page numbers from the Japanese text. Dirk de Graeff van Polsbroek, a Dutch diplomat who was staying in Nagasaki at the same time as Pompe, shared the same sentiment by saying that as far as he could see, the West was forcing its culture and religion on the peaceful Japanese who, he felt, possessed a higher culture than any people in Europe. He was filled with regret and could not help thinking about what effects encroachments from the West would have on this country and its people. He lamented that only time would tell. (Polsbroek will appear later in this book.)

14 Friedrich August Lüdorf, *Acht Monate in Japan nach Abschluß des Vertrages von Kanagawa* (Bremen, 1857). No English translation of Lüdorf work exists, so passages that appear in this book have been translated from the Japanese version. See Ryūdoruhu [Lüdorf], *Guretagō Nihon tsūshōki* [Records of Trade with Japan Aboard the Greta] (Yushodo Shuppan, 1984), 285. Subsequent citations will appear as Lüdorf, *Acht Monate*, and will list page numbers from the Japanese text.

15 Chamberlain, *Things Japanese*, 6–7. Chamberlain wrote this in 1905. Therefore, he thought that the great reforms of modern Japan began in the middle of the eighteenth century.

16 Félix Régamey, *Japon* (Paris, 1903). No English translation of Régamey's work exists, so passages that appear in this book have been translated from the Japanese version. See Regame [Régamey], *Nihon sobyō ryokō* [Sketches of a Jouney to Japan] (Yushodo Shuppan, 1983), 23. Subsequent citations will appear as Régamey, *Japon*, and will list page numbers from the Japanese text.

17 Chamberlain, *Things Japanese*, 4.

18 Chamberlain, *Things Japanese*, 2.

19 Chamberlain, *Things Japanese*, 2–3. Edwin Arnold is a forgotten poet these days, but he was famous at the time for being editor in chief for *The Daily Telegraph* and for his epic poem, *The Light of Asia*. Arnold came to Japan in November 1889 and spoke at both the Tokyo Club and the Imperial University before the end of the year. Chamberlain was on hand to interpret for Arnold at the university. Both talks featured details from Arnold's book, *Sea and Lands*. Based on what Chamberlain is mentioning in this quotation, the details come from the Tokyo Club talk.

20 Chamberlain, *Things Japanese*, 6.

21 Edward W. Said, *Orientalism* (India: Penguin Books, 2006), 176, 278, 3, 46, 40.

22 Said, *Orientalism*, 1.

23 Said, "Orientalism Reconsidered," *Cultural Critique*, No. 1 (Autumn 1985): 95.

24 Ludovic marquis de Beauvoir, *Pekin, Jeddo, and San Francisco: The Conclusion of a Voyage Round the World*, trans. Agnes and Helen Stephenson (London: John Murray, 1872), 128, 122, 196.

25 Yokoyama Toshio, *Japan in the Victorian Mind: A Study of Stereotyped Images of a Nation, 1850-80* (London: Palgrave Macmillan UK, 1987), 2.

26 Sherard Osborn, *A Cruise in Japanese Waters* (Edinburgh and London: William Blackwood and Sons, 1859).

27 Laurence Oliphant, *Narrative of the Earl of Elgin's Mission to China and Japan in the Years 1857, '58, '59* (Edinburgh and London: William Blackwood and Sons, 1859).

28 Yokoyama, *Victorian Mind*, 56.

29 Osborn, *Cruise*, 151.

30 Osborn, *Cruise*, 174.

31 Yokoyama, *Victorian Mind*, 54.

32 Osborn, *Cruise*, 151.

33 Osborn, *Cruise*, 173.

34 Oliphant, *Narrative*, 112.

35 Osborn, *Cruise*, 149.

36 Osborn, *Cruise*, 163.

37 Osborn called this temple the "Temple of Tetstze," while Oliphant called it the "Dai Cheenara Temple." The translator of Oliphant's work, Okada Akio, understood this to be Daishigawara temple in Kawasaki City, so I chose to use this name.

38 Osborn, *Cruise*, 171.

39 Osborn, *Cruise*, 172.

40 Osborn, *Cruise*, 164.

41 Osborn, *Cruise*, 153–4.

42 Osborn, *Cruise*, 176. Oliphant also mentions this in his book.

43 Osborn, *Cruise*, 39.

44 Oliphant, *Narrative*, 393.

45 Oliphant, *Narrative*, 331.

46 Oliphant, *Narrative*. This passage comes from the Translator's Notes section of the Japanese version of Oliphant's text. See Orifanto [Oliphant], *Eruginkyō kennichi shisetsuroku* [Narrative of the Earl of Elgin's Mission to Japan] (Yushodo Shuppan, 1968), 291. The original Japanese has been translated into English here.

47 Osborn, *Cruise*, 184.

48 John Reddie Black, *Young Japan: Yokohama and Yedo* (London: Trubner and Co., 1880), Vol. 2, 97.

49 Yokoyama, *Victorian Mind*, 52.

50 Yokoyama, *Victorian Mind*, 52.

51 Osborn, *Cruise*, 167.

52 Yokoyama, *Victorian Mind*, 53.

53 Osborn, *Cruise*, 40–1, 167.

54 Samuel Wells Williams, *A Journal of the Perry Expedition to Japan 1853–1854* (Kelly and Walsh, 1910), 209.

55 Richard Mounteney Jephson and Edward Pennell Elmhirst, *Our Life in Japan* (London: Chapman and Hall, 1869), 382–4.

56 Ivan A. Goncharov, *The Frigate Pallada*, trans. Klaus Goetze (New York: St. Martin's Press, 1987), 305.

57 Erwin von Bälz, *Awakening Japan: The Diary of a German Doctor: Erwin Baelz* (Indiana University Press, 1932), 377.

58 Yokoyama, *Victorian Mind*, 99–100.

59 Ota Yuzo, *Rahukadio Hān* [Lafcadio Hearn] (Iwanami Shinsho, 1994).

60 Aoki Tamotsu, *Bunka no honyaku* [Cultural Translation] (Tokyo University Press, 1978).

61 Lafcadio Hearn, *Japan: An Attempt at Interpretation* (London: Macmillan and Co., 1904).

62 Aoki, *Honyaku*, 50–1.

63 Hearn, *Japan: An Attempt*, 6–7.

64 Ota, *Lafcadio Hearn*, 45.

65 Jephson and Elmhirst, *Our Life*, 5.

66 Oliphant, *Narrative* Vol. 2, 8.

67 Émile Guimet, *Promenades Japonaises* (Paris, 1878, 1880). No complete English translation of Guimet's work exists, so passages that appear in this book have been translated from the Japanese version. Guimet published this work in two volumes. The first volume details events in Kanagawa and was published in 1878, while the second volume details events in Tokyo and Nikko and was

published in 1880. The former was translated into Japanese and published under the title *1876: Bon Jour Kanagawa* (Yurindo, 1977), and the latter was translated and published as *Tōkyō Nikkō sansaku* [A Ramble through Tokyo and Nikko] (Yushodo Shuppan, 1983). For citation purposes, the earlier work shall appear as *Promenades-Kanagawa*, and the latter shall appear as *Promenades-Tokyo-Nikko*. Félix Régamey drew the illustrations that appear in this work.

68 Guimet, *Promenades-Kanagawa*, 33.

69 Guimet, *Promenades-Kanagawa*, 134–6.

70 Régamey, *Japon*, 206–7.

71 Rutherford Alcock, *The Capital of the Tycoon: A Narrative of a Three Years' Residence in Japan* (New York: The Bradley Co., 1863), Vol. 2, 259–60.

72 Black, *Young Japan*, Vol. 1, 19.

73 Alcock, *Tycoon*, Vol. 2, 288–90.

74 Edwin Arnold, *Seas and Lands* (London: Longmans, Green, and Co., 1892), 287.

75 Arnold, *Seas and Lands*, 275.

76 Lin Yutang, "How to Understand the Chinese," in *The Little Critic, Second Series: 1933-1935* (The Commercial Press, 1935), 15.

77 Lin, *Little Critic*, 7.

78 Alcock, *Tycoon*, Vol. 2, 264.

79 Goncharov, *Pallada*, 283.

80 Kattendijke, *Uittreksel*, 70.

Chapter

2

Cheerful People

The first thing that Westerners who set foot in Japan in the middle part of the nineteenth century saw was how truly happy and content the Japanese people appeared to be. Even Rutherford Alcock, who was oftentimes scathing in his criticism of Japan, wrote, "A good-humoured and contented, as well as a happy race, the Japanese seem, whatever may be their imperfections."[1] Matthew Perry, meanwhile, felt that "the people seem happy and contented"[2] when he landed at Shimoda during his second expedition to Japan. Sherard Osborn, who visited Shimoda four years after Perry, remarked that "Every one looked as happy and free from care as any people could do" despite the fact that they were rebuilding their town in the wake of a massive tsunami that had recently wreaked havoc on their lives.[3]

Others shared this sentiment. Henry Arthur Tilley (dates unknown), for example, was an Englishman who served on the Russian fleet from 1858 and accompanied them on their voyage to Japan in 1859. His impression of Hakodate was that "Health and content were written in the face of man, woman, and child."[4] George Smith (1815–1871), the bishop of the Anglican Church in Hong Kong, came to Japan in 1860 and wrote:[5]

> On reading the accounts of writers who described Japan a century ago, and comparing their estimate of the national character with the spectacles and exhibitions of native customs and usages now to be commonly observed in the streets of Nagasaki, the inference is unavoidable either that those writers limited in their opportunities of observation, gave an exaggerated and overdrawn picture in favour of the native character, or that the Japanese of the present day have in some important particulars degenerated from the Japanese who lived a hundred or two hundred years ago.

As we can see in this writing, Smith was not swayed by the illusions of Japan that had been built up before he visited the country, but even he had to recognize the following:[6]

> If the Japanese do not enjoy the blessings of what is called in the West constitutional freedom, and know little about theories of civil and religious liberty, they contrive to make daily life flow smoothly in the stream of time, and are content to be borne along on the tide of present sensual enjoyment and careless ease.

Members of the Prussian Eulenburg expedition, which came to Japan to conclude a treaty of commerce in 1860, also noted the contentment of the Japanese. The expedition report stated that no matter how one viewed them, they seemed to be a healthy and content people and could probably do without the presence of visitors to Japan.[7]

Meanwhile, Count Joseph Alexander Hübner (1811–1892), a senior Austrian diplomat who visited Japan in 1871, gave another example by saying the following:[8]

> But whatever people may say or think of the feudal system in general, and of the institutions which have hitherto prevailed in Japan, there is one point on which everyone is agreed. At the time of the arrival of the Europeans, and until very lately, the people were happy and contented.

As you can see, there were a great many accounts detailing how content the Japanese seemed to be, and these records continued until the 1880s. For example, Henry Spencer Palmer (1838–1893) was a Briton who made a name for himself by designing waterworks in Yokohama, Tokyo, Osaka, Kobe, and other cities in Japan, and he wrote the following about bathers at the Ikaho Hot Springs in the *Times* in 1886:[9]

> Happiness, contentment, and good temper are stamped on every countenance—the impress of their sunshiny natures, and aptly harmonizing with the spirit of the place. Except at moments given to a hushed admiration of some fresh beauty in the view of a rare product of forest or field, they keep up a constant flow of chat and laughter.

Isabella Lucy Bird (1831–1904) was a British woman who visited Japan in 1878 and gave examples about how happy the Japanese were. Bird traveled on horseback across the Tohoku region, an area in which visitors to Japan had yet to set foot in at the time, and when she arrived at Kuroishi in Aomori, she was surprised by the primitive state of the farmers, especially their homes, which she likened to smoking brick kilns that dotted the landscape. She also noted how the walls looked like they had been haphazardly coated in mud by hand. Despite the rather primitive conditions, however, she went on to say

Farmers in Akita (from Bird, *Unbeaten Tracks*)

that people who sat in front of their homes naked to the waist "were all placidly contented."[10]

If we return to Sherard Osborn's observations, meanwhile, he wrote that he did not encounter "a single cross or sullen look,"[11] and this appears to be a Japanese characteristic that almost every Western observer witnessed at the time. Ludovic de Beauvoir, for instance, said, "these people delight in laughing and enjoying themselves."[12] Rudolf Lindau (1829–1910), a Prussian who came to Japan in 1859 as the Swiss Commerce Commissioner and who served as the Swiss consul in Japan in 1864, said that no other race of people gives over to merriment as easily as the Japanese do, and they laugh at any joke be it good or bad. He also stated that the Japanese were almost like children in that once they started laughing, they would continue to do so for no reason whatsoever.[13] Albert Berg (dates unknown), one of the authors of the Eulenburg expedition report, saw the same characteristics in which the Japanese had an innate zest for jokes and laughter while they were discussing things.[14]

William Gray Dixon (1854–1928), a Scotsman who came to Japan in 1876 and worked as an instructor at the Imperial College of Engineering (now the Faculty of Engineering at the University of Tokyo), described scenes he saw on the streets of Tokyo, and then stated:[15]

One fact is at once apparent; there is a universal air of good humour. Nothing is more noticeable among the crowd than this. The cares of the world evidently press lightly upon them; they seem less alive than Europeans to the stern realities of life. None wears that distracted look so common in a Western city throng. They form a smiling, contented crowd, from the shaven-headed old grand-dame to the crowing baby. To look at them—man, woman, boy, girl alike—one might fancy there was no such thing as sorrow in the world.

Dixon went on to say that, naturally, the Japanese were not without misery and sadness, "but the fact remains, that among this people there is nothing which so strikes and so wins a stranger as this aspect of geniality."

Lev Ilich Metchnikov (1838–1888), also known as Léon Metchnikoff, taught Russian at the Tokyo School of Foreign Languages (now the Tokyo University of Foreign Studies) from 1874–1875 and could not help but be fascinated by laborers who told jokes and laughed all the time.[16] Gustav Kreitner (1847–1893), a lieutenant in the Austrian army who came to Japan as a member of Count Béla Széchenyi's expedition in 1878, already felt during his brief stay in Nagasaki that the Japanese were favorable, kind, and pleasant, and that the extremely charming people often erupted in childish laughter, a quality that literally diffused like electricity.[17] Kreitner then went to visit a dye factory in Osaka and said the following:[18]

When we entered the facility, one of the girl workers laughed, and this spread to the girl next to her, and soon the entire factory was filled with a loud, ceaseless laughter that almost shook the rickety wooden building we were in. I knew that this explosion of cheerfulness came from the girls' hearts and that they were not being sarcastic in any way, but I was fraught with confusion and dismay.

Before Beauvoir visited Japan, he traveled to Australia, Java, Siam (Thailand), and China, but he felt that Japan was the highlight of the trip.[19] He also noted that the best things to view in this wonderful country were not the arts, performance arts, or scenic spots, but "that of every-day life, that of the streets or the country during the first few days, when you find yourself in contact with a people whose customs are so peculiar." He also sighed and thought of "the courtesy, the liveliness, and frivolity of this nation of puppets amusing themselves amongst the warblings of this city of bird cages." The true sight for him to behold was the good-naturedness of the people. He gave the "bright, good-tempered lively expression [of the Japanese] which attracts you at once" as an example, and also mentioned that the ladies are "charming; smart and smiling, bright and fresh" and their sashes "on the back like a cartridge box...gives a little air of pertness, which is delightful."

When Beauvoir went to see Heikenji temple in Daishigawara (located in present-day Daishi, Kawasaki City, Kanagawa Prefecture), two girls at the teahouse served as guides for his party. He noted the following about them:

Two of the young ladies acted as our guides; they went on in front, laughing and playing arm-in-arm, clattering on their little wooden clogs, with their blue flowered robes and scarlet petticoats amidst the corn and the corn-flowers, with no fear of the fresh breeze disarranging the artistic erection of their beautiful ebony locks.

Meanwhile, little girls fishing in the rice fields called out *"Ohayō!"* ("Good morning!") in cheerful voices while carrying their little brothers, who were about the same height as they were, on their backs. The greetings of *"Ohayō,"* the smiles, the "invitations to stop at every door to drink tea with the family," and "offerings of flowers" moved Beauvoir. He stated the courtesy and amiability of all the people was beyond description, and thought the Japanese were the "gentlest and most polished" people on Earth. He also felt the Japanese were a bit childish, but they were a kind, simple, and trustworthy people.

Beauvoir was a young man of twenty-one, so we should keep in mind that his descriptions were likely the musings of a youth finding it hard to contain his excitement with what he was seeing. Despite this, however, he had definitely found the true Japan. Other observers would echo his observations.

Rudolf Lindau, for example, stated the following about his experience in a farming village outside Nagasaki:[20]

I will never forget the wonderful way the farmers always welcomed me. When I stood in front of a farmhouse to request fire, a boy or girl would always hastily bring out a brazier right away. When I entered a house, the father would always ask me to sit down, and the mother would greet me politely and serve tea…The boldest person would touch the fabric of my clothes, and little girls often touched my hair, and then they would run away laughing with embarrassment. I would give them some metal buttons…and everyone would line up and repeatedly thank me with a *"Taihen arigato!"* ["Thank you so much!"]. Then, they would kneel and bow their cute little heads and gently smile. Coming across such attitudes among people of the lower class was a complete surprise to me. When I took my leave, they would see me off to the edge of the road, and I could still hear their warm, friendly voices yelling *"Sayonara, mata myonichi!"* ["Goodbye. See you tomorrow!"] when they were almost out of sight.

Members of the Eulenburg expedition often visited villages surrounding Yokohama while they were staying in the city, and everywhere they went they were met with warm hospitality, even receiving tea, eggs, oranges, and other goods on several occasions. They were also surprised that just a few groschen coins were enough to cover the cost for such services. The Japanese people trusted their newfound guests and never treated them with disrespect, and sometimes they would even guide the expedition on their journey by following them along the road for considerable distances with a hospitable yet reserved tone. Sometimes they would even have their children serve as escorts. The children often screamed and ran away when they came across the Eulenburg expedition, but when they grew more accustomed to being around the foreign visitors, they would welcome them kindly and gather together and greet the party with an *"Ohayō!"* The children were constantly intrigued by the clothes of the party members, and they often touched them.[21]

Aimé Humbert (1819–1900), who came to Japan in 1863 as the leader of the Swiss delegation, wrote the following about coastal dwellers in Yokohama at the time:[22]

All the good people who compose the population of the beach accost me in the friendliest manner. The children bring me beautiful glistening shells, and the women do their best to make me understand the culinary properties of the hideous little marine monsters which they pile up in their baskets. This spontaneous kindliness and cordiality is a characteristic common to all the lower classes of Japanese society.

Humbert also described an episode in which he was invited into one of the farmhouses while walking through a village in the countryside. The farmers cut and brought him the most-beautiful flowers from their garden and they refused to accept any monetary compensation from him. Refusing to accept money for kindness seems to have formed part of the moral makeup of the common people at the time. During her great journey on horseback across the Tohoku region in 1878, Isabella Bird also encountered and was moved by people showing her kindness and expecting nothing in return. This happened so often that it more than made up for the many unpleasant experiences she had on the trip.

On one such occasion, Bird had arrived at her lodging for the night after a busy day of traveling and sightseeing when she realized she had lost one of the leather straps for her horse. She wrote, "though it was after dark, the man went back a *ri* [about four kilometers] for it, and refused to take some *sen* which I wished to give him, saying he was responsible for delivering everything right at the journey's end.[23] In a miserable village in the mountains along the border between Niigata Prefecture and Yamagata Prefecture, she remarked that "a woman in this unseemly costume firmly refused to take the 2 or 3 *sen* which it is usual to leave at a place where you rest, because she said that I had had water and not tea, and after I forced it on her, she returned it to Itō [Bird's interpreter]."[24] She also related the following about her experience at a transport office in Tenoko, a village in Yamagata:[25]

When the women of the house saw that I felt the heat they gracefully produced fans and fanned me for a whole hour. On asking the charge they refused to make any, and would not receive anything…Not only that, but they put up a parcel of sweetmeats, and the man wrote his name on a fan and insisted on my accepting it. I was grieved to have nothing to give them except some English pins…I told them truly that I should remember them as long as I remember Japan, and went on, much touched by their kindness.

Bird also wrote about the difficulties she experienced when she encountered flooding in the northern part of Akita Prefecture:[26]

I like to tell you of kind people everywhere, and the two *mago* [pack horse drivers] were specially so, for, when they found that I was pushing on to Yezo for fear of being laid up in the interior wilds, they did all they could to help me; lifted me gently from the horse, made steps of their backs for me to mount, and gathered for me handfuls of red berries, which I ate out of politeness, though they tasted of some nauseous drug.

A Tohoku farmer (illustration by Otto, from *Bigō ga mita seikimatsu Nippon* [Late Nineteenth-Century Japan Seen through the Eyes of Georges Ferdinand Bigot], Heibonsha, 1996)

Bird also acknowledged the following:[27]

The *mago* are anxious that I should not get wet or be frightened, and very scrupulous in seeing that all straps and loose things are safe at the end of the journey, and, instead of hanging about asking for gratuities, or stopping to drink and gossip, they quickly unload the horses, get a paper from the Transport Agent, and go home…They are so kind and courteous to each other, which is very pleasing.

Bird did not just mention the *mago*. She also wrote that "the kindliness and courtesy of the coolies [rickshaw drivers] to me and to each other was a constant source of pleasure to me."[28] After Bird's journey to Tohoku and Hokkaido, she headed for Kansai. In Miwa Village in Nara Prefecture, three rickshaw drivers asked her to hire them to take her to Ise. Bird refused as they did not have any references and she did not know much about them, but the oldest among them said, "We also wish to worship at Ise." Bird was touched by this and said she would hire them except for the weak one in their group, but they begged her to hire him as well, saying he had a large and poor family and that they would help him. In the end, Bird hired all three of them, and she said, "These faithful fellows are the comfort of our tour with their unwearable good nature, strict honesty, and kindly, pleasant ways."[29] When her trip to Ise was over, the time for them to part ways in Otsu City came. She had this to say about the "tall and very ugly man," who was their leader:[30]

I cannot tell you how sorry I am to part with this faithful creature, or how I will miss his willing services, hideous face, and blanket-swathed form. But no, he is not hideous! No face, beaming with honesty and kindness, can ever be so, and I like to look at his, and to hope that one day it may be said of him, as of a child, 'of such is the kingdom of heaven.'

Bird also said the following:[31]

In many European countries, and certainly in some parts of our own, a solitary lady-traveller in a foreign dress would be exposed to rudeness, insult, and extortion, if not actual danger; but I have not met with a single instance of incivility or real overcharge.

Rickshaw driver; this is a sketch of a rickshaw driver in Tokyo, but he apparently looked nearly identical to the driver mentioned here (from Bird, *Unbeaten Tracks*)

Georges Hilaire Bousquet (1846–1937) was a Frenchman who stayed in Japan from 1872 to 1876 as an advisor to the Ministry of Justice. He noted that whenever he felt hot, hungry, or tired while hunting or walking in the countryside, he would often stop by a farmhouse and be treated to the hospitality of the farmers. He also said that every time he did so the entire family would welcome him and he struggled to make them accept payment for their services. He felt the warm-hearted nature of a simple and sociable people who were a bit uncouth yet friendly.[32]

Bousquet also related the following about the men who carried the palanquin he rode in on his way to Nikko. There were three palanquin bearers, but only two carried the palanquin at one time while the other man rested, and they would take turns so as to give each other a break. However, Bousquet noted that he never heard them say anything when they switched jobs. One time, the man who was supposed to take over in the back mistakenly took the position at the front and apparently said, "Oops. I am not supposed to be here." Then he laughed out loud. Bousquet attributed this laughing to the nature of the Japanese. In the end, the bearers carried the palanquin for more than ten *ri* over a difficult road and were extremely tired by the end of the day. Bousquet was in awe by what he saw, and he said the following:[33]

They desire little, are always happy and content, are not impulsive, and although on the outside they appear to be rough and rude, they clearly appear to be the most wholesome of all the Japanese people. Even the lower castes of society in this country have impeccable manners.

Meanwhile, John Reddie Black had this to say about the Japanese:[34]

Their innocent, open-hearted cordiality, their undisguised but not offensive curiosity, their jovial willingness to amuse or be amused, rendered the men agreeable; while the pretty manners and the merriment of the women-kind were simply charming. Then there was the welcome almost universally accorded to foreigners who in passing sought to rest themselves, and the cheerful greeting "Ohai-o," that was never wanting from those who were met on the roads, or from the labourers in the fields or the inhabitants of the villages.

This Japanese characteristic of amusing themselves and others can also be seen in the writings of Peter B. W. Heine (1827–1885). Heine, a painter traveling with Commodore Perry's fleet, was received by a company of women chosen by the Magistrate of Shimoda. Heine's interpreter told him there were not any beautiful ladies from this area, but Heine said every woman he met was quite lovely and he was particularly struck by the way they tied up their hair. The ladies were not shy or embarrassed at all, so he pressed his luck and played with their kimonos and soon even touched their chins, pinched their cheeks and cavorted with them in other ways. The Japanese lords, samurai and family members who were also in attendance all laughed out loud when they saw him.[35] Naturally, they probably did so because they thought it was amusing that every man, even one from the West, had a weakness for women. Whatever the case, they were happy to see Heine enjoying his time in Japan in such an innocent way. It should also be noted that the ladies were not giving themselves to him. They also enjoyed seeing the reactions of the foreign guest they were entertaining.

There is also an endless list of examples of what Black deemed "undisguised but not offensive curiosity." Others had similar observations.

For example, Francisco Diaz Covarrubias (1833–1889), a Mexican astronomer who came to Japan for a joint international project to observe the planet Venus in 1874, wrote about a woman he met at a store in Yokohama who stared at his clothes, gloves, as well as his sword and watch, and finally even touched his beard. Covarrubias went on to describe the Japanese women who often interacted with visitors to Japan at work as not being that sophisticated from an intellectual standpoint, but he also mentioned how they were almost child-like in their obedience and innocence.[36]

A village beauty (illustration by Wirgman, from Alcock, *Tycoon*)

Naturally, observers did not always depict the curious Japanese as being completely innocent. While Isabella Bird was traveling in Tohoku, for example, she was continuously hounded by curious onlookers who gathered to see her. In Aizutakada, a crowd surrounded her lodging, one person even climbed onto the roof of the neighboring house, and children climbed onto the fence and caused it to collapse under their weight. In Bange, meanwhile, over 2,000 people gathered to see her leave. When she pulled out her telescope, the people mistook it for a gun and started a huge stampede to get away. Adults even pushed and trampled over children in the process. In Yuzawa, Akita Prefecture, observers climbed onto the roof of the building next to Bird's lodging and caused it to collapse. When she stayed at a lodging in Jinguji, another village in Akita, a crowd of people disturbed her slumber in the middle of the night. About forty men and women had apparently removed the sliding doors to her room and were quietly watching her sleep. Later, Bird crossed over to Hokkaido and wrote that the Ainu she met there did not show any of the curiosity the Japanese did. Depending on the situation, the curiosity of the Japanese sometimes showed signs of immodesty, impudence, and insensitivity, but in Bird's case, she noticed these curious crowds were never rude to her. They also never pushed or shoved each other around.

Aimé Humbert said the characteristics of the lower classes in Edo were "an instinct of sociability…good humour, and repartee" while also mentioning that the most-notable characteristics of the Japanese working class were cheerfulness, a relaxed temperament, and the tendency to not dwell on things, and their child-like innocence.[37] In fact, Humbert wrote how curious and even absurd the adults looked playing *kitsune-ken* and other children's games. He went on to write the following:[38]

> The lower classes are passionately fond of listening to story-tellers and singers. Every day at the cessation of labour and of traffic, groups of persons of both sexes may be seen about the workshops, or at an angle of the cross roads, ranged in a semicircle around the professional *raconteur*.

There are numerous accounts that the Japanese valued their children and that this is the reason why foreign observers like Humbert felt Japan was a paradise for children. Actually, however, many of the observers viewed everyone in the country as a child. They often saw truly strange sights of not just young people, but even respectable adults mixing together with small children to fly kites, play with Japanese tops, and play games of shuttlecock.

William Elliot Griffis (1843–1928), an instructor at the Fukui domain school and the Daigaku Nanko (also known as Kaisei College, the precursor to the Tokyo Imperial University) from 1870 to 1874, was surprised that "We frequently see full-grown and able-bodied natives indulging in amusements which the men of the West lay aside with their pinafores, or when their curls are cut." He also said the following:[39]

It might be said that during the last two centuries and a half,...the main business of this nation was play...Among a nation of players such as the Japanese may be said to have been, it is not always easy to draw the line of demarcation between the diversions of children proper and those of larger growth.

Griffis, who originally sought to be a missionary and studied at a seminary to become one after returning to his homeland, did not view these child-like tendencies of the Japanese favorably. However, in the eyes of Black, who was a naval instructor, merchant, and journalist, Japanese adults marking each other's faces, as they are apt to do in the shuttlecock game, was a delightful sight to behold. He stated:[40]

Naught but mirth and jollity could be seen among them. Laughter is always catching; but Japanese laughter on such occasion surpasses anything of the kind to be heard elsewhere; and such is their heartiness and kind nature that the good folk are only too happy to see others enjoy their games as well as themselves.

Edward Morse summarized the child-like innocence of the Japanese quite well in the following passage that appears in his book *Japan Day by Day*:[41]

The more I see of these gentle people the more they remind me of a set of overgrown, good-natured, kind-hearted, laughing children. In many ways they are childish, in precisely the same way that our children are childish, and some of the resemblances are striking. In lifting a load or doing any arduous work they grunt and make a great noise with their mouths in a tone which seems to say, "See what a big thing I am doing!"

Raphael von Koeber (1848–1923), who was a lecturer of philosophy at Tokyo Imperial University in the Meiji period, also noted that the most charming point of the Japanese was their naiveté and child-like nature.[42] In 1918, he wrote that Japan was continuing to lose its fresh principles, child-like nature, and wildness, qualities that were so endearing to him when he first arrived in the country.[43]

Josef von Hübner agreeing with the consensus that "the Japanese…are gentle, merry, and very affectionate"[44] and Henry Palmer asking whether "for happiness, gentleness…no other country can even profess to show the match of…Japan"[45] are judgments these men made based on actual proof, not overembellished descriptions or illusions, upon comparing their observations with the examples above. Moreover, if the Japanese people at the time truly were this gentle and cheerful, and this was indeed Hübner's belief, then it is only natural to think that this was close to the reality of the situation.

Of course, this does not mean that Japan at the time was heaven on Earth. Arguments that use Western records describing Japan as a paradise as proof that these authors were simply seeing an illusion do not know the literature of that time very well. If we examine all of the texts, there are amazingly few examples that unconditionally praise Japan as a paradise. The term paradise, rather, often evokes negative connotations. For example, Black said, "It is sometimes thought that Japan was a paradise before foreigners came to it. In reality it was not more so than other countries."[46] Robert Fortune (1813–1880), an English botanist who came to Japan in 1860, said:[47]

> Scenes of debauchery and drunkenness are common, and even murder is not infrequent. Over such matters one would willingly draw a veil; but truth must be told in order to correct the impression which some persons have of Japan—namely, that it is a very Garden of Eden, and its inhabitants as virtuous as Adam and Eve before the fall.

Rutherford Alcock, meanwhile, was highly critical of Laurence Oliphant's travel diary, particularly the fact that Lord Elgin's delegation "had only to extort certain privileges on paper." He then went on to say:[48]

> It was the business of the resident Ministers to make these paper concessions realities, [but]…there was not, and never could be, any real accord, whatever the outward professions of good faith and amity. Hence, also it naturally followed that, although the original negotiators were received with smiles, and their path was strewn with flowers; their successors had only the poisoned chalice held to their lips, thorns in their path, and the scowl of the two-sworded bravos and Samourai to welcome them, whenever they ventured to leave their gates.

In other words, Alcock was trying to say that the shogunate was tricking Lord Elgin's mission by only showing them the good qualities of the Japanese. However, these were just superficial attributes and Elgin's mission failed to see the dark underbelly of Japan. Alcock even stated in the preface to his book *The Capital of the Tycoon* that he wrote this treatise in order to present an opinion that contrasted with Oliphant's *Narrative of the Earl of Elgin's Mission to China and Japan.*

Rutherford Alcock

Alcock was a staunch critic of feudal Japan and constantly looked down on the dissemination of the image that Japan was a paradise. It was his belief that "Utopian views of Japan long prevalent" should be "somewhat rudely destroyed upon closer acquaintance."[49] According to Alcock, Japan looked like a paradise from far away, but actually living here made people "feel disposed, on larger experience, to depict it as a pandemonium." Even as he said, "I will try, as much as in me lies, to avoid both extremes,"[50] he was plagued by the deception of the shogunate officials and the threats of nationalistic ronin (masterless samurai) on a daily basis, so he may have actually viewed Japan somewhat negatively. However, he did use the phrase "garden of Eden" during his visit to the Izu region, when he was moved by the richness and beauty of the villages there.[51]

I hate to come back to this point again, but I am not concerned with whether there is enough proof to call old Japan a paradise or whether the notion was all just an illusion created by foreign observers during their stays. I do not even care if it is an illusion that completely differs from reality. The most important issue in my mind is trying to figure out why the observers viewed Japan as a paradise.

One of the reasons is that the framework of their minds made them see things this way. There is obviously some validity in their labeling Japan as a paradise due to viewing it as a strange place. Culture shock plays a role in this. More importantly, however, is that everything they saw was reality. This gap between the West and Japan, or, more specifically, the gap between the modern industrial society they were living in and the relatively premodern nature of Japan, is actually what made them feel that Japan was different and unique. In addition, the look of contentment on Japanese faces, combined with the gentle and cheerful nature of the people, probably caused many of the observers to call Japan "heaven on Earth" even though the reality was clearly not the case.

People's expressions and behavior have to support the corresponding reality. So how, exactly, did the foreign observers interpret the Japanese people's feelings of contentment that truly looked real and the reality they were constantly seeing? It is, after all, only through their eyes that we can recreate the old Japanese civilization that disappeared, or, rather, that the Japanese caused to disappear. Naturally, we sometimes have to look through the rose-tinted glasses of those who left these accounts, and this is not just limited to descriptions written by visitors to Japan from this time period. The writings, literature, records, and testimonials that historians use are all products of certain systems of thought. We obviously must consider bias whenever we use such resources, as this is the logical basis for dealing with historical texts.

Fortunately, many of the Western writers were not tourists who were simply interested in Japan, but rather individuals who came to the country on business or to carry out political assignments. Even among the tourists, however, many of them had a keen eye for observations and were highly intelligent. They certainly praised Japan to a certain degree, but this did not cloud their critical eye. After Basil Chamberlain called his book "the epitaph for old Japan," he said it was for "recording the many and extraordinary virtues of the deceased—his virtues, but also his frailties."[52] Furthermore, according to scholar Edward R. Beauchamp, William Griffis, who wrote dozens of books about Japan and served as a bridge to the country, wrote the following letter to Japanese Ambassador to the United States Takahira Kogorō when he was awarded the Fourth Class Order of the Rising Sun from the Japanese government in 1909, for which he expressed both his joy and surprise:[53]

I have never ceased to criticize Japan and the Japanese…I have never flattered the Japanese or Have (sic) I defended them in a mere partisan spirit. In endeavoring to be an interpreter of the Orientals to the Occidentals I have proceeded in the spirit of the scientific student, my aim to break down the wall of prejudice, ignorance and bigotry whether ethnic, religious and social, and express the truth, without fear or favor. Hence I have criticized all things Japanese as freely and unreservedly as I should my own country and people.

We should be thankful for having a critic such as Griffis.

However, sympathy is just as important as criticism and is arguably the best way to reach an understanding. Chamberlain teased Morse for praising Japan by identifying it with his homeland by saying "The only drawback is the author's [Morse's] parti pris of viewing everything through rose-coloured spectacles, which makes those who would fain be instructed by him feel that they are listening to a special pleader rather than to a judge."[54] When Chamberlain wrote this, Morse's Japan Day by Day had yet to be published, and he was thinking of an earlier book by Morse, titled Japanese Homes. After reading Japan Day by Day, however, Chamberlain was even more assured of his conviction.

It should be noted, however, that Chamberlain took the critical comment "rose-colored spectacles" from Morse's own words. Morse wrote the following in the introduction to *Japanese Homes*:[55]

Edward Sylvester Morse when he was in Japan

> In the study of another people one should look if possible through colorless glasses; though if one is to err in this respect, it were better that his spectacles should be rose-colored than grimed with the smoke of prejudice. The student of Ethnology as a matter of policy, if he can put himself in no more generous attitude, had better err in looking kindly and favorably at a people whose habits and customs he is about to study.

In other words, Morse had a solid methodology and self-awareness. He even professed that "I may have erred in looking through spectacles tinted with rose; but if so, I have no apology to make," and he believed that "such an investigation must be approached in a spirit of sympathy, otherwise much is lost or misunderstood."[56] This is close to the methodology of contemporary cultural anthropology. We should also give a word of thanks to a sympathizer such as Morse.

Notes:

1 Alcock, *Tycoon,* Vol. 1, 124.

2 Matthew C. Perry, *The Japan Expedition 1852-1854: The Personal Journal of Commodore Matthew C. Perry*, ed. Roger Pineau (Washington: Smithsonian Institution Press, 1968), 216.

3 Osborn, *Cruise*, 112.

4 Henry Arthur Tilley, *Japan, the Amoor, and the Pacific: with Notices of Other Places, Comprised in a Voyage of Circumnavigation in the Imperial Russian Corvette "Rynda" in 1858-1860* (London: Smith, Elder, and Co., 1861), 112.

5 George Smith, *Ten Weeks in Japan* (London: Longman, Green, Longman, and Roberts, 1861), 84.

6 Smith, *Ten Weeks*, 122.

7 Albert Berg, *Die Preussiche Expedition nach Ost-Asien nach amtlichen Quellen* (Berlin, 1864). No English translation of this work exists, so passages that appear in this book have been translated from the Japanese version. See Beruku [Berg], *Oirenburuku Nihon Enseiki* [Record of the Eulenburg Expedition to Japan] (Yushodo Shuppan, 1969), Vol. 1, 344. Subsequent citations will appear as Berg, *Eulenburg Expedition*, and will list page numbers from the Japanese text. It is unclear who actually wrote this expedition report, but it is believed that Berg wrote at least the second volume of the four-volume set. The original text was published in Berlin in 1864 as an official report of this expedition. Other articles on Japan written by Eulenburg and other members of the Eulenburg expedition, such as Gustav Spiess, Werner von Reinhold, and Max von Brandt, were translated into Japanese. Some of these works appear in subsequent sections of this book.

8 Alexander F.V. Hübner, *A Ramble round the World*, trans. Lady Herbert (London: MacMillan, 1878), 420. The original French text is titled *Promenade Autour du Monde, 2 Vols* and was published in Paris in 1877.

9 Henry Spencer Palmer, *Letters from the Land of the Rising Sun* (Yokohama: Japan Mail, 1894), 9. Palmer was a correspondent with the *Times*, and this book is a collection of his articles on Japan.

10 Isabella Lucy Bird, *Unbeaten Tracks in Japan, Vol. 1-2* (New Yok: G.P. Putnam's Sons, 1894), Vol. 1, 397.

11 Osborn, *Cruise*, 150.

12 Beauvoir, *Pekin, Jeddo, and San Francisco*, 130.

13 Rudolf Lindau, *Un Voyage Autour du Japon* (Paris, 1864). No English translation of Lindau's work exists, so passages that appear in this book have been translated from the Japanese version. See Rindau [Lindau], *Suisu Ryōji no mita Bakumatsu Nihon* [Japan at the End of the Edo Period Seen through the Eyes of a Swiss Consul] (Shinjinbutsu Oraisha, 1986), 211. Subsequent citations will appear as Lindau, *Un Voyage Autour*, and will list page numbers from the Japanese text.

14 Berg, *Eulenburg Expedition*, Vol. 1, 103.

15 William Gray Dixon, *The Land of the Morning* (Edinburgh, 1882), 194–5. Dixon also cautioned that the good-natured Japanese could invite unsuitably high praise from visitors to Japan, which could lead to disillusionment later on.

16 Lev Ilich Metchnikov was known as "Léon Metchnikoff" in France, and he wrote a book on Japan, titled *L'empire Japonais: Pays, Peuple, Histoire* (Geneva, 1881). However, the passage here does not come from this text, but rather a serial that he wrote from 1883 to 1884 for the *Русскій Вѣстникъ* [The Russian Messenger], a Russian magazine. No English translation of Metchnikoff's work exists, so passages that appear in this book have been translated from the Japanese version. See Mēchinikohu [Metchnikoff], *Kaisō no Meiji Ishin* [Memoirs of the Meiji Restoration], trans. Watanabe Masashi (Iwanami Bunko, 1987), 126. Subsequent citations will appear as Metchnikoff, *Kaisō*, and will list page numbers from the Japanese text.

17 Gustav von Kreitner, *Im fernen Osten* (Vienna, 1881). No English translation of Kreitner's work exists, so passages that appear in this book have been translated from the Japanese version. See Kuraitonā [Kreitner], *Tōyō kikō 1* [An Account of a Voyage to the Far East 1] (Heibonsha Toyo Bunko, 1992), 214. Subsequent citations will appear as Kreitner, *Im fernen Osten*, and will list page numbers from the Japanese text.

18 Kreitner, *Im fernen Osten*, 229.

19 Beauvoir, *Pekin, Jeddo, and San Francisco*, 144, 121, 151, 174, and 131.

20 Lindau, *Un Voyage Autour*, 33–4. Incidentally, there are several records that have survived from the time, and they also mention the Japanese affinity for buttons. For example, artist William Heine, who accompanied Commodore Perry, mentioned someone even trading him a plump fox for his buttons in Shimoda.

21 Berg, *Eulenburg Expedition*, Vol. 1, 153.

22 Aimé Humbert, *Japan and the Japanese Illustrated*, trans. Cashel Hoey (London: Richard Bentley and Son, 1874), 24–5. The original work is titled *Le Japon Illustré* and was published in Paris in 1870.

23 Bird, *Unbeaten Tracks*, Vol. 1, 185.

24 Bird, *Unbeaten Tracks*, Vol. 1, 254–5.

25 Bird, *Unbeaten Tracks*, Vol. 1, 259.

26 Bird, *Unbeaten Tracks*, Vol. 1, 353.

27 Bird, *Unbeaten Tracks*, Vol. 1, 185.

28 Bird, *Unbeaten Tracks*, Vol. 1, 101.

29 Bird, *Unbeaten Tracks*, Vol. 2, 267.

30 Bird, *Unbeaten Tracks*, Vol. 2, 290.

31 Bird, *Unbeaten Tracks*, Vol. 1, 184.

32 Georges H. Bousquet, *Le Japon de nos jours et les échelles de l'extrême Orient* (Paris, 1877). No English translation of Bousquet's work exists, so passages that appear in this book have been translated from the Japanese version. See Busuke [Bousquet], *Nihon kenbunki 1* [Experiences in Japan 1] (Misuzu Shobo, 1977), Vol. 1, 64. Subsequent citations will appear as Bousquet, *Le Japon*, and will list page numbers from the Japanese text.

33 Bousquet, *Le Japon*, Vol. 1, 251.

34 Black, *Young Japan*, Vol. 1, 148–9.

35 Wilhelm Heine, *Reise um die Erde nach Japan* (Leipzig, 1856). No English translation of Heine's work exists, so passages that appear in this book have been translated from the Japanese version. See Haine [Heine], *Sekai shūkō Nihon e no Tabi* [A Cruise around the World: Traveling to Japan] (Yushodo Shuppan, 1983), 140–1. Subsequent citations will appear as Heine, *Reise*, and will list page numbers from the Japanese text.

36 Francisco Diaz Covarrubias, *Viaje de la Comission Astronomica Mexicana al Japon* (Mexico, 1876). No English translation of Diaz Covarrubias's work exists, so passages that appear in this book have been translated from the Japanese version. See Diasu Kobarubiasu [Diaz Covarrubias], *Nihon ryokōki* [A Record of a Trip to Japan] (Yushodo Shuppan, 1983), 198. Subsequent citations will appear as Diaz Covarrubias, *Viaje*, and will list page numbers from the Japanese text.

37 Humbert, *Japan and the Japanese*, 229, 268.

38 Humbert, *Japan and the Japanese*, 257.

39 William E. Griffis, *The Mikado's Empire* (New York, 1876), 452–3.

40 Black, *Young Japan*, Vol. 1, 262.

41 Edward Sylvester Morse, *Japan Day by Day* (Boston: Houghton Mifflin, 1917), Vol. 1, 228–9.

42 Raphael von Koeber, *Kleine Schriften: Philosophische Phantasien, Erinnerungen, Keitzerein, Paradoxien 1918-1925* (Iwanami Bunko, 1928). No English translation of Koeber's work exists, so passages that appear in this book have been translated from the Japanese version. See Kēberu [Koeber], *Kēburu Hakase zuihitsushū* [A Collection of Essays by Dr. Raphael von Koeber], trans. Kubo Tsutomu (Iwanami Bunko, 1957), 81. Subsequent citations will appear as Kreitner, *Kleine Schriften*, and will list page numbers from the Japanese text.

43 Koeber, *Kleine Schriften*, 78–9.

44 Hübner, *Ramble*, 231.

45 Palmer, *Letters*, 188.

46 Black, *Young Japan*, Vol. 1, 151.

47 Robert Fortune, *Yedo and Peking: A Narrative of a Journey to the Capitals of Japan and China* (London: John Murray, 1863), 38.

48 Alcock, *Tycoon,* Vol. 1, xv. However, Oliphant thought that the shogunate official's pleasant demeanor was a mask. He stated, "The cordiality of our reception at Yedo was, in certain quarters, the mask which a somewhat shallow diplomacy led them to assume, in order to avert a danger they deemed imminent, and which they dared not meet." (Quote taken from Oliphant, *Narrative*, 464.)

49 Alcock, *Tycoon*, Vol. 1, 86.

50 Alcock, *Tycoon*, Vol. 2, 229.

51 Alcock, *Tycoon*, Vol. 1, 384.

52 Chamberlain, *Things Japanese*, 8.

53 Edward R. Beauchamp, *An American Teacher in Early Meiji Japan* (Hawaii: University of Hawaii Press, 1976) 140.

54 Chamberlain, *Things Japanese*, 65.

55 Edward Sylvester Morse, *Japanese Homes and Their Surroundings* (Boston: Ticknor and Company, 1886), 22.

56 Morse, *Japanese Homes*, 22–3.

Chapter 3

Simplicity and Wealth

Japan was never supposed to be a paradise, yet the Japanese people truly looked happy and content. The question is: Where is the proof that this was the case? The answer lies in descriptions made by Western observers at the time, and their testimony to the richness of the Japanese people's lives, particularly their access to the basic needs of food, clothing, and shelter, is extremely surprising. This is stunning because it completely differs from more conventional and bleaker images of the time, which see the Japanese people suffering under crushing restrictions imposed by the Tokugawa shogunate.

As a case in point, Townsend Harris arrived in Japan and took his post in Shimoda in August 1856. During his stay, he visited Kakizaki, a village near Shimoda, and said, "Kakizaki is a small and poor fishing village, but the people are clean in person and civil in manner. You see none of the squalor which usually attends poverty in all parts of the world. Their houses are as clean as need be."[1] Of course, Harris did not imply that this village was well off. He was simply stating that even though the people were poor, the village was not dirty.

As the days went by, however, Harris's observations became more meticulous. The following passage is from his October 23 diary entry:

> Took a walk of some five miles. The country is very beautiful—is broken up in steep volcanic cones, but every possible spot is terraced and cultivated like a garden. The labor expended in cutting down the rock to form some of these terraces is something wonderful.

On October 27, meanwhile, he walked ten miles and found new admiration for "the patient industry of the Japanese." Then he wrote the following upon visiting the village of Suzaki on October 28:

> I came on the village of Sazaki [Suzaki]—a very ancient place, to judge by the vast number of heavy stone terraces for supporting temples, houses and gardens. The aggregate labor is very great, and all this among a village population of five hundred to six hundred souls.

Harris acknowledged that the success of unremitting labor over several generations succeeded in creating the scene he saw before him and that this was due to the endurance of a culture that had built up over the years. Of course, about 230 years of shogunate regulations is actually what made this possible.

Shimoda Harbor in 1853 (from Hawks, ed., *Narrative of the Expedition of an American Squadron to the China Seas and Japan*)

Harris also noticed he could not find a garden in Shimoda like the one that Engelbert Kaempfer (1651–1716) wrote about in his book *The History of Japan*. Harris thought the reason for this was "this is a poor place, where all are poor and have enough to do to live without looking to the ornamental." After saying this, however, he had to add a few more eye-opening lines. He said, "But they live comfortably, are well fed according to their wants, and are abundantly clad, and their houses are clean, dry, and comfortable. In no part of the world are the laboring classes better off than at Shimoda." This was a description that Harris wrote in November 1856, but he also wrote the following in June 1857 when he set off to explore the area to the southwest of Shimoda:

> I have never seen a person that had the appearance of want marked on his countenance. The children all have faces like "full moons," and the men and women are quite fleshy enough. No one can for a moment suppose (after seeing the people) that they are not well fed.

What was Harris trying to say with these descriptions? The people living in and around Shimoda were certainly not that high on the social ladder as the first thing he noticed was that they were by and large very poor. However, they exhibited none of the tragic signs associated with poverty and appeared to be happier than poor people from other parts of the world in terms of their access to food, clothing, and shelter. This was the second and most admirable point that Harris made in his descriptions. Incidentally, Harris had first-hand knowledge to support and compare his observations, as his six-year travels as a merchant took him to various regions across the globe, such as India, Southeast Asia, and China, before arriving in Japan.

Prussian merchant Friedrich Lühdorf, meanwhile, came to Shimoda a year earlier than Harris and stated the following about the rice fields he saw near Shimoda:[2]

The fertility of the lands surrounding Shimoda exceeds every description. Beautiful rice fields go all the way up to the tops of mountains and the land is cultivated all the way to the sea. Japan could even be a country blessed by the heavens, a paradise on Earth. Everything a person could ever want can be found in this happy country.

Lühdorf had only been staying in Shimoda for half a year when he wrote this passage. Therefore, his observations did not delve into finding out whether the landowners were exploiting the farmers tilling the beautiful rice fields or not. However, his statements corroborate with those of Harris. If he had assumed the people were leading miserable lives, why would he have described Japan as a heaven on Earth?

Willem Kattendijke provided similar evidence about the city of Nagasaki in the latter half of the 1850s (the Ansei era). He stayed in the city from 1857 to 1859, during which he also made trips to Kagoshima, Tsushima, Hirado, Shimonoseki, and Fukuoka. He stated:[3]

The greatest proof that this country is happy is the prosperity you see everywhere you look. As far as I can see in Nagasaki, anyway, even lowly farmers and day laborers all have sufficient clothing to wear, and even among the lower classes there is no want or complaint about food.

Kattendijke's observations also effectively endorse Harris's descriptions. In other words, he backs up the notion that the people of Japan may have been well off in terms of both clothing and food.

However, we actually encounter an issue with the phrase "even lowly farmers" in Kattendijke's description. Consider the following passage he wrote in another section of his book:[4]

The farmers have to bear heavy taxation. Therefore, their lives are truly miserable. If this were not the case, then we may never discover the reason why the frugal and diligent Japanese famers, who work on the rich soil this country is blessed with, are so poor.

The issue is that, as Rutherford Alcock also saw it, differences between lands held by the shogunate and those owned by the daimyo, or domain lords, may have influenced Kattendijke's description. At any rate, however, it is certain that Kattendijke believed that the people greatly flourished under this system and lived very happy lives.[5]

Meanwhile, Alcock, who assumed his position in Japan in 1859, visited a number of farm villages in the Kanagawa countryside, and almost everywhere he looked he saw that "cottages and farm-houses are rarely seen out of repair—in pleasant contrast to China, where everything is going to decay." He also saw that in autumn, "the men and women…are well and comfortably clad." He also momentarily perceived that "there is no sign of starvation or penury in the midst of the population, if little room for the indulgence of luxury or the display of wealth."[6] This observation is almost identical to the one made by Harris.

Upon actually seeing Japanese farmland while climbing Mount Fuji in September 1860, however, Alcock's observations took on a tone of admiration. He said, "Nothing could exceed the beauty of the road" between Odawara and Hakone, and he noted how the fields they passed were filled with signs of a promising harvest. He also described what can be found in Japan, in general: "A fruitful soil, a fine climate, and an industrious people, make a list which seems to contain nearly all that can be desired for any country in the way of material prosperity."[7]

On the way home from this excursion, Alcock passed through a small village in the Izu region that had fertile soil, a variety of crops, mountains covered in pine forests, and comfortable surroundings. When he passed by the residence of Egawa Tarōzaemon, the magistrate of Nirayama, he felt that the official had an "existence not unlike that of a wealthy landowner in England, whose pleasure it is to spend his days on his own estates and among his tenants."[8] He also mentioned undulating fields of rice, tobacco and cotton, eggplants (which he said tasted good in curry), succulent taro, and sweet potatoes. He also wrote that the "persimmon with its red fruit, and the orange trees with their golden produce, were grouped round the different hamlets and villages." Alcock then went on to describe another small village he visited, hidden by great Japanese cedar trees over 100 feet (about 30 meters) tall. His party even measured the girth of one of the trees and found it to be 16 feet 3 inches (about 5 meters) thick. Then, Alcock's party passed through a gorge, and he noted the pink hydrangeas blooming on the banks and also related how, as they climbed higher, harebells appeared everywhere with their graceful flowers. When they were in the heart of the mountains, they "came upon a pretty secluded village of about a hundred houses." He wrote the following about what he saw:[9]

> Much has been heard of the despotic sway of the feudal lords, and the oppression under which all the laboring classes toil and groan; but it is impossible to traverse these well-cultivated valleys, and mark the happy, contented, and well-to-do populations which have their home amid so much plenty, and believe we see a land entirely tyrant-ridden, and impoverished by exactions. On the contrary, the impression is irresistibly borne in upon the mind that Europe can not show a happier or better-fed peasantry, or a climate and soil so genial or bounteous in their gifts.

Alcock also stayed for a while in Atami. He mentioned that he had never lived among a more primitive or easily satisfied population and doubted whether all but twenty out of the 1,400 or so residents who made their living by fishing or farming in the area had ever left their homes. This reminded Alcock of meeting an old man with hair as white as snow in a village twenty miles (about 32 kilometers) outside of Burgos, Spain. The old man said he had never been to the city, and this made Alcock believe that what he witnessed in Japan was the same situation that existed in Britain before the railroads appeared. He also thought that the villagers "lead, to all appearance, a happy life enough, after a fashion of their own…as the mole and the oyster in their respective elements may be happy." With this Alcock sank into reflection and asked himself what feudalism actually entailed. On one hand he stated that "the feudal lord is everything and the lower and laboring classes nothing," but he also said that all he saw was "peace, plenty, [and] apparent content, and a country more perfectly and carefully cultivated and kept, with more ornamental timber everywhere that can be matched even in England."

Almost two centuries before Alcock, Engelbert Kaempfer stated that Japan "was never in a happier condition than it now is, governed by an arbitrary monarch, shut up and kept from all commerce and communication with foreign nations." Alcock seems to have agreed with Kaempfer's assessment. Even though the country was "governed by an arbitrary monarch" and laws of "less advanced stages of civilization," he felt that the people were extremely happy based on their seemingly content nature and simple customs. The following passage is a fitting epilogue to Alcock's observations concerning this issue:[10]

> At all events, be the connection of cause and effect what it may, taking

the despotic and oligarchic constitution of these realms, with its rude and sharp administration of justice, which admits neither public pleading, appeal, nor extenuations, but takes a man's head off as certainly for a theft as a murder; and, on the other hand, the material prosperity of a population, estimated at thirty millions, which has made a garden of Eden of this volcanic soil, and has grown in numbers and in wealth by unaided native industry, shut off from all intercourse with the rest of the world, it is impossible to pass any sweeping condemnation either on them or the institutions under which they live, and where such results are possible.

According to Albert Berg of the Eulenburg expedition, Alcock jovially spoke about his return trip from climbing Mount Fuji by saying the plains were fertile and filled with farm fields and the mountains were covered with fantastic well-groomed forests of Japanese cedar trees that were unbelievably tall. Alcock also said the people were healthy and well-to-do, and the laborers were in good spirits and kind.[11] This may well have been the height of Alcock's favorable impression of Japan.

In the spring of 1861, Alcock briefly traveled to Hong Kong to serve judgment on the Michael Moss case,[12] and, after returning to Nagasaki, he embarked on a journey to Edo by land to demonstrate the right of passage that the Anglo-Japanese Treaty of Amity and Commerce guaranteed to foreign diplomats. His itinerary essentially followed the trip to Edo made by the Dutch Nagasaki trading house supervisor. This took him through the Ōmura, Hizen, Chikuzen, Buzen and other domains in Kyushu, and he felt that "the extreme richness and fertility of the soil were in striking contrast with the apparent poverty of those who lived on it." We also cannot overlook the fact that he wrote that "the villages looked poor and the peasant's home (bare of furniture at all times) more than usually void of comfort, yet all the people looked as if they had not only a roof to cover them, but rice to eat." He concluded that "although the fertility of the soil is great, and turned to the best account by a plentiful supply of the cheapest labor, yet little superfluity is left to those who have to live by the cultivation of the land." If this were the case, the cost of land was likely quite high. Therefore, he remembered hearing that tribute collected in lands held by the shogunate was usually set at forty percent but could be as high as sixty to eighty percent in the domains.[13]

Opinions were mixed, however, as to whether this was true. In 1858, three years before Alcock traveled on this road, a member of the Dutch trading house named Dirk de Graeff van Polsbroek (1833–1916) saw beautiful fields and well-tended farmland and a number of prosperous villages. He wrote that he was especially impressed by the wealth and order of Hizen Province (located in present-day Nagasaki Prefecture and Saga Prefecture).[14]

Raphael Pumpelly (1837–1923), who was summoned by the shogunate to serve as a mining technician and to conduct mine inspections in Hokkaido from 1862 to 1863, saw evidence to the contrary when he passed through shogunate-held lands into the Tsugaru domain (present-day western Aomori Prefecture) during his second exploratory journey and could not help but be amazed by the difference in the conditions of the people. He wrote:[15]

> I was struck by the more flourishing condition of the inhabitants of the imperial domain, as compared with those of the territory of the Prince of Tsungara [Tsugaru]. There was a general air of dilapidation in the villages, and of thriftlessness among the people, in the region we were now passing through, which spoke of the imposition of burdens disproportionate to the sources of revenue. The line of demarcation between the two conditions was as sharply drawn as the geographical boundary. The cause could not lie in nature, for the sea, which is in both the only source of revenue, offered its treasures alike to both.

Pumpelly claimed the "tycoon" system was the basic reason why the regions were so different. Namely, he thought shogunate policies to impoverish the various domain lords, such as the *sankin kōtai* system, caused them to exact higher tributes in order to procure more revenue.

Now is not the time to discuss whether Pumpelly's theory was right or wrong. In addition, now is not the time to point out the historical irony of how the shogunate fell into chronic financial distress by loosening its control over the people and making practical attempts to preserve their happiness and eventually fell to domains in the southwest (Satsuma and Chōshū), which had built up considerable wealth by exploiting their respective populaces. For now, I just want to touch on the differences between the shogunate and domain territories and focus on generalizations like the ones made by Alcock. Pumpelly mentions one of these generalizations in the following:[16]

> The government of the Empire is best described by calling it a feudalism of the most despotic kind, while at the same time it is doubtful whether any other people ever before prospered and lived as happily under a feudal and despotic government as the Japanese.

However, we know from Algernon Mitford's descriptions of the Kaga domain (present-day Ishikawa and Toyama Prefectures) that we need to be aware of careless generalizations concerning differences between shogunate and domain lands. In 1867, Mitford visited Nanao Port on the Noto

Peninsula with British Consul-General Harry Parkes to help him attempt to open it to international trade. Later on, however, Parkes ordered Mitford to travel from Kaga to Osaka via the Echizen domain (present-day Fukui Prefecture). Mitford wrote the following about his travels:[17]

> Wherever we went we were met with the same gracious and unexpected kindness that had made our stay at Kanazawa so pleasant. We could not help being struck by the great prosperity of the country. We passed through such towns as Matto, with two thousand houses, Komatsu, with two thousand five hundred, all under the mild rule of the Prince of Kaga, and a happier people it would be difficult to find.

This quite clearly shows how wealthy the Kaga domain was (over a million *koku*).

It was also hard for George Smith, the Anglican bishop of Hong Kong, to see differences between shogunate and domain lands in terms of wealth and living conditions:[18]

> As we proceeded further into the country, the view changed from the bold scenery of mountain and sea landscape to a rich and verdant panorama of fertile valleys teeming with agricultural produce and covered with growing crops of rice, wheat, rye, and rape-seed extending from the low level over the gradually rising acclivities to the summits of hills of moderate height. Coppices of cedar and fir were interspersed like emeralds of fairest setting amid the smiling beauty of Nature's golden aspect. Camellias, roses, and evergreens of every variety hung in drooping festoons over our pathway which widened in this more frequented part into the broad dimensions of a well-paved road. The villagers welcomed us in every direction, interchanging signs of goodwill and offering us sweetmeats, hot tea, or cold water. On our return many of the women and boys were standing outside their cottages, offering flowers to ourselves and holding out bunches of green fodder for our horses. Some asked us if this were our Zondag (Sunday); others proffered their importunate request for the much-prized ornament of a gilt button. In the narrower parts of the road the females whom we met sometimes hastily leaped aside out of our way, apparently through fear of our restive horses more than of the riders, and giving way to loud laughter amid their manifestations of alarm.

In the first part of his book, Smith writes about points that leftist historians in postwar Japan embraced, such as how the domains aligned with the shogunate to create an oligarchy that exploited farmers throughout the country. However, his descriptions about the people he saw in Togitsu give the opposite impression:[19]

> The people seemed everywhere to possess a fair amount of material comfort; and the signs of prosperity and contentment generally prevailed. Stout limbs and moderate strength of physical frame were the preponderating characteristics in their appearance, and told no tale of want of food in sufficient quantity to preserve health and sustain bodily labour.

If Smith had not noticed a sign posted on the guardhouse, he probably would have never even realized he had passed from shogunate lands into those held by the Ōmura domain. In other words, as far as he could tell, there was no discernable difference between farming villages in the Ōmura domain and those in lands held by the shogunate in terms of the livelihoods of the people. The villages in Ōmura were prospering.

Smith would later visit Edo, and along the way he also saw prosperous villages near Kanagawa. He mentioned well-kept farmland with fertile soil that appeared to be plowed to the very last inch, along with abundant vegetation, and he also noted the following:[20]

> Cottages and refreshment-houses succeed each other at short intervals, indicating by their general appearance the prevalence of contentment and moderate plenty among the inmates. Flowers too lent their charm in cheering the poor man's dwelling and diffusing abroad the poetry of nature.

The rich atmosphere of the rice fields near Kanagawa also moved Alcock. He wrote:[21]

> The tall, well-kept hedges and fences are still thickly covered, cut and trimmed in the Dutch manner of gardening, and how admirably they are planted and trimmed! Nowhere out of England can such hedges be seen, and not in the British Isles can be found such variety. Here is a low hedge, or border rather, made of the tea-plant, two or three bushes deep, and growing about three feet high, not unlike the ordinary flowering camellia, of which it is a species. Now we have come to an inclosure fenced in with nectarines, and there is a hedge of pomegranate. Inside a tall orange-tree is laden with its golden fruit; and, stranger still, a cherry tree in full blossom this 25th day of November! Oh happy land and pleasant country!

Robert Fortune, meanwhile, thought the overall scene of well-kept rice paddies and farm fields of Japan "resembles more that of a garden than a farm."[22] He also wrote:[23]

> We are told that he is but the serf of the great land proprietor, and that he is heavily taxed and kept in a state of complete degradation. I am not in a position to deny these statements, but I can affirm, from personal observation in many parts of the country, that the farmers and their families live in good comfortable-looking houses, are well clothed, well fed, and appear to be happy and contented. It is just possible, however, that they may be a wealthier class in the territory adjoining the Imperial cities, such as Nagasaki and Yedo, than in that of the vassal princes and feudal lords of the soil.

It goes without saying that expanding agricultural production is what supported these rich and beautiful farming villages. Of course, not everyone believed this was the case. Smith, for example, said, "Japanese agriculture is still practised in a very primitive style."[24] We have to consider, however, that he was simply comparing Japanese "tools of the most homely construction" with the standard of capital-intensive "experimental farming" in Great Britain at the time. He was not the only observer to make this mistake. British doctor and missionary Henry Faulds (1843–1930), who came to Japan in 1874 and stayed for nine years, also saw the wooden plows that the Japanese farmers were using and compared them to primitive tools used by the ancient Greeks,[25] but this was also a superficial observation.

Kattendijke and Alcock, however, knew from their observations that Japanese agriculture was superior in almost every respect. Kattendijke, for example, said that Japanese agriculture was close to perfection and could feed the extremely large population despite the small size of the country, when one considered how high the level of agricultural production had become.[26] According to Alcock, meanwhile, "Nowhere in the world, perhaps, can the Japanese farmer be matched for the good order in which he keeps his farm."[27] He also noted that "everywhere unmistakable signs of skilled agricultural labor and wealth may be seen."[28] Others echoed Kattendijke and Alcock, including Harris, who praised Japanese agriculture and gazed in particular wonderment at their magnificent rice fields. He said, "I never saw such fine crops of rice, or rice of so good a quality as here."[29] Meanwhile, Germain Felix Meijlan (1785–1831), who headed the Nagasaki Dutch trading house from 1827 to 1830, also said that Japanese agricultural techniques were extremely efficient and probably of the highest level.[30]

Demographic historian Hayami Akira (1929–) used the unique term "industrious revolution" to clearly explain advancements in agricultural production during Tokugawa times. This term differs from the industrial revolution, and, according to Hayami, refers to the agricultural revolution in eighteenth-century Britain that increased both labor and land productivity through the expansion of farm acreage and the introduction of large numbers of livestock and large-scale tools. Technological development took a capital-intensive direction, or, in other words, saw an increase in the capital to labor ratio, and what made this possible was a high arable land to population ratio, or, namely, a large amount of space available for raising livestock.

Edo-period Japan, however, had a low arable land to population ratio, which means there was not nearly enough land to raise livestock at the same level as Britain. Consequently, livestock-raising never really took hold in Japan, and the country soon saw increases in invested labor. In other words, Japanese agriculture became more labor-intensive. Hayami stated that in any case, Japanese agriculture did away with old-style plows pulled by livestock and began relying on the physical power of humans and the hand plows and spades they wielded. Meanwhile, increased fertilization meant that more weeding operations were necessary, and the need for additional purchasing capital forced many of farmers to find employment during the off-season. He also went on to say that improvements in land use frequency led to a growth in labor investment for the farmers and their families.[31]

Hayami argues that this choice was logical under the circumstances because production per person had definitely increased a great deal, although he also recognizes that a number of issues resulted from these developments. However, we can say that the "industrious revolution" definitely brought about the highest economic and material prosperity seen in a pre-industrial country—a fact that nearly every foreign observer of Japan from the end of the Edo period to the beginning of the Meiji period could attest to. This is because they witnessed the characteristics of Edo-period farm villages almost immediately: scenes of crops covering the land from the plains all the way to terraces in the hills, well-maintained irrigation facilities and elaborate fertilization, little to no livestock, and intensive plowing and weeding operations.

Weed removal was particularly impressive. Carl Peter

Plowing the fields (from Alcock, *Tycoon*)

Thunberg (1743–1828), a Swedish doctor who worked at the Dutch trading house in Nagasaki, was also a botanist versed in the teachings of Carl Linnaeus and excited about coming across unknown plant species in Japan when he made the journey overland to Edo. However, he would end up being rather disappointed with what he found. In fact, he "could not discover the least trace of weeds," and noted that "the industrious farmers pull them diligently up, so that the most sharp-sighted botanist can hardly discover any uncommon plant in their well-cultivated fields.[32]

Naturally, there were enormous differences in the living conditions of the people from region to region. Edward Morse, for instance, wrote the following:[33]

> The villages vary greatly in their appearance: some are extremely trim and pretty, with neat flower-plats in front of the houses, and an air of taste and comfort everywhere apparent; other villages present marked evidences of poverty, squalid houses with dirty children swarming about them. Indeed, the most striking contrasts are seen between the various villages one passes through in a long overland trip in Japan.

Samuel Wells Williams (1812–1884) accompanied Commodore Perry on his journeys and served as his Chinese interpreter. Upon the expedition's second voyage to Japan in which they docked at Yokohama, which was still a small village at the time, Williams wrote in his diary about seeing the "dress and miserable habitations" of the people which showed "plainly their low condition."[34] However, this may have just been a casual impression on Williams's part, for he still remembered the beautiful rows of houses with well-built fences of coral that he saw in Naha during their visit to Okinawa. In Yokohama, meanwhile, Williams saw miserable dwellings "built of dried mud and straw supported by cross joists and beams," and he decried that "the village was rendered unsavory by the numerous vats, thatched over to retain urine, compost, and other manuring substances from evaporating, which lined the waysides." Williams was essentially comparing two places that could not be compared, namely, that of a poor village on the coast of Honshu and the main city of Okinawa, which was still the rich kingdom of Ryukyu at the time. Despite this, however, Williams also wrote that "the men looked healthy and well-fed," so the question that I have is what happened to "their low condition" that he mentioned earlier?

Even if we ignore the significance of Williams's descriptions for the time being, we still need to consider a number of factors that determined the standard of living for the Japanese people at the time, such as regional differences and the characteristics of local villages. For example, fishing villages seem to have been miserable places. When Alcock's party landed on the coast near Hyōgo on their way back from Nagasaki, for example, he wrote that "nothing could well be poorer or more miserable-looking than the few fishing hamlets we saw."

Furthermore, there were poor rural areas in every Japanese province. When Isabella Bird entered the mountains of Fukushima Prefecture on her way north from Nikko during her journey across the Tohoku region, she noticed all of the mountain villages looked poor and unclean. She even wrote, "I was entirely unprepared for the apparent poverty and real dirt and discomfort that I have seen since leaving Nikko."[35] At the same time, however, she had to admit the following:

> With us poverty of the squalid kind is usually associated with laziness and drunkenness, but here the first is unknown, and the last is rare among the peasant proprietors. Their industry is ceaseless, they have no Sabbaths, and only take a holiday when they have nothing to do. Their spade husbandry turns the country into one beautifully kept garden, in which one might look vainly for a weed. They are economical and thrifty, and turn everything to useful account. They manure the ground heavily, understand the rotation of crops, and have little if anything to learn in the way of improved agricultural processes.

Therefore, Bird came to the conclusion that these villages appeared to be poor because the people did not follow the Western standards of comfortable living and did not concern themselves with cleanliness. However, a mountain village she saw near the Fukushima-Niigata border appeared to be tragically poor. She wrote:[36]

> There was not a house clean enough to rest in, so I sat on a stone, and thought about the people for over an hour. Children with scald-head, scabies, and sore eyes swarmed. Every woman carried a baby on her back, and every child who could stagger under one carried one too. Not one woman wore anything but cotton trousers. One woman reeled about "drunk and disorderly." Ito [the interpreter] sat on a stone hiding his face in his hands, and when I asked him if he were ill, he replied in a most lamentable voice, "I don't know what I am to do, I'm so ashamed for you to see such things!"

However, when Bird entered the plains of Yonezawa, her tone changed completely. There she discovered "an enchanting region of beauty, industry, and comfort," and wrote:[37]

The plain of Yonezawa, with the prosperous town of Yonezawa in the south, and the frequented watering-place of Akayu in the north, is a perfect garden of Eden, "tilled with a pencil instead of a plough," growing in rich profusion, rice, cotton, maize, tobacco, hemp, indigo, beans, egg plants, walnuts, melons, cucumbers, persimmons, apricots, pomegranates; a smiling and plenteous land, an Asiatic Arcadia, all its bounteous acres belonging to those who cultivate them, who live under their vines, figs, and pomegranates, free from oppression—a remarkable spectacle under an Asiatic despotism…Everywhere there are prosperous and beautiful farming villages, with large houses with carved beams and ponderous tiled roofs, each standing in its own grounds, buried among persimmons and pomegranates, with flower gardens under trellised vines, and privacy secured by high, close-ly-clipped screens of pomegranate and cryptomeria.

Observers met people of various levels of wealth and poverty, even within the same city or province. Shiba Kōkan (1747–1818) left Edo on a journey to Nagasaki in 1788 and kept a journal, which he would later title *Saiyū nikki* (Diary of a Journey to the West), to record the details of his journey, which would continue through the following year. A passage in his journal gives us truly fascinating information about the very poor and simple people he met in Totomi Province (present-day western Shizuoka Prefecture), not far from the exciting and prosperous city of Edo. Specifically, this involved an episode in which Kōkan was sitting down for lunch by a river in the mountains during his pilgrimage to Akiba Shrine. An old woman was sitting next to him and asked, "And where might you be from?" Kōkan answered "I'm from Edo." The old woman responded by telling him the following story:[38]

Well, now. How fortunate for you! Edo is a good place. I'll tell you about this place. We have not one grain of rice to eat and just fill our bellies with millet and potatoes. What's more, our salt is in short supply, miso is hard to come by, and no one here has ever even seen raw fish. We have to keep an eye out for monkeys during the daytime, and when night falls, we have to run off wild boars. As you can see, our fields are surrounded by fences. The monkeys jump over them and destroy our wheat and millet.

Four or five children were sitting next to the old woman, so Kōkan gave them what was left of his rice. He noticed that they reacted with the joy of children getting something sweet to feast on.

Later on in the same mountain district, Kōkan came across some laborers.

They asked him what Edo was like, so he pulled out the *nozoki megane* glasses, a kind of primitive stereoscope, that he had in his pack and showed them views of Ryōgoku Bridge and Edo Bridge. Kōkan was a painter and became well-known amongst Dutch scholars for his interest in Western paintings. He often made a little money on his journeys by showing people copper plates that he made of famous spots in Edo. They could view these with the special *nozoki megane* glasses that he also made. Kōkan did not intend to take money from these laborers at first, but he changed his mind after seeing them gazing in awe at the majesty of Edo and said, "I cannot let you see this for nothing. It's thirty-two copper pieces for each one of you." He was surprised that the laborers paid him right away and wrote "The people are simple in this way."[39] Naturally, people living in the mountainous rural areas that Bird and Kōkan passed through, not to mention the farming villages that Morse saw, showed various degrees of wealth and poverty, but from what we can gather from the testimony of Westerners, almost all the people in Japanese farming villages at the time were happy and looked content.

This means that the first thing we have to do is examine the established theory that farmers living in the Edo period were subjected to crushing taxes. This theory has gone unchecked for a long time, but it may have started to wobble to some degree recently as testimony provided by observers disagrees with this notion quite a bit. Economic historian Thomas C. Smith, for instance, shed a clear light on this point when he wrote the following in the introduction to one of his journal articles:[40]

> Few notions are so widely held among students of Japanese economic history as that the land tax during the Edo period was cruelly oppressive. It is thought to have left the peasantry no significant surplus after production costs and to have become heavier as time passed.

Smith believed this theory was completely wrong and gave clear proof that over time, the farmers actually built up a surplus of wealth.

Until now, historians have drawn the conclusion that the people were severely taxed because the rate of taxation was high in relation to the crop yield assessed by land surveys. However, if we focus on gaps between crop yield assessments and the actual yield taken, Smith claims that "the figures cited mean very little and may even be misleading." Generally speaking, land surveys hardly took place after 1700, and Smith says that "by the middle of the nineteenth century, therefore, taxes were based on assessments a century to a century and a half before." It is not hard to understand why the government failed to conduct land surveys, however. For one thing, implementing surveys required a great deal of time and effort, but more importantly, the fear of rebellion prevented governments from acting.

Even though crop yield assessments ceased, agricultural productivity continued to grow, and the number of crops also increased. According to Smith's figures, it was clear there was a general growth of productivity since population in the cities increased significantly without the need for food imports during this time period. Meanwhile, the tax rate did not change much over the long term and actually dropped. For these reasons, there is little doubt that the farmers were steadily increasing and saving up surpluses of wealth. As Smith described it, taxation in the later Edo period did not lead to the confiscation of goods or the forfeiture of property and became less severe over time.

Now we have another issue to tackle. Since taxation became less oppressive for the people and as the agrarian population continued to increase, it would make sense that they would have started to eat into the surplus they had stockpiled. However, agricultural laborers soon found work in the cities and villages due to the rapid development of commerce and industry, so this never happened. There were actually extreme shortages of agricultural labor in the farm villages. Smith was also cautiously aware that the surplus of wealth did not equally spread to the farmers, creating a huge gap between the haves and have-nots. In addition, he could not rule out that causes other than taxation, such as natural disasters and the monetary economy, may have led to poor conditions for the people. Despite these factors, however, Smith basically believed that a large number of farmers in the Edo period made a living tilling the land. In a way, this gives us some insight into why so many Western observers wrote about the image of happy and content Japanese farmers.

However, it is not entirely clear how the image of the Japanese people having enough in terms of food, clothing, and shelter relates to the fact that they led simple lives, a point described by almost all of the foreign observers. Kattendijke, for example, said the following:[41]

> The Japanese have simple desires…At best their idea of luxury is just using some money to buy a kimono. Whatever the case, the ban against luxury has traditionally been very strict and the basic necessities for living are cheap…Meals eaten by aristocratic families are also simple and do not differ that much from those of the poor…Avoiding luxury is one of the characteristics that distinguishes the Japanese from other Asian countries, and even the homes of the most noble individuals are simple and plain. Even in large halls, there is not one chair, desk, bookshelf or other piece of furniture provided.

Every Westerner noticed that Japanese homes had hardly any furniture almost as soon as they landed in Japan. Beauvoir also wrote the following upon observing the Japanese town of Yokohama three days after he landed in the country:[42]

> Of furniture there is hardly any; a small stove in one corner, a curtained wardrobe for the sleeping-mattresses, and a small set of shelves to hold the lacquered saucers for rice or fish, comprise all that is necessary for the little houses where they live in the sight of everyone, like the Roman who desired nothing so much as to live in a glass house. Nothing is hidden from the neighbours!

Alcock actually envied this way of living without furniture to a certain degree. He wrote the following:[43]

> If European joints could only be made supple enough to enable their owners to dispense with sofas and chairs, and, par conséquence, with tables, and we were hardy enough to lie on clean mats…the possibility of marrying on £400 a year might certainly be predicted with something like unanimity in favor of matrimony. The upholsterer's bill never can offer any impediment to a young couple in Japan.

Naturally, Alcock was being a bit sarcastic with this statement. He was implying that a Japanese family could live quite well in a house with a matted floor, a futon and a wardrobe the whole family could use, and a cooking pot, a half dozen rice bowls and plates, and a large wash basin. He went on to write "I think this is the nearest approach to Arcadian simplicity that has yet been made." However, he really wanted to say that the Western notion of living a comfortable life was completely absent from the lives of the Japanese.

As for Harris, he wrote, "No sofa, chair, table, sideboard, or other furniture is to be found in the rooms."[44] Harris left the U.S. consulate in Shimoda for Edo in November 1857 and became the first Western diplomatic representative from a country other than the Netherlands to visit the city. After passing through Kanagawa, a post town on the Tōkaidō road located in present-day Yokohama, he began seeing more and more onlookers. Harris wrote the following about that day in his diary:[45]

> They are all fat, well clad and happy looking, but there is an equal absence of any appearance of wealth or of poverty—a state of things that may perhaps constitute the real happiness of a people. I sometimes doubt whether the opening of Japan to foreign influences will pro-

mote the general happiness of this people. It is more like the golden age of simplicity and honesty than I have ever seen in any other country. Security for person and property, universal frugality and contentment seem to be the apparent condition of Japan at present.

On the day Harris entered the city of Edo, meanwhile, he estimated that 185,000 onlookers had lined up to watch him as he traveled from Shinagawa to the Kudan Sakashita area of Edo. His lodgings were actually set up at the former site of the Bansho Shirabesho, an institute in Edo for the study of foreign texts. As he traveled, he noted that "The people all appeared clean, well clad and well fed; indeed, I have never seen a case of squalid misery since I have been in Japan."[46] Harris also had an audience with Tokugawa Iesada, the thirteenth Tokugawa shogun, at Edo Castle. He wrote the following about this experience:[47]

> The dress of the Tykoon was made of silk, and the material has some little gold woven in it. But it was as distant from anything like regal splendor as could be conceived. No rich jewels, no elaborate gold ornaments, no diamond hilted weapon appeared, and I can safely say that my dress was far more costly than his. The Japanese told me his crown is a black lacquered cap, of an inverted bell shape…The material [of his breeches] was far inferior to the glorious "kincabs" of the Benares looms. I did not see any gilding in any part, and all the wooden columns were unpainted. Not an article of any kind appeared in any of the rooms, except the braziers and the chairs and tables brought for my use.

Harris used this series of descriptions to imply that the people seemed happy and content. However, he also wanted to say that the Japanese lived plain and simple lives from the shogun at the very top of the hierarchy all the way down to the commoners at the bottom. This is what he meant by the "equal absence of wealth and poverty" he saw. The heart of what he was trying to say was that this simple lifestyle, which provided just enough security in terms of food and clothing, created "the real happiness of a people." Once Harris realized this, he began to feel disappointment and dismay in thinking that his mission was to destroy this happiness.

There were also some observers who could not hide their dismay for this plain and simple civilization. For example, William Griffis was invited by the Echizen domain (present-day eastern Fukui Prefecture) to come to Fukui as a chemistry instructor. He visited the city in February 1871 and noted that it was "simply a dark, vast array of low-roofed houses, colossal temples, gables, castle-towers, tufts of tobacco, and groves of trees" when viewed from afar, and "there were no spires, golden-vaned; no massive pediments, façades, or grand buildings such as strike the eye on beholding a city in the Western world."[48] He also wrote the following about his experience in the city:[49]

> I realized what a Japanese—an Asiatic city—was. All the houses of wood, the people poor, the streets muddy, few signs of wealth, no splendid shops. Talk of Oriental magnificence and luxury! What nonsense! I was disgusted. My heart sunk. A desperate fit of the blues seized me.

The sorry state of the shops Griffis saw in Kanagawa just after landing in the country had already shocked him a great deal. He even doubted whether the goods on sale were worth five dollars altogether. Therefore, the images he saw in Fukui likely made him "realize the utter poverty and wretchedness of the people and the country of Japan" even further.

Isabella Bird wrote about similar conditions that she saw during her visit. She wrote:[50]

> Japan is beyond the limits of "Oriental magnificence." Colour and gilding are only found in the temples; palaces and cottages alike are of grey wood; architecture scarcely exists; wealth, if there be any, makes no display; dull blues, browns, and greys, are the usual colours of costume; jewelry is not worn; everything is poor and pale, a monotony of meanness characterises the towns.

What saddened these observers was that "Oriental magnificence and luxury" never existed in Japan. Luxury was a word that described the despotic dynasties of China, India, and the Middle East, not Japan.

For Harris and Alcock, it was quite clear that the material civilization of Japan at the time was simply poorer than the West, which had been supported by modern industry, and nothing more. Harris, for example, stated, "In criticizing Kaempfer's description I must bear in mind the difference there is in the standards of splendor, etc., as they existed in 1696 and 1857. What was splendor when he left Holland in 1685 would not be entitled to any adjective of praise in 1857."[51] In other words, Harris wanted to say that the castles, palaces, and temples that Kaempfer praised were now boring and decrepit. Members of the Dutch trading house found much to praise about Japan's material civilization around the time of Kaempfer's trip to Edo from 1691 to 1692, and even around the time of J. F. Overmeer Fischer's (1800–1848) 1822 trip and Philipp Franz van Siebold's (1796–1866) 1826 trip. By the mid-nineteenth century, however, the gap between Japanese and Western civilization had opened considerably. Based on the standards of material civilization that their respective countries had reached, for Westerners at the time, Japan was not wealthy. There were different dimensions of wealth, and gifted individuals like Harris and Alcock, who knew a great deal about Asia, understood this quite well.

After Alcock depicted the simple nature of the daily necessities used by everyone from the domain lords all the way down to the common people who were living day to day, he stated that "There is something to admire in this Spartan simplicity of habits, which seems to extend through all their life."[52] At first, Alcock wanted to say something sarcastic about the simplicity of the lives of the Japanese, but we should note the serious tone he took here. Alcock continued by writing that "Certainly so much austerity, and such universal absence of luxury must go far to enable all to live upon little, [and] preserve to each his independence of action." In essence, he stated that competition based on obtrusiveness, which is usually a source of misery rather than happiness and often brings about ruin, did not exist in Japan. He also quoted a poem about "happy peasant-life" that seems to fit Japan quite well:

Lead a careless life,
With naught to wish and naught to spare.

Alice Mabel Bacon (1858–1918), an American who visited Japan in 1888 as an instructor at a school for noble girls, wrote the following when she saw the interior of a small house used by a gatekeeper:[53]

In the living-room, there was a god-shelf, containing the family idols, with flowers set before them, and a little china cupboard, in which were the cheap but prettily decorated pieces of china that form the table service of any ordinary workingman's family. These things, with the omnipresent hibachi and tea-kettle, formed all the furniture in the room.

However, Bacon thought that "the independence of furniture displayed by the Japanese is most enviable, and frees their lives of many cares," and went on to write:

Babies never fall out of bed, because there are no beds; they never tip themselves over in chairs, for a similar reason. There is nothing in the house to dust, nothing to move when you sweep; there is no dirt brought into the house on muddy boots; and it makes no difference whether the meals are served hot or cold, so long as there is hot water enough to make tea. The chief worries of a housekeeper's life are absolutely non-existent in Japan, except as they have been imported from abroad lately.

George Smith described the hills in eastern or southeastern Nagasaki by writing "The villages on these hills showed no sign of wealth or affluence; and the farming peasantry seemed to be a poorer class of population, though not necessarily on that account to be regarded as destitute of the principal necessaries of life."[54] This shows that the Japanese did indeed live in poor and miserable conditions, but this was separate from the idea that they were unhappy as they maintained the lowest limit of satisfaction. Earlier, we saw how Bird had made the distinction between these two kinds of wealth. Georges Bousquet, who served as an advisor to the Ministry of Justice, said that even though almost all the people living in this simple and pure country were poor, he did not see one wretch.[55]

However, Edward Morse probably depicted this division in the most vivid detail. In 1877, he wrote that, while the people he met in a poor village in Tochigi Prefecture on his way back from Nikko "were the very lowest, and their faces were coarse and the children were very dirty, and the houses were poor, there was no trace of brutality or maliciousness in their looks or any expression of haggard despair."[56] He also mentioned a woman who sat down next to his party while they were eating and "grinned and laughed at us whenever we took a mouthful." In other words, she was definitely vulgar, but maintained an indifferent cheerfulness.

Morse generalized this knowledge even further in his book *Japanese Homes*. He wrote:[57]

> In the cities the quarters for the wealthier classes are not so sharply defined as with us...In nearly all the cities, however, you will find the houses of the wealthy in the immediate vicinity of the habitations of the poorest. In Tokio one may find streets, or narrow alleys, lined with a continuous row of the cheapest shelters; and here dwell the poorest people. Though squalid and dirty as such places appear to the Japanese, they are immaculate in comparison with the unutterable filth and misery of similar quarters in nearly all the great cities of Christendom. Certainly a rich man in Japan would not, as a general thing, buy up the land about his house to keep the poorer classes at a distance, for the reason that their presence would not be objectionable, since poverty in Japan is not associated with the impossible manners of a similar class at home.

Morse also wrote, "As an American familiar with houses of certain types, with conditions among them signifying poverty and shiftlessness, and other conditions signifying refinement and wealth, we were not competent to judge the relative merits of a Japanese house."[58] He then went on to say that he did see some magnificent houses in Japan, but these often numbered one among hundreds of poor, small dwellings that looked like nothing more than shelters from the rain. He also wrote, "Though the people that inhabit such shelters are very poor, they appear contented and cheerful notwithstanding their poverty."[59] In other words, he stated that "In Japan, at least, poverty and constricted quarters are not always correlated with coarse manners, filth, [and] crime." Morse was deeply impressed by the fact that poverty in Japan was markedly different from that of the West at the time. Chamberlain echoed Morse by asserting that "though poverty exists, pauperism does not."[60] In other words, he was saying that being poor did not turn the Japanese people into inhuman wretches. Rather, they could be poor and still live happy lives.

Count Friedrich Albert Graf zu Eulenburg (1815–1881), who led the Prussian expedition to Japan in 1860, shed light on one aspect of this by saying that the Japanese have few needs and wants and live frugal lives every day. He gave the following example to explain how frugal they could actually be. He related how Henry Heusken, the interpreter for the American legation, had a ten-year-old boy as his servant. The boy's monthly stipend was only six silver pieces, and he would use three of these to cover monthly meals and maintain his physical appearance with haircuts and the like, while sending the remainder to his parents for them to live on. Incidentally, three silver pieces in Japan at the time was worth about one thaler and 15 groschen in Prussian currency (about US$1.10 based on 1870 conversion rates). Eulenburg admired this, but he also wondered if it were possible to live in a house in his country on this meager monthly salary.[61]

The low cost of living in Japan at the end of the Edo period shocked the Western observers. Henry Tilley, who landed in Nagasaki and Hakodate as a member of the Russian fleet in 1859, said that "from the price I paid [for cloth] soon after our arrival in the country, I should judge that foreign manufactures could not compete with them."[62] In 1867, Beauvoir bought cakes at a shop in Yokohama and related that "for two 'tempos' (a large copper coin, with a hole in the center, worth a penny) we bought enough to bring on indigestion."[63]

Count Eulenburg

Alcock, meanwhile, stopped for lunch in the Nara countryside and was surprised that for just three tempo coins, which he equated to the outrageously low price of three pence, he received a veritable feast of bamboo shoots, salted fish, rice, and even a glass of Japanese wine.

George Smith also stated the following about the low cost of living:[64]

> The material condition of the poorer classes of laboring population, as compared with other countries, is sometimes difficult to determine. A Chinese acquaintance for some time resident at Nagasaki and well acquainted with the neighbourhood of Shanghae and Ningpo, stated to me as a result of his observations that the cheapness of rice and fish (the two main necessaries of life to an oriental) enabled the lower orders of Japanese to live on their small wages, and placed a larger portion of material comfort within their reach than is enjoyed by the same classes of working people in China. He qualified his remarks however by the assertion that, all classes of society taken together, the Chinese lived in a state of greater comfort and plenty.

Smith's Chinese friend's comment suggests something important. Namely, he touched on what Chamberlain called "the comparative social equality of all ranks and stations in this country." Chamberlain also stated that "the Japanese and Far-Easterners generally are at bottom more democratic than Anglo-Saxons on either side of the Atlantic,"[65] and "the rich not being blatant, the poor are not abject;…a genuine spirit of equality pervades society."[66] Chamberlain made these statements because he observed that there were no snobs in Japan, or any nobility in the true sense of the word, whereas snobbery was rampant in Britain, and Americans held a strange affinity for wealthy families. He even noted how the people even called Prince Okuma Shigenobu, "Monsieur Okuma."[67]

Eliza Ruhamah Scidmore (1856–1928), an American who first came to Japan in 1884 and who became well-known as a Japanese correspondent through her frequent visits to the country, also wrote, "The poor in Japan are very poor, getting comparative comfort out of smaller means than any other civilized people in the world." She also went on to say:[68]

> A few cotton garments serve for all seasons alike. The cold winds of winter nip their bare limbs and pierce their few thicknesses of cloth, and the fierce heat of summer torments them; but they endure these extremes with stoical good-nature, and enjoy their lovely spring and autumn the more. A thatched roof, a straw mat, and a few cotton wadded futons, or comforters, afford the Japanese laborer shelter, furni-

ture, and bedding, while rice, millet, fish, and sea-weed constitute his food…Perfect cleanliness of person and surroundings is as much an accompaniment of poverty as of riches.

Much can be said, therefore, about how the low cost of living and simple ways of life allowed the Japanese to live comfortably. These were not the only reasons, however. Scidmore, for example, wrote about a coastal village in Kamakura which vividly shows that poverty did not necessarily mean abandoning luxury. The villagers may have even found the true meaning of life. She wrote:[69]

> On bright spring mornings men, women, and children gather sea-weed and spread it to dry on the sand…Barelegged fisher-maidens, with blue cotton kerchiefs tied over their heads, and baskets on their backs, roam along the shore; children dash in and out of the frothing waves, and babies roll contentedly in the sand; men and boys wade knee-deep in the water, and are drenched by the breakers all day long…Women separate the heaps of sea-weed, and at intervals regale their dripping lords with cups of hot tea, bowls of rice, and shredded fish. It is all so gay and beautiful, every one is so merry and happy, that Kamakura life seems made up of rejoicing and abundance, with no darker side.

Mary Fraser (1851–1922), wife of British Envoy to Japan Hugh Fraser (1837–1894), offered a similar description when she wrote the following about net fishermen she saw along the coast of Kamakura in 1890:[70]

> It is a beautiful sight as the brown men, their loins girded with twisted blue cotton stand in the water, stretching out the lengths of the net full of dancing silver fish, behind them the sunset sea, and before, the dusky velvet sands. This is the time when the children glean their harvest; and not the children only, but poor widows, who have no man to send a-fishing, and very old people, whose sons are dead, all gather round the fishermen, holding out little bowls and baskets for what they will give; and all that is fit for food and yet not good enough for the market goes to them…It is good to see that there is never a rough word said to the beggars, who, though as poor as the grey grasses on the dunes, do not look despairing or dirty or unhappy.

Now we can see why Chamberlain said, "though poverty exists, pauperism does not." The look of contentment that everyone could see on the faces of the Japanese derived from a society that guaranteed people freedom and independence through mutual interactions with nature and their fellow man. The coast belonged to the people who lived there and everyone, including widows and the elderly, shared the bounties of the sea. Everyone in the village, both rich and poor, enjoyed what Ivan Illich called "Commons," or spaces in which people share and live off of what they produce themselves.

Simply stated, poverty in Japan at the time was of the preindustrial variety and differed completely from the poverty many considered a dismal social problem in early industrial societies. Siebold actually pointed this out before anyone else when he stated the following about the salt production he saw in the Chugoku region of Japan on his way to Edo:[71]

> I have repeatedly stated that general prosperity can be seen in some nationalized industries in Japan in regions where large-scale or mass production takes place, yet the sort of poverty seen in European commercial centers, the human misery and disgraceful behavior of which has exhausted me in both body and soul, does not exist. The same is true for this area [the Chugoku region]. In addition, there are no industrial barons in Japan who brandish their untold riches over those classes of people who are half-starving to death. There is a stricter sense of formalism that exists between the laborer and the factory owner in Japan than in Europe, but they are more closely tied through mutual respect for and courtesy toward their fellow countrymen.

Now we know what the Western observers saw to make them express their praise and admiration for the rich lifestyle of old Japan. They were comparing it to slums found in their countries, as well as the dismal poverty and moral degradation associated with these areas, brought about by early industrial society. Edward Morse's earlier quote is a good example of this, but I think Laurence Oliphant paints a better picture. When he said that beggars, thievery, child abuse, and vulgar ladies did not exist in Japan, he was probably using the world Friedrich Engels (1820–1895) depicted in his 1845 classic work *The Condition of the Working Class in England* as a backdrop to this comparison.

Friedrich Engels, meanwhile, wrote the following about the weaving industry in Britain prior to the arrival of industrialization:[72]

> The workers vegetated throughout a passably comfortable existence, leading a righteous and peaceful life in all piety and probity; and their material position was far better than that of their successors. They did not need to overwork; they did no more than they chose to do, and yet earned what they needed.

With the appearance of large factories run by machines, however, the peaceful and simple lives of the workers changed completely. The young Engels depicted the resulting misery of the early industrial society in the following manner:[73]

> They [the poor] are given damp dwellings, cellar dens that are not waterproof from below, or garrets that leak from above…They are supplied bad, tattered, or rotten clothing, adulterated and indigestible food…They are stirred up like game, and not permitted to attain peace of mind and quiet enjoyment of life. They are deprived of all enjoyments except that of sexual indulgence and drunkenness, are worked every day to the point of complete exhaustion of their mental and physical energies, and are thus constantly spurred on to the maddest excess in the only two enjoyments at their command.

Engels also detailed the contents of an 1833 industrial commission report:[74]

> The report of the Central Commission relates that the manufacturers began to employ children rarely of five years, often of six, very often of seven, usually of eight to nine years; that the working-day often lasted fourteen to sixteen hours, exclusive of meals and intervals; that the manufacturers permitted overlookers to flog and maltreat children, and often took an active part in doing so themselves.

Engels gives a bleak assessment of the situation, but today's historical standards do not back up the notion that the so-called industrial revolution caused the working class in Britain to lose their peaceful way of life and plunge into hell. In fact, the main current of thought in today's British historical circles is that the industrial revolution did not pan out the way we have traditionally believed. For one thing, there is a theory that states that people's lives improved due to increases in wages. Another reason is that, according to historian Kitagawa Minoru, British industrialization was by no means that drastic and was not even a watershed moment in history. He also stated:[75]

> The rate of economic development during the era of industrialization did not increase at an amazing speed and the ratio of industrial salaries to all salaries and the population of people engaged in industrial labor were both low. Industrial systems and steam engines were by no means widespread, and the propagation of techniques was still commonly the apprentice system…Therefore, industrialization only had

an effect in a small number of areas and among a small number of people. Macroscopically speaking, Britain had hardly changed.

According to Kitagawa, moreover, poverty and filth in the cities did not just suddenly appear along with the industrial revolution, but actually existed as early as the mid-seventeenth century.[76] The problem was already well-known by the time William Hogarth (1697–1764) created the famous work *Gin Lane*, a print that depicts a tragic city scene in eighteenth-century Britain. That being said, however, the brutal conditions of an industrial city in the 1840s as depicted by Engels were nonetheless true. Historian Muraoka Kenji also pointed out that poor sanitation expanded along with the advancement of industrialization in the developing cities, and this caused the death rate to rise in the 1830s and finally level off in the 1840s and 1850s.[77]

Now we have a better idea of why Harris felt that he had to write about the poor people he saw in Shimoda wearing neat and tidy clothes, living in clean houses with good sunlight, and having children who were plump and well-fed. He even stated, "In no part of the world are the laboring classes better off than at Shimoda." In reality, however, there really was not anything worth praising in Japan. Observers like Harris were just caught up in how much better off the Japanese poor looked than poor people in their own countries did.

Thomas Carlyle (1795–1881) had already stated in his work *Past and Present* (published in 1843) that the wastelands brought about by the industrial revolution were a terrible sight likely not even seen in the most barbaric regions of the world.[78]

Thus, much of what the Westerners witnessed in Japan, particularly the well-known Japanese attribute of cleanliness, left a strong impression on them and became the target of their attention not just because they were observing traditional Japanese customs, but rather because Japanese society contrasted so dramatically with the early industrial society in their own countries at the time. A lot of what they saw may have even shocked them. Consider what Engels wrote about the slums of London in the following passage:[79]

> A vegetable market is held in the street, baskets with vegetables and fruits, naturally all bad and hardly fit to use, obstruct the sidewalk further, and from these, as well as from the fish dealers' stalls, arises a horrible smell...The filth and tottering ruin surpass all description. Scarcely a whole window pane can be found, the walls are crumbling, doorposts and window frames loose and broken...Heaps of garbage and ashes lie in all directions, and the foul liquids emptied before the doors gather in stinking pools.

If we take the terrible filth of these slums into account, then it should come as no surprise that the Western observers were moved by how clean the poor people's clothing and homes were in Japan. Albert Berg wrote that the cleanliness of Japanese homes was such that he felt bad about entering with dirty boots on. Isabella Bird, meanwhile, even felt bad about walking with her dirty shoes on a road in Nikko that looked like it had been swept clean. She felt the same way when she was on a road in Niigata. What these observers seem to be saying is that "Japanese cleanliness" was due to a preindustrial social custom in which the people constantly swept and made their roads look like mirrors.

We also need to consider another contrast in the minds of the Western observers whenever they emphasized the cleanliness of the Japanese, namely, China. While Kattendijke was stationed in Nagasaki, for example, he took some time off and visited Shanghai. He gave an honest assessment of his visit to China by saying that even during his stay there, he thought about how saintly Japan was numerous times and felt that there was no comparison between the countries or the people.[80] Kattendijke was not the only person who felt this way. In fact, there were innumerable examples of Westerners who felt that Japan was like Heaven compared to China.

A young Beauvoir, for instance, said, "Oh! When one leaves that dirty ignoble Celestial Empire, what a pleasure it is to see Japan where everything glistens with brilliant colours!" He even went on to say that China was a "plain of coffins." Oliphant, meanwhile, wrote, "We had just passed a year in China, and all comparisons made with that Empire were in favour of Japan." Scidmore also believed Japan was a "dream of Paradise" when she visited the country after coming from China and Korea. Perhaps the best example, however, was given by Portuguese writer Wenceslau de Moraes. He stated:[81]

> For people who have lived in China for a long time and are used to seeing the dull scenery, the barren coast, and that ugly and detestable group of people, whom the Europeans loath and Pierre Loti termed the "Yellow Peril," living in the squalid lowly hamlets of China, the contrast with Japan comes as a complete shock.

Needless to say, it is not my intention to use Moraes and the other observers' quotes as to satisfy any sense of Japanese nationalism or patriotism on my part. In fact, there are quite a few positive descriptions of China written by Europeans who loved the country. For example, Samuel Williams, who accompanied Perry on his voyage, stated that people who had lived in Canton and Macao as missionaries thought Japanese kimonos were hideous and that long clothes in China were much more pleasant, and he also wrote that he doubted whether the Japanese enjoyed their lives as much as the Chinese did. In addition, Ernest Mason Satow (1843–1929), who was famous for his work *A Diplomat in Japan*, reminisced on his time in Beijing, his first post as a student interpreter, saying it "will never be effaced from my memory."[82]

J. M. Tronson (dates unknown) was a member of the fleet commanded by Admiral James Stirling that visited Japan in 1854 to sign the Anglo-Japanese Treaty of Amity and Commerce. Tronson had a very favorable impression of Shanghai and its surroundings because the people were friendly and peaceful. He also mentioned how they were different from the people living in the south who brandished guns to keep the populace in line and wrote, "One feels a pleasure in walking through the country, where the people are kind and civil, and a fine hardy race." However, when he entered the city of Shanghai proper, he saw that "in all directions were stagnant pools, noisome smells, squalid beggars, cripples, itinerant musicians, and gamblers." He called it a "scene of misery."[83]

What we can conclude is that observers to China likely did not see the glorified civilization that existed before the arrival of Marco Polo, but rather the chaotic end of a despotic empire collapsing in on itself due to provocations made by the European powers. When Alcock said that "everything is going to decay" in China, his remark rings true when one considers that he served as consul in each area of China from the end of the Opium War until the Taiping Rebellion, episodes that involved the British and brought about extensive damage to the country. Beauvoir, meanwhile, compared the Chinese people "who wish to massacre us with stones and pikes" to the Japanese, who he felt were "the gentlest and most polished nation on the face of the earth," but he does not seem to realize that the incursions by Europeans like himself caused the Chinese to react this way.

One reason why many of the observers felt Japan was a salvation compared with China had to do with the climatic conditions of the southern Chinese coast. Richard Jephson and Edward Elmhirst of the British Ninth Regiment wrote the following:[84]

> We landed on the 9th of May, 1866, after having been a year in Hong-Kong, where we had had the bad fortune to drop in for a particularly sickly season, the bitters of which only served to heighten our appreciation of the lovely, sunny land in which we found ourselves, on this bright spring morning.

While standing on the deck of their ship and remarking that the green plains and mountains they saw in Japan reminded them of their homes in

Britain, Jephson and Elmhirst were also saddened by remembering their comrades who lay buried in Hong Kong's "Happy Valley." There were a great many soldiers from the Ninth Regiment who remained in that "last home." According to Tronson, meanwhile, during his stay in Nagasaki, "The health of the squadron was considerably improved by the visit. On board of the *Barracouta*, when arriving at Nagasaki, there were twenty-eight sick, and on leaving the port but five."[85] He wrote that those who succumbed to disease along the Chinese coast should be sent to Japan with its climate, which was conducive to good health.

It might have also been the case that Chinese culture was simply too different for Westerner sensibilities to put up with. Beauvoir mentioning the "plains of coffins" hints at this. In other words, China was an inscrutable mess of chaos and vanity for the Westerners, and their senses probably could not bear the country's Baroque sordidness, as it were. Marguerite Duras (1914–1996), a modern French writer, sculpted in her work *The Vice Consul* the Western European ambivalence toward, for example, an Indian nothingness by depicting a French youth who shot Hansen's disease patients that had gathered in the square. However, what exactly invited Chinese madness and chaos into the lives of nineteenth-century Western Europeans?

No matter how Japan and China compare with one another, it is an undeniable fact that Western visitors to Japan in the nineteenth century saw an enjoyable country with beautiful land. Now, we need to undertake a more versatile analysis to prove that this is true.

Notes:

1 Harris, *Complete Journal*, 203, 243.

2 Lühdorf, *Acht Monate*, 166.

3 Kattendijke, *Uittreksel*, 123.

4 Kattendijke, *Uittreksel*, 19.

5 Kattendijke, *Uittreksel*, 126.

6 Alcock, *Tycoon*, Vol. 1, 267.

7 Alcock, *Tycoon*, Vol. 1, 354.

8 Alcock, *Tycoon*, Vol. 1, 377.

9 Alcock, *Tycoon*, Vol. 1, 376–7.

10 Alcock, *Tycoon*, Vol. 1, 383–8. Alcock's quoting of Kaempfer appears on p. 391.

11 Berg, *Eulenburg Expedition*, Vol. 1, 158–9.

12 Michael Moss was a British man who shot and severely injured a government official who reproached him for violating hunting laws and other issues. Alcock gave him a three-month prison sentence and fined him 1,000 dollars, but Moss appealed the case to the Hong Kong Supreme Court. Moss won the case and received 2,000 dollars in compensation.

13 Alcock, *Tycoon*, Vol. 2, 70–89.

14 Herman J. Moeshart, *Journaal van Dirk de Graeff van Polsbroek 1857-1870* (Netherlands, 1987). No English translation of Moeshart's book exists, so the passages that appear in this book are

taken from the Japanese version. See Mūsuharuto [Moeshart], *Porusuburukku Nihon hōkoku 1857-1860* [Dirk de Graeff van Polsbroek's Report on Japan 1857-1860] (Yushodo Shuppan, 1995), 62. Subsequent citations will appear as Moeshart, *Journaal*, and will list the page numbers from the Japanese text.

15 Raphael Pumpelly, *Across America and Asia* (New York: Leypoldt and Holt, 1870), 186.

16 Pumpelly, *Across America*, 118–9.

17 Hugh Cortazzi, ed., *Mitford's Japan* (London: Routledge, 2013), 53.

18 Smith, *Ten Weeks*, 181–2.

19 Smith, *Ten Weeks*, 183–4.

20 Smith, *Ten Weeks*, 265–6.

21 Alcock, *Tycoon*, Vol. 1, 264.

22 Fortune, *Yedo and Peking*, 56.

23 Fortune, *Yedo and Peking*, 269.

24 Smith, *Ten Weeks*, 190.

25 Henry Faulds, *Nine Years in Nipon* (Boston: Cupples and Hurd, 1888), 79.

26 Kattendijke, *Uittreksel*, 123.

27 Alcock, *Tycoon*, Vol. 1, 283.

28 Alcock, *Tycoon*, Vol. 1, 121 and Vol. 2, 101.

29 Harris, *Complete Journal*, 235.

30 Iwao Seiichi, *Gaikokujin no mita Nihon dai ikkan: Nanban torai igo* [Japan in the Eyes of Foreigners Volume 1: After the Arrival of the Barbarians] (Chikumashobo, 1962), 328.

31 Hayami Akira, "Kinsei no Keizai Hatten to 'Industrious Revolution' ["Modern Economic Development and the 'Industrious Revolution'], in Saitō, Sugiyama eds., *Tokugawa shakai kara no tenbō* [Views from Tokugawa Society] (Dobunkan, 1989).

32 Carl Peter Thunberg, *Travels in Europe, Africa, and Asia Performed between the Years 1770 and 1779* (London, 1795), Vol. 3, 136.

33 Morse, *Japanese Homes*, 4.

34 Williams, *Perry Expedition*, 115–6.

35 Bird, *Unbeaten Tracks*, Vol. 1, 170.

36 Bird, *Unbeaten Tracks*, Vol. 1, 254.

37 Bird, *Unbeaten Tracks*, Vol. 1, 266–7.

38 Shiba Kōkan, "Kōkan saiyū nisshi" ["Shiba Kōkan's Diary of a Journey to the West"], in *Nihon Shomin Seikatsu Shiryō Shūsei* [Lives of the Japanese People] (Sanichi Shobō, 1969), Vol. 2, 273.

39 Shiba, "Kōkan saiyū nisshi," 275.

40 Thomas C. Smith, *Native Sources of Japanese Industrialization, 1750-1920* (University of California Press, 1988), 50–53.

41 Kattendijke, *Uittreksel*, 126–7.

42 Beauvoir, *Pekin, Jeddo, and San Francisco*, 129.

43 Alcock, *Tycoon*, Vol. 1, 107.

44 Harris, *Complete Journal*, 330.

45 Harris, *Complete Journal*, 428–9.

46 Harris, *Complete Journal*, 441.

47 Harris, *Complete Journal*, 479–80.

48 Griffis, *Mikado's*, 423–4.

49 Griffis, *Mikado's*, 415–30.

50 Bird, *Unbeaten Tracks*, Vol. 1, 7–8.

51 Harris, *Complete Journal*, 418.

52 Alcock, *Tycoon*, Vol. 1, 268.

53 Alice Mabel Bacon, *A Japanese Interior* (Boston and New York: Houghton Mifflin Co., 1894), 41–2.

54 Smith, *Ten Weeks*, 192.

55 Bousquet, *Le Japon*, Vol. 1, 125.

56 Morse, *Day by Day*, Vol. 1, 106–7.

57 Morse, *Japanese Homes*, 5–6.

58 Morse, *Japanese Homes*, 6.

59 Morse, *Japanese Homes*, 49–50.

60 Chamberlain, *Things Japanese*, 449.

61 Friedrich Eulenburg, *Ost-Asien 1860-1862 in Briefen des Grafen zu Eulenburg* (Berlin, 1900). No English translation of Count Eulenburg's book exists, so the passages that appear in this book are taken from the Japanese version. See Oirenburuku [Eulenburg], *Dai ikkai Doitsu kennichi shisetsu Nihon taizaiki* [Record of the First German Expedition to Japan] (Toko Shoin, 1940), 190–1. Subsequent citations will appear as Eulenburg, *Ost-Asien*, and will list the page numbers from the Japanese text.

62 Tilley, *Japan, the Amoor*, 91.

63 Beauvoir, *Pekin, Jeddo, and San Francisco*, 131.

64 Smith, *Ten Weeks*, 222–3.

65 Chamberlain, *Things Japanese*, 383.

66 Chamberlain, *Things Japanese*, 449.

67 Chamberlain, *Things Japanese*, 356.

68 Eliza Ruhamah Scidmore, *Jinrikisha Days in Japan* (New York, 1891), 40–1.

69 Scidmore, *Jinrikisha*, 40, 1.

70 Mary Fraser, *A Diplomatist's Wife in Japan: Letters from Home to Home* (London: Hutchinson and Co., 1899), 335–6.

71 Philipp Franz von Siebold, *Nippon: Archiv zur Beschreibung von Japan* (Wurzburg & Leipzig, 1897). No English translation of Siebold's book exists, so the passages that appear in this book are taken from the Japanese version. See Jiboruto [P.F. Siebold], *Edo sanpu ryokō* [Travels to Edo] (Heibonsha Toyo Bunko, 1967), Vol. 1, 127. Subsequent citations will appear as Siebold, *Nippon: Archiv*, and will list the page numbers from the Japanese text. This particular quote comes from Chapter 2 of the first volume of Siebold's work.

72 Friedrich Engels, *The Condition of the Working Class in England in 1844*, trans. Florence Kelley Wischnewetzky (New York: John W. Lovell Co., 1887), 3.

73 Engels, *Condition*, 65.

74 Engels, *Condition*, 101.

75 Kawakita Minoru, "Igirisu kindaishi no uchi to soto" ["The Ins and Outs of Modern British History"], in Chizuka Tatami and Kondō Kazuhiko, eds., *Sugisarō to shinai kindai* [The Modern Age Lingers on] (Yamakawa Shuppansha, 1993), 12–13.

76 Tsunoyama Sakae and Kawakita Minoru, eds., *Rojiura no Daiei Teikoku* [Backstreets of the British Empire] (Heibonsha, 1982), 18–9.

77 Tsunoyama and Kawakita, *Rojiura*, 92–3.

78 Tsunoyama and Kawakita, *Rojiura*, 35.

79 Engels, *Condition*, 20.

80 Kattendijke, *Uittreksel*, 157.

81 Wenceslau de Moraes, *Tracos do Extremo-Oriente* (Lisbon, 1895). No English translation of Moraes's book exists, so the passages that appear in this book are taken from the Japanese version. See Moraesu [Moraes], "Nihon no tsuibo" ["Memories of Japan"], in *Meiji bungaku zenshū, Dai 49-kan* [Complete Works of Meiji Literature, Vol. 49] (Chikumashobo, 1968), 168. Subsequent citations will appear as Moraes, *Nihon no Tsuibo*, and will list the page numbers from the Japanese text.

82 Ernest Mason Satow, *A Diplomat in Japan* (London: Seeley, Service, and Co., Ltd., 1921), 20.

83 John M. Tronson, *Personal Narrative of a Voyage to Japan, Kamtschatka, Siberia, Tatary, and Various Parts of Coast of China: in H. M. S. Barracouta* (London: Smith, Elder and Co., 1859), 173–5.

84 Jephson and Elmhirst, *Our Life*, 2.

85 Tronson, *Personal Narrative*, 21.

Chapter
4

Friendliness and Courtesy

It certainly stands to reason that the first impressions that foreign observers had of Japan were not always favorable. Gustav Spiess (dates unknown), a delegate with the Saxony Commerce Association, which accompanied the Eulenburg expedition, was almost feverish with anticipation at seeing the mysterious country of Japan, but when he finally landed and saw the city of Edo with his own eyes, he was shocked to see how drab it actually was and stated that the streets were filthy everywhere he looked. He also stated that half-naked townspeople, obviously from the working class, stood on both sides of the roads. He mentioned they were extremely stout and ugly in appearance and were made even uglier by the pockmarks that dotted their faces.[1] Spiess would later discover that he had been walking through one of the poorest districts in Edo, but he would never forget these negative images of Japan that he saw when he first arrived.

Meanwhile, Algernon Mitford, who was appointed secretary to the British Legation, felt a deep sense of loss when he landed in Yokohama during a rainstorm in October 1866. He had read Laurence Oliphant's travel accounts and had high hopes that he would find the "fairy land of whose beauties we had heard from earlier travelers," but after he landed he noted that the front of what appeared to be the customs house was inundated with water, the officers standing in front of the building all looked angry, and the laborers covered in their straw raincoats looked like "animated haycocks sodden in an unpropitious season." He also mentioned women splashing through the puddles with their clogs while carrying babies with severe skin diseases on their backs. As Mitford said, it was a "melancholy arrival, in all truth, and sufficiently depressing."[2]

Mitford's dashed hopes and negative impressions of Japan would linger for some time. In a letter addressed to his father he wrote "I hate the Japanese. The Chinese are a much pleasanter people to have to deal with." He was also unimpressed with Edo and said that the city was "pretty in detail," but he could not find any grand or magnificent buildings, and the low, narrow structures he did find were like "cattle sheds in interminable parallel lines."[3] Thus, Mitford did not have a favorable view of Edo at first and only began to feel the charm of the city and to view the Japanese more favorably in 1867, and he would look back at Japan with rose-tinted glasses when he wrote *Memories* in his later years.

Pompe van Meerdervoort, a Dutch doctor who opened a hospital in Nagasaki, also had a negative impression of the Japanese at first, particularly with the skin diseases that seemed to plague the people. In fact, he wrote that no other country had as many people with pockmarks derived from smallpox as Japan and even believed that a third of the residents suffered from this affliction.[4] Naturally, Pompe may have been exaggerating to a certain degree. If we look at photographs of people taken at the end of the Edo period, we can see that Shioda Saburō, who served as a French interpreter for the shogunate, clearly has a pockmarked face, but it is hard to believe that a third of all Japanese people had facial features such as these. Other foreign observers also back this claim. Based on the observations Sherard Osborn made on his trip to and from the temple at Kawasaki Daishi, for example, he found that "Pockmarks were common, but by no means general."[5]

Pockmarks may not have been as common as Pompe claimed them to be, but there are quite a few descriptions that testify to the spread of skin diseases. Isabella Bird, for example, often saw this reality during her trip across Tohoku. Rutherford Alcock, meanwhile, noted:[6]

> Among the working classes, various forms of cutaneous eruptions are common—perhaps to be accounted for by their habit of washing together in crowds...Itch, too, is a common malady—common to a distressing degree—and inveterate beyond anything known in Europe! It is almost impossible to get a domestic servant free from this loathsome disease—or keep him so.

In defense of the Japanese, however, it should also be noted that Alcock made these observations after recognizing that "as to general conditions of salubrity Japan certainly appears to be greatly favoured."

Skin diseases were widespread, but there were also quite a few people suffering from eye diseases. Pompe, for instance, said no other country in the world had as many blind people as Japan and that the cause for most of these cases was the Japanese not knowing how to treat eye disease.[7] However, the true dark side of this country in which even the poor appeared to be happy lay in the unbridled spread of sexually transmitted diseases associated with public prostitution. Pompe pointed out this reality by saying that Japan was a beautiful island nation for a number of reasons, but on closer inspection there was a deep sense of moral degradation among its people.[8]

Naturally, Anglican bishop George Smith also saw the reality of things. He said, "Maladies originating in personal vice or hereditary taint are the great universal scourge...One half of the female sex at some period of their lives and one quarter of the infants at the time of birth, are visited with its marked effects."[9] For Smith, who adhered to a strict sense of morality, the worst offenses committed by the Japanese were their sexual indulgences and drinking. He even stated, "Never in any portion in the East have I witnessed so large a proportion of cases of drunkenness as in Japan." He also heard Pompe say that "about one-half of the whole adult population are more or less inebriated by sakee at nine o'clock every morning," and he frequently saw drunk men in the streets and came across bars and liquor stores wherever he went.[10]

The bishop also heard Pompe mention that the food consumed by the lower classes was of the lowest quality and that as their diet consisted of rice, fish, and pickles, it not only reduced their stamina, but also induced their skin diseases. Smith also related from Pompe that even though the laborers and workers appeared to be physically strong, their diet caused them to age prematurely with many thirty-somethings appearing to be in their mid-to-late forties.[11] In Smith's eyes, the Japanese were both morally and physically impoverished.

It should also be noted that Smith came across beggars during his stay in Nagasaki. He initially believed Oliphant and Osborn when they said there were few to no beggars in Japan, so he may have felt as if he had made an important discovery. He said, "Ordinary beggars form a spectacle by no means uncommon in Japan" and being a bishop may have moved to him to offer them help in some way. However, Smith's Japanese acquaintance stopped him from "affording relief even to the sick and diseased, the halt and maimed, the blind and aged, who frequently threw themselves in our way." He also mentioned the following:[12]

> They dissuaded us from giving eleemosynary relief by the assertion that there was no such thing as pauperism in Japan—that a feeling of clanship and the duties of family-relationship were a sufficient safeguard against the prevalence of real destitution and want—that helpless strangers overtaken with disaster or afflicted with sickness are immediately sent back at the public expense to their native districts—and that consequently every beggar in the public streets might reasonably be suspected as being an idle, worthless or dishonest man.

Smith recognized that the "ordinary beggars" he saw were primarily of the religious variety, such as begging monks, mountain priests, and wandering mendicants. He also saw beggars while he was in Edo. It is unclear whether these were religious beggars on a pilgrimage, but it is certain that he witnessed that "One poor mendicant was in close vicinity to a Daimio's palace wall, sitting on a mat by the roadside with his toes eaten away by disease, and silently holding out his hand in mute entreaty for alms," and that "a woman and child were similarly seated on a mat awaiting the casual gift from the passers-by."[13]

It should come as no surprise that Japan had its fair share of beggars. The reason it became an issue definitely related to the widespread notion that Japan was a paradise. In some cases, such as with the British, there was a strong desire to correct the misleading descriptions made by Oliphant and Osborn. Robert Fortune stated:[14]

> Kaempfer informs us that in his time "multitudes of beggars crowded the roads in all parts of the empire, but particularly so on the Tokaido." Some of the members of Lord Elgin's embassy, if I remember right, seem to doubt the truth of this, as they did not meet with any on the occasion of their visit to Kawasaky; but on this occasion beggars were probably kept out of the way by the authorities. Truth compels me to state that at the present day, as in the days of Kaempfer, the beggars in Japan are numerous and importunate. As I rode along the road, there were many who "sat by the wayside begging." These were "the maimed, the halt, the lame, and the blind," who, as I passed by, prostrated themselves on the ground and asked for alms.

Alcock also took note of the beggars. According to him, "A few noisy beggars generally take up their position by the wayside" in the open space near Zōjōji temple.[15] He also said the "many species of them [beggars] which may be studied along the public road to Kanagawa and elsewhere" were beggars by vocation. He continued by saying:[16]

> Then, there is the unsightly, diseased, and generally lachrymose beggar, who seeks to make the desired impression upon you by exhibiting as much misery as possible, bodily and mental, and these are generally crouched on all-fours on a mat by the roadside, in tatters, with uncut hair, their face but a little raised from the ground, unless it be necessary to expose some loathsome limb covered with sores.

Alcock also mentioned something he saw near Fujisawa on the way back from an otherwise pleasant trip to Izu.[17]

> We...passed a dead man on the road, evidently a beggar; so destitution does exist, however rare, and men die on the high roads—at least this one instance seemed to show such things were, even in Japan, though somebody has said or written there were no beggars in Japan.

Rudolf Lindau, however, saw something a little different. He wrote about the beggars with leprosy that approached him at the temple at Kawasaki

Daishi (Heikenji) by saying that, generally speaking, there were hardly any poor people in Japan. He went on to mention that people did not need much money for their material needs, so even the beggars did not have to worry about acquiring the basics. He also said that he rarely saw beggars on the street or along large roadways and almost always saw them hanging around Buddhist temples.[18] In other words, beggars settled down and lived on holy ground.

A similar situation existed near bridges. In 1871, for example, Leroy Lansing Janes (1838–1909), an instructor who went to Kumamoto to teach English, was accosted by beggars who gathered at each bridge he crossed over.[19] Thus, it can be said that the bridges were similar to temples, as well as crossroads, in that they were a type of religious sanctum.

Lindau said the beggars belonged to a special class seen as being impure, so to speak. In other words, outcasts and beggars had a culturally characterized existence and surrounded specially designated areas such as temples, streets, and bridges, and did not regularly wander through cities and villages. If this were truly the case, then we can see why John Reddie Black wrote that the most pleasant characteristic of Japan was its absence of beggars. Black initially believed that an outcast system was in place whereby the police could seize every beggar and keep them in holding facilities hidden from the public eye. Additional research may be needed to determine whether there was some truth to this theory, but at any rate, beggars from Edo-period Japan existed within a different sociocultural context than their counterparts in industrialized societies, as was familiar to Western observers in their own countries. It is also clear this social dissociation process existed in identifying differences between beggars in China and Japan, as Alcock said, "Beggars they certainly are…, but they are far from being either so numerous, or so frequently to be seen at the point of starvation as in the neighboring country of China." According to Alcock, the beggars in Japan seemed to be saying "We are beggars and must live, but there is no need to be miserable about it," based on their demeanor.

Fortune quoted Kaempfer as proof that beggars had existed in great numbers in Japan since long ago, but the people that Kaempfer was talking about were certainly not beggars in today's sense of the word. They were actually wanderers.[20] The first example he gave of beggars gathering on the Tōkaidō were pilgrims on their way to Ise Shrine. In addition, he also categorized pilgrims, ordained Buddhist nuns, mountain priests, and traveling entertainers as beggars. It is true that all of these people depended on alms to complete their journeys, but it goes without saying that their lives as beggars differed from the modern notion of the term, namely that their existence was associated with poverty. Conversely, they were more like the religious wanderers prevalent in much of Western Europe in the Middle Ages. Many observers who visited Japan at the end of the Edo period took a similar view to Kaempfer and simply labeled any religious wanderer they saw as a beggar.

Naturally, we cannot deny the existence of true beggars. Philipp Franz von Siebold, for instance, indicated the existence of a class of outcasts and said that they did not have houses to live in, slept on the

Traveling entertainers (from Alcock, *Tycoon*)

side of the roads they begged on, and asked passersby for charity with their heads down. When they asked for alms, Siebold went on, they would show their deformity or sickness as a way to invite disgust and, consequently, pity.[21] The sights Alcock witnessed, meanwhile, had already been recorded as early as the 1820s. Janes and his wife Harriet, meanwhile, saw the poverty in Kumamoto in 1871. Harriet wrote about her first impression of Kumamoto by saying that "The people looked more miserable and much poorer than in the open ports…It made my heart ache to see the expression of hopelessness on so many faces."[22] We cannot forget that these tragic souls existed in a different context from poor people in industrialized societies, but they certainly made up one part of the dark side of old Japan.

On a side note, Janes, like Pompe, was critical of the Japanese diet.[23] He did not hide his disdain for *sashimi* (raw fish), beans he said were as hard as flint rocks, seaweed stewed in soy sauce, tofu, and foul-smelling *takuan* pickles, and he mentioned that even lords and high officials ate this food. Janes believed eating habits were related to human morality, as well as mental and physical stamina, and went on to say a "diet of dirty sea salt—salt fish, salt radish, salt egg-fruit, salt plums, and salt soy—means a briny and pickled moral state and a desiccated, scurvied condition of every organ and tissue of the body." He also thought the Japanese affinity for raw fish was one of the causes of Hansen's disease.

In addition, Janes was also critical of other Japanese customs. He disliked the practice of heating homes with hibachi braziers, for example, attributing it to cold rooms and, consequently, the onset of tuberculosis. Meanwhile, when Janes returned to Japan again some years later, he was asked by Inoue Kowashi, the Japanese Minister of Education at the time, for advice on how to reform the education system. Janes stunned Inoue by saying that first and foremost, the quality of the kitchens and food at the boardinghouses, as well as student clothing and unheated rooms, needed to be improved.[24] In a way, Janes was like the American occupation forces in Japan at the end of the Second World War in that he proposed reforming every aspect of Japanese society starting with the basic needs of food, clothing, and shelter.

Examples like those listed above clearly show that Western observers were critical of the old Japanese civilization and often even opposed it with disgust. However, it is still remarkable to see how the same critics also admired Japan with great passion and even awe. The mysterious civilization they encountered still managed to pull them in with its charm, and this led them to praise it even though they were well aware of its dark underbelly. Their descriptions tell us that, as Gustav Spiess put it,[25] there was indeed a serpent in this garden of Eden. We can also see why many of them felt Japan was an "elf-land."

Above all, the foreign observers were impressed by the aforementioned politeness and courtesy of the Japanese people. James Curtis Hepburn (1815–1911), a missionary who visited Japan in 1859, stated immediately after arriving in the country that the people were polite and friendly.[26] Samuel Robbins Brown (1810–1880), who also came to Japan in 1859 and lived in the same temple as Hepburn, echoed much of what Hepburn had to say.[27] This shows that it was common knowledge that the Japanese were polite and courteous. However, the observers did not stop there. As we have already seen, they also wrote that the Japanese were pure and childlike, affable, good-natured, curious, and had a zest for life.

An example of the Japanese curiosity occurred when a number of people noticed that Jephson and Elmhirst's summer uniforms differed from those of the regiment they had replaced. They wrote that "The lower orders of the Japanese are wonderfully inquisitive and observant" and described this episode by saying, "This fact was soon made the subject of endless inquiries. The next stage was the manipulating one, when we all had to submit to being turned round and round, and having every part of our dress examined minutely."[28] Jephson and Elmhirst may have found this experience a bit strange, but certainly not unpleasant.

Meanwhile, I mentioned in an earlier chapter that the kitchen at the lodging where Sherard Osborn's party stayed became the target of the people's curiosity. He wrote about this episode by saying, "It would indeed have been unreasonable to have resented their inquisitiveness; and if we ever did so, they immediately recalled us to our senses by a good-humoured laugh."[29]

There were also descriptions attesting to the childlike innocence and open nature of the Japanese. For example, many Japanese people apparently thought the foreign visitors could understand and speak Japanese. As Albert Berg mentioned, the Japanese thought their language was the only one in the world and did not grasp the concept of foreign languages.[30] Morse also mentioned this fact, saying:[31]

Inquisitive people (illustration by Régamey, from Guimet, *Promenades Japonaises*)

> In meeting people at the teahouses along the road it is impossible to make them comprehend that you do not understand a word they say; they keep talking to you, and generally in a louder tone, imagining you are deaf, or they have an expression on their faces as if they considered you an idiot or mentally weak. In vain you say "Wakarimasen," the Japanese for "I do not understand"; finally, I would say to them earnestly, "What is your opinion of the Kansas and Nebraska Compromise?" at which they would look at me inquiringly and then grunt or laugh heartily, appreciating the point.

In other words, the Japanese opened their hearts to the foreign visitors and, as Chamberlain said, identified with them as fellow human beings. Much of this may have related to the free and open way of life in Edo society, an important characteristic of the city and its people. The complete openness of Japanese homes even shocked the foreign observers at first. Alcock, for instance, stated:[32]

> All the shops have open fronts, and give a view right through the interior to the inevitable little garden at the back, and the inmates of the house sit, work, and play in full view, whatever may be the occupation in hand—the morning meal, the afternoon siesta, or the later ablutions, the household work of the women, the play of their nude progeny, or the trade and handicraft of the men—each house is converted into a microcosm where the Japanese may be studied in all their aspects.

Morse, meanwhile, said, "Nothing illustrates more clearly the simple and open character of the common people than the sketch which I got in my ride from Yokohama." He went on to describe the scene he saw when he entered a Japanese home at night:[33]

I wandered into a house to sketch the *kamidana* with its light burning at night, when I observed the woman of the house sound asleep and the child she had been nursing sound asleep also. I could not resist making an illustration of the fact that the houses are literally open to any one who has the impertinence to intrude.

Incidentally, Morse's sketch actually shows a topless woman wearing only a waistcloth.

Henry Holmes (dates unknown), the captain of a British trading ship who came to Nagasaki in 1859 to

Sleeping woman (illustration by Morse, from Morse, *Day by Day*)

seek trade relations, gave another example of this openness. During his stay, he often went out into the city in the early morning and entered houses in which the occupants were still sleeping. He said that "To enter a house I had only a sliding door to push back. There were no locks or bolts." He also went on to say, "If I disturbed the sleepers it was taken in good part," and "I enjoyed in rolling and tumbling with the whole family on the floor, not in one house, but in many."[34] Even setting Holmes's somewhat unbelievable adventures aside, it is an undeniable fact that Japanese homes were completely open to the outside world, and, as Hübner described, if someone did wander into a house unannounced, the intruder was granted free rein to look at and fiddle with things. Hübner went on to state:[35]

> They [the buildings] are completely open towards the street and the court…In walking along the streets, the eye takes in all the details of the interior of these houses. Domestic life is entirely open to the inquisitive passers-by. There is nothing to hide.

Having free and open homes meant that the Japanese people could easily view their neighbors' lives and this led to a strong sense of friendliness and solidarity with each other. The same could also be said for their lives on the street, at the wells, and at areas for bathing and washing. Every aspect of society was open. Children only went inside when it was time to eat or sleep and spent most of their time playing in the streets. Henry Faulds wrote:[36]

> A great deal of Japanese life is passed in the streets, and can best be seen there. In the good times for which old-fashioned Japanese people sigh, much more of the domestic doings were visible to the public than would now be considered comely or proper…The houses are open from floor to roof in warm weather, and concealment is nearly

impossible; and at night, when the paper windows are drawn closely together, you may see a painful tragedy or side-splitting comedy enacted in shadow by the unconscious inmates.

Edouard Suenson (1842–1921), a Dane who traveled to Japan as a member of the French navy and stayed there from 1866 to 1867, also mentioned that the happenings of a Japanese household were almost always open for the world to see. Therefore, he reasoned, if one were to remain standing in front of any given Japanese home from morning until evening, he or she could get an accurate view of how the occupants lived. This would include anything from arguments between husbands and wives to every other kind of conflict imaginable. The combatants simply ignored anyone who may have been watching. Meanwhile, half-naked women putting on makeup never showed any sign of embarrassment even if they made eye contact with Westerners passing by outside.[37]

We can also say that the Japanese not only opened their homes to visitors that they had never met before, but also their hearts. In 1862, during a stay in Kanazawa—just a village in the countryside outside Yokohama at the time—Rudolf Lindau said that he saw bright lights and heard the lively sound of shamisen and koto coming from the second floor of a home on the opposite side of the canal from his inn. It appeared that the people were celebrating something, so Lindau decided to visit the home and investigate. He wrote:[38]

> The occupants of the house were quite startled to see this unexpected guest, and I think they even felt a little uneasy with me at first. However, after I explained that I wanted to cross the canal to get a closer look at the house from which this music was coming from, they finally laughed and welcomed me into their abode.

Lindau mentioned there were four married couples and two children on the second floor along with four Japanese entertainers. They welcomed him with food and drink and allowed him to join their happy gathering for over an hour. The Japanese were not nervous around the foreign visitor, approached him with innocent curiosity, and enjoyed watching him fumble with his chopsticks. They even went out of their way to walk Lindau back to his inn after the festivities had ended.

Vittorio F. Arminjon (1830–1897), an Italian navy commander who visited Japan in 1866 to sign a trade agreement between the two countries, also commented on the openness of the Japanese and felt that there was no other country in the world in which the people of the lower classes looked so satisfied and content. We should pay attention to the following description he gave:[39]

Poverty hardly appears as a dark and tragic entity in the lives of the Japanese. The people are friendly and willingly help others. Therefore, no one suffers from hunger at any level of society except unknown individuals who do not deserve the compassion of society.

In other words, Arminjon said the common people of the Edo period lived satisfied lives due to members of the same community helping each other. Naturally, this mutual willingness to help others had something to do with the conventions and systems in place in Japan at the time, but strong ties with neighbors brought about by the free and open way of life mentioned above had a more-significant effect.

This open and friendly society was also peaceful and safe. We know from Holmes's aforementioned description that people in the Edo period usually did not lock their doors at night. In fact, this custom remained relatively common all the way up to the second world war in small cities in the Japanese countryside. Moreover, farmers living in small villages never locked their doors. Arthur Crow wrote the following about his experience on Nakasendō Road in 1881;[40]

> Most of the villages were deserted, their inhabitants, men, women, and children (above ten years) being away in the muddy rice-fields. It says a great deal for the honesty of the people that they are not afraid to leave their houses for the whole day without lock and key or protection of any sort.

Pompe backed up this claim. During his five years (1858–1893) living on Dejima in Nagasaki, for example, he never gave any thought to locking the door to his home.[41] Oliphant also related the following about his party staying on the grounds of Saiōji temple:[42]

> As locks and keys did not exist, our rooms were open to the incursions of any of the numerous attendants who swarmed about our lodgings, and though we left the most tempting English curiosities constantly displayed, yet we never had to complain of a single article missing, even of the most trifling value.

Meanwhile, Carl Munzinger (1864–1937), a German missionary who came to Japan in 1890, wrote that he never locked up any of his belongings, including small sums of money, but never once had anything stolen.[43] Naturally, the Japanese used locks on storehouses and other buildings to protect their goods, but as Morse described in his famous book *Japanese Homes*, usually "the only night-lock the house possesses is attached to them [the *amado* shut-ters]." Morse added that "So feeble are these devices that they would hardly withstand the attack of a toothpick in the hands of a sneak-thief. To a Japa-nese our houses must appear like veritable prisons with locks, bolts, and automatic catches at every opening."[44] Over the course of his stay in Japan, Morse enjoyed living in a country in which he did not have to constantly keep an eye on his pocketbook. He was also pleasantly surprised by the fact that an umbrella or other article he may have left on a bench somewhere would turn up again unscathed. He wrote:[45]

It is delightful to be in a country where the people are so honest. I never think of keeping my hand on my wallet or watch. On my table, with my door unlocked, I leave my small change, and the Japanese boy or man coming in fifty times a day leaves untouched everything he should not touch. He took my ulster and spring overcoat to clean, and soon came back with some small change which he found in one of the pockets; then he returned again bringing three San Francisco horse-car tickets.

In addition, the owners of Japanese shops were often absent from their estab-lishments. On one occasion, Morse waited twenty minutes for one shop owner to return before getting angry and going to the neighboring store to relay the message that he wanted to buy something when he came back. It appalled to him that shoplifters hardly ever wreaked havoc in these unmanned stores.[46] On another occasion, Morse stayed at an inn in Hiroshima and decided to stay at the same one on the way back from his travels. Therefore, he decided to leave his watch and some money there. The female servant just placed his belongings on a tray. Morse was worried and asked the innkeeper if he could store them somewhere safe, but the proprietor casually replied that the tray was just fine and that the inn did not have a safe anyway. When Morse came back a week later, "every bit of change to the last cent, and the watch, of course, were in the open tray as I had left them."[47]

Despite all of these reports, however, thieves naturally existed in Japan and burglary was quite common. James Hepburn, for instance, penned a letter just after landing in Japan that said thieves were rampant in Japan and he insisted that Nagasaki, which he visited before traveling to Kanagawa and staying at Jōbutsuji temple, was the worst.[48] George Smith was also caustic on this point. He said that stealing was the "most unamiable part of their [the Japanese] character" and mentioned that they could easily hide stolen goods in the sleeves of their kimonos. He also mentioned that even a guardsman at the temple he stayed at in Nagasaki was in the habit of steal-ing firewood and rice.[49]

However, we have to consider what Rudolf Lindau said in relation to Hepburn and Smith's observations. Lindau claimed that in Japan, as in China, the good and friendly native society had completely disappeared in areas controlled by the Europeans. He said that the laborers in Dejima had all gone bad and the merchants in Yokohama were becoming more difficult to deal with every day.[50] Whatever may have happened to the Japanese character, it is clear the Western observers were impressed by how safe Japanese society was in the nineteenth century. Bird's writings attest to this because she stated that Japan was safe enough for a woman to traverse on her own. She reinforced this point with two such trips to the Japanese countryside.

Japanese society was extremely open, and the people were friendly, but it was also peaceful and did not see much fighting among the people. Henry Palmer wrote the following about a group of pilgrims that he saw in Yamada on their way to Ise Shrine at the beginning of 1887:[51]

> The people, after all, are the great charm of Japan…Surely, for happiness, gentleness, and sobriety, for soft-voiced and always smiling chatter, for the blessed faculty of inhaling healthful enjoyment from the simplest things, and for the lucky possession of bodies and limbs that hours upon hours of weary tramping and sight-seeing are utterly unable to exhaust, no other country can even profess to show the match of a festival crowd in Japan. Police in such a throng, it seems to us, can have nothing to do…Happy-hearted and kindly poor of Japan! How contented they look, how cheery, and always how clean!

As I mentioned earlier, Palmer lived in Japan for eight years. Thus, such an observation is significant coming from someone who lived in the country for so long. Morse also wrote about the gentle and orderly nature of peaceful Japanese crowds. When he went to see the Sumida River festival, for instance, he noted that even though the boats floating here and there created a congested mess, there was "not a cross word in all this confusion," and he only heard "Arigato" ("Thank you") and "Go men na sai" ("Excuse me"). He continued by saying "Such a lesson in refinement and gentleness, and from boatmen too! Little by little the realization of why the Japanese have always called us barbarians is dawning upon us."[52] Morse also thought, "A book might be written on the lower working classes of Japan; their honesty, frugality, politeness, cleanliness, and every virtue that in our country might be called Christian."[53]

In addition, Morse attended a sumo bout and noted the "perfect quiet and order prevailing" among the spectators and that "when the show was over and they all came swarming out, there was no crowding, pushing, or loud talking, no rushing to whiskey saloons," behavior that he attributed to Americans back home. He also said, "The Japanese may be considered a temperate race" and that "Thus far, I have seen no staggering drunkards." During Morse's stay in Japan, he also witnessed one fight, an episode he considered unique and remarkable. He described the situation as follows, contrasting it with fights in his home country:[54]

> To describe our street fight would be unnecessary, as all know that from the smallest boy to the old man a crowd instantly gathers, forms a ring, and watches the combat with excited interest, admiring the punches and regretfully departing when the battle is finished or the police interfere. In the Japanese affair the men were simply pulling hair! I was the only one that watched. Every one else showed disgust or horror at such a breach of good manners, and a wide berth was given the fighters, people actually turning aside in passing.

Morse also noticed that foreign visitors who had been in Japan for a few months were surprised and disappointed to find that "those virtues or attributes which, under the name of humanity are the burden of our moral teaching at home, the Japanese people seem to be born with." He backed this up by saying these attributes were "characteristic, not only of the more favored classes, but the possession of the poorest among them."

Thus, Morse lauded the morals and good manners of the Japanese people. This is a bit confusing because on one hand we have records that describe how well the Japanese behaved, while others decried the rampant drunkenness they saw. Smith, for example, often saw staggering drunkards in Nagasaki, and Pompe noted how after 9 p.m., half the people walking through the streets of Nagasaki were drunk. Fortune also said, "All Yedo gets drunk after sunset." He continued by saying:[55]

> This is, of course, an exaggeration; but, no doubt, drunkenness prevails to a degree happily unknown in other countries at the present day. Even before the evening closes in, the faces of those one meets in the streets are suspiciously red, showing plainly enough that saki has been imbibed pretty freely.

Meanwhile, if we look at the journal kept by Kawai Koume, wife of Kishū domain Confucian scholar Kawai Baisho, the entry dated August 1, 1849 reads: "2.7 liters of sake were ordered and cost 2 monme in silver. Citron sake was also made there. The place soon became quite noisy and the patrons somewhat wild and unrestrained." If we read even further, we can see that sake was actually consumed on a daily basis at this house. Kawai wrote that the amount of sake needed for the year came to about 345 liters, which means that about two liters were consumed every two days.[56]

Furthermore, other descriptions written by Westerners show us that they felt their lives were in danger from drunken samurai who strode about. Shinagawa was a particularly notorious place. In fact, Raphael Pumpelly was passing through Shinagawa one day when he ran into eight to ten drunken samurai who "dashed into the street just ahead of us, flourishing their drawn swords and acting like devils."[57] It was clear to Pumpelly and he could not help writing that drinking was a major vice among the Japanese.

Morse himself later said that "during the Tokugawa shogunate the drinking of sake was much more common than at present. At that time sake was always offered to a friend when calling, and it was considered an offense to refuse it."[58] If this were the case, then in just a dozen years or so, there must have been a dramatic change in the basic custom of drinking sake. Or it could be that Morse's descriptions about drinking simply testified to the austere character of the Meiji people. Street fights, after all, were one of the "spectacles" of the Edo period, along with fires (We will see how group fighting in the Edo period led to bloodshed and even death in a later chapter of this book). In Morse's case, what he described may also have been the result of the new Meiji government providing education to the masses. It may sound like Morse was joking when he said that the Japanese were "inclined to sing instead of to fight, as is the common impulse with the Anglo-Saxon and the Irish, and particularly the Irish," but he was, in fact, quite serious.

In addition, Morse also saw and wrote about how Japanese crowds did not push each other, but Katherine Sansom (1883–1981), who was the wife of famous Japanese historian George Sansom and lived in Tokyo in the early Shōwa period, said, "But here in Japan the pushing and scrambling goes on regardless of whether there is any need for it." She also wrote:[59]

> Well then, you get past the ticket examiner in due course and make your way to the train in company with these urgently pushing people. And who are they? The worst offender is quite likely some elderly woman with gentle eyes and mouth, so small that you feel you might pick her up and carry her without any trouble.

Did Morse spoil us with exaggerated observations, or did a huge change in the Japanese moral character actually take place between his time and Sansom's time? Before pondering this question, we have to take note of the testimony of other foreign observers that strongly supported Morse's descriptions. Mexican astronomer Diaz Covarrubias, for example, said the following:[60]

> The most fascinating thing about the Japanese is that they are an extremely modest and intrinsically obedient and orderly people. During the celebrations that took place when the Emperor and a lady of the court had their first daughter and when Ambassador Okubo returned with reparations from China concerning the Taiwan issue, as well as many other events, the 60,000 to 70,000 people living in Yokohama, a city of Kanagawa, did not engage in any kind of fighting or drunkenness, and I was blessed with being able to see and enjoy light displays, fireworks, strange silent plays performed by actors in animal costumes, and other festivities. I did not come across a single drunkard in the streets at any of the festivals I attended.

Meanwhile, John Russell Young (1840–1899), who accompanied U.S. General Ulysses S. Grant on his visit to Japan in 1879, wrote the following about the crowd in Ueno Park on the day of the welcome party for the American entourage:[61]

> What you note in a Japanese crowd is the lightness and gayety of the people, the smiling faces, the fun-loving eyes. Moreover, you know the good order, the perfect order, the courtesy, the kind feeling…The good-humor and patience of the crowd seemed to have no end.

Palmer had the same feeling about a celebration he witnessed on the day the 1889 Meiji Constitution was issued. He wrote:[62]

> Pleasant also, and again peculiarly Japanese, is the behavior of the crowd. That there is much crushing is, in the nature of things, inevitable. But nowhere else, assuredly, than in Japan could be seen the perfect patience, politeness, and gentleness, and good-humour that mark the vast throngs which press this evening through the streets of Tokio.

One could argue and, indeed, there is a tendency to accept these descriptions as historical documents that prove how powerfully the Meiji government controlled the people at these national events. However, Rudolf Lindau provided older testimony about the orderly nature of crowds at festivals, countering the notion that it was a Meiji phenomenon. In Lindau's case, he viewed the Nagasaki guardian deity festival in 1861 and wrote that the crowd was quiet and there were no fights. A strange liveliness pervaded throughout the city, but at the same time, perfect order was maintained.[63] In addition, police officers were not responsible for maintaining this order.

Isabella Bird, meanwhile, saw a festival at Akita's Tsuchizaki Harbor in 1878 and wrote:[64]

> The police told me that there were 22,000 strangers in Minato, yet for 32,000 holiday-makers a force of twenty-five policemen was sufficient. I did not see one person under the influence of sake up to 3 p.m., when I left, nor a solitary instance of rude or improper behavior, nor was I in any way rudely crowded upon, for even where the crowd was densest, the people of their own accord formed a ring and left me breathing space.

This alludes to another point, namely that Japanese commoners viewed the foreign observers as a distinct class of nobles. Moreover, the shogunate allowed them to ride horses across the country, a right typically reserved for the warrior class, the highest rank in Japanese society at the time. All of the observers who rode horses in Japan also hired grooms, which, according to Pumpelly, was another "luxury permitted only to officers." Pumpelly also went on to say that the Japanese "look with wonder on a European merchant riding in a saddle and keeping running footmen."[65] If this were the case, then we have to consider that the Japanese yielded to Lindau and Bird as they passed along the road during the festivals because they viewed them as nobles. Based on what Bird saw, however, the Japanese crowds were "quiet and gentle," did not push against each other, and made way for everyone, not just those at the top of the social hierarchy.[66]

We can also see strong support for Morse's descriptions in a number of passages written by Léon Metchnikoff, an instructor who taught Russian at the Tokyo School of Foreign Languages from 1874 to 1875. When Metchnikoff was taken to the two theaters competing for first place among all of the playhouses in Edo, he saw a great many people packed like sardines into the buildings, women baring their breasts to nurse their babies, and men who were just wearing loincloths. He thought the scene resembled a direct democracy from ancient Greece, but he also noted there was no chaos or pushing at these gatherings. He also stated:[67]

> In this country, even the poorest and most exhausted laborer does not stray from courtesy and etiquette… Even though I lived in the district of Edo with the largest number of commoners per capita for two years, I never once saw any Japanese arguing with each other. What's more, fistfights are almost never seen in any part of the city. There aren't even curse words in the Japanese language! Words like *"baka"*

["idiot"] and "*chikusho*" ["damnit"] are the extreme limit by which the Japanese insult others.

Bousquet's descriptions also fell in line with Morse's writings. He said:[68]

> Looking down from one of the many wooden bridges that span the Okawa River, one can see the ships riding the rising tides with their sails up and slowly coming in from the sea. This organization of boatmen, namely sailors, is one of the most unimpressive groups of laborers I have ever seen. However, they do not show any roughness in appearance, and they work together to steer their boats by barking orders at their respective crews. Calling other people names is extremely rare even among the lower classes... Fighting, arguing, and assaults do not exist at all in the conventional sense. There is none of the violence or restlessness exhibited by similarly busy throngs of people in my homeland.

Bousquet also noted that, even after the fireworks display on the river was over and the crowds began to disperse, there were no violent boat accidents among those that were trying to steer out through the confusion and no harsh words were exchanged.

Harsh critics of Japan even praised the peaceful amiability of the Japanese. George Smith, for instance, claimed there were "no fights, quarrels, or violence in the streets."[69] Meanwhile, Carl Munzinger, who built upon the stereotypical images of Japan in his initial criticisms of the country, remarked that the violent beer-fueled fights that often broke out in his native Germany did not occur that often in Japan. He also noted that the people hardly ever insulted one another and curse words were all but unknown. In addition, he mentioned that even when rickshaw drivers collided with each other, they would gracefully bow to one another and politely ask for forgiveness for any offense they may have caused.[70]

Furthermore, Walter G. Dickson (dates unknown), a Briton who visited Japan both before and after the Meiji Restoration, wrote that "during all my travels in Japan, I do not recollect of seeing two men really angry or quarreling, with high words, and certainly never once saw (what one sees daily in China) two women quarreling or using very questionable words to each other."[71] Therefore, as Morse and many other observers described, it certainly seemed like the Japanese from the end of the Edo period until the middle of the Meiji period were an extremely peaceful and courteous people who hardly ever argued or quarreled with one another and did not push each other in theaters or other throngs.

There are obviously examples that can be found to counter this view, however. According to Émile Guimet, for instance, a rickshaw driver insulted another such driver pulling his own rickshaw through a crowd of people enjoying a festival in Nihonbashi. This incensed Guimet's driver, who attacked the other driver without caring about what happened to either his rickshaw or its occupant. However, we cannot read into this too deeply because no society is completely free from arguments and other squabbles. Thus, this is not the best example to counter the argument that the Japanese hardly ever fought with each other.

Aimé Humbert, on the other hand, provided an argument to the contrary. He wrote that the laborers, sailors, and grooms living on both sides of the Sumida River were quite boorish and they constantly engaged in fights and power struggles. He also mentioned these quarrels were solved by tug of war battles on bridges. He wrote:[72]

> The highlight of this contest is the end. This is because the men on the losing team get pulled, roll over, and come tumbling down together in a heap. Even more amusing is when the rope suddenly breaks and members of both teams all cry out in loud voices and hit the ground at the same time. The indescribable sound is almost deafening, and everyone starts wandering around this way and that in a fit of dizziness and confusion. Then, they pick themselves up, stretch and shake out their bodies, and erupt in laughter. Finally, when all is said and done, the opponents go and meet each other on the bridge, break off into twos and threes, and find their way into one of the tea-houses that dot the area. This is when the sake drinking begins in earnest and when the competitors make amends with each swig of their drinks. The referees, rope-pullers, women, and passersby, as well as people from both sides of the river, take part in the festivities, which continue until the district gates close for the night.

As we can see in Humbert's example, there was indeed a fight, but the combatants had solved their problems in the end. Thus, Humbert's description actually does more to prove the innocence and goodwill among the Japanese people. According to sociologist Kato Hidetoshi, meanwhile, the Japanese seldom used violence even in fights, one of the "spectacles" of Edo, and would, more often than not, put their pride to the test in competition. As we shall see in a later chapter, street gang violence that caused deaths was a completely different problem that went far beyond social disputes within certain communities.

Others mentioned the peaceful nature of the Japanese. Diaz Covarrubias, for example, said no one ever stole any of his things during his stay at the observatory established in Nogeyama. He also said that he often went out into the middle of nowhere at night unarmed and guided by rickshaw drivers that he did not know, but he was never mugged or insulted by anyone. He praised Japan by saying it was the only country in which he could do this and come out unscathed.[73]

Diaz Covarrubias was also impressed by how rickshaw drivers never fought over customers and how they decided who would get a job via lots or straws. Morse had an almost identical experience. He wrote:[74]

> In coming from the University I walked up to a group of four jinriki-sha men and wondered if they would all rush for me as do our hack-men back home; but, no, one of them stooped down, picked up four straws of various lengths, and then drew lots. No feeling was shown as the lucky one drew me away to the station. Time had to be made to catch the train and during the ride the wheel of my jinrikisha bumped into the hub of another one ahead. The men simply smiled their apologies for getting in the way, and kept on. I instantly contrasted this behavior and the customary swearing resulting from a similar accident back home.

William Dixon also wrote about a similar experience he had, writing:[75]

> Throughout the city [of Tokyo] there are regular stances, at each of which there may be four or five to a dozen men. Instead of quarreling over a "fare," their plan is to draw lots by means of a bundle of cords of unequal lengths. This they may do on a chance of an engagement from some one they see approaching. If the expected fare passes without taking a *kuruma*, his mind having already been made up to walk, the laugh is turned upon the poor *jin-riki-ya* who has drawn the successful cord, a laugh in which he is fain to join.

Pierre Loti (1850–1923), who visited Kyoto in 1885, had a different experience in which he was suddenly assailed by a group of rickshaw drivers when he came out of the station. He also wrote that they argued with and pushed each other in an attempt to get him to ride in their vehicle.[76] Perhaps society had changed by Loti's time. However, there is evidence that rickshaw drivers still used lots to choose customers as late as 1891 in Kyoto, as E. Cavaglion, a French tourist, described in his writings.[77]

Cavaglion and many other observers felt the Japanese were a peaceful people who were not prone to fighting, but they also admired how courteous and graceful they were. Beauvoir, for instance, was impressed by the elegant manners of a woman who offered him tea and tobacco at the store he entered. Seeing this "simple womanly graciousness" caused him to "acknowledge the right this people has of calling us barbarians." In the streets he saw "all the men in greeting and bowing low to one another have always a smile on their lips." He also wrote the following about his travels into the countryside:[78]

> There, as elsewhere along the road, it is impossible to express how we were surprised at the civility and amiability of the entire population. "Anāta! Ohāio!" (good day, I salute you) the young girls called out smilingly as we passed their tea-houses at a gallop. "Ohāio," said all the labourers, who left their pitchforks in the rice-field to run and look at us, and smile at us from the edge of the path. "Ohāio, omedetto!" such were the words of all the travellers, men and women, who crossed our route. Yes, you must come to Japan to see how the traveller is received, feted, and made much of, by the country people. They certainly are the most polished people on the earth.

Even Morse felt that the polite demeanor and kindness the Japanese displayed when interacting with others was an intrinsic virtue of their character. He was surprised to find that "You buy some trifle in a shop, and passing the place a week after, the shopkeeper recognizes you and thanks you again."[79] Morse would later move to Enoshima to set up a coastal laboratory and he was deeply impressed by the fact that the poor fishermen and merchants living there were "so sweet and gentle that it is impossible to swear or show the slightest impatience." He wrote:[80]

That others also feel this is shown by a remark made by an American who belongs to the highest rank of society at home. We were at a country inn for a few days. After a polite concession to some of our mistakes by one of the maids, he said, 'The manners and refinement of these people are equal, if not superior, to those of our best society at home.'

A rickshaw driver (illustration by Régamey, from Guimet, *Promenades Japonaises*)

One day, Morse also traveled into a rather squalid district in Tokyo. The Japanese officials who accompanied him even said the slums they were entering were one of the worst parts of the city. However, he wrote, "I heard no loud cries or shouting, [and] saw no blear-eyed drunkards or particularly dirty children." He went on to write:[81]

> For a hundred children picked from what might be called slums, though slums they were not, I would venture that they were more polite and graceful in manner, less selfish, more considerate for the feeling of others than a hundred children picked at random from upper Fifth Avenue, New York.

William Dixon commented on the good manners he often saw when rickshaw drivers would come and help others struggling to pull their carts up steep hills. Those who helped received a bow and a word of thanks as a reward. This even happened between runners who had never met each other before. Dixon also related how a medical missionary living in Tokyo was approached by a rickshaw driver who respectfully asked if he could give him a ride to his home. Once they arrived, the runner refused to accept the missionary's money when he tried to pay. Apparently, the missionary had cared for the runner's friend when he was sick, so he wanted to return the favor. After saying this, the runner simply bowed and was on his way again.[82]

Edwin Arnold also mentioned the following about the kindness of rickshaw drivers:[83]

> When you send out to your Kurumaya a cup of tea and a saucer of boiled rice, and hear afterwards his grateful words, you wonder whether he is of the same race as that which you left quaffing half-and-half and eating rump-steaks on the banks of the Thames.

Arnold also wrote the following about the crowds he saw in Nakadōri and Ginza in 1889:[84]

> A happier looking population can nowhere be studied; they go chattering and laughing along, the porters singing between their balanced burdens, the air all full, far or near, of pretty salutations—"O hayo! O hayo gozaimas!" or "Sayonara! sayonara!" and at evening, "O yasumi nasai!" ("Condescend to take honorable repose!") The deep reverences these little people make to each other in the street are charming for grace and general goodwill—the commonest coolie bends with the air

of a finished teacher or deportment when he meets a friend or accepts an engagement.

Arnold mentioned that people living in the countryside were no different. He continued by writing the following:[85]

> As you pass through the villages lining the high roads, the little ones, waddling about on wooden pattens, with their smaller brothers and sisters strapped upon their backs, wag their shaven heads and bend low—shaking the baby altogether out of position—uttering cheerful and friendly *Ohayos*! The very baby, if he can say anything at all, blinks with his tiny almond eyes, and nods his small poll, and babbles "*Hayo! Hayo!*" to the passing wayfarer. At the tea-houses, when all is paid, and there is nothing more to expect, the girls will offer the departing guest a bunch of chrysanthemums, or a red or a white camellia, and to whatever expressions of thanks you employ, the pretty answer is, "What have I done?" ("*Dō itashimashita?*")

Arnold also said:[86]

> I feel how utterly indescribable it all is, even while trying to describe this unique, unparalleled, unspoiled, astonishing, fascinating, sweet-tempered Japan. After two months spent in their midst, I have to repeat what I ventured to say after two weeks, that nowhere, for the lover of good manners, is there a country so reposeful, so refreshing, so full of antique grace, and soft, fair courtesies as this "Land of the Rising Sun." Only go among them with goodwill and sympathy, and—whatever your blunders of deportment and language—you will meet here from all ranks of the people a refinement of politeness and a charm of intercourse nowhere else experienced.

As we can see, the Japanese displayed good manners in almost every corner of society. Diaz Covarrubias, for example, said he was always pleasantly surprised to see Japanese travelers at the train station because they would never crowd up around a ticket booth or by the door of a train, and when they got in line they always remained where they were and never tried to cut in front of others.[87] Naturally, we cannot deny the fact that the Japanese acted this way because the railroads had just come to Japan and they approached the experience as if they were going out on the town. In other words, they were on their best behavior.

Later observations contrasted with what Diaz Covarrubias saw. Chamberlain, for example, said that "a railway journey in this country is apt to be anything but a joy." His reason for saying this was that "the Japanese who, when abiding in their own native ways, are the very pink of neatness, become slipshod, not to say dirty, when introduced to certain conditions of European life."[88] He went into the details of this by mentioning the orange peels and used cigar butts that littered the floor of the train, passengers with disheveled clothing, passengers brazenly changing in front of everyone, and even one passenger who had removed his false teeth and proceeded to clean them. Chamberlain was a bit disturbed by what he saw and concluded that the Japanese abandoned all sense of shame when they traveled. In a way, the scenes he saw resembled the way some people relax in Japanese-style rooms found on special "parlor trains" today, which have tatami mats and low tables.

Not everyone shared Chamberlain's views, however. Isabella Bird, for instance, painted a completely different picture of the Japanese travelers. In 1878, she boarded a train bound for Kyoto in Kobe and rode in a third-class car. She wrote the following about her experience:[89]

> We travelled third class, as I was most anxious to see how the "common people" behaved. The carriage was not divided higher than the shoulders, and was at once completely filled with Japanese of the poorest class. The journey lasted three hours, and I unweariedly admired the courtesy of the people to each other and to us, and their whole behaviour. It was beautiful—so well bred and kindly, such a contrast to what one would probably have seen near great seaport cities at home; and the Japanese, like the Americans, respect themselves and their neighbours by travelling in decent and cleanly clothing. Respect to age and blindness came out very prettily on the journey. Our best manners fall short of theirs in grace and kindliness.

Henry Faulds also described a station scene he saw in 1874. He wrote that Japanese people standing in line to board the train would often stand to the side and bow deeply to the station workers in their golden-laced uniforms. He mentioned how they would sometimes even take off their clogs before boarding the train and joked that they expected "to find them lying there when he should arrive at his destination!"[90] Faulds may have been poking fun at the people getting on the train, but he was actually witnessing the mannerisms of a beautifully simple and honest people.

Sugimoto Etsuko, also known as Etsu Inagaki

On the train (from Régamey, *Japon*)

Sugimoto (1873–1950) actually wrote about taking her own clogs off prior to boarding a train in her book *A Daughter of the Samurai*. Sugimoto was born in 1873, so this episode took place when she was in her early twenties. She was on her way to Tokyo to enter a mission school and first traveled from Echigo Nagaoka to Takasaki. There she saw a train for the first time in her life. She wrote:[91]

> I have little recollection of anything except a scolding from Brother, because I, feeling that I was entering some kind of house, stepped out of my wooden shoes, leaving them on the platform. Just before the train started, they were handed in at the window by an official whose duty it was to gather all the shoes from the platform before the starting of every train.

Passengers on boats and ships exhibited similar behavior to those on the trains. W. G. Dickson, for example, boarded a steam ship on the Tone River for part of his journey to Nikko in 1873. He had to stay overnight in a small cabin on the boat, so he was advised to charter the room for himself. He wrote:[92]

> As we never found anything but courtesy from the Japanese, and in their company one is not exposed to the objectionable practices of Chinese in belching, spitting, hawking, blowing their noses with one finger, and other minor annoyances to ear and eye and nose, I determined to go in the first-class cabin, and to take only my share of it.

Dickson went on to say the cabin was small, yet clean, and was occupied by a dozen or so passengers. He also added that "in everything and from every one there was nothing but civility and good-nature."

The foreign observers were well aware that the Japanese people were courteous and composed themselves with excellent manners, but what surprised the observers more than anything was the way the Japanese bowed back and forth to one another for extended periods of time on the street and in buildings. Kattendijke wrote:[93]

> The courtesy of the Japanese truly exceeds the bounds of reason and enters the realm of the absurd. First-time visitors to Japan may see two normal, run-of-the-mill Japanese meet each other in the street and start bowing to one another back and forth, all the while blabbing away in incessant chatter. When the visitor sees how long this goes on, they may even grow irritated and angry.

A Japanese salutation (from Alcock, *Tycoon*)

When Alcock first landed in Nagasaki it was a holiday, so many people in the streets were wearing nice clothes. However, Alcock immediately tuned in to the way the people were "exchanging grave and courteous salutations as they met." He went on to say they bent over "with their hands sliding down to their knees, and uttering their greetings with a deep-drawn inspiration."[94]

Tronson encountered a similar scene as soon as he landed in Hakodate. He wrote:[95]

> When two persons, acquaintances, meet, on approaching they both make a low bow, passing the hands down the legs, and bending the body so as to rest the hands below the knees; they also make a deep inspiration, sounding some aspirate, something like 'Oh' slowly pronounced, and pass on their way.

Jephson and Elmhirst, meanwhile, described the bowing they saw in Yokohama in the following way:[96]

> Instead of the Japanese being the uncivilised barbarians that Englishmen are apt to imagine them, no people in the world are more polished in their manner, not only towards strangers, but each other. Even among the lower classes, two friends meeting in the street never approach until after bowing low two or three times in succession, while making that peculiar hissing noise that they use to convey a greeting. On parting, the same process is repeated, with the addition of compliments, good wishes, etc. Indeed, when two officials come into each other's presence on a visit of ceremony, the interchange of mutual homage is almost ludicrous to watch.

Tilley's depiction of people bowing in Nagasaki is quite detailed. He wrote:[97]

> The common mode of salutation is to bend nearly double and remain so for some time in conversation…It is a most amusing sight to see two old women bobbing thus, and chattering for half an hour before either one or the other will give in. The men generally salute one another in the same manner, but they pass the hands down the knee and leg, and give a strong inhalation of pleasure while performing these gymnastics…In [inferiors saluting their superiors] a low bend from the inferior till the fingers touch the ground, a curt yet affable bend from the superior.

It should be noted that lower-ranking individuals were not necessarily the only ones who bent over until their fingers touched the ground. Sometimes the roles would reverse and the superior would salute an inferior in a similar fashion. As we can see in a passage written by Ernest Satow, when his party visited the Tosa domain (located in present-day Kōchi Prefecture), they were met by Yamauchi Yōdō (1827–1871), the fifteenth head of the domain. According to Satow, Yamauchi "met me at the threshold, and saluted me by touching the tips of his toes with the tips of his fingers."[98]

Other observers also wrote about bowing among the Japanese. Aleksei Vladimirovich Vysheslavtsov was a doctor who accompanied the Siberian Military Flotilla of the Russian Pacific Fleet, which was commanded by General Nikolay Muravyov-Amursky, to Edo in 1859 to discuss issues related to national borders on Sakhalin Island (known as "Karafuto" in Japan). When Vysheslavtsov was at a kimono store, he saw how drawn out the exchange of bows between the owner and customers was, writing:[99]

> Watching from the side, I saw the two gentlemen engage in a series of salutations that bordered on the ridiculous. First, both men lined up and bent their upper bodies, slid their hands down to their knees, and deeply bowed their heads. While they were doing this, they were sucking in air through their teeth with all their might. Then, the owner offered the customer a pipe, which also prompted a sucking sound. The owner looked exhausted, embarrassed, and in a dreamlike state when he saw the ecstatic look on the face of his customer. Finally, the two exchanged a few words and sat down, the customer taking the pipe. A full fifteen minutes had already passed during this exchange, and soon they began prostrating to one another on the floor, the sucking sound becoming so loud and violent that it made me nervous. It was like there was a living air pump in the room trying to suck the

breath out of us innocent bystanders. I would have waged a fortune to know what exactly they were talking about.

According to Vysheslavtsov, all of the shogunate officials who visited the corvette, the ship he rode on, also bowed and sucked in air through their teeth in this fashion.[100]

Léon Metchnikoff also wrote about the sucking sound. He shared a cabin with a Japanese merchant named Genjirō on his journey by ship to Japan, and he wrote about what happened when the Japanese man reunited with his brother and employees when they arrived:[101]

> They stretched their hands down to their knees and bent their bodies at their waists to almost right angles, and then they sucked in air as if they were sniffling and blew it back out in huffs. They repeated this exercise over and over. They looked like startled geese making an aggressive display. Once they were finished, each person remained in a prostrated position, chattering away with what seemed like long words and nasal voices.

The observers were greatly taken aback by the aspiration sounds the Japanese made while bowing, and there are countless descriptions that depict this phenomenon.

Henry Tilley also wrote about his experiences with Japanese bowing. As I mentioned in a previous chapter, Tilley was a Briton serving in the Russian navy as a member of Muravyov-Amursky's fleet and landed with them in Edo. One day, he was able to explore the city. He was particularly interested in the guard houses set up in each district, and whenever he entered these buildings, they would serve him tea and provide him with tobacco. He wrote:[102]

> What ceremonies, prostrations, etiquette I there observed! What bending of backs, what rubbing of knees, strong whistling inhalations of the breath, and untiring jabber of tongues! The change of guard was a long job, each party trying to outdo the other with obsequious politeness before they came to business; when that was completed, the raiment had to be arranged, the two swords placed jauntily in the obi or silk scarf worn round the waist, the various under dresses folded more gracefully over the naked bosom, the target hat placed on the head, or the fan outspread; and then the gallant gentleman would take up his book, spend another five minutes in salutations to his successor, ere he shuffled off to report, and then home, or to the tea house.

Arthur Collins Maclay (1853–1930), who worked as an instructor at the Tōō Gijuku School in Hirosaki (located in western Aomori Prefecture) in 1874, also noted how it took four samurai warriors five minutes just to leave a room. They were bowing back and forth in a bid to outdo each other with politeness and let each other leave first. In this case, Maclay reasoned that the samurai acted this way in order to avoid offending each other, something which could quickly escalate into a fight to the death.[103] This is an interesting theory, but we cannot really say if it was true.

Incessant Japanese bowing still caught the attention of the foreign observers as late as the middle Meiji period. In 1891, for example, a French tourist, Cavaglion, saw a graceful young man in a suit take off his hat and speak to an old woman with rotten teeth at a shrine in Kyoto. When they bade farewell to one another, the young man bowed to the ground and lowered his head to his legs, making a sort of semicircle with his body.[104]

Scenes such as these invited praise and admiration from the observers, but they did not always see it this way. Even in the aforementioned examples, it often went too far and looked ridiculous in many peoples' eyes. Others even decried what they saw. Vysheslavtsov, for example, looked down on what he called a peculiar Japanese affability, labeling it a behavioral esprit created by a yoke tied around the neck of the country since long ago. In other words, he was willing to argue that Japanese courtesy was the result of pressure placed on the people throughout history, consuming the best parts of their courage and turning them into mere puppets. He acknowledged he was being a little stereotypical in his analysis, but he felt he had to be in criticizing what he saw.[105]

However, John La Farge (1835–1910), an American painter who came to Japan in 1886, felt Japanese courtesy maintained a "great feeling of a certain freedom" or "something of what we might call democratic."[106] This closely resembles what Chamberlain felt. However, we should avoid going too far in exploring this reverse theory that claims the chivalric manners embedded in feudalism or the Japanese class system led to a certain kind of freedom and independence among the people. The bigger issue is that Japanese courtesy surprised the foreign observers, and all of them recognized innocence, cheerfulness, and kindness as the central virtues of the Japanese. Edwin Arnold clearly understood this point, writing:[107]

> I cannot express to you the subtle pleasure I have derived from contact with your common people in cities and railroad stations, in villages, and tea-houses, and country roads. I have nowhere passed without learning lessons of finer manners than I knew before, and without being constructed in that delicacy of heart which springs from true goodwill and lies above all precept.

"Your bill, sir." (from Arnold, *Japonica*)

Arnold was compelled to say this at a club in Tokyo because he had already seen the true nature of Japanese courtesy firsthand. He even viewed it as a beautiful social contract to live an easy life in this world. He also wrote:[108]

> There is a universal social compact in Japan to make life pleasant by politeness. Everybody is more or less well-bred, and hates the man or woman who is *yakamashu*—noisy, uncivil, or exigent. People who lose their temper, are always in a hurry, bang doors, swear, and "swagger," find themselves out of place in a land where the lowest coolie learns and practices an ancient courtesy, from the time when he wobbles about as a baby on his mother's back.

Arnold also asked:[109]

> Where else in the world does there exist such a conspiracy to be agreeable; such a wide-spread compact to render the difficult affairs of life as smooth and graceful as circumstances admit; such fair decrees of fine behavior fixed and accepted for all; such universal restraint of the coarser impulses of speech and act; such pretty picturesqueness of daily existence; such lively love of nature as the embellisher of that existence; such sincere delight in beautiful artistic things; such frank enjoyment of the enjoyable; such tenderness to little children; such reverence for parents and old persons; such wide-spread refinement of taste and habits; such courtesy to strangers; such willingness to please and be pleased?

Arnold commented that "The universal silent social contract to make existence as agreeable for everybody as possible, includes in Japan the custom of never seeming to take personal woes to heart; above all, of never saddening other people with them."[110] Now we can probably understand why he said:[111]

> As for the people, I am, and always shall be, of good Saint Francis Xavier's feeling: "This nation is the delight of my soul!" Never have I passed days more happy, tranquil, or remonstrative than among Japanese of all classes, in the cities, towns, and villages of Japan.

Arnold came to Japan in November 1889, rented a house in Azabu, and lived there with his daughter. He left Japan in January 1891 and married a Japanese woman in 1897. Some records indicate his praise for Japan turned into disenchantment in his later years, but I am not sure if this is true or not, and to tell the truth, I do not really care. What is important in my mind is that, as Arnold believed, the old Japanese civilization that had long faded into memory, was, in fact, an agreement enacted to make human existence as pleasant as possible. In a way, old Japan was a deeply affectionate society. People could frankly and sincerely communicate their emotions while also maintaining politeness. Thus, people living in this era had every reason to be happy and content.

Raphael von Koeber gave an example that supports this. Koeber was a teacher, so he was primarily thinking about his university students when he said the most-favorable attributes of the Japanese were their child-like nature and almost lovable sense of wildness. He felt his students displayed this naive, child-like nature of the Japanese more than any other group because they lived free lives yet treated their superiors with an innocent sense of trust and respect. Koeber praised the strong ties between teachers and students and noted the mutual sense of love and respect they held for one another.

There are other examples that speak of this affection between Japanese teachers and students, but perhaps the best example is a scene that Yamakawa Kikue (1890–1980) wrote about from an important memory in her childhood, namely, the death of her grandfather, Aoyama Nobutoshi.[112] Nobutoshi was the fourth son of Aoyama Nobuyuki, a famous historian from the Mito School, a discipline focused on history and Shinto studies that began in the Mito domain (located in present-day Ibaraki Prefecture). When Nobutoshi passed away at the age of 87 in 1906, Yamakawa noted that many of his students from long ago, who were now gray-haired and balding, came to pay their respects. She also wrote that they gathered around his coffin and started crying out "Sensei!" ["Teacher!"] like young children. Then, Nobutoshi's nephew Isamu, who was himself an old man around seventy years old and suffering from paralysis, lamented that his uncle was like a father to him and gave a long, moving eulogy. Meanwhile, elderly scholar Tezuka Yoken, another nephew and student of Nobutoshi's, got a little drunk and began joking around to make everybody laugh.

This episode paints the perfect picture of how the Japanese behaved in ages past. No matter how old they were, the Japanese still had the tendency to act like children and obediently showed affection to those around them. Yamakawa went on to say that all of the people who came to see her grandfather became his students when they were seven or eight years old and they had kept in touch with him both publicly and privately, struggled together during the hard times before and after the Meiji Restoration, and were more like blood relatives than teacher and students.

Yamakawa wrote about another episode that truly shows the warmhearted love of people living in old Japan.[113] Yamakawa's mother, Chiyo, started to learn sewing under a teacher at age thirteen in accordance with the custom at the time. Her teacher's name was Ishikawa, the wife of a low-ranking samurai from the Mito domain. Mr. Ishikawa was a towering bald man, and he was extremely proud of the seamstresses at his home and loved them like they were his own children. Whenever Chiyo or another seamstress would complete a kimono, their teacher would show it to the man, and he, apparently touched by the efforts the young girls made in perfecting their craft, would bathe her in congratulations on a job well done. He also promised to iron out the kimono for her, thus putting the final touches to the garment. To her delight, steam from his iron wafted into the air like white translucent silk.

Sometimes Ishikawa's wife pestered him to take out and help prepare cloth for the girls to use, but he would often use this chance to have some fun with the girls. Instead of taking out an *uchikake* skirt or another garment for a kimono, he would put pajamas on his head, hold a long stick in his right hand and an umbrella in his left, and tried his best to be Ono no Komachi from the Noh play, *Sekidera Komachi*, by saying "Hello? Please let me in the gate" in a cute, falsetto voice. Having fun with his "family" was far more important than the kimono and everything else in his life, and he was always laughing when he was home. Mr. and Mrs. Ishikawa grew up in the carefree Bunka-Bunsei era (1804–1830) and were gifted in the performance arts. In addition, Mr. Ishikawa was a notoriously daring young man, even flirting with danger on one occasion when he argued down an arrogant superior.

Strong ties between superiors and inferiors could also be seen in the example of Utsunomiya Saburō (1834–1903), a chemist who had considerable influence on the Meiji-period kiln industry. In his younger days, Utsunomiya often visited the Katsuragawa family, the head of which served as a shogunate physician. He went there so often that it was almost like he lived there. This family was called the "leader of Dutch studies" due to producing successive generations of eminent *rangaku* (Western studies) scholars. The head of the family at the time was Katsuragawa Hoshū (1826–1881), the seventh head of the family. Utsunomiya loved Hoshū, and the two would often play together. Hoshū would also recite the nursery rhyme, "This is Lord No and that is Lord No" to Utsunomiya whenever he took him to the bathroom so that the boy would not get scared. Hoshū became bedridden in his later years due to illness, and Utsunomiya was always by his side. One day, something cold fell and hit Hoshū on the face, waking him up. When he opened his eyes, he realized tears were falling from Utsunomiya's face.[114]

Naturally, foreign observers of Japan also noticed this deep sense of affection among the Japanese. Rutherford Alcock, for example, had a dog named Toby that died while he was staying in Atami. He said, "Some of the best traits of the Japanese character came out very favorably on this occasion." He wrote:[115]

> My head betto [stable attendant], as soon as he learned of the death, came himself to put him in his basket-shroud and under the sod. I asked the proprietor's leave to bury him in his pretty garden under the shade of a tree, and he instantly came himself and helped to dig the grave. A group of assistants of all ranks gathered round with mournful faces, as though one of their own kind had passed away. He was folded up in a mat, some of the beans he was so fond of were put in the grave with him, and a bunch of evergreens inserted at the head, which was scrupulously laid to the north. The priest of the temple brought water and incense sticks to burn, and then a rough tombstone to mark the spot was laid on his grave. They are really a kindly people when not perverted by their rulers and prompted to hostility.

Samuel Brown also related an episode in which he experienced the love and affection of the Japanese. After he started living in Kanagawa, he was always suspected by the shogunate of trying to spread the teachings of Christianity as a missionary. One day, however, he was walking through the town when he met a senior police officer and his men. Brown stated that when he was walking across the street, the officer surprisingly took his hand and saluted him, told him that he was transferring to Edo, as his duty in Kanagawa was finished, and said he was truly sorry that he did not have enough time to come and say farewell. This officer apparently repeated the same greeting to other missionaries.[116] Brown was not entirely sure why this shogunate official got so emotional in saying goodbye since he had scrutinized Brown for so long, yet he truly appeared to be channeling warm-hearted feelings.

Brown realized the officer hated saying goodbye to anyone, even a missionary from another country.

Griffis, meanwhile, described an episode of his own. Griffis had found himself in a bit of a quandary after he resigned from his position of instructor at the Fukui domain school because he had not even completed one year on his three-year contract. However, he had a strong desire to move to Tokyo, and eventually the domain school gave in to his wishes. Even though there were strong opinions on both sides of the issue, his farewell party was a huge affair. He wrote a letter to his younger sister that read, "All day yesterday, my house was filled by my pupils, officers, citizens, and everybody generally, who came to bid me farewell. All bring presents in money, lacquer ware, confectionary, curios, etc. My tables are filled with all kinds of things."[117] The day he left, meanwhile, about fifty students and townspeople walked with him for three miles to see him off, while the school director Murata Ujihisa (1821–1899) and twelve others traveled with him for twelve miles before finally bidding farewell. Murata was actually the most fearsome and vocal opponent standing in the way of Griffis's desire to leave.

Arthur Maclay detailed a similar episode when he left the Tōō Gijuku School after ten months and moved to Tokyo. When he left on November 11, 1873, his students walked with him for two miles until they reached the countryside. When they finally bade him farewell, a student representative made him a speech expressing their thanks. Twenty-one-year-old Maclay was touched by this gesture, and tears filled his eyes when he looked down at their upturned faces from his horse and thought of what to say in return. He also wrote "I shall never forget that scene. There they stood in a semicircle, ankle deep in the mud, and shivering with the cold."[118]

French painter Félix Régamey, who succeeded in visiting Japan again for the first time in twenty-three years in 1899, wrote about his own experience. One day, he left the settlement in Tsukiji and enjoyed a brisk walk through Honjo, a district inhabited by craftsmen. Their way of life fascinated Régamey, and he praised the fact that the craftsmen and their families accepted him into their homes yet were not selfish and did not expect any money from him in return. One of the artisans Régamey met, a nail-maker, even smiled and let him take a handful of nails. Régamey wrote:[119]

> I was deeply moved and bowed my head. Such kindness moved me to the bottom of my heart, and I grew impatient with the fact that I could only talk with these sincere people with hand gestures. It appears that the motto of these wonderfully cheerful and hardworking people is to have courage and be in high spirits. The women are gentle and kind, and the children run around and laugh in high spirts yet can

be extremely attentive when need be… I don't think they know just much I love them.

One who is happy is one who can make others happy. This was the last shining light of the common people in old Japan.

In closing this chapter, I want to reconsider the issue that Yokoyama Toshio brought up in his book, namely that the policy of the Japanese government in the 1870s was to issue warnings to and control the people. To support his position, Yokoyama used the actual example of Admiral Cyprian Arthur George Bridge (1839–1924) visiting Kyoto in the latter half of the 1870s and being impressed by the city's order. According to Yokoyama, the Kyoto government ordered the people of the city to thoroughly clean the drainage system and ditches in order to make it look pleasing to foreign visitors who were coming to attend the exposition taking place there. In addition, he said that the national and local governments admonished the people to keep them from engaging in ugly behavior in front of foreign visitors. He wrote:[120]

> During the 1870s, not only in Kyoto but in many country districts of Japan, the authorities were trying hard to prevent trouble between the inhabitants and foreigners. But the foreigners were unaware of these efforts and innocently enjoyed their excursions to these newly opened areas and encounters with well-instructed citizens and villagers.

In other words, Yokoyama wants to say that the cleanliness and courtesy of the Japanese, which greatly impressed the foreign observers, was actually the result of government efforts to influence the people and present Japan in this light. As we saw in chapter one, this repeats the argument that Yokoyama made in response to Oliphant and Osborn's observations. However, I completely disagree with his assessment.

First, Bridge lauding how orderly and compact Kyoto was had absolutely nothing to do with whether the drainage channels and ditches were clean or not. Likewise, Kyoto's straight and wide streets had nothing to do with the small, wooden houses that looked like dollhouses. Even if we take it that the people cleaned Kyoto to make it look presentable to visiting foreign visitors, this certainly was not the case in other parts of Japan. When Bird visited the town of Nikko and commented on how the streets were so clean that she felt bad about walking on them with her boots, no one had told the residents that a British woman was planning to visit them. Bird felt the same way when she visited Niigata, but again, they had no prior knowledge of her arrival. The towns were simply clean. I also find it hard to believe that the cheerful girls on their way home from school, whom Bridge saw and said brightened up an otherwise dull and gloomy town, had anything to do with orders imposed by the Kyoto government.

Now, I do admit the authorities influenced the Japanese people to a certain degree and instructed them to avoid creating trouble with foreign visitors. When Bird was in Tsugawa in Niigata, for example, she encountered a child who shouted insults at her, but the police quickly scolded him and made him apologize.[121] However, this would happen in any society, not just in Japan. We have to look at the bigger picture and see if Yokoyama was right to argue that the authorities had almost complete control over the populace.

There are two issues I have with this point. First of all, the foreign observers were not fools. They would easily be able to tell if the Japanese feelings of goodwill, kindness, and courtesy were superficial attributes instrumented by the authorities or whether they truly came from the heart. As I mentioned earlier, we also have to consider the fact that the Westerners looked like nobles to the Japanese, so they often treated the visitors the way they would any other high-ranking official. The government had no need to tell them to act this way. Meanwhile, if the Japanese were just following the custom of submitting to high-ranking officials, then the foreign observers would not have praised the Japanese to the degree they did. As we have already seen, there were innumerable accounts praising the kind and courteous people of old Japan. It is nonsensical to think that government policy and manipulation was responsible for creating such a huge pool of these testimonies.

Secondly, no matter how many times the government warned and instructed the people, they did not have complete control over the situation. Bird gave an example involving rickshaw drivers while she and her entourage were in Akita. It was quite hot, so the three men who were pulling her cart were almost completely naked. When they suddenly came across a police officer, they quickly tried putting on the *hanten* coats they had hung on the bar of the cart. Bird noted she "never saw such a picture of abjectness" in the way the oldest runner acted and that "He trembled from head to foot." Naturally, he was afraid of being arrested for indecent exposure. However, when the policeman went away, "the two younger men threw their clothes in the air and gambolled in the shafts, shrieking with laughter!"[122] Gustav Kreitner came to Japan in 1878, the same year as Bird, and experienced a similar situation. He stated that when his party approached a police station, the rickshaw drivers pulling their carts immediately covered their naked bodies with worn-out *happi* coats or rested them on their shoulders when they saw a policeman crossing the street.[123] In both of these cases, the runners were just pretending to obey the law.

In addition, the police could not prevent trouble from occurring between locals and foreign visitors no matter how much notice they gave to the people. When Henry Faulds visited Kami Yoshida at the base of Mount Fuji, for example, he received a rather rough welcome, to wit, a mob of people started throwing mud and rocks at him when he arrived. He asked the young man who looked like the leader why they were treating a peaceful foreign visitor who just wanted to see the beauty of the area so poorly, and this finally seemed to calm them down. Faulds later discovered that French naval officers had recently visited the area and their bad behavior was the cause of the problem.[124]

The incidents above occurred in the 1870s, but more disturbances took place at the beginning of the 1880s. One notable episode took place when Joseph Cook, a clergyman from Boston, visited Kyoto. Cook grew irritated with his rickshaw driver because it was hot and he felt the man was going too slow, so he decided to poke him with his umbrella. Infuriated, the runner immediately pulled Cook out of the rickshaw, stripping off his hat and clothes in the process.[125]

Returning to instances of people throwing stones, Russian sailors from General Muravyov-Amursky's fleet said a crowd of Japanese people that they met in Edo treated them in this manner in 1859. The mob apparently followed and surrounded the visitors and then bathed them in stones, and they did this with the police watching the whole time.[126] As I mentioned earlier, Henry Tilley was also a member of this fleet and said that people threw stones at him whenever he went shopping. Children would usually start but the adults would join in soon enough. On one particular occasion, Tilley and the others felt their lives were in danger when a fourteen-year-old boy samurai pulled out a sword "which was almost as big as himself" and saved them. When the mob saw the stick he wielded, they fell back and dispersed. From then on, the boy protected Tilley and his party every time they went shopping in the city.[127]

There were many other instances as well. According to Alcock, Lord Elgin's party was also pelted with stones in the "great commercial centre of the city" in 1858. Alcock decided to set foot into this infamous place and see what would happen, but the people only threw a piece of dried mud at him. He did go on to say, however, that "They offered no insult, but there was a good deal of shouting and hooting, which was certainly not intended to be either respectful or complimentary."[128] Meanwhile, Siebold's oldest son Alexander (1846–1911) came to Edo with his father in 1861. When they went to Ryōgokubashi, a rushing mob suddenly surrounded them screaming "Barbarian girl! Barbarian girl!" They had to make a quick getaway. Alexander was only fifteen years old at the time and apparently the Japanese mistook him for a girl. Ryōgokubashi was a notoriously dangerous place for foreign visitors, as the local people would not only pelt them with rocks, but also spat at them.[129]

Yet another incident occurred in 1867 when Dutch Consul General Polsbroek went to Asakusa with fellow countryman and Kaiseijo Institute chemistry instructor Koenraad Wolter Gratama (1831–1888). There they met a mob of about 1,000 Japanese commoners who proceeded to pelt them with stones. Their bodyguards did nothing to help them, and Polsbroek was afraid of being trampled to death. Luckily, the two men escaped with their lives, but Gratama badly injured his back.[130]

Nagasaki also had its fair share of incidents. According to Dutch Consul Albert Bauduin (1829–1890), locals there frequently threw rocks at foreign visitors, sometimes causing serious injuries and even deaths. In a letter that Bauduin wrote to his older sister in 1859, he mentioned that fights between Westerners and the Japanese occurred on a daily basis. Usually, the Japanese person would end up getting shot, and the matter would be settled. Bauduin went on to say that, during the same week he wrote the letter, two dead bodies had already been found. He sarcastically quipped that Japan was a lovely country and that loaded pistols made wonderful bedfellows.[131]

Rocks were not the only thing the Japanese hit foreign visitors with. They were also quite lethal with their verbal insults. Many Westerners who came to Japan at the end of the Edo period remarked about how Japanese children constantly hounded them with cries of "Tōjin baka." Members of the Eulenburg expedition often heard this in Edo's Shitamachi, and they knew that it meant "Stupid foreigner."

Even so, Albert Berg wrote that the people were not being altogether hostile when they hurtled such insults their way.[132] Reinhold Werner (1825–1909), who was the commander of the transport ship *Elbe*, one of the four ships in the fleet used by the Eulenburg expedition, also mentioned that children insulted him and his men, but that they did not seem to be antagonizing him. He stated that hundreds of Japanese children followed his party while yelling "Tōjin! Tōjin!" "Tōjin" was the epithet the Japanese used to label Chinese people. Thus, Werner ascertained the children, in their innocence, thought their party had come from China. All innocence aside, however, the yelling children must have contrasted with his image of the Japanese people's peculiar sense of good manners.[133]

Rudolf Lindau, incidentally, also found himself surrounded by children screaming "Tōjin!" in Kamakura in 1862. He said there was a noisy mob, but no harm came to him or his entourage.[134] The same year, Raphael Pumpelly met a throng of people in Hachiōji screaming "Tōjin! Tōjin!" in a deafening tone. However, he wrote, "There was no intention to insult us, as often happened in the fishing villages where men and children would run after us, yelling 'bacca! bacca!' (fool! fool!)."[135]

It is worth noting that "Tōjin baka" was actually an insult that the

Japanese used as far back as the early Edo period. In 1613, for example, John Saris (1579–1643), who was dispatched to Japan by the British East India Company, was hounded by "the boyes, children, and the worser sort of idle people" wherever he went during his stay in Edo, and they constantly hurtled insults at him such as "'Coré Coré, Cocoré, Waré,' that is to say 'You Coréans with false hearts!'"[136] In addition, Olof Eriksson Willman (1620–1673), a Swede who accompanied the Dutch mission to Edo in 1652, said children yelled "Bye-bye Toshin" at his party, particularly when they were in Edo and Osaka. Willman was offended when he took what they were saying as "We're here to play tricks on you, Mr. Adventurer."[137]

All of these examples show that police and government intervention had little to no influence on how the Japanese people acted. In other words, they were not forced to laugh in the presence of foreign visitors. On the contrary, they interacted with foreign visitors any way they wanted. As a result, foreign visitors encountered the Japanese people in a myriad of situations, many of which were troublesome and unpleasant. This forced them to rethink and create new images of the Japanese that included not only the positive aspects of kindness, goodwill, and courtesy, but also many negative qualities.

In closing, the following passage by Edouard Suenson serves as an excellent and unembellished example of foreign observers encountering the Japanese:[138]

> Westerners who visit this place [Gankirō, a brothel in Yokohama] for the first time unconsciously feel a sense of security when they find out that the surrounding areas, which tend to feel unsafe, are duly guarded by the police. The crowds are truly intense and it seems a disturbance could break out at any moment… You cannot really understand what they are saying, but they often yammer about something in dirty voices. They are a stocky people with dark complexions and suspicious eyes. Everyone covers their faces and cheeks so that all you can see is their two dark shiny eyes. They seem to do this to avoid showing their faces. However, your wariness disperses like the fog after only staying here for a short time. You will finally see that underneath their disguises, these people are actually pleasant and peaceful craftsmen who hide their honest and good faces under their wrapped cheeks, and their vulgar voices are nothing more than capricious utterings that they use to make those around them laugh. At times, they even let foreigners in on their mischief.

Notes:

1 Gustav Spiess, *Die Preussiche Expedition nach Ost Asien während der Jahre 1860-1862* (Leipzig, 1864). No English translation of Spiess's work exists, so passages that appear in this book have been translated from the Japanese version. See Supīsu [Spiess], *Supīsu no Puroshia Nihon enseiki* [Gustav Spiess's Record of the Prussian Expedition to Japan] (Okugawa Shobō, 1934), 266. Subsequent citations will appear as Spiess, *Die Preussiche Expedition*, and will list page numbers from the Japanese text.

2 Cortazzi, *Mitford's Japan*, 19.

3 Cortazzi, *Mitford's Japan*, 29–30.

4 Pompe, *Vijf Jaren*, 331.

5 Osborn, *Cruise*, 174.

6 Alcock, *Tycoon*, Vol. 1, 190–1.

7 Pompe, *Vijf Jaren*, 329.

8 Pompe, *Vijf Jaren*, 346.

9 Smith, *Ten Weeks*, 224–5.

10 Smith, *Ten Weeks*, 86, 223.

11 Smith, *Ten Weeks*, 223.

12 Smith, *Ten Weeks*, 58.

13 Smith, *Ten Weeks*, 311–2.

14 Fortune, *Yedo and Peking*, 64–5.

15 Alcock, *Tycoon*, Vol. 1, 116.

16 Alcock, *Tycoon*, Vol. 2, 275.

17 Alcock, *Tycoon*, Vol. 1, 394.

18 Lindau, *Un Voyage Autour*, 161.

19 Leroy Lansing Janes, *Kumamoto, An Episode in Japan's Break from Feudalism* (University of California Press, 1970). The handwritten manuscript of this work, as well as other notes kept by Janes, is available at the Princeton University Library (see rbsc.princeton.edu/collections/leroy-lansing-janes-papers for more information), but it can only be accessed in person by request. In addition, the University of California Press edition is extremely hard to find. Therefore, passages that appear in this book have been translated from the Japanese version. See Jēnzu [Janes], *Kumamoto Kaisō* [Memories of Kumamoto] (Kumamotonichinichi Shimbun, 1978), 16. Subsequent citations will appear as Janes, *Kumamoto*, and will list page numbers from the Japanese text.

20 Engelbert Kaempfer, *The History of Japan* (New York: Macmillan Co., 1906). See Vol. 2, Part 3, Chapter 5. In other chapters of his book, Kaempfer also mentions that all of the beggars he came across were religious wanderers.

21 Siebold, *Nippon: Archiv*, Vol. 1, 142–3.

22 F.G. Notehelfer, *American Samurai: Captain L. L. Janes and Japan* (Princeton University Press, 1985), 121.

23 Notehelfer, *American Samurai*, 125.

24 Janes, *Kumamoto*, 20.

25 Spiess, *Die Preussiche Expedition*, 52.

26 Takaya Michio, ed., *Hebon shokanshū* [The Letters of Dr. J.C. Hepburn] (Toshin Shobō, 1955), 15.

27 Takaya Michio, ed., *S. R. Buraun shokanshū* [The Letters of S.R. Brown] (United Church of Christ – Japan Publishing Section, 1965), 56.

28 Jephson and Elmhirst, *Our Life*, 74.

29 Osborn, *Cruise*, 175.

30 Berg, *Eulenburg Expedition*, Vol. 1, 153.

31 Morse, *Day by Day*, 169–70.

32 Alcock, *Tycoon*, Vol. 1, 90–91.

33 Morse, *Day by Day*, 176.

34 Henry Holmes, *My Adventures in Japan, before the Treaty Came into Force, February, 1859* (London: King and Co., Ltd., 1904), 18–19.

35 Hübner, *Ramble*, 279.

36 Faulds, *Nine Years*, 46.

37 Edouard Suenson, *Skitser fra Japan* (Copenhagen, 1869–1870). No English translation of Suenson's work exists, so passages that appear in this book have been translated from the Japanese version. See Suenson [Suenson], *Edo Bakufu taizaiki* [A Record of a Visit to Japan at the End of the Edo Period] (Shinjinbutsu Oraisha, 1989), 43. Subsequent citations will appear as Suenson, *Skitser*, and will list page numbers from the Japanese text.

38 Lindau, *Un Voyage Autour*, 204–6.

39 Vittorio F. Arminjon, *Il Giappone e il Viaggio della Corvetta Magenta nel 1866* (Genova, 1869). No English translation of Arminjon's work exists, so passages that appear in this book have been translated from the Japanese version. See Aruminyon [Arminjon], *Itaria shisetsu no Bakumatsu kenbunki* [Record of the Italian Expedition to Japan at the End of the Edo Period] (Shinjinbutsu Oraisha, 1987), 96. Subsequent citations will appear as Arminjon, *Il Giappone*, and will list page numbers from the Japanese text.

40 Crow, *Highways and Byeways*, 77.

41 Pompe, *Vijf Jaren*, 183.

42 Oliphant, *Narrative*, Vol. 2, 204–5.

43 Carl Munzinger, *Japan und die Japaner* (Berlin, 1898). No English translation of Munzinger's work exists, so passages that appear in this book have been translated from the Japanese version. See Muchingā [Munzinger], *Doitsu senkyōshi no mita Meiji shakai* [Meiji Japanese Society Seen through the Eyes of a German Missionary] (Shinjinbutsu Oraisha, 1987), 101. Subsequent citations will appear as Munzinger, *Japaner*, and will list page numbers from the Japanese text.

44 Morse, *Japanese Homes*, 248–9.

45 Morse, *Day by Day*, Vol. 1, 37.

46 Morse, *Day by Day*, Vol. 1, 316–7.

47 Morse, *Day by Day*, Vol. 2, 266.

48 Takaya, *Hebon*, 183.

49 Smith, *Ten Weeks*, 101–2.

50 Lindau, *Un Voyage Autour*, 62.

51 Palmer, *Letters*, 188–191.

52 Morse, *Day by Day*, Vol. 1, 131.

53 Morse, *Day by Day*, Vol. 1, 125, 19, 38, 43.

54 Morse, *Day by Day*, Vol. 2, 370–1.

55 Fortune, *Yedo and Peking*, 118.

56 Kawai Koume, *Koume nikki* [Diary of Koume] (Heibonsha Toyo Bunko, 1964), Vol. 1, 3, 30.

57 Pumpelly, *Across America*, 132.

58 Morse, *Day by Day*, Vol. 2, 316.

59 Katherine Sansom, *Living in Tokyo* (London, 1937), 68–9.

60 Diaz Covarrubias, *Viaje*, 200.

61 John Russell Young, *Around the World with General Grant* (New York, 1879), Vol. 2, 572–3.

62 Palmer, *Letters*, 143.

63 Lindau, *Un Voyage Autour*, 50.

64 Bird, *Unbeaten Tracks*, Vol. 1, 337–8.

65 Pumpelly, *Across America*, 102.

66 Bird, *Unbeaten Tracks*, Vol. 1, 182.

67 Metchnikoff, *Kaisō*, 111–2, 123.

68 Bousquet, *Le Japon*, Vol. 1, 72–4.

69 Smith, *Ten Weeks*, 88.

70 Munzinger, *Japaner*, 76–7.

71 Walter G. Dickson, *Gleanings from Japan* (Edinburgh and London: Willian Blackwood and Sons, 1889), 24. Not much is known about Dickson, but he did visit Kamakura with Fortune when he came to Japan in 1860 (Fortune, *Yedo and Peking*, 221). Fortune called him Dr. Dickson from China in his book, so he likely worked as a physician in that country. The first time Dickson came to Japan he stayed until 1862 and he remained in Japan from 1883 until 1884 on his second visit. This book is a record of Dickson's second visit. I would appreciate learning more about Dickson's career from someone who knows about the doctor's life.

72 Humbert, *Japan and the Japanese*. Certain sections of Humbert's book have not been translated into English. In such cases, passages have been translated from the Japanese version. See Anbēru [Humbert], *Bakumatsu Nippon zue* [Illustrations of Japan at the End of the Edo Period] (Yushodo Shuppan, 1969), Vol. 2, 73–4. Subsequent citations for passages that have no English translation will appear as Humbert, *Japan and the Japanese*, and will list page numbers from the Japanese text.

73 Diaz Covarrubias, *Viaje*, 200–1.

74 Morse, *Day by Day*, Vol. 1, 33.

75 Dixon, *Land of the Morning*, 217–8.

76 Pierre Loti, *Japoneries D'Automne* (Paris, 1889). Although excerpts of this book have been translated into English by Lafcadio Hearn (see Hearn, *Stories by Pierre Loti*, Tokyo: Hokuseido Press, 1933) and other authors, no complete English translation of Loti's work exists. Therefore, passages that appear in this book have been translated from the Japanese version. See Roti [Loti], *Aki no Nihon* [Japan of Autumn] (Kadokawa Bunko, 1953), 11. Subsequent citations will appear as Loti, *Japoneries*, and will list page numbers from the Japanese text.

77 E. Cavaglion, *254 Jours Autour du Monde* (Paris, 1894). No English translation of Cavaglion's work exists, so passages that appear in this book have been translated from the Japanese version. See Kavariyon [Cavaglion], "Meiji Japan-1891," in Monburan (Montblanc), et al., *Monburan no Nihon kenbunki* [Record of Count Charles du Montblanc's Visit to Japan and Other Records], trans. Morimoto Hideo (Shinjinbutsu Oraisha, 1987), 137. Subsequent citations will appear as Cavaglion, *254 Jours*, and will list page numbers from the Japanese text.

78 Beauvoir, *Pekin, Jeddo, and San Francisco*, 132, 136.

79 Morse, *Day by Day*, Vol. 1, 328, 139.

80 Morse, *Day by Day*, Vol. 1, 44.

81 Morse, *Day by Day*, Vol. 2, 370.

82 Dixon, *Land of the Morning*, 220–1.

83 Arnold, *Seas and Lands*, 270.

84 Arnold, *Seas and Lands*, 177–8.

85 Arnold, *Seas and Lands*, 204.

86 Arnold, *Seas and Lands*, 285–6.

87 Diaz Covarrubias, *Viaje*, 201.

88 Chamberlain, *Things Japanese*, 407.

89 Bird, *Unbeaten Tracks*, Vol. 2, 230.

90 Faulds, *Nine Years*, 36.

91 Etsu Inagaki Sugimoto, *A Daughter of the Samurai* (New York: Doubleday, Page and Company, 1926), 117.

92 Dickson, *Gleanings*, 62–3.

93 Kattendijke, *Uittreksel*, 205.

94 Alcock, *Tycoon*, Vol. 1, 92.

95 Tronson, *Personal Narrative*, 361.

96 Jephson and Elmhirst, *Our Life*, 378.

97 Tilley, *Japan, the Amoor*, 86.

98 Satow, *Diplomat*, 268.

99 Aleksei Vladimirovich Vysheslavtsov, *Ocherki perom i karandashem iz krugosvietnago plavaniia v 1857, 1858, 1859 i 1860* [Sketches in Pen and Pencil from a Trip around the World in the Years

1857, 1858, 1859 and 1860] (Saint Petersburg: M.O. Wolf, 1867). No English translation of Vysheslavtsov's book exists, so the passages that appear in this book are taken from the Japanese version. See Vishesurahutsohu [Vysheslavtsov], *Roshia Kantai Bakumatsu raihōki* [Record of the Russian Fleet Visit to Japan] (Shinjinbutsu Oraisha, 1990), 124–5. Subsequent citations will appear as Vysheslavtsov, *Ocherki perom*, and will list the page numbers from the Japanese text.

100 Vysheslavtsov, *Ocherki perom*, 38.

101 Metchnikoff, *Kaisō*, 48.

102 Tilley, *Japan, the Amoor*, 182.

103 Arthur Collins Maclay, *A Budget of Letters from Japan* (New York: A.C. Armstrong and Son, 1886), 75.

104 Cavaglion, *254 Jours*, 137.

105 Vysheslavtsov, *Ocherki perom*, 49.

106 John La Farge, *An Artist's Letters from Japan* (New York: The Century Co., 1897), 200, 237.

107 Arnold, *Seas and Lands*, 277.

108 Edwin Arnold, *Japonica* (London, 1891), 34–7.

109 Arnold, *Japonica*, 94–5.

110 Arnold, *Japonica*, 124.

111 Arnold, *Japonica*, 94.

112 Yamakawa Kikue, *Buke no josei* [Samurai Women] (Iwanami Bunko, 1983), 8.

113 Yamakawa, *Buke*, 40–9.

114 Imaizumi Mine, *Nanokori no yume* [Remains of a Dream] (Heibonsha Toyo Bunko, 1963), 10–1, 15.

115 Alcock, *Tycoon*, Vol. 1, 379.

116 Takaya, *S. R. Buraun*, 55–6.

117 Beauchamp, *American Teacher*, 77.

118 Maclay, *Budget*, 127.

119 Régamey, *Japon*, 258–60.

120 Yokoyama, *Victorian Mind*, 153.

121 Bird, *Unbeaten Tracks*, Vol. 1, 195.

122 Bird, *Unbeaten Tracks*, Vol. 1, 304–5.

123 Kreitner, *Im fernen Osten*, Vol. 1, 268.

124 Faulds, *Nine Years*, 127–9.

125 Robert S. Schwantes, *Japanese and Americans: A Century of Cultural Relations* (New York: Harper and Brothers, 1955), 11.

126 Vysheslavtsov, *Ocherki perom*, 94, 98–9.

127 Tilley, *Japan, the Amoor*, 158–9.

128 Alcock, *Tycoon*, Vol. 1, 158–9.

129 Alexander Siebold, *Fr. Von Siebold's Letzte Reise nach Japan* (Berlin, 1903). No English translation of Siebold's work exists, so passages that appear in this book have been translated from the Japanese version. See A. Jīboruto [A. Siebold], *Jīboruto saigo no Nihon ryokō* [Philipp Franz von Siebold's Last Trip to Japan] (Heibonsha Tōyō Bunko, 1981), 130–1. Subsequent citations will appear as A. Siebold, *Letzte Reise*, and will list page numbers from the Japanese text.

130 Moeshart, *Journaal*, 209–10.

131 Bōdovan (Albert Bauduin), *Oranda Ryōji no Bakumatsu Ishin: Nagasaki Dejima kara no tegami* [Letters from the Dutch Consulate at Dejima from the Late Edo to Early Meiji Periods] (Heibonsha Tōyō Bunko, 1981), 130–1. The original letters were translated from Dutch into Japanese. Passages that appear in this book have been translated from Japanese into English.

132 Berg, *Eulenburg Expedition*, Vol. 1, 104, 168.

133 Reinhold Werner, *Die Preussiche Expedition nach China, Japan und Siam* (Leipzig, 1863). No English translation of Werner's work exists, so passages that appear in this book have been trans-

lated from the Japanese version. See Verunā [Werner], *Erubagō Kanchō Bakumatsuki* [Japan at the End of the Edo Period as Recorded by the Captain of the Elbe] (Shinjinbutsu Oraisha, 1990), 89. Subsequent citations will appear as Werner, *Die Preussiche Expedition*, and will list page numbers from the Japanese text.

134 Lindau, *Un Voyage Autour*, 211.

135 Pumpelly, *Across America*, 105.

136 Ernest M. Satow, *The Voyage of Captain John Saris to Japan*, 1613 (London, 1900), 121.

137 Olof Eriksson Willman, *The Journal of Olof E. Willman: From His Voyage to the Dutch East Indies and Japan, 1648-1654*, trans. Catharina Blomberg (Global Oriental, 2013). This particular passage has been translated from Japanese into English. See Viruman [Willman], *Nihon taizaiki* [Record of a Stay in Japan] (Yushodo Shuppan, 1970), 70.

138 Suenson, *Skitser*, 55.

Chapter
5

Fullness and Variety

In 1889, Mary Fraser, wife of newly appointed British Minister Plenipotentiary and Envoy Extraordinary to Japan, Hugh Fraser, never went a
day without enjoying a ride through the city of Tokyo by carriage. For her,
"Every step of the way brings me to some new picture or new question,
reveals some unimagined poetry or bit of fresh fun in daily life." She also
mentioned that Japanese commoners were "the most picturesque and amusing lower classes that Heaven has yet created." She went on to write the
following:[1]

> There are parties of little acrobats, children in charge of an older boy,
> who come tumbling after the carriage in contortions which would be
> terrible to see did one not feel convinced that Japanese limbs are made
> of india-rubber. Then there are the pedlars; the old clothes-sellers;
> the pipe-mender, who solemnly clean a pipe for one rin as they sit on
> the doorstep; the umbrella-makers, who fill a whole street with enor
> mous yellow parasols drying in the sun. Here a juggler is swallowing a
> sword, to the delight and amazement of a group of children; there the
> seller of *tofu*, or bean-curd, cuts great slabs of the cheesy substance, and
> wraps it in green leaves for his customer to carry away. I love watching
> the life of the streets, its fullness and variety, its inconvenient candour
> and its inexplicable reticences. I am always sorry to come in, even to
> our lovely home with its green lawns and gardens in flower.

Fraser found Japan to be a wonder. Even before she set foot in the country,
she was anxious to uncover the truth of its mysteries and hoped to avoid
becoming another traveler who just kept "all their lives one silly memory of
the strangest country in the world." Japan did not disappoint. Upon landing
in Nagasaki and later traversing the Seto Inland Sea, Fraser stated that her
experiences "upset all my wise resolutions about first impressions." She also
related the following:[2]

> The only thing that came to me as I stepped on shore at Nagasaki
> was a fit of really light-hearted laughter—laughter of the joyous and
> unreasonable kind whose tax is mostly paid in tears. Life suddenly
> presented itself as a thing of fun and joy…For sixpence I would have
> changed places with a seller of cakes whom I met in the road. His
> clothes were of the impressionist kind, some rather slight good inten-

tions carried out in cool blue cotton, the rest being brown man and sandals. He carried a fairy temple made of snowy wood and delicate paper…At a distance one might have mistaken him and his shrine of sweets for a bundle of lotus blooms on two brown stems.

Mary Fraser

One might be tempted to tease Fraser and tell her to go ahead and switch places with the cake seller, all the while knowing she would grow to hate doing his job in less than a day. What she was trying to say, however, was that she could feel the merriness and frolicking nature of the people in this land. She also found amusement and beauty in the nooks and crannies of Japanese life.

Women may have sensed the peculiarities of this civilization better than men. Eliza Scidmore, for example, was an American woman who had often visited Japan since her first visit in 1884. She said, "Japan is so inexhaustible and so full of surprises that until the last day of his stay the tourist and the resident alike are confronted by some novelty that is yet wholly common and usual in the life of the Japanese."[3] Scidmore clearly indicated one of the most-important characteristics of old Japanese civilization with this assertion. She also wrote:[4]

Every-day life looks too theatrical, too full of artistic and decorative effects, to be actual and serious, and streets and shops seem set with deliberately studied scenes and carefully posed groups. Half consciously the spectator waits for the bell to ring and the curtain to drop.

The "stage effects" Scidmore spoke of were likely tea utensils, tobacco pipes, hibachi braziers, *byōbu* screens, bonsai trees, and many other ornamental implements. What she probably wanted to say, however, was that like Fraser, she viewed these things as part of the merriness and amusement that pervaded the lives of the Japanese.

This is a bit of an understatement, however, because Fraser's and Scidmore's observations went much further than this. Fraser was overflowing with excitement at seeing the streets and the interesting people who filled them. Scidmore also talked about groups of people in the streets and shops. In other words, they indicated that the streets were overflowing with variety. There were almost as many professions as there were people, and the streets were teeming with performances.

Edward Morse also wrote about experiences that were nearly identical to those of Fraser. For example, he stated that "A ride through the streets and to the University, back and forth, again and again, is always a novel and delightful experience. You are sure to see something new and never tire of seeing the old." The following description gives us an indication of what he saw:[5]

Children running across the path of your jinrikisha with their long sleeves flying; women with their highly dressed hair and always bareheaded, the older women waddling like ducks and the younger ones scuffing along; women nursing their children in the streets, in the shops, and even while riding in the jinrikishas; peddlers of all kinds; traveling shows; restaurants; stationary and peripatetic hawkers of fish, of toys, of candy; pipe-repairers; shoe-menders; barbers with their ornamental box—all with different street cries, some like the call of a strange bird; blind men and women strolling along the street blowing whistles; two old women and a girl, with cracked voices and a cracked guitar, singing; a bald-headed man with a bell who prays in front of your house for a tenth of a cent; another man reciting stories with a laughing group about him; jinrikishas rushing by in every direction, drawn by two men, with a dignified officer in uniform,…another a woman with a large-sized child in her lap, the child holding in her hand a half-consumed sweet potato and tugging away at the maternal font for the milk to go with it,…and all the while such a clatter of wooden clogs on the hard roadway and a continual hum of voices. People profoundly bowing to one another; the interminable shops lining the streets, all open from side to side and all the activities fully exposed.

Naturally, the customs and behaviors one sees on the streets of a different country will all appear rare and interesting at first. However, something more than novelty is needed to believe, as Morse did, that "all these sights are bewildering and absorbing." What Morse found "absorbing" was likely the variety found among the throngs of people in the streets. This probably meant there was also a great variety of lifestyles. The streets were not simply a means of transport— lives were lived in the streets, from mothers

Toy peddler in Nagasaki (from Régamey, *Japon*)

nursing their infants to peddlers hawking their goods. Vendors, repairmen, traveling entertainers, and people of religious faith, meanwhile, had highly specialized professions, and this led to the diversification of unique clothes and tools as a way to identify one's specialty to others. Morse noted that the modern crowds of people he saw on the streets of Boston and New York, which displayed their modern professions and societal rank in a simplified and unified fashion, completely differed from those in Japan. The streets were full of variety. Fraser's "fullness and variety" could be found there.

An *amma-san* in the streets (from Arnold, *Seas and Lands*)

In considering the civilization of old Japan, we must constantly keep in mind that this variety divided and subdivided portions of the cities and towns into unique enclaves where people lived and others found refuge. If we adopt the ideas of Nietzsche's ecology, then the old Japanese civilization was at the peak of this paradigm if we believe, as Nietzsche did, that a richness of variety that differentiates individuals is essential for a civilization to succeed. If a pipe-repairer chose to specialize and focus on becoming a pipe-cleaner, he or she could make a living based on this extremely limited and exclusive profession.

People with disabilities, meanwhile, were not placed into institutions and could make a living on their own without any specialized care. Edwin Arnold wrote:[6]

> One of the most ordinary figures in the Japanese streets and lanes is the *Amma-san*, or shampooer. By daytime you will see him wending his slow way—for he is quite blind—through the throng, guiding himself and warning others to keep clear of him, by the bamboo staff which he carries, and with which he constantly touches the ground a little in advance of his footsteps. By night you hear rather than see him, tootling a melancholy note, something like the cry of a plover, upon a little reed flute, which he bears with him…and his profession,

as one who practices the scientific "massage," is the great resource of blind men and women in Japan, who would otherwise prove a burden on their families, but are here a source of support, very often, indeed, amassing wealth, and adding the profession of money-lending to their original vocation. The blind shampooer would not be possible where wheel-traffic existed. His plaintive cry would be drowned in the uproar of hooves and wheels, and he himself would be run over a hundred times. But in Tokio there is nothing for him to fear except the *jinrikishas*, which make no noise, and scrupulously avoid colliding with children and the *Amma-san*.

Imagine yourself on the streets of Tokyo with Arnold in the late 1880s. You might see four men walking by, carrying a white, square-shaped box on their shoulders—a coffin. As Arnold said, "The dead gets to see Tokyo for the last time." However, he also had this to say:[7]

You need not be too melancholy about it; nobody greatly dreads or dislikes dying in Japan, where religion has been defined as "a little fear and a great deal of fun." The clog-maker, the girl grinding ice in the *Kori-mizu* shop, the hawker with fried eels, the little naked boys and girls at play; the priest, the policemen in white, and the pretty, tripping *musumë*, look at the cortége a little, but with their laughter and chat only half suspended...The street, which had stood aside a little for the procession, fills anew with *misoku*, i.e. "coolies," or "leg-men," toiling at wheeling timber, assisted heartily by old ladies in light blue trousers; students in flat caps and scarlet socks; wandering *etas*, the Japanese pariahs; perambulating shopkeepers, such as the moji-yaki, or "letter-burner," who bakes sweet paste into characters, animals, or baskets; his fellow, the *ame-ya*, or jelly-man, who, from barley-gluten, will blow you, by a reed, rats, rabbits, or monkeys.

Arnold also described ragpickers, sparrow handlers, boys carrying medicine chests for doctors, fortune-tellers, tofu-makers, sand artists, and, of course, the *amma* masseurs that he saw in the streets. He listed a great variety of examples of the people he saw, and each one of them had a place to live, albeit modestly. Yet the people filled the streets with vigor and happiness. As Arnold also said, "The somber color of the houses, and their black and white heavy roofs and ridges, would give a too subdued and almost somber look to a Japanese street, if it were not for the gay contents of the shops, and the bright, good-tempered busy throngs in the roadway."[8]

Now, imagine following Arnold down a side street to see all of the small shops huddled there. There are so many, but the one that stands out is the liquor store. It has a sign made with the branches of a Japanese cryptomeria tree, and letters and pictures adorn the beautiful sake barrels. There are many other stores as well, including a cabinet maker, a clog and straw sandal maker, a lamp store, a china store, a rice store, a flower shop, a tin seller, a tofu store, and a Buddhist altar store. At the fish market we can see gargantuan shellfish, blue and yellow prawns, octopus and dried cuttlefish, bonito flakes, smoked salmon, squid, dried sardines, seaweed, oysters, abalone, and every other kind of seafood known to man. The last place we come to is the bath house.[9] The details in Arnold's descriptions are nothing short of remarkable.

Isabella Bird described the stores that she saw when she visited Niigata in 1878 in similarly great detail in a chapter fittingly titled, "The Shops."[10] While stating that "'The gorgeous east' is not a phrase which applies to anything in Japan except to a few temples" and pointing out the shabby nature of Japanese stores that hid their most magnificent goods in the back, she was nonetheless drawn in by the various types of businesses displayed there. She wrote:

> The coopers' and basket-makers' shops contain articles of exquisite neatness of workmanship and singular adaptability. I never pass a cooper's without longing to become a purchaser. A common tub, by careful choice of woods and attention to taste and neatness of detail, is turned into an *objet d'art*. The basket-work, coarse and fine, is simply wonderful, from the great bamboo cages which are used to hold stones in their place for breakwaters, down to the grasshoppers, spiders, and beetles of such deceptively imitative art that you feel inclined to brush them off the fine plaited fans to which they are artificially attached. Shops of the same kind herd together; thus, in one long street, one sees little except for toy-shops with stuffed and china animals on wheels, windmills and waterwheels, toy idols and idol cars, battledores and shuttlecocks, sugar toys of all kinds, and dolls of all sizes. A short street contains few but barbers' shops, another is devoted to the sale of wigs, chignons, toupées, and the switches of coarse black hair which the women interweave dexterously with their own. An adjacent street is full of shops where all sorts of pins for the hair are sold, from the plain brass or silver pin costing a trifle, to the elaborate tortoise-shell pin with a group of birds or bamboos finely carved, costing 8 or 12 *yen* at least. I counted 117 different kinds of ornamental hair-pins!

Bird went on to mention that there were stores that specialized in goods used to tie one's hair in a topknot, clog stores, paper umbrella stores, rain umbrella and parasol stores, paper raincoat and wrapping paper stores, stores that sold straw sandals for horse riders, straw raincoat and hat stores, and stores that sold packsaddles. There were also lacquerware and Buddhist altar stores on the main street. There were used clothing stores, fan stores, stores that sold hanging scrolls, *byōbu* screen stores, stores that sold cords for *haori* coats, stores that sold boiled and dried baby sardines, handkerchief stores, tobacco pipe stores, stores that only sold writing brushes, stores that only sold ink, stores that only sold inkstone boxes, and, of course, there were bookstores. Furthermore, "The number of shops for the sale of paper is enormous," according to Bird, and there were also stores that only sold hibachi braziers and stores that only sold chopsticks. There were paper lantern stores, oil lampstand stores, teakettle stores, sewing kit stores, kitchenware stores, teapot stores, and liquor stores, and there were china stores everywhere. Speaking of china, Bird also stated that "Everywhere in the interior[11] one sees horses loaded with it, and there is hardly a wayside teahouse at which I have not seen morsels, some of them very old, which I longed to buy." Many shops sold hemp string and rope and the food stores were always crowded. However, Bird noted these locales were not as noisy as similar places in her homeland.

What is surprising about Bird's descriptions is the incredibly specialized nature of the goods sold at each store. It is hard to imagine that someone could make a living by running a store that only sold cords for *haori* coats or inkstone boxes. Naturally, such establishments were probably small in size. This means that the number of people living off of a fixed volume of trade was actually quite large. In other words, stated in ecologic terms, there was an extremely specialized and diverse differentiation of labor. There were also spaces in which the poor could make a modest living.

Furthermore, dealing in one specialized type of item bred a specialized attachment to and knowledge of these goods. Goods took on a sort of personality, and the shop owners, conversely, took on the nature of their goods, be it calligraphy brushes, chopsticks, or fans. This tendency occupied a fixed position in the general flow of society, increasing the responsibility and amplifying the contentment of the shop owners. This is what the division of labor entailed. At the same time, moreover, many of them were also master craftsmen. In other words, coopers sold the barrels they made themselves, and so on. Stores were essentially workshops. As Morse stated, "The interminable shops lining the streets, all open from side to side and all the activities fully exposed; the umbrella-maker, fan-painter, seal-cutter, every craft being practiced in open daylight, all seem like a grotesque dream."[12] In other words, the streets were like an exhibition hall showing off the products and creations of society.

As Arnold said, meanwhile, the side streets had the ecology of an extremely diverse set of stores. Thus, the common people did not live in simple residential habitats. Rather, they led diverse lives interspersed among the various small shops and could see the diversity in handicrafts and other goods displayed in the streets near their homes. This made the daily lives of the people as diverse as the division of labor. In other words, every social activity and profession became part of one revolving beacon that was reflected in the eyes of people walking in the streets. These places were varied and diverse, and conjured up the very idea of fullness.

Percival Lowell (1855–1916), who is known for founding the Lowell Observatory, felt this way when he said the shops lining the "Broadway of Tokio" in 1877 made for a "shopper's paradise." He noted that beautiful chinaware, pocket books, and fans lined the streets awash in "a fairy-like vista of illumination," and customers could not help but gaze at these wares even though they were common household goods. He also said, "The street vendors revealed their charms and magnificent antiques shone above the garden." There were also flower shops. Everything gave Lowell "an acute case of shopping fever." He found himself following along with a crowd of adults and children clad in picturesque clothing and stated, "And you, carried along with the current, wander for miles with the tide of the pleasure-seekers, till, late at night, when you at last turn reluctantly homeward, you feel as one does when wakened from some too delightful dream."[13]

Foreign observers in Japan at the end of the Edo period only had limited contact with the lives of the Japanese city dwellers due to the closed nature of big cities such as Edo. Thus, their observations of commercial districts in Edo and Nagasaki never really delved into discovering the level of economic prosperity in Japan. When Robert Fortune stepped into Edo's central commercial district, he was disappointed to find that nothing of any worth could be seen lined up in front of the shops. Westerners would later find out that Japanese merchants kept their most valuable goods inside their stores and only brought them out at the customer's request, but Fortune did not know this when he made his trip into the shopping district. However, he did notice that a great many daily goods such as silk and cotton clothing, lacquerware, bronzeware, porcelain, umbrellas, tobacco pipes, toys, and paper products were on display. Edo was neither an industrial center nor a trade hub, so he believed it was only natural that the shops dealt with these daily necessities.[14]

Vysheslavtsov had a similar impression when he visited Edo's commercial district. He stated that there were shops on every street and alley as far as the eye could see, and these locales were packed with an incredible number of handicrafts. Upon considering Edo's population of two million people (this was the number that Vysheslavtsov heard at the time), however, this made sense. He went on to say that the basic necessities, such as straw sandals, braided straw hats, ready-made apparel, ironware, weapons, religious instruments, groceries, books, paintings, and other daily commodities were usually sold, and that as one walked past the front of hundreds of different stores, he or she might suddenly find the need to scream.[15] However, Vysheslavtsov did not see any of the luxurious lacquerware and porcelain he had seen beautifully displayed in Yokohama. He even wondered whether the common people had any connection at all with these artistic works. Henry Tilley noticed the same phenomenon while he was in Nagasaki. He stated that "I often wondered what became of the rich and decorated utensils and furniture displayed in the shops, as I never once saw any such in use among the people, nor even at the feasts of the higher classes."[16]

However, some of the observers noticed that there were extremely unique and remarkable articles that the Japanese used in their everyday lives. Sherard Osborn stated:[17]

It was wonderful to see the thousand useful as well as ornamental purposes to which paper was applicable in the hands of these industrious and tasteful people; our papier-maché manufacturers, as well as the Continental ones, should go to Yedo to learn what can be done with paper. We saw it made into material so closely resembling russian and morocco leather and pig-skin, that it was difficult to detect the difference. With the aid of lacker-varnish and skillful painting, paper made excellent trunks, tobacco-bags, cigar-cases, saddles, telescope-cases, the frames of microscopes; and we even saw and used excellent waterproof coats made of simple paper, which *did* keep out the rain, and were as supple as the best Mackintosh.

These lightweight and effectively waterproof raincoats only cost eighteen pence apiece according to Oliphant. Reinhold Werner, one of the members of the Eulenburg expedition, also said that the Japanese wrapped themselves in raincoats made of oiled paper in the winter rain and snow and that every member of his party was able to receive a tailor-made, completely waterproof raincoat for a total of only nine marks.[18]

Perhaps we should take a brief sidetrack and delve a bit deeper into the excitement that Japanese handicrafts aroused in foreign observers. Laurence Oliphant, a member of the Earl of Elgin's mission to Japan in 1858 to conclude the Anglo-Japanese Treaty of Amity and Commerce, wrote the following about the bazaars he saw in Shimoda:[19]

These bazaars are the most tantalising of resorts. There is so much displayed, and it is all so beautiful and new that one walks through avenues of brilliant novelties in a stupefied condition of mind, and with a strong sensation of overwhelming responsibility. If anybody would only come and tell one which to choose, and what was most likely to be admired at home. Alas! everybody else is buying furiously…all the best things are being bought up under your nose, and there you stand bewildered and dismayed; so you finally determine to buy recklessly and indiscriminately, until your pocket is emptied of its contents.

Osborn, a member of the same party, related the following:[20]

We found the Dutch bazaar at Decima [Dejima] filled with porcelain and lacker-ware in a thousand tasteful forms; we had fancied ourselves perfectly *blasé* about all "curiosities," but such impenetrability gave way rapidly with the temptation before us. The first feeling was a desire to buy up everything, where all was so pretty. Tables, curiously inlaid with mother-of-pearl—representations of birds and animals, which our papier-maché manufacturers, or those of France, would give anything to be able to imitate—cabinets, on which golden fish or tortoise stood out in most truthful relief—wonderful little gems in ivory, bone, or wood, fifty times more replete with originality, skill, and wit than anything China ever produced—porcelain so delicate, that you were almost afraid to touch it—in short, a child in a pastry-cook's shop never ran from sweet to sweet more perplexed to know which to invest in, than we that morning in Decima bazaar!

The feverish excitement that gripped Lord Elgin's mission also claimed members of the Prussian Eulenburg expedition, which visited Japan two years later. According to Reinhold Werner, the coffers of the *Elbe*, the ship he commanded, were nearly empty after just five days during their stay in Nagasaki, and rooms on the ship were filled with boxes of pottery and lacquerware.[21]

These are perhaps the earliest examples of excitement surrounding Japanese handicrafts among the Japonists in the West. In 1885, Edward Morse described how widespread Japonism had become in the U.S. in the following manner:[22]

Within twenty years there has gradually appeared in our country a variety of Japanese objects conspicuous for their novelty and beauty,-lacquers, pottery and porcelain, forms in wood and metal, curious shaped boxes, quaint ivory carvings, fabrics in cloth and paper, and a number of other objects as perplexing in their purpose as the inscriptions they often bore. Most of these presented technicalities in their work as enigmatical as were their designs, strange caprices in their ornamentation which, though violating our hitherto recognized properties of decoration, surprised and yet delighted us...Gradually, yet surely, these arts, at first so little understood, modified our own methods of ornamentation, until frescos and wall-papers, wood-work and carpets, dishes and table-cloths, metal work and book-covers, Christmas cards and even railroad advertisements were decorated, modelled, and designed after the Japanese style...Not only our own commercial nation, but art-loving France, musical Germany, and even conservative England yielded to this invasion.

Morse even stated that due to the wonderful effects of this Japonism, "it was a relief...to have driven out of our dwelling the nightmares and horrors of design we had before endured so meekly."

Perhaps the first person to have sold these handicrafts discovered in Japan was Captain Henry Holmes. In 1858, he loaded his ship, the *Troas*, with coal and set sail from London to Shanghai. There, the talk of the town was how Japan was going to open its ports to the rest of the world in six months due to the recent trade agreements that the country had concluded. Holmes met with the Jardine Matheson Trading House and worked out a deal to load 200 tons of sugar onto his ship for them and set sail for Nagasaki. Holmes borrowed the nautical maps that Captain Osborn had used to visit Japan the previous year, but according to the captain, these charts were by no means complete, and he had to be on his guard. Holmes arrived in Nagasaki in February 1859, about six months before the conditions stipulated by the agreement went into effect. He was aware of the risk that, depending on the situation, foreign ships were sometimes seized and impounded by the shogunate, but when he arrived, the shogunate officials simply asked conventional questions such as where he had come from and why he was visiting Japan, as well as his name and the name of his ship. Thus, he was able to safely land and unload his cargo without incident.

I introduced a portion of Holmes's "adventures" during his forty-four-day stay in Nagasaki earlier. However, the captain did not just enter peoples' homes in the early morning or, as we will touch on later, stare at a completely naked young woman he almost bumped into on the street. He had a mission, as it were. In his words, he "ransacked every nook and corner in the town" in his search for strange and unique Japanese products to buy. He wrote:[23]

I entered house after house, ransacked it from top to bottom, turning out the contents of boxes, cabinets and drawers, and covering the floor with them, with the family looking on and as much amused as I was myself. What would an English family think of a Japanese entering their home and doing the same? to say nothing of entering a house with the family at rest, arousing them and commencing a morning romp on the floor.

After his stay in Japan, Holmes loaded his ship with two to three tons of sea-weed at the request of the Jardine Matheson Trading House representative traveling with him, and they set sail for Hong Kong. On the night they landed, Holmes was interviewed by a newspaper reporter because his visit to Japan before the trade agreement took effect was an enticing story. The interviewer started by asking Holmes his opinion of the country of Japan and its people. "My opinion of the people is that they will surprise the world," he replied.

At around five o'clock the next morning, four or five gentlemen paid Holmes a visit. Even though the captain asked them to come back at a more reasonable hour, they refused to leave. Holmes reluctantly went to meet them, thinking it a matter of great importance if they could not wait until later, but he discovered they just wanted information about Japan and to see what he had brought with him from that fascinating land. Holmes mentioned he indeed had his own collection of things and could show the pieces to them at a later date, but they begged to see something right away. He saw it was no use and asked the ship steward to unpack and bring out some of the things he had stowed away. When the items appeared, the gentlemen could only gasp.

"How beautiful; is that for sale?" one of them asked.

"I do not wish to sell anything at present," Holmes replied. However, this only made the men more determined to buy something. One of the gentle-men set his heart on a pair of bronzes that were brought out and repeatedly beseeched the captain by saying "Tell me the price and book them for me." Reluctantly, Holmes gave a price of twelve pounds, and the man bought them on the spot. Holmes had obtained the bronzes in Japan for five *ryo*, or about twenty-five shillings, thus selling them for nearly ten times the original amount.[24]

After landing in Hong Kong and finishing his business with the Jardine Matheson Trading House, Holmes returned to his ship and "found a motley group of Europeans and Chinamen all waiting the return of the showman to exhibit the collection of Japanese skill in works of art, manufactures and samples of products of the country." He also noted that he was "besieged by an excited throng of sightseers, collectors of curiosities, scientific men, all eager to inspect and purchase." He found this spectacle somewhat peculiar and even said that "Had I come from the Moon or some unknown world there could not have been more excitement." Holmes also wrote that he owed the newspaper reporter a debt of gratitude for making him rich by using his "fertile brain" and writing "such a flaming account from the little information I gave him."

On the second day, "there were connoisseurs, doctors, lawyers, and Government officials mixed up with a superior class of Chinamen." Everything remaining in his collection, namely, "swords, cabinets, temples, bronzes, gold coins, rare porcelain, specimens of silk and embroidery," was sold. Holmes also noted that "the general opinion was that the Japanese must be a clever people." He went on to say that "The Governor of Hong Kong bought the swords...Chinamen the gold coins, willingly giving me 100 per cent profit."[25]

It goes without saying that the valuable pottery, lacquerware, bronzes, and other artifacts that visitors to Japan were in a frenzy over had little to do with the lives of Japanese commoners. Albert Berg, for instance, was likely describing a samurai home when he praised the fact that everything, from wash buckets to ladles used to give water to horses, was covered in lacquer. However, Westerners did not just aim their praise at the beauty of the superior Japanese arts and handicrafts, but also the fact that such articles of good taste managed to penetrate the daily lives of ordinary Japanese citizens.

Aimé Humbert, for instance, noticed consistent shapes in handicrafts exhibited in front of shops in the commercial district of Edo, all of which his countrymen would likely have labeled works of *bon gout*, or good taste. He said the craftsmen in Edo were true artists. He also noticed that packages sold at seed stores had the names and colored pictures of the plants on them, illustrations he likened to small masterpieces that looked like they had been copied out of booklets about Japanese plants. However, they were actually the work of young shop owners who simply drew and painted the pictures on paper sprawled out on tatami mats.[26] Humbert also could not help noticing the Japanese middle-class dining ware he saw when he was surrounded by trays during a simple lunch. When he saw how deftly and masterfully the people used this beautiful dining ware, which included bowls, sake cups, plates, small boxes, lacquered trays, bottles, rice bowls, and savory teapots, he thought the people looked more like oversized children playing house than having a meal.[27]

Facecloths also drew the attention of foreign observers. Émile Guimet, for example, described small sheets of cloth colored in bright indigo with an elegant white design that could be used as facecloths to wipe away sweat, as well as bandanas that people could wear on their heads. He went on to say that no one wore the sheets on their heads in exactly the same way. He described it as a unified sense of variety.[28]

Alice Bacon, meanwhile, wrote:[29]

I cannot see exactly why the Japanese keep on making the cheapest things so pretty, for many of them are never chosen at all for their beauty, but simply considered for their quality. For instance, there is a kind of blue and white toweling, very coarse, that comes at from one to five cents a yard, that is used by all the coolies and jinrikisha men, and never regarded as pretty or decorative in any way; but still it comes in the loveliest designs, and when freed from its association with coolies might be used for almost any purpose of house decoration.

Americans like Bacon considered "cheap" and "nasty" to be synonyms, but even the cheapest articles in Japan had beautiful and artistic designs on them. Bacon also stated the following:[30]

The cheap prints, the blue and white towels, the common teacups and pots, the great iron kettles in use over the fire in the farmhouse kitchen; all these are things as pretty and tasteful in their way as the rich crêpes, the silver incense burners, the delicate porcelain, and the elegant lacquer that fill the storehouse of the daimiō.

Bacon explained the reason why cheap goods in Japan were so beautiful in the following passage:[31]

The instinct of beauty is so strong in the Japanese artisan that things come from his hands beautiful, whether he makes anything pecuniarily by it or not...The china stores which contain nothing but the cheapest earthenware used by the commonest of the people are one blaze of beauty in color, form, and decoration.

Bacon felt that "here [in Japan] every poor man's table service is dainty and delicate in the highest degree." She was also certain that "in this country there is no need of the various missions (flower missions and the like) that have been started in England and America to cultivate the aesthetic sense of the poor in the great cities." In other words, she felt the Japanese people were "more civilized" than Americans. What is even more surprising is that she said, "The word 'civilization' is so difficult to define and understand, that I do not know what it means now as well as I did when I left home." For Bacon, the concept of culture was changing from something ideal and moral into something trivial and commonplace.

This cultivated and artistic nature also spread to the kitchens and dining halls across Japan. During Isabella Bird's trip across Tohoku, she was impressed by how clean and orderly everything looked when she was served food at inns. She stated that "However dirty the clothing and even houses of the poorer classes are, I have never seen anything but extreme cleanliness in the cooking and serving of meals." Jephson and Elmhirst of the Ninth Regiment also stated the following about eating in Yokohama:[32]

> We may mention that on more than one occasion, when returning home late at night, we have partaken of the delicate seaweed soup that is hawked about in the streets of every town, and *that* without any fear of either the materials of the soup itself, of the cups we drank out of, being less clean than at our own table.

They also stated that "Extreme cleanliness characterises not only their dwellings, but their food, manner of cooking, serving it, &c." Bird was impressed even more by the beauty of utensils used in the kitchen, saying:[33]

> Each cooking utensil has its special beauty and fitness, and the people take a pride both in their cleanliness and antiquity. Many an inn kitchen contains articles in bronze and iron which are worth all the gaudy and tasteless rubbish of many a Yokohama curio shop, specially iron and bronze kettles of antique and elaborate workmanship, in design at least equal to those in the Imperial Treasury at Nara, and even exceeding in grace of form and delicacy of execution the cooking utensils in the Pompeiian room of the Naples Museum.

The same could be said for other tools and implements used in the home and elsewhere. Bird also visited Kyoto and marveled at the articles lined up outside the small, dingy-looking stores that lined the streets. She stated that "It is not alone the costly things which connoisseurs buy, but household furnishings made for peasant use, which are often faultless in form, colour, and general effect…The highest art and some unspeakably low things go together." She also thought that "An English workman who 'scamps' his work…should see what honest, careful, loving labour does here in perfection of finish for one shilling a day."[34]

Arnold, meanwhile, said, "Nothing is ugly in the very humblest Japanese home. From the rice-tub to the hairpins, all domestic and personal articles are more or less beautiful and becoming."[35] He thought the common furnishings looked like jeweler's work, the tatami mats looked as if woven with silk, and the buckets and baskets as delicate as ivory work. Hübner also summed up what he saw:[36]

A taste for the fine arts is common among the very lowest classes, and to a degree which is not found in any country in Europe. In the humblest cottage you will find traces of this…With us…this kind of art is the privilege of the rich and of people in easy circumstances. In Japan it is everyone's property.

It goes without saying that good taste also appeared in clothing. Oliphant, for instance, felt "The Japanese are remarkable for the simplicity and elegance of their taste in matters of dress and ornament, as a general rule avoiding gaudy patterns, or any thing which, in the vernacular of the day, is known as 'loud.'"[37] He was not the only one to feel this way, as many other foreign observers at the time shared this sentiment. Diaz Covarrubias, for instance, noticed that women's clothes were usually vivid and showy on the bottom, but a bit plain on top.[38] Naturally, this was a chic sense of fashion at the time. As early as the sixteenth century, however, Luís Fróis (1532–1597) actually noticed that the Japanese wore good clothing on the bottom and poor clothing on top.[39]

According to Vysheslavtsov, meanwhile, Japanese women's clothing was not disparaging, and the uppermost clothing was usually a plain color, such as deep purple, brown, or navy blue, replete with a detailed damask pattern, no matter how magnificent the material may have been.[40] When Arnold met the wife of Count Kuroda Kiyotaka, he felt her kimono was "quiet in colour and cut, almost to Quakerism," even though the material was so luxurious.[41] Of course, not every woman wore kimono with subdued colors. It was widely known that young women and girls wore kimono with bright, vivacious colors. Vysheslavtsov even noted how brightly the silver and golden embroidery on the clothes of geisha and other women who sat along the latticed windows glittered in the light, illuminating the night.[42]

The extremely simple Japanese rooms and furnishings became the subject of surprise and ridicule to most Westerners. Even Morse said that when he stepped into a Japanese room for the first time, he was surprised it "appeared absolutely barren" and that a "search for an object aside from the bare rooms seemed fruitless." He went on to say that "one got the idea that the house was to be let." He also wondered how one could decorate a room with no mantel, no cabinet, and no desks or chairs with beautiful decorations, antiques, paintings, drapes, and other decorative furnishings. After making several observations, however, he realized that "Absolute cleanliness and refinement, with very few objects in sight upon which the eye may rest contentedly, are the main features in household adornment which the Japanese strive after." He went on to say that the tatami mats, the papers of the *fusuma*, the walls, and the cedar board ceilings—the neutral colors of which created a restful atmosphere, "all combine to render the room quiet and refined to the last degree." Therefore, Morse reasoned, "Such a room requires but little adornment in the shape of extraneous ornaments." Furthermore, Morse stated, "The general tone of the room sets off to perfection the simplest spray of flowers, a quiet picture, a rough bit of pottery, or an old bronze...and yet the harmony is not disturbed."[43]

Morse also stated that the stuffiness and maze-like nature created by furnishings and decorations in an American room would have likely driven the Japanese crazy. Georges Bousquet embraced the exact same sentiment as Morse on this point. He stated that the Japanese still faithfully maintained their homes in the classical style and that even though they were simple and modest, the insides of the wonderfully plain rooms contained none of the eyesores that almost always cheapened the look of bourgeois salons in the West.[44]

In his book *Japanese Homes and Their Surroundings*, Morse reinforced the point that Japanese rooms, which at first glance appeared haphazard, were actually detailed and rich and contained a plethora of intricate designs and decorations. He particularly praised the *ramma*, or transom window, design and included several illustrations in his book to show readers examples of its beauty. He included the *ramma* found in old family homes in Gojō Village, Yamato Province (located in present-day Gojō City, Nara Prefecture) and Yatsushiro Town, Higo Province (located in present-day Yatsushiro City, Kumamoto Prefecture). In both cases, Morse found it deeply impressive that "the work had been done by a local artist." He went on to say:[45]

> It is a remarkable fact, and one well worth calling attention to, that in the smaller towns and villages, in regions far apart, there seems to be artistic workmen capable of designing and executing these graceful and artistic carvings—for such they certainly are.

Morse grew angry when he thought about the "hundreds of towns and thousands of villages in our country where the carpenter is just capable of making a shelter from the weather." He wondered why this was possible in Japan and reasoned that Japanese workmen "have learned their trades—

Ramma design, above: Gojo Village, Yamato Province; below: Yatsushiro Town, Higo Province (from Morse, *Japanese Homes*)

not 'served' them—and are employed at home." Morse also noted that "the people everywhere appreciate artistic designs and the proper execution of them; and, consequently, men capable in their various lines find their services in demand wherever they may be." In other words, Morse came to the conclusion that the affinity for good taste that had even spread to the level of the common people in Japan was proof that Japanese workmen maintained a certain artistic eagerness that went beyond just hammering nails into wooden planks. This was what civilization entailed. In this case, Morse's views came very close to those of British socialist activist William Morris (1834–1896).

Morse also knew that the Japanese were collectors of a wide variety of beautiful and curious items. It surprised him that "Within these plain and unpretentious houses there is often to be seen marvels of exquisite carving, and the perfection of cabinet work."[46] However, Morse noticed that whereas Americans "parade in the most unreasoning manner every object of this nature in our possession," in Japanese homes "these [objects] are rarely exposed" and were usually kept in a *kura*, or storehouse. He also saw that pictures in the *tokonoma* were changed regularly, something Morse found much more rational than the Western custom of displaying every single handicraft in one room and leaving the same pictures on the wall for ages.[47] Sugimoto Etsuko, who was born into the home of a former advisor to the Nagaoka domain and who married Sugimoto Matsuo, a Japanese man who ran a business in the eastern United States, remarked about the experience she had with this. After arriving in the United States, she lived for a while in an American home cramped with furnishings and decorations, a domicile that she said "reminded me of godowns." She also said, "It was several months before I could overcome the impression that the disarranged profusion of articles was a temporary convenience, and that very soon they would be returned to the godown."[48]

Conversely, around the time Alice Bacon started living in Japan, she thought it "most enviable" that Japanese homes were all but absent of furniture, which freed them from cleaning and maintaining such articles. She also could not help being moved by the fact that the simple Japanese furnishings were "much better than many of our modern conveniences and inventions." She even praised the hibachi, the Japanese braziers that often became the target of American ridicule for being the weakest of heaters. She stated:[49]

> The arrangement is very far superior to an alcohol lamp, as well as much cheaper, and why we do not use it in America I cannot imagine, except that we are not bright enough to think of such a simple thing; and, besides, we like the more complicated and expensive ways better.

As I mentioned earlier, Eliza Scidmore wrote, "Every-day life looks too theatrical, too full of artistic and decorative effects, to be actual and serious." She probably felt this was true in every aspect of Japanese life. For example, a room with hardly any furniture could have been taken for a stage, and hibachi braziers and tea ceremony utensils that appeared could have easily passed for stage props. Bacon, meanwhile, had seen the roughly five square meter room of the girl who married the chauffeur that Bacon retained, and she noted the girl's utensils looked like children's toys. In other words, tools that the Japanese used in their daily lives did not look real, but rather appeared as surrealistic implements that looked more like stage props or toys.

If the Japanese were leading lives that looked more like stage plays to visitors to Japan, this means that it was common practice among everyone in society to focus on beauty, refinement, and good taste in order to lessen the real struggles of life. Morse stated the following in regard to this point:[50]

> One of the many delights in riding through the country are the beautiful hedges along the road, the clean-swept walks before the doors, and in the houses everything so neat and the various objects in perfect taste; the dainty teacups, teapots, bronze vessels for holding the burning charcoal, beautiful grained panels, odd knots from trees, and woody fungus hollowed out to hold flowers. And all these beautiful things are in the houses of the common country farmers.

Morse also gave another example to illustrate this point. While on his way home from his trip to Nikko, he stopped at an inn in a dingy-looking town. When he stepped inside, however, he was quite moved by the *tokonoma*, noting its "rough, worm-eaten wood for a shelf, the natural trunk of a tree for the mid-post, a simple kakemono. The details were solidly constructed." When he recalled "the things that decorate the walls of similar places at home—prize fights, burlesque horse race, or naked women," he felt the Japanese were far superior in "refinement" than his fellow countrymen.[51]

The variety, refinement, and everything else the foreign observers had seen were all elements of a separate and distinct Japanese civilization, one that abundantly supplied its people with tools and other implements to make life easier while also focusing on the notion of good taste. As Chamberlain eloquently phrased it, "The charm here is in the street life of the lower classes…the delicate art adorning each common object of every-day life."[52]

Notes

1 Fraser, *Diplomatist's Wife*, 27–8.

2 Fraser, *Diplomatist's Wife*, 2.

3 Scidmore, *Jinrikisha*, iii.

4 Scidmore, *Jinrikisha*, 2.

5 Morse, *Day by Day*, Vol. 1, 262–3.

6 Arnold, *Seas and Lands*, 457–8.

7 Arnold, *Japonica*, 65–6.

8 Arnold, *Japonica*, 64.

9 Arnold, *Japonica*, 48–50.

10 Bird, *Unbeaten Tracks*, Vol. 1, 225–33.

11 "The interior" was a term that frequently appeared in English writings during the early-to-mid Meiji period and referred to communal inland dwellings outside the range of the treaty ports established by the Ansei Treaties of 1858. Visitors to Japan could not travel into these areas without a passport. "The interior" later disappeared due to treaty revisions.

12 Morse, *Day by Day*, Vol. 1, 263.

13 Percival Lowell, *The Soul of the Far East* (Boston and New York: Houghton, Mifflin, and Co., 1888), 114–7.

14 Fortune, *Yedo and Peking*, 121.

15 Vysheslavtsov, *Ocherki perom*, 43.

16 Tilley, *Japan, the Amoor*, 96.

17 Osborn, *Cruise*, 181–2.

18 Werner, *Die Preussische Expedition*, 144.

19 Oliphant, *Narrative*, Vol. 2, 76–7.

20 Osborn, *Cruise*, 41.

21 Werner, *Die Preussische Expedition*, 29.

22 Morse, *Japanese Homes*, 25–26.

23 Holmes, *My Adventures*, 31–2.

24 Holmes, *My Adventures*, 33–6.

25 Holmes, *My Adventures*, 37–9.

26 Humbert, *Japan and the Japanese*, Vol. 2, 10 (translated from the Japanese version).

27 Humbert, *Japan and the Japanese*, Vol. 2, 14–5 (translated from the Japanese version).

28 Guimet, *Promenades-Kanagawa*, 68.

29 Bacon, *Japanese Interior*, 226.

30 Bacon, *Japanese Girls and Women, Revised and Enlarged Edition* (Boston and New York, 1902), 236–7.

31 Bacon, *Japanese Interior*, 227–8.

32 Jephson and Elmhirst, *Our Life*, 381.

33 Bird, *Unbeaten Tracks*, Vol. 1, 241–2.

34 Bird, *Unbeaten Tracks*, Vol. 2, 254–6.

35 Arnold, *Seas and Lands*, 340–1.

36 Hübner, *Ramble*, 265–6.

37 Oliphant, *Narrative*, 387.

38 Diaz Covarrubias, *Viaje*, 50–1.

39 Luís Fróis, *Kulturgegensätze Europa-Japan* (Tokyo: Sophia Universität, 1955). No English translation of Fróis's work exists, so passages that appear in this book have been translated from the Japanese version. See Huroisu [Fróis], "Nichiō bunka hikaku" ["A Cultural Comparison of Japan and Europe"], in *Daikōkai Sōsho Dai-11-kan* [Great Voyages Series, Vol. 11] (Iwanami Shoten, 1965), 507. Subsequent citations will appear as Fróis, *Europa-Japan*, and will list page numbers

from the Japanese text.

40 Vysheslavtsov, *Ocherki perom*, 130–1.

41 Arnold, *Seas and Lands*, 203.

42 Vysheslavtsov, *Ocherki perom*, 131.

43 Morse, *Japanese Homes*, 309–16.

44 Bousquet, *Le Japon*, Vol. 2, 715.

45 Morse, *Japanese Homes*, 171–2.

46 Morse, *Japanese Homes*, 9–10.

47 Morse, *Japanese Homes*, 309, 316–7.

48 Sugimoto, *Daughter*, 182.

49 Bacon, *Japanese Interior*, 42, 36–7.

50 Morse, *Day by Day*, Vol. 1, 54–5.

51 Morse, *Day by Day*, Vol. 1, 107–8.

52 Chamberlain, *Things Japanese*, 439.

Chapter
6

Labor and the Body

Aimé Humbert, who led the Swiss delegation to Japan, arrived in the country in April 1863, and after a difficult round of negotiations that lasted for about ten months, he finally concluded a treaty of amity and commerce between the two countries in February 1864. Over the course of these proceedings, Humbert was able to escape the negotiating table from time to time and experience the real Japan. He was particularly impressed by the fact that "for centuries they [the Japanese] had enjoyed the pleasures of an easy and simple life." He went on to write the following:[1]

> I witnessed the last days of the age of innocence, in which, with the exception of some great merchants whom fortune had obstinately pursued with its favours, no one worked except to live, and no one lived except to enjoy existence. Work itself had the place in the category of the purest and deepest enjoyments. The artizan had a passion for his work, and, far from counting the hours, the days, the weeks, which he gave to it, it was with reluctance that he drew himself away from it till he had at length brought it—not to a certain saleable value, which was less the object of his care—but to that state of perfection which satisfied him. If he were tired, he left his workshop and rested himself for as long or as short a time as he pleased, either in his house, or in company with his friends at some place of amusement.

In this case, Humbert likened Swiss workers he remembered seeing in his youth to the Japanese commoners he was currently observing. This is actually what he meant by "the pleasures of an easy and simple life."

Rutherford Alcock, meanwhile, touched on this reality by writing that "This is not a country in which...time [is], apparently, estimated as a valuable commodity,"[2] and "In truth, the Japanese in general seem to take life and its labors very easily, and are never too busy to collect in vast crowds to see any thing novel."[3] Thus, the lives of the Japanese were simple, leisurely, and carefree. Morse felt the Japanese people, who appeared to be busy but actually took a relaxed approach to their duties, were "a good-humored and contented, as well as a happy race" for this reason.

However, whereas Humbert and Alcock saw the Japanese leading easy-going and comfortable lives, Rudolf Lindau viewed them as incorrigible idlers. Lindau first set foot in Japan in 1859 and visited the country again in 1861, and he published records detailing his impressions of these visits in the Parisian literary magazine *Revue des Deux Mondes*. He was then able to come to Japan for a third time in 1864, this time as the Swiss consul. He published his book *Un Voyage Autour du Japon* in 1864, which, along with Alcock's *The Capital of the Tycoon*, was one of the most popular books among Westerners who visited Japan during this time period. In his book, Lindau wrote:[4]

> The number of people who do not do anything in Japan is stagger-ing. Most of them just squat around a hibachi, drink tea, and smoke tobacco with a small pipe, and they all seem to have the most contented looks on their faces. They also sit and talk with each other for hours on end. One can truly sense the gentle nature of the Japanese as well as get a feel for their courtesy and graceful manners upon approaching them when they gather in this fashion, but such occasions also showcase their incurable sense of laziness. Not many Japanese seem to possess the virtue of being diligent and showing love for their work. There-fore, they appear to be unbelievable slouches in the eyes of Europeans who have never lived in the Orient.

Lindau may have gone a bit too far when he said there was no universal passion among the Japanese for their work if we consider that almost every Westerner lavished praise on the diligence of the Japanese farmers and the fastidiousness of the craftsmen. The diligence and perseverance of the Japa-nese agricultural workers was particularly pronounced, and the fruits of their labor often became the target of unified praise among Westerners.

Despite this, however, there was some truth to the Japanese being unbe-lievable slouches and taking life and its labors very easily during this time period. In fact, the incomprehensible paradox prevalent in such observations made by people from the modern industrial age is what made the character-istics of pre-industrial society stand out so vividly. Therefore, Lindau uncon-sciously made an important point about the differences between modern and pre-modern society. Wage labor, a system ingrained into society as a strict, almost militaristic labor discipline, along with the establishment of modern industry and measured by a strict adherence to time, was an as-yet unknown idea in Edo-period Japan. People were free to work whenever they had to and were also free to loaf around whenever they wanted to. As Humbert said, Europe at the beginning of the nineteenth century was similar to Japan in this regard as people there also worked and rested when they wanted to.

We can say, therefore, that Lindau was not trying to admonish the Japa-nese in the passage above. He was simply amazed by what he saw, and the certain sense of helplessness he felt translated into a kind of praise in its own right. This is because the unique sense of Japanese kindness and courtesy shone even brighter whenever the people exhibited idleness to this degree. Moreover, Lindau did not need to lament the Japanese "slouches" he saw. Their laziness and idleness would soon be "corrected" in the "trial by iron fire" that was the explosion of modern industry that occurred in the new Meiji period.

Edward Morse gave perhaps the most vivid account of the realities of this leisure and easy-going way of life that existed before modern wage labor was introduced to Japan. Morse, who had already made a name for himself as a biologist in the United States, came to Japan in 1877 to research brachiopods, but he was immediately commissioned to be a professor of zoology and physiology at Imperial University in Tokyo. He stayed in Japan until 1879 before returning home, but he visited the country again in 1882. During this time, he travelled to various places throughout Japan and wrote "thirty-five hundred pages of journal" detailing his experiences. He organized these notes and records and finally published the book *Japan, Day by Day* in 1917. Morse decided to publish this record of his travels at the recommendation of his friend William Sturgis Bigelow (1850–1926), who was a famous collector of Japanese art and who had accompanied Morse on his 1882 trip to Japan. It was actually Bigelow who had persuaded Morse, who was engrossed in his brachiopod research, to publish this work. He made his case in a letter addressed to Morse, a portion of which appears below:[5]

> Drop your damned Brachiopods. They'll always be there and will inevitably be taken care of by somebody or other as the years go by, and remember that the Japanese organisms which you and I knew familiarly forty years ago are vanishing types, many of which have already disappeared completely from the face of the earth, and that men of our age are literally the last people who have seen these organisms alive. For the next generation the Japanese we knew will be as extinct as Belemnites [an extinct group of cephalopods that only remain as fossils today].

We can thank Bigelow for asking Morse to publish his book because it is filled with scenes that depict Japanese workers. The day after Morse landed in Yokohama, for instance, he saw the following:[6]

> At the entrance to the canal a new wall is being built, and one could watch with interest for hours the curious human pile-driver. The staging is lashed together with ropes of straw. The men at their work are nearly naked, and, in one case, with the exception of the loincloth, absolutely so. The pile-driver is a curious contrivance. A hay weight

is attached to a long pole which is guided by a workman who sits on a plank of the stage, while others pull ropes which are attached to the weight below and run through pulleys above…There were eight men in the circle…An odd, monotonous chant was sung, and at the end of the stanza all pulled together, and then suddenly letting go, the weight dropped with a thud. It seemed a ridiculous waste of time to sing the chanty, for such it was, without exerting the slightest effort to raise the weight. Nine tenths of the time was devoted to singing.

Morse came across a similar scene during his trip to Nikko. He could hear a chorus of chanting that sounded like a sutra as he approached a temple, leading him to believe that some sort of religious service was taking place. In reality, however, a large group of laborers was turning a windlass and hoisting some lumber. Morse wrote:[7]

> It was an odd sight to see this crowd of naked, brown-skinned carpenters all howling a chorus for some time before making the slightest effort at pulling. At another place a double truck was being dragged and pried along by a crowd of workmen, and in the same way they would sing lustily, one man standing out from the crowd singing a chanty, and when they all joined in the chorus a simultaneous effort would move the clumsy affair about six inches.

Morse soon realized that "Japanese workmen hum or sing at their work." Then, he came to think "It is a curious trait in their character to lighten the burden of their labors by some pleasant sound or rhythm." However, he also questioned the usefulness of the singing by saying "It strikes us as a great waste of time to sing for a full minute or more before the slightest movement or effort is made." He was hard-pressed to find the answer to his question, though.

In these instances, Morse witnessed the nature of Edo-period Japanese labor that still remained intact in 1877. Without a doubt, of course, the Japanese could have easily improved their work efficiency several times over by focusing more of their efforts on the job at hand and shortening the singing time. However, this would end up just creating work for the Japanese, plain and simple. In the aforementioned examples that Morse gave about group labor, singing during long pauses in work operations did, in fact, serve the purpose of creating a rhythm that made it easier for the laborers to pound the earth, hoist lumber, and transport heavy loads, but more importantly, it served an intrinsic purpose of boosting worker morale by adding some enjoyment and steering the group to complete tasks that would otherwise be extremely tedious and tiring. In other words, work that included singing, which modern industrial circles decry as an extremely inefficient form of labor, rejected the units of time calculated by wage labor and made it a custom to promote self-operational aspects of the workers' mental and physical lives. In terms of Ivan Illich's philosophy, labor had not yet become "work."

Naturally, the laborers received daily wages. However, these differed from the modern meaning of the term because labor still retained the aspect of being the main activity in their lives and had not yet entirely become the notion of hard work that we are familiar with today—paying in cash and demanding high attention to detail. Moreover, this definition of hard work does not entail overworking. Even the safe and high-paying modern job of simply monitoring a measuring instrument is not an activity we base our lives around, but rather the price we have to pay to earn money. As long as this is the case, it is considered hard labor. Perhaps the merchants and lords who used this inefficient group labor system that was universal in the Edo period wanted to improve it and make it more efficient. However, they would have found it impossible to make changes. This is because the labor system was a customary practice established by one distinct civilization, one that even they could not ignore or break.

Leisure was also demonstrated in the broadest sense of the word when people worked and performed their duties. Kattendijke, who presided over the Naval Training Center in Nagasaki, was well aware of this. It is well-known that Katsu Kaishū (1823–1899) attended and was an outstanding student at this institution. One day, Katsu ran a new cutter aground on a reef. Therefore, Kattendijke needed to build a slip in order to implement repairs to the ship. After a number of efforts, Kattendijke selected a suitable place to conduct operations and finally reached the stage where they could lift the ship onto the repair platform, but it turned out the lumber had not yet arrived, and they had to wait for the next high tide. In this case, Kattendijke was overwhelmed with awe by the leisurely nature of the Japanese.[8] In the minds of the Japanese, however, they probably wondered why it was necessary to rush things. Just making the cutter usable again was all that mattered to them, no matter how long it took.

Meanwhile, it was often necessary for Kattendijke to negotiate with the shogunate officials about managing the training center. At first, however, he often lost his patience and got irritated in his dealings with them, no matter how hard he tried to remain calm. One day, Katsu even wrote the following about Kattendijke, although he inserted Commodore Perry in place of his name. He wrote that "Perry" was a good person, but an ill-mannered and quite irritable man.[9] Katsu was secretly insinuating that this was the case with Kattendijke, and the Dutchman immediately realized this. Kattendijke received counsel in this way and made more of an effort to be patient with the Japanese, but taking part in the negotiations with the sho-gunate officials was a pain he had to endure. Kattendijke, after all, related that the Japanese kept sitting there, smoking and surveying the scene as if they were getting ready to go on a trip or partake in some form of recreation even though the negotiations were almost ready to begin. In addition, they had a carefree attitude in which they continued to drink tea and eat cakes throughout the proceedings. On top of this, they told the most-unimag-inable jokes with straight faces. In essence, Kattendijke could not handle the situation. He later reminisced that, in order to organize and conduct negotiations so that they would not fail, normal patience and perseverance were not enough.[10]

George Smith also wrote about the leisurely attitude of the Japanese. When he visited the ironworks in Nagasaki, which were overseen by Dutch technicians, he heard the story of how a Dutch man-of-war had lost its rud-der and remained chained to the harbor for several weeks while the crew waited for the Japanese to find a replacement. He stated:[11]

Each week the same style of despatch from the governor of the city informed the Dutch officials that the tree had been felled in the forest; then, that it had been lopped of its branches and stripped of its bark; then, that it had been squared and planed into shape; until the patience of the Dutch captain had wellnigh been exhausted.

Foreign observers could also see that this leisurely attitude permeated every aspect of Japanese society during their travels. John Reddie Black, for instance, wrote the following about travelers on the old Tōkaidō road:[12]

The commonalty, men, women and children, on foot, all with their dresses turned up for facility of movement, and for the most part tak-ing the journey pretty easily; frequently stopping at the numberless tea-houses or resting sheds by the way, and refreshing themselves with the simple cup of weak green tea, and a cheery chat with whomsoever might stop like themselves to rest. It used to seem that distance was no consideration with them. They could go on all day, and day after day, if only they were allowed (which they generally were) to take their own time and pace. The value of time never entered into their thoughts; and even in business operations, one of the greatest annoy-ances of European merchants was the difficulty, I may say impossibil-ity, of keeping them up to time in fulfilling their engagements.

The way Black saw it, the rhythm of society followed a leisurely beat.

Meanwhile, Georges Bousquet, who came to Japan as a law advisor to the Meiji government in 1872 and stayed in the country for the next four years, gave the following evaluation of the Japanese work ethos:[13]

> The Japanese laborers, namely the farmers and city laborers, are generally sensible, skillful, gentle, and also cheerful, and they are definitely more sociable than the majority of people in similar environments in many of the civilized countries of the world. They are active more than they are diligent and perseverant more than energetic. They do what is necessary when they need to earn money for food and other daily needs and complete their tasks without uttering that many complaints. However, their efforts end there...They get what they need and do not think of earning anything more. They do not work themselves to exhaustion to earn huge profits, and when they finish one job, they do not necessarily move on to the next one. Try giving a laborer an order to do some work and see what happens. He will likely require more time than is necessary every time. Then, threaten to cancel the order. He will likely quit the job outright rather than subject his body to work he deems unnecessary. Now, go to any workplace in the country. You will see the workers smoking, laughing, and talking amongst themselves. Sometimes they wield their hammers and lift stones and do a good job, but then they stop to discuss how to approach the task before beginning again. Soon the sun goes down and quitting time eventually comes. Now the day is done. They always have an excuse ready in order to take a break, be it the heat, the cold, rain, but most especially a festival...Only a little is needed to support a household.

According to Bousquet, an adult living in a Japanese city during this time period could make a living on two *yen* and seventy-five *sen* (fourteen francs) per month, while someone living in a farm village only needed twenty *yen* (100 francs) per year. What is surprising about this passage is that Bousquet's complaint, in which he laments the difficulties of a so-called "developing country" modernizing, is very similar to those uttered by today's technocrats in developed countries. He went on to say the following:[14]

> From a societal standpoint, the Japanese are not unhappy by any means. They live cheerful lives outdoors and in the sunlight. Their circumstances are a hundred times better than those of workers at a factory in Manchester, who just earn enough to put food on the table, or laborers in London, who are worn out from being overworked and live dark, miserable lives by candlelight.

However, Bousquet did concede that Japanese industry was far from advanced and not very productive, and, therefore, could not hope to compete with Europe. For this reason, he believed Japan failed in its attempts to industrialize and modernize. However, this issue does not concern us now. The issue is that, according to Bousquet, the labor customs of the Japanese people and their work ethos were not conducive to industrialization and modernization.

Based on the theory that the introduction of modernization took place in Japan from the 1860s onward, the foundation for the success of modernization in the Meiji period was due to the establishment of a work ethos among the people that developed through Shingaku, a religious teaching founded by Ishida Baigan (1685–1744) that blended elements of Buddhism, Shintoism, and Confucianism, along with other movements in the Edo period. In addition, as we saw with Hayami's view in chapter 3, the Edo period was one in which farmers knew the meaning of work.[15]

While realizing the legitimacy of these opinions on one hand, I want to stress that we also need to weed some of them out. The Japanese people certainly were hard workers, but this by no means blocks the fact that, as Humbert said, the Japanese worked and rested when they wanted; as Alcock and Black said, they did not know the value of time; and, as Morse said, they frolicked and slacked off while they worked. Therefore, the old Japanese style of labor likely comes across as lazy, lethargic, and undisciplined if we evaluate them based on the standards of modernization. However, from Bousquet's point of view as a modern legal advisor, it is the aspects of this labor that appear as a dull self-sufficiency that lacks incentives for advancement. Therefore, who can negate Illich's statement about the convivial symbiosis of the people? Modernized labor was the agent of change that took the original nature of this style of labor away from the Japanese people and set them on the correct course of modernization by bathing them in the "flames of hell."

Naturally, work that could be called hard labor existed in Japan at the time. Isabella Bird, for instance, witnessed merchants who had carried loads that weighed anywhere from forty to sixty or more kilograms up into a mountain village in southern Yamagata Prefecture from Yamagata City in 1878. She wrote:[16]

> It is sickening to meet these poor fellows struggling over the mountain passes in evident distress. Last night five of them were resting on the summit ridge of a pass gasping violently. Their eyes were starting out; all their muscles, rendered painfully visible by their leanness, were quivering.

Morse also wrote the following about an observation he made in 1877:[17]

One notices with sympathy the painful endurance of a class of men who take the places of horses or bulls in dragging and pushing a two wheeled cart [a large hand-drawn cart called *daihachiguruma* in Japanese] with heavy loads of merchandise. In their efforts they bark or grunt out a series of short sounds and so loudly that they may be heard a considerable distance…The beads of perspiration pouring down their faces and water dripping from their mouths are evidences of the painful efforts they are making.

When Morse was in Otaru in Hokkaido, he met an old woman there with incredible strength. She was selling scallops and shouldering a carrying pole that was so heavy that neither Morse nor his entire Japanese entourage could lift it. When they finally gave up, the old woman silently lifted the pole, politely said farewell, and left at an "absolute trot." Then, Morse wrote, "Though this little dried up woman had already carried the load for a mile or more, she had breath enough left repeatedly to cry out her market stuff."[18] Naturally, this old woman was probably an unusually strong "fishwife" among other vendors in Otaru at the time.

Even so, labor was decorated with song. On his way from Kobe to Arima Hot Springs in 1878, Austrian Lieutenant Gustav Kreitner met some villagers from the mountains who were transporting pottery and foodstuffs. He wrote:[19]

The people who were carrying the loads were almost completely naked. They held bamboo supports on their shoulders and loaded these with incredibly heavy transport baskets, the weight of which even now looks like it could cause the supports to break. Their bodies were somewhere in between running and walking. Sweat poured down from their sun-tanned necks. However, no matter how difficult their job is, these laborers are always in good spirits and greet others pleasantly. Even while they walk, they hum a tune from their constricted chests. Songs they sing while gasping arouse the strength to push forward and take a stride with their right legs after their left legs hit the earth.

At the time, Yokohama Harbor did not have any wharves for large ships to dock at. Passengers had to board small, Japanese flatboats from their ocean vessels anchored offshore. The captains of these boats would

Pulling the cart (from Bird, *Unbeaten Tracks*)

then take them to the jetty. For many foreign visitors to Japan, their first experience was the short trip on these wobbly flatboats, which were called *sampan*. Therefore, the appearance of half-naked boatmen chanting while they rowed often appears in their descriptions. For example, Beauvoir stated the following:[20]

> Nothing could be more eccentric than this tapering craft, manned by six sturdy fellows, who, with their bodies thrown forward, standing up on a board, intoning a curious rhythmical song, give their boat, by the quiet and regular movement of the oars, the appearance, rapidity, and quivering motion of a fish.

Beauvoir noted the "curious song" the men were singing. Morse, meanwhile, heard a "peculiar series of grunts." He wrote:[21]

> And such a peculiar series of grunts they made, keeping time with each other with sounds like *hei hei cha*, *hei hei cha*, and then varying the chanty, if it were one, putting quite as much energy into the grunts as they did into the sculling. The noise they made sounded like the exhaust of some compound and wheezy engine. I felt a real sympathy for them in seeing the intense energy they gave to each stroke, and they never let up in the entire two miles.

Their labor was unquestionably intense enough to win sympathy from Morse, but was this no more than a simple example of Japanese boatmen engaging in hard labor? The answer is no. Whether they were singing a chanty or grunting, their voices became one with the boat, a living organism that helped them smash through the crests of the waves, but it may have also been the sounds of happiness that they developed themselves. Bird recorded that even when the boatmen bumped into other *sampan* boats, they did not shout or swear at each other.[22] This also shows us that they paddled their boats in extremely high spirits. Alcock, meanwhile, heard the boatmen "rising to the oar with a loud monotonous chant,

Paddling the *sampan* (illustration by Régamey, from Guimet, *Promenades Japonaises*)

but, wonderful to relate," when he was in Hakodate in 1859.[23]

For the Japanese workers, who were praised by Alcock for achieving excellence in every artistic skill, it goes without saying that labor was a source of happiness and pride. Morse marveled how even though the interiors of Japanese homes looked simple at first, in "many places in their apparently naked rooms the ingenuity and art-taste of the cabinet-maker could be expended." In his opinion, Japanese carpenters not only excelled at their work, but also possessed "much ingenuity of construction and an infinite amount of artistic talent." According to Morse, Japanese carpenters had more skill than similar craftsmen in the United States. After considering the fact that American carpenters had a number of expensive machines at their disposal compared with the rather primitive tools of the Japanese, Morse could not help thinking the issue lay in the realm of intelligence and insight. He also said that not that many Americans were serious about becoming a carpenter whereas the Japanese craftsmen carried on the traditions of their families for generations and children were raised among the smell of wood shavings drifting off the lathes. He also stated:[24]

> It is a startling sight to a nervous man to see a carpenter standing on a stick of timber, hacking away in a furious manner with this crooked-handled instrument [an adze] having an edge as sharp as a razor, and taking off great chips of the wood within an ich of his naked toe.

However, Morse never saw anyone suffer an injury with these adzes, and he took this as the soundest evidence of the "unerring accuracy" and steady hands of the Japanese carpenters.

Henry Tilley, who landed at Edo as a member of the Muravyov fleet, also saw firsthand the hard work of the carpenters at his lodging at Daichūji temple in Mita. He wrote:[25]

> Scores of half-naked carpenters were busy in the yard, sawing up planks, and transforming them like magic into various articles of European comfort, such as chairs, tables, &c., of which they had models before them. They are, I believe, the most expert joiners and workers in wood in the world. I long watched them and saw with pleasure their expertness in making chairs and tables, and other things which they had never perhaps seen before.

Edouard Suenson was also moved by the skill of Japanese carpenters when he visited Osaka as a member of French Ambassador to Japan Léon Roches's delegation. Roches's delegation was a huge party of around 100 people, so the Japanese authorities had to make last-minute modifications to provide makeshift lodgings for everyone. Suenson noted the following when the carpenters went to work:[26]

> In about an hour, the interior of the main building changed a great deal. By moving the *fusuma* to suitable locations, the workmen split the two large halls into several smaller rooms, all of which were quite spacious and comfortable. The skill and agility of the Japanese craftsmen who completed this job deserve our attention, and even though they did not employ the best tools, they quickly completed the task with a level of accuracy and good taste that craftsmen from the West could not even hope to match.

This scene is additional proof that the Japanese carpenters were by no means slouches and could be quite agile when the time came for them to be so.

Foreign observers painted the Japanese style of labor with a mixture of praise and disdain, but the strong, muscular bodies of Japanese physical laborers were often the target of their praise. Émile Guimet, for instance, depicted the physique of typical physical laborers such as rickshaw drivers and cart pullers in the following manner. He said that the rickshaw drivers were tall and slim, and their slightly well-built upper bodies were supported by strong, muscular legs. He stated that the cart pullers, meanwhile, were incredibly strong and muscular, had strong shoulders that were relatively wide, and their constantly naked legs rippled with muscles every time they moved.[27] Hübner also praised the "masculine strength and beauty" of the Japanese boatmen and said, "One must have travelled in Japan during the summer to understand the Greek statuary of the golden age." According to Hübner, the sculptors of ancient Greece were always surrounded by men who worked with little to no clothes on and, therefore, could see the movements of their muscles and bodies. He reasoned he had a similar experience every time he viewed the bodies of the Japanese workers, although I am sure they would have been embarrassed by being compared to Greek sculpture. Nevertheless, Hübner did add that the Japanese had short legs.[28]

Like Hübner, American artist John La Farge, who visited Japan in 1886, associated the bodies of the rickshaw drivers that he hired for his trip to Nikko with images of ancient Greece. He wrote:[29]

> From under my umbrella I tried to study and occasionally to draw the motions of the muscles of our runners, for most of them were naked, except for the complicated strip around the loins—a slight development of the early fig-leaf. The vague recall of the antique that is dear

to artists—the distinctly rigid muscles of the legs and thighs, the rippling swellings of the backs—revived the excitement of professional study and seemed a god-send to a painter.

Laborers (from Humbert, *Japan and the Japanese*)

La Farge also noted the "clear streams of sweat varnishing their bronze nakedness."

Many other observers felt this way about the rickshaw drivers, including Guimet. At first, he felt guilty riding in carts pulled by human beings. However, it was a comfortable ride, and the rickshaw drivers were cheerful. Therefore, he felt his regret disappear and be replaced by enjoyment. Meanwhile, the rickshaw drivers were not poor by any means. In fact, driving a rickshaw earned a certain rank in society, and when the runners arrived at an inn for the night, they almost always indulged themselves in luxury. In addition, Guimet mentioned their carts were coated with lacquer that gleamed in the light, had colorful designs depicting golden flowers or other legendary scenes painted on them, and were decorated with silver pegs and bronze frames.[30]

Along with the rickshaw drivers, the physical laborers that attracted the attention of the foreign observers were the *betto*, or stable attendants. The *betto* would prepare the horses for their master and lead in front. Beauvoir wrote the following about his "faithful and indefatigable runner, with his graceful and nervous limbs, who rivals his horse:"[31]

> When he started, his dress was magnificent; he wore a dark blue robe with enormously large sleeves, and tight trousers which defined the most exquisite legs. As he ran through the rice fields, his sleeves streaming in the wind, he looked like a great blue butterfly racing after the tall flowers.

There were also several accounts left by the Eulenburg expedition that provide details about the *betto*. Albert Berg, for instance, wrote the following:[32]

> The stable hands called *betto* are a strange race of people…They are energetic and skillful young men who are good at what they do, but they do present some problems when one employs them. Interacting with these natural souls is like fostering a friendship with an animal.

They have majestic bodies complete with wide chests and iron muscles, and they are always funny and good-natured people filled with enthusiasm and vivacity. Whenever we rode our horses, they instinctively ran here and there to the utmost limit of their strength, and they often wore themselves out and were dripping with sweat. Even so, they always spoke with cheerful voices…At home, they were not very useful at all. Our party had to take care of the stables, otherwise the *betto* would take all the money we needed to buy food for the horses and blow it on drinking and cavorting about. They also frequently got angry and argued. We had to pay each one of them on separate days. This was because they often took the money and disappeared for two to three days at a time to prowl the bars and did not return until they had spent all the money.

My running groom (*betto*)
(from Beauvoir, *Pekin, Jeddo, and San Francisco*)

The *betto* were also proud of their position and if something happened to hurt their pride, they would disappear with their comrades and completely abandon the stables. They had ringleaders as well. These leaders would quickly collect tributes from the other *betto*, but, in turn, they served as their employer and looked after them, and they also had to feed them when they were out of work. On one occasion, the Eulenburg expedition let one of their *betto* go and tried to hire a man with a loan horse who just happened to come walking by, but the other *betto* refused to work with him and derided him as a "merchant *betto*." In other words, the *betto* were servants to the samurai, the highest rank in Edo-period Japan.

Jephson and Elmhirst, meanwhile, wrote:[33]

> One word about the bettoes…a separate caste of their own, they are looked upon by their countrymen almost as a distinct tribe. Capital grooms *if they choose*, they will face and handle the most dangerous horse…but you never know when they will take it into their heads to shift their quarters and leave you without the slightest warning. They are quick and intelligent, but the greatest thieves in the universe.

Based on the scenes depicted in the records listed above, we can probably associate laborers such as the cart pullers, rickshaw drivers, and *betto* with the masculine beauty traits of strong, dashing good looks and chicness. These examples can also be used to show that they performed their duties well when they wanted to, but they were still subject to idleness and hooliganism depending on the situation. More than anything, however, the Westerners probably saw them as strong individuals who were full of vitality.

Western observers who visited Japan years later often recorded that Japanese men and their bodies looked "ugly." This dramatically differed from their almost universal praise of Japanese women, and we can find the most representative examples of these images in the works of Moraes. However, observers who visited Japan from the end of the Edo period until the beginning of the Meiji period did not always think Japanese men who worked were ugly.

Bettoes (from Humbert, *Japan and the Japanese*)

Guimet, for instance, likened them to the ancient Greeks. This episode occurred when he was on a ship that weighed anchor in Yokohama Harbor in 1878. On the same ship, there was a Japanese man who was returning to Japan after getting his engineering license in the United States. Guimet's eye was drawn to a group of Japanese men who had boarded the ship. He stated the following:[34]

> What is this illusion of ages past that has appeared on the deck of the ship? A group of Romanesque young men majestically approaches. They don long Latin clothes, have their hair cut in the style of Titus, and they have slender faces. How graceful they are. They do not even appear to be Asian. They look like the sons of Brutus as they approach.

Actually, the men on the boat were the servants of the Japanese engineer who had just returned from the United States and were coming to greet their master. Guimet went on to say that the young Japanese men looked like a bas-relief sculpture etched into their master's luggage as they bowed low to him. The beautiful pleats on their clothes, their fixed outline, the pose of their naked arms, their well-composed feet, their lowered heads, and the lines of their bodies that fell into harmony with their clothes all reminded Guimet of the solemn beauty of an ancient sculpture. He also wondered why the master was so ugly while his servants were so beautiful. Naturally, the "Mongolian engineer," the name Guimet gave to the master, had dressed for the occasion with a frock coat and silk hat.

Many foreign observers noticed huge physical differences between members of the upper and lower classes. Chamberlain was quite candid about this point when he said, "The lower classes are mostly strong, with well-developed arms, legs, and chests. The upper classes are too often weakly."[35] Léon Metchnikoff also noticed the reality that the physical laborers in Japan were far more beautiful in terms of their clothing and physical frames than members of the middle and upper classes.[36] For Reinhold Werner, he could tell the difference between the upper and

Master and servants (illustration by Régamey, from Guimet, *Promenades Japonaises*)

lower classes by looking at their noses. He said members of the upper classes had Roman noses while the common people had stout noses that bulged upwards a bit. He also said that upper-class individuals maintained a graceful appearance, but people of the lower classes that he met all reminded him of gymnasts, as they were tall and had extraordinarily well-developed muscles.[37] As the differences were this pronounced, Werner said that the members of the upper classes were clearly conquerors from abroad, an expression that sounds as if he were preoccupied with the theory that nomadic tribes had entered Japan from the Asian continent.

Suenson was not particularly fond of the appearance of many Japanese, but he felt his negative views instantly float away after seeing the wisdom that emanated from their chestnut brown eyes and the goodwill and cheerfulness that oozed from every one of their facial expressions. Before long, he even embraced sympathy for these people. He also noticed the obvious differences between the upper and lower classes and stated that the laborers of the lower classes had strong, muscular bodies while the men of the upper classes were thin and often quite weak, as they did not develop their muscles through hard labor. Members of the upper classes often flaunted these conspicuously ugly Japanese traits, but he also noticed they made efforts to keep their hands and feet neat and tidy.[38] Metchnikoff also said there was a rich variety of appearances among the Japanese and, therefore, this is what caused contradictions to appear in records made by foreign observers. He went on to say:[39]

When one looks at a man and thinks of his drooping ears and low nose, his huge mouth and almost perfectly square face, one might be surprised to see that standing right next to him is a fine and elegant slender face, usually that of a woman, which evokes images of lovely ladies from Lombardy or Leonardo Da Vinci's Madonna...One may come across some city dwellers with sunken chests, slightly protruding stomachs, and narrow crooked legs, but at the same time and in the same vicinity, one may see short commoners that possess truly symmetrical proportions. Their powerful limbs look like those on a bronze statue and their dashing looks resemble the handsome men of Seville.

If we take it that the human body is a unique aspect of society and an expression of the spirit structured by this, then the reality of the beautiful and active bodies of the *betto*, rickshaw drivers, boatmen, and servants that Westerners observed at the time means that, to a certain degree, Japanese laborers were, in fact, free and independent and could choose to perform any job they wanted within the society of old Japan, a hypothesis that could be considered blasphemous from the standpoint of conventional Japanese history. What we have to be aware of, however, is that these surprising records that describe the Japanese laboring classes only fall within the period stretching from the end of the Edo period to the beginning of the Meiji period. For this reason, only the laborers from the Edo period

Teahouse girl in Enoshima (illustration by Régamey, from Guimet, *Promenades Japonaises*)

were truly free. The question we are now faced with is: why, exactly, were their bodies so free and active? To answer this question, we have to shift the focus of our investigation to the framework of status that existed in society during this time period.

Notes:

1 Humbert, *Japan and the Japanese*, 268.

2 Alcock, *Tycoon*, Vol. 1, 396.

3 Alcock, *Tycoon*, Vol. 2, 117–8.

4 Lindau, *Un Voyage Autour*, 44.

5 Morse, *Day by Day*, Vol. 1, 9–10.

6 Morse, *Day by Day*, Vol. 1, 3–4.

7 Morse, *Day by Day*, Vol. 1, 77; Vol. 2, 292; Vol. 1, 115.

8 Kattendijke, *Uittreksel*, 56–7.

9 Kattendijke, *Uittreksel*, 53.

10 Kattendijke, *Uittreksel*, 60.

11 Smith, *Ten Weeks*, 230–1.

12 Black, *Young Japan*, Vol. 1, 163–4.

13 Bousquet, *Le Japon*, Vol. 1, 143.

14 Bousquet, *Le Japon*, Vol. 2, 778–9.

15 Hayami, "Kinsei no Keizai," 19.

16 Bird, *Unbeaten Tracks*, Vol. 1, 256.

17 Morse, *Day by Day*, Vol. 1, 9.

18 Morse, *Day by Day*, Vol. 1, 437–8.

19 Kreitner, *Im fernen Osten*, 237.

20 Beauvoir, *Pekin, Jeddo, and San Francisco*, 120.

21 Morse, *Day by Day*, Vol. 1, 1.

22 Bird, *Unbeaten Tracks*, Vol. 1, 16.

23 Alcock, *Tycoon*, Vol. 1, 242.

24 Morse, *Japanese Homes*, 40.

25 Tilley, *Japan, the Amoor*, 152.

26 Suenson, *Skitser*, 188.

27 Guimet, *Promenades-Kanagawa*, 24.

28 Hübner, *Ramble*, 269.

29 La Farge, *Artist's Letters*, 45–9.

30 Guimet, *Promenades-Kanagawa*, 55.

31 Beauvoir, *Pekin, Jeddo, and San Francisco*, 133.

32 Berg, *Eulenburg Expedition*, Vol. 1, 115-6.

33 Jephson and Elmhirst, *Our Life*, 46.

34 Guimet, *Promenades-Kanagawa*, 11–2.

35 Chamberlain, *Things Japanese*, 251.

36 Metchnikoff, *Kaisō*, 48.

37 Werner, *Die Preussiche Expedition*, 71.

38 Suenson, *Skitser*, 71.

39 Metchnikoff, *Kaisō*, 85–6.

Chapter

7

Freedom and Status

Among the many unexpected surprises that Japan had in store for Western observers, by far the biggest discovery they made was the reality that the Japanese commoners lived truly satisfied lives. This was unexpected and strange in their minds because, until they actually experienced Japan and saw the country with their own eyes, they continued to hold the preconceived notion that Japan was under the despotic rule of the shogun and that every aspect of the people's lives was controlled and under the surveillance of government spies. In other words, they believed individual freedom did not exist. When they actually visited and observed the realities of Japan, they found that strict regulations existed to a certain degree, but they were also taken aback by how happy the people seemed to be. Laurence Oliphant, for example, had to acknowledge that, although "The more we investigate the extraordinary system under which Japan is governed, the more evident does it become that the great principle upon which the whole fabric rests is the absolute extinction of individual freedom," he was surprised that "It is a singular fact, that in Japan, where the individual is sacrificed to the community, he should seem perfectly happy and contented."[1]

No matter how strange or paradoxical this may have seemed to the observers, they could not mistake the obvious look of happiness and contentment that appeared on the faces of the Japanese people. As almost every observer recognized with surprise that the Japanese people were kind and courteous, they had to have realized that the Japanese only acted this way because they were happy and satisfied with their lives. For this reason, many of the observers immediately set out to solve the origin of this paradox.

Oliphant was not the only one preoccupied with this issue. Descriptions in the *Eulenburg Expedition*, the report that detailed the proceedings of the Prussian expedition to Japan, also mentioned in great detail the paradox that, even though the people should have been oppressed and distrustful of one another under the ceaseless surveillance of government spies, in reality the opposite was true. According to the report, the people looked cheerful and lively, and they openly engaged with others.[2] Daniel J. Macgowan (1814–1893), an American missionary who came to Japan in 1859, shared the same view. He stated the following as quoted by Alcock:[3]

Japan, it must be confessed, furnishes the best apology for despotism that the world affords. The Government is omniscient, and consequently strong and stable. The bondage is absolute and pressing on all sides alike; society is scarcely conscious of its existence.

Alcock and Kattendijke, both of whom excelled at making and vividly describing their observations of Japan, actually investigated this issue in earnest. As we can see from their observations of commoners prostrating themselves in front of daimyo (domain lord) processions, they noticed an obvious and insurmountable gap between the hereditary nobility and the common people. However, Alcock thought "for that very reason there may be more real liberty among the mass of people than we can imagine." This is because, as it was the case during the feudal age in Europe, it was rare for violence by a monarch or the nobility to trickle all the way down to the common people, who were their subjects. It is analogous to a powerful storm harming a tall tree. Branches at the top may break and suffer injury, but the shrubs and bushes at the base of the tree usually remain unharmed. The same situation existed in feudal Japan. Alcock wrote:[4]

> The outward show of servility may be but skin deep, and the body of the industrial population, in town and country, may be left with a larger share of freedom and greater immunity from individual wrong, or meddling legislation brought to bear upon them by those who wield the chief power of the state, than in many countries having the form and show of popular freedom and more democratic institutions.

Kattendijke's opinion was quite similar to Alcock's assertion. He stated, for example, that the Japanese lower classes, as far as he could see, enjoyed individual freedoms a great deal more than their counterparts in any other country in the world. He also expressed surprise at the rights they were given.[5] This rather unexpected observation may sound surprising and confusing at first, but Kattendijke elaborated on his argument. He felt that the Japanese lower classes were free because they had absolutely nothing to do with members of the upper classes. The warrior class, which sat at the top of the hierarchy in Edo-period society, hid themselves from the public eye and were abject slaves to custom and formality. This also became more pronounced the higher their position on the social ladder. Meanwhile, the townspeople enjoyed individual freedoms at a level that was not even seen in many of the so-called "free" European countries. Kattendijke admitted that the rules that governed

Willem Huyssen van Kattendijke

Japanese society were quite rigid, but judgments were fair, and there was no danger to the people—provided that they respected the laws and customs of the day.[6]

Kattendijke's remarks were likely influenced to some degree by the writings of J.F. van Overmeer Fischer (1800–1848), an agent of the Dutch East India Company (VOC) whom we shall touch on in a subsequent section of this chapter. However, Kattendijke based on his own experience the surprising argument that the Japanese government, namely, the shogunate, held little actual power over the common people.[7] For example, he said that when Jan Hendrik Donker Curtius (1813–1879), the Dutch Commissioner in Japan, proposed reclaiming land in the canal that delineated the border between Dejima and Nagasaki as a means to enlarge the island, Magistrate Okabe Nagatsune (1825–1866), who was also the governor of Suruga Province, rejected the proposal on the grounds that people living in the neighborhood would lose the space where they kept all of their barges. According to Kattendijke, Okabe's written reply stated that it was his duty as magistrate to protect Japanese laws and honor the rights of the people. Kattendijke used this and many other examples to show how the government respected the rights of its subjects.

Captain Reinhold Werner of the Prussian expedition also mentioned an example in which the people living in Japan, a country under the rule of absolute despotism, sometimes had more rights as individuals than people living in the constitutional states of Europe. He stated:[8]

> During our stay in Nagasaki, the shogunate devised plans to build a hospital. Major Pompe, a Dutch military doctor working for the shogunate, found a suitable place to build this facility and Magistrate Okabe approved the site. The area in question was a field about 1,000–2,000 square meters in size at the top of a hill. However, a poor farmer lived and worked on this land. The magistrate asked the farmer to transfer this land to the shogunate for the price of the land as well as the cost of the harvest. However, the farmer flatly rejected the shogunate's request, claiming that he wanted to harvest the seeds he had planted first. The magistrate then offered to pay him double, and then even tripled the price, but the farmer still refused and, in the end, actually decided that he did not want to give up his land for any reason at all. The magistrate was in no position to enforce his will on the farmer. There are no laws of expropriation in Japan, and the shogunate had to purchase land elsewhere, a site that proved much less conducive for a hospital.

Naturally, an honest historian would hesitate to use this anecdote. First of all, this statement was hearsay, as Werner had heard it from a Dutch official. Secondly, if we take it that a Dutchman related this episode to Werner, he was probably just hearing an excuse by the shogunate official to refuse use of the land. However, I think it is quite possible that what Werner was saying was true. The Nagasaki magistrate during this time period was Okabe Nagatsune, an official praised by every Westerner for his enlightened nature and graceful attitude. It would make perfect sense if Okabe were the official that both Kattendijke and Werner mentioned in the aforementioned examples.

Furthermore, based on Kattendijke's experience, shogunate officials were extremely weak against visitors to Japan who committed acts of violence. Even in cases in which Dutch sailors committed crimes, Kattendijke saw the officials handle the incidents peacefully to the point where he actually wanted the officials to punish the criminals more severely. At one point, he even questioned why they bothered to carry two swords with them.[9]

In addition, the shogunate officials were not just weak when it came to dealing with visitors to Japan. They were also helpless to prevent disturbances from erupting among the local people. Kattendijke stated that if, for example, there were a dispute between residents living in towns A and B, horrible fights would often occur throughout the town, and several bodies would be found after the dust settled. The officials could not do anything to stop this.

Kattendijke also remarked:[10]

> I actually witnessed one such instance in which a fight erupted between groups of people flying kites, a popular pastime in Nagasaki. The offenders were prosecuted after the incident was over, but the fight lasted for hours without any outside interference. Some government officials appeared and calmed the angry youths and finally ended the fight. In another incident that occurred just before I arrived in Japan, about 200 to 300 Chinese apparently spilled out into the streets in the strictly monitored Chinatown and plunged the city of Nagasaki into chaos for several days, but even then, the magistrate made no effort to send them back to their designated area. The Chinese finally grew weary of drinking and rioting and went back home on their own accord...The police officers in Japan are simply outrageous. One could even say that police do not exist in Japan.

Kattendijke's testimony may sound hard to believe at first since it differs so much from our long-held images of the Japanese people being oppressed under the Japanese feudal system of the shogunate and the domains. However, Humbert also offered testimony to the exact same point.

Humbert described an incident that occurred at a Yokohama brothel called "Gankirō" in which one of the prostitutes working there refused to serve the leader of a group of *betto*, the grooms mentioned in an earlier chapter. This angered the leader, so he summoned his underlings and they surrounded Gankirō, essentially besieging the establishment for thirty-six hours until the woman eventually killed herself. As it turned out, the woman was actually with her lover, and he forced her to stay in a small room, an instigative action that the owner of Gankirō simply overlooked. It makes sense that the *betto* leader got angry, but his men caused a destructive riot, plain and simple. Aimé Humbert related the incident:[11]

The underlings formed a tight unit behind their leader, and they pushed until they reached the edge of the moat surrounding the enclosure. However, as they had to cross the only bridge that leads to Gankiro, the police forestalled them by tearing planks off of the bridge and closing both doors of the only gate. Therefore, no matter how violent or noisy the rioters became, it was all for naught. Realizing this, the mob of bettoes organized themselves to attack the police, who were actually stronger in numbers yet remained calm and reserved throughout the entire incident. The main force of bettoes armed themselves with bamboo spears and established a foothold from which they could launch an attack. The rest of them lined the canal and surrounded the establishment. All night long and well into the following day, they spent time preparing for battle and finally raised a war cry. This seemed to be the signal to start the attack, but suddenly the gate to Gankiro opened just a bit, and a representative from the police came out and walked up to the mob. The two sides then exchanged two or three pleasantries to which the riotous bettoes raised a happy cheer of victory and dispersed as if by magic.

Aimé Humbert

It was actually the police who had persuaded the prostitute and her lover to throw themselves into a well. This sounds like the end to a tragic love story, but due to this turn of events, the officials ended the disturbance in a way that also allowed the *betto* to save face. From start to finish the police just served as intermediaries, and they left it to the parties involved to negotiate a solution to the problem. In addition, on the same day, only the brothel owner and his subordinates were called to the Kanagawa magistrate's office to be interrogated. This incident definitely happened, as Humbert said he actually witnessed it during his stay in Japan in 1863.

Humbert probably related this incident to Dirk de Graeff van Polsbroek, the man he deemed the most senior European staying in Japan. Polsbroek then gave a similar example showing the tolerant stance that the shogunate took in regard to the passions and violence that sometimes erupted among the common people. From atop a gallery of a Japanese-style restaurant in Nagasaki, he claimed to have witnessed residents from neighboring districts form ranks and engage in a great battle. Humbert related what Polsbroek said, as follows:[12]

> Even though the people were armed with bamboo spears and fighting each other in battle lines, the police brigade simply closed the surrounding gates to confine the battle to a limited area and let them run amok for two hours while they looked on with their arms crossed. After two hours, the magistrate dispatched a representative to mediate and hear what each side had to say. Having apparently reached a settlement, the official then ordered the police to tell everyone to peacefully disperse and return to their homes. As a result, this command was easily executed.

This is probably the same incident that Kattendijke wrote about, but Humbert went on to say that it was fascinating that this particular episode made him remember that animosity also existed between factions living in similarly big cities in Europe during the Middle Ages and the revolutionary period, and there were also battles between villages. In other words, these kinds of incidents only became punishable crimes after the state deprived various communities within society of their right to autonomy and established itself as a modern unified state authority. Premodern state powers, even in cases of absolute monarchies, did not have the will or the actual power to enter and impose controls over residential areas governed autonomously by the community.

The shogunate and the domains wielded centralized and authoritarian control at the national and regional level in terms of collecting tributes and taxes, preventing peasant revolts, and suppressing the Christian population, but the price they had to pay for this, as it were, was staying out of the daily lives of the common people as much as possible, with the exception, of course, of the rather ineffective sumptuary laws that they had to impose. On the contrary, there were many areas governed by communities of commoners, and, as one of their customary rights, this autonomy gave them the authority to refuse any interference by the shogunate and the domains they deemed unreasonable. The same situation existed among the absolute monarchies of Western Europe in the Middle Ages in which the authority of a centralized bureaucracy was limited, and it was actually difficult to impose the will of the state on the autonomy maintained by various communities within society. In recent years, the shogunate and domain system has often been compared with the absolute monarchies of Western Europe, and the freedom of the people living in the Edo period was most likely very similar to that of Europeans living in the Middle Ages and the early modern era.

Even so, why did the government officials respond to the aforementioned incidents in ways Westerners deemed incomprehensible? In the case of Nagasaki, for example, the battle between two neighborhood districts resembled the orgy the Japanese people often engaged in at festivals and other wild and crowded events, and such incidents were never handled by the Nagasaki magistrate's office, but rather by the local elders. Furthermore, the people never directed these disputes at the bases of shogunate control, and they never left their designated residential areas. It was actually their customary right to battle other districts, and the shogunate officials recognized the autonomy of everyone involved in a given dispute. However, they still had to consider the overall security of Nagasaki. Therefore, they closed the gates to prevent the incidents from spreading to other areas, and if anyone were killed in the disputes, they had to punish criminals under shogunate law. The guilty parties were usually prosecuted after the incident subsided.

The same thing probably happened at the Gankirō incident in Yokohama. The prostitute refused to serve the *betto*, and the brothel owner overlooked her actions, something considered unacceptable and even illegal in the minds of the people. The *betto* leader had been shamed, and his underlings organized a party to attack the brothel, and, perhaps, they had every right to do so. In this case, moreover, it was also the widely accepted custom to negotiate a solution between the parties involved without waiting for shogunate intervention. As we saw in the previous chapter, the *betto* had ringleaders and were a very proud group in society. Their demonstration against Gankirō was their proper societal right. The shogunate officials did not have the authority to deny their rights, and they had no desire to get involved in negotiations. However, they could not allow these fights to go overboard and lead to more serious security issues such as arson and murder. These crimes violated shogunate law. Therefore, they responded by implementing measures to separate the parties, such as removing the bridge to prevent them from attacking each other, rather than putting pressure on the group of *betto* and forcing them to disperse.

What we need to be aware of, however, is that the *betto* force also showed signs of attacking the government officials. In other words, they viewed the measures taken by the officials as unlawful acts that denied their right to reach a settlement to the problem amongst themselves. Here, the government officials had to take arbitrary measures in order to reach a solution quickly. Humbert stated that the shogunate officials were the ones who coaxed the prostitute and her lover into killing themselves. Thus, they fulfilled their role as intermediary and judged in favor of the group of *betto*. In addition, the brothel was the only side to receive a warning from the magistrate's office. As we can see from these examples, the authority of the shogunate and the domains permitted designated social groups in proper residential areas to exercise their customary rights through violence.

Humbert also stated, "There are two societies in Yeddo; one, armed and privileged, lives in a state of magnificent imprisonment, in the vast citadel; the other, disarmed, and subject to the dominion of the first, seems to enjoy the advantages of liberty."[13] Now we can see what he meant by this, and it also shows the reason why, as Kattendijke saw it, that the Japanese townspeople enjoyed a level of freedom not seen in Europe. Naturally, the freedom that Humbert saw in the lives of the Japanese commoners was not the same as the freedom enjoyed by modern citizens today. Rather, the people earned freedom by being a member of a village or town community or belonging to a social community based on their social position or occupation. It also developed due to the unique government structure of the shogunate and domain authority, which did not interfere in town and village life and which respected the custom of autonomy among the villagers and townspeople. The freedom that Kattendijke saw did not exist in Europe any longer because the same kind of community autonomy so prevalent in Japanese society had long since vanished from the vast majority of European countries.

As stated earlier, the right to face off against opposing groups was recognized in farm villages, and this concerned several interests and honor among communities. Specifically, these involved disputes over land and water. In the late Middle Ages, self-governing villages literally armed themselves and battled rival villages over natural resources and the rights to rivers, and deaths were common in these clashes. These armed groups of farmers were strictly prohibited in the Edo period, but such regulations did not deny a village from claiming and protecting its rights to wildlands and rivers via its own power. It was also common for villages engaged in disputes to forcefully clash with rival villages and use guns and spears as a means to threaten their adversaries. In such cases, villages looked down on cowardice and forced their fellow villagers to fight. They also had provisions on hand to treat and compensate for injuries. However, if any villagers were killed, this would violate shogunate and domain laws and would fall under said jurisdiction.[14]

In recent years, historians have emphasized the reality that the north and south magistrate's offices in Edo were only manned with a limited number of *yoriki* and *dōshin*, two ranks of police deputies in the Edo period, yet maintained excellent security in a large city of one million people. Naturally, shifting the functions of the police and judges to the people is what made this possible. Local societies handled and settled small crimes and disputes by themselves throughout the big cities and farming villages. Bishop George Smith's experiences in Nagasaki attest to this reality.

George Smith found lodgings at Sōfukuji temple, where missionary Channing Moore Williams (1829–1910) lived, and Smith described how one day, someone stole Williams's wallet, which had an *ichibugin*, a silver coin worth about thirty dollars, in it. Williams did not know who the culprit was so he asked his Japanese friend for help, and when his friend arrived, he instantly deduced who the criminal was and forced him to confess. Williams got his money back. The criminal turned out to be a servant who worked for one of Williams's fellow missionaries. Williams's Japanese friend solved the crime in the following manner. First, he investigated recent spending habits of the people who lived around the temple. He instantly discovered there was a man who was spending money far too extravagantly, and, as Smith related, he "seized upon the culprit and turned a deaf ear to his indignant denials. By main force he had him stripped to nudity; and at length drawing forth from his interior garments a secreted sum of money." Smith went on to write the following:[15]

> By species of a Lynch-law often practised in a land where the forms of justice are sometimes slow, and willingly endured by a criminal under a code of laws visiting such offences with a more than Draconic severity of punishment, the thief was bound and mercilessly beaten by our Japanese acquaintance.

Who exactly was this Japanese acquaintance "acting in the threefold capacity of police-detective, judge and executioner?" He was none other than a district chief of Nagasaki. Smith understood that the law called for the capital punishment of lynching for the crime committed, but naturally this was the rule of law in place before the separation of public and private matters of the town community acknowledged by the authority of the shogunate. The amount the thief stole was equivalent to over twenty *ryo* in terms of Japanese currency at the time, and this was an age when stealing ten *ryo* meant your head would fly off the chopping block.[16] In this case, however, we should be aware that the issue was settled with flogging after being handled by the people.

Punishment in the Edo period was sometimes quite severe, so in theory, we can see how some people believe it was an age of very little freedom. However, there is a huge dissociation between theory and reality, and the belief that the people were not free has lost support in recent years due to descriptions like the one Smith relayed above. Oliphant, meanwhile, noticed another point in which there were various loopholes in the "conventional rules of the most precise and rigid description." He wrote, "There is, indeed, a practice which exists in Japan, and which may have extended to other countries, of doing things 'nayboen,' as it is called here; in other words, in a recognized incognito."[17] This term, "nayboen," seems to have left a strong impression on Oliphant, and he often jokingly used it to describe the actions of his party throughout his book.

However, the freedom people enjoyed in the Edo period, in which lower-class communities were given autonomous control and access to an incredibly flexible system of law, finally met with complete destruction in the Meiji period, a time when the highly puritanical state did not recognize such concepts as "nayboen." In contrast to the freedom of modern citizens living in Europe, which actually grew and developed from the seeds of freedom that various premodern communities had planted, the traditional autonomy of Japanese premodern communities was completely severed by the Meiji Restoration. As a result, freedom for modern Japanese citizens was cultivated in the minds of intellectuals as a foreign ideal rather than in the lives of everyday people. This means that we should reconsider and re-evaluate the autonomy of premodern communities, as this formed the basis of the people's freedom in the Edo period.

As I mentioned in an earlier chapter, Alexander Siebold was the oldest son of the famous Philipp Franz von Siebold and accompanied his father when he revisited Japan in 1859, and he stayed in Japan until 1887. Alexander wrote about the farming villages in the areas surrounding Nagasaki and said that the system of governance in the towns and villages was extremely free and the people who owned land had the right to elect their town elders and *shōya*, or village chieftains. In addition, he also mentioned that there were absolutely no police constables or government officials from the magistrate's office stationed in the local areas. Alexander was also pleased to find that Buddhist priests did not extend their influence over the villagers. In addition, he believed the Japanese farmers were better off than people living in most of the countries in Europe.[18]

Today's Japanese historical circles have finally reached the stage in which they do not need testimony like that of Siebold to counter the absurdities that other foreign observers wrote in their superficial descriptions of conditions in Japan that they knew nothing about. Historian Satō Tsuneo, for example, said that, unlike Western Europe, the feudal system of the Edo period realized a separation between villages and cities. In principle, therefore, members of the warrior class did not enter the farm villages. This means that the typical village in the Edo period was populated by a group of simple producers in the agricultural, forestry, and fishery industries who governed themselves and did not answer to a lord. At the very least, Satō reasoned, the village was usually spared the violent controls of armed samurai. The shogunate and the domain lords did not interfere in the inner workings of the village and depended on the local community to implement a self-governing system of taxation. Satō also said that under the logic of this self-governing system, the villagers took on the characteristic of a self-governing organization designed for the people and run by the people.[19] Concerning the relationship between the farmers and Buddhist temples, meanwhile, Satō said that the *shūmon ninbetsu aratamechō*, which were records that the shogunate and domain lords kept as a type of religious census, could, at first glance, look like strict religious controls imposed by the shogunate and the domains. In reality, however, the religious census was a skeleton of what it once was, and the farmers often changed temples or Buddhist sects whenever they wanted. Thus, the farmers were free from various religious ties and, so long as they did not violate conventions, were free to operate their farms and live their lives as they saw fit.[20] In 1871, Hübner said, "There is not even in Europe an example of a more liberal municipal council" as existed in the Japanese farm villages,[21] certainly not a baseless claim by any means. In fact, this freedom was a legacy of the Edo period.

There was actually a precursor to Alcock's opinion that the people were free and content under the despotism of the shogunate. J. F. van Overmeer Fischer (1800–1848), who worked at the Dutch trading house at Dejima from 1820 to 1829, had already stated the following in *Bijdrage tot de Kennis van het Japanische Rijk* (Contributions to the Knowledge of the Japanese Realm), a book he published in 1833:[22]

> The Japanese live under complete despotism, and, therefore, the common impression is that they do not enjoy happiness or contentment. However, I have experienced the complete opposite through my interactions with the Japanese people. Despotism is just a word in this country and does not actually exist…The Japanese, who work hard and carry out their duties, are completely free and independent. They do not know the concept of slavery, and they do not even serve their lord without compensation. Diligent workers earn considerable respect, and the lower classes are generally content…In Japan, even the poorest people can afford to buy food. In addition, relationships between the upper and lower classes are polite and warmhearted, and when one sees this, there is a general sense that all of the people are content and trust each other.

From Fischer's standpoint, he did not envy the position of the shogun, the domain lords, and the upper-class warriors. The shogun and the domain lords were bound by the rigid formality of courtesy, knew very little about their own lands and ministers, and, moreover, had to delegate their authority to the lower classes. Therefore, the upper classes just gave off a show of dignity and did not have any true power.[23] In addition, everyone was equal under the law in Japan, and no one, not even the members of the upper class, were above the law.[24] Furthermore, the sumptuary laws applied to everyone, restricting lavish decorations and luxury among the lowliest servants and the shogun alike.[25] Therefore, Fischer said the following about the ruling class in Japan:[26]

> There was not much for the townspeople of relatively low social status to be jealous about, for many of them led happy lives by working hard and running their own business, be it the merchants, storeowners, or individuals engaged in other business ventures. These people were obliged to kowtow to the so-called shogunate government officials, but no one prevented them from working and creating profit for themselves, and they enjoyed the highest level of freedom.

In other words, shogunate controls over people of relatively low social class were extremely loose.[27] Previous generations of historians likely derided and ridiculed Fischer's assertion. Today, however, we have reached a point in which historians have to accept many of his points. For example, historian Kasaya Kazuhiko's latest research has provided detailed evidence to support the claim that the shogun and the domain lords actually delegated authority to various groups of their advisors.[28] Concerning Fischer's point that the shogun, domain lords, and the upper-class warriors did not live enviable lives, meanwhile, correspondence from Donker Curtius to his homeland of the Netherlands provides additional proof that this was the case. He stated the following in an 1854 report:[29]

> People who do not have a position of public office certainly enjoy a free way of life, while those who belong to the ruling class make a living by bearing the brunt of strict ties and adherence to ceremony. In Europe, sovereigns and people of power are seen as public servants at the highest level of the state, while those in Japan are even called "slaves" to laws and customs.

If we read into Fischer's thoughtful argument, then we should be able to see that the observations of Alcock, which seem to contrast with the common sense of conventional Japanese progressive history, are actually not that out of the ordinary, and are, conversely, an extremely important and fresh look at the unique nature of the state and society in the Edo period. We also cannot overlook the fact that so many people made the same observation. If I could add something, it is also clear that Alcock did not read anything written by Fischer. It is hard to imagine that Alcock, who specifically quoted and commented on the works of Carl Thunberg, the Swedish naturalist who stayed at Dejima in the 1770s, would never have mentioned Fischer if he read any of his works.

There is another passage written by Fischer that I would like to quote. He stated the following:[30]

> Based on both outward appearances and character, there are huge differences between the pompous officials, who act politely and with a sense of pride when they interact with others, and the townspeople, who have strong bodies, always positively approach their work with a fresh and leisurely attitude, and have the heart to share the profits they earn with their families.

This statement gives us the answer to Guimet's question about why the Japanese master he saw on the ship looked so ugly while his servants looked so beautiful. In fact, the stable hands, messengers, and laborers that appear in the numerous illustrations in Humbert's *Japan and the Japanese Illustrated* all have truly beautiful and strong bodies.

Fischer stated that relationships between the upper and lower classes were polite and warmhearted, but Alcock noticed something else about this point. He wrote:[31]

> There is also, upon the whole, so far as I have had opportunities of observing, less cringing servility in the inferior classes, lay and official, and much less official hauteur in the dealings of the higher with the lower classes, than the accounts in Commodore Perry's narrative had led us to suspect.

Alcock also said that higher-ranking officials always spoke with lower-ranking counterparts politely and with a peaceful air. In addition, he stated that the Japanese were extremely sensitive to insults and looking down on others, and "for just in proportion as they are conscious of sensitiveness on these points, is their scrupulousness in avoiding any provocation or ground of offense to others."[32]

As a case in point, Commodore Perry's narrative detailed the incident involving "Sam Patch," a Japanese man who had drifted all the way to the

United States and was accompanying Perry on his expedition to Japan. Perry wrote the following:[33]

> He fell on his knees before them after the manner of his country, and would have remained in that position if Lieutenant Bent, who was determined that no such obsequiousness should be shown on the deck of an American man-of-war, and under the flag of the United States, to anything wearing the human form, had not peremptorily ordered him immediately to rise to his feet.

Commodore Perry's Chinese interpreter Samuel Williams also detailed this incident in his journal, but he also described the experience he had when they made landfall. He wrote, "I gave a few cash to a girl who brought the water, but our official conductors made her give them back. The people were respectful to these officers, yet not cringing."[34] Edouard Suenson, who often accompanied French Envoy Roches as a member of the French navy, also wrote that the Japanese almost never looked fearful when they were in the presence of high-ranking officials. On one occasion he even saw a young man enjoying a pleasant conversation with the domain lord and his ministers as if they were friends. As Suenson saw it, the young man had been taught to respect higher-ranking individuals and senior officials, but he had also been taught to assert himself and demand respect from them in turn.[35]

Suenson's description goes against conventional views of Edo Japan and, therefore, makes us doubt the author to a certain degree. We have been taught that there were strict relationships between the upper and lower classes under the class system during this time period, and, in fact, many other observers at the time recorded that Japanese interpreters remained kneeling the entire time and prostrated themselves before the higher-ranking officials during international negotiations. Therefore, who exactly was this young man that Suenson wrote about?

Ivan Goncharov might help us solve this mystery. When he met with shogunate officials in Nagasaki, he knew that the lower-ranking individuals had the custom of putting on an air of foolishness when they interacted with their superiors. Even when he joked around with the interpreters that he had befriended, he noticed that they became quite serious in the presence of their superiors. Even so, Goncharov did not feel like they were slaves. He stated, "in their [the younger lower-ranking officials] deference to the old people I did not observe any fear or subservience; with them this appears to be simple, sincere, warm, almost an act of love, one might say, and therefore it is not unpleasant to watch."[36]

Alcock, meanwhile, felt that the lower classes of Japanese were a warmhearted and courteous people that tried to make others feel happy. They were far from being slaves even when he saw them bow their heads to their lords and listen to their orders. One of the reasons why Alcock hesitated to agree with the popular belief among the Westerners that the Japanese did not enjoy freedom probably had to do with him actually experiencing peaceful relations between the upper and lower classes on a number of occasions. Suenson, meanwhile, stated the upper classes in Japan respected and took care of the lower classes a great deal. He went on to say that there was always a close and friendly relationship between the lord and the servant, and this kind of relationship was as yet unknown in the free countries of the West.[37]

Another example actually comes from the middle of the Meiji period. Alice Bacon wrote the following in her book *A Japanese Interior*:[38]

> It is a curious thing, though, that in spite of all of this prostration and groveling before their masters, servants here are on much more easy and friendly terms with their employers than they are in America, and their position is much more independent and responsible. They take out their servility in manners, and retain their real independence in a way that is quite surprising. So far as I am able to judge, personal and domestic service here occupy a much more desirable position among employments than with us.

Bacon also realized that "The Japanese servant generally does, not what you tell him to do, but what he thinks is for your highest good, a characteristic that is quite exasperating at first," but through repeated experiences the servants were usually correct.[39]

Bacon discussed this topic more in depth in another book she wrote, namely, *Japanese Girls and Women*.[40] She wrote the following:[41]

> To the foreigner, upon his arrival in Japan, the status of household servants is at first a source of much perplexity. There is a freedom in their relationships with the families that they serve, that in this country [the United States] would be regarded as impudence, and an independence of action that, in many cases, seems to take the form of direct disobedience to orders...Every servant in your establishment does what is right in his own eyes, and after the manner that he thinks best. Mere blind obedience to orders is not regarded as a virtue in a Japanese servant; he must do his own thinking, and, if he cannot grasp the reason for your order, that order will not be carried out. Housekeeping in Japan is frequently the despair of the thrifty American housewife, who has been accustomed in her own country to be the head of every

detail of household work, leaving to her servants only the mechanical labor of the hands. She begins by showing her Oriental help the work to be done, and just the way in which she is accustomed to having it done at home, and the chances are about one in a hundred that her servant will carry out her instructions. In the ninety-nine other cases, he will accomplish the desired result, but by means totally different from those to which the American housekeeper is accustomed…And as she finds that her domestics will take responsibility upon themselves, and will work, not only with their hands, but with the will and intellect in her service, she soon yields to their protecting and thoughtful care for herself and her interests…Even in the treaty ports, where contact with foreigners has given to the Japanese attendants the silent and repressed air that we regard as the standard manner for a servant, they have not resigned their right of private judgment, but if faithful and honest, seek the best good of their employer, even if his best good involves disobedience of his orders.

Bacon thought this characteristic of Japanese servants originated in the relationship between lords and vassals under the feudal system. Vassals found satisfaction by serving their lords over several generations in the feudal system, and they knew the history of the family they served as well as the intricate characteristics of each family member. Therefore, they could use their heads and serve their masters to the best of their ability without waiting for any orders. As Bacon put it, "The servant in many cases knew his master and his master's interests as well as the master himself, or even better, and must act by the light of his own knowledge in cases where his master was ignorant or misinformed."[42]

Bacon had her students at the school for noble girls read Frances Burnett's *Little Lord Fauntleroy*, and when she explained the scene in which a servant disgraced himself by laughing at something odd the young lord had said, she stated, "My little peeresses were amazed beyond measure to learn that in Europe and America a servant is expected never to show any interest in, or knowledge of, the conversation of his betters, never to speak unless addressed, and never to smile under any circumstances." In Japan, servant girls joined the families they served in the sitting room with the hibachi and could even ask the master about words they did not know in books they might have been reading. Furthermore, if one visited a home and the woman of the house happened to be out, the head handmaiden would take her place and greet the guest and engage him or her in conversation.[43]

Basil Chamberlain also wrote something nearly identical to Bacon's description. While prefacing that "Personal intercourse with this people for more than thirty years has convinced the present writer that it is *la politesse qui vient du coeur*—something deeper than mere bows and smiles—that it is rooted in genuine kindliness," he stated that the courtesy of the Japanese appeared to "offend glaringly against the canons of courtesy, as understood in the West." He went on to say:[44]

> The most fundamental and all-pervading breach of courtesy (from the European standpoint) is displayed in the way servants and other inferiors behave towards their superiors...You order your cook to buy mutton. He goes straightway and invests in beef—he knows beef to be cheaper, and thinks to spare your pocket. Disobedience, in fact, is the rule—not disobedience from malice prepense, but from an ineradicable assumption on the subordinate's part that he can do better for his master than his master can do for himself.

If this were the case, then the lord was worshipped by his retainers, but they also forced their will over him from time to time. One could say the phenomenon of supplanting field-officers who led the military despotism in the early Shōwa period was deeply rooted in this aspect.

However, in the passage under the heading "Politeness" in his book *Things Japanese*, Chamberlain based much of what he wrote on the words of Bacon. Chamberlain, for example, wrote "You tell a jinrikisha-man to set you down, that you may walk a hill. You probably have to do so four times before he obeys." Bacon, meanwhile, wrote:[45]

> It is a point of honor with him [a rickshaw driver] to pull his passenger up the steepest and most slippery of hills, and never to heed him if he expresses a desire to walk in order to save his man. I have had my *kurumaya* stoutly refuse, again and again, my offers to walk up a steep hill, even when the snow was so slippery under his bare feet that he fell three times in making the ascent. "*Dai jobu*" (safe) would be his smiling response to all my protestations.

Bousquet, meanwhile, said the following about how superiors, in this case a master craftsman, were not in complete control over their subordinates, in this case an apprentice:[46]

> Being an apprentice does not mean losing one's authority. The apprentice is closely tied to his master, especially if he is the master's son, but he does not hesitate to state his opinion even when the master does not ask for it. He slides towards his master and offers him some tea, then bows and

touches his forehead to the ground as he receives an order. But in the next instant he tells a crude joke, which the master responds to with a smile.

Such observations and opinions lead us back to John La Farge's idea that a certain sense of democracy lay in the courtesy of the Japanese people. A closer look at his views may be in order. He stated:[47]

> The weakness, the insufficiency of the individual, has been stiffened by the importance of the family, of the clan, as a basis of society; and I could almost say I discern in this one main-spring of the peculiar courtesy of this nation, which seems to go along with a great feeling of a certain freedom, so that the obedience of the inferior does not seem servile. The servant who has done his duty of respectful service seems afterward ready to take any natural relation that may turn up.

In another section of his book, La Farge stated that the "provincial feeling" and the "rule of the idea of the family" formed "the basis of a certain dignity and personal independence." He continued by writing:[48]

> Within this courtesy I see all about me, I feel something of what we might call democratic, for want of a better name. I recognize it in the manner of the subordinate, who takes an apparently personal interest in things, after his duty of politeness and obedience is paid.

La Farge was not the only one to feel this way. Metchnikoff also professed that even the poorest, most-exhausted laborers followed the propriety of courtesy to the letter, but he did not feel that this was slave-like or servile in any way.[49]

With this in mind, now we can understand what Chamberlain wrote in the following passage:[50]

> He [the visitor to Japan] will then begin to realise a truth which the existence of an almost absolute government [Chamberlain was refer- ring to the absolute government of the Meiji period here] and of an elaborate code of manners at first tends to conceal, namely, that the Japanese and Far-Easterners generally are at bottom more democratic than Anglo-Saxons on either side of the Atlantic.

Courtesy shown by the lower classes to those of the upper class, which included prostrating oneself, may have looked subservient at first glance but was really nothing more than a lubricant to keep the cogs of the class system moving smoothly. As long as the people of the lower classes honored this courtesy, they secured their personal independence. This is because those of the upper classes actually depended on the lower classes and were influenced by them. The class system did not mean subservience in the face of despotism. Rather, it established the range of what each class could and could not do and actually guaranteed personal dignity and independence within each respective social standing.

One's class also meant one's role in society and ability to do work, and this ability made pride essential. Historian Bitō Masahide presented an epoch-making idea in which he argued that the "hierarchy of roles" was the structural principle of Edo-period society. He argued that one's "role" was the overall duty that an individual or a family owed to society. He also believed that society organizing itself around the "roles" associated with class or, in other words, the ability to do work, developed sympathy between each social class in the Edo period and created the collective consciousness in which each class was an equal member of the state.[51] In addition, this class system, based on a hierarchy of roles, was by no means static, and fluid interchange between the classes was quite high. The opinions of foreign observers were not superficial or absurd in any way in regard to this point.

In addition, when Chamberlain reinforced the belief that democracy and equality were at the roots of Japanese society, he was likely comparing the carefree nature of Japanese society with the dramatically different and strict class system in Britain. Democracy in Britain was nothing more than the idea of a parliamentary government under the rule of a noble class of gentlemen. Conventional history, which prescribed the so-called people's revolutions, such as the Puritan Revolution and the Glorious Revolution, and which regarded nineteenth-century British society as a "civil society" led by the bourgeoisie, completely crumbled under the advocacy of gentlemanly capitalism. Now, there is an established theory that states that nineteenth-century Britain was a society under the strong rule of "gentlemen," the core of which consisted of landowning nobles.[52]

Naturally, the display of democracy and equality as seen by foreign observers did not conform with modern ideas of democracy and equality as-is. Nonetheless, based on these modern ideas, it is important to consider that traits that could only be called "democratic" developed within a class system that was not supposed to be democratic or equal in any way. As mentioned earlier, evidence shows that the people were independent, and there are a number of statements attesting to the roles inherent in each class that back up the reality of this democracy. More than anything, however, the observers felt this existed in the "roots" of society.

Metchnikoff used Japanese performance art as an example to support this claim. He said that the Japanese enjoyed and interacted with stage performances in a particularly informal way and pointed out that even audience members entered the dressing rooms during an intermission as if they were part of the show and busily helped set up props and other installations for the next scene. According to Metchnikoff, however, this affable enjoyment was the characteristic of every aspect of life in Japan, not just the stage.[53] He also said that what surprised him most as a European was the extremely democratic system prevalent in the Japanese way of life. The fact that he did not expect to see this in the remote corner of the Far East likely meant that the open friendliness that pervaded throughout Japanese society as a whole touched his heart.[54]

Metchnikoff went on to say that, when thinking of the Orient, Europeans immediately imagined the riches and luxury of tyrants rarely seen around the world as well as the conversely subservient nature of the lower classes and the poverty often depicted in paintings. However, Metchnikoff then contrasted this by saying that he visited the home of a high-ranking Meiji government official and found it to be no different than the simple homes of the common people that he saw in Edo. It was even simpler than houses owned by low-ranking Swiss government counselor-level middle-class bourgeoisie.[55] Metchnikoff said that the idea of class system equality in Japanese society was already fully developed, and he probably experienced this during this visit. Many other observers who visited Japan at the end of the Edo period also had the impression that the houses of the upper and lower classes were no different when compared.[56]

Metchnikoff also said Japanese farmers enjoyed greater independence than the majority of European farmers. He likely described the basis for this assertion in the following passage:[57]

> Generally, the farmers of this land take an indifferent attitude toward everything that occurs outside the sphere of their lives, and they create an isolated world in which they live and are cautious about reacting against any new system or creating a disturbance, but once they are moved to act, they can protect their own rights until the end.

These are words that Metchnikoff used to describe the farmers that he saw at the beginning of the Meiji period, but it is likely that he was also referring to the independence that people enjoyed in the Edo period. Saint Nicholas of Japan, the Russian Orthodox priest whose real name was Ivan Dimitrovich Kasatkin (1836–1912) and who is known for founding the Tokyo Holy Resurrection Cathedral in Kanda, held a view very close to that of Metchnikoff. Metchnikoff related what Nicholas said in the following:[58]

You should visit the farmers in the remote countryside. You will most likely be amazed by how sound and independent their ideas about the government are...If I could say something about the Japanese people, it is that they live in far better circumstances than those in many countries in Europe, and they seem to be aware of their civil rights. However, despite these realities, the people are still completely unsatisfied with the order they maintain among themselves! The merchants complain about taxes on this and that (even though in reality the taxes are not that high), and the farmers complain about the collection of the annual rice tribute. Furthermore, everyone shows contempt for the government officials by saying, "They all take bribes. They are not decent at all." What's more, almost all of the people deride the shogunate, blaming them for the impoverished nature of the country. Hearing them say such things is extremely fascinating. Furthermore, you hardly see any beggars in this country at all, and in every big city, the entertainment districts are filled with singing and dancing every night. Are these people truly the slaves of the Orient who quietly prostrate themselves in front of their rulers?

Nicholas said that the Japanese people criticizing the shogunate even though they were blessed with good living conditions and actually being able to utter these complaints without any repercussions was proof of their independence. In 1861, he moved to Hakodate as the parish priest to the church attached to the Russian consulate. He wrote the previous remarks when he returned to Russia on leave in 1869, so these episodes were, in the end, based on his experiences in Hokkaido at the end of the Edo period. In any case, we cannot discard his testimony as an isolated example nor can we treat it as something made up by an outsider who did not fully understand the situation he was in, as the testimony overlaps and agrees with so many other descriptions.

The Japanese people that Nicholas saw were not slaves who bowed down to their rulers. If this were the case, then we have to address contrasting examples such as instances of people being told to "bow down" in the presence of a daimyo procession. Albert Berg of the Eulenburg expedition certainly mentioned an infamous daimyo procession screaming at people to "stay down," but he never actually saw anyone do so. This means that the people avoided the processions as much as possible and that, as Berg saw it, they never gave much care to those in power, and most of them just continued with their work as usual.[59] Furthermore, George Smith said that the procession of the lord of Owari Province (present-day Aichi Prefecture) took two hours to pass the Kanagawa lodging area on the Tōkaidō road, but the people only bowed to the lord himself and the four or five vehicles that followed him. After these had passed, however, "the people considered themselves absolved from the necessity of kneeling and rose to a standing posture to witness the remaining part of the spectacle."[60]

Ernest Satow, a member of the British Legation, visited Nikko in 1872 and entered the mountainous land to the south. There he was greeted by a group of villagers who gathered at a temple and cried out the commands "Shitaniro!" ("Down!") and "Kaburimono o tore!" ("Remove your hats!") as a show of respect for the first foreign visitors to ever pass on this road. They followed the village chief, who was clad in a *kamishimo*, the formal attire of a samurai, and the children began copying him by crying out "Shitaniro!" and clearing the path ahead of them even though the only thing surrounding them were trees.[61] As we can see in the way that "Shitaniro!" became a cute children's game, although troublesome at times, the people were not ashamed of bowing to dignitaries, and engaging in such courteous behavior even helped to enliven their lonely mountain village. One can even get a sense of how nervous they were in meeting the village chief in a *kamishimo*. In this greeting of "Shitaniro," we can read into the hearts of these warmhearted villagers. This can also help us explore the depths of the hearts of the Japanese people as a whole.

Remarks by other observers point out other important characteristics. Humbert, for instance, said, "The mobility of expression and the great variety of physiognomy, which we remark among the Japanese, seem to me the result of an intellectual development more spontaneous, more original, and in short more free, than is to be met with amongst any other people in Asia."[62] Isabella Bird described the charm of the streets of Tokyo and noted "the personal independence and liberty enjoyed by all classes shown by a demeanour neither servile nor self-assertive."[63] Jephson and Elmhirst said, "They—the yakonins [government officials], of course, in a greater, the lower classes in a lesser degree—carry themselves as becomes men, fearlessly and uprightly, look you straight in the face, and consider themselves inferior to none."[64] Henry Holmes said, "Even the lower classes have a self-reliance that I have not seen in other Eastern nations."[65] George Smith said, "They [the palanquin bearers] are somewhat independent in their bearing and have begun to adopt the unpleasant habit of deeming a foreigner a fair victim for their extortions."[66] Historians cannot ignore this variety of testimony about the attitudes and physiognomy of the independent Japanese mind that existed from the end of the Edo period to the beginning of the Meiji period.

In other words, Westerners found an unexpectedly equal society and an independent people in Edo-period Japan. In fact, it was their preconceived notions of "despotism" that was the problem. They most likely imagined vicious Oriental tyranny in Japan, but as such ideas and images were just preconceived notions of the Orientalism they held against the Far East, the system of rule in the Edo period could not have been further from this notion. What they saw was the reality that, although there was a separation between armed rulers and

Palanquin bearers (from Jephson and Elmhirst, *Our Life*)

unarmed subjects, it was, on the whole, an affable civilization in which the rulers were extremely relaxed and the subjects were free to live their lives within the scope of their social class. The gap between the rich and the poor, meanwhile, was not that wide, and there was little to no class discrimination, and even though there was a clear distinction between class differences, it never led to animosity or dissatisfaction.

Notes:

1 Oliphant, *Narrative*, 392–3.

2 Berg, *Eulenburg Expedition*, Vol. 1, 341.

3 Alcock, *Tycoon*, Vol. 1, 82.

4 Alcock, *Tycoon*, Vol. 1, 229.

5 Kattendijke, *Uittreksel*, 19.

6 Kattendijke, *Uittreksel*, 125.

7 Kattendijke, *Uittreksel*, 158.

8 Werner, *Die Preussiche Expedition*, 56.

9 Kattendijke, *Uittreksel*, 64.

10 Kattendijke, *Uittreksel*, 64–5.

11 Humbert, *Japan and the Japanese*, Vol. 2, 75 (translated from the Japanese version).

12 Humbert, *Japan and the Japanese*, Vol. 2, 75–6 (translated from the Japanese version). This senior resident was likely Polsbroek, the vice consul of the Netherlands at Kanagawa.

13 Humbert, *Japan and the Japanese*, 187.

14 Fujiki Hisashi, *Toyotomi heiwarei to sengoku shakai* [Toyotomi Hideyoshi's Peace Ordinances and Warring States Society] (Tokyo Daigaku Shuppankai, 1985). See Chapter 2, titled "Sonraku no Heiwa: Kenka Teishirei" ["Peace in the Villages: Orders to Stop Fighting"].

15 Smith, *Ten Weeks*, 39–40.

16 Hiramatsu Yoshirō, *Edo no tsumi to batsu* [Edo Crime and Punishment] (Heibonsha, 1988). According to Hiramatsu, even in cases in which the serious crime of stealing over ten *ryo* occurred, it was often written down as nine *ryo* three *bu* two *shu*, an amount just below ten *ryo*, which the officials usually overlooked. Naturally, this was done to avoid the severity of the death penalty as prescribed by law.

17 Oliphant, *Narrative*, 391–2.

18 A. Siebold, *Letzte Reise*, 98–101.

19 Satō Tsuneo, *Binnō shikan o minaosu* [Reviewing Historical Views of Poor Farmers] (Kodansha Gendaishinsho, 1995), 92–4.

20 Satō Tsuneo, *Binnō*, 133.

21 Hübner, *Ramble*, 419.

22 J.F. van Overmeer Fischer, *Bijdrage tot de kennis van het Japanische Rijk* [Contributions to the Knowledge of the Japanese Realm] (Amsterdam, 1833). No English translation of Fischer's work exists, so passages that appear in this book have been translated from the Japanese version. See Fisseru [J.F. Fischer], *Nihon fūzoku bikō* [Notes on Japanese Customs] (Heibonsha Toyo Bunko, 1978), Vol. 1, 66–8. Subsequent citations will appear as Fischer, *Bijdrage*, and will list page numbers from the Japanese text.

23 Fischer, *Bijdrage*, Vol. 2, 34–6.

24 Fischer, *Bijdrage*, Vol. 1, 87.

25 Fischer, *Bijdrage*, Vol. 2, 33.

26 Fischer, *Bijdrage*, Vo. 2, 37.

27 Fischer, *Bijdrage*, Vol. 2, 34.

28 See Kasaya Kazuhiko, *Shukun: "Oshikomi" no kōzō* [Lords: The Structure of "Force"] (Heibonsha, 1988), and Kasaya Kazuhiko, *Kinsei buke shakai no seiji kōzō* [The Political Structure of Warrior Society in Modern Times] (Yoshikawa Kobunkan, 1993).

29 Foss Miyako, *Bakumatsu Dejima mikōkai bunsho: Donkeru Kuruchiusu oboegaki* [Unreleased Writings about Dejima at the End of the Edo Period: Notes on Jan Hendrik Donker Curtius] (Shinjinbutsu Oraisha, 1992), 110.

30 Fischer, *Bijdrage*, Vol. 1, 89.

31 Alcock, *Tycoon*, Vol. 1, 187.

32 Alcock, *Tycoon*, Vol. 1, 164.

33 Francis Hawks, ed., *Narrative of the Expedition of an American Squadron to the China Seas and Japan, Performed in the Years 1852, 1853, and 1854 under the Command of Commodore M.C. Perry, United States Navy* (Washington, 1856), 486. This scene of Sam Patch prostrating himself before the Japanese also appears on page 342 of the narrative, but Captain Adams is the officer who orders Patch to stand up.

34 Williams, *Perry Expedition*, 140.

35 Suenson, *Skitser*, 85.

36 Goncharov, *Pallada*, 304.

37 Suenson, *Skitser*, 86.

38 Bacon, *Japanese Interior*, 105.

39 Bacon, *Japanese Interior*, 212.

40 As described above, Bacon built on her experiences staying in Japan for a year and two months (1888–1889) and published this work in 1891. She received assistance in her writing from Tsuda Umeko, who, as fate would have it, was staying in the United States at the time. In addition, Bacon returned to Japan in 1900 to serve as an instructor at the English school that Tsuda had established and stayed for another two years. She used her additional experiences to publish the 1902 supplementary version of her book. Furthermore, the Bacon family also let Yamakawa Sutematsu stay at their home during her study abroad trip to the United States as one of five girls who accompanied the Iwakura Mission in 1871. Therefore, Bacon taught Sutematsu like a sister and actually dedicated this book to her. The name appears as Ōyama Sutematsu, as she had since married Ōyama Iwao. This information comes from the notes of Hisano Akiko's translation of Bacon's *A Japanese Interior*. See also Hisano's *Rokumeikan no kifujin: Ōyama Sutematsu* [A Noble Lady of the Rokumeikan: Ōyama Sutematsu] (Chuko Bunko, 1993).

41 Bacon, *Japanese Girls*, 299–301.

42 Bacon, *Japanese Girls*, 302.

43 Bacon, *Japanese Girls*, 304–7.

44 Chamberlain, *Things Japanese*, 382–3.

45 Bacon, *Japanese Girls*, 319–20.

46 Bousquet, *Le Japon*, Vol. 1, 96–7.

47 La Farge, *Artist's Letters*, 200.

48 La Farge, *Artist's Letters*, 220.

49 Metchnikoff, *Kaisō*, 122.

50 Chamberlain, *Things Japanese*, 383.

51 Bitō Masahide, *Edo jidai to wa nani ka* [What Is the Edo Period?] (Iwanami Shoten, 1992).

52 See P.J. Cain and A.G. Hopkins, *British Imperialism* (Routledge, 2016); Mizutani Mitsuhiro, *Eikoku Kizoku to Kidai* [British Nobility and the Modern Age] (Tokyo Daigaku Shuppankai, 1987); Kawakita Minoru, *Igirisu: Hanei no atosaki* [Britain: The Reversal of Prosperity] (Daiyamondosha, 1995); and Kawakita Minoru, *Kōgyōka no rekishiteki zentei* [The Historical Premise of Industrialization] (Iwanami Shoten, 1983).

53 Metchnikoff, *Kaisō*, 114–5.

54 The passage here comes from another serial that Metchnikoff wrote from 1876 to 1877. No English translation of Metchnikoff's work exists, so passages that appear in this book have been translated from the Japanese version. See Mēchinikohu [Lev Ilich Metchnikov], *Bōmei Roshiajin no mita Meiji Ishin* [The Meiji Restoration Seen through the Eyes of a Russian Exile], trans. Watanabe Masashi (Kodansha Gakujutsu Bunko, 1987), 91. Subsequent citations will appear as Metchnikoff, *Bōmei*, and will list page numbers from the Japanese text.

55 Metchnikoff, *Kaisō*, 119, 129.

56 Metchnikoff, *Bōmei*, 64.

57 Metchnikoff, *Bōmei*, 125–7.

58 Nicholas Kasatkin (Nikolai), *Dnevmiki Sviatogo Nikolaia Iaponskogo* [Diary of Nikolai] (St. Petersburg, 2004). No complete English translation of Kasatkin's work exists, so passages that appear in this book have been translated from the Japanese version. See Nikorai [Nikolai], *Nikorai no mita Bakumatsu Nihon* [Japan at the End of the Edo Period Seen through the Eyes of St. Nikolai] (Kodansha Gakujutsu Bunko, 1979), 12–3. Subsequent citations will appear as Nikolai, *Diary*, and will list page numbers from the Japanese text.

59 Berg, *Eulenburg Expedition*, Vol. 1, 107.

60 Smith, *Ten Weeks*, 246–7.

61 Ernest Satow, "Travel in the Interior: Yedo to Nikko and Back," in *Collected Works of Ernest Mason Satow Part 2: Collected Papers* (Tokyo, 2001).

62 Humbert, *Japan and the Japanese*, 38.

63 Bird, *Unbeaten Tracks*, Vol. 2, 204.

64 Jephson and Elmhirst, *Our Life*, 377.

65 Holmes, *My Adventures*, 20.

66 Smith, *Ten Weeks*, 101.

Chapter

8

The Naked Body and Sex

It is widely known that the Japanese customs of public nudity and mixed bathing astonished the Westerners who came to Japan at the end of the Edo period, which, in turn, even made them question the morality of the Japanese people. Japan was also a paradise in the sense that naked women, who could only be seen in designated places in the West, were visible in the streets on an almost daily basis.

Samuel Williams, who accompanied Commodore Perry on his expedition and served as his interpreter, made the following judgment based on his experiences in Shimoda in 1854:[1]

> Of all heathen nations I have ever heard described, I think this is the most lewd. Modesty, judging from what we see, might be said to be unknown, for the women make no attempt to hide the bosom, and every step shows the leg above the knee; while the men generally go with the merest rag, and that not always carefully put on. Naked men and women have both been seen in the streets, and uniformly resort to the same bathhouse, regardless of all decency. Lewd motions, pictures and talk seem to be the common expression of the viler acts and thoughts of the people, and this to such a degree as to disgust everybody.

Williams also had the grit to write in the same text, "I hope and pray that the gracious designs of Providence in thus favoring this Expedition will be still further developed, and the light of revealed truth be permitted to shine upon the benighted and polluted minds of this people," thus reflecting his innocent, yet arrogant stance as a solemn Christian missionary. For this reason, it makes sense that he distorted and misread the openness of Japanese clothing, or lack thereof, as much as he did. In fact, we can probably even sympathize with the disgust this Puritan felt at seeing pornography and mixed bathing, to some extent.

However, in the case of Peter Heine, a German painter who also accompanied Perry, he did not wear the glasses of Puritanism, thus his descriptions carry an indifferent objectivity that allows us to view things in a different light. He stated the following:[2]

> The bathhouse is communal, with men and women, both young and old, and children all mixing and squirming about together. Even when we enter the bathing area, these naked people do not show a sin-

Mixed bathing in Shimoda (from Hawks, ed., *American Squadron*)

gle sign of surprise, or, at most, just cry out as if they are having some
fun with us. From what I witnessed in the baths, such cries seemed to
come from one or two women rushing to jump into the bathtub with
a splash to avoid being seen by a foreigner who may have just come
in, or women who crouched and hid themselves with their hands in a
pose not unlike the Venus de' Medici.

If we read into this description, we can see that Heine himself was not at
all surprised by what he saw. All he did was depict a bathing scene that
illustrated the extreme fondness for cleanliness on the part of the Japanese.
Because of this subdued viewpoint, the bathing scene Heine conveyed came
to show the broad-minded and natural characteristics of the Japanese people
instead of painting them, as Williams did, as depraved souls who constantly
gave into their lust.

What actually surprised Heine, rather, was the extreme heat of the bath
water. For example, he was startled to see a man using water he had just
boiled in a wooden tub and continued to look on in awe at seeing the man
stand up, his body as red as that of a boiled crab, while another man kept
building up the fire. He truly thought the people were boiling each other
alive and compared them to martyred saints who had likewise suffered this
fate prior to the Middle Ages in the West. However, the man in the bath
looked like he was enjoying himself, and when he finally got out of the tub,
he unabashedly stood completely naked in front of Heine and proceeded

to wipe himself off with a washcloth. The Japanese affinity for hot water would later become a favorite topic among other foreign observers, but Heine's description may be one of the earliest examples.

At age twenty-one, Heine took part in the May Uprising in Dresden, one of the European Revolutions of 1848, along with composer Richard Wagner, and later fled to the United States, where he lived in exile. Therefore, he likely avoided embracing many of the Christian prejudices that formed the framework of the sensibilities of Westerners living in the nineteenth century. Like Williams, many of them were critical. For example, Heine's fellow countryman, Friedrich Lühdorf, the Prussian merchant introduced in earlier chapters, also witnessed a bathhouse scene during his stay in Shimoda in 1855 and said that in no other country in the world do men and women live together under such obscene methods as they do in Japan.[3] Officers on American ships docked at Shimoda asked Lühdorf where the bathhouses were, so it probably did not take long for most foreign observers to know where they could see these now infamous scenes of mixed bathing. Anglican bishop George Smith was also sharply critical of this custom, stating:[4]

> All ages and both sexes are intermingled in one shameless throng of bathers without signs of modesty or of any apparent sense of moral indecorum. Some persons palliate this custom of promiscuous bathing in public by assuming the innocent simplicity of their primitive habits, and dwelling on the wide difference of every country in the conventionalities of moral right and wrong. The obvious reply to this charitable theory is that the Japanese are one of the most licentious races in the world.

Critical as they may be, Williams and Smith's responses actually do little more than show how their adherence to the taboos of the Christian faith or, rather, their stereotypes transformed into a unique hypocrisy of modern civil society. Moreover, such descriptions even seem to highlight their own obsession with the naked body. At any rate, it seems they were completely unaware of the rudeness they exhibited upon intruding upon others who were naked and taking a bath while they themselves were fully clothed. The Japanese commoners saw how conceited they were, but they just laughed and let it pass.

Not all of the foreign observers brazenly intruded upon the bathhouses, however. According to Count Eulenburg, for instance, many of these facilities faced the street and only had latticed doors and windows. Therefore, people walking by outside could easily see into the bathing area if they were close enough.[5] Mixed bathing was on display for everyone to see.

Naturally, when Harris assumed his position in Shimoda in 1856, he knew about this custom. Despite his strict Puritanical beliefs, however, he wrote, "I cannot account for so indelicate a proceeding on the part of a people so generally correct."[6] Meanwhile, shogunate officials assured him that "this very exposure lessens the desire that owes much of its power to mystery and difficulty" and, therefore, mixed bathing "is not considered as dangerous to the chastity of their females." Harris seemed to have found this to be true, but only after he visited an *onsen*, or hot spring bath. When he visited one particular establishment, he witnessed a woman taking a bath with her child. He stated, "She was not in the least discomposed, but gave me the usual 'Ohio' (good-morning) with a smiling face." Harris probably did not find the experience altogether bad as he wrote "Her skin was very fair, nearly as white as a Circassian."[7]

Tronson, a naval officer on board the British HMS *Barracouta*, also visited a bathhouse soon after he landed at Hakodate in 1856. Naturally, he had heard much about this "strange establishment." There he saw men, women, and children squatting down and making ample use of the bath water, and even when he and his party entered the bathing area, they carried on as usual without any embarrassment of being seen. He went on to say that "We are astonished at the primeval simplicity of the Japanese, and would imagine that such exposures would have a demoralising influence on the young of both sexes."[8]

Rutherford Alcock, who always reflected on civilization with a critical tone, said the Japanese "may daily be seen 'naked and not ashamed,'" but he actually felt this custom was simply associated with the climate and nothing more. However, he did point out that "If this great institution of the bath be the source of the public opinion…It certainly has a recommendation wanting in all other parliaments, of acknowledging to the fullest extent the rights of both sexes, and their equality."[9] In other words, he wanted to say the bathhouse was a true democracy in that women also could take part in the chatter and gossip that took place among the bathers. Alcock did not scorn mixed bathing or nudity anywhere in his treatise, *The Capital of the Tycoon*.

Robert Fortune, meanwhile, had a hard time making up his mind about the issue. He stated:[10]

> In one of the villages through which we passed we observed what appeared to be a family bathing-room. The baths at the time were full of persons of both sexes, old and young, apparently of three or four generations, and all were perfectly naked…Bathing-houses or rooms, both public and private, are found in all parts of the Japanese empire-in the midst of crowded cities, or, as we here see, in country villages.

The bath is one of the institutions of the country…The stern moralist of Western countries will no doubt condemn the system of promiscuous bathing, as it is contrary to all his ideas of decency; on the other hand, there are those who tell us that the custom only shows simplicity and innocence such as that which existed in the Garden of Eden before the fall of man. All I can say is, that it is the custom of the country to bathe in this way, and that, if appealed to on the subject, the Japanese would probably tell us that many of the customs amongst ourselves- such, for example, as our mode of dressing and dancing, are much more likely to lead to immorality than bathing, and are not so useful nor so healthy; at any rate, the practice cannot be attributed to habits of primitive innocence in this case, as no people in the world are more licentious in their behaviour than the Japanese.

As you can see, the end of this passage repeats the judgment made by George Smith.

Henry Tilley, meanwhile, asked "What is the right definition of the word 'modesty?'" He went on to say:[11]

Such was the question I put to myself when I first, this day, entered a Japan bathing-house. There were men of all ages, women, girls, and children, standing by dozens washing themselves, with as much unconcern as though they were drinking tea, and, to tell the truth, the European visitor looked on as much unconcerned as any. "The immodesty is in the remark," said Madame de Staël, to a young officer, who asked her if she did not think some statue of Hercules, or Venus, which they were looking at, was very immodest. So I resolved to think no evil of the naked modesty of Japan.

Like Tilley, Reinhold Werner was also one of the more tolerant observers regarding the nakedness of the Japanese people. While in a public bathhouse he naturally hesitated and embraced moral doubts about the men, women, wives, old people, young girls, and boys all bathing together without any sign of embarrassment. He was also taken aback by the fact that wives would often have their bodies washed by male bathhouse attendants even though they were not wearing swimsuits or bathrobes while doing so. He wondered why

Woman washing her hair (from Wirgman, *A Sketchbook of Japan*)

the Japanese, who were highly educated and graceful, lacked any sense of shame. Like Alcock, he believed shame, or the lack thereof, was influenced by the weather. On hot summer days in Japan, it made sense that people took off their clothes. Werner said that Africans, Indians, and Malaysians removing their clothes was not that strange, as they lived in warmer climates and had different body types, but it shocked him to see naked Japanese people because he found their mental and physical attributes nearly identical to those of Westerners. They also interacted with others in a European manner, were generally refined and graceful, and were well-mannered. After learning more about the Japanese, he found they held vastly different ideas about modesty and shame and no longer found the custom to be odd or unpleasant.[12]

Rudolf Lindau, meanwhile, went even further in defending the Japanese on this issue, stating:[13]

> There is a huge difference between the degradation of the people and the absence of shame. Children know no shame, but the adults do. Therefore, the people are not completely shameless. As Rousseau rightly said, shame is a "social system."…All the various races of people have created standards that they believe are suitable, or unsuitable, and that determine courtesy and decency in the areas of moral education and their customs. Plainly stated, we should not label someone who never breaks one of these social promises in the country in which they are born, raised, and educated as shameless. Among these most delicate and most solemn Japanese, it is hard to be offended by the sight of a girl washing herself in front of her house, even if it so happens that she is naked and everyone can see her. The behavior among the men and women of all ages who gather at public bathhouses is also almost never shameful.

Lindau's description was an excellent example of cultural relativism. In addition, he also had the chance to discuss the issue with an extremely well-to-do Japanese man who did not understand why nudity and mixed bathing bothered Europeans so much nor why Lindau hesitated to explain the custom to others. The Japanese man explained that he never looked away from a naked woman he met in the bath and asked what was wrong in doing so.

Edouard Suenson also defended the body consciousness of Japanese women in the following passage:[14]

> The lack of modesty on the part of Japanese women has been highly criticized by Western Europeans, as it strays so far from the ideals of

decency that they are accustomed to in their homelands. Even so, this seems to be more of a natural childishness on the part of the Japanese rather than any sense of ethical immorality…One has to remember that Japanese women are never purposefully seeking the chance to expose the appealing parts of their bodies. They just do not have scruples whenever they bathe, put on makeup, or engage in other similar actions. They innocently believe these actions are normal and natural…In my opinion, I believe criticism should not be directed at their lack of modesty but rather at the shameless foreigners who, instead of avoiding the sight of their naked bodies, frequently go and stare at them in a lewd manner.

Raphael Pumpelly also shared his experience at a bathhouse. When he entered a nearby facility during his stay at a Hokkaido mine in 1862, he ran into the wife of the mine chief and their children all taking a bath together. Pumpelly turned around to leave, but then the woman got out of the bath and kindly asked him to stay and enjoy himself as she and her family could go to a different bathing room. Naturally, she was completely naked. Pumpelly was initially shocked because "The whole thing was done so gracefully, and without the slightest embarrassment on her part." Then, he drew the conclusion that "*Honi soit qui mal y pense* [Shame be to him who thinks evil of it] is perhaps as applicable in a Japanese public bath as in the galleries of sculpture of the Vatican." In essence, Pumpelly noted the custom of mixed bathing, "shocking as it seems to an European, appears to be perfectly compatible with Japanese ideas of modesty and propriety."[15]

As Lindau said, moreover, the veiled sense of modesty that Japanese women displayed when they were naked did not necessarily mean they were completely shameless. Guimet, who lavished praise on almost every aspect of Japan, understood this point quite well. He stated the following:[16]

> I came across women who knew nothing of rudeness nor what constituted shocking behavior—veritable Eves before the fall of mankind. Therefore, it was only the curious looks of gentlemen and the cries of shock uttered by [foreign] ladies that revealed to them the sin they never knew. I will state it clearly: shame is a horrible feeling to have. The Japanese did not possess this negative trait before we gave it to them.

For a young Beauvoir, who had a weakness for the pleasures of life, the Japanese custom in which "everyone lives in the light of day, and modesty, or rather immodesty, is unknown," was worthy of praise and joy. The Japanese did not feel shame, and Beauvoir called this "the innocence of an earthly paradise." He also wrote the following in 1867 about the sights he saw on a side street of Benten-dōri in Yokohama, which was a "street of baths:"[17]

Bathing (illustration by Régamey, from Guimet, *Promenades Japonaises*)

> The most splendid tattooing on the men stands out amidst the rosy tints of the delighted nymphs, whom the professional rubbers soap and wipe. The good people do all this with such utter *sang-froid*, and appear to think it all so perfectly natural, that I believe for very little we should have formed one of the party, without fearing to wound that social prejudice which says "so shocking!"

Meanwhile, the description Crow made about the night he spent in a fishing village near Odawara in 1881 gives us a heartwarming and natural glimpse of Japan. He wrote:[18]

> Here and there in front of his cottage stood a father, fresh and tidy after his hot bath, nursing his little child, and appearing the picture of happiness and contentment…Numbers of men, women, and children are bathing in their wooden tubs, either behind the house or in front, and even in the village street, one large tub sometimes containing a happy family perfectly oblivious of their ridiculous appearance.

In 1859, Captain Holmes, the merry man who visited Nagasaki before its ports officially opened to international trade, witnessed an amorous young woman run out of her house completely naked and jump into "an oblong tub which stood about twelve feet in front of the house." The woman almost bumped into the surprised captain, but she did not blush and just "giggled and laughed" at him from her bath. Holmes did not get angry the way Smith did. In fact, he said, "I…filled my sails and proceeded on my course, leaving the fair nymph to enjoy her gambols in the noonday sun, and reflecting upon the strange sights to be seen in the public streets."[19]

As we can see from these descriptions, mixed bathing was a controversial topic among the foreign observers. However, shocking scenes of people using washbasins to bathe themselves in front of their homes also attracted their attention. John Reddie Black, for example, made the following observation:[20]

Those who published their Japanese experiences in those early days, speak of the public tubbing of females which came under their observation in Yedo; whilst later writers have called their statements into question: one, in particular, who has been among the most largely read and quoted, declaring, that although he had traversed the streets of Yedo at all hours of the day he had never seen anything of the kind. It is very likely not, for he arrived in Japan at the time foreign influences had had their effect. As late as 1862 such things were seen in the vicinity both of Yedo and Yokohama; and within five years from this present writing, i.e. as lately as 1874, such a sight might have been, and was, seen every evening by passers-by, in the immediate neighbourhood of the settlement. I have seen it repeatedly both on one of the pathways leading from Homura to the Bluff, and also in the surrounding villages. By excursionists in all directions, what is called "indiscriminate tubbing" is so commonly seen, that they soon come to think nothing of it.

This testimony shows that Westerners got used to seeing women exposing themselves while bathing. Thus, they naturally came to understand that such behavior had no sexual implication whatsoever and, therefore, was not obscene in any way. As Basil Chamberlain stated in his introduction as the editor of the Japan Mail, "The nude is seen in Japan, but is not looked at."[21]

Edward Morse also provided testimony to this effect. During his trip to Nikko, he agreed to help his traveling companion, Dr. Murray, measure the temperature of several hot springs they came across. While they were making observations at one particular site, he heard a cheerful "Ohayo" and turned to see two modest girls he had met the day before. Of course, now they were completely naked and Morse was a bit ruffled at seeing them so. Morse and Murray then continued to measure the temperature at several other several hot springs and soon discovered that a number of men and women both young and old had started to follow them, curious to know what they were doing. Morse said, "They did not mind the bathers nor did the bathers mind them, as indeed they should not." He continued:[22]

> With ten times the graceful politeness that we have, with gentleness of manner and sweetness of disposition, yet they are wholly lacking in appreciation that nakedness is immodest, and, utterly lacking it, you are no more abashed by it than are the Japanese, and therefore conclude that what would be immodest for us is not for them. The only immodesty displayed is the behavior of foreigners in looking at nakedness, and this behavior the Japanese resent and turn away from.

As he was passing through a village on the way back from Nikko, Morse saw, from atop his rickshaw, "In front of one house and almost directly on the road was a woman bathing in one of the deep wooden tubs." He mentioned "She contemplated us as we passed without once ceasing her operations," and "Not one of our jinrikisha men turned his head to look." After Morse called Dr. Murray's attention to her, the woman noticed and "turned partly away." He went on to say the woman probably thought they were "country bumpkins or barbarians."

Morse also wrote in the same text, "On the streets of the city or country I never saw a man looking at the ankles or legs of a girl; I have never seen a low-necked dress." He could not help comparing this with the ways of his homeland, in which there were "girls with the tightest of bathing costumes with legs and contour exposed, in full sunlight, lounging about in the sand with men having still less on." He also could not help asserting that "There are a few acts of theirs that seem very immodest to us; there are many of our acts which seem very immodest to them."

Morse felt this way in 1877, but Aimé Humbert had already been staying in Japan for four years in 1863 when he understood that no matter how strange Japanese nakedness and the custom of mixed bathing might seem to a foreign visitor, he did not think the Japanese deserved to be criticized for such reasons. He also had little to complain about from a moral standpoint as he saw the complete harmony that such customs played in the Japanese way of life. He also noted that some Japanese giggled whenever Europeans entered a bathroom and, therefore, reasoned that what the Japanese used to see as plain and natural had suddenly become something shameful and reprehensible in their minds. Meanwhile, Humbert also recorded an incident involving a Japanese man who had attended the Paris World's Fair in 1867. He wrote that the man publicly engaged in behavior in the middle of Paris during the daytime that Parisians would not normally even be allowed to see at night.[23]

As we can see, both mixed bathing and the indiscriminate bathing that people engaged in outside their homes surprised the foreign observers a great deal, but many of them were also surprised to find the custom of Japanese nudity spread beyond the confines of the bathing areas. For example, they found male laborers wearing only a *fundoshi*, a kind of loincloth, and women shamelessly baring their skin in front of others to be "shocking" behavior. For example, Beauvoir saw a woman guarding the gate to a residence near Kanazawa (located in present-day Yokohama City) while he was on his way to Kamakura. He had to note, however, that this woman, who was brushing her hair, was wearing nothing but the light of the sun. Naturally, she was probably topless.

William Griffis also wrote about this subject. He stated the following about the penchant for Japanese women to remove their clothing in hot weather:[24]

> The laborers often strip to the loin-cloth, the women to the waist. Even the young girls and maidens just rounding into perfection of form often sit half nude…They seem to be utterly unaware of any impropriety. Certainly they are innocent in their own eyes. Is the Japanese virgin "an Eve before the fall?"

Even Isabella Bird, who made efforts to intrinsically understand the lives of the Japanese, felt some surprise at seeing women in the farming villages of Tohoku who were "unclothed to their waists," even though it was, in fact, July. At one of the inns she stayed at, "A coolie servant washed some rice for my dinner, but before doing so took off his clothes, and the woman who cooked it let her kimono fall to her waist before she began to work, as is customary among respectable women." Bird had to judge that the Japanese "standard of foundational morality is very low, and that life is neither truthful nor pure."[25]

On his way to Nikko, John La Farge stopped to rest at a teahouse and noticed that his "feminine grooms, stripping to the waist, wiped and sponged their sweating arm-pits and bosoms, in unconcernedness of sex." However, he went on to say that when they noticed him sketching their naked bodies, they reacted "as if I did not take their nakedness for granted, sleeves and gowns were rapidly pulled over the uncovered flesh."[26] La Farge was probably surprised by the grooms' lack of scruples, but he did not view their naked bodies with suspicion or disgust, as he was an artist by nature. He also stated, "Japanese morals are not affected by the simplicity of their costumes, and…to the artist it seems a great pity that the new ideas should be changing these habits [particularly the habit of not feeling shame in one's nakedness] in a race so naturally law-abiding."[27]

Metchnikoff, meanwhile, said the following:[28]

> The Japanese commoners never wear any pants, and this appearance adds to the surprise of Europeans, most likely due to the loincloths. In this way, the cruelty of fate has made it so that the most graceful ladies from Britain who are brought to this remote region of the world blush and cover their eyes whilst screaming, "How shocking!" wherever they go.

Metchnikoff also mentioned that police officers only chased after naked rickshaw drivers because the missionaries and their wives were clearly pushing the government to do so. However, Metchnikoff believed there was no direct connection between nudity and morality.

Wenceslau de Moraes agreed with Metchnikoff to some extent. He believed it was foolish and even libelous to criticize the Japanese for being naked or half-naked and claim the country was one in which the women knew no shame. He felt Japanese women were elegant and graceful, calm, serious, and simple, and he went on to state:[29]

> The Japanese do not feel the shame of being naked when the conditions of their lives cause them to be so. What is embarrassing is when these conditions do not exist and people just show off their bodies to spark sexual desires. Japanese women breastfeed their children in public. When it is hot and they are working hard inside their homes, they may appear to be almost naked to passersby looking in from outside. However, they never expose their arms from the sleeves of their kimono to attract and seduce a gentleman.

Alice Bacon also described an experience she had. While spending a week at an inn along the coast one summer, she noticed a small woman clad in a blue kimono who appeared every day, carrying a pole and baskets filled with fruit she intended to sell. One day, Bacon was staring out at the ocean when she noticed that the unmistakable carrying pole, the baskets, and the blue kimono had been left on the beach. The woman had apparently finished selling her goods and taken a refreshing dip in the sea. Eventually, the woman reappeared and began drying herself off. Suddenly, a man appeared and began to approach her, but she apparently knew him and remained calm and leisurely continued to dry herself. When the man was almost right next to her, she raised herself up and bowed to him, and they exchanged greetings while smiling. Naturally, the woman was in her birthday suit the entire time. Bacon discussed this in the following passage:[30]

> As one travels through rural Japan in summer and sees the half-naked men, women, and children that pour out from every village on one's route and surround the *kuruma* at every stopping place, one sometimes wonders whether there is in the country any real civilization, whether these half-naked people are not more savage than civilized; but when one finds everywhere good hotels, scrupulous cleanliness in all the appointments of toilet and table, polite and careful service, honest and willing performance of labor bargained for, together with the gentlest and pleasantest of manners, even on the part of the gaping crowd that shut out light and air from the traveling foreigner who rests for

a moment at the village inn, one is forced to reconsider a judgment formed only upon one peculiarity of the national life, and to conclude that there is certainly a high type of civilization in Japan, though differing in many important particulars from our own…According to the Japanese standard, any exposure of the person that is merely incidental to health, cleanliness, or convenience in doing necessary work, is perfectly modest and allowable; but an exposure, no matter how slight, that is simply for show, is in the highest degree indelicate. In illustration of the first part of this conclusion, I would refer to the open bath-houses, the naked laborers, the exposure of the lower limbs in wet weather by the turning up of the *kimono*, the entirely nude condition of the country children in summer, and the very slight clothing that even adults regard as necessary about the house or in the country during the hot season. In illustration of the last part, I would mention the horror with which many Japanese ladies regard that style of foreign dress which, while covering the figure completely, reveals every detail of the form above the waist, and, as we say, shows off to advantage a pretty figure. To the Japanese mind it is immodest to want to show off a pretty figure. As for the ball-room costumes, where neck and arms are freely exposed to the gaze of multitudes, the Japanese woman, who would with entire composure take her bath in the presence of others, would be in an agony of shame at the thought of appearing in public in a costume so indecent as that worn by many respectable American and European women. Our judgment would indeed be a hasty one, should we conclude that the sense of decency is wanting in the Japanese as a race, or that the women are at all lacking in the womanly instinct of modesty.

Japanese living in the Edo period did not see anything sinful in the natural state of the human body. This completely differs from the culture of Christianity. Naturally, the human body can be a powerful sex symbol, especially for women, and the Japanese have stories that depict this point, such as the *Tale of Kume no Sennin*, in which the protagonist is distracted by the sight of the calf of a fair maiden washing clothes in a river, causing him to fall down from Heaven. However, this is just a comical tall tale. In this case, there is no allusion to sin but rather the allure of women.

Putting on makeup (illustrated by Wirgman, 1864)

Japanese culture in the Edo period did not repress the allure of women and was quite open about the subject. Therefore, this allure lost its strength as a sexual symbol. As stated earlier, meanwhile, the Japanese at the time also did not believe that the customs of mixed bathing and public nudity were obscene. Conversely, we have to read them as signs of openness and affinity during the Edo period.

As Edwin Arnold said, "The Japanese are not in the least ashamed of the body,"[31] and the common people maintained this tolerant awareness of the body until at least the late 1880s. Moraes stated the following:[32]

> Until about thirty years ago, men and women shared the same tubs at the numerous bathhouses spread throughout the city. Later, however, criticism from foreigners, especially the moral philosophers, led to the placement of partitions within the tubs to separate the sexes, with men on one side and women on the other. Believing this did not go far enough, many of the foreigners continued with their moral criticism, and soon the baths were blocked by walls, completely separating the men and women into two bathing areas.

When Moraes said "thirty years ago," it is a bit unclear what year he was actually referring to, but despite frequent regulations imposed by the government, mixed bathing had not completely disappeared when he first visited Japan in 1889. Descriptions made by other researchers support this claim. For example, Adolf Fischer (1856–1914), an Austrian art researcher who visited Japan in 1892, was surprised by two women who had entered the same bath he was using at an inn in Muroran, Hokkaido. Fischer tried to make his presence known to the women, but they failed to take notice. He even said they treated him as if he were the wind.[33] According to Fischer, he often saw mixed bathing in the "interior" of Japan during this time period.[34] Henry Palmer, meanwhile, wrote about his experiences at Ikaho Hot Springs when he visited the area in 1886. He mentioned the men and women bathed separately and then wrote, "In the public baths men and women of the lower orders often bathe together, in half-open sheds at the street side, yet with a degree of modesty and decorum, and a quiet unconcern about one another's presence or the stray glances of passers-by."[35] According to Weston's writings, when a certain foreigner visited a hot spring after a day of mountain climbing, he entered the bathing area and was greeted by a Japanese acquaintance who proceeded to introduce his wife and children to him one after another.[36]

Despite all of these examples of the Japanese feeling little shame for nudity, even the fact that, as Pompe wrote, men and women would often leave public bathing houses completely naked if their homes were nearby,[37] running from the bathhouse without any clothes on, just to catch a glimpse at a red-haired foreigner, shows that they were far from being innocent and open. Kattendijke mentioned something to this effect when he wrote that the lower classes of the Japanese knew absolutely nothing about mutual courtesy. He said that if anyone in his party walked by a bathhouse, the Japanese would jump out of the bath and stand in the doorway as naked as the day they were born to watch them.[38] Kattendijke often wrote about the otherwise courteous nature of the Japanese, so this experience must have been a huge shock to him.

As I mentioned in an earlier chapter, Laurence Oliphant actually had a similar experience in which the townspeople were jumping out of the baths in Edo to see his party when he visited the city in 1858. He described "bathers of both sexes, regardless of the fact that they had nothing on but soap, or the Japanese substitute for it, crowding the doorways." If we restate this Victorian euphemism, however, either he or the women were completely naked. This is an almost wholly unbelievable scene, but Christopher Pemberton Hodgson (1821–1865) described an identical experience he had in this regard. Hodgson came to Japan to serve as the acting director of the British consulate in Nagasaki in 1859, and after spending three months and completing his duties there, he travelled to Yokohama and Edo on his way to Hakodate to accept the position of consul. He wrote the following about his experience in Edo:[39]

> When the bathers of both sexes sallied out to see us pass, from some twenty of their common cells, in all the natural simplicity of our first parents' costume before the expulsion, I cannot remember but one other occasion on which I was so fearfully horrified…All the bathers of both sexes came out, unabashed and without the slightest idea that they were naked, to gratify their curiosity by a good long gaze on the novel spectacle.

Even in 1878, the same scene could be seen in Yokote, Akita Prefecture. Isabella Bird wrote, "As I rode through on my temporary biped, the people rushed out from the baths to see me, men and women alike without a particle of clothing."[40] Some may argue that all of these scenes show the child-like innocence of the Japanese. However, we can also get a sense of vulgarity and idiocy in some cases.

There is also some debate about the belief that the common people at the time did not hide their naked bodies because they were not particularly obsessed with sex. This means they were not sexually repressed and were quite open about the issue. At the same time, however, this tolerance likely also meant there was a dangerous and vulgar realism in relation to sex. In fact, according to one certain Westerner, mixed bathing, which many of the observers had defended as being the furthest thing from indecent, actually had an extremely sexual aspect to it. Meanwhile, Matsura Seizan (1760–1841), the ninth lord of the Hirado domain (located in present-day Nagasaki Prefecture), wrote the following:[41]

> In the bathhouses of Edo, until I was a boy, sometimes the men's and women's baths were separated, but most of the time men and women would take baths together. Therefore, I have heard that fornication was quite rampant when others were not looking, such as in the dark recesses of the bathhouse or in the middle of the night.

Matsura said divisions between men's and women's baths became quite strict after the shogunate implemented the Kansei Reforms, a series of reforms issued in the 1790s, but according to Negishi Shizumori (1737–1815), the upper part of the partitions were solid siding panels while the lower sections were latticed. Thus, bathers could easily see people on the other side. Negishi even heard from one of his young acquaintances that, while he was taking a bath, he saw a woman enter the women's side of the facility, apparently unaware that men could see her from the adjacent room. The young man peeked and saw her facing the lattice, taking great care in washing her vulva. Being in the prime of his manhood, the young man got an erection and, unable to control himself, finally jumped into the bath, nearly fainting when he hit the water.[42]

Another aspect that shocked foreign observers visiting Japan at the end of the Edo period was the rampant spread of erotic pictures and pornographic books. As Reinhold Werner said earlier, he accepted the fact that the Japanese were not ashamed of nudity, but he could not sympathize with the claim that this was due to Japan being an innocent paradise. He went on to say:[43]

> Innocence in the Western sense of the word has never existed in Japan…The most licentious images seen in paintings and sculptures are displayed as toys for everyone to see in almost every shop one ventures into. Fathers buy them for their daughters, mothers for their sons, and brothers for their younger sisters. Ten-year-old children already know more about the intricacies of sexual love than most elderly ladies in Europe have known or will ever know.

Others echoed Werner's position. Vysheslavtsov, for example, noted that the illustrations in pulp novels he often saw at bookstores lacked anything that could be called graceful. He also said these picture books often found themselves in the hands of children and that they seemed to be perfectly aware of what the pictures conveyed.[44]

Meanwhile, Heinrich Schliemann (1822–1890), an archeologist famous for his work on the excavation of the city of Troy, wrote about his experiences with Edo-period pornography. Schliemann visited Japan in 1865, stayed in Yokohama and Edo for just one month, and wrote a book about his travels. In this work, most of which plagiarized previous literature on Japan, he mentioned that women and girls of every age greatly enjoyed looking at lewd pictures.[45] Henry Tilley seems to have seen the same sight in Nagasaki. He wrote, "Obscene picture books and prints are very common; and it is no unusual occurrence for a young girl to offer them for sale quite as a matter of course, and as though there was nothing disgusting about them."[46] Luo Sen, a Cantonese man who accompanied Perry's expedition to Japan, also mentioned an experience he had in Shimoda in which none of the natives found it odd or wrong for young girls to look at pornographic books.[47]

Edward B. de Fonblanque (1821–1895), a British military logistics officer who came to Japan in 1860 to purchase horses to be used in military exercises in China, also encountered goods he considered obscene. He wrote the following:[48]

> In shopping in Japan, the greatest care must be exercised to guard against the acquisition of indecencies which are found not only in books and pictures, but are painted on their porcelain, embossed on their lacquer, carved in their ivory, and surreptitiously conveyed into their fans. Mr. Alcock made a purchase of illustrated books destined for some children in England, and it was only by a fortunate accident that he discovered among them, before they were despatched, pictures which would have disgraced Holywell Street. I was deeply grieved to learn that even the sacred character of the Bishop of Victoria, who had neglected the precaution of minute examination, could not save himself from a similar outrage. Had not an acquaintance providentially examined his porcelain cups, they would, in all probability, have been stopped and confiscated at the English Custom-House as inadmissible, even as the private property of a bishop.

Incidentally, Holywell Street was a notorious corner of London known for its numerous bookstores that sold pornographic materials.

There were even more shocking scenes. Vysheslavtsov, for example, witnessed the chef at a *monjayaki* restaurant take the soft, sweet batter and make curvy body shapes that one would normally never see outside an anatomy class right in front of the customers.[49] Furthermore, Hübner saw the licentious work of a sand artist at a teahouse in Odawara in 1871. He said the artist "contrived to draw and paint at the same time strange ornaments, flowers and birds" at first, but then "amidst the loud laughter of the company, erotic subjects worthy of the secret chamber of Pompeii." Hübner finished by describing the "enjoyment" the women and young girls took in seeing the artist's works.[50] Satow, meanwhile, saw children's confectionery in the shape of a penis when he visited Kawara, a small town near Senju that he said had thirty-three brothels, in 1872.[51] Naturally, this probably had some relation to a local belief.

There are countless examples that show that the Japanese had a relaxed awareness of sex, but I should probably mention one more: a vulva-shaped stone found on the grounds of Kamakura's Tsurugaoka Hachimangū shrine, which, even today, is famous for apparently helping women conceive children. There are a number of descriptions about this stone, but Lindau's is the perhaps the most poignant. He wrote:[52]

> It is a stone of just some ninety centimeters, and on the top, there is a woman's sexual organ that has been roughly carved into the stone by the elements of nature over time. The stone is surrounded by and stands in the shadow of old trees. This strange idol is revered throughout the land and is called "Lady Vagina." People from all over come here as if on a pilgrimage and leave considerable donations at the stone. In particular, women who cannot bear children come here to pray for fertility and to free themselves from the shame of not being able to conceive. Newlyweds, young girls, and even children come here to pray.

At first glance, such a stone sounds magical and majestic. The worship of sexual organs was a custom practiced in almost every country long ago, but this particular example is a positive and complete public awareness of sex.

Other encounters were not so positive, however. As I mentioned in an earlier chapter, a party of Japanese men gave Perry's sailors pornographic books and even threw some onto his ship. According to one of Perry's lieutenants, however, they also followed the boat and invited the sailors ashore to have sex with their women, all the while making unmistakably suggestive gestures. A woman who had accompanied this Japanese procession even lifted up her kimono to expose herself.[53] The Japanese were probably just teasing Perry's men as this was actually a common occurrence in fishing villages and other areas of Japan, but their behavior truly shocked the American sailors.

Vysheslavtsov also wrote about the appalling conduct displayed by the townspeople in Edo who had gathered to see his party. He wrote:[54]

> Some Japanese girls unabashedly smiled down on us from above, and, seeing this, some Japanese men near us looked up and pointed at them with bemused looks on their faces and said, "Nihon Musume," which means "Japanese girls." Sometimes the Japanese add indecent gestures to otherwise sinless behavior, and because of this, other adults, and even some children who seem to lose the innocence associated with their age, laugh out loud.

One can imagine what kind of indecent gestures these Japanese men used. The point is, however, that the Japanese of the Edo period generally found sex to be a source of laughter. One could even say this was based on how they tolerated and dealt with the realities of human life. This may have also been why the Japanese officials laughed at Heine when he hesitated to touch the Japanese woman sitting next to him. However, the Japanese may have walked a fine line between the realism of viewing human desire as a natural aspect and a vulgar cynicism toward human life.

Ivan Goncharov wrote the following anecdote about Kawaji Toshiakira (1801–1868), a high-ranking minister for the shogunate. At a banquet held by the Russian delegation, Kawaji wrapped up some leftover cake, hid it in his bosom, and jokingly said, "Don't think that I take this to some beauty… this is for my subordinates." Goncharov went on to write, "On this occasion the talk drifted onto the women. The Japanese here showed a certain cynicism. They, like all Asiatic people, are given to sensuousness and neither hide nor censure this weakness."[55] Incidentally, Goncharov praised Kawaji for his intelligence.

Townsend Harris had a similar experience. One day, he was invited by Inoue Kiyonao (1809–1867), the magistrate of Shimoda, to a banquet. After the meal, Inoue skillfully served tea and eventually, "The conversation now took the usual Japanese turn." Harris went on to write the following:[56]

Kawaji Toshiakira

> The lubricity of these people surpasses belief. The moment business is over, the one and only subject on which they dare converse comes up…Bingo-no-Kami [Shimoda Magistrate Okada Tadayasu] informed me that one of the Vice-Governors was specially charged with the duty of supplying me with

female society, and said if I fancied any woman the Vice-Governor would procure her for me.

This incident disgruntled the solemn and celibate Harris, a man who remained single his entire life, and it is not hard to imagine that such incidents caused him to secretly loathe the Japanese. However, Inoue was Kawaji's actual younger brother, and he was known for being a distinguished and capable official who was one of the most prominent individuals in Japan at the end of the Edo period.

The Japanese during this time period simply did not follow the Christian concept that places spiritual love far above sexual attraction. Most Westerners believed this kind of love was sublime, yet it seemed to be almost non-existent in Japan. Many of the foreign observers also believed that the Japanese did not marry for love. Reinhold Werner, for example, wrote:[57]

> Based on what I have seen and learned about the spiritual lives of the Japanese, love is almost never a motivation for them to get married. Therefore, I have the impression that love is an unknown emotion for many Japanese wives and young girls. I have definitely seen Japanese parents dote over their children and their children longing to embrace them in return, but I have never seen any sign of love between married couples. There are several Europeans who have lived in Kanagawa and Nagasaki for long periods of time and have taken Japanese wives. Their opinions perhaps carry the greatest weight in supporting this issue, as even they believe that Japanese women have no knowledge of love in the noblest sense of the word.

It is fairly clear that the Japanese did not know or understand this Western notion of love, the "love in the noblest sense of the word." As Werner said, education, a good upbringing, the law, and religion leads to this spiritual love which, in turn, causes sexual love to be more graceful and stimulating. In short, Werner claimed this was the result of Christian culture and the moral taboos associated with it. He went on to say:

> True love is not possible without a sense of refined shame. Girls who do not feel shame for any reason can never truly feel love, nor can they ever truly love someone else. In addition, the Japanese marriage laws, which allow men to take as many wives as they want, prevent feelings of love from awakening in the people.

If we follow Werner's standpoint, which claims that the Christian view of sexual intercourse between a man and a woman is the culmination of "love in the noblest sense of the word," then what he said is reasonable. We must reconsider the height of nineteenth-century Western European civilization standards that allowed this Prussian naval officer to make a so-called high-level judgment. However, we also have to reconsider how many fugitives of love this Christian idea of the opposite sex created in Western literature stretching from the latter half of the nineteenth century to the first half of the twentieth century. This can help us deal with the issue in a different light.

Returning to Edo-period Japan, however, Japanese men and women at the time fell in love together. In other words, sexual intercourse is what prescribed their relationship. Naturally, sex oftentimes strengthened mutual love between Japanese couples and helped define familial duties for new mothers and fathers. They did not seek guarantees in ideas such as "love in the noblest sense of the word," which may not last forever, as relationships between husbands and wives formed the cornerstone of familial intercourse. The ability to compromise, as well as preserve a natural sense of mutual forgiveness, maintained ties between husbands and wives no matter how difficult their lives may have become, and at the heart of this, sexual activity guaranteed this love. One could even say the Japanese at that time were true realists in seeing the logic in such a relationship between the sexes. Therefore, the Japanese came to find marriage and sex to be normal, everyday activities they could enjoy naturally. They had no reason to be ashamed of sex because it guaranteed the union between a man and a woman and created joy. There is a famous senryu poem that reads as follows:

Benkei ya
Komachi wa baka da
Naa kaka

Benkei and Komachi are stupid,
Right, honey?

The author of this poem was poking fun at Benkei and Komachi for their inability to enjoy sex. As we can see in this famous, albeit vulgar, poem, the sexual act was the most enjoyable pastime in the world. Meanwhile, sex also invited generous laughter. Pornographic books from the Edo period captured readers with its various depictions of the union between men and women, as well as their sometimes-comical views of sex. During the Bunka-Bunsei era (1804–1830), interest in the bizarre and in sadism also appeared, but this did not go overboard or instill any fear of sex in the people. Therefore, there were very few depictions of sadomasochism, and so on. Even when strange fetishes were shown, they were still based on an indifferent and cheerful awareness of sex. Now we can see why Oliphant felt that the Japanese were "a somewhat frivolous and pleasure-loving race."[58]

Nevertheless, the Western European ideas of noble love and the sexual awareness of the Edo-period Japanese, or, in other words, Harris's rigorism of love and the realism of shogunate officials that bordered on cynicism, both have their good and bad points, and it is impossible to judge which is ideologically superior. Poet and novelist Itō Sei (1905–1969) discussed this issue in a famous paper, titled "The Falsehood of 'Love' in Modern Japan." I do not want to go too deeply into this work, but we cannot close our eyes to the fact that during the Edo period, the Japanese had immense sexual desires and almost never found love to be sublime, and this caused the foreign observers to assume that the Japanese were somewhat vulgar and obscene in their attitudes toward sex.

Despite this however, I cannot emphasize enough the fact that a peaceful openness concerning sex pervaded Japanese society at the time. Willem Kattendijke stated the following about the experience he had in Hirado while he was busy instructing some students in the ways of ocean navigation:[59]

> We gave some young women rings, and they came to us with breasts exposed. From what I could see, the girls did not realize how nervous this made us. When they discovered that we had given the most beautiful ring to the most beautiful girl in their group, many of them unabashedly came right up to us, flashed their bare breasts and even made us touch them. Apparently, each one of them was trying to tell us why she had the right to receive the most beautiful ring. I have never seen innocence to this degree before.

Kattendijke also added that, based on this reality, it would be a big mistake to conclude that these girls had no sense of honor.

Count Eulenburg had an experience in which he shared the same sentiment. As a means to recuperate from the difficult, and one may dare say depressing, negotiations with the shogunate, Eulenburg decided to take a long ride to Ōji (located in present-day Kita Ward, Tokyo), a famous tourist spot, for a bit of relaxation. Once he arrived, his party paid a visit to a teahouse where the owner and four women who had powdered the napes of their necks and their chests white lavished them with some of the most-candid service they had ever received. Meanwhile, two girls in the neighboring house treated them to a more tantalizing delight. Namely, they had suddenly entered a small river completely naked and began bathing under the watchful gaze of the Prussian entourage. Eulenburg could not help being moved by the extreme innocence he was witnessing.[60]

Based on what Kattendijke, Eulenburg, and others had written, we can see that Japanese women from long ago had no problem looking at and even innocently smiling at foreign visitors who passed them while they bathed. Old Japan, an age in which many Westerners believed Japanese attitudes toward sex were too realistic and hedonistic, was also a time when the Japanese were not particularly conscious of sex, and they lived their lives filled with a peaceful sense of openness. It should be noted that even Werner, who made the critical yet reasonable judgment that the Japanese knew nothing about spiritually noble love, thought that, since no one seemed to be shocked by the custom of Japanese women stepping out of the bath to talk with passersby while fanning themselves off naked, the Japanese had turned this openness to their advantage.[61]

However, there were both positive and negative issues associated with sexual awareness and intimacy in the Edo period. It was widely known, for instance, that systemized prostitution existed in Japan, and this often became the target of curiosity and controversy among the Westerners. After the solemn George Smith expressed his outrage at mixed bathing and nudity among the Japanese, he wrote the following:[62]

> I abstain also from making a more than passing allusion to another of the national institutions of Japan, the government regulation of houses of infamy and the public revenue accruing from the systematic licensing of these resorts of the dissolute. Young females of handsome appearance are sold by their venal parents, and consigned at an early age to a life of degradation. At the expiration of their term of service, they are not unfrequently taken in marriage by the middle class of Japanese, who regard it as no disgrace to select their wives from such institutions.

According to Raphael Pumpelly, meanwhile, "Japan is a country full of contradictions." He felt this way because even though "It is pretty certain that female virtue stands quite as high among that people as among any other, and higher than in some western countries," he also said, "we find parents selling their daughters to licensed houses of prostitution, which abound to a great extent." At the same time, however, he also had to recognize that this licensed prostitution system, as we should call it, "carries with it mitigating circumstances which are wanting in other countries." He went on to explain this point in the following:[63]

The victims, who are always from the lower classes, are sold from poverty, and being themselves entirely irresponsible for their position, none of the disgrace attaches to them which drags the unfortunates of the West into the lowest depths; on the contrary, they are sold in childhood for a limited number of years, and as the proprietors of the establishments are obliged to have them instructed in every branch of female education, they often marry into the class in which they were born.

Kattendijke also noted the fact that prostitutes working at brothels in Japan differed from those in Europe, as did the social stigma attached to them. This is because the Japanese people did not treat them as social outcasts. Kattendijke even saw that prostitutes were allowed to visit temples during festivals, etc., and they could also settle down and start a family after the term of their service had ended.[64] Pompe echoed what Kattendijke said by stating that prostitutes often returned to society as respectable housewives when they turned twenty-five, and in most cases, these turned out to be happy marriages.

Meanwhile, the brothels received government approval when they opened, which means they were legitimate establishments, and the women working there never became the target of societal scorn. In fact, the Japanese accepted much of what occurred at these establishments. For example, they did not believe extramarital sex was disgusting or immoral. Furthermore, many understood that the women who worked there were often sold when they were children in order to help their impoverished parents. Pompe went on to say:[65]

> The girls are more than happy to leave their parents' homes for the brothels. They even look like overly excited school girls getting ready to enter a boarding house at school because they get to eat delicious food, wear beautiful kimonos, and lead exciting and enjoyable lives... Both the parents and their daughters simply believe they are victims of fate. The parents can visit their daughters at the brothel, and, conversely, these girls find the greatest joy in being able to visit their parents on days they are allowed to go out into the city. Mothers can also immediately go to care for and console their daughters if they happen to get sick.

Carl Thunberg, who lived at Dejima and served as a medical officer for the Dutch Trading House from 1775 to 1781, actually reported this long before Pompe did. He wrote that the brothel in Nagasaki, the town in which the Dutch Trading House was located, was "protected by the laws and the government." He also went on to say, "Houses of this kind therefore are not considered as an infamous resort, or improper places of rendezvous," and that high-ranking officials often treated their guests to a trip to these locales as a means to show hospitality. Meanwhile, prostitutes who completed their term of service "are by no means considered as being dishonoured, and often married extremely well."[66]

Thunberg's description definitely had an influence on Pompe, but Pompe supported his own opinion with convincing evidence that he obtained through his observations and experiences. He was stationed in Nagasaki during the Ansei and Bunkyū eras (1854–1864), a time in which Dutch confinement to the island of Dejima had loosened considerably. Thus, he had more chances to view and interact with the Japanese. Moreover, he could also directly observe the actual physical conditions of the prostitutes since he had opened a hospital with the support of the Nagasaki magistrate and had treated many of these women. In other words, he was not simply repeating hearsay.

Pompe followed the code of modern Western ethics, so naturally he could not accept acts that he deemed barbaric, namely, that of the shogunate protecting prostitution and Japanese society seemingly accepting this without any sense of shame. He also felt these barbaric acts were the complete opposite of the elegance and grace that the Japanese displayed in many other areas. In addition, Pompe also attributed this system to the alarmingly rampant spread of sexually transmitted diseases. He even issued a warning that this was a sign that the decadence exhibited by the Japanese as a whole had gone too far and needed to be stopped right away.

Despite Pompe's warning cries, however, we have to admit the strange truth that a defensive tone is also apparent in his view of the prostitution issue. In other words, Pompe himself mentioned how prostitution was both good and bad. More than this, however, he came to the realization that he was viewing scenes of a unique civilization in which evil was limited to certain places.

Returning to the point that prostitutes re-entered society when their terms had expired, there were many other observers, such as Lindau, who repeated Pompe's relatively favorable view of this aspect. Hübner, however, was highly critical of this view. When he wrote at length about Yoshiwara, he said that even though "It is asserted that, according to the ideas of this country, this horrible trade [prostitution] is not looked upon as disgraceful…and that honourable men do not hesitate to choose their wives among them," such views were all "absolutely false." For one thing, he heard such claims from "Persons living in Edo…whose witness cannot for a moment be called in question." He went on to write with assurance that "There [in Japan], as elsewhere, these unhappy girls are considered lost and dishonoured…An official man who should be known publicly to frequent them, would be dismissed the service and degraded without mercy."[67] Of course, some may argue that Hübner was trying to defend Japan and vindicate it against what he saw as a stream of disgraceful and false charges levied at the country. Furthermore, he came to Japan in 1871, when Yoshiwara had already lost its once honorable standing, so there may indeed be some truth to the descriptions of the Japanese and foreign visitors he saw. However, it is probably also true that he simply failed to grasp the unique nature of brothels that were prevalent and accepted in old Japan. After all, Lindau did not have any reason to lie and even gave three concrete examples of retired prostitutes who had found honorable marriages.[68]

Alcock was unexpectedly calm in regard to this issue. He wrote:[69]

> So far as I can ascertain, there is nothing very peculiar, or sufficiently distinctive in the form the evil takes, or even the action of the Government in licensing establishments, to make it worthy of such particular notice. The law recognizes the establishments maintained (as it does in some Christian countries), and protects both parties to the contract; while public opinion so entirely recognizes the absence of any free will in the unfortunate victims, generally brought up from infancy to their vocation, that when freedom comes, as it does by law after a certain period of servitude, no indelible stain appears to attach to them, and they may consequently, and, it would seem, often do in effect, find husbands.

Alcock also said, "No doubt there is something very much opposed to our idea of the true foundations of morality and national life in this easy transition from the depth of pollution to the sanctity of married life and domesticity." While acknowledging that "To us it seems as if the great barrier between virtue and vice was thrown down," he reserved judging the Japanese, as he felt that "We vainly speculate upon the influence such social habits may exercise in the inner life of the nation." Alcock was intelligent enough to know that the Japanese at that time did not know of such bourgeois ideas as "the sanctity of married life and domesticity" and, therefore, did not reproach them for failing to recognize the evil of prostitution in the Western sense of the word. In other words, like Pompe, he had correctly realized that he had encountered a separate and unique civilization. He was also aware that if he forced himself to apply his own ethical standards to the people living in this civilization, "We should probably fail entirely in arriving at a right conclusion" in understanding them.

As we have seen in this chapter, prostitution, a cultural item that existed equally in both Japan and Western Europe, had two completely different meanings within each respective cultural system. Alcock was one of the first to come to this cultural anthropological understanding. When he said, "Polygamy and slavery, as both have existed in the East from the days of the patriarchs down to the present time, do not apparently carry with them all the consequences we should a priori expect," cultural anthropology, which in time developed as a byproduct of the British Empire's global domination, was likely already blooming in the minds of speculative diplomats such as Alcock long before Fraser arrived on the scene.

Even so, this system of prostitution in Japan did have its share of harmful effects and tragedies. We can quote William Willis (1837–1894) to reinforce this point. Willis assumed the position of medical officer at the British Legation in 1862 and wrote the following in a report he submitted to the Foreign Office in 1867.[70] He stated that prostitutes were generally released from service when they turned twenty-five, but as many of them owed money to the brothel owners, in many cases their terms of service actually stretched on much longer. One third of the women died from syphilis and other diseases before their terms of service were up. Apparently, ten percent of the prostitutes in Edo suffered from syphilis, and the rate was twice as high in Yokohama. Syphilis was rarely seen in the countryside, but a third of all thirty-year-old men living in big cities suffered from this affliction. Such data provided the anti-prostitution proponents, like George Smith, with the proof they needed to denounce this practice.

However, numerous House of Lords Special Committee reports from the 1860s made it clear that conditions in Smith's homeland of Britain strayed quite far from his saintly and ethical sensibilities. These reports also estimated there were 45,000 prostitutes in London and 368,000 nationwide. Smith was certainly vocal about how dirty and shameful it was for a government, in this case, the shogunate, to protect prostitution, but as Alcock said, public prostitution systems also existed in Europe, and he could not judge whether licensed or unlicensed prostitution was more morally repugnant. Regarding the age of prostitutes in Britain, meanwhile, some writers at the time argued that less than one in ten of these women actually lived until the age of twenty-five and a quarter of them died every year. Naturally, these arguments claimed that prostitutes hardly ever returned to society or assumed the role of housewife.[71] Meanwhile, the publication of a famous pornographic book, *My Secret Life*, clearly exposed the fact that the strict sexual morality of the Victorian era was nothing more than a veneer. For these reasons, the Japanese did not deserve to be criticized as the most-licentious people in the world by the likes of Smith and Fortune.

Furthermore, the tragedies of prostitution in Japan did not actually surprise the foreign observers. Rather, they were surprised by the fact that the

Japanese viewed prostitution in a relatively positive light, almost as if it were an element of society and a natural consequence of life. Naturally, the Japanese did have some issues with prostitution on moral grounds. Some Japanese writers even described them as evil institutions. However, they still mentioned that these places were free and open. In other words, just like with the case of nudity, prostitution meant something completely different to Japan and Western Europe.

We have known how open and commonplace prostitution was in Japan since the end of the seventeenth century, when Kaempfer mentioned in his travels that he noticed "numberless wenches, the great and small Inns, tea-booths, and cookshops, chiefly in villages and hamlets, in the great Island Nipon, are abundantly and at all times furnish'd withal." He stated that Akasaka and Goyu, lodging districts along the Tōkaidō road, were especially notorious areas and that all the inns had prostitutes. Thus, these two locales earned the lowly names of "great storehouse of Japanese whores, and by way of banter, the common grind-mill." It goes without saying that Kaempfer was referring to maids at the inns who worked as prostitutes, something other foreign visitors had also described in their travel logs. What he was really trying to say, however, was that prostitution went far beyond the walls of the licensed brothels. According to him, "There is hardly a publick Inn upon the great Island Nipon, but what may be call'd a bawdy-house."[72] Siebold also mentioned a brothel in Shinagawa in the diary he kept during his trip to Edo in 1826. He wrote that, generally, people viewed these facilities as if they were restaurants and served a necessary purpose for people. He also mentioned that prostitutes walked out of these places like someone walking out of a café in his home country, yet no one seemed to take issue with this.[73]

Meanwhile, when Dirk Polsbroek accompanied Jan Hendrik Donker Curtius on his visit to Edo in 1858, a town elder invited him to the Itō family residence in Shimonoseki. For generations the Itō family allowed directors of the Dejima Dutch Trading House to stay at their residence on their way to Edo. The previous head of the family, who even received the Dutch name Hendrik van den Berg from Trading House Director Hendrik Doeff (1777–1835), was well-known for welcoming Siebold and Fischer during their trips to Edo. At first, the current head of the family invited Polsbroek to a brothel where he was welcomed by beautiful girls the likes of which he had never seen before. Then, they moved to the Itō residence where the village chief's wife, an extremely graceful Japanese woman, asked him whether he thought the brothel and the girls who welcomed him were beautiful. He was quite taken aback by this because she asked him this question in front of her son and mother-in-law.[74] In other words, even the village chief's wife had no qualms with bringing up the issue of a brothel in front of others.

William Griffis, meanwhile, wrote the following about Shinagawa and Yoshiwara in 1871:[75]

> We...drive on through the narrow road past fine, large houses, clean, shining, and pretty. What business is carried on in those edifices, splendid in Japanese eyes, charming to a foreigner, and appearing, beside the ordinary citizen's dwelling, as palaces beside cottages! Scores of them are ranged along the road. Shinagawa is the home of the harlots, and here is the resort, not only of the ruffian, the rake, and the robber, but of the young men of the land. The finest houses in Japan belong to the woman in scarlet. The licensed government brothel, covering acres of land, is the most beautiful part of the capital. Oriental splendor, a myth in the streets, becomes reality when the portals of the Yoshiwara are crossed.

It goes without saying that this description is critical on moral grounds. Apart from this, however, it also mentions the differences between the Japanese and Western European views of prostitutes. Such differences unexpectedly show us that we cannot simply deal with this phenomenon through moral criticism. Willis stated the following in his aforementioned report:

> Brothel-keepers are looked upon often as very good citizens, and if kind to the inmates of their establishment deserving of praise. They are married and lead ordinary lives and are not shunned as a degraded class, in many places they are wealthy and an interest in a brothel is considered a good steady source of income, and not in any way incompatible with respectability.

Furthermore, the Westerners also acknowledged the difficulty in morally judging government protection and supervision of the brothels. Pompe, for instance, clearly stated that the government was not only evil for accepting prostitution, but also for guaranteeing and protecting the rights the brothel owners held over the children in their service. However, he contradicted himself by writing that the women selling their bodies looked happy to do so. He was even moved by what he saw as devoted behavior. If the government protected its contract with a given brothel, then this guaranteed that parents who sold their daughters to this institution could rely on their children's devotion to escape the clutches of poverty. Pompe also had a favorable view of the shogunate officials who inspected the brothels and stated that they frequently visited these establishments to hear complaints from the prostitutes and determine whether any laws had been broken. Nevertheless, Pompe added that many of the women chose not to say anything for fear of retribution from the owners.[76]

Reinhold Werner wrote that Japan was the only country in the world in which the government controlled the brothels. However, we have to doubt his judgment as well because he was writing about Gankirō in Yokohama, a unique establishment in a treaty port that served as a kind of experiment for the shogunate. According to Rudolf Lindau, Gankirō was built to respond to demands from certain foreign consular officers to do something about the bloody fights between the Japanese and European sailors that repeatedly erupted in the streets of Yokohama. He wrote that, on the morning of the day Gankirō opened, almost every foreigner received goods advertising the brothel from the owner. The man even explained to them in English that Gankirō had been established for their enjoyment.[77] Naturally, prostitution existed here, but dancing was also famous. Major W. H. Poyntz of the British garrison in Yokohama enjoyed watching about twenty young dancers who chanted "Yah, Yah, Yah!" in between songs and played a kind of game in which they took off their clothes one garment at a time. It was an exhilarating sight, and the other officers in attendance, all the way up to Admiral Vincent King, thoroughly enjoyed themselves.[78] Naturally, this was a scene they could never see in their homeland.

In 1885, the *Triomphant*, a French naval ship commanded by Captain Louis Marie-Julien Viaud, also known by his pen name Pierre Loti, weighed anchor at Mihara (located in present-day Hiroshima Prefecture) on the Seto Inland Sea at 1:30 in the afternoon. Viaud's diary read as follows:[79]

> Behold what a strange town this is. It is like a large cave of harlots. The ship was literally invaded by all the women of the town. They boarded the ship, bowed, and without any sign of shame, came right out and asked us why we had come. We just let them rush on board. They scattered between the battery and the crew, and the "battle" waged on until evening. The ship was filled with small cries and laughter.

What was the captain doing during this "battle?" Naturally, all the women of Mihara were likely prostitutes awaiting the arrival of a foreign ship to their port. Even so, why did Viaud, aka Loti, paint this scene in the bright and indifferent light of a festival? Where was the obscurity and reclusiveness associated with prostitution?

Isabella Bird even experienced the pain of visiting Ise Yamada (located in present-day Mie Prefecture) and seeing the brothels there, lining almost the entire three-mile-long road between the outer and inner shrines.[80] It did not take much investigation for her to report that "Vice and religion are apt to be in seeming alliance in this country," and that "the great shrines of pilgrimage are nearly always surrounded by the resorts of the dissolute." The fact that brothels surrounded holy sites was related to the habit of pilgrims failing to maintain their abstinence, but this was also accepted. Paying for sex was not a dark and dirty trade done in the underbelly of society, and likewise, selling sex was also an honorable trade, even in the vicinity of sacred institutions. Sex was a ritual of rejuvenation and fertility, and it certainly had deep connections with religion in Japan, connections which could even take us back to the shadows of ancient Japan. For this reason, the foreign observers, clinging to their modern ideas of prostitution, could not dig through these layers of sexual history and come to grips with what they saw.

Notes:

1 Williams, *Perry Expedition*, 183–4, 225.

2 Heine, *Reise*, 133.

3 Lühdorf, *Acht Monate*, 101.

4 Smith, *Ten Weeks*, 104.

5 Eulenburg, *Ost-Asien*, 142.

6 Harris, *Complete Journal*, 252.

7 Harris, *Complete Journal*, 372.

8 Tronson, *Personal Narrative*, 256–7.

9 Alcock, *Tycoon*, Vol. 1, 92, 358.

10 Fortune, *Yedo and Peking*, 93–4.

11 Tilley, *Japan, the Amoor*, 118.

12 Werner, *Die Preussiche Expedition*, 78–80.

13 Lindau, *Un Voyage Autour*, 42–3.

14 Suenson, *Skitser*, 94.

15 Pumpelly, *Across America*, 137.

16 Guimet, *Promenades-Kanagawa*, 36–8.

17 Beauvoir, *Pekin, Jeddo, and San Francisco*, 129–30.

18 Crow, *Highways and Byeways*, 252–3.

19 Holmes, *My Adventures*, 22.

20 Black, *Young Japan*, Vol. 1, 115.

21 Basil Hall Chamberlain, *Things Japanese, Complete Edition* (Meicho Fukyukai, 1985), 60.

22 Morse, *Day by Day*, Vol. 1, 97–101.

23 Humbert, *Japan and the Japanese*, Vol. 2, 111–2 (translated from the Japanese version).

24 Griffis, *Mikado's Empire*, 529.

25 Bird, *Unbeaten Tracks*, Vol. 1, 192, 194.

26 La Farge, *Artist's Letters*, 179.

27 La Farge, *Artist's Letters*, 35.

28 Metchnikoff, *Kaisō*, 80–1.

29 No English translation of Moraes's work exists, so passages that appear in this book have been translated from the Japanese version. See Moraesu [Moraes]. "Nihon seishin" ["Japanese Spirit"],

in *Meiji bungaku zenshū, Dai 49-kan* [Complete Works of Meiji Literature, Vol. 49] (Chikuma shobō, 1968), 239. Subsequent citations will appear as Moraes, "Nihon seishin," and will list page numbers from the Japanese text.

30 Bacon, *Japanese Girls*, 257–9.

31 Arnold, *Japonica*, 51.

32 Moraes, "Nihon seishin," 238.

33 Adolf Fischer, *Bilder aus Japan* [Images of Japan] (Berlin, 1897). No English translation of Fischer's work exists, so passages that appear in this book have been translated from the Japanese version. See Fisseru [A. Fischer], *100 Nenmae no Nihon bunka* [Japanese Culture 100 Years Ago] (Chuo Korinsha, 1994), 313–4. Subsequent citations will appear as Fischer, *Bilder*, and will list page numbers from the Japanese text.

34 Fischer, *Bilder*, 85. Fischer was referring to the "interior," or, in other words, lands outside the treaty ports.

35 Palmer, *Letters*, 9–11.

36 Walter Weston, *Mountaineering and Exploration in the Japanese Alps* (London, 1896), 148. William Dixon heard something similar from a foreign visitor working at a university in Tokyo. According to what he heard, this Japanese man was a servant for a family affiliated with the university. See Dixon, *Morning*, 651. Weston may have taken this story from Dixon's work.

37 Pompe, *Vijf Jaren*, 306. Naturally, they were also wearing *yumoji* undergarments under their loincloths.

38 Kattendijke, *Uittreksel*, 124.

39 Christopher P. Hodgson, *A Residence at Nagasaki and Hakodate in 1859-1860* (London, 1861), 251–2.

40 Bird, *Unbeaten Tracks*, Vol. 1, 295.

41 Matsura Seizan, *Kasshi yawa* [Kasshi Night Stories] (Heibonsha Toyo Bunko, 1977), Vol. 2, 283.

42 Negishi Shizumori, *Mimibukuro* [Essays] (Heibonsha Toyo Bunko, 1972), 347–8.

43 Werner, *Die Preussiche Expedition*, 79.

44 Vysheslavtsov, *Ocherki perom*, 117–8.

45 Heinrich Schliemann, *La Chine et Le Japon au Temps Présent* (Paris, 1867). No English translation of Schliemann's work exists, so passages that appear in this book have been translated from the Japanese version. See Shurīman [Schliemann], *Nihon Chūgoku ryokōki* [A Record of a Voyage to Japan and China] (Yushodo Shuppan, 1982), 97. Subsequent citations will appear as Schliemann, *La Chine*, and will list page numbers from the Japanese text.

46 Tilley, *Japan, the Amoor*, 91.

47 Luo Sen, "Journal of the Second Visit of Commodore Perry to Japan," in Hawks, ed. *Narrative of the Expedition of an American Squadron to the China Seas and Japan, Performed in the Years 1852, 1853, and 1854 under the Command of Commodore M.C. Perry, United States Navy*, trans. Samuel Wells Williams. (Washington, 1856). Luo Sen was Cantonese. Williams wrote about him in his book and often called him "my teacher." After returning to China, Luo wrote *Riben riji* [Diary of my Trip to Japan].

48 Hugh Cortazzi, *Victorians in Japan* (London, 1987), 275. Fonblanque's book is titled *Niphon and Pe-che-li* (London: Saunders, Otley, and Co., 1862). Incidentally, the Bishop of Victoria (Hong Kong) was George Smith.

49 Vysheslavtsov, *Ocherki perom*, 118.

50 Hübner, *Ramble*, 239.

51 Ernest Satow, *The Diaries and Letters of Sir Ernest Mason Satow, 1843-1929: A Scholar in East Asia* (Edwin Mellen Press, 1998), Vol. 2.

52 Lindau, *Un Voyage Autour*, 210.

53 Williams, *Perry Expedition*, 349. This quote is an excerpt from the Japanese translation of Williams's book that appeared in the translator's notes. It has been translated into English here. The page number is from the Japanese version of the book.

54 Vysheslavtsov, *Ocherki perom*, 47.

55 Goncharov, *Pallada*, 418.

56 Harris, *Complete Journal*, 308.

57 Werner, *Die Preussiche Expedition*, 82–3.

58 Oliphant, *Narrative*, Vol. 2, 207.

59 Kattendijke, *Uittreksel*, 86.

60 Eulenburg, *Ost-Asien*, 89.

61 Werner, *Die Preussiche Expedition*, 79.

62 Smith, *Ten Weeks*, 104.

63 Pumpelly, *Across America*, 135.

64 Kattendijke, *Uittreksel*, 46–47.

65 Pompe, *Vijf Jaren*, 336–44.

66 Thunberg, *Travels*, Vol. 3, 75, 77.

67 Hübner, *Ramble*, 278.

68 Lindau, *Un Voyage Autour*, 63.

69 Alcock, *Tycoon*, Vol. 3, 95–6.

70 Hugh Cortazzi, *Dr. Willis in Japan*, 1862-1877 (London: Bloomsbury, 2013), 242–244.

71 See Watarai Yoshiichi, *Vikutoriachō no sei to kekkon* [Sex and Marriage in Victorian Britain] (Chuko Shinsho, 1997).

72 Engelbert Kaempfer, *The History of Japan* (New York: Macmillan Co., 1906), Vol. 2, 345–6.

73 Siebold, *Nippon: Archiv*, Vol. 1, 187.

74 Moeshart, *Journaal*, 66–7.

75 Griffis, *Mikado's*, 362.

76 Pompe, *Vijf Jaren*, 343.

77 Lindau, *Un Voyage Autour*, 147–8.

78 Cortazzi, *Victorians*, 277.

79 Roti (Loti), *Rochi no Nippon nikki* [Pierre Loti's Journal of Japan] (Yurindo, 1979), 107.

80 Bird, *Unbeaten Tracks*, Vol. 2, 276. Smith also used the euphemistic "the resorts of the dissolute" to describe the brothels.

Chapter
9

The Status of Women

One of the discoveries made by foreign visitors to Japan when the country reopened itself to the world at the end of the Edo period was the unique charm of Japanese women, particularly that of young, unmarried girls. The Japanese term of *musume*, which means "young girl" or "daughter," soon became a part of the English and French lexicons, and they appeared in numerous descriptions written by the foreign observers.

One such observer was Max von Brandt (1835–1890). He was a German who first set foot in Japan in 1860 as a member of the Eulenburg expedition, returned to the country in 1862 to serve as consul, and served as the German ambassador to Japan from 1872 to 1875. In his mind, the *musume* were an essential part of the Japanese scenery and brought life and luster to the country.[1] When the Eulenburg delegation visited Ōji (located in present-day Kita Ward, Tokyo), along the way they rested at a gardener's home in Somei Village (located in present-day Toshima Ward, Tokyo), and, according to Albert Berg, the most beautiful flower in the garden was the young woman of the house. Berg went on to write that she was an incredibly graceful and charming woman, and when the party arrived, she was working in the garden wearing simple and casual clothes, but she stopped her work to serve tea to the delegation. She had a modest and kind demeanor and charmed everyone in the party.[2] According to Count Eulenburg's own memoirs, meanwhile, the young girl who served tea was pretty and always blushed when she spoke to the men, and soon all of the young members of the delegation were smitten with her. In fact, Eulenburg wrote that it took considerable effort to make them leave.[3]

Willem Kattendijke also commented on the Japanese *musume*. One example he gave came from the time when he oversaw navigation training on the *Kanrin-maru*, Japan's first steam warship, and visited Kagoshima in 1858. There, he saw women with exuberant black hair that covered their shoulders, and they were wearing fascinating summer clothes that were silky and almost see-through. Their looks were enough to arouse the sailors on the ship, and some of them even whispered to Kattendijke that they had never seen such beauty before and expressed their wish to weigh anchor here and never leave. Kattendijke and his men had visited Kagoshima the year before, an occasion that had also left them deeply impressed by the incomparably beautiful hair of the women.[4]

Returning to Berg's descriptions, the day after his party entered Edo, they observed the central city for the first time and were escorted to a teahouse by the shogunate officials who served as their guides. Naturally, this was a normal everyday teahouse that served tea and sake—it was not one of the brothels that we discussed in the previous chapter, but even so, Berg was struck with admiration at the beauty of the server girls.[5] Captain Werner, who brought the Eulenburg expedition to Edo on the Prussian fleet, also felt that the Japanese women he saw were attractive and pleasing to look at no matter where he went. He even said they were so beautiful that one could fall in love with them anywhere in the country.[6]

Rudolf Lindau, meanwhile, wrote:[7]

A woman at a teahouse (illustrated by Wirgman, from Alcock, *Tycoon*)

The *musume*, or young women, have the most beautiful teeth in the world, their eyes look generous and kind, and their eyebrows look like black bows. They also have pretty, egg-shaped faces on slender, graceful bodies, and a modest yet sometimes extremely graceful demeanor. It is a sight to see a *musume* bow deeply and approach you with a gentle smile on her face. It is so wonderful to hear them say "Mappira Gomen-Nasai" ["Good day to you"] when you pass them on the street.

And Edouard Suenson said:[8]

Japanese women are far and removed from the ugliness of the men. They are the epitome of beauty, with their clean white skin, which has a tinge of red, their rich black hair, their dark brown eyes that seem to be filled with sorrow, and their lively faces... They are short but have an excellent physique, and the section stretching from their neck to their shoulders and bosom looks like it could be used as a model for sculptors. They also have well-shaped hands and feet that are amazingly petit. Seeing them, one can understand and even tolerate the excessive sexual desires of the Japanese men.

A Japanese *musume* (illustration by Bigot, from Bessatsu, *Bigō ga mita Seikimatsu Nippon* [Late Nineteenth Century Japan Seen through the Eyes of Georges Ferdinand Bigot])

Dirk Polsbroek also wrote about his observations of Japanese women. While he was in Edo, for instance, he saw a domain lord surrounded by young women in the palanquin he was riding in. When one of the women lifted the bamboo curtain on the palanquin and made ready to leave, Polsbroek noticed her hand and arm were more beautiful than any he had ever seen in Europe.[9]

L.F. Maurice Dubard (1845–?), a French naval officer stationed in Japan from 1874 until the following year, also said:[10]

> Japanese women do not have yellow skin, as the rumors in the West say, at least not while they are young. Particularly in the north, it is not uncommon to meet girls with pink or white skin, and even the petit Parisian girls would likely be astonished by their beauty. The section above their bosom that can be seen from the collars of their native dresses is almost perfect, and the women have an erotic voluptuousness whether you look at the napes of their necks, the roundness of their shoulders, or their chests.

There were some detractors, however. According to Dubard, for instance, he regrettably found the waists and lower bodies of the *musume* to be infantile and felt they did not match the splendor of their upper bodies. Suenson added to this by saying Japanese girls were beautiful until they turned thirty, after which wrinkles would appear on their faces, their complexion would turn yellow, and their appearance would soon start to sag. He attributed the cause of this to their excessive bathing, and many others stated the same opinion, including Lindau. Furthermore, it is noteworthy that Suenson wrote that Japanese women were already fully developed at age thirteen or fourteen,[11] so it was only natural for some Japanese daughters to leave their homes and get married at age fifteen. Of course, in Japan there used to be a custom in which people added an extra year to their age with the turn of the new year, a concept called *kazoedoshi* or "age reckoning," so in this case, fifteen-year-old girls were actually thirteen or fourteen.

Quotes such as those mentioned above cannot possibly be renounced as Japonist illusions. Rather, such statements are more akin to anthropological musings.

Servant girl at a Kanazawa inn, Kanagawa Prefecture (illustration by Régamey, from Guimet, *Promenades Japonaises*)

Dubard even sharply criticized the French view that Japan was a paradise of eternal spring, mysterious flowers, and women who could not say "No." He found these to be myths and compared the country to the mythical city of El Dorado.[12]

As I mentioned in an earlier chapter, Henry Tilley was a Briton who visited Japan in 1859 as a member of the Russian fleet, and passages from his travel logs, such as the one below, could also be called early examples of detailed anthropological reports. He wrote:[13]

> The women are as fair of skin as most Europeans, and are well formed; their arms, hands, and feet being well-moulded; were it not for their awkward manner of walking, owing to their sandals, they would be graceful; when sitting and conversing, the movements of their hands and arms are particularly so. Their abundant black and rather coarse hair is bound up into thick masses at the back of the head, and a number of little arrows made of gold, silver, or ivory are passed through it, something in the same manner as with the peasant girls on the Rhine. Their coiffure once made, and the hair plastered with wax, it remains untouched for many days; care being taken not to disorder it in sleep. The teeth are an object of much attention; the young girls and the men have them white and even; the married women still even, but glossy black…Though a young girl be like an angel at fourteen, she will be worn out, old and ugly at twice that age…The sandals worn by both sexes are of straw, fastened by a thong which passes between the great toe and its neighbor. To keep these sandals on in walking requires a depression of the heels, which of course causes a corresponding depression in other parts of the body, and gives the wearer an awkward appearance: a woman walking quickly has to shuffle along at a step something between a toddle and a trot.

Suenson also wrote about this "toddling" in the following passage:[14]

> These small, dressed-up girls blush when they walk the street and toddle as if looking for a hole to climb and hide inside of. They wear high clogs to protect their feet from the dirty mud in the road. With each step they take, their knees rub against each other, and they wobble about as if they might fall. Their large coiffured hair looks heavy, causing those around them to worry that the balance of their bodies might cause them to flip over. However, these girls seem oblivious to such worries and continue to totter along, all the while blushing and laughing loudly. And when they finally arrive safe and sound at the

harbor, they show signs of being surprised at themselves for making it in one piece, but do not seem to realize how equally surprised it makes Westerners who, for the first time in their lives, might be observing Japanese girls crossing the town in such a fashion.

Isabella Bird, meanwhile, saw Japanese women in the following light:[15]

> Tottering with turned-in feet on high wooden clogs, with limbs so tightly swathed that only the shortest steps are possible, a heavy chignon on the head, and the monstrous bow of the *obi* giving the top-heavy wearer the appearance of tumbling forward, the diminutive Japanese women look truly helpless.

Japanese women did not necessarily look beautiful in the eyes of Westerners from a figurative standpoint, although they still found much to admire. Tilley, for instance, said that Japanese women were not beautiful in the strict sense of the word, but they were pleasant and likable.[16] Kattendijke, meanwhile, said he had only seen a few truly beautiful women during his stay in Japan.[17] Hübner also stated his opinion in the following passage:[18]

The little, girlish steps of a *musume* tripping down the street (from Arnold, *Japonica*)

They [Japanese women] are not exactly beautiful, for they are wanting in regularity of feature. Their cheek-bones are too prominent. Their beautiful, large, brown eyes are too decidedly of an almond shape, and their thick lips are wanting in delicacy; but that does not destroy them…They are gay, simple, and gracious, full of natural distinction, and…extremely easy to live with.

Alice Bacon, an American who taught at a school for noble girls from 1888 to 1889, held the following opinion about "beautiful" women in Japan:[19]

Foreigners who have lived a great deal among the Japanese find their standards unconsciously changing, and see, to their own surprise that their countrywomen look ungainly, fierce, aggressive, and awkward among the small, mild, shrinking, and graceful ladies.

There were also some aspects that Westerners had a hard time tolerating. The customs of Japanese women blackening their teeth and essentially plastering their faces white with face powder, for instance, drew scorn. Tilley referred to the former custom when he mentioned that married women had glossy black teeth. Members of the Dutch Trading House also described this infamous custom, after which almost every Western observer wrote about how much they despised it. For example, Rutherford Alcock said that the blackened teeth of such women looked "like open sepulchres."[20] Suenson also wrote about how he could not help retreating whenever the women opened their lips and brandished their disgusting teeth. He went on to mention that some of them even realized how hideous they looked and described how a few of the younger ladies would strangely distort their lips in an almost pitiful effort to hide their teeth whenever they laughed.[21]

Some of the observers tried to explain in their writings that Japanese women shaved off their eyebrows and dyed their teeth black as a way to make themselves more attractive, but Laurence Oliphant could not believe this. He felt the women purposely made themselves look ugly as a sign that they were married and, therefore, taken. Many other Western observers also believed this was an expression of a woman's sincerity toward her man. However, as Oliphant himself also doubted, a woman who made herself look ugly in the eyes of men other than her husband also looked ugly to him. He questioned whether the husbands were satisfied with this. Perhaps they took mistresses because they were not satisfied. This is the conclusion that Oliphant had reached.[22]

Alcock had an incredible habit of speculating about things and also troubled his subordinates at the British Legation with his lengthy and often digressive reports, and he was extremely verbose on this issue as well. He not only defended the custom of teeth-blackening but also the lipstick that Japanese women wore, and he thought women who made themselves ugly in this way "must have sirens' tongues or a fifty-horse power of flattery" to hold their charm over their husbands and children. He also stated, "If this be a sacrifice offered on the shrine of conjugal fidelity…either the men are more dangerous or the women more frail than elsewhere." Even so, if the husband "has any sense of beauty in him," he was sacrificing quite a bit. Nevertheless, the husband may have also preferred this, as it was customary and possibly fashionable at the time, but if this were the case, then other men would also have preferred it which would make doing so to preserve fidelity utterly meaningless.[23] The way that Alcock carried on about this point soon reached the level of ridiculousness. We might even laugh at the thought of a diplomat, who normally deals with serious issues that need to be solved, mobilizing his power of reason and arguing for the customs of women from a foreign country. At any rate, Oliphant and Alcock missed the point in thinking women practiced this custom to preserve fidelity in terms that were too materialistic. However, they were not completely wrong. Before we can discuss this, however, we have to touch on the other custom that foreign observers disliked, namely, the use of too much makeup.

Albert Berg said that sometimes girls who were old enough to get married painted their faces with large amounts of makeup, completely erased their natural looks and became something grotesque, with only their eyes being accentuated.[24] According to Alcock, women who put on makeup looked "like painted Twelfth-night Queens done in pastry and white lead." He also stated that, with their penchant for "painted cheeks and lips…the Japanese matrons may certainly claim unrivaled pre-eminence in artificial ugliness over all their sex" and claimed that this was a "perverse ingenuity in marring nature's fairest work."[25] Just like with the custom of blackening teeth, there were countless examples that spoke of young Japanese women putting on too much makeup, but we should focus on one more aspect. Reinhold Werner stated:[26]

> Chinese women just put on red rouge. In contrast to this, Japanese women paint their entire face, as well as their neck, throat, and shoulders, with white powder, and color their cheeks and lips in crimson. It certainly has an effect when seen from afar, but as one approaches one of these young ladies, it becomes a bit too much to bear.

Young women putting on too much makeup and wives shaving their eyebrows and staining their teeth black were, as Suenson discovered, all a part of one societal phenomenon. As he saw it, the young women enjoyed doing as they saw fit, and he noted the elegant way they killed time, which included laughing and chatting with one another, drinking tea, smoking tobacco, putting on makeup, and also going to and taking part in a great many festivals. However, he also saw that this lavish lifestyle ended when the women got married, and they immediately dedicated themselves to fulfilling the dual role of wife and mother. In other words, Suenson felt shaved eyebrows and blackened teeth were signs the women used to prove that they had completely given up their vanity and their enjoyment of life's pleasures.[27] In other words, young women putting on makeup and married women blackening their teeth were both expressions of an age-rank system that existed within this unique civilization. Young people who roamed free and lived their lives to the fullest, and whose deviant behavior was often even tolerated, eventually came to a point in their lives in which they became adults who preserved order among their people through the way they spoke and conducted themselves. This custom was essentially the same as the age-rank system of the Maasai people, an ethnic group that lives in Kenya and Tanzania. Teeth-blackening was not supposed to be an effective guard against a woman's infidelity. It was nothing more than a symbol that Japanese wives used to show that they belonged to a fixed age group in society, and, naturally, even if this implied moral virtue, this was not systematically guaranteed.

According to sociologist Abe Toshiharu (1935–), the Western African age-rank systems, such as those that typically appear among the Maasai and Guji Oromo people, are social systems that separate life stages into several divisions, assign unique behavior patterns, rights, and duties to each stage, constantly connect each stage to one's entire life, and relate to mutual dependence among members of the society. In other words, life follows a process of consistent advancement in the system.[28] Teeth-blackening and shaved eyebrows did not achieve the actual function of distancing married women from the temptations of other men, which many Westerners thought these customs were used for. In fact, we can see in erotic pictures by Kitagawa Utamaro, a famous ukiyo-e artist, that women who blackened their teeth and shaved their eyebrows did so to achieve an eroticism that was alluring to men. The entire system was certainly, as Suenson correctly surmised, the advancement of a girl going from the *musume* stage in her life to that of wife or mother. In other words, it was a symbolic expression of one step closer to the conclusion of the overall process of life.

Abe also said that it is normal for young Maasai girls to have three lovers at the same time and that this never causes friction or other problems within the tribe. However, the girls only enjoy this freedom until they undergo female circumcision. After undergoing this rite and getting married, they start a chaste family life as a wife and mother.[29] If we read into this description and compare it with what Suenson witnessed in Japan, we can likely come to a fairly accurate understanding of the behavior of young women and the custom of teeth-blackening among married women in Edo-period Japan. All of this was the expression of the Japanese-style age-rank system that still existed in Edo-period society. In rural districts in which the habit of sneaking into someone's room at night to have sex was prevalent, it is well-known that young women actually enjoyed sexual freedom until they got married. Furthermore, groups of young Japanese men were also part of conventional age-rank systems, and they shared many things in common with the young warrior Maasai men known as the "morans."

Naturally, there are differences regarding this issue depending on one's level in society, so the topic cannot be discussed uniformly in every area. Suenson said the following:[30]

> How, exactly, can we Westerners, who have only known about the country of Japan for a little while, accurately and intricately depict the general nature of the Japanese and their unique characteristics with only the brief amount of time that we have interacted with the people? Even knowing that a completely homogenous society is difficult to deal with, when we focus on a country such as Japan, which, on the whole, has incredibly non-conforming elements, the difficulty increases a great deal more. Clear boundaries are laid down between the social levels of the residents, and these various levels of status are completely different, and it is only natural that various characteristics are set into the nature of the people in order for the benefits of each group to remain mutually exclusive, but this is true for only a few sections of the country and not for other areas.

This is one of the most-surprising examinations of the age-rank system, and we can probably see that "non-uniformity" was more commonly rooted at the base of society even though customs such as celebrating one's coming of age were also widely seen among the ruling class. Even so, the meaning of this age-rank system and how it fit within Edo-period society still remains unsolved for the most part.

Another mystery was the overall status of women. Women dying their teeth black and shaving their eyebrows while their husbands were free to keep one or more mistresses were customs that made the observers question the standing of women in Japan. Suenson even said the status of women was the most tragic part within the otherwise orderly Japanese society.[31] According to Christopher Hodgson, "There is much real family affection in these islands: old age and old people are respected, and children are spoilt and petted," but "The only one of the family connection in the domestic circle to be pitied is the wife."[32] This is because she had to live together with the husband's mistress or mistresses. Vittorio Arminjon shared the same opinion and wrote that it was lamentable that the wife's position in the marriage was so low.[33] Basil Chamberlain, meanwhile, devoted an entire entry in his book *Things Japanese* to the status of women, and he stated that "the way in which they [Japanese women] are treated by the men has hitherto been such as might cause a pang to any generous European heart." This was because "a woman's lot is summed up in what are termed 'the three obediences,'" and they could be "divorced almost at his [the husband's] good pleasure." However, Chamberlain added that, "We would not have it thought that Japanese women are actually ill-used. There is probably very little wife-beating in Japan." He also stated that unlike in Islamic countries, the zenana, a separate room for the wife and other women of the household, did not exist, and the women did not cover their faces with veils.[34]

Quite a few observers believed that the status of Japanese women was high compared to China and the Islamic nations. Griffis was one such individual. He stated:[35]

> The student of Asiatic life, on coming to Japan, however, is cheered and pleased on contrasting the position of women in Japan with that in other countries. He sees them treated with respect and consideration far above that observed in other quarters of the Orient. They are allowed greater freedom, and hence have more dignity and self-confidence…No woman's feet are ever bound, and among the middle and lower classes she is almost as much at liberty to walk and visit as in our own land.

Kattendijke had the same opinion. He stated that unlike in other Asian countries, Japanese women were commonly treated with the utmost respect and received the honor deserving of women. Nevertheless, they did not meddle in other people's affairs like European women and were content to remain humble in relation to men, but even so, Kattendijke said they were never looked down upon.[36]

Oliphant also said, "There is probably no Eastern country in which the women have so much liberty or such great social enjoyment." He had a sense the status of Japanese women was closer to that of the West than the East. However, he was wrong in saying "Polygamy is not permitted"[37] to support this claim. On the other hand, Tilley wrote, "Polygamy, if allowed by law in Japan, is not practised; for although the great generally have a number of concubines, still one woman only is the wife, and she alone has the honour of being a hostage for her lord."[38] If this were the case, then the observers felt that taking several concubines and polygamy were two completely different concepts. Berg also stated that the best example showing the relatively high status of Japanese women was likely their open-minded freedom and using this in their work or when helping men with their work. He went on to say that this did not exist in other Asian countries and that Japanese women behaved gracefully and modestly, but at the same time they were not viewed as being naive. Berg concluded that this was probably the only point seen as a matter of equal rights.[39]

Proponents who gave Japan high marks for the status of women naturally did not give the country a passing grade upon considering how free European women were. In other words, they judged the status of Japanese women was much better than that of other Asian countries, but it was still far from being worthy of praise based on their own modern European standards. As mentioned earlier, there were many observers who saw this as a tragedy, and in most cases, they were basing their judgments on modern European standards. Edward Morse, for example, stated, "In entering a carriage or jinriki-sha, the man will enter before his wife; in walking along the street the wife lags behind, at least four or five feet," and noted that "in various ways one observes the inferior position of women." In other words, as Chamberlain also felt, it pained Morse to know that women were veritable slaves to men. He felt "The absence of that deference and courtesy to women, so universal in our country…is very marked here."[40] In other words, as Kattendijke also said, courtesy was hardly ever bestowed on Japanese women.

Part of the problem could be that Japanese women were sometimes viewed as immature and unworldly. Chamberlain stated, "Women are all their lives treated more or less like babies" in Japan.[41] He was likely using such words to compare Japanese women with their Western counterparts, the latter of whom had independent personalities and could take part in the advancement of society on equal terms with men. When Pierre Loti stated that Japanese women in the 1880s never took on a serious tone, depicted them as foolish puppets who laughed even during the most solemn moments, and then emphasized their simple brains and sly, pampered eyes,[42] he was not far off from what Chamberlain was saying. However, Chamberlain harshly criticized Loti for taking a "self-centered, unsympathetic attitude" in his books *Madame Chrysanthème* and *Japoneries d'Automne* for failing to grasp a holistic view of Japan. Upon returning to Japan in 1901, Loti himself stated in his diary that he finally understood the charm of the Japanese *musume* that he could not see fifteen years earlier.[43] This shows that his view of Japan greatly changed. However, it was probably only natural for him to view the women who were "all their lives treated more or less like babies" as frivolous and foolish dolls who just laughed all the time.

Loti lived a "married life" with a Japanese *musume* for a short time in Nagasaki in 1885, but naturally this was nothing more than paying the woman to live with him. This might have actually been common practice. After Japan opened itself to the rest of the world, quite a few Japanese parents had their daughters serve as mistresses to the foreign visitors at the so-called "treaty ports," and we can see this in a description written by George Smith in which he stated, "Frequent visits were paid to the dwelling of the two earliest Protestant missionaries on their first arrival by fathers and mothers anxious to gain a temporary settlement for their daughters and to hire them out for monthly wages."[44] At any rate, Loti quickly grew wearisome of this "marriage." His partner was simply a doll who did not have one original idea of her own, and when he stripped off her kimono, he saw she had a frail body. Thus, it makes sense why he wanted to run away from her.

Austrian art researcher Adolf Fischer, who visited Japan twice during the 1880s and 1890s, also recorded a story identical to Loti's in his own famous book. A German whom Fischer named Kurt in the book had grown wearisome of the Japanese after staying in the country for seven years. Therefore, he was trying to return to his homeland. He had had three children with a Japanese woman, but he wanted to discard her and his "substitute family" in the hopes of finding a "real family" back in Germany. Kurt complained to Fischer that Japanese women were like dolls and did not make good conversational partners. He questioned what one could talk with them about and what they could actually understand. Fischer agreed with these complaints, as he also thought that Japanese women were more like decorations.[45]

Some came to the defense of these childlike women, however. Chamberlain thought Japanese women who were treated as babies all their lives had at the same time "solid—we had almost said stern—qualities unsuspected by the casual observer." He went on to say, "These delicate-looking women have Spartan hearts." Can "babies" have Spartan hearts? In other words, Chamberlain had clearly contradicted himself. Moreover, he also recognized that "the subjection of women has never been carried out in the lower classes of Japanese society to the same extent as in the middle and upper." He went on to write:[46]

> The peasant women, the wives of artisans and small traders, have more liberty and a relatively higher position than the great ladies of the land. In these lower classes the wife shares not only her husband's toil, but his counsels; and if she happen to have the better head of the two, she it is who will keep the purse and govern the family.

A woman who manages the family finances and governs the household cannot be a baby. During his stay in Atami, Alcock went shopping and "exhausted all the shops, and all the amusement that could be extracted out of the operation of bargaining with their puzzle-headed owners." Basically, he was saying that the Japanese men all over the country were bad with numbers. However, he said, "The women, strange to say, are much better than their lords at figures; and when it came a question to addition or multiplication, we always had recourse to the more ready wit of the wife."[47] Meanwhile, Williams could see the influence women in Shimoda in 1858 had over trade. He said, "I...have been surprised to see how much the women do in the management of trade." He then went on to write, "I got a crowd at the door in a state of great merriment by ridiculing a dull fellow with a shrewd wife for being forced to ask her opinion on the prices of things we wished to buy. In every shop, almost, a woman comes to the board, and in all she is present."[48]

William Dixon saw the same sort of thing. He wrote:[49]

> Many of these shops are managed by women, the wives of the proprietors and very business-like these wives often are, much more so in some cases than their easy-going husbands. Their acuteness may take unexpected forms. For instance, after finding the price of some single article to be 20 *sen*, one may be surprised, on wishing to buy seven of them, to be charged a *yen* and a half, an excess of 10 *sen* over the combined price of seven at 20 *sen* each. The first idea likely to occur to one in such circumstances is, that there has been a miscalculation. But no, the tidy saleswoman is too sharp for that. Her idea evidently is, that if the demand increases so should the price.

Chamberlain was not the only one who was aware that the status of common women was much higher than that of the wives of the ruling class. Georges Bousquet, for instance, said that women in farming villages did the same work as wives living in the European countryside and had a say in everything associated with this work.[50] Walter Weston, meanwhile, stated, "Of the rural life of Japan is the all-important part played in it by women." He went on to state:[51]

> It is not surprising, therefore, that these useful and inexpensive helpers enjoy far more freedom and consideration than that normally placed on their more-conservative, upper-class counterparts. A farmer's wife does not just help her husband with the work, she is also someone he can talk to. The wife also keeps the household finances, so it is she who really controls the house.

Bousquet came up with his opinion in the first year of the Meiji period, and Weston came up with his in the late-Meiji period, and Alexander Siebold penned his own opinion in the following passage during his stay in Nagasaki from 1859 to 1861. He described what appears to be a scene of him and his father entertaining some villagers at their new home in Narutaki, a district in Nagasaki in which the elder Siebold had opened a school. The younger Siebold wrote:[52]

> All of the women down to the last elderly lady appeared, and we treated them to soba noodles and fish. We also heated and served sake, that drink enjoyed all over the country. After a while, the women grew "cheerful," and their leader approached my father and uttered a few words of courtesy, and then she wrapped her arm around him and tried to carry him around the village…People in the countryside almost always practice monogamy, so the status of the wife here is better than that of the wives of wealthy merchants or nobles, and they play a role in the home similar to that of German housewives.

Alice Bacon, meanwhile, said, "There seems no doubt at all that among the peasantry of Japan one finds the women who have the most freedom and independence." She went on to write:[53]

> Among this class, all through the country, the women, though hard-worked and possessing few comforts, lead lives of intelligent, independent labor, and have in the family positions as respected and honored as those held by women in America. Their lives are fuller and happier

A young woman from Enoshima working on shell handicrafts (illustration by Régamey, from Guimet, *Promenades Japonaises*)

than those of the women of the higher classes, for they are themselves bread-winners, contributing an important part of the family revenue, and they are obeyed and respected accordingly.

Bacon also said that, after a woman of the higher class got married, she "lays aside her independent existence," and as the years and months went by, "her face…shows how much she has given up." Meanwhile, the face of a peasant woman, who "works side by side with her husband…shows more individuality, [and] more pleasure in life." Based on Bacon's observations, "The wife of the peasant or merchant is much nearer to her husband's level than is the wife of the Emperor." She also mentioned that "whichever of them [the husband or the wife] happens to be the stronger in character governs the house, regardless of sex." Clearly, what raised the status of wives was the importance of their labor.

When Bacon was in Tokyo, meanwhile, she often saw scenes of entire families pushing heavy carts in the morning. She only realized that the wives were helping when she noticed their smaller size and babies tied to their backs. "But when evening comes, and the load of produce has been disposed of," Bacon explained, "the woman and baby are seen seated on the cart, while the two men pull it back to their home in some neighboring village."[54] Obviously, the wife had helped unload the goods they were transporting.

Furthermore, when Bacon visited Nikko, she saw that women were employed as *mago*, the stable hands that I mentioned in an earlier chapter, in the area. She recorded the following in the late 1880s:[55]

> When we would hire ponies for a two days' expedition to Yumoto, a little, elderly woman was the person with whom our bargains were made; and a close bargainer she proved to be, taking every advantage that lay in her power. When the caravan was ready to start, we found that, though each saddle-horse had a male groom in attendance, the pack-ponies on which our baggage was carried were led by pretty little country girls of twelve or fourteen, their bright black eyes and red cheeks contrasting pleasantly with the blue handkerchiefs that adorned their heads; their slender limbs encased in blue cotton, and only their red sashes giving any hint of the fact that they belonged to the weaker sex.

Among the many foreign observers who visited Japan, Alice Bacon undertook perhaps the most comprehensive examination of the status of women in Japan. According to her, they led happy childhoods. However, they were more like pets that their parents and older brothers cared for. In addition, they had been taught since they were children to always maintain a pleasant attitude and hide any signs of sadness or anger, all in the hopes of pleasing those around them with the self-control and manners befitting a woman at the time. However, their happiness ended with marriage, and every woman in Japan was expected to get married.

Married life was unpleasant for a Japanese woman because she became little more than the head servant to her husband, but she also had to endure the pain of entering her husband's family. In other words, she had to move from the home in which she was born and raised to a new environment that was oftentimes quite harsh. Her husband's parents lived at this new home, and her mother-in-law made the early years of her married life particularly unpleasant. For example, the mother-in-law would make the new wife do every household chore while she continued to maintain actual power over family affairs. If the young woman did not pass the test that her new parents, especially her mother-in-law, created for her, her destiny often ended in divorce no matter how much she and her husband were in love. There was an unusually high rate of divorce in Japan at the time, and this was caused by the fact that the nature of marriage entailed the rulers of the household, namely the husband and his parents, adopting a dependent servant to continue their family line and did not relate to any kind of spiritual connection between husband and wife. Meanwhile, divorce was a tragedy for the woman. She would often lose her children as they remained at the husband's home, and an environment of shame awaited her when she returned to her own home.

In addition, there was also the custom of wives living in the same home as their husband's mistress. Sometimes, the wife even had to welcome the mistress into the home. Therefore, she had to maintain her grace, submit herself to her husband's wishes, and do away with her individuality. Nevertheless, this custom of self-sacrifice gave birth to the quiet and dignified demeanor of Japanese women and the charm of self-restraint that they used to deal with any circumstance.[56]

It goes without saying that Bacon's description above depicts the married life of upper-class households in Meiji-period Japan and the ideal type of such, especially among noble families and other households with strong family ideals or that of high-ranking officials from warrior families, wealthy merchants, and wealthy landowners. Bacon's range of contacts in Tokyo was naturally limited to elite families from Meiji-period Japan, due to her position as an instructor at a school for noble girls. There are unquestionably a number of variations even if we limit ourselves to the reality extracted from this ideal type, but by far the biggest problem that we face is likely what percentage of the population actually occupied this ideal household type in Japan at the time. The reality is that this occupied less than ten percent of all Japanese homes. The vast majority of Japanese people were naturally influenced by the ideology of male dominance over women and led married lives that had no relation to this ideal type. Therefore, Bacon also had to mention the free and happy framework of the married lives of farmers and other commoners to supplement her treatise.

As a case in point, if we focus on the divorce issue, the following example that Bacon introduced shows the level of freedom of women at the time. Among Bacon's contacts was a female servant named Okiku who worked for an upper-class family. She left the family to get married, but returned after a little over one month had passed. Bacon mentioned this to a friend of hers who asked if "she [Okiku] had found her husband unkind." Bacon replied by saying, "No, her husband was very nice, very kind and good, but his mother was simply unbearable; she made her work so hard that she actually had no time to rest at all." Okiku knew her mother-in-law was a strict woman before she got married, but the man who became her husband had promised his mother would move out and live with his older brother and that they would have a separate home. She agreed to marry him based on these terms. However, her husband's older brother's wife was lazy and impossible to live with, so his mother moved into their new home, knowing that Okiku was much easier to get along with. Soon Okiku's life grew unbearable. She asked for and obtained a divorce.[57]

Where in this story are the binds of the family system and the dominance of the man? It appears to be a fight between women with the man stuck staggering in between. It is clear from seeing how the old woman was forced out of her older son's home by his wife that the stronger woman won the battle. In addition, Okiku was not run out of her house by her mother-in-law. She asked for a divorce because she could not tolerate the marriage any longer. As Bacon also recognized, divorce did not hinder women who wished to remarry whatsoever. If the home she entered displeased her, she could leave at any time. This was the right women had at the time.

Naturally, this story took place in the world of Japanese commoners, which greatly deviated from the ideal type that Bacon depicted. However, even in the case of typical upper-class households, Bacon recognized that "the dependence is in many cases a happy one" for wives who serve their husbands and their parents. She also mentioned that, "The wife's position, especially if she be the mother of children, is often pleasant."[58] Thus, a woman could only curry favor with her husband and his mother with the power of her self-restraint, and this means that it was up to her to determine whether the home would be a happy one or not. In other words, while she was indeed like a servant, her self-sacrifice reflected on her as the source of happiness in the home. Bacon even equated this self-sacrifice for their loved ones on the part of Japanese women, especially those from warrior families, to "the old-fashioned New England conscience, transmitted through the bluest of Puritan blood."[59]

As I mentioned in an earlier chapter, Sugimoto Etsuko was raised by the family of a former advisor to the Nagaoka domain, studied at Aoyama Gakuin College, and married a Japanese man who lived in the United States, the country she eventually moved to and lived in for a long time. She embraced a strong sense of rebellion when she was young because those around her had told her she had to be submissive because she was a woman. At the same time, however, she could not help thinking it strange that her mother, who withstood anything fate had in store for her, and a servant girl she liked named Ishi, submitted themselves "not only dutifully and patiently...but with pride." She also questioned why women were not allowed to touch treasures stored in the mud-walled storehouse and asked her father why the women in her family, even her honorable grandmother, were deemed unclean just because they were female. Etsuko asked, "It cannot be...You honour her [grandma] too greatly for it to be true." Her father just patted her on the head and answered, "Continue to believe so, little Daughter. And yet do not forget the stern teachings of your childhood. They form the current of a crystal stream that, as it flows through the ages, keeps Japanese women worthy-like your grandmother." After she moved to the United States, Sugimoto had deep doubts about American housewives who constantly nagged their husbands for money, or, in some extreme cases, had to steal money out of his pockets even though they had the necessary monetary expenses. This was because, in Japan, the wife was the husband's "banker" and was entrusted with everything related to the household budget, while the husband had to ask the wife for money whenever he needed some.[60]

We have touched on the appearance and status of both young and married women, but what about their elderly counterparts? Bacon, for instance, devoted an entire chapter to the peace that visited women in their old age. Japanese women commonly aged early in their lives and often had wrinkles after they reached thirty-five. Old ladies whose faces were covered with wrinkles and walked around hunched over had their own unique and unforgettable charm. The life of a Japanese woman was often called a series of submissions to others, but this was nothing but a name for the latter part of their lives. If a woman's children all grew up and one of her sons got married, she could retire and enjoy a free and happy life in her old age. Even though her new daughter-in-law did most of the household duties, she maintained control over the house and led a pleasant life by being waited on by her son's family. She was also free to go out, something she could not do when she was younger. Her days were filled with happiness, watching plays, visiting shrines and temples, and enjoying other pleasures. The struggles she endured during the first part of her married life were all for the freedom and happiness she now enjoyed.[61] However, if this were the case, what exactly was the unpleasantness that women encountered under the household system that Bacon wrote about? Setting aside having an autocratic husband, the source of a new bride's struggles had to be her mother-in-law. Bacon even stated that girls were fortunate if they found a husband without parents. However, the mother-in-law used to be a young wife who was treated poorly by her own mother-in-law. In other words, the household system for women entailed a cycle that repeated every generation in which they endured the hardships of the first half of their lives and then enjoyed the latter half.

In addition, even childless widows were not unhappy. According to Bacon, even widows who moved in with their brothers or nephews lived happy lives in their old age. She wrote:[62]

> Many such old ladies I have met, whose short hair or shaven heads proclaim to all who see them that the sorrow of widowhood has taken from them the joy that falls to other women, but whose cheerful, wrinkled faces and happy, childlike ways have given one a feeling of pleasure that the sorrow is past, and peace and rest have come to their declining years. Fulfilling what little household tasks they can, respected and self-respecting members of the household, the O Bā San, or Aunty, is not far removed in the honor and affection of the children from the O Bā San, or Grandma, but both alike find a peaceful shelter in the homes of those nearest and dearest to them.

Bacon introduced the following example of one such "Aunty," in a story about "one of the happiest old ladies I have ever seen." She had many children, but they had all died. Therefore, she decided to move in with her younger brother in order in avoid being a burden on her husband's family. Many children lived there, so she took on the duties of watching them along with their mother. From the oldest child to the youngest, she took care of them one by one. They slept on her back and sought her advice whenever something was troubling them, and they found joy walking with her in the town and were delighted by the toys and candy that she would suddenly and unexpectedly pull out of drawers. When she reached the age of seventy, all of the children had grown up and found homes of their own. The sight of her bent form and wrinkled face was welcomed by all of them, and they took turns looking after her as a way to repay her for all the love she had shown them throughout the years. Bacon said, "It was a joy to see her childlike pride and confidence in them all, and to know that they have filled the place left vacant by the dead with whom had died all her hopes of earthly happiness."

As an enlightened American woman with the spirit of independence, Bacon naturally viewed the family system that forced Japanese women to be obedient in a negative light. However, if we read into her detailed examinations and the frequent examples that she introduced, it seems as though this family system may have appeared to be male-centric on the surface, but in reality, it was one in which the woman played the central figure, and it guaranteed the woman her happiness.

A farmer's wife near Nikko in 1876: her husband was a warrior who became a farmer. (illustration by Régamey, from Guimet, *Promenades Japonaises*)

More than anything, Japanese people at the time placed importance on harmony within the family. Customs such as wives and concubines living together were nothing more than aspects of a system only seen in the homes of the domain lords or high-ranking warriors that ensured the continuation of the family line. If a man wanted to spend time with a concubine, Bacon noted that it was normal for him to avoid doing so in the same house that his wife and children lived in, and she also realized that such a luxury was only permitted among a small number of men. She also stated that Japanese women had no concern with the world outside their homes. However, this was also apparently the case for a large number of men, so they also led happy or unpleasant lives within the area of their homes until prosperity and success became their concern in the Meiji period. Women were the ones who decided whether the men's lives were happy or unpleasant. If this were the case, then testing new wives and teaching them the family traditions as the newest member of the family was a natural step for her to preserve peace and happiness in the household that she would herself be a part of until she died. The woman showed subservience and self-sacrifice to make her home a happy one, and as a result, she could return to happiness herself. As Bacon also realized, even if she became dependent on another home by marrying into it, she would come to govern it in her old age. Self-control and self-sacrifice gave her a silent sense of dignity. The strict nature of Japanese women that Chamberlain mentioned came from the self-discipline they had learned since childhood.

In 1860, Albert Berg wrote that the grace and appearance of many older wives attested to their moral mission in life and their peaceful way of life.[63] After reading Bacon's descriptions, we can now clearly see what this entailed. Likewise, when Morse visited Wakayama Prefecture in 1882 and wrote, "I notice the remarkably good looks of the older women, very sweet, motherly, and intelligent faces; indeed, I may say that in the many places I have visited in Japan I never saw so many fine and intelligent old ladies as here."[64] we can clearly see the reason for these "good looks." It was not just due to the old traditions of the Kishū domain (located in present-day Wakayama Prefecture), one of the three houses of the Tokugawa family.

However, Japanese women were not always subservient. One of the strongest impressions that foreign observers had at first was their incredible vivacity. Friedrich Lühdorf, for instance, wrote about his impression of Japanese women in Hakodate in 1855 in which he described how they were generally healthy and active.[65] Furthermore, according to the book, *Narrative of the Expedition of an American Squadron*, the young women of Shimoda had "much of that vivacity and self-reliance in manners."[66] In other words, Japanese women, or at least the commoners, did not always give off the impression that they were being oppressed.

The lack of timidity toward foreign visitors on the part of Japanese women also left a huge impression on people visiting from overseas. J.M. Tronson, who landed in Hakodate in 1856, wrote the following:[67]

> They [Japanese women] are not so shy and reserved before strangers as the Chinese; should you enter a house and sit down on the elevated floor, the good wife, or one of the daughters would approach and offer a cup of tea (*Tchà*), poured from a bright brass or porcelain tea-pot (*To-shin*).

Sherard Osborn, meanwhile, wrote the following about a Japanese family he saw on a boat that approached his party on the day they landed at Edo in 1858:[68]

> A lady is seated with her children; her dress betokens that she is of the better order…She sits abaft in the most matronly manner, and points out to one of her daughters what she deems most worthy of notice in our unworthy selves, our boat, and our boat's crew. The young lady, we are glad to observe, without being unladylike, showed none of that suspicious fear of the genus Man so general in the excessively modest East.

Customs official and his family (from Humbert, *Japan and the Japanese*)

Robert Fortune also wrote the following about the Umeyashiki (Mansion of Plum Trees), the famous teahouse he stopped at on his journey from Yokohama to Edo in 1860:[69]

> The Japanese ladies differ much from those of China in their manners and customs. It is etiquette with the latter to run away the moment they see the face of a foreigner; but the Japanese, on the contrary, do not show the slightest diffidence or fear of us. In these tea-houses they come up with smiling faces, crowd around you, examine your clothes, and have even learnt to shake hands!

Even women from the warrior class were more extroverted and freer than we might imagine. A little while after Aimé Humbert arrived and settled in at the Dutch Legation, he was visited by the wives of shogunate officials working at the *unjosho*, or customs house. Their party consisted of four married women, two daughters who were of marriageable age, and a number of other children both big and small. They had all received permission from their husbands to make the visit. At first, they acted quite modestly, hesitating while taking off their clogs, but once they passed in front of the mirror in the sitting room, they burst into laughter. It was rare for them to see their entire body reflected so. Then, they unleashed a flood of questions, inquiring about who painted the pictures on the walls, how to use each piece of furniture, and so on. They even entered Humbert's private room. Their eyes glittered with curiosity at seeing the buttons, toiletries, and sewing implements there, and they finally left his room after receiving some of the buttons and some prints as presents.[70] They could apparently communicate quite well with hand gestures and broken English.

Christopher Hodgson, who was also stationed in Hakodate, said that Japanese wives had a sad existence, but it is hard to find anything that could be called sad in his records detailing his interactions with the wife of the Hakodate magistrate. During his time in Hakodate, for example, Hodgson's family invited her family to numerous functions, and vice versa, and he said that she had a beautiful dress and was adorned "rather like 'Marie Stuart.'" At one dinner that Hodgson and his family attended, she was the one who served sake, and when everyone was finished eating, she escorted Hodgson's wife and daughter to a separate room and began inspecting their clothing along with her servant girls. In return for this, she gave them a tour of the magistrate's mansion and showed them some of her own kimonos. Meanwhile, at a dinner at Hodgson's residence, she wanted to try on some of Hodgson's wife's clothing and was quite pleased to see herself wearing Western-style clothes. She was also intrigued by illustrated newspapers that showed views of London. Hodgson allowed her to have some old copies that she told her servants to carry home with them.[71]

Several other observers also noted how free Japanese women were. Berg mentioned that Japanese wives from the middle class and their daughters did not wear veils when they went out and did not walk the streets with male escorts.[72] George Smith said, "A married woman seems to be admitted among the lower and middle classes to an intimacy and familiar intercourse with strangers, visitors and customers, which presents an appearance of approximation to the ideas and habits of European society."[73] Both Berg and Smith made these observations around 1860, but J. F. van Overmeer Fischer had already recognized this freedom among Japanese women in the 1820s. He wrote that wives enjoyed social intercourse with their friends and were always happy to visit each other. They could also be seen taking pleasure trips and thoroughly enjoyed savoring Japan's beautiful nature. Fischer also saw that wives and daughters from good homes were constantly accompanied by their servants.[74]

Essayist and feminist Yamakawa Kikue (1890–1980) wrote about women from warrior families in the Mito domain. She stated that wives from good homes only went out to visit their hometowns during the Bon festival and the New Year's holidays, their relatives if something good or bad happened to them, their family grave on the date their mother or father passed away, or a shrine to pray to the gods. However, if a woman had an attendant, she was able to go out whenever she wanted. When Yamakawa's mother, Chiyo, was a girl, for example, a local dowager often went out with her.[75] In this case, an elderly woman was visiting a shrine to pray, but it goes without saying that this was a favorite pastime for women at the time. Meanwhile, Chiyo's sewing instructor and her husband, who I mentioned both came from a warrior family, would often take their sewing girls out on sunny spring or fall days, and they always went to the banks of the Naka River, where the girls could run and frolic in the fields. After they finished playing, the couple would take them to a big farmhouse owned by a family they knew for tea and a picnic lunch.

Yamakawa also described how her grandfather Aoyama Nobutoshi's older brother, Nobumitsu, who became the head of the main branch of the Aoyama family, remarried, and his new wife was a fierce woman who earned the nickname, "Nun Shogun." Not only did she completely control her husband, but she also drove each woman that her son married out of their house, something she ended up doing four times. Alcock said that there was an "unprecedented and in every way extraordinary authority given to mothers over their sons," and this "redresses the wrong" of the treatment women receive throughout their lives, but this "Nun Shogun" did not receive any ill treatment and was actually a complete autocrat in the Aoyama family. When a former retainer of the family came to offer his greetings, he apparently did not come right away, so the woman scolded the man and asked him why he stayed the night at another house when her family had more than enough food to feed him. Yamakawa judged that it was not uncommon in such cases for even women to take on a boastful air and address others using the language of men.[76] In fact, there was clearly little difference between the language of men and women among the Edo commoners if we read works by Jippensha Ikku (1765–1831), an Edo-period author and artist, and Shikitei Sanba (1776–1822), an Edo-period comic writer.

Yamakawa also wrote about the trouble that her grandmother's aunt encountered at a bathhouse while she was touring Edo.[77] According to this record, the woman found a tub filled with hot water and immediately splashed her body with it, all the while thinking how considerate the people of Edo were, especially the owner who had prepared the bath for her. However, she soon realized that the bath was for someone else. A woman came into the bath and saw that someone was using her tub, for which Yamakawa's grandmother's aunt quickly apologized. The woman was kind and said feel free to use the tub, but then she violently berated the bathhouse owner, screaming, "Hey, there's no water for me!" The owner responded by saying, "But I prepared your bath over there," to which the woman cried, "I'm not blind, woman! I don't see my bath anywhere!" If such words were truly used by the women of Edo, then we have to do away with the conventional image of their calm and obedient nature.

Another example of this involved a woman who recalled an episode that occurred in the younger days of Yasuda Zenjirō (1838–1921), an extremely wealthy businessman from the Meiji period. She was fifteen years old at the time, and, according to her story, she was washing her clothes at a well when Yasuda came up behind her and poked her on the shoulder. She did not know it was him and ostentatiously screamed, "Picking on me again, eh Kiyokimi? You little brat!" in the language of men.[78] This is a story from the end of the Edo period, but the common women from the Bunka-Bunsei era (1804–1830) used the same rough Edo dialect that men did. I cannot name any actual sources here, but erotic books from the time period clearly show that this was the case.

Relationships with husbands were also equal. According to Mary Fraser, wife of diplomat Hugh Fraser, one of her housekeepers lamented why "she married such a fool," and constantly scolded her husband. The husband always endured her words, and then asked her to clean his tobacco pipe and serve him some tea.[79] After Jephson and Elmhirst finished their work with the regiment in Yokohama for the day, they would often spend time at one of the antique shops that lined the streets. One day, they passed in front of one of these stores and saw an old woman they knew sitting there, asking her "where her husband was." She answered "'He was after the girls,'" and laughed "as if delighted at the idea of having such a gay old dog for a spouse." The next time they visited the store, they tried teasing this old lady-killer, but he did not seem happy with the name his wife gave him and eagerly tried to cast it off. Jephson and Elmhirst soon understood that the old woman was bragging about her husband.[80]

The badge of the Ninth Regiment, which Jephson and Elmhirst belonged to, was the goddess Britannia, the symbol of Great Britain. When Jephson and Elmhirst visited a teahouse, the Japanese there asked them who the young woman on their badges was. During the conversation, word came up that the ruler of Britain was a woman. The women in the teahouse raised their heads and screamed at their husbands, "Aha! You see there *are* countries where women are treated with respect. These tojins aren't such barbarians after all!" The men looked confused and asked, "Do your women, then, fight?" Jephson and Elmhirst's party all responded that of course they did, the voices of two or three of the married men being particularly noticeable.[81] However, the Japanese women seemed to be an even match for British women when it came to fighting. According to Yamakawa, the wife of one Mito-domain scholar was famous for her strength, and Yamakawa remembered a story in which this woman apparently climbed on her husband like a horse and repeatedly beat him with her fists.[82]

Before Kiyokawa Hachirō (1830–1863) had become a well-known *shi-shi*, a group of warrior activists who were influential at the end of the Edo period, he embarked on a trip to western Japan with his mother in 1855. They stayed at an inn in Niigata, and the owner not only accompanied them to Yutagami but also decided along the way to go with them to visit Zenkōji temple. She stayed with them multiple nights before they finally came to Izumozaki. The woman sent one of her servant girls home to tell her husband what she had planned to do, so it was evident this woman had a high level of freedom. She was in her thirties and did not appear to desire having a love affair, but it was clear she was attracted to Hachirō. When they were in Izumozaki, the woman's mother sent a servant for her and she soon abandoned her journey and returned home.

In the end, however, it did not appear that her actions were scandalous or out of the ordinary. Hachirō similarly did not feel embarrassed and said that the wife of Matsukiya was a respectable lady, but she was emotional, did not get tied down to things, was extremely open, and had the air of a young boy. Nevertheless, he did not see any diffident behavior on her part. It is also interesting that Hachirō's mother essentially welcomed the woman into her family and showed no sign of stopping the woman with common sense.[83]

From the time when Shinoda Kōzō (1871–1965) worked as a reporter for the *Hochi Shimbun*, a Meiji-period newspaper known today as *Sports Hochi*, he documented gossip from the end of the Edo period until the first year of the Meiji period. One woman that he interviewed talked about her mother and said that, when she was young, she served a wealthy *hatamoto*, a samurai under direct service to the shogun, as his page. She was a remarkable woman who often went to Shinjuku with her friends and paid prostitutes for their time. One of her companions was a lovely *oiran* courtesan who was only eighteen years old, and they would smoke tobacco together while they gossiped and talked about their lives. After they had fun talking, the woman's mother would even walk the *oiran* home.[84] The woman said that her mother was quite strange, but it seems that dynamic and open-hearted women like her were fairly common in the Edo period and in the first year of the Meiji period, in which, of course, the traditions of the previous age still lingered.

Even if women of the Edo period came from the warrior class, they were apparently free to drink alcohol and smoke tobacco. When Hodgson's wife, who, incidentally, was a French woman, was invited to the home of the Hakodate magistrate, his wife offered her some tobacco. Mrs. Hodgson declined the offer, something the magistrate's wife found surprising.[85] Berg, meanwhile, wrote that in no other country was the use of tobacco as prevalent as in Japan. He said that almost every adult carried tobacco and a pipe with them and that many wives and daughters smoked in their homes.[86] Werner echoed this by saying that the women, like the men, were heavy users of tobacco.[87] Regarding the consumption of alcohol, meanwhile, Yamakawa said that even though her grandfather hardly ever took a sip of sake, her grandmother had been raised on it and enjoyed a bottle every night.[88] According to the diary left by Iseki Takako (1745–1844), an Edo-period writer and wife of *hatamoto* Iseki Chikafusa, when her daughter-in-law's mother came to visit the Iseki residence, Takako's husband prepared alcohol for her to drink.[89] Iseki also mentioned in her diary many other examples of women drinking alcohol.

Women of the Edo period had to show on the surface that they were bound by the *san-ju*, or the "three obediences" (obedience to one's father, one's husband, and one's children after the husband dies), by women's education, and by other systems, and probably did appear to be slaves to men to a certain degree, but in reality, they were surprisingly free and were apparently equal to and independent from their male counterparts. The fact that many foreign observers recognized that, in comparison to other Asian countries, Japanese women had the air of a certain kind of freedom shows they had unconsciously discovered the existence of a reality that only appeared to be judged on the moral front that women put on in their subservience to men. The lives of women from the Edo period, whether they came from warrior or common families, were actually not that rigid and formal, and were apparently lives worth living since they were born. If we *do* view certain parts of their lives as tragic, then we are only looking at such aspects through our modern eyes, something that could be called "intellectual arrogance."

The way in which women of the Edo period were free and active seemed to have greatly diminished in the Meiji period. However, even in the mid-Meiji period, the premodern nature of women's freedom still lingered in the air. With the exception of a few examples, foreign observers unanimously praised the women of old Japan. Some of them, notably Wenceslau de Moraes and Edwin Arnold, even wrote that Japanese men were ugly but that the women were so beautiful that they were like a different race of people. Richard Gordon Smith (1858–1918), a libertine who stayed in Japan during the late 1890s and early 1900s, also wrote on his sixth day in the country that, "I never saw a single good-looking native man; it is quite astonishing what a contrast they are to the women."[90]

Herbert George Ponting (1870–1935), a British photographer who also visited Japan in the late 1890s to the 1900s, was another observer who praised Japanese women. To Ponting, the country of Japan was one in which the "woman is a great power." He said, "The home is woman's province: so is the inn," and went on to say that even though foreign visitors did not particularly care for the food, they still wanted to stay at Japanese-style inns instead of international hotels for this reason. Ponting explained that "It is because you feel the sweet authority of woman the moment you enter a Japanese house." He went on to say, "She is an autocrat, and a clever one, for she rules even where she does not really pretend to rule; but she does it so tactfully that, whilst the husband holds the reins, he does not see…that his little wife has got the bit firmly between her teeth, and he is simply following wherever she chooses to lead."

The scene that left the biggest impression on Ponting, however, was the behavior of the nurses he saw during the Russo-Japanese War (1904–1905). He observed the Japanese army hospital in Hiroshima and the Russian prisoners' hospital in Matsuyama, and wrote the following:[91]

> The Japanese nurses were veritable ministering angels of mercy…At Matsuyama the Russians could not sound the praises of their gentle Japanese nurses loud enough. The looks with which the fallen followed every movement of their little guardians told a plain and simple tale, and more than one gallant fellow, when he left his bed, was pierced by an arrow that wounded him far deeper than the bullet which had laid him low…She [the Japanese woman] was sagacious, strong, and self-reliant, yet gentle, compassionate, and sweet; a very ministering angel of forgiveness, tenderness, and mercy.

I will say what every Japanese intellectual in the present day must feel rising in his or her heart at reading the passage above: What an empty and unsteady sense of praise! Japanese intellectuals have already been taught to respond to any praise for Japan with a sneer and distrust. But think about it for a moment. Who today praises the women of a given ethnic group so ardently?

Moreover, Ponting was not a unique and isolated example. Moraes and Arnold, for instance, both continuously wrote about their almost-embarrassing praise for Japanese women, and even among more cool-headed descriptions of praise that hold back criticism, with the exception of a few examples, almost every Western observer shared the same feelings. Such praise was no more than momentary inspiration, however. In fact, Westerners who lived with Japanese women even found that the charm that had initially moved them faded and inherently became problematic, and in some cases, as with Loti or the aforementioned Kurt, their praise soon reverted to disappointment and hatred. Ponting and other observers like him read the works of Alice Bacon, the woman who comprehensively discussed the unreasonable subservient status placed on Japanese women, and they knew of Pierre Loti's derision and disgust for Japanese women quite well. However, they had been raised on the modern values of the West and could only think and function under these standards. Therefore, they clearly perceived unique characteristics of women living in a separate civilization built on values that differed from their own. We cannot overlook the fact that this caused a certain kind of praise to spring into their hearts, even if it did not reach the extreme levels exhibited by Ponting.

There is probably also a feminist counter-argument that states this praise entailed the sexism of a male-dominated culture that reached its peak in the nineteenth century and that all of their praise for the virtue of Japanese women centered on those aspects that were favorable to men. From an ultramodern standpoint, such proponents are content to deny outright the premodern characteristics that observers such as Ponting had discovered and pondered about, and they believe in justice and advancement.

Mary Fraser, the wife of the British ambassador to Japan, held a meeting "every two weeks...alternately with my English one" in order to get a little closer to Japanese women, "both from the interest and sympathy I feel for them." She also felt that it was good way to repay them for their kindness, and she was certain there were many things she could learn from them. But what, exactly, did she hope to learn? As the meetings went on, some of the women in attendance began to speak their mind. One of the them said to Fraser, "'Hearts are alike in Europe and Japan. English ladies are very brave and true to their duties—that is what we admire.'" Fraser "sighed" and replied, "'You could teach us more than we can teach you on that point.'" It was at that moment that Fraser thought of "what we Western women could make of our world, had we the heroic humility, the faithfulness to duty, the divine unselfishness of our Eastern sisters."[92]

Fraser then went on to say that naturally, "The exaggeration of a virtue is revenged in Nature's exacting balances by the formation, somewhere, of a fault." She felt Japanese husbands unfairly treated their wives with coldness and indifference. Then, she could not help mentioning, "The truth is that marriage is not...the supreme relation of life, as it is in Europe. Love, in our sense of the word, has nothing to do with the matter." She went on to say:[93]

> Her [the Japanese woman's] marriage is the passing from childhood's happy careless life to the responsibilities of reason. Body and soul, mind and spirit, must all tend to one thing—the giving entire satisfaction to the new master and his family. This seems very dreary and cold to us; and the best European woman, educated in the full consciousness of her own value, would feel that she lost her integrity by entering such bondage...And yet all English history can show no record of higher, stronger love than the Japanese wife has again and again laid at her

lord's feet. It would seem as if that rare passion of which I spoke just now may, in fact, be born in what we call bondage.

Fraser felt this way and thought that her readers would "exclaim, as you hear of some amazing piece of heroism, 'How the woman must have loved the man!'" However, she followed this by saying, "And your friend, your little Japanese friend, looks up into your face with her childlike smile and some surprise in her dark eyes: 'Oh no, it was her duty; he was her husband.'"

While Sugimoto Etsuko was attending the mission school, she found that "love as pictured in Western books was interesting and pleasant…but not to be compared in strength, nobility, or loftiness of spirit to the affection of parent for child, or the loyalty between lord and vassal." Sugimoto would later reflect that she had "warped ideas on this unknown subject," and this was due to Japanese girls being strictly trained in warrior homes to "regard duty, not feeling, as the standard of relations between man and woman."[94] This is exactly what Fraser encountered.

We have to hand it to Fraser when she said:

> It seems to me that the common amusement called "falling in love" has absolutely nothing to do with the affectionate and caring fulfilment of the duties of married life, and that the crown of worship of one human being for another may be, and often is, granted without that passing preliminary ailment having been contracted at all.

In other words, Fraser understood why her Japanese friend told her it was not love. Her Japanese friend took love to be a romance, and as the husband was the protagonist in the story, the wife did not sacrifice herself as a way to express any romantic feelings. It was deeper than that. Is there any deeper sense of love than duty, which is completely unrelated to the romantic "disease" of falling in love? Love was separate from romance and implicit in the woman's duty to her family. This is what Fraser discovered, although she still felt that it was impossible for her to do away with romance, a tradition that has existed in Western Europe since the troubadours and the fate of lovers, e.g., the tale of *Tristan and Isolde*. As Fraser explained, the old Japanese civilization brought the curtain down on the death of these lovers, a scene that had nothing to do with the real lives of the Japanese people.

Notes:

1 Max von Brandt, *Dreiunddreissig Jahre in Ost-Asien: Erinnerungen eines Deutschen Diplomaten* [*Thirty-three Years in East Asia: Memories of a German Diplomat*] (Leipzig, 1901). No English translation of Brandt's work exists, so passages that appear in this book have been translated from the Japanese version. See Buranto [Brandt], *Doitsu Kōshi no mita Meiji Ishin* [The Meiji Restoration Seen through the Eyes of a German Diplomat] (Shinjinbutsu Oraisha, 1987), 241. Subsequent citations will appear as Brandt, *Dreiunddreissig*, and will list page numbers from the Japanese text.

2 Berg, *Eulenburg Expedition*, Vol. 1, 129.

3 Eulenburg, *Ost-Asien*, 88.

4 Kattendijke, *Uittreksel*, 98, 114.

5 Berg, *Eulenburg Expedition*, Vol. 1, 17.

6 Werner, *Die Preussiche Expedition*, 77.

7 Lindau, *Un Voyage Autour*, 52.

8 Suenson, *Skitser*, 92–3.

9 Moeshart, *Journaal*, 96.

10 L.F. Maurice Dubard, *Le Japon Pittoresque* [Picturesque Japan] (Paris, 1879). No English translation of Dubard's work exists, so passages that appear in this book have been translated from the Japanese version. See Dubāru [Dubard], *Ohanasan no koi* [A Love for Flowers] (Yurindo, 1991), 55. Subsequent citations will appear as Dubard, *Pittoresque*, and will list page numbers from the Japanese text.

11 Suenson, *Skitser*, 93.

12 Dubard, *Pittoresque*, 40.

13 Tilley, *Japan, the Amoor*, 83–5.

14 Suenson, *Skitser*, 44.

15 Bird, *Unbeaten Tracks*, Vol. 1, 40.

16 Tilley, *Japan, the Amoor*, 84.

17 Kattendijke, *Uittreksel*, 48.

18 Hübner, *Ramble*, 222–3.

19 Bacon, *Japanese Girls*, 60.

20 Alcock, *Tycoon*, Vol. 1, 231.

21 Suenson, *Skitser*, 95.

22 Oliphant, *Narrative*, Vol. 2, 114.

23 Alcock, *Tycoon*, Vol. 1, 180–3.

24 Berg, *Eulenburg Expedition*, Vol. 1, 105.

25 Alcock, *Tycoon*, Vol. 1, 180.

26 Werner, *Die Preussiche Expedition*, 76.

27 Suenson, *Skitser*, 91–92.

28 Abe Toshiharu, *Afurikajin no Seikatsu to Dentō* [The Lives and Traditions of African Peoples] (Sanseido, 1982), 114.

29 Abe, *Afurikajin*, 91.

30 Suenson, *Skitser*, 82.

31 Suenson, *Skitser*, 91.

32 Hodgson, *Residence*, 241.

33 Arminjon, *Il Giappone*, 169.

34 Chamberlain, *Things Japanese*, 500–1.

35 Griffis, *Mikado's Empire*, 551, 554.

36 Kattendijke, *Uittreksel*, 47.

37 Oliphant, *Narrative*, Vol. 2, 115.

38 Tilley, *Japan, the Amoor*, 87.

39 Berg, *Eulenburg Expedition*, Vol. 1, 199.

40 Morse, *Day by Day*, Vol. 1, 282–3.

41 Chamberlain, *Things Japanese*, 501.

42 Roti [Loti], "Nihon no fujintachi" ["Japanese Ladies"], in *Rochi no Nippon nikki* [Pierre Loti's Journal of Japan] (Yurindo, 1979). This originally appeared as an article in the French newspaper, *Le Figaro*, in 1891.

43 Loti, *Nippon Nikki*, 137.

44 Smith, *Ten Weeks*, 113.

45 Fischer, *Bilder*, 334–43.

46 Chamberlain, *Things Japanese*, 502, 508.

47 Alcock, *Tycoon*, Vol. 1, 384.

48 Williams, *Perry Expedition*, 219.

49 Dixon, *Morning*, 228.

50 Bousquet, *Le Japon*, Vol. 1, 257.

51 Weston, *Wayfarer*, 22. Part of this passage is also translated from the Japanese version. See Wesuton [Weston], *Wesuton no Meiji kenbunki* [Walter Weston's Travels in Meiji Japan] (Shinjinbutsu Oraisha, 1987), 53.

52 A. Siebold, *Letzte Reise*, 98–9.

53 Bacon, *Japanese Girls*, 260–1. The contents of Bacon's *Japanese Girls and Women* are as follows: Chapter 1: Childhood; Chapter 2: Education; Chapter 3: Marriage and Divorce; Chapter 4: Wife and Mother; Chapter 5: Old Age; Chapter 6: Court Life; Chapter 7: Life in Castle and Yashiki; Chapter 8: Samurai Women; Chapter 9: Peasant Women; Chapter 10: Life in the Cities; Chapter 11: Domestic Service; Chapter 12: Within the Home; and Chapter 13: Ten Years of Progress. This work could be called a one-of-a-kind outline of the lives of women in the 1880s and 1890s, but it is actually a vivid account of not only their lives, but also life in general at the time. Together with Bird's *Unbeaten Tracks in Japan*, this is one of the two best accounts about Japan from the time period. With their attention to detail, these women described the reality of the situation better than any of their male counterparts.

54 Bacon, *Japanese Girls*, 107–9.

55 Bacon, *Japanese Girls*, 245.

56 Bacon, *Japanese Girls*, see Chapters 1–4.

57 Bacon, *Japanese Girls*, 73–4.

58 Bacon, *Japanese Girls*, 86–7.

59 Bacon, *Japanese Girls*, 219.

60 Sugimoto, *Daughter*, 140, 143, 178.

61 Bacon, *Japanese Girls*, see Chapter 5: Old Age.

62 Bacon, *Japanese Girls*, 123–25.

63 Berg, *Eulenburg Expedition*, Vol. 1, 199.

64 Morse, *Day by Day*, Vol. 2, 290.

65 Lühdorf, *Acht Monate*, 54.

66 Hawks, *American Squadron*, 397.

67 Tronson, *Personal Narrative*, 258.

68 Osborn, *Cruise*, 148–9.

69 Fortune, *Yedo and Peking*, 69–70.

70 Humbert, *Japan and the Japanese*, 19–22.

71 Hodgson, *Residence*, 211–8.

72 Berg, *Eulenburg Expedition*, Vol. 1, 199.

73 Smith, *Ten Weeks*, 107.

74 Fischer, *Bijdrage*, Vol. 2, 117.

75 Yamakawa, *Buke*, 23.

76 Yamakawa, *Buke*, 116–9.

77 Yamakawa, *Buke*, 68–9.

78 Shinoda Kōzō, *Bakumatsu-Meiji onna hyakuwa* [A Hundred Tales of Women from the Bakumatsu-Meiji Era] (Iwanami Bunko, 1997), Vol. 2, 200.

79 Fraser, *Diplomatist's Wife*, 122.

80 Jephson and Elmhirst, *Our Life*, 180.

81 Jephson and Elmhirst, *Our Life*, 74–5.

82 Yamakawa Kikue, *Oboegaki: Bakumatsu no Mito Han* [Memoir: The Mito Domain at the End of the Edo Period] (Iwanami Shoten, 1974), 102.

83 Kiyokawa Hachiro, *Saiyūsō* [Trip to the West] (Iwanami Bunko, 1993), 55–66.

84 Shinoda, *Onna hyakuwa*, Vol. 1, 155.

85 Hodgson, *Nagasaki*, 212. Evidence that Hodgson's wife was French can be seen in Alcock's *Tycoon*, Vol. 2, 22.

86 Berg, *Eulenburg Expedition*, Vol. 1, 268.

87 Werner, *Die Preussiche Expedition*, 75.

88 Yamakawa, *Buke*, 77.

89 Iseki Takako, *Iseki Takako nikki* [Diary of Iseki Takako] (Buneisha, 1978), 168.

90 Richard Gordon Smith, *Travels in the Land of the Gods, 1898-1907: The Japan Diaries of Richard Gordon Smith* (London, 1986), 22.

91 Herbert George Ponting, *In Lotus-land Japan* (London: Macmillan and Co., 1910), 231–2, 247–51, 238.

92 Fraser, *Diplomatist's Wife*, 516–21.

93 Fraser, *Diplomatist's Wife*, 521–4.

94 Sugimoto, *Daughter*, 131.

Chapter

10

A Children's Paradise

Rutherford Alcock was the first person to pen the expression, "a very paradise of babies," to describe Japan.[1] When he first landed at Nagasaki, he felt this way because "Groups of half, or wholly naked children…you meet every where." This expression would come to be used by a great many Westerners who visited Japan.

It is a fact that the streets of Japanese cities were overflowing with children. According to Edouard Suenson, when Japanese children reached a certain age, their parents forced them to play outside all day long, so it was common to see them tumbling about in the streets with their friends from early in the morning to late at night.[2] Curt Adolph Netto (1847–1909), a German who lived and worked in Japan from 1873 to 1885, echoed Suenson's observations by depicting the following scene in *Japanischer Humor*, a book he coauthored with Gottfried Wagener (1831–1892):[3]

The children's primary playground is the street…They do not pay attention to traffic and jump headlong into their games. They know well enough to clear a small path for pedestrians, jinrikisha runners, and the porters who shoulder heavy loads to pass through because they know these adults will not disturb them while they play with their tops, bat at their flying shuttlecocks, or pull on the strings of their kites. Even when a horse comes galloping toward the children, they just stare at the riders and coach drivers with an eerie calmness and continue to play, completely absorbed in whatever game they might be enjoying.

Georges Bousquet, another foreign observer who, like Netto, stayed in Japan to work from 1872 to 1878, wrote the following:[4]

In front of the houses, children of the lower classes play games like shuttlecock and fly kites of various shapes and sizes. Such activities startle any horses that may be nearby, making it hard for the riders to pass through. Parents just let their children roam free, so the streets are seething with them. The bettoes, or stable-hands, that lead the horses, constantly pick up children who run in and around the legs of the horses with both hands and gently set them down at the threshold of the entrance to their homes.

According to Mary Fraser, scenes such as this were apparently quite common even in the late 1880s and early 1890s. On one occasion, she took a carriage ride through the city and saw the *betto*, or groom, leading their procession and "lifting fat babies out of the middle of the road where they sat confidingly, leading deaf old women politely to one side, and apparently saving a life once in every ten yards."[5]

Edward Warren Clark (1849–1907), an American summoned to Japan in 1871 as an instructor for a school in Shizuoka, moved to Tokyo at the end of 1873 and said, "The most interesting sights in the streets are the games and the sports of the children." He mentioned the girls, whose "faces are powdered with a little rice flour, their lips are tinted crimson, and their hair is done up in a most extraordinary fashion," made circles of about a half dozen to play Japanese shuttlecock and sang songs to help their shuttlecocks go straight. Meanwhile, he stated the boys were engrossed in flying kites. At first, he did not know what the "peculiar humming sound" and "strange noises…from the sky" were. He also saw the boys racing each other on stilts and six-year-olds having wrestling matches. He said, "Their bodies were stout and chubby, and their rosy cheeks showed signs of health and happiness."[6] Naturally, Clark was viewing scenes from the New Year's holidays.

Edwin Arnold, meanwhile, came to Japan in 1889, rented a house in Azabu with his daughter, and stayed in the country for a year and two months. He felt "The streets, almost entirely, belong to them [the Japanese children]." He went on to say:[7]

> There is practically no horse traffic in Tokio; a very few pony drags are to be seen, and tram-cars run in such main thoroughfares as the Ginza and the Nihombashi, while now and then you will meet a Japanese officer riding on horseback, with a betto running at his saddle-flap, to or from the barracks. But these are the exceptions; and, consequently, the *Kuruma*-men can trot in safety round every corner, and the children disport themselves in the street without causing the slightest maternal anxiety. They are charming to see, these small Japanese, in their dignified wide sleeves and flowing *Kimono*, as they are gentle and demure in manners; with beautiful feet and hands, and bead-like black eyes, which stare at you without fear or shyness.

According to Netto, the children never got out of the way of passing horses and vehicles because they were so used to the adults keeping them out of harm's way. He also said that in no other country were the children looked after as meticulously as they were in Japan, even those from the lower classes. He added that Japanese children, with their small sizes, precociousness, and small topknots, pretty much became tyrants over their whole family.[8]

Bousquet also saw that Japanese children were fawned over and spoiled more than children from any other country.[9] Edward Morse added to this, saying:[10]

> Again I must repeat that Japan is the paradise for children. There is no other country in the world where they are so kindly treated or where so much attention is devoted to them. From the appearance of their smiling faces, they must be happy from morning till night.

I will refrain from quoting Morse too much on this subject, but he literally repeats this opinion throughout his book, *Japan Day by Day*.

Meanwhile, Isabella Bird wrote the following about her experience in Nikko in 1878:[11]

> I never saw people take so much delight in their offspring, carrying them about, or holding their hands in walking, watching and entering into their games, supplying them constantly with new toys, taking them to picnics and festivals, never being content to be without them, and treating other people's children also with a suitable measure of affection and attention. Both fathers and mothers take a pride in their children. It is most amusing about six every morning to see twelve or fourteen men sitting on a low wall, each with a child under two in his arms, fondling and playing with it, and showing off its *physique* and intelligence. To judge from appearances, the children form the chief topic at this morning gathering.

In Bird's eye, the love that Japanese adults gave to their children was tantamount to child worship.

Scenes of men holding children in their arms also attracted Alcock's attention. He wrote:[12]

Japanese children (from Régamey, *Japon*, 1899)

It is a very common sight, in the streets and shops of Yeddo, to see a little nude Cupid in the arms of a stalwart-looking father, nearly as naked, who walks about with his small burden, evidently handling it with all the gentleness and dexterity of a practiced hand.

A sketch by Charles Wirgman appears at the end of this passage in Alcock's book. Morse also wrote about the remarkable sight of fathers holding their children's hands, and "if anything of interest is going on, [they] will hold the children high on their shoulders to see the sight."

Based on his experiences in Nagasaki during the late 1850s, Willem Kattendijke felt that the education that young Japanese children received was quite similar to what Jean-Jacques Rousseau advocated in his book, *Emile- or On Education*. Kattendijke stated that Japanese parents generally caressed their children a great deal, and this love pervaded Japanese homes at all levels of society. Parents often kept a close eye on their children, but they also let them go free and run around the street almost completely naked. No matter how bad the children may have behaved, Kattendijke never saw parents scold or chasten them. The love parents showed almost reached the level of doting, and he said that he had never seen children as happy and pleasant as those in Japan.[13]

The reality that the Japanese did not scold or punish their children had existed since at least the sixteenth century. Spanish merchant Bernardino de Avila Girón, who lived primarily in Nagasaki between 1594 and 1619, wrote that Japanese children were adorable creatures and that that they were remarkably able to understand the world and see the reason in things by age six or seven. However, he went on to say that Japanese mothers and fathers had nothing to do with this, as even parents of well-behaved children neither punished nor educated their little ones. Furthermore, he found it odd that the Japanese had no qualms about decapitating people with swords, yet found punishing their children to be cruel and unusual punishment.[14]

Luís Fróis also described this. He said that Europeans usually punished their sons by whipping them, but this hardly ever happened in Japan. On the contrary, Japanese parents just reprimanded their children with a few words.[15]

The paternal nurse, left: summer costume, right: winter costume (from Alcock, *Tycoon*)

Members of the Dutch Trading House also witnessed such a reality as described by Girón and Fróis. Carl Thunberg, for instance, wrote, "I observed every where that the chastisement of children was very moderate. I very seldom heard them rebuked or scolded, and hardly ever saw them flogged or beaten, either in private families or on board of the vessels."[16] When he mentioned being on "the vessels," Thunberg was referring to traveling to Edo by boat. Meanwhile, J.F. van Overmeer Fischer stated that Japanese parents were overly tolerant of their children's innocent behavior, as they never slapped them even when it might have been necessary.[17] Fischer attributed this to the nature of the Japanese. In the eyes of some of the observers, therefore, such leniency made it seem like the parents were abandoning their duties and spoiling their children.

Others, however, viewed things differently. As mentioned earlier, for example, Kattendijke compared the behavior of Japanese parents to Rousseau's style of free education. Alcock, meanwhile, felt that "the children in Japan have a merit the tendency of modern education is to deprive ours of at home, namely, they are natural children, are well amused with the pleasures proper to their age, and have no wish to be thought above them."[18]

Count Eulenburg had an even more-fascinating experience in this regard. During his stay in Japan, his delegation went on an excursion to Ikegami (located in present-day Ōta Ward, Tokyo), the location of the famous Honmonji temple. At first, the resident priest refused to open the gate to let the delegation in to view the temple grounds. Once the shogunate officials who had accompanied Eulenburg gave the priest a silver *ichibugin* coin, the delegation finally gained admission to see the sights, but while they were negotiating, hundreds of children had come and gathered behind Eulenburg's party and some of them even ran past the entourage and into the temple grounds where they started playing and ringing the temple bell. Eulenburg noted how neither the priest nor the officials tried to stop the children and, in fact, looked amused by the scene before them. The Japanese did not hit their children. Therefore, Eulenburg never heard a child crying, save for the few times they fell and hurt themselves or were alarmed by the sight of Eulenburg's party suddenly galloping toward them on their horses.[19]

Almost every Westerner who visited Japan during this time period was aware of the fact that Japanese children did not cry. Edward Morse, for instance, wrote, "A rare thing is to hear a baby cry, and thus far I have never seen the slightest sign of impatience on the part of the mother."[20] Isabella Bird had the exact same opinion. She wrote "I am very fond of Japanese children. I have never yet heard a baby cry, and I have never seen a child troublesome or disobedient...The arts and threats by which English mothers cajole or frighten children into unwilling obedience appear unknown."[21]

In 1899, Félix Régamey succeeded in visiting Japan again, and he described his experience when he was invited to the home of a Frenchman in Kobe. He wrote:[22]

> After dessert, there was much ado about putting the girls to bed. There were four girls, and the youngest was seven years old. The master told his Japanese maid to "Take this girl to bed." There was a shout, and suddenly the girl came back crying…Later on, I heard from the master's wife that the Japanese cannot frighten children or force them to obey their commands. Rather, they cherish children and give in to their every demand.

In other words, Japanese adults like the maid that Régamey described did not know the skills and tricks of getting children to listen to them, especially those who were particularly stubborn. Free as they may have seemed, Japanese children never ignored their parent's orders or threw a tantrum. Therefore, the Japanese maid in this case did not know how to take care of this French girl. As we shall also see later on in this chapter, Japanese children were never sent to their rooms when the adults were having a party.

In the words of Morse, children probably did not cry due to "no punishment, no chiding, no scolding, [and] no nagging" from the adults. However, there was also the fact that children obeyed their parents, did nothing that would necessitate scolding, and, therefore, had no need to cry. As Morse put it, "No nation possesses children that can approach the Japanese children in love of parents and respect for the aged."[23] In addition, Bousquet also felt that Japanese children were certainly spoiled, but they were far more disciplined than lower-class children in France. Meanwhile, Arthur Maclay said, "Their parents fondle and spoil them most effectually, and, at the same time, never lose their control over them,"[24] and Mary Fraser said, "All that is desirable in the little people's deportment can be attained without snubbings or punishments or weary scoldings." Fraser went on to write:[25]

Bell tower at Honmonji temple in Ikegami (from Berg, *Eulenburg Expedition*)

The love showered upon children simply wraps them in warmth and peace, and seems to encourage every sweet good trait of character without ever fostering a bad one. Japanese children are never frightened into telling lies or hiding their faults. Open as the day, they bring every joy or sorrow to father or mother to be shared or healed, and their small likes or dislikes are quite as much taken into account as those of their elders.

Fraser also stated, "The children rule everything in the little homes," but went on to say that they "are not a bit spoilt. When they come to what is considered the age of reason (anywhere between six and ten), they abdicate their sovereignty of their own accord, and seem to grow up in a day."[26]

Moreover, Japanese parents did not let their children do as they please all the time. As Aimé Humbert testified, parents were primarily concerned with their children's education and taught them proper manners and etiquette from a very young age. Children may have seemed spoiled and free to do whatever they wanted, but as Humbert also said, this was because parents were "prodigal of toys, and games, and entertainments, as much for their own enjoyment as in the interest of his [their child's] education."[27] Bird, meanwhile, was always ready to hand out "sweeties" to children, but she noted that "not one has ever received them without first obtaining permission from the father or mother." Once their parents gave them permission, they would smile and bow their heads in thanks for the treats, and then they would divide the presents up among the other children. Bird felt that they were "gentle creatures, but too formal and precocious." On the other hand, however, she admired "the way in which children are taught to be independent in their amusements." She went on to write:[28]

Part of the home education is the learning of the rules of the different games, which are absolute, and when there is a doubt, instead of a quarrelsome suspension of the game, the fiat of a senior child decides the matter. They play by themselves, and don't bother adults at every turn.

In other words, Japanese children maintained an independent world that was just for them, and, apart from watching over the safety of their children, adults had little say in their affairs. It was for this reason that Morse felt that Japanese children "have more liberty…than the children of any other people."

Some Japanese observers also commented on this point. For example, Noda Shigesuke, also known as "Noda Senkoin," was an ascetic from the Sadowara domain in Hyūga Province (located in present-day Miyazaki Prefecture). During his ascetic training in 1812, in which he went on a pilgrimage to all of the sacred mountains in Japan, he wrote the following about his experience in Hinagu Village in Higo Province (located in present-day Kumamoto Prefecture):[29]

> There is a statue of Jizo-sama [Ksitigarbha, the guardian bodhisattva that protects children] in this village. It is a wooden statue only about thirty-three centimeters tall. The children use it as a toy. In summer, they take it into the river to cool it off, and in winter they keep it under a heated *kotatsu* table to keep it warm. They take the statue with them everywhere, even into the rice fields, yet this does not seem to offend anyone. The adults do not scold them for fear they might anger Jizo-sama.

Noda was not describing a unique or exceptional custom. Rather, he was just talking about one facet of the civilization that he lived in. Namely, he was pointing out that the worlds of children and adults were separate and completely different entities. In other words, civilization in the Edo period drew unique dividing lines between the worlds of the adults and the children, and this custom still existed as late as the middle of the Meiji period.

It should also be noted, however, that although the old Japanese civilization created separate and independent worlds between the children and the adults, it was also characterized by the children playing a part in every aspect of the adults' lives. Perhaps the best example of this was the way in which children maintained their own world of independence while taking part in festivals. Morse, for example, depicted the scene of children pulling their own floats in a festival parade. He wrote the following:[30]

> Along came two carts dragged by children holding light-colored paper lanterns. The carts were rude two-wheeled vehicles built up roughly with boards and packed full of children beating drums, screaming, and laughing as only children will. The framework above was elaborately decorated with paper figures, colored cloth, and a liberal supply of lanterns.

There were a number of adults who helped direct the float, but the children, even the little ones, had decorated it with lanterns and were now pulling it through the streets by themselves. Morse sketched the float in his book, and this illustration shows that the float consisted of bamboo poles on top of a small cart with a number of lanterns attached to the poles. Therefore, Morse could see how even small children were able to pull it.

In addition, Morse found particular joy in discovering that the adults played together with the children not only at festivals, but in almost every situation in daily life. He was also amazed to discover that parents never left their children at home alone. Morse said that they "are tied to the back of the mother or one of the older children and have delightful rides, fresh air, and see everything that is going on."

Many other observers described this custom of carrying children. According to Bousquet, for instance, when both the mother and father went out to see an event, it was common to see them carrying one or two children on their backs or taking them along for a ride in a rickshaw.[31] Curt Netto, meanwhile, said:[32]

> In Japan, mothers put their babies in a bag attached to their backs and take them everywhere, just like a kangaroo carrying its baby in its pouch. They do this whenever and wherever they go and in every situation, be it doing chores at home or going out to see a show. The children are as snug as bookmarks in between their mothers' dresses and skin, and they often peek out from their covers as happy as can be. One can see how these little ones, with their small, almond-shaped eyes, stay so happy in their little hideaways heated by the bodies of their mothers.

Netto continued by saying that no matter where one looked in Japan, there were always two or three children mixed in with the crowd. He went on to say that even when a mother went to the theater or other locale, she would never think to leave her children at home. She would continue to play the role of kangaroo for them no matter what. Thus, mothers would take them to temples, to cherry blossom festivals, and even on long pilgrimages across the country. Alcock, meanwhile, was astonished by what he saw at a playhouse he visited in Osaka. Namely, both adults and children were watching a performance that was quite lewd and certainly not intended for children to see.[33] As I explained in an earlier chapter, Japanese children viewed pornographic books and pictures and sexual toys quite freely because no efforts were made to separate them from such elements.

Part of Alcock's surprise may have had to do with cultural differences. As a case in point, Westerners have been delighted by the tale of *Peter Pan* for years now. One scene of particular note is the night Wendy and Michael's parents leave them at home while they go out to a dinner party. This is when Peter Pan visits them for the first time and takes them on their fantastic adventure to Neverland. We can interpret the deeper meaning of parent-children relationships, or the lack thereof, that emanates from this episode in several ways, but at any rate, Japanese children had no need for such a story because they always went out with their parents.

As we can see, therefore, the division between adults and children in Edo-period Japan was much different than what exists today. Philippe Ariès (1914–1984) said that, until the modern era, it was also common in Europe for children to be treated as adults and that there was no definitive life stage known as "childhood."[34] There are some doubts as to whether this assertion is true, however. Based on the universal nature of age-rank systems throughout human history, there has never been a civilization that did not establish dividing lines between children and adults. Ariès was simply saying that the unique modern division between adults and children that began to take shape in the latter half of the eighteenth century did not exist prior to that.

Support for the Ariès argument can be found in Japanese clothing at the time. Basil Chamberlain, for example, said that "Children's dress is more or less a repetition in miniature of that of their elders."[35] Isabella Bird wrote something to the same degree when she said, "They have no special dress. This is so queer that I cannot repeat it too often. At three they put on the *kimono* and girdle...and childish play in this garb is grotesque."[36] Jephson and Elmhirst also said:[37]

> As to the children, the fact of their being dressed exactly like the grown-up people, gave them, in our eyes, at first, an intensely comical appearance. The child of two years of age and the old person of seventy wear precisely the same description of clothes; the former looking very much like the latter seen through an opera-glass reversed.

As we can see from these descriptions, Japanese children were almost identical to images of children that appear in the paintings of Pieter Bruegel. Ariès based his argument on these works to show that children living in medieval and modern Europe had no unique clothing and wore what resembled adult clothing in miniature.

Chamberlain also said that "Japanese girls do not, like ours, remain in a sort of chrysalis state till seventeen or eighteen years of age, and then 'come out' in gorgeous attire. The tiniest tots are the most brilliantly dressed."[38] Perhaps he caught sight of some young girls dressed up for their visit to a shrine to commemorate turning three or seven years old, a tradition known as *Shichi-Go-San* in Japan. What he wanted to say was that, in Japan, the girls wore smaller versions of clothing donned by their adult counterparts. In other words, they did not go through the rite of passage that Natasha Rostova experienced in *War and Peace* in which she wore girl's clothing that resembled pajamas throughout her childhood until the night she donned a grown woman's gown for the first time as a debutante. There is some evidence, however, that such unique modern divisions between adults and children did not exist in Russia prior to the reign of Peter the Great (1672–1725, and who reigned as monarch from 1682–1725).

During the Girl's Festival on March 3, 1890, Mary Fraser was invited to the home of a noble family. The family's five-year-old daughter, who Fraser dubbed the "heroine of the moment," asked her, "'Would you like to see the dolls? Pray forgive me for putting you to the trouble of going to another room.'" Then, "with perfect gravity," the girl took Fraser's hand and led her into the back room. Fraser described her attire on that day in the following passage:[39]

> She was dressed in sapphire-coloured crape, shading from pale blue at the foot to dark purple at the shoulder, embroidered in gold in lovely patterns, and girdled with royal scarlet and gold; her hair, gathered in a shining knot on the top of her head, was held in place with jeweled pins; and there was a distinct touch of rouge on either round cheek.

If we look at the picture in Fraser's book with the caption that reads, "My little hostess," we can see she is wearing a *furisode* (hanging sleeves) kimono, which shows her family crest, together with an intricately designed kimono skirt. She is also following the convention of holding a folding fan in her right hand, and there is a dagger inserted into her kimono near her chest. In other words, this five-year-old girl is dressed up exactly like an adult from the same time period.

However, this aspect was not limited to clothing. While Bird was staying in the home of the mayor of Irimachi Village in Nikko in 1878, for instance, she saw one of the "formal children's parties" held for "Haru," the twelve-year-old daughter of the family. Bird said the girl put on makeup and a *furisode* kimono, and then made her way to some stone steps where she greeted her guests, other girls who were wearing the same style of dress, "with very formal but graceful bows." At the party, meanwhile, they "played at very quiet and polite games until dusk," and Bird was completely surprised by the "dignity and self-possession of these children" in their imitation of funerals, weddings, dinner parties, and other events in the lives of adults.[40] Bird also saw the "dignity and self-possession" of children at a festival at the Tsuchizaki Port in Akita. She wrote about girls around eight or nine years old

My little hostess (from Fraser, *Diplomatist's Wife*)

who were wearing white makeup and wigs and performing dances on top of carts that were being pulled through the city. Bird was moved and even distressed by their "perfect dignity and self-possession," claiming they performed as well as "the actors in the Shintomi Theatre at Yedo."[41]

After returning from her trip to the Tohoku region of Japan, Bird was invited to a party hosted by Ernest Satow. The occasion featured music from a Japanese orchestra, which Bird described as peculiar and excruciating to the point where it gave her a headache, but she also felt a complex set of emotions that lay somewhere between excitement and sadness at seeing the "dignity and abstraction" in the dance of a nine-year-old girl who was the daughter of one of the nobles. Bird wrote the following:[42]

> The perfect self-possession with which this little "princess" went through the dance was most remarkable, and the bow at the end, which once more included the whole audience, was a work of art. The dignity was painful, not ludicrous. I often wished that the small maiden would falter a little, or be embarrassed, or show some consciousness of our presence. Nor when it was over and she had received our thanks, was there the slightest relapse into childhood. Mr. de Saumarez,[43] who is passionately fond of Japanese children, vainly tried to win her into friendliness, but she scarcely spoke; she was absolutely indifferent; the face remained motionless; the dignity was real, not a veneering.

Despite her qualms, I am not sure if Bird had any reason to be pained by seeing the self-possession that did not befit a young girl. After all, Werner said even children between the ages of ten to twelve had the sensibility and calmness of fully grown adults,[44] and he made this observation at the end of the Edo period, long before Bird came to the country. This adult-like self-possession of Japanese children surprised Westerners who visited Japan from the end of the Edo period until the late 1880s to early 1890s to this degree because Rousseau's concept of "children's discoveries," or, namely, childhood innocence, had created a modern obsession in Europe. In the old Japanese civilization, however, the concepts of a child-like mindset and innocence did not exist. As anyone could recognize, Japanese children were lovable and innocent and did, indeed, behave like children quite often. As Alcock said, they did not know about the affectations of adults. However, nothing prevented them from showing a dignity and self-possession that rivalled that of the adults if it became necessary for a time. At any rate, they learned when and what to do in any situation by constantly interacting with and watching the adults around them.

Sometimes children copied the vices of adults as well. When Léon Metchnikoff came to Japan in 1874, for instance, he soon paid a visit to the home of Takasaki Masakaze, a senior government official. However, Takasaki was not at home, but a boy of around fifteen came in his place and treated Metchnikoff with the utmost respect and hospitality. He also brought out a tray of tobacco and asked Metchnikoff to partake while also preparing a pipe for his own personal use. In no time he had taken two puffs.[45] This did not surprise Metchnikoff because he had already seen children smoking together with adults at a theater. In addition, a boy of fifteen was already considered an honorable man who had come of age in the civilization at the time.

Bird, meanwhile, saw that the children in Nikko's Irimachi Village stayed up as late as their parents and took part in all of their conversations. The adults were aware that these children had their own worlds in which they played, but they also considered them to be friends and companions, even the youngest ones. It also goes without saying that children helped their parents with their work. Morse, for example, saw a little boy going back and forth sprinkling water from a bucket to clean the street in front of a local establishment, an action that appeared to be a way to help his parents, the business owners. Townsend Harris also wrote in a May 1857 diary entry that children in the areas surrounding Shimoda did not play games, either individually or in groups, and they did not toss rings, jump rope, or spin tops, nor did they have the toys to do so. This makes sense, however, because the children living in farm villages were needed in the fields, and May was an especially busy time for them, so they likely did not have any time to play. Harris was relieved when he finally saw some children flying kites.

According to Netto, however, the first job that children had after coming down from the backs of their mothers was babysitting their younger brothers and sisters. Therefore, he saw children carrying other children in the streets. He also said the ones being carried were not much smaller than the ones doing the carrying.[46] According to Bousquet, meanwhile, as soon as Japanese children were able to walk, they soon learned how to carry their younger brothers and sisters. He said that they shouldered their younger siblings no matter what they did, be it playing, running, walking, or running errands.[47] Naturally, Bousquet had observed a common custom among the people of the lower class. Chamberlain, meanwhile, wrote, "Nothing perhaps gives the streets a more peculiar aspect" than children carrying their younger siblings on their backs.[48] In addition, Morse saw farmers planting the rice fields soon after he arrived in Japan, and he noticed that whole families worked together with the parents and older children working in the rice paddies while smaller children with babies on their backs looked on from the neighboring ridges. He wrote that "five children out of six [were] lugging babies upon their backs."[49]

When Émile Guimet landed in Yokohama in 1876, he saw women grip-
ping their knees and dragging their feet while walking, thus allowing them
to move their upper torsos in such a way as to balance their bodies, and he
said they bobbed their heads like pigeons with each step they took. However, this did not surprise him because he had already seen images of women
walking like this on folding screens. He was surprised, though, to see that all
women he met, both young and old, were carrying children on their backs.
In addition, he also saw children shouldering babies who were almost as big
as they were and wondered if such children could be found anywhere else
but in Japan.[50]

In other words, as Netto said, Japanese children who could not stand up
straight almost never left the little "thrones" on their mothers' backs, but
once they had learned to stand up and walk, they no longer needed their
mothers to carry them, although they still needed to be breastfed.[51] Alice
Bacon echoed this by saying "The Japanese baby…is not weaned entirely
until the age of three or four years."[52] Bird, meanwhile, stayed at an inn in
a rural town in Fukushima Prefecture and saw a five-year-old boy there
who was still drinking his mother's milk. The woman looked like she was
around fifty, but when Bird asked her how old she was, she was shocked
to learn the woman was still only twenty-two.[53] Netto theorized that this
custom of nursing a child for a long time caused the mother's body to age
quickly, and he also mentioned it had contraceptive effects.

The important point to consider here is that so-called "spoiled" children
eventually had to leave their mother's back
and, as Guimet and Netto saw it, almost
immediately start carrying their younger
brothers and sisters around, even though
they were not that much different in size.
Bacon, meanwhile, stated:[54]

> Babies of the lower classes, within a
> few weeks after birth, are carried about
> tied upon the back of some member of
> the family, frequently an older brother
> or sister, who is sometimes not more
> than five or six years old. The poorer
> the family, the earlier is the young
> baby thus put on someone's back, and
> one frequently sees babies not more
> than a month old, with bobbing heads
> and blinking eyes, tied by long bands

Babysitting (illustration by Régamey,
from Guimet, *Promenades Japonaises*)

of cloth to the backs of older brothers and sisters, and living in the streets in all weathers. When it is cold, the sister's *haori*, or coat, serves as an extra covering for the baby as well; and when the sun is hot, the sister's parasol keeps off its rays from the bobbing bald head. Living in public, as the Japanese babies do, they soon acquire an intelligent, interested look, and seem to enjoy the games of the elder children, upon whose backs they are carried, as much as the players themselves.

Arnold also added the following about Japanese babies who were strapped to someone's back:[55]

> [The babies] see everything, share everything, take part in agriculture, kite-flying, shopping, cooking, gossiping, washing, and all that goes forward and around, which perhaps gives them their extraordinary gravity and worldly wisdom, mingled with gladness, as soon as they reach the mature age of four or five.

Bird saw another example of precocious children in a stilt race that took place in Ikarigaseki, Aomori Prefecture. She said, "I have…never seen what we call child's play, that general abandonment to miscellaneous impulses, which consists in struggling, slapping, rolling, jumping, kicking, shouting, laughing, and quarrelling."[56] Thus, Japanese children were quiet even when they played games. Willem Kattendijke and a few other observers thought Japanese children were the worst-behaved in world, with the boys being particularly naughty in their minds,[57] but their views seem to be the exception. Overall, the games that Japanese children played were quite calm and silent. Morse repeatedly reinforced the reserved nature of Japanese children and said, "There is not a boy in Japan who would not be called a 'sissy' if brought in contact with the usual run of our boys."[58] In fact, the only "bad boys" that appeared in Meiji-period literature were bullies and the boys they bullied, the latter of which would one day decide to stand up for themselves and fight back and easily make the bully cry. There were few, if any, truly vicious and unruly children in old Japan.

Dirk Polsbroek assumed the post of Dutch vice-consul in Kanagawa in 1859, and he, too, described the silent nature of Japanese children. He wrote the following:[59]

> Almost all of the Japanese who lived in my neighborhood were fishermen, but they were always polite and courteous. Meanwhile, they were also pleased with me because I would open my garden up three times a week and let their children play there, and I also provided

them with some toys. I have never seen such well-mannered and disciplined children in my life. They always play silently and never argue or shout, and when it is time for them to go, they put the toys away neatly and repeatedly thank me in the most courteous way.

William Griffis gave a lecture about Japanese children's games and races at the Asiatic Society of Japan in 1874, a speech in which he mentioned New Year's games of Japanese shuttlecock, kite-flying, spinning tops, hide and seek, tag, stilts, peashooters, snowball fights, and indoor games. With the obvious exception of snowball fights, all of these games likely seemed calm and harmless in the eyes of the Westerners. Griffis also mentioned the group battle game, called "Genji and Heike," that was played at Japanese schools. This was originally a game that samurai played in which they reenacted the battles between the Taira and Minamoto clans, and it had just been introduced as a school sporting event in the Meiji period.[60]

Captain Henry Holmes also wrote about children that he saw in Nagasaki playing games of shuttlecock, flying kites, spinning tops, and walking around on stilts. He wrote the following the day he landed in the city on February 9, 1859, just before the trade treaty went into effect:[61]

> To our great astonishment the first thing we observed was many children enjoying themselves in the following manner: Boys spinning tops, flying kites, walking on stilts; girls playing battledore and shuttlecock. This was a surprise, for the tops, kites, and battledores were all of a superior make to what I had to handle in my boyhood's days.

The date that Holmes landed, February 9, corresponded to the 7th of the first month in the lunar calendar. Therefore, he was witnessing the sights and sounds of the New Year's holidays.

Griffis mentioned another game called "daimio's procession." This was a game in which the players had "forerunners, officers, etc., and imitating, as far as possible, the pomp and circumstance of the old daimio's train." Thus, it was quite popular with boys. In other words, the primary games that children played were those in which they imitated the actions of adults. Griffis also said:[62]

> Many of the amusements of the children indoors are mere imitations of the serious affairs of adult life. Boys who have been to the theatre come home to imitate the celebrated actors, and to extemporize mimic theatricals for themselves. Feigned sickness and "playing the doctor," imitating with ludicrous exactness the pomp and solemnity of the real

man of pills and powders, and the misery of the patient, are the diversions of very young children. Dinners, tea-parties, and even weddings and funerals, are imitated in Japanese children's plays.

In other words, children were small adults and imitated what they did. In addition, games of shuttlecock, flying kites, spinning tops, and the card game known as *karuta* were not just for children. Adults also took part in these amusements and often played along with their younger counterparts. Children, meanwhile, were a part of and became familiar with every aspect of the adults' lives, and making games out of imitating their parents was a way for them to experience the lives of adults on a smaller scale. Children who were free from adult interference conversely created stronger bonds with their parents and other adults.

Griffis also said, "We do not know of any country in the world in which there are so many toy-shops, or so many fairs for the sale of things which delight children."[63] However, the examples he gave, such as street performances, *nozoki megane* glasses, story-tellers, edible figures made out of rice-flour dough, and other sights, were pastimes enjoyed by both children and adults alike. Alcock also wrote that the adults who watched such sights often did so awe-stricken, with their mouths wide open. According to Suenson, meanwhile, the toy-shops in Japan had a huge selection of articles and even rivalled the great toy stores of Nuremberg. He also said all of the toys were simple implements, but they had been created with incredibly clever designs such that even the adults could play with them for hours on end.[64] Hübner, meanwhile, said the following:[65]

> The shops where they sell toys excited my greatest admiration. One asks oneself how it is possible to expend so much wit, invention, and taste, to amuse children, who are incapable of appreciating these real *chefs-d'oeuvre* of art? The answer is simple enough. It is, that in this country every one spends his leisure in playing like children. I have seen three generations—a grandfather, father, and son—absorbed in the operation of flying a kite.

Robert Fortune was also moved by the fact that "All sorts of toys were abundant, and some of them were most ingenious and pretty." He went on to say that "This large trade in toys shows us how fond the Japanese are of their children."[66] Sherard Osborn saw the same thing. The following passage is a description he made of the area surrounding Shinagawa during his party's long trek to the temple at Kawasaki Daishi:[67]

A domestic scene (from Humbert, *Japan and the Japanese*)

Among the many pedestrians thronging the road-side, peasants were to be seen hastening back to their homes from market, carrying some purchase from the big city, and it was generally remarked that few of these good fellows were without some child's toy in their hands. We had noticed the number of children's toyshops, and these seemed proofs of how much love is expended upon the younger members of the community by these kind-hearted people.

Griffis said that if we were to study the subject of children's games more closely, it "leads one to respect more highly, rather than otherwise, the Japanese people for being such affectionate fathers and mothers, and for having such natural and docile children."[68] Morse also stated, "The Japanese have certainly solved the children problem, and no better behaved, kinder children exist, and no more patient, affectionate, and devoted mothers are found."[69]

When Griffis landed in Yokohama and saw Japanese children for the first time, he said, "What pretty children! Chubby, rosy, sparkling-eyed."[70] Suenson, meanwhile, said every child he saw was healthy and full of life and shone with the joy of living. He was truly fond of them and even expressed sadness that they would soon grow up, almost as if he were lamenting a puppy becoming a dog. In addition, he could almost immediately tell that the children were raised in a happy environment.[71] Henry Palmer also said, "As for the children, they swarm, they are delightful, and they present veritable nosegays of colour…When you know them better you also find that, with all the attractions and virtues of children, they have very few of their faults."[72] Eliza Scidmore, meanwhile, said, "Nothing could be gentler or sweeter than these Japanese children" who wore the same long-sleeved kimonos as their mothers.[73] Even Carl Munzinger, who was highly critical of Japan, said most of the Europeans he knew disliked the Japanese people, but they had all been taken in by the country's children.[74] Meanwhile, it was Chamberlain's opinion that "children's petty ways and children's games add much to the picturesqueness of Japanese life." He also said, "The [Japanese] babies are indeed generally so good as to help to make it a paradise for adults."[75] According to Moraes, Japanese children were the most adorable in the world.[76] Many Japanese people living today find it heartwarming that Japanese children from ages past were so charming and lovable.

Morse provided more examples of their charm. For example, he mentioned the children he met on their way home from school and how they always bowed and let him pass by on the street. This happened in the suburbs of Tokyo, in Kagoshima, and in Kyoto. Morse also mentioned how he would give the cooking girl at his home and her playmates an earthenware teapot and teacups for them to have tea together, and that they would return his kindness with bows befitting noble ladies. He said, "They were not older than nine or ten years old, dressed poorly, and were the children of the servants in the yashiki." Morse also took two of the girls for a walk to a fair that was taking place on Hongo Street. He gave each of them ten *sen* to see how they would spend the money, and was surprised when "We passed a poor woman sitting on the ground dolefully playing a samisen, a beggar, in fact, and each of the children without a hint from me dropped a cent into her basket."[77] Where, exactly, did these courteous, merciful, and lovable children go?

Actually, however, the question should be where did the parents who cared for these children with loving hearts go? Where are the mothers and fathers who did such a good job raising them to be like this? Bird also said:[78]

> Poor though the homes are, the men enjoy them; the children are an attraction at any rate, and the brawling and disobedience which often turn our working-class homes into bear-gardens are unknown here where docility and obedience are inculcated from the cradle as a matter of course.

In essence, we can ask the same question about where this way of life in the Japanese household that Bird described went.

The charm of Japanese children, which attracted the attention of Westerners, was a reflection of their parents' love, and this would also become a target of the Westerners' praise. In addition, the Japanese not only expressed an almost abnormal level of interest in their own children but also in young people who came from other countries and who had different skin or eye color.

Christopher Hodgson probably knew this better than anyone else. In June 1859, Hodgson was appointed as consul at the British consulate in Nagasaki and moved there with his wife and two daughters. When Nagasaki Magistrate Okabe Nagatsune found out about this, he had a present delivered to Hodgson's elder daughter, Eva. Hodgson's wife wrote the following about her daughter's gifts:[79]

> [The first,] a very pretty Japanese doll, nicely dressed up, whose head, arms, and legs had joints and articulations like our own; two boxes covered with "crèpe," one containing a quantity of little buds, tied up at the end with a thin gold wire, which, being undone and put into water, expand into elegant flowers; the second consisting of a dozen little tiny dolls in miniature, not larger than one's thumbnail, and a "rouleau" of curious paintings.

Despite the luxurious nature of the presents, they were not meant to be a diplomatic gesture on the part of Okabe in any way because he was not the only one who sent Eva gifts.

Another example occurred when Mrs. Hodgson landed in Nagasaki for the first time, an experience she found most dreadful at first. On the day she landed, there was a festival happening, and the streets were crowded with people; and once the throng saw a Western woman and her daughters, they immediately rushed over to them, creating a veritable stampede. Mrs. Hodgson said there were about 5,000 people who surrounded them, and they proceeded to touch Eva's overcoat and hat, eventually making the girl cry. In addition, a man stalked Mrs. Hodgson for "several hundred yards" in the hopes of "lifting my gown and flounces in order to take portraits of them," although she would later hear that he was a famous artist from Nagasaki. When Mrs. Hodgson and her daughters finally made it safely on board their ship, she wrote to her mother that "Consequently, my first impressions of Nagasaki are far from pleasant. I cannot tell you much of what I saw, but I saw enough to disgust any woman of delicacy; quite revolting. I could perhaps describe it, but certainly dare not write it."[80]

However, the Hodgson family settled in at the temple that was designated to be their home and soon made several excursions into the city. These trips gradually caused Mrs. Hodgson to change her mind about Japan. The following passage described her third trip to the city:[81]

Nobody can imagine the delight my little girl caused both to young and old. Every old woman, and many old men, too, would rush from their shops to admire her; then, half crawling on their knees, rush to give her cakes, cups, and so many presents, that my husband's pockets and the sleeves of the two officers and interpreter could carry no more. I cannot understand as yet why a child has so much attraction with them.

Old people in the city were not the only ones who wanted to give her daughters presents. The elderly priest and his family, who oversaw the temple that the Hodgson family was staying at, also "ruined themselves by presents of cakes and bonbons" to Eva and Sarah.

Such admiration for the Hodgson girls could be seen elsewhere as well. Before the end of the year, Hodgson left Nagasaki and assumed the post of consul in Hakodate. After settling into his new surroundings, Hodgson decided to invite some officials from the magistrate's office to a dinner party. The "two Governors, the Lieutenant-Governor, three Vice-Governors, and their suite" ate quite a bit and even enjoyed some champagne. After the meal, the "Lieutenant-Governor, who has a big family" kept asking about Hodgson's daughter, as he found it hard to believe that she was not at the party. As I mentioned before, this was because Japanese people often took their children with them wherever they went. Hodgson continued by writing the following:[82]

He asked so much for her that at last we were obliged to send for her, and when she made her appearance, and had made her bow to the two Governors, the Lieutenant-governor, who sat at the far end of the table, filled his hands with cakes and sweetmeats, and came the whole length of the room to offer her them. Eva was rather shocked, but on the sign from her mother, received with a "petit salut" the well-intentioned compliment of the Governor, when she soon after retired.

The government officials were following the customs of a separate and unique civilization—that of old Japan. In addition, both the magistrates and the elderly people of Nagasaki were deeply taken by a girl who had crossed the ocean to visit Japan from a distant land. It actually took skill to dote over children in this way, and the Japanese wielded it exceptionally well when interacting with their own children as well as those from other countries. However, individuals did not possess this skill on their own. Rather, the old Japanese civilization, which had long since disappeared at this time, fostered this skill among the Japanese people as a whole.

More examples occurred in Hakodate, this time involving an "O-bās-săn" (old woman or grandma) that the Hodgson's had hired to look after Eva and Sarah. One day, Hodgson discovered Eva smoking tobacco with some other children and ordered the old woman to be vigilant and prevent it from happening again. However, he related the following:[83]

> A suspicious volume of smoke, however, was seen to issue from her [Eva's] paper window soon afterwards: as approaching footsteps were heard, a pipe was thrown out of the same convenient aperture. The child had been smoking again, but the O-bās-săn, rushing to the rescue, declared that she only had been smoking, whereas it was too evident, from the guilty face of the true culprit, and the odour, which even Eau-de-Cologne, lavishly resorted to, could not quite efface, that the nurse was affectionately endeavouring to screen the child at the expense of a kindly intended fib.

On another occasion, Eva was collecting insects and water plants from a pond in the garden. Suddenly, a snake appeared, and the old woman tried to keep Eva from grabbing it. Eva said, "If you will not let me catch it, go and catch it yourself" and pushed the old woman into the pond. Hodgson heard the splash and rushed out to help her. He wrote the following:[84]

> There was poor Nurse up to her waist in water. Of course we suspected the guilty one, and after helping out the O-bās-săn, were going to punish her, but the kind old creature, though wet through and dripping, declared upon her honour that it was her fault, that she was drunk, that she had slipped and was very stupid, begging pardon for the trouble she had caused, and saying and doing all she could think to save the child…She was again affectionately protecting the delinquent from confinement and dry bread. These are two instances of a good heart in a Japanese, and of love of children. The child and the nurse were inseparable, the one always making the nurse do whatever she pleased, and the other delighted to obey the slightest wish.

There is no limit to the suggestions that these two anecdotes elicit. What needs to be said for now, however, is that, from the perspective of the aforementioned French housewife that Félix Régamey met in Kobe, the love and affection that this old woman gave to the child she was looking after may have seemed to be ridiculous and an unwanted sense of blind devotion that did nothing but spoil the child. Hodgson may have shared the same viewpoint to a certain degree, but he was moved by the level of affection he saw. In other words, the Japanese of days past often showered their children with these pure feelings of love, for better or worse. Hodgson also realized that Japanese children, especially the girls, liked Eva a great deal and would "do anything she wished, give her everything, and follow her in admiration."

However, Eva was just one example. When Bird visited Niigata in 1878, she met a three-year-old British girl named Ruth who was the target of the people's affection. Bird wrote the following:[85]

> I have walked about a great deal in Niigata, and when with Mrs. Fyson, who is the only European lady here at present, and her little Ruth, a pretty Saxon child of only three years old, we have been followed by an immense crowd, as the sight of this fair creature, with golden curls falling over her shoulders, is most fascinating. Both men and women have gentle, winning ways with infants, and Ruth, instead of being afraid of the crowds, smiles upon them, bows in Japanese fashion, speaks to them in Japanese, and seems a little disposed to leave her people altogether. It is most difficult to make her keep with us, and two or three times, on missing her, and looking back, we have seen her seated, native fashion, in a ring in a crowd of several hundred people, receiving a homage and admiration from which she was most unwillingly torn.

The reason why Ruth wanted to be with the Japanese more than people from her own country is clear. The strong feelings of love and affection that the Japanese lavished on children was something she had experienced for the first time. Her fellow countrymen thought such unbridled affection spoiled children. Bird added that "The Japanese have a perfect passion for children, but it is not good for European children to be much with them, as they corrupt their morals, and teach them to tell lies."

What, exactly, was Bird referring to here? What bad morals and lies did the Japanese teach Ruth? Eva's elderly nanny certainly did not teach her how to smoke, but there is some evidence that she helped foster it. One reason for this is that Japanese adults were friends with their children, so they did not think they were doing anything wrong when they allowed their little ones to enjoy jokes, tell lies, smoke, and drink alcohol. In other words, the Japanese at the time did not yet know the concept of "pure and innocent children" who were supposed to remain separate from the impure world of adults. Naturally, such a concept was the product of Western modernism. Bird was a superior observer who showed very little bias, but the terms "corrupt morals" and "lies" as used by her clung strongly to this neurotic obsession created by Western modernism. Incidentally, Ruth's father was Philip Kemball Fyson (1846–1929), a British missionary who came to Japan in 1874 and preached in Niigata for seven years.

Blind devotion probably entails pure love, and *Gin no Saji* (Silver Spoon), a book by Japanese author Naka Kansuke (1885–1965), does a good job depicting this aspect. The book gives several examples of the blind devotion that the main character, a woman called "Oba-san" ("Auntie"), shows to Naka. According to the book's timeline, this woman was Naka's mother's oldest sister and she came to stay at his house around the time he was born. She raised Naka with great love and affection as if she were his mother. We can probably even imagine her to be one of the ladies that Bacon described as being happy no matter how miserable their lives were.

The first part of *Silver Spoon* consists of memories involving Naka's Auntie. Her husband was small in stature, but he was a domain official for the Imao domain in Mino Province (located in present-day Gifu Prefecture). They were a good-natured couple who had very little money due to the husband having his stipend withheld by the domain, and they were in debt to many people. Later, the husband would succumb to cholera and pass away, so Naka's Auntie moved in with the Naka family, which had previously moved to Tokyo, as a retainer to the former Imao domain head.

Whenever Naka went outside, he did so on Auntie's back, and he almost never touched the ground until he was five years old. Naka was afraid of other people, so his day usually involved being carried on his Auntie's back and playing in the neighborhood, or they would banish themselves to the inside of the house and play together there. She had a set of weapons and other implements, and she would often put a *karasu-boshi*, a kind of hat that Japanese nobles used to wear, on Naka's head and equip him with a sword while brandishing herself with a *naginata* spear and a headband. Then, in the hallway, they would act out the Battle of Yamazaki, a battle that took place in Kyoto in 1582. Naka played Katō Kiyomasa, and Auntie played Shioten Masataka, the governor of Tajima (located in present-day Hyōgo Prefecture), and the game would end with Kiyomasa taking Shioten's head. Sometimes they played so hard that she would get dizzy and lose her breath and not be able to stand up for a while. She was probably in her fifties, after all. Her eyes were also bad, so she put bells on Naka whenever they went outside so she would not lose track of him. Naka was weak and had a very small appetite. Therefore, she sometimes pretended that the hill in the garden was the Tōkaidō Road and took Naka for a walk around it as if they were making the pilgrimage to Ise Shrine. When they reached the end of their journey, she would clap her hands in prayer in front of a stone lantern and open up a boxed lunch for both of them to enjoy. Then, she would distract Naka with a story while getting the normally finicky eater to eat bamboo shoots and clams. Naka could not hold chopsticks by himself, so she raised a small bowl to his mouth and got him to eat while murmuring, "There now, little sparrow."

Naka's Auntie could not read Chinese characters, but she was quite knowledgeable and had a good memory, and she told Naka every kind of story. He eventually learned the pilgrimage song, *Sai no Kawara* (Children's Limbo), and the tale of Minamoto Yoshitsune's drum, known as "Hatsune"—a story that originated in the *Tale of the Heike* and was later adapted into a play known as *Senbon Zakura* (A Thousand Cherry Trees). He also memorized lines from the *Hyakunin Isshu* card game simply by listening to his Auntie read them out loud. She was also a religious person and very superstitious. She taught Naka how to see Monju (Manjusri, the bodhisattva of wisdom) and Fugen Bosatsu (Samantabhadra, the bodhisattva of meditation) in the shapes of the summer clouds. This does not mean she was particularly concerned with Naka's education. She was simply caring for the weak and sickly boy with blind devotion. She poured everything into him. She was a sensitive woman who would even cry if she saw someone with a disability, and she reacted to everything in the world she lived in with either love or tears. It was a world in which only she and the boy lived.

In 1900, Naka was a third-year student in junior high school, and he visited his Auntie who was now living a lonely life in her hometown. She had become a decrepit old woman who was almost completely blind. Despite the limitations of her body, however, she was able to walk to the local fishmonger and buy fish so as to make Naka a delicious dinner. There were thirty-two flounders on his plate, which means she bought every flounder at the store for him. She would pass away soon after this episode. I will repeat what I said earlier. Doting over children in this way took a certain level of skill. However, this woman was not the only one who possessed this power. Each and every person in old Japan had it, and this civilization has long since vanished.

This love and affection for children that bordered on blind devotion made it possible to stabilize children's basic emotions and self-consciousness, but it also created a different kind of problem. As Kattendijke stated earlier, he praised the way Japanese adults treated Japanese infants and compared their child-raising techniques to what Rousseau described in *Emile, or On Education*, but, on the other hand, he felt their education ended too quickly. Parents would let their children roam free in the streets once they reached a certain age, and Kattendijke concluded that this incomplete education hampered their character development and, as a result, created a general characteristic of conceit among all the Japanese of any given social strata.[86] In addition, Chamberlain praised Japanese children, but then went on to write, "Pity only that a little later they are apt to deteriorate, the Japanese young man being less attractive than his eight or ten-year-old brother, becoming self-conscious, self-important, sometimes intrusive."[87] In other words, in the eyes of Westerners visiting Japan at the time, child-raising was so lenient that it appeared to lack any kind of training or discipline whatsoever.

Finally, I would like to introduce some opposing positions. Naturally, these were made by Japanese people living at the time, which countered the Western view of Japan as a "paradise of babies." Japanese folk historian Hagiwara Tatsuo (1916–1985), for example, stated that Morse frequently called Japan "a paradise for children," but Hagiwara felt that Morse was simply expressing too much praise for the country. He also quoted Japanese social educator Miyamoto Tsuneichi, most notably from his book *Kakyo no Kun* [Guiding Principles of the Homeland], to counter claims made by Morse and other foreign observers. In particular, he quoted the fact that the infant mortality rate in the Meiji and Taishō periods was extremely high.[88] However, this argument is terribly flawed. For one thing, the issues of a high infant mortality rate and doting over children are on completely different levels. Specifically, the infant mortality rate was also much higher in premodern Europe and even into the early modern era. Meanwhile, through contacts made in Japan during the sixteenth to seventeenth centuries, visitors to Japan already knew that the Japanese did not hit their children. High infant mortality rates in Edo-period Japan and modern Europe were the unavoidable will of the gods, and there was no connection between this and how the children were treated and whether they were happy or not.

Japanese historian Ujiie Mikito (1954–) raised another counterpoint. He gave a number of examples to prove that, even in the city of Edo (and the Edo period, in general), which was associated with the boisterous laughter of the lovely, fairy-like *musume*, obvious cases of child abuse took place on an almost daily basis. He also repeatedly claimed that, at least in Edo, kind-hearted visitors to Japan were only in the country for a brief time, and this means that the scenes they depicted were based on a limited exposure to Japan and their own personal bias. Therefore, the country was by no means the "children's paradise" that they claimed it to be. It was a highly developed society with numerous, often graphic examples of child abuse that Ujiie said were like cries for "Help."[89] Whether or not the foreign observers were kind-hearted certainly does not weaken their arguments, however, and some of them definitely stayed in Japan for extended periods of time.

However, Ujiie's argument does not hold up even if we set these points aside. We should accept the fact that child abuse existed in the Edo period, but using this to say that Japan was not a paradise for children is an argument that gets too caught up in the rhetoric of "Heaven." Heaven has never existed on Earth, so it is a waste of time to say so, and one cannot use it as a counterargument because foreign observers are trying to support their position with the same rhetoric. Every example that Ujiie gives is a crime against children, but are there any countries in this world that are truly crime-free? When foreign observers say, for example, that the Japanese do not hit their children, they are describing the general reality and are not denying that examples of crimes against children do exist.

In the case of the foreign observers who witnessed the civilization of old Japan, they were simply implying two key points: that child-raising in Japan was extremely tolerant and that there was a spirit among the entire society that cared for and respected children. In addition, the foreign observers not only praised this reality, but also viewed it with disdain at times. Since their arguments were based on the normal behavior of Japanese society as a whole, specific examples of child abuse can do little to counter it.

Notes:

1 Alcock, *Tycoon*, Vol. 1, 94.

2 Suenson, *Skitser*, 96.

3 Curt Adolph Netto and Gottfried Wagener, *Japanischer Humor* [Japanese Humor] (Berlin, 1901). No English translation of Netto and Wagener's work exists, so passages that appear in this book have been translated from the Japanese version. See Nettō [Netto] and Wāgunā [Wagener], *Nihon no yūmoa* [Japanese Humor] (Toko Shoin, 1971), 177. Subsequent citations will appear as Netto and Wagener, *Japanischer Humor*, and will list page numbers from the Japanese text.

4 Bousquet, *Le Japon*, Vol. 1, 98.

5 Fraser, *Diplomatist's Wife*, 10.

6 Edward W. Clark, *Life and Adventure in Japan* (New York: American Tract Society, 1878), 154–6.

7 Arnold, *Japonica*, 44, 47.

8 Netto and Wagener, *Japanischer Humor*, 176.

9 Bousquet, *Le Japon*, Vol. 1, 99.

10 Morse, *Day by Day*, Vol. 1, 351, 297.

11 Bird, *Unbeaten Tracks*, Vol. 1, 143.

12 Alcock, *Tycoon*, Vol. 1, 125.

13 Kattendijke, *Uittreksel*, 202–3.

14 Bernardino Avila Girón, *Relación del Reyno del Nippon que Lamoron Corumptamente Jappon* (1615). No English translation of Girón's work exists, so passages that appear in this book have been translated from the Japanese version. See Hiron [Girón], "Nihon Ōkokuki" [Record of the Kingdom of Japan], in *Dai Kōkaijidai Sōsho dai jūikkan* [Great Voyages Series Vol. 11] (Iwanami Shoten, 1965), 60, 64. Subsequent citations will appear as Girón, *Reyno del Nippon*, and will list page numbers from the Japanese text.

15 Fróis, *Europa-Japan*, 537.

16 Thunberg, *Travels*, 125.

17 Fischer, *Bijdrage*, Vol. 2, 125–6.

18 Alcock, *Tycoon*, Vol. 2, 281–2.

19 Eulenburg, *Ost-Asien*, 108–9, 146.

20 Morse, *Day by Day*, Vol. 1, 10.

21 Bird, *Unbeaten Tracks*, Vol. 1, 373.

22 Régamey, *Japon*, 203.

23 Morse, *Day by Day*, Vol. 1, 41.

24 Maclay, *Budget*, 347.

25 Fraser, *Diplomatist's Wife*, 497.

26 Fraser, *Diplomatist's Wife*, 183.

27 Humbert, *Japan and the Japanese*, 44.

28 Bird, *Unbeaten Tracks*, Vol. 1, 373.

29 Noda Shigesuke, "Nihon kyūhō shūgyō nikki" [Diary of a Pilgrimage to the Nine Peaks of Japan], in Suzuki Tōzō, ed., *Nihon Shomin Seikatsu Shiryō Shūsei* [Lives of the Japanese People] (Sanichi Shobō, 1969), Vol. 2, 13.

30 Morse, *Day by Day*, Vol. 1, 298–9, 351.

31 Bousquet, *Le Japon*, Vol. 1, 99.

32 Netto and Wagener, *Japanischer Humor*, 176–7.

33 Alcock, *Tycoon*, Vol. 2, 112.

34 Philippe Ariès, trans. Robert Baldrick, *Centuries of Childhood: A Social History of Family Life* (New York: Vintage, 1965).

35 Chamberlain, *Things Japanese*, 125.

36 Bird, *Unbeaten Tracks*, Vol. 1, 373.

37 Jephson and Elmhirst, *Our Life*, 68.

38 Chamberlain, *Things Japanese*, 125.

39 Fraser, *Diplomatist's Wife*, 267–68.

40 Bird, *Unbeaten Tracks*, Vol. 1, 134–35.

41 Bird, *Unbeaten Tracks*, Vol. 1, 339.

42 According to the translator's notes in the Japanese translation of Ernest Satow's *A Diplomat in Japan*, James St. Vincent Saumarez (1843–1933) was a diplomat who served as the Second Secretary at the British Legation from 1876 to 1880.

43 Bird, *Unbeaten Tracks*, Vol. 2, 211–2.

44 Werner, *Die Preussiche Expedition*, 98.

45 Metchnikoff, *Kaisō*, 134.

46 Netto and Wagener, *Japanischer Humor*, 176.

47 Bousquet, *Le Japon*, Vol. 1, 99.

48 Chamberlain, *Things Japanese*, 92.

49 Morse, *Day by Day*, Vol. 1, 10.

50 Guimet, *Promenades-Kanagawa*, 24–5.

51 Netto and Wagener, *Japanischer Humor*, 176.

52 Bacon, *Japanese Girls*, 11.

53 Bird, *Unbeaten Tracks*, Vol. 1, 173.

54 Bacon, *Japanese Girls*, 7–8.

55 Arnold, *Seas and Lands*, 207.

56 Bird, *Unbeaten Tracks*, Vol. 1, 373.

57 Kattendijke, *Uittreksel*, 203.

58 Morse, *Day by Day*, Vol. 1, 362.

59 Moeshart, *Journaal*, 111.

60 Griffis, *Mikado's Empire*, 452–65. Edward Clark also wrote a detailed description of the game "Genji and Heike," which Clark called the "The Reds Versus the Whites," which took place at the school in Shizuoka. See Clark, *Life and Adventure*, 63–7.

61 Holmes, *My Adventures*, 12.

62 Griffis, *Mikado's*, 464, 460.

63 Griffis, *Mikado's*, 453–4.

64 Suenson, *Skitser*, 97.

65 Hübner, *Ramble*, 294.

66 Fortune, *Yedo and Peking*, 35–6.

67 Osborn, *Cruise*, 163–4.

68 Griffis, *Mikado's*, 465.

69 Morse, *Day by Day*, Vol. 1, 351–2.

70 Griffis, *Mikado's*, 354.

71 Suenson, *Skitser*, 45, 96.

72 Palmer, *Letters*, 16–17.

73 Scidmore, *Jinrikisha*, 54.

74 Munzinger, *Japaner*.

75 Chamberlain, *Things Japanese*, 92.

76 Moraes, "Nihon Seishin," 173.

77 Morse, *Day by Day*, Vol. 2, 347, 369.

78 Bird, *Unbeaten Tracks*, Vol. 1, 361.

79 Hodgson, *Residence*, 109–10.

80 Hodgson, *Residence*, 103–4.

81 Hodgson, *Residence*, 119, 122.

82 Hodgson, *Residence*, 203–6.

83 Hodgson, *Residence*, 247.

84 Hodgson, *Residence*, 248.

85 Bird, *Unbeaten Tracks*, Vol. 1, 223–4.

86 Kattendijke, *Uittreksel*, 203.

87 Chamberlain, *Things Japanese*, 92.

88 Yanagita Kunio, ed., *Meiji Bunka 13: Fūzoku* [Meiji Culture Vol. 13: Manners and Customs] (Hara Shobō, 1979), 283–4. This work was originally published in 1954.

89 Ujiie Mikito, *Edo no Shōnen* [The Youth of Edo] (Heibonsha Library, 1994), 74–96.

Chapter

11

Scenery and Cosmology

It is quite evident that one of the main reasons why Western observers felt that Japan seemed like a paradise was the natural beauty that the country was blessed with—they showered unanimous praise on the wonderful sights they saw. Many Westerners first landed at Nagasaki, and the beauty that they saw there almost immediately caught their eye and became the subject of many a conversation. For example, Reinhold von Werner, the captain of the Prussian transport ship, the *Elbe*, had already heard about Nagasaki's beauty when he entered its harbor, but he wrote that the scene that lay before him surpassed all his expectations. Werner had visited Rio de Janeiro, Lisbon, and Constantinople, which many considered to be the three most beautiful harbors in the world at the time, but he felt that Nagasaki was even more beautiful than those.[1] Meanwhile, Pompe van Meerdenvoort wrote that everyone on his ship was in awe at seeing how beautiful nature could be when they first saw the view of Nagasaki Bay in 1857. Pompe came to Nagasaki to serve as an officer at the Dutch Naval School, and he wrote that he had absolutely no complaints about his surroundings even though he would have to live there for two to three years.[2] Rudolf Lindau also said that he did not know any Europeans who had landed in Nagasaki and had not been struck by the ideal location of the city and the attractive beauty of its panorama of views.[3]

The suburbs and other areas surrounding Nagasaki were also beautiful. Albert Berg, who, like Werner, was a member of the Eulenburg expedition, wrote that the beauty of the suburbs was incomparable and that wherever one went, there was lush and wonderful scenery.[4] Willem Huyssen van Kattendijke, the commandant of the Nagasaki Naval Training Center, also related the following about the suburbs of Nagasaki:[5]

How many times have I thought to myself that I would love to spend the rest of my days in this beautiful country if it were possible to do so? For example, I will never forget the names of such places as Nihongi, Urakami, Hokkayama, Konpira, Mikanyama, and Mikata. Their beauty even made me think that the people who lived in these areas were the most fortunate on Earth.

One of the reasons why Westerners were so sensitive to the natural beauty of Japan may have had to do with the fact that their home countries shared the same natural characteristics and temperate climate. John Russell Young, a journalist who visited Japan as a member of General Grant's party in 1879, recalled scenes in his home country upon seeing the beauty of Nagasaki when his ship entered the harbor. After enjoying their trip through Europe, Grant's party had visited India, Southeast Asia, and China before coming to Japan, and Young said, "We were weary of the cocoa-nut and the brown, parched soil, of the skies of fire and forests with wild and creepy things." However, he was moved by the greenery that he saw everywhere in Nagasaki. Young explained that "the green that I had not seen since leaving England [was] our old-fashioned green of the temperate zone." He also said that "the green is an honest, frank, chaste green, running from hill-top to water-side, and throwing upon the waters long, refreshing shadows."[6]

Basil Chamberlain, meanwhile, found great charm in Japan, notably "the street life of the lower classes," but his heart was particularly taken in by the "enchanting" scenery. He wrote the following:[7]

> Those giant cedars that overshadow moss-grown shrines, those volcanic cones of ineffably graceful logarithmic curve, those torrents to be crossed warily on stepping stones or on "hanging bridges" stretched like a spider's thread and trembling at every step, and the breezy uplands carpeted with wild flowers and re-echoing with the carolling of nightingales and larks, and the summer hills around which the vapours trail in grey semi-diaphanous garlands, and the valleys of mingled scarlet maple and deepest green, whose pinnacled rock-walls zigzag the sky with their sharply serrated line. Surely the catalogue of Japan's perfections is sufficiently long and goodly.

Max von Brandt, who stayed in Japan from 1862 to 1875 and served as the Prussian consul and later as the German ambassador to Japan, was an oftentimes harsh critic of the country, but even he found its natural beauty to be a constant source of happiness and the greatest sense of comfort. He was deeply impressed by snow on the branches of blooming camellia trees and palm trees and cycads staring out from thick forests of coniferous trees, and he was also intrigued by the peculiar mixture of plants from both the colder climates of the north and the tropics that he had found. Whenever he strapped his hunting rifle over his shoulder and went into the wild, he saw that the creeks and rice paddies were framed with blue and white irises and that yellow, white, and marmalade lilies filled the meadows. Colorful azaleas also adorned the hills, and forests of pine trees, bamboo thickets, maple forests awash in the autumn shades of pale yellow and deep red, and many other sights took his heart and would not let go. The countryside of Japan could charm the hearts of wanderers at any time of year.[8]

Autumn views of Japan also cast a spell on Count Eulenburg when he was bogged down by stalled negotiations with the shogunate. He wrote in his diary on November 17, 1860 that he only went for a short ride with Henry Heusken and Ferdinand von Richthofen, but mentioned that it was a very pleasant experience. He even stated that he had never seen trees or a place as beautiful as this in autumn in his entire life and could never grow weary of the views. Then, he stated the following in his diary on November 26:[9]

> Winter has come…in the past few days the leaves have rapidly fallen from the trees and they are all but bare, but this has not tarnished the beauty of the area whatsoever. Quite the contrary. Now we can see through many of the thickets on both sides of the road we travel on, giving us splendid views of fields, hills, and evergreen forests in the distance. Crisp, clean air and a pleasant ride…What more could one ask for? I can see now how one could truly find happiness living here among these pleasant people and surrounded by such beautiful nature.

Of course, there was also spring. Aimé Humbert asked himself "Where can there be found a more luxuriant spring vegetation, more rich in beautiful details?"[10] He felt that only the views in Switzerland could compare with Japan's beautiful scenery, but he also wrote that "in Japan, nature is over-cultivated" and lacked any sort of "melancholy attraction."

A village on the outskirts of Edo

Berg, meanwhile, was struck by the beauty of the countryside in the outskirts of Edo and even said that it was perhaps the most beautiful region in Japan. He also stated that farmhouses, villages, and temples could be seen everywhere, as could plentiful water and tilled land. He added that the fields were tended like flower gardens such that not even a single weed could be seen. He described farmhouses in bamboo forests, roads shaded by tall cryptomeria trees, and shrines hidden by green groves of trees, as well as camellias and podocarp hedges. He concluded that there was an almost limitless variety of plant species.[11]

Robert Fortune, meanwhile, wrote the following about his long journey to the southwestern outskirts of Edo:[12]

> Never in my wanderings in any other country did I meet with such charming lanes as we passed through on this occasion. Sometimes they reminded me of what I had met with in some of the country districts of England; but I was compelled, notwithstanding early prejudices, to admit that nothing in England even could be compared to them. Large avenues and groves of pines, particularly of *Cryptomeria*, were frequently met with, fringing the roads, and affording most delicious shade from the rays of the sun. Now and then magnificent hedges were observed, composed sometimes of evergreen oaks of various species, sometimes of *Cryptomeria japonica* and other evergreens. These were kept carefully clipped, and in some instances they were trained to a great height, reminding one of those high hedges of holly or yew which may frequently be met with in the parks and gardens of our English nobility. Everywhere the cottages and farm-houses had a neat and clean appearance, such as I had never observed in any other part of the East…The scene was always changing and always beautiful—hill and valley, broad roads and shaded lanes, houses and gardens, with a people industrious, but unoppressed with toil, and apparently happy and contented.

Margaret T.K. Ballagh (1840–1909), the wife of an American missionary who had come to live in Yokohama in 1861, was also a fan of these hedges. She wrote:[13]

> Near the suburbs of Yokohama, we passed some magnificent hedges. These I think, are the prettiest feature of the country. We saw often miserable farmers' dwellings so prettily enclosed and surrounded, as to produce, notwithstanding their own ugliness, a pleasing effect.

Japanese homes were commonly one-story dwellings, so the rows of houses in villages tended to be a bit drab. According to Edward Morse, however, the otherwise dull "Japanese house owes its picturesque appearance" to thatched roofs.[14] Fortune also mentioned the thatched roofs he saw on temples and wrote "Never, in any other part of the world, have I seen such beautiful thatching. Indeed this is a subject of admiration with every foreigner who visits Japan."[15]

Eliza Scidmore depicted the farmhouses that she saw in the Yokohama suburbs in the following passage:[16]

Farmhouses near Edo, with irises on the roofs (Fortune, *Yedo and Peking*, 57)

> The farm-houses....are so picturesque that one cannot believe them to have a utilitarian purpose. They seem more like stage pictures about to be rolled away than like actual dwellings. The new thatches are brightly yellow, and the old thatches are toned and mellowed, set with weeds, and dotted with little gray-green bunches of "hen and chickens" while along the ridge-poles is a bed of growing lilies.

It appears that the lily that Scidmore was describing was actually a species of perennial iris (*Iridaceae*) known as *ichihatsu*, or roof iris. According to the *Kojien* Japanese dictionary, there used to be a folk belief that planting these flowers on straw roofs could prevent fires. A number of Westerners also described flowers growing along the ridges of thatched roofs, and they usually called them "lilies" or "irises." However, Morse specifically stated, "The ridge-poles of many of the roofs in the north of Japan are covered with red lilies," while "Around Tokyo the blue iris seems to be the favorite flower for this decoration." Thus, we can see that lilies were definitely planted on roofs in some instances.

Whatever the case, the homes looked beautiful. Morse went on to state that "One has no idea how beautiful these roofs appear: grand old thatched roofs, high and broad, with a splendid sweep to the eaves and surmounted by a waving fringe of red lilies."[17] Ludovic de Beauvoir also saw roofs decorated with "blue lilies" in the western suburbs of Yokohama. He stated "All these houses, scattered amidst thickets of azaleas and camellias, had the upper part of their thatched roofs covered with a slight layer of earth, from which rose like a thick crown, blue lilies in full bloom," and went on to say that "these gardens [were] hanging like wreaths of azure."[18] Naturally, these "blue lilies" he saw were roof irises. Aimé Humbert also stated:[19]

Inaka, in a word, seen from a birdseye view, looks like a park, or a continuous garden dotted with rural habitations…These charming retreats [tea-houses], rich with the beauties of nature, are innumerable…The roof…rises to the summit, where we see long lines of iris in full flower.

The roads that the Westerners traveled on were also quite beautiful. Joseph Hübner, for example, traveled to the northeastern base of Mount Fuji in 1871 and noted that every village he passed was "clean, tidy, and evidently prosperous," and that "Fine and flourishing villages succeed one another at short intervals." On the way back, he noted that the small village he stopped at in Shizuoka Prefecture was "coquettishly placed between two wooden mountains; a limpid stream runs through it, and its banks are lined with beautiful flowers." When he arrived at the mayor's house, he thought "It was a perfect gem." He stated, "The road [connecting the villages] is but a path, well kept, and full of people."[20]

Morse also stated that the road to Nikko was "a much better road than I ever saw in New England outside the cities."[21] Oftentimes, both sides of the road were lined with trees that the locals had planted. During his trip to Edo, for example, Philipp Franz von Siebold described a road lined with cherry trees that stretched for a mile or more and sported a fantastic view of Ōmura Bay (located in Nagasaki Prefecture).[22] Émile Guimet, meanwhile, rode in a rickshaw on the Reiheishi Kaidō Road, which led to Nikko, and upon seeing the beautiful sight of the trees lining the road, he felt that roads in Japan were like something out of a dream.[23]

In addition, when people traveled the roads in old Japan, the scenes would change as if they were walking around a revolving lantern. Siebold, for example, wrote the following about what he saw in Tatsuno, Harima Province (located in present-day Tatsuno City, Hyōgo Prefecture):[24]

Here we stood in a wide road and gazed at the glorious scenery. There were seed beds and vegetable gardens on both sides, and the well-kept road, which passes through pine forests and villages, resembled a path we might find in a park back home. The road looked like it was made so that travelers would be pleasantly surprised by each new sight waiting for them around the next bend.

The sea and other bodies of water also caught the eye of many observers.

J. F. van Overmeer Fischer was particularly taken in by the charm of Japan's nature and called the country a veritable "Heaven on Earth." He felt his descriptions could not truly convey just how beautiful the scenery in Japan was, but he did say that a lake he saw near Kyoto during his trip to Edo was more beautiful than Italy's Lake Maggiore. He also stated that in summer, hundreds of sails could be seen raised on countless boats that were scattered and floating on the lake, and he also commented that the light of evening was particularly beautiful, and this, along with the sound of music, drew people to the area like a magnet and provided the perfect backdrop for an evening stroll. Fischer felt it was a wonderful way for the people to amuse themselves.[25] Edouard Suenson, meanwhile, thought the Japanese sailboats were incredibly beautiful and picturesque.[26]

Now, let us fast-forward our way to 1889, the year that Mary Fraser travelled across the Seto Inland Sea while accompanying her husband (the newly appointed British ambassador) to Japan. Over the course of the cruise, she suddenly found her ship surrounded by a large group of boats with white sails. She wrote:[27]

> The deep was suddenly covered with what seemed like a flotilla of white nautilus shells, with sails all set, closing in round us with a flutter of wings, and the cool music of a hundred prows rushing through the water in the sun…The warm sheen of the junk sails…held together in a thousand lovely patterns…gave the impression of a web of silver against the blue.

Fraser went on to say the ships "pressed in on every side" like "the white lotus blooms that smother the marble bridge in the pond of the Summer Palace," and when the wind changed, "they all floated away in a wide half circle, which became a fringe of stars on the water after the night came down." Fraser was also struck by the unique beauty of Japan's mountains, writing:[28]

> Of all the things that I have seen none are so individually and weirdly beautiful as these pine-fringed hills of Japan, with their delicate, daring profiles rising in curves and points that no Western mountain ever knew, crowned with pines following each other in leisurely succession, and holding out dark-green branches for the mists to tear on, or coppery golden arms for the sun to strike.

Fraser was born in Rome and had lived in such countries as the United States, Britain, Switzerland, Prussia, Austria, China, and Chile. Therefore, she had a wide range of countries to compare Japan with.

A flock of birds in flight

Many of the foreign observers also noticed that Japan's forests were well preserved. Friedrich Lühdorf, for example, visited Hakodate and Shimoda in 1855 and wrote:[29]

> There are wonderful forests everywhere in Japan, and, it is worth noting, the people make considerable efforts to grow, maintain, and preserve the trees. For this reason, one must receive permission from the authorities if he desires lumber. In addition, if a tree does get chopped down, a young tree must be planted in its place. The forests make views of the land all the more beautiful.

Birds were also protected in Japan. Lühdorf noted with surprise that birds did not fly away from people in fear. For example, he saw wild ducks come right up to his boat and sparrows often darting in and out of people's homes. He reasoned that this had to do with the fact that hunting was outlawed in Japan. It was strictly forbidden to shoot wildlife in the countryside.[30]

Actually, the Dutch stationed at Dejima knew this long before Lühdorf's time. Carl Thunberg, for instance, wrote that birds "are never feared away by the gun…not even of me, who was their daily butcher," and that they appeared in "such numbers, that at a distance they appeared as large islands."[31] When Siebold made his journey to Edo, meanwhile, he saw thousands of wild ducks gathered on the shoal of the Sunako River in Owari Province (located in present-day Aichi Prefecture). He asked the locals why this was the case and discovered that the domain lord had ordered them to be protected. Just before Siebold reached the Chiryu post station on the Tōkaidō Road, he also spotted several ibises in the rice fields. He asked a local chief if he could hunt these rare birds, to which the man replied that firearms were outlawed by the domain lord.[32] We can even go back in time to the days of Olof Eriksson Willman, who traveled to Edo as a member of the annual journey (*hofreis*) by Dutch officials to the court in 1651, to find evidence of this. Over 100 years before Thunberg and Siebold, Willman discovered that birds in Japan were not afraid of people and flocked together in surprisingly large numbers near the roads.[33]

In April 1863, Humbert entered the Seto Inland Sea via Hirado, and according to his accounts, it was clear that Japan was a paradise for birds simply by viewing the country from the sea. He wrote the following:[34]

> One of the most unique aspects of the scenery in the Japanese islands is that there are thousands of birds screaming and fluttering about. Here one might see eagles and vultures circling over the rocks and then be startled by a crane suddenly darting out from a forest of Cryptomeria. In the distance, cormorants and herons forage for fish in reed bushes or the incoming tides of quiet inlets. Wild geese and ducks can be seen everywhere, gliding over the waves and soaring into the sky in perfect order, and seagulls and stormy petrels gather near the capes and reefs and then fly off in flocks.

Hunting was prohibited in and around Edo at a radius of about forty kilometers. Therefore, the city was a veritable paradise for birds. Berg gave perhaps the best account of this aspect in the *Eulenburg Expedition*, the book he coauthored with other members of the mission. He stated that the moats of Edo Castle spread out into large ponds in some places, with magnificent trees lowering their branches to the top of the shallow pools filled with lotus flowers. It was on these ponds that thousands of wild ducks made their home. In the fir trees on the castle walls, meanwhile, countless birds and even birds of prey built their nests. Berg also related that no one ever hunted any of these birds. Hunting was typically a right only enjoyed by the shogun himself.

Berg then went on to say that traveling west from Ikegami and passing over the hills brought one to a small lake called Senzoku Pond (located in present-day Ōta Ward, Tokyo). In autumn, thousands of wild ducks could be seen here, but just like in the areas surrounding the city, people were not allowed to catch any of the waterfowl. Berg also mentioned this area was home to a rich variety of bird species, most notably herons and cranes, which often walked through the muddy rice paddies while searching for frogs and fish to eat. In winter, meanwhile, large flocks of geese gathered here. Sometimes, the farmers accidentally snagged them with fishhooks.

Berg also wrote that access to the garden surrounding the northern cemetery of the shogun's family (Kaneiji temple's mausoleum) was off-limits, but it appeared quite charming from what he could see from the outside. A large flock of gray herons and countless numbers of wild ducks made their home in the lake adjacent to the mausoleum, and Berg said that the scene was indescribably beautiful in the glow of the setting sun.[35]

Vittorio Arminjon also touched on the hunting ban mentioned above, and he also said how strange it was that the farmers did not worry or even complain about any damage that these small birds may have inflicted on their crops. He reasoned that the farmers let them be because the humid summers in Japan bred a multitude of insects, which the birds ate.[36]

Visitors to Japan knew quite well that Edo was the largest and most-populous city in the world at the time. However, when they arrived and saw the city for themselves, they found it to be a place that almost completely deviated from what their idea of a metropolis was. They were also taken aback by its stark differences with other Asian cities, more so, even, than its differences with cities in their own countries. Edo was a strange place for them because nature permeated and became a part of the great city, making it one in which urban areas were interspersed with elements of the countryside. In other words, based on their standards, it was like a very large village.

Henry Tilley, the British officer who accompanied Muravyov-Amursky's fleet during their visit to Japan in 1859, wrote the following about the view he observed from a berth that lay some four miles away from the center of Edo:[37]

From the anchoring place, a spectator would have no idea that he was in the neighbourhood of one of the most populous cities in the world. Vainly he would look for wharves, lofty buildings, spires, or pagodas. None such exist in Japan; there is only a low shore, broken by little eminences, and covered with verdure, gradually increasing in elevation inland, and a high range of mountains for a background, conspicuous over which towers the magnificent cone of the volcano, about 12,000 feet high, and distant 40 miles. A low line marks the head of the bay a few miles farther up, and the opposite coast is quite lost sight of over the broad lake here formed by its waters. But at night the truth would break upon the gazer when he saw, for miles along the shore, light after light peeping out from darkness, or by day when he marked through a glass the long unbroken line of low houses along the shore, and the sharp roofs of the temples amid the trees at a greater distance. Then the numbers of junks coming and going, and the busy fleets of fishing-boats scattered in groups over the bay, would remind him he was in the vicinity of a largely populated district.

Werner also felt that Edo could not be compared with the big cities in Europe, or could even be called a city at all, even though it was a city of one million people. Rather, he felt it was more like a large, prosperous village. The skyline in Edo lacked any kind of towering structure, and Werner believed that people suddenly arriving in Edo would only see elements of a city in the immediate vicinity of the shogun's castle. Werner went on to say that visitors would no doubt confuse every other part of the city with one of the hamlets found in the suburbs or in other such areas outside the city.[38]

Georges Bousquet came to Japan and visited the city in 1872, just after Edo underwent the name change to "Tokyo." He wrote the following about his first impression of what he saw:[39]

> One would have at least expected to find a grand city, large gates, or magnificent houses and bridges spread throughout the area, but upon arriving here via the Tokaido Road, one only finds, upon hiring a dirty jinrikisha to traverse the uneven streets, low, dingy houses made of wood or sometimes just empty lots. Such sights would likely betray any new visitor's high hopes for the city.

In other words, Bousquet also viewed Edo as an endless village of wooden houses. However, if we free ourselves from the conventional idea of a city, in which the area carries a certain sense of monumental splendor and there exist distinct divisions between urban and rural elements, then we can see the unique charm of Edo as a city. After Bousquet stated his aforementioned disappointing first impression of Edo, for example, he pondered the following:

> Why, then, after living here for some time, does one find it so difficult to leave the city? Why does it remain so fascinating here even after walking on all its streets and exploring every nook and cranny? The answer is that even though it has the guise of a city made up of a simple arrangement of meager houses, Edo actually shows a great deal of variety in terms of its structures. One can find new places that look like they came right out of a painting on a daily basis.

Bousquet also mentioned green hills, rivers flowing through valleys, gardens, temples and shrines, forests, and meadows. In essence, he thought that Edo looked like an extension of the countryside.

Berg also realized that Edo was characterized as a city that included elements of the countryside. He stated that many temples were built on the tops of hills, hidden by evergreen trees, and surrounded by wide cemeteries. He also noted that lands owned by the domain lords had magnificent parks and gardens, and that there were green trees, sparkling rivers, and a truly diverse variety of buildings everywhere one looked. Then, he went on to say that homes were clustered together on the main roads, but if one traversed the backstreets, he or she would immediately be treated to sights of the countryside. Sometimes, elements of the country even mixed in with the more densely populated districts of the city, and Berg decried that this made it difficult to define clear boundaries between urban and rural areas.[40]

Hübner, meanwhile, stated the following:[41]

> You go out of the hotel of the legation, which is situated in a very gay street; you descend a little alley which by degrees takes the look of a village. A few steps further on and you find yourself in the midst of a complete solitude. Go on a little further, and there you are come back into a town.

Alfred Roussin (1839–1919), a French naval officer who came to Japan in 1863, stated that if one stepped outside the crowds of people and the hustle and bustle of the city streets, he or she would suddenly find themselves on a long, quiet road or sometimes even in a farm field or orchard.[42] Brandt gave an almost identical description when he said the following:[43]

> Even in Edo, we would just take a few steps away from the lively main street and find ourselves at a quiet temple in a dark and gloomy forest, or the houses would disappear and be replaced by fields and lakes and a ridge of continuous green hills. We almost always spotted a temple roof and a vermilion-lacquered pagoda towering into the sky at the top of each of these hills, and we could see Mt. Fuji towering over them in the distance.

Speaking of Mount Fuji, Algernon Mitford wrote the following the day after he landed in Yokohama for the first time and initially had a bad impression of the country:[44]

> Walking out that afternoon and suddenly coming in full view of Mt. Fuji, snow-capped, rearing its matchless cone heavenward in one gracefully curving slope from the sea level, I too was caught by the fever of intoxication which the day before had seemed quite inexplicable—a fever which burns to this day, and will continue to burn in my veins to the end of my life.

Lindau, meanwhile, wrote that countless numbers of parks and gardens essentially buried the city of Edo in green such that when viewed from afar, it looked like one large park stretching out into eternity. He went on to write:[45]

> Edo is a garden town with greenery that stretches as far as the eye can see—it is a town washed by the ocean, cut by large rivers, and decorated with second homes. In many neighborhoods you can see endless rows of houses that line up and form orderly streets. Yet, whenever you turn and look around, a temple, or a garden, or a large house catches your eye and seems to break the monotony of the streets. This distinguishing aspect is what makes Edo the most unique city in the world and what creates the strongest, yet most comfortable, sense of surprise among travelers who see the city for the first time.

Koenraad Wolter Gratama (1831–1888), a Dutch chemistry professor at Bunseki Kyūrisho, a scientific research institution established by the shogunate in Nagasaki, visited Edo for the first time in 1866. He thought that the city looked like the countryside, stating:[46]

> Japanese towns all look alike for the most part...but Edo is the exception and I had a much different impression of it than other places I visited...There are large gardens, so large, in fact, that they could be called parks, scattered here and there throughout the city; it makes me feel like I am in a country village...The view is splendid—townhouses, roofs, gardens, and the roads come together to create a veritable tapestry of scenic delights. One part of the city may stretch off into the distant horizon while another part overlooks a swarm of countless fishing boats floating in Edo Bay.

As mentioned in earlier chapters, George Smith, the Anglican bishop of Victoria (Hong Kong), was a vocal critic of customs in Japan that he deemed immoral, particularly in the entertainment industry, but even he seemed to relax a bit when he saw "the Bellevue of Edo," a glorious view of the city from the top of a hill. He stated:[47]

> It is sometimes difficult to realise in such a spot the fact of being in the heart and centre of a couple of millions of people. The whole surrounding aspect is that of a succession of Hyde Parks or Kensington Gardens—a city of green slopes and overhanging groves, with broad spacious roads sometimes expanding to the dimensions of an open field and everywhere lined with a succession of sparsely diffused dwellings.

Towards the south a fine view of the distant harbour with its fleet of native craft stretched far away to the dimly decried hills over the bay. There was little to denote the existence of a thickly crowded capital except the glittering white exterior of the houses and the interspersed temples with a slightly dim obscuration of the atmosphere from the smoke of the more densely packed streets of the trading quarter. I have heard the opinion expressed by a friend who has visited all the capitals in Europe but one, that in the external beauty of its well-wooded scenery and the general picturesque appearance of the surrounding view Yeddo surpasses every city of western countries.

Beauvoir, meanwhile, was captivated by hedges of camellias and laurels that rose from the tops of ramparts in the city. He wrote "Surrounded by the giddy flight of the sacred white-plumaged birds; it seemed to me more brilliant and more fairy-like than anything my imagination had pictured of the hanging gardens of Babylon!" Then, when he climbed up to Sengakuji temple (located in present-day Minato Ward, Tokyo), he said, "From the top of the terraces nothing is seen but tangled thickets and green valleys which, even in the midst of a town containing several hundred thousand inhabitants, breathes the tranquil air of the woods sung of by Virgil."[48]

Rutherford Alcock may have said it best in an ode he penned to the unique city of Edo. He wrote:[49]

No capital in Europe presents so many striking features of a type altogether peculiar; nor, upon the whole, can any boast of so much beauty in the site and surrounding country, and this for leagues in every direction…The capital itself…can boast what no capital in Europe can—the most charming rides, beginning even in its centre, and extending in every direction over wooded hills, through smiling valleys and shady lanes, fringed with evergreens and magnificent timber. Even in the city, especially along the ramparts of the official quarter, and in many roads and avenues leading thence to the country, broad green slopes and temple gardens, or well-timbered parks gladden the eye, as it is nowhere else gladdened within the circle of a city.

Alcock also felt that the suburbs of Edo were beautiful, and he saw hedges that "only [those in] England could rival, either for beauty or neatness." He went on to say that "Over all an Eastern sun, through the greater part of the year, throws a flood of light from an unclouded sky, making the deep shadow of the overarching trees doubly grateful with its ever-varying pictures of tracery, both above and below."

Fortune, meanwhile, likely stated the general consensus that many Westerners had reached regarding this unique capital city with the following words:[50]

> Although Yedo is a large city, and remarkable in many ways, it cannot be compared with London, Paris, or any of the chief towns in Europe, either in the architecture of its buildings, the magnificence of its shops, or in the value of its merchandise. It has no Woolwich or Greenwich, no St. Paul's or Westminster Abbey, no Champs Elysées or Versailles; it has nothing to show like the Boulevards in Paris or like Regent Street in London…But, nevertheless, Yedo is a wonderful place, and will always possess attractions peculiarly its own in the eyes of a foreign visitor.

Ōji, a town located in the northern suburbs of Edo (located in present-day Kita Ward, Tokyo), was a popular tourist destination that foreign visitors staying in Japan visited at least once. There was a famous Inari shrine here, and it was a popular tourist spot even among the locals in both spring and autumn, but shogunate officials probably preferred taking Western diplomats to this area to show off its beautiful teahouses. Humbert called Ōji a garden that combined utility and pleasure as well as the secular and the divine. He said that the local people loved the area and went on to say:[51]

> The Gardens of Odji-Inari…are situate at the opening of a mountain gorge on the northern side of Yeddo. A small river forming several cascades winds gracefully through the valley. On the bank above its limpid waters, rises the long galleries and pavilions of the tea-house, which enjoys the coolness of the water and the shade of the great trees. The guest chambers, the verandahs, the partitions, and the mats are kept in a state of dazzling cleanliness. The whole establishment is distinguished by elegance and simplicity.

Shogunate officials also guided the Earl of Elgin's mission on their long journey to Ōji, and Laurence Oliphant detailed this trip in his writings. At first, he was surprised by how wide Edo was and said that the streets "seemed interminable." He went on to say that "Many of the streets and roads which we traversed were lined with peach and plum trees," and he reasoned that "at the period of the year when these are in full blossom, they must form a most charming and fragrant avenue." Even though they were still in the city, parks and country homes began to appear. Oliphant continued:[52]

These charming little cottages, raising their thatched roofs amidst the

A view of Ōji in northern Edo (from Tilley, *Japan, the Amoor*)

fruit-trees and creepers which threatened to smother them in their embraces, were surrounded by flower-beds tastefully laid out, resplendent with brilliant hues, and approached by walks between carefully-clipped hedges.

Oliphant related that "We were filled with astonishment and delight at the exquisite taste displayed in the gardens and cottages upon the roadside." He went on to say, "No model estate in England can produce 'cottages ornées' comparable to those which adorn the suburbs of Yedo." What he found particularly fascinating, moreover, was the fact that "As we got further from town the cottages became more scattered, but the country did not lose its air of civilization." Finally, they descended into a valley "where a charming village lay embosomed in a wood." This was Ōji. Surrounded by glorious scenery, the members of the Elgin mission relaxed at a teahouse and enjoyed the hospitality of the "graceful and respectful" young women who served them.

Beauvoir also visited Ōji where, as Count Eulenburg had also experienced, he saw that "half a hundred young girls and boys were playing in the sparkling waters of the torrent." He wrote the following about the natural beauty that he saw on the way to the area:[53]

> We passed imperceptibly from the town to the country, the streets turning gradually into lanes shaded by flowering westerias; the water,

which just now was filling the moats of the fortresses, here ran in winding rivulets under bowers of azaleas; nothing can be conceived more charming than these meanderings amid an Eden of verdure. How beautiful and smiling nature is in Japan!

Aleksei Vysheslavtsov, meanwhile, was also deeply impressed not only by Ōji, but also by the journey there. He wrote that, after riding off from his accommodations at Mita Daichūji temple, it took him about three hours to leave the city. He went on to praise the scenery and said that it was like passing through a magnificent park. He also wondered if every suburb of Edo were as beautiful as Ōji. He also had his curiosity piqued by the extremely diverse variety of plants he encountered. After climbing a hill and stopping to rest at a teahouse, he suddenly saw a scene before him that he said etched itself into his soul and would remain with him until death. He told his readers that this was Edo: scenes of sparkling silver rivers, emerald green rice fields, villages and wooded groves, garden trees swaying in the wind, and a thin haze hovering over the horizon. He said words were not enough to describe the everlasting beauty of Japan's nature.[54]

Now we can finally see what Alcock meant when he said, "No capital in Europe presents so many striking features of a type altogether peculiar" as Edo. It was not a city like Paris, Rome, London, or Vienna, all of which were magnificent cities with tall buildings and famous monuments. Any observer who was hoping to see structures such as these when he or she arrived in Edo would have been deeply disappointed. Edo's uniqueness was characterized by the fact that elements of the countryside permeated and mixed with the city. For this reason, Westerners could not tell the difference between Edo and its suburbs. Moreover, as they walked through the city, observers often found themselves suddenly surrounded by country scenes without even realizing it. What is important to remember, however, is that even when the scenery changed and took on the tone of a farm village, it was still the city of Edo. This is what Oliphant indicated when he said that "the country did not lose its air of civilization." In other words, Edo was by no means a "big village." It was a truly unique urban center that could be called a "city with rural elements," or a "rural village with urban elements." This was a unique urban concept that did not exist in any other part of the world at the time, at least not in Europe, China, or the Islamic countries. Later on, when the city became Tokyo, the locals were a bit embarrassed that their capital city had been labeled a "big village" or a conglomeration of hamlets, but Westerners who visited Japan at the end of the Edo period recognized the unique nature of this urban concept and could not hide their excitement about it. In other words, it was the nature of this unique city that proved that

Japan at the time had built up a separate and unique civilization that had the power to show its individuality to the rest of the world.

Nature permeated Edo, but it did not encroach upon the city. Berg testified to this.[55] He described the gardens that decorated the streets of Edo by saying they were similar to seventeenth- to eighteenth-century French flower gardens, as both contained bowers and finely trimmed bushes. Naturally, Japanese gardens were not that much more orderly than French gardens. However, they were oriented similarly with a Baroque artificiality. Gardens that faced homes did not have naturally shaped trees or bushes, and plants shaped like fans, sailboats, and partition screens grew there. There were also bonsai trees and potted flowers placed on beautiful gravel roads, goldfish ponds and small, manmade streams with moss-covered rocks sticking out, and small shrines built in the corners of gardens. In other words, nature was being used fashionably as it was in a European salon. Berg said that these gardens were beautiful and pleasant to look at, comparing them to elegant noble ladies dressing themselves up in the latest fashion. In other words, they emanated beauty no matter how unnatural they may have appeared. It is also worth noting that Berg added that the gardens possessed the same traditional sophistication and customs of upstanding Western social meeting places. In other words, he was saying the countrified aspects displayed in the city of Edo were a product of a separate and unique civilization.

Humbert wrote that since there were hills to the south, west, and north of Edo Castle, these areas were blessed with beautiful rocks and "pretty valleys and grottoes, springs and ponds."[56] These were the natural conditions. However, when Humbert said these elements had been used skillfully to alter the landscape, and, moreover, when he said, "If nature has not isolated the demesne by means of hedges or natural palisades of bamboo covered with climbing plants, industry supplies the deficiency," he was saying that nature was being shaped by an urban countryside. He also said:

> When the garden is approached from the street, a rustic bridge is thrown across the canal before the door, and hidden with tufts of trees and thick-leaved shrubs. On crossing the threshold, the visitor might believe himself to be in a virgin forest far from all human habitations.

Humbert may have felt this to be the case, but this was really just an imitation of nature. Nature, here, was also being dressed up. Humbert also mentioned the view from the hills and said, "The whole landscape and all its details wrap the mind in calm, and leave it no other impression than the vague pleasure of perfect rest." Thus, he said that Edo was countrified, but also unmistakably urban at the same time. Suenson, meanwhile, said

Entrance to a residence in Edo (from Humbert, *Japan and the Japanese*)

the only criticism he had about scenery in Japan, particularly views in the suburbs, was that they were too regular and straightened out. He felt the Japanese were not letting nature be nature.[57] Likely, he was hinting at the custom of taming nature, a custom that was associated with the civilization of old Japan.

This unique charm of Edo almost completely disappeared due to changes and rebuilding in the Meiji period, however. After the shogun and the domain lords had abandoned Edo, their large estates were left to degenerate into wastelands. Edmond Cotteau (1833–1896), a French travel writer who came to Japan in 1881, wrote that due to such changes, much of the strange beauty that attracted previous visitors to Japan had disappeared from the city.[58]

It was not just the natural beauty of Japan and the charm of the harmony with nature in Edo that caught the eye of the foreign observers. They could not help being surprised by and praising not only this beauty, but also the way the Japanese at the time lived closely together with nature. Guimet was not the only one to be moved by the fact that the Japanese seemed to have great affection for nature. He mentioned how they knew how to use the beauty of nature well. He also said they lived a comfortable and quiet life, did not have reckless desires, never competed against each other, and somehow knew how to effectively live with peaceful sensibilities and maintain a modest material sense of satisfaction.[59]

A rural teahouse in the suburbs of Edo; note the irises on the roof. (from Humbert, *Japan and the Japanese*)

Some of the observers even discovered good examples of the affinity that the Japanese had for nature at teahouses, which were famous abodes in the Japanese countryside. Suenson, for example, said that the Japanese were fervent nature-worshippers where even ordinary laborers enjoyed viewing the lovely scenery while savoring a cup of tea. Therefore, he reasoned, the Japanese carefully selected the locations for these teahouses the purpose of which was to please the eye.[60] Beauvoir, meanwhile, said the following:[61]

> I do not know whether there exists any people more susceptible to the beauties of nature than the Japanese: everywhere in the country where there is a fine view, everywhere where a beautiful tree and the retirement of delicious shade seem to invite the traveler to repose, even in the almost hidden paths across the fields, a teahouse is to be found.

Richard Jephson and Edward Elmhirst said, "We don't recollect ever having seen a Japanese who had the heart to pass a tea-house." They went on to say, "If he has any money, he will have a drink, either tea or saki, generally the latter; if he has not, he will sit on one of the benches, and apparently derive much satisfaction from watching others engaged in their potations."[62]

Bousquet, meanwhile, postulated that the Japanese love for nature, which was, quite simply, almost too excessive, was one of the dominant characteristics of the Japanese psyche. Nevertheless, he did not view this favorably. He felt that their love for nature was blind, as they never criticized any aspects of the scenery, even in cases where he felt it was warranted. In his mind, it lacked the function of a psyche that tries to bring order to the disorder in nature. However, even Bousquet had to admit that only Japanese architects understood the mutual beauty that art and nature gave each other.[63]

Hübner, meanwhile, commented:[64]

> The Japanese are wonderful lovers of nature. In Europe a feeling for beauty has to be developed by education. Our peasants will talk to you of the fertility of the soil, of the abundance of water, so useful for their mills, of the value of their woods, but not of the picturesque charms of the country. They are not perhaps entirely insensible to them: but if they do feel them, it is in a vague, undefined sort of way, for which they would be puzzled to account. It is not so with the Japanese labourer. With him, the sense of beauty is innate. Perhaps, also, he has more time to cultivate it. He is not so overworked as our English or German labourers.

Hübner was an Austrian noble and a diplomat who was once the right hand of Klemens von Metternich, the first state chancellor of the Austrian Empire. One could ask, therefore: how much did he truly know about the farmers in his homeland to make such an assertion? Furthermore, what knowledge did he have to allow him to write, "The fertility of the soil, the soft rains, the warm sun, do half the business" for the Japanese farmer and then go on to say that "There are many hours when he can rest, lying on his mat at his cabin door...while his eyes are feasting on the beautiful scenery around him, which he thoroughly enjoys"? We can only guess at how he came up with these ideas. However, even if he heard them through some idle gossip, the reality of what he felt remains. He may have truly been dazzled by the beautiful appearance of the villages he witnessed at the base of Mount Fuji, but it was clear that he understood that natural beauty was one of the key components used to create the appearance of Japanese villages at the time.

Hübner also mentioned the natural beauty that he saw while he was staying at a lodge in Hata Village in Hakone, including one particular occasion when he had to stay inside all day to weather the rain. Hata Village was a hamlet that often appeared in travel logs written by Edo-bound members of the Dutch Trading House, and Hübner also said it was "celebrated for the beauty of its site, and for its famous tea-house and gardens." He wrote:[65]

Can you conceive greater bliss than to lie on a scrupulously clean matting, in a lovely little room completely open to the garden, while a fine close rain falls from morning till night, giving a delicious freshness to the whole earth, and making you conscious of a renewal of health and strength?

In other words, Hübner had experienced what every Japanese person knew at the time, namely that life was exposed within nature, and this, in turn, gave one a deep sense of contentment and ease. With this in mind, it is worth noting the following description that Hübner made about his experience riding in a palanquin:[66]

When one travels in a cango [*kago*, or palanquin], one shaves, as it were, the very soil. During the morning, when crossing the meadows, the grass, moss, and flower stems tickled my face. My eyes pierced through those mysterious regions which the pedestrian treads under foot, but which escape his sight. It was to me like a revelation. The sun sparkled amidst the shadows cast by the broad leaves. I watched the bees, the butterflies, and millions of little insects gliding and fluttering through the blades of grass or sucking the calyx of the flowers. And what flowers! Great blue-bells gently inclining their heads over magnificent pinks; exquisite lilies, blossoming under a dome of long, thin leaves; and an endless variety of shades, and colours, and plants unknown in other hemispheres. Everything smiles in this country, the vegetation as well as the human beings.

As we can see, this passage vividly shows what the world looked like to the Japanese of yesteryear who travelled in palanquins.

It goes without saying that the Japanese of the late Edo period enjoyed going out during each of the four seasons. Naturally, this attracted the attention of the foreign observers, including Sherard Osborn, who quickly observed this upon visiting Edo in 1858. He wrote the following:[67]

Judging by the number of places adapted for public amusement in Yedo, we should write the people down as a most holiday-making set. The whole city was surrounded with gardens, tea-houses, and temples, which were all resorted to by the old and young of both sexes for recreation.

Berg, meanwhile, stated:[68]

The Japanese townspeople find considerable enjoyment in relaxing with their families and friends on a fine day in lovely natural surroundings during a holiday or similar event. They spend time in cemeteries and on the grounds of shrines, and they also go to teahouses located in beautiful scenic spots. Old people enjoy pleasant conversations with each other, and the young play together with their friends, go fishing, or shoot targets with small bows and arrows. Even the girls enjoy fishing and archery.

Naturally, Westerners at the time also practiced the custom of spending a peaceful day in a park or the pastoral landscape of the suburbs. We can see this in the affinity that French painters Jean-Antoine Watteau and François Boucher, both of whom were representative artists of the mid-eighteenth-century Rococo era, had for pastoral landscapes. In Europe, however, only nobles enjoyed this custom. Thus, Berg noted with surprise that even Japanese people from the lower classes were relaxing and frolicking in nature in this way. Morse echoed this by saying, "It is interesting to see how much enjoyment the people seem to take in beautiful scenery. Without exaggeration I see a hundred times as many people in this country enjoying beautiful cloud effects, lotus blooming, the parks and garden, as I do at home."[69]

Meanwhile, George Smith wrote the following based on his experiences in Nagasaki:[70]

On every fine day numbers of the middle class of tradesmen may be seen going forth in family groups and gay holiday attire to rusticate on their picturesque hills and to enjoy a refection in the public houses of refreshment...They seem to regard it a religious duty to keep holiday and make merry.

Smith also noted how, whenever he and his party rode out into the countryside, the villagers would ask them if "this day were Zondag (Sunday)." The Japanese had learned this word from the Dutch and simply assumed that it meant "holiday."

It goes without saying that the seasonal pastime that the Japanese enjoyed most of all was *hanami*, or flower-viewing (most often cherry blossom viewing). Scidmore experienced this in the late 1870s to early 1880s and wrote about Sugita Village, a suburb of Yokohama famous for its plum blossoms, saying:[71]

Sugita's plum-trees bud in January...During the rest of the year little heed is paid to Sugita's existence...With the blossoms Sugita puts on its holiday air, tea-houses open, tateba spring from the earth, and scores of low, red-blanketed benches are scattered through the grove, signals of tea and good cheer...Strings of sampans stream into shore, lines of jinrikishas file over the hills, zealous pilgrims come on foot...The tiny hamlet often has a thousand visitors in a day...Notwithstanding the crowds, everything is decorous, quiet, and orderly, and no more refined pleasure exists than this Japanese beatitude of sitting lost in revery and rapturous contemplation of a blossoming tree, or inditing a verse to *ume no hana*, and fastening the bit of paper to the branches.

According to Japanese architectural critic Kawazoe Noboru (1926–2015), cherry blossom viewing in Edo began at Kaneiji temple in Ueno, and by the Kanbun-Enpo era (1661–1681), the pastime had already become one met with much fanfare and oftentimes drunken merrymaking. However, in the 1680s, such merrymaking in Ueno was greatly restricted by sumptuary laws and other restrictions and was moved to other areas. Later on, festival-like cherry blossom viewing events sprang up in such locales as Asukayama (located in present-day Kita Ward, Tokyo) in the Genbun era (1736–1741), Nippori (located in present-day Arakawa Ward, Tokyo) in the Kansei era (1789–1801), and Mukojima (located in Tokyo's Sumida Ward) in the Tenpō era (1831–1845). Kawazoe stated that flower-viewing in the Kansei era was lively, but it was the furthest thing from an orgy. This is because the event featured a number of cultural events such as singing, *joruri* musical dramas, dancing, *haikai* poetry, and *kyoka*, or comic *tanka*, poem readings. Meanwhile, Asukayama, an area famous for cherry blossoms that is located four kilometers from Nihonbashi, attained fame by receiving 1,270 cherry trees from Tokugawa Yoshimune, the eighth Tokugawa shogun, who had the trees transplanted from Edo Castle's Fukiage Palace (the current site of the Fukiage Ōmiya Palace at the Imperial Palace in Tokyo) between the years 1720 and 1721. Kawazoe added that until Yoshimune had the trees transplanted, Asukayama was a simple forest of zelkova trees. In addition, Asukayama was not the only place that the shogun helped establish. He also created famous cherry blossom viewing areas at Shinagawa's Gotenyama, along the banks of the Sumida River, and along the banks of the Tamagawa Aqueduct in Koganei (the current site of Tokyo's Koganei Park).[72]

Of course, there were incidents of drunkenness and fighting at flower-viewing events. Alcock, for example, said:[73]

It is one of the great delights of the Japanese at Yeddo, during all April, to make picnics to these suburban gardens and temples. Groups of men, women, and children, by families, may be seen trooping along the shady roads on their way to enjoy the beauty of the opening spring...It is sad enough that this Arcadian scene is so often marred by intemperance. Not content with inhaling the freshness of the opening flowers, the men drink deep of saki; nor is this practice altogether confined, as one would fain have hoped, to the rougher sex. The latter make the streets unsafe on their return.

Iseki Takako, meanwhile, visited Asukayama in March 1840. She wrote the following about what transpired there in her diary:[74]

> I saw a man named Yabe take a graceful woman with him to Koshinzuka and when they both came back at nightfall, they encountered a group of men who were staggering drunk. The men saw the woman and approached, looking as if they were ready to start a fight. Everyone ran away at the commotion, but a male servant with a small child could not get away in time. The drunkards caught him and beat him severely, and it looked like both he and the child were going to get killed. That is when Yabe came back and tried to reason with and apologize to the men, but they did not listen to him and pulled out their swords. Yabe realized he had no choice but to fight and pulled out his own sword, killing one of the men and severely injuring another. With that, the remaining drunkards scattered off in terror.

Iseki also added that these drunken men, who had come from a distant province and served the governor there, had, in their drunkenness, seen Yabe and the woman flirting with each other and grew restless with jealously. Apparently, this was the trivial point that led to the fight. Now we can see what Alcock meant when he said, "They [The Japanese] are as much given to drunkenness as any of the northern races of Europe, as quarrelsome as the worst, and far more dangerous in their cups."

Despite such incidents, however, Morse and many other observers praised the good manners that the Japanese exhibited during holidays and other festive events. Scidmore also commented on the joy and cheerful foolishness of people enjoying flower-viewing at Mukojima in the late 1870s and early 1880s by saying "natural actors, orators, and pantomimists every one of them." She added, "With all this intoxication, only glee and affection manifest themselves. No fighting, no rowdyism, no rough words accompany the spring saturnalia."[75] This view may have been a bit too favorable, but it truly expressed what she felt. Thus, it appears that there were both good and bad aspects to the Japanese of yesteryear.

We have kind of strayed off course here and gone into the nature of Japanese drinking habits, but as it was so eloquently described in so many detailed examples of these flower-viewing events, the Japanese enjoyed and found amusement in each of the four seasons, and this was unquestionably tied to flowers in general. This is basically the view that Scidmore had, even devoting an entire chapter in her book to "Flower Festivals." She said, "The calendar is divided into the time of the camellia, the plum, the cherry, the wistaria, the lotus, the chrysanthemum, and the maple," and she also mentioned peonies and azaleas. She also listed the best times and places to view all of these flowers in Tokyo in the late 1870s and early 1880s.[76] It is worth noting that highly skilled floricultural techniques produced these seasonal flowers, as we can clearly see in the life-sized chrysanthemum figures of Dango-zaka (located in present-day Bunkyō Ward, Tokyo) and other examples.

Siebold stated the following in a passage, titled "The Floral Calendar," in his magnum opus, *Nippon*:[77]

> Even under the thatched roofs of impoverished village homes, one can see branches with green leaves and flowers occupy what little space there is. Surely this must please the gods of the home. Under fragrant cherry trees and trellises made of blooming wisteria, meanwhile, people hold cheerful parties from which emanate feelings of joy and happiness, and one can hear music and poetry fill the air in celebration of the world of plants…Bountiful nature gives the natural people of this climate a continuous calendar; there are plants and flowers that embody the four seasons, and there are flowers and fruit that come into season each month. Thus, the Japanese have created what could be called the "floral calendar."

Siebold listed a number of floral species and the respective months in which they appeared based on such works as the *Chaseki sōkashū* (Collection of Tea Ceremony Flower Arrangements), a book published in Edo in 1810, the *Kinototori hanagoyomi* (Floral Calendar of 1825), a work published in 1825, and a floral calendar featuring pictures that was published in Osaka.

Nature provided the springboard for these flowering trees and grasses as enjoyed by the people, but it was the high level of floricultural skill during the Edo period that ultimately created and perfected them. According to botanist Nakao Sasuke (1916–1993), the primary centers of floriculture in the world were initially western Asia and China, while Japan was a secondary center that derived much from the Chinese. In the Edo period, however, Japan had already surpassed China and had advanced far beyond western Europe, which was another secondary center. In other words, Japanese floriculture in the Edo period was one of the most-unique and most-flourishing times in history. Nakao also stated that floriculture began spreading to the masses in the Genroku period (1688–1704), 200 years before similar movements would take place in western Europe. He went on to say that there was a development of floricultural events that everyone could enjoy and take part in, such as flower viewing and chrysanthemum figures, and that numerous floricultural groups formed, floricultural experts such as gardeners and landscapers appeared, and books on gardening began to be published. Nakao also stressed the point that Japan pioneered all of these developments. Selective breeding of camellias and cherry trees, meanwhile, began as early as the Muromachi period (1392–1573), but in the Edo period, camellias were introduced to Europe where they were met with considerable praise, and Japanese horticulturalists from this time period had created anywhere from 400–500 varieties of cherry trees and 200 varieties of plum trees. Nakao stated that this high level of selective breeding on flowering trees only took place in Japan.[78]

This flourishing floriculture of the Edo period was widely introduced to the rest of the world through the writings of Engelbert Kaempfer, Thunberg, Siebold, and other observers. Their writings attracted Fortune, who traveled from Britain to hunt for rare plants in Japan, a mission he carried out twice in the years 1860 and 1861. His goal was to collect plants, "many of which were entirely new to Europe, and of great interest and value." For this reason, he mainly visited Dango-zaka and Somei (located in present-day Toshima Ward, Tokyo), which were both famous floricultural centers at the time. He wrote the following about the latter:[79]

> Park-like scenery, trees and gardens, neatly-clipped hedges, succeeded each other; and my attendant yakoneens [yakunin, or shogunate officials] at length announced that we had arrived at the village of Su-mae-yah [Somei]. The whole country here is covered with nursery-gardens. One straight road, more than a mile in length, is lined with them. I have never seen, in any part of the world, such a large number of plants cultivated for sale. Each nursery covers three or four acres of land, is nicely kept, and contains thousands of plants, both in pots and in the open ground. As these nurseries are much alike in their features, a description of one will give a good idea of them all.

Fortune found an abundance of sophisticated garden plants in Dango-zaka and Somei that were as yet unknown in Europe, and he bought them all. Japan was a literal treasure trove for him. However, he did not limit the scope of his quest to Dango-zaka and Somei. Gardeners throughout Edo, for example, brought many rare species to the British Legation where he was staying, thus helping him to grow his collection. He also continued his search for plants while he was on his way to the lodging station in Kanagawa, during which time he had hired a Japanese assistant to help him find rare plant varieties at temples and farm villages in the suburbs.

Fortune was a member of the Royal Horticultural Society of London and had originally been dispatched to China to collect garden plants on their behalf. He sent a number of newfound species to his home country, but soon this vocation became almost an obsession for him. Namely, he made it his undying mission to bring unknown flower varieties from around the world back to Britain and, in turn, disseminate them to the rest of Europe. He first set foot in Japan in Nagasaki. Siebold, who had succeeded in visiting Japan for a second time, lived in the Nagasaki suburbs at the time, so Fortune soon paid him a courtesy call so as to view his gardens. The elder Siebold was out at the time, but his son Alexander was there to receive Fortune, and he said that the British plant hunter snapped branches and picked flowers off all of the new plants without even asking for permission. The elder Siebold, upon hearing about this, quickly grew nervous as he suspected Fortune's actions were those of a jealous academic looking to claim some of his specimens.[80] Naturally, Fortune made no mention of this incident in his book, *Yedo and Peking*.

In 1860, Fortune surveyed and, as he put it, ransacked all the flora he could find in the autumn and winter. However, his tenacity as a plant hunter brought him back to Japan the following year, this time to observe flora in the spring and summer. At the time, the only foreign visitors who could enter the city of Edo were diplomats from the various treaty nations. An invitation from Alcock, therefore, is what allowed Fortune to stay there in 1860. However, Alcock was summoned back to Hong Kong due to the Michael Moss incident and was no longer in Japan when Fortune came back the second time. The chargé d'affaires was Fredrick Gerhard Myburgh (1838–1868). Fortune did not wish to deal with Myburgh, so he found favor with Townsend Harris, the United States ambassador to Japan, who welcomed him with open arms. As a result, Fortune was able to see Somei and Dango-zaka in May. He stated:[81]

> The Su-mae-yah [Somei] gardens…presented quite a different appearance from what they had done in the autumn before. They had put on their summer dress; the trees were covered with leaves, and many flowering shrubs and herbaceous plants were in full bloom.

In both Dango-zaka and Somei, Fortune found rare plant species he had not seen the previous year, and he bought them one after another. As he put it, "every corner was examined." According to Nakao, this allowed Fortune to bring several plant varieties back to Britain, including male spotted laurel trees and Japanese primrose. Nakao went on to say that trees with speckled leaves were almost never seen in European gardens, with the notable exception of spotted laurel trees. However, there were no male trees in Europe, so they could never bear fruit. After Fortune introduced male spotted laurel trees from Japan, they could be seen bearing fruit all over Europe in the autumn and winter. In addition, the Japanese primrose differed greatly from the European primrose, but after Fortune transfused it to his home country, it met with much praise and fanfare among the people. A number of new variants have been developed since then and are now being imported back to Japan.[82] As fate would have it, however, Fortune soon stirred up controversy by being a British citizen staying at the United States Legation. Myburgh wrote a letter to Fortune and demanded his immediate withdrawal from Edo to which Fortune had no choice but to obey. Nevertheless, he had acquired more than enough of what he wanted and could gracefully avoid fighting with Myburgh. Fortune was able to send a sarcastic reply to Myburgh at the legation, however.

According to Kawazoe Noboru, meanwhile, Fortune had gone from Dango-zaka to Somei, but did not seem to be aware of the equally brilliant trees and flowers growing in Sugamo (located in present-day Toshima Ward, Tokyo), nor did he realize that such specimens were on display over a much wider area. Kawazoe even stated that Somei and Sugamo literally comprised the largest center of flower and tree cultivation in the world.[83]

According to Kawazoe, the reason why Edo-period floriculture was the best in the world at the time was apparently due to gardens established at daimyo and *hatamoto* residences or at temples and shrines, all of which were of a truly high caliber. There were 1,000 gardens among the daimyo residences alone, and there were 300 on the same level as Koishikawa-Kōrakuen, and Rikugien—two famous gardens located in present-day Bunkyō Ward, Tokyo. In addition, there were probably thousands of gardens in Edo if we include those at *hatamoto* residences and on temple and shrine grounds. Thus, the city likely looked just like Lindau described it, namely, that it was buried in so many parks and gardens that it resembled one big, endless garden.

Naturally, gardens need beautiful plants for people to look at, and I mentioned earlier that, in order to fulfill this need, a center of horticulture developed in the northern suburbs of Edo. Edo's floriculture was led by the warrior class. There were several proponents, including the aforementioned example of Tokugawa Yoshimune transplanting trees from his own palatial garden. First and foremost, the warriors used gardening as a form of leisure. The azaleas of Ōkubo, Tokyo, for example, soon surpassed those of Somei as a result of gun regiment warriors living there spending a lot of their spare time in the pursuit of plant and flower cultivation. Meanwhile, the officials of the Kumamoto domain (located in present-day Kumamoto Prefecture) created the famous series of flowers known as the *Higo Rokka*, or the "six flowers of Higo Province."

We also cannot ignore contributions from temples and shrines. When Fortune was hunting for rare plant species in the areas surrounding Kanagawa, for example, he set his sights on one of the temples there. It was here that he found and obtained the seeds of his dream tree: the *asunaro*, or hiba arborvitae.

Many Japanese writers also described the nature of gardens at warrior homes. In September 1840, Iseki Takako was invited to the home of her daughter-in-law's older brother, Toda Ujiyoshi. Toda was a *hatamoto* with a stipend of five thousand *koku* who would later be one of the officials who received Commodore Perry during his first visit to Japan. Incidentally, Iseki was born in 1785 and entered the Iseki family as the second wife of another *hatamoto* named Iseki Chikafusa. Therefore, she was fifty-five years old when she made this visit. Her husband had already died, and her son was actually the child of her husband's first wife. She was a learned scholar of classical Japanese and was leading a calm, comfortable life in her retirement.

When Iseki arrived at the Toda residence and saw the garden, she said that the family had an affinity for trees and had set up a ledge on the opposite side of the garden for numerous plants and trees planted in flower pots. In addition, there were a number of *Ezo-giku* (China asters) in full bloom at the time on the left and right sides of the garden. Iseki's hosts had set up several seats in the garden for a party, and Iseki sat there and began reciting poems about the China asters. In the end, however, she said that she was too drunk to remember anything when night had fallen and when it was time to go home. When she woke up the next morning at her own home, she saw that there were China asters now blooming in her garden as well. She said that there were so many in her garden that they had to have come from somewhere else because they did not grow in the wild. She wrote that they had grown in number after several officials had gone to the island of Ezo (Hokkaido) for a year and brought them back, hence the name *Ezo-giku*. She enjoyed looking at the purple flowers, which could be mistaken for irises or wisteria, and she wrote that she was intrigued by Ezo after thinking about how such lovely flowers bloomed on that as-yet-undeveloped island.[84] This whole episode relates to the love of floriculture on the part of shogunate officials from Edo.

The officials that Iseki said went to Ezo for a year were likely government surveyors sent to inspect the land of Ezo (Hokkaido) during the Tenmei era (in the 1780s) under orders from Tanuma Okitsugu, a *rōjū*, or senior counsellor to the shogun, at the time. The survey mission made several trips to Ezo, and Mogami Tokunai (1754–1836), who was a famous geographer and explorer around the time when Iseki was born, was also a member. Some

China asters were brought to Edo as a byproduct of these expeditions, and fifty years later, this beautiful flower had taken root and was blooming in gardens across the city.

However, affectation for flowers soon trickled down to the middle and lower classes. As I mentioned earlier, the Japanese of the Edo period used the floral calendar as a guide for gathering at famous flower viewing spots and temples and shrines throughout the year and in each of the four seasons. As Nakao stated, however, the custom of flower-viewing was by no means a universal human characteristic. Rather, this unique aspect developed when floriculture spread to the masses in the Edo period. Humbert, meanwhile, saw that the people's fervor for the floral calendar was also linked to cultural tastes. He stated the following:[85]

> When the orchards are in flower, the citizen, the painter, and the student, are seized with rural fancies: they fly from the labours and the pleasures of the capital, and hide themselves for a day, or for many days, if it be possible, among the rustic roofs of the tea-houses.

Eliza Scidmore, moreover, noticed elderly men sitting under plum trees at the Kameido Tenjin Shrine (located in Tokyo's Kōtō Ward), sipping on some tea and smoking tobacco while slowly and quietly writing some words down on pieces of paper with ink brushes. She said, "Then, with radiant face and cheerful muttering, the ancient poet will slip his toes into his clogs and tie the little slip to the branches of the most charming tree."[86] Naturally, the elderly poet had composed a haiku verse or a *tanka* poem. John La Farge also heard from a friend that he saw "in cherry-blossom time some old gentleman, with capacious sakè gourd in hand and a big roll of paper in his girdle, seat himself below the blossom-showers, and look, and drink, and write verses, all by himself, with no gallery to help him."[87] Hearing this, La Farge wondered, "Where else would be possible the charming absurdity of [this] story?" This happened in the early Meiji period, but already by the beginning of the nineteenth century Siebold had written the following about Japan:[88]

> In Japan, a love of flowers and poetry go hand in hand. The plum and cherry trees attract the eyes of people with their snow-like flowers, and when the wisterias, in full bloom, thickly cover the wisteria trellises, the Japanese poet relaxes under the shade of the flowers he holds so dear, writes down what is on his mind with a light brush on a small piece of paper sprinkled with gold dust, and then ties this paper to the very tree to which he composed the verse.

As a love for flowers disseminated itself into every corner of society, popular trends in flowers repeatedly became commonplace in the late Edo period, particularly for such varieties of herbaceous flowers as chrysanthemums, morning glories, primrose, irises, and Japanese rohdeas. Naturally, this came about due to the demands of townspeople of the middle-to-lower class who did not have the ability to keep large-scale gardens. However, even in these cases, the warriors maintained constant initiative, as seen in the *Rohdea japonica* trend during the Kaei era (1848–1854). According to Kawazoe, retired *hatamoto* warriors and lower-ranking vassals skillfully cultivated the *Rohdea japonica* to increase their income, a point the *Machi Bugyō Jōshinsho* [Town Magistrates' Reports] of 1853 actually lamented about a great deal. Naturally, this was the same year that Perry landed in Japan, so the report criticized the *hatamoto* for getting too caught up in battling for profits with the townspeople rather than focusing more of their attention on Perry's black ships, an event which was turning Japan on its head at the time.

In addition, the flower and tree culture in Japan at the time was by no means run only by the warriors, upper-class townspeople in the big cities, or master gardeners. Fortune, for instance, wrote the following about the farm villages near the lodging station in Kanagawa:[89]

> As we rode onwards we passed many snug little suburban residencies, farm-houses, and cottages, having little gardens in front containing a few of the favourite flowering-plants of the country. A remarkable feature in the Japanese character is, that, even to the lowest classes, all have an inherent love for flowers, and find in the cultivation of a few pet plants an endless source of recreation and unalloyed pleasure. If this be one of the tests of a high state of civilization amongst a people, the lower orders amongst the Japanese come out in a most favourable light when contrasted with the same classes amongst ourselves.

Isabella Bird, meanwhile, wrote the following about what she saw as she passed through the southern suburbs of Kyoto on her way to Nara:[90]

> We travelled through seven miles of continuous streets before we got into the country, much of the distance being among the dwellings of the poorest classes; but it is industrious poverty, without vice or squalor, and nearly every mean, contracted, dingy abode is displaying at least one great, bulging chrysanthemum, such as would drive the Temple gardener wild with envy.

Henry Faulds, who came to Japan in 1874 and operated a hospital at the foreign settlement in Tsukiji, wrote the following about his excursion to the base of Mount Fuji:[91]

> The Japanese are passionately fond not only of beautiful scenery, but of flowers; and I was not quite surprised when the sober looking coolie laid down the shafts of his rickety "hansom," and rushed amid the tall flowers with open arms like a school-boy. After his fit of enthusiasm had somewhat subsided, he returned with an armful of bright yellow and white compositae, orange lilies, and some graceful sprays, on which shone numbers of beautiful large crimson scarlet brambles, or rather raspberries, with which he adorned his vehicle.

Nevertheless, this medical missionary also had to express some displeasure about this experience, adding that "Thanks to the aesthetic culture of my drawer, we lost our way twice on this lava plain."

All of the examples above show just how important flowers were for the civilization of old Japan. However, flowers were not the only scenic objects that decorated each passing season and created rhythm for the year. There were also places famous for snow and for insects, for example. Humbert said:[92]

> In winter, if the snow should fall, it is considered a duty as well as a pleasure that whole families should go and contemplate the strange aspect of the statues in the enclosure of Kanda-Miōdzin [Kanda Myojin shrine, located in present-day Arakawa Ward, Tokyo], in the high pagoda of Asaksa [Asakusa]; but above all, no one must fail to retire to certain tea-houses in the faubourgs, such as those of Niken-Tschaïa, in the neighbourhood of Foukagawa [Fukagawa, located in present-day Koto Ward, Tokyo], to admire the spectacle of the bay and the country under the novel decoration. In summer, it is agreed that the concert of grasshoppers must be listened to upon the heights of Dökwan-yama [Dokan-yama, a hill located in Arakawa Ward, Tokyo], and a good family man would never fail to take his children thither, plentifully supplied with little wicker cages, in order to bring back some of these sweet songsters.

According to Kawazoe, Dōkan-yama, a continuous hill stretching from Ueno to Nippori and then on to Asukayama, was the best scenic spot in Edo. It was also famous for larks and its autumn insects.[93] When Humbert mentioned "grasshoppers," he was, of course, referring to the crickets and other singing insects there.

In Japan, there was, and still is, a custom of viewing the moon on the fifteenth night of the eighth month in the lunisolar calendar, which falls on September in the Western calendar. Although people still celebrate this custom to some degree today, the Japanese of yesteryear had particular affection for this time period, with their hearts abeat with the poetic rhythm of the season. In Iseki Takako's diary, her entry for 1840.8.13 (lunisolar) shows that she could not wait to see the moon on the night of the fifteenth:[94]

> In the evening, the moon soon rises and shines its light like a beautiful flower. I have heard people say that since long ago, one cannot get to sleep on nights when the moon is so beautiful, and I now think they are right. While it is still evening, the moon passes just over the thick forest of fir trees and immediately floods its light into this lowly cottage, making the inside of the dwelling as bright as day and illuminating all of the futons on the floor. There is no way to describe how calm and cool this unbridled light makes you feel.

Iseki went on to imagine that, if friends gathered together to watch the moon on this occasion and if they drank a fair amount of sake without getting too out of hand, talking with each other all night long, they would never get tired of this long sleepless night. Of course, on the night of the fifteenth, people offered rice cakes and sake to the moon and placed blades of pampas grass into bottles.

Musashino is an area in the Kanto region of Japan famous for viewing the moon. Long ago, this area was so rustic that even villages and buildings were hard to find. On one particular night, the moon used to rise up from behind the mountains instead of from behind the houses, which had by now grown in number. It was a scene from an age that has long since passed, and now, the pampas grass was the only reminder of the past, when the moon would emerge from and rise above the grass and then disappear beneath the grass again. Iseki felt truly blessed to have lived in this age and could not help but write a poem, which read:

> The moon shines down,
> Lighting the heavens and all the land.
> The plains of Musashi.

Sadly, the moon no longer brightens up the insides of homes like it used to, and no one loses sleep over the peak season for viewing the moon in Japan today. Even though some people do continue to follow this custom, it is usually just done for show and is a far cry from the way it used to create rhythm in the lives of the people. In Iseki's age, however, people longed to see and pass the night with the autumn moon, a tradition that became synonymous with their very existence.

There were even religious connotations attached to the moon. The lodging stations at Takanawa and Shinagawa were a case in point. All night long on the 26th of the seventh month (August 23 in the Western calendar), these areas were apparently bustling with people anxious to see the moon. Iseki wrote:[95]

> The people just want to see the instant the moon rises rather than engage in any graceful or refined ceremony...Some lowly commoners even lay their mats down by the river, rubbing their sacred beads in prayer to the Buddha as they wait for the moon. Families of high standing, meanwhile, hang glowing lanterns from the eaves of their houses, indulge in sake, and sing along with the sounds of the koto as they wait for the moon to rise on that special night. Vendors also gather along the main roads, which are bustling with passersby.

According to Iseki, the events that took place on the night of the fifteenth were based on a folk belief in which people viewed the light of the moon shining just above the surface of the sea as the Amida triad (the Buddha Amida flanked by bodhisattvas Kannon and Seishi) and prayed to them. People would watch the sea intently, and when the surface of the ocean lit up, the masses would begin invoking the name of Amida, creating a veritable uproar. Iseki's residence was in Kudan-zaka (located in present-day Chiyoda Ward, Tokyo), so she could easily see people, many of whom gathered along the coast, as well as the fires from vending stalls and people's homes lighting up the night sky. Iseki was a scholar of classical Japanese literature, and she looked down on Buddhist priests who preached that both the sun and moon were the Buddha.

Speaking of the moon, Noda Shigesuke, the mountain ascetic I mentioned earlier, had a strange experience when he entered shogunate lands in Hida Province (located in present-day Gifu Prefecture) from Kaga Province (present-day Ishikawa Prefecture) in the fifth month of 1815. He wrote:[96]

> The Hida guard station is in Nakayama, and, as these are the lands of His Lordship, the Shogun, the guards also belong to the central government. I took out and showed a ticket to pass through here. But the guard at this station was an eccentric man, and told me that I could not use the ticket. He said, "You need to recite a verse of poetry to go through." This presented us with a problem, as many of us were so uneducated that we could not even create half a poem, let alone a

full verse. When we respectfully declined and asked for his mercy, the guard said he could not let us pass because even a merchant from Osaka had written a poem earlier in the day and been granted permission to pass, so they could not make an exception for us. Therefore, I decided to present a poem about the bright moon as viewed the night before. He gave me some paper and an inkstone. Even though this was a shogunate guard station, I did not hesitate to write down my poem and present it to them. It met with much praise and a long discussion.

Naturally, this is a historical document that shows just how widespread the fervor for poetry was at the time, but this is not all it shows. As mentioned earlier, Siebold stated that the Japanese love for flowers and poetry went hand in hand, but this was not necessarily limited to flowers. Other scenic objects of the four seasons, including the moon, invoked poetry in the hearts of the people at the time. The guard who met Noda may have been a bit eccentric, but he was simply following the old Japanese custom of reading and listening to poetry about scenic objects. Noda came to the same conclusion and, therefore, decided to write a poem about the moon. According to historian Ujiie Mikito (1954–), moreover, in the Edo period, there was a custom by which traveling performers could receive permission to pass if they put on a performance for the guards should they fail to have a ticket to go through such a checkpoint.[97] Noda's experience was probably similar to this. Even so, Noda actually did have a pass to get through the guard station.

Naturally, these scenic objects of the four seasons belonged to a nature that civilization had tamed, a concept depicted in the somewhat notorious Japanese word *kachō fūei*, which means "living with the beauties of nature." However, human beings cannot live in raw nature. The natural world is actually chaos, and we cannot exist within it. The actual state of the natural world has, from the beginning of time, gone beyond the human realm of understanding. Thus, human beings have to use a meaningful cosmology to humanize nature into a world that they can inhabit. Creating a meaningful framework within this chaotic world is the concept that we call "civilization," and it is our destiny, as human beings, to restructure this meaningless world into one with a meaningful cosmology. The issue, then, becomes whether this restructured world proves to be one in which people can find truly meaningful lives. The civilization of the later Edo period organized the world into a cycle of seasonal scenic objects and incorporated them into the lives of the people from all ranks, both rich and poor. As this cycle repeated itself over the years, it allowed people to identify the happy and sad aspects of life and provided them with guidance throughout their entire lives. Moreover, the people created stronger bonds with each other through the flowers, snow, birds and insects, and the moon. It may be easy to criticize this civilization, but the people who lived within it were by no means unhappy, as we can see in the way Iseki aptly stated that she was thankful to be born in the Edo period.

Nakao Sasuke was keenly aware that scenic objects of the four seasons meant everything to the Japanese at the time. There was a particular group of potted plants, which people today call *koten engei shokubutsu*, or classical garden plants, and this group included whisk ferns, spikemoss, Japanese rohdeas, sekkoku orchids, wind orchids, and other species. As Nakao stated, these flowers were developed and reached the height of their popularity in the Edo period, but then declined from the Meiji period onward to the point where today, such plants are only grown and preserved among a small niche of farmers. These plants received a high level of breeding based on unique aesthetics, but Nakao stated that Westerners did not find them attractive at all. Nevertheless, we should remember that speckled species within this group were viewed differently, as was the case with Fortune's specific interest in speckled plants, which were almost nonexistent in the West at the time. He wrote the following:[98]

> The most remarkable feature in the nurseries of Su-mae-yah [Somei] and Dang-o-zaka is the large number of plants with variegated leaves. It is only a very few years since our taste in Europe led us to take an interest in and to admire those curious freaks of nature called variegated plants.

According to Nakao, Westerners did not show an interest in classical garden plants because, as even children could see, such plants lacked any discernable beauty upon viewing them for the first time. In other words, education and knowledge were required to appreciate their beauty. For this reason, middle-class warriors and merchants, as well as village chiefs and landowners in rural areas, had the knowledge to grow and preserve such plants. Nakao went on to state that these groups understood their innate social standing, as coined by Kaibara Ekiken (1630–1714), a Japanese Confucianist and herbalist. Namely, they were not overly concerned with success, and they led stable and peaceful lives. People who followed these teachings found cultivating classical garden plants to be an enjoyable pasttime.[99]

Nakao called these classical garden plants "living witnesses" to this unique time in Japanese culture. The current climate in Japan, which champions rising to the challenge of whatever life brings and brandishing one's individuality, would likely have viewed the cultivation of whisk ferns and Japanese rohdeas as an unadventurous hobby enjoyed by retirees. However, such plants contained the mentality of the Edo period, namely, a mentality in which people poured their efforts into otherwise unappealing plants and tried to find goodness and beauty that corresponded with the world, no matter how minute or plain that existence may be. The meaning of life did not require fame or success. People of this age valued the cosmology they used to determine how they fit in with scenic objects from the four seasons, or, in other words, the cycle of life. Whisk ferns and Japanese rohdeas were a part of this cosmology. It is only natural for us to oppose the mentality of this unique time in Japanese culture, but we cannot deny that it brought some happiness to the people.

Whatever the case, the natural views of this time period, which the people helped to create, were likely quite beautiful. Iseki, for instance, never forgot the memories of playing with her family at Futako-Tamagawa (located in present-day Setagaya Ward, Tokyo) when she was a young girl. She wrote:[100]

> In the eighth month, we pass along the road where thousands of flowers bloom on both sides to reach the wide riverbank, where we lay a mat. People gather and gaze at the Tamagawa River, which truly looks like a pearl. The water is as clear as a mirror, and the grains of sand in the gardens are as pure as if they have been polished. Rare grasses grow and flowers bloom on the riverbank, and on the gently sloping hill to the side, where young pine trees form a dense forest, small children collect hatsutake mushrooms. On the opposite side of the river, a range of mountains stretches off into the distance. What an incredible day.

Iseki also recalled that her family hired some fishermen from a nearby village. The fishermen placed their nets in the river and, with Iseki and her family's help, caught some sweetfish. Iseki said the grilled sweetfish tasted better than anything else she had ever eaten.

She had also tried goby fishing at Haneda long before. The dawn was still dark when she set out on a boat, but soon the sun rose, and she said that it had never looked so big before. She went on to say that the day was so clear and bright that she could see the mountains beyond the sea in the distance and that the scattered ships with their sails raised looked like they had been painted there, and she said the fishing boats coming and going truly looked like fall leaves floating to the ground.[101]

In addition, when Iseki was a child, she went to Komabano (located in present-day Meguro Ward, Tokyo) with some other children to catch crickets, and she spent the whole day playing there. This was the shogun's hunting grounds and was normally off limits to the public, but someone in her group knew the shogun's falconer and they were allowed to enter. She wrote:[102]

> When we entered the wide plain, it felt indescribable. The grasses and other plants constantly served as grazing fodder and did not grow that high, the landscape was completely covered in green as far as the eye could see, and we saw flowers of the bush clover and yellow valerian mixed together with pampas grass. But the seven autumn flowers were not the only plants growing here. Elated, we picked flower after flower, snapping off branches and stems until we grew tired of doing so. I never had so much fun in my life as I did in this place. Meanwhile, the boys started rummaging through the miscanthus in their hunt for some bugs, whereby some of the winged creatures, including crickets and grasshoppers, fluttered off into the sky.

In addition, Iseki and her party could see Mount Fuji in the distance from this field of flowers.

In her later years, Iseki went to stay with her stepson's family, who cared for her in her old age, and she often went out to meet with her classical Japanese literature and poetry friends. Her life seemed to be happy, but it had not always been so. Her first marriage failed, and she eventually married into the Iseki family, becoming Iseki Chikafusa's second wife. Thus, she likely experienced the misfortunes and struggles of life just like everyone else, but she had these beautiful memories of nature that constantly brightened up her life and actually supported the central portion of her being.

Imaizumi Mine (1855–1937) was another person who could not forget the sights she saw when she was young. In her case, it was the beauty of the Sumida River, which she knew and loved since she was little. Mine was born to the Katsuragawa family, whose heirs were famous for their excellence in Dutch studies and for serving as personal physicians to the shoguns, their family, and their concubines. Mine led a happy childhood as a popular girl among the students who gathered at her home. However, after the Tokugawa shogunate collapsed, the Katsuragawa family also declined, and the man she eventually married, Imaizumi Toshiharu, was often imprisoned for being affiliated with Etō Shinpei and Saigō Takamori, officials who had stirred up rebellions against the new Meiji government. Therefore, her life was filled with great hardship. However, in *Nagori no Yume* (Remains of a Dream), a book she dictated and which was eventually published three years after her death in 1940, the splendor of Edo glows on every page:[103]

The Sumida River in my youth was truly beautiful...It was almost like a crystal flowing across the land...Among the many childhood memories I have of stretching up to gaze through the fence from my window, I will never forget the beautiful sight of the houseboats floating on quiet, mirror-like water, a vision that even now seems like an illusion...The boats glided past the bridges and the sounds of shamisen love songs reverberated on the river, completely taming the water with its tone and resonance. The boatmen usually only wore a yukata, such that their hands just barely passed through sleeves blowing in the wind, and they also wore tightly twisted headbands...They looked dashing. Drops of water from the oars they branded plopped into the river like beads.

Imaizumi also wrote the following about her experiences viewing flowers:[104]

There is water in Mukojima in which one can see the reflection of the flowers on its surface. The beauty of the flowers amplifies the beauty of the water, while the water, in turn, makes the flowers look even more beautiful. It was truly remarkable seeing the reflection of the flowers in the Sumida River...The flowers in Ueno were also beautiful, and there I heard the sound of a bell ringing. Was the bell causing the cherry blossoms to scatter about or were the flowers causing the bell to ring? It was almost a divine experience.

She went on to say that "some time ago" someone showed her a "recently taken" picture of Ryōgoku. She was probably referring to a picture taken around 1935, but all she could do was gasp in awe.[105] She did this because she knew the scenery that she had cherished in her heart and that she wanted to last forever had completely disappeared. However, the beautiful elegance of that view could not be erased from her memory, and because of this memory, her life was worth living.

The meaning of a civilization lies in its framework of views that works its way into the hearts of human experience and provides evidence for the meaning of life. As Westerners typically say, Japan is most definitely blessed with beautiful natural conditions. However, the Japanese natural beauty they praised was, in the end, the product of a separate and unique civilization. For example, pine forests were second-growth forests that replaced laurel forests that had been destroyed, and bush clovers were plants that accompanied second-growth forests rather than primordial forests.[106]

The so-called "scenes of Japan" that Westerners wanted to praise were, with the exception of virgin lands deep within the mountains, those created by interactions between the Japanese and nature, or, in other words, by the way in which the Japanese lived. In fact, we do not even have to mention certain elements of this scenery, such as the houseboats, sailboats, the headbands of the boatmen, pristine riverbanks, and thatched roofs with irises blooming on top of them. In other words, Japan's natural beauty was not only a product of interactions between its unique civilization and the country's topography, but also the cosmology that the civilization built to acclimate within it an awareness of the four seasons. In addition, the Edo-period Japanese tasted the fulfillment of life within this cosmology, and they internalized the cycle of cosmologic time within their individual lives. Moreover, the fulfillment of life that was created by opening their awareness to nature and being aware of its correspondence with everything bred a strong sense of fellowship and feelings of sympathy among the people, even in the dimension of society. Such feelings did not just apply to relationships between people, either. It also included every living creature.

Notes:

1 Werner, *Die Preussiche Expedition*, 24.

2 Pompe, *Vijf Jaren*, 273.

3 Lindau, *Un Voyage Autour*, 31.

4 Berg, *Eulenburg Expedition*, Vol. 2, 116.

5 Kattendijke, *Uittreksel*, 49.

6 Young, *General Grant*, Vol. 2, 473–4.

7 Chamberlain, *Things Japanese*, 439.

8 Brandt, *Dreiunddreissig*, 239–40.

9 Eulenburg, *Ost-Asien*, 147, 150.

10 Humbert, *Japan and the Japanese*, 9, 25–7.

11 Berg, *Eulenburg Expedition*, Vol. 1, 118–9.

12 Fortune, *Yedo and Peking*, 94–5.

13 Margaret T.K. Ballagh, *Glimpses of Old Japan 1861-1866* (Tokyo, 1908), 91.

14 Morse, *Japanese Homes*, 77.

15 Fortune, *Yedo and Peking*, 50.

16 Scidmore, *Jinrikisha*, 12.

17 Morse, *Day by Day*, Vol. 2, 53.

18 Beauvoir, *Pekin, Jeddo, and San Francisco*, 201.

19 Humbert, *Japan and the Japanese*, 340.

20 Hübner, *Ramble*, 251, 254, 267, 251.

21 Morse, *Day by Day*, Vol. 1, 47.

22 Siebold, *Nippon: Archiv*, Vol. 1, 50.

23 Guimet, *Promenades-Tokyo-Nikko*, 135.

24 Siebold, *Nippon: Archiv*, Vol. 1, 145.

25 Fischer, *Bijdrage*, Vol. 1, 102, 116.

26 Suenson, *Skitser*, 131.

27 Fraser, *Diplomatist's Wife*, 4.

28 Fraser, *Diplomatist's Wife*, 3.

29 Lühdorf, *Acht Monate*, 259.

30 Lühdorf, *Acht Monate*, 55.

31 Thunberg, *Travels*, 128.

32 Siebold, *Nippon: Archiv*, Vol. 1, 169–71.

33 Willman, *Journal*, 27, 28, 32, 35 (translated from the Japanese version).

34 Humbert, *Japan and the Japanese*, Vol. 1, 11 (translated from the Japanese version).

35 Berg, *Eulenburg Expedition*, Vol. 1, 110, 127, 169–70.

36 Arminjon, *Il Giappone*, 90.

37 Tilley, *Japan, the Amoor*, 144–5.

38 Werner, *Die Preussiche Expedition*, 43, 45.

39 Bousquet, *Le Japon*, Vol. 1, 68–9.

40 Berg, *Eulenburg Expedition*, Vol. 1, 71.

41 Hübner, *Ramble*, 285.

42 Alfred Roussin, *Une Campagne Sur le Côtes du Japon* (Paris, 1866). No English translation of Roussin's work exists, so passages that appear in this book have been translated from the Japanese version. See Rusan [Roussin], *Huransu Shikan no Shimonoseki kaisenki* [A French Officer's Record of the Battle of Shimonoseki] (Shinjinbutsu Oraisha, 1987), 180. Subsequent citations will appear as Roussin, *Une Campagne*, and will list page numbers from the Japanese text.

43 Brandt, *Dreiunddreissig*, 240.

44 Cortazzi, *Mitford's Japan*, 20.

45 Lindau, *Un Voyage Autour*, 165, 171–3.

46 Koenraad Wolter Gratama, *Leraar onder de Japanners: Briven van Dr. K. W. Gratama Betreffende Zijn Verblijf in Japan, 1866-1871* (Amsterdam, 1987). No English translation of Gratama's work exists, so passages that appear in this book have been translated from the Japanese version. See Haratama [Gratama], *Orandajin no mita Bakumatsu-Meiji no Nihon: Kagakusha Haratama shokanshū* [Bakumatsu and Meiji-era Japan Seen through the Eyes of a Dutchman: The Letters of Koenraad Wolter Gratama, Chemist] (Saikon Shuppan, 1993), 51. Subsequent citations will appear as Gratama, *Leraar*, and will list page numbers from the Japanese text.

47 Smith, *Ten Weeks*, 303–4. Naturally, Smith was exaggerating when he stated the population of Edo was two million, but this was one of the population estimates made for the city at the time.

48 Beauvoir, *Jeddo, Pekin, and San Francisco*, 164–6.

49 Alcock, *Tycoon*, Vol. 1, 137, 130.

50 Fortune, *Yedo and Peking*, 201–2. Woolwich, a district in West London, was a military center complete with a dockyard, an armory, and the Royal Military Academy.

51 Humbert, *Japan and the Japanese*, 348–9.

52 Oliphant, *Narrative*, 407–12.

53 Beauvoir, *Pekin, Jeddo, and San Francisco*, 172–3.

54 Vysheslavtsov, *Ocherki perom*, 156–8.

55 Berg, *Eulenburg Expedition*, Vol. 1, 255–6.

56 Humbert, *Japan and the Japanese*, 268–9.

57 Suenson, *Skitser*, 110.

58 Edmond Cotteau, *Un Touriste dans l'Extreme Orient* (Paris, 1884). No English translation of Cotteau's work exists, so passages that appear in this book have been translated from the Japanese version. See Kotō [Coutteau], *Bon Jūru Japon* [Bon Jour, Japan] (Shinhyoron, 1992), 64. Subsequent citations will appear as Cotteau, *Un Touriste*, and will list page numbers from the Japanese text.

59 Guimet, *Promenades-Kanagawa*, 155.

60 Suenson, *Skitser*, 110. Suenson divided the teahouses into two groups: those that offered relatively immoral amusement and those that provided travelers with a convenient place to stop and rest. He actually called the latter tea shops to distinguish the two, but both were called *cha-ya*, or teahouse, in Japanese.

61 Beauvoir, *Pekin, Jeddo, and San Francisco*, 135.

62 Jephson and Elmhirst, *Our Life*, 73.

63 Bousquet, *Le Japon*, Vol. 2, 663–4.

64 Hübner, *Ramble*, 265.

65 Hübner, *Ramble*, 260–1. In describing the delicate charm of the teahouses in the fields, Hübner said that "In the photography of Beato I do not find the least trace of resemblance." Felice Beato was an Italian photographer who came to Japan in the early 1860s and took pictures of Japan from the end of the Edo period to the beginning of the Meiji period. We should pay attention to not only Hübner's comments about Beato, but also photography in general.

66 Hübner, *Ramble*, 242–3.

67 Osborn, *Cruise*, 179–80.

68 Berg, *Eulenburg Expedition*, Vol. 1, 196.

69 Morse, *Day by Day*, Vol. 1, 355.

70 Smith, *Ten Weeks*, 115–6.

71 Scidmore, *Jinrikisha*, 31–3.

72 Kawazoe Noboru, *Tōkyō no genfūkei* [Scenic Spots in Historic Tokyo] (NHK Books, 1979), 22–3.

73 Alcock, *Tycoon*, Vol. 1, 123.

74 Iseki Takako, *Nikki*, Vol. 1, 98–9.

75 Scidmore, *Jinrikisha*, 74.

76 Scidmore, *Jinrikisha*, 65, 77.

77 Siebold, *Nippon: Archiv*, Vol. 3, 362.

78 Nakao Sasuke, *Hana to ki no bunkashi* [The Cultural History of Flowers and Trees] (Iwanami Shinsho, 1986); see Chapter Three: "Nihon no hana no rekishi" ["History of Flowers in Japan"].

79 Fortune, *Yedo and Peking*, 109–10, 106.

80 A. Siebold, *Letzte Reise*, 95.

81 Fortune, *Yedo and Peking*, 193–4.

82 Nakao, *Bunkashi*, 83–4.

83 Kawazoe, *Genfūkei*, 51.

84 Iseki, *Nikki*, Vol. 1, 287–9.

85 Humbert, *Japan and the Japanese*, 340.

86 Scidmore, *Jinrikisha*, 69.

87 La Farge, *Artist's Letters*, 30.

88 P. Siebold, *Nippon: Archiv*, Vol. 3, 367.

89 Fortune, *Yedo and Peking*, 92–3.

90 Bird, *Unbeaten Tracks*, Vol. 2, 261–2.

91 Faulds, *Nine Years*, 131–2.

92 Humbert, *Japan and the Japanese*, 341.

93 Kawazoe, *Genfūkei*, 35.

94 Iseki, *Nikki*, Vol. 1, 274–8.

95 Iseki, *Nikki*, Vol. 1, 262–3.

96 Noda, *Shūgyō Nikki*, 132–3.

97 Ujiie, *Shōnen*, 323.

98 Fortune, *Yedo and Peking*, 114.

99 Nakao, *Bunkashi*, 177–78.

100 Iseki, *Nikki*, Vol. 1, 259–60.

101 Iseki, *Nikki*, Vol. 1, 330–1.

102 Iseki, *Nikki*, Vol. 1, 265–6.

103 Imaizumi Mine, *Nagori no yume* [Remains of a Dream] (Heibonsha Toyo Bunko, 1963), 148–9.

104 Imaizumi, *Nagori*, 152–3.

105 Imaizumi, *Nagori*, 159.

106 Nakao, *Bunkashi*, 110.

Chapter 12

Living Things and Cosmology

Christopher Hodgson's wife had finally settled in at the temple assigned to the British consulate in Nagasaki, but one morning, she woke up, put her feet on the floor, and noticed there was a snake just a few inches away from her. She screamed and called a Japanese servant to get rid of the serpent, but the man refused to kill it. On another occasion, a different snake had entered the guest room and coiled itself up when she came across it. It stared at her before slithering off, "as much as to say, 'I will call again.'" Mrs. Hodgson then went on to say "it kept its promise," as a few nights later it slid right past her daughter Eva's pillow and escaped again. Mrs. Hodgson often saw the snake in the garden, but she could not get anyone to kill it. It was almost as if the snake were the lord of the temple.

Japan was, as Friedrich Lühdorf said, a paradise for insects and reptiles. Mrs. Hodgson may have been quick to agree with his assessment because she was not only troubled by snakes, but also centipedes. She mentioned how she could never let her guard down after she found one of the creatures crawling on her shoulder and several others in her dresses and shoes. On one particular night when she had knelt down in prayer, she saw a big one right next to her. She grabbed a sword and repeatedly struck it, eventually killing it with the blows and, as she put it, "almost fainting with fear and horror at what I was doing." Mrs. Hodgson also mentioned how every night, "Rats, as huge as cats, danced and squeaked over my head." She lamented how "Very often have I been awakened at night by fear."[1]

Margaret Ballagh, meanwhile, came to live at Jōbutsuji temple in Kanagawa with her husband in 1861 and was disgusted by "the ceaseless buzzing, chirping and whirring of bats, birds and insects, and the yelping of hungry, wolfish dogs, and the cawing of black, cunning crows which are very daring in robbery." She even stated that because of the crows, "a servant going to market dare not bring his basket home on his head." She also mentioned that rats running around this old temple at night caused "the rafters to tremble like an earthquake," and that "Poor pussy flies in terror at the sound of a Japanese rat." In a subsequent section of her book, Ballagh also said, "Most of the cats here are…large, glossy, fat and lazy, and do not get their living by catching rats. In fact, the rats are nearly as large as they are, so pussy knows better than to attack them, so we are left to their mercy and we find them very merciless."[2]

Aimé Humbert, meanwhile, said that Japanese cats were "exceedingly bad mousers, very idle, and very affectionate."[3] According to Lühdorf, the adorable cats of Japan never caught mice or rats because they were overly pampered by Japanese women who doted over them like pets.[4] Speaking of mice, the "Auntie" in Naka Kansuke's book *Silver Spoon* said that part of her family's decline in good fortune was attributed to white mice, which the woman claimed were divine servants of Daikokuten (a household deity in Japan called "Mahakala" ["Shiva"] in Sanskrit), which lived in her home. Because of this, the woman and her family cared for and fed the mice, so much so that they bred and multiplied to extraordinary numbers. In the end, the tiny creatures ate all of the rice in the storage bins.

Dogs were also prominent. Edo, for instance, was a city filled with stray dogs. Laurence Oliphant wrote the following:[5]

> The streets of Yedo are infested with dogs…sleek, well-fed, audacious animals, who own no masters, but who seem to thrive on the community, and bid it defiance. They trot proudly about, with ears and tail erect, and are most formidable to meet in a by-lane. These animals are held in as high veneration and respect as they were in former times in Egypt…It is only due to them to say that, as a race, they are the handsomest street-dogs I ever saw.

In other words, most of the dogs in Edo did not actually have owners per se and were usually raised by neighborhood communities. One could even say, therefore, that the dogs were members of the community themselves. Oliphant felt a much greater affinity for these ownerless dogs of Edo than the "wretched, mangy curs of Constantinople or the pariahs of India" and pointed out their defiant nature regarding human beings. Despite this, however, I am curious to know how, exactly, they stacked up against dogs from other parts of the world at the time. Were they truly that formidable? Lühdorf, for example, had a Newfoundland named Faust that he kept on his ship. One day, Faust went ashore with his master at Hakodate and got into a series of fights with local dogs, all of which he won. It got to the point where the Hakodate magistrate even had to ban Faust from coming ashore.[6]

Robert Fortune gave perhaps the most-comprehensive depiction of the dogs of Edo writing:[7]

> The dogs were the only animals which showed their enmity to us, and this they did in a manner not to be mistaken. They rushed out of the houses, and barked at us in the most furious manner; but they are cowardly withal, and generally keep at a prudent distance…Old Dutch writers inform us that these street dogs belong to no particular individual, but they are denizens of particular streets—public property, as it

were—and that they are regarded with a kind of superstitious feeling by the natives...I think these statements may be received as doubtful, or only partially true. Although some of these dogs may have neither home nor master, yet by far the greater portion have both; and if the inhabitants look upon them as sacred animals, and have any superstitions regarding them, they certainly show these feelings of reverence in a peculiarly irrelevant manner. On a warm summer afternoon these animals may be seen lying at full length in the public highway, apparently sound asleep; and it was not unusual for our attendants to kick and whip them out of our road in a most unceremonious way.

In addition, Fortune mentioned seeing dogs with cuts on their backs from the swords of the "yakoneens" (*yakunin* officials), and George Smith also wrote that many dogs had cuts and gashes they had suffered from the swords of daimyo retainers. Smith also stated that the *betto* who led their procession whipped dogs that were napping in the road out of the way. This was exactly the same thing that Fortune mentioned above, so Fortune may have stolen this quote from Smith's book, which came out two years earlier. At any rate, Engelbert Kaempfer's notion that the Japanese revered dogs and interacted with them with a certain sense of reserved superstition seems to have been completely dispelled by the reality that Smith discovered.[8]

Rutherford Alcock also wrote about the injured dogs he saw. He said, "many a poor crippled animal is to be seen limping about slashed over the back, or with more hideous evidences of brutality."[9] Alcock attributed this to the warriors he detested so much, namely, the two-sworded samurai, who often tested out their weapons on the pitiful animals. Alcock's opinion seems to ring true upon reading a passage in *Bakumatsu no Mito-han* [The Mito Domain at the End of the Edo Period], a book by essayist and feminist Yamakawa Kikue (1890–1980). She wrote the following:[10]

> The viciousness of boys from this period [the Edo period] is something that those living today cannot even imagine...They had no qualms about testing their swords on dogs. My mother often remembered seeing bloodied dogs yelping and running around in Mito when she was a young girl.

However, it might be a bit rash to think that dogs were abused in the Edo period upon reading descriptions such as these. After all, the fact that many dogs had cuts and gashes means the samurai did not actually kill them, and no matter how many times the warriors and *betto* grooms yelled at and kicked the dogs out of their way, the animals still found places in the middle

Puppies at Ōyama Shrine (1873); the correspondent who visited this shrine was surprised by the number of puppies that had gathered to eat food that some pilgrims had given them. There were apparently over thirty puppies.

of the road to lie down in. Conversely, it could be that the dogs angered the samurai and caused them to brandish their swords because of their apparent defiance and pampered laziness. More than anything, however, if dogs were truly being persecuted and run off the streets, the foreign observers would never had seen so many of them. This was not just the case in Edo, either. For example, James Curtis Hepburn, who lived at a temple at a Kanagawa lodging station, wrote:[11]

> Whenever I go for a stroll, I try my best to avoid the Tokaido road as well as the city streets as much as possible because of the various nuisances one encounters in these areas. Namely, I refer to the dogs. There are a great number of these animals, all of which have no master. Even so, they are well-fed and are accustomed to being near people. As soon as they see a foreigner walking by, however, they start barking and run away. Their barking and howling soon spreads like wildfire to other dogs in the area, and the whole town seems to resonate with the din. I try to avoid this ruckus.

James and Margaret Ballagh lived in the same temple as Hepburn, and Margaret also wrote, "Whenever a native dog sees a foreigner, he barks at him, and the towns are usually infested with the ugly, wolf-like creatures."[12]

In the Meiji period, dogs did not have to worry about being slashed by samurai swords anymore, so, apparently, they started lying down in the streets with a greater sense of peace. Arthur Maclay said the following about the dogs he encountered during his trip to Nikko in 1874:[13]

> Japanese dogs are spoilt. They lie right in the road, and never think of getting out of the way. The kind-hearted coolies never think of hurting them, and always pull their vehicles to one side. Then they scold the dog, and he wags his tail. Jack [Maclay's friend] takes a load of pebbles and keeps distributing them in advance. Effect good. One pampered hound, however, refuses to stir. The coolies turn to one side. But the wheel of Jack's vehicle passes over the gently wagging tail. Dog went to the top of the embankment at one leap.

Edward Morse, meanwhile, said, "In my numerous rides I have noticed how carefully they [the rickshaw drivers] turn out of the way for a cat, dog, or hen that may be in the road, and thus far I have never noticed the slightest evidence of impatience or ill treatment of animals." He went on to say that he based this judgment not only on his own limited experience in Japan, but also "the testimony of those who have lived in the country for many years." Morse also wrote:[14]

> The other morning I flung a piece of stone at a dog under the window; he watched the stone as it went by him, but showed no fear. I hurled another, which went between his legs; still he wondered at it without showing the slightest concern. Later, I met another dog in the street, and deliberately stooped, picked up a stone, and threw it at him; he did not run away or growl at me, simply watched the stone as it went by him. Since boyhood I have observed that the mere movement of picking up a stone will cause a dog to slink or even to run away. Such experiences here prove that cats and dogs are not stoned at sight.

The Japanese did not worship dogs by any means. Fortune and Smith were correct in considering Kaempfer's claim to be a thing of the past. However, when Kaempfer said, "The Dogs also deserve to be mention'd among the Inhabitants of Nagasaki...the streets lie full of these animals, leading a most easy and quiet life, giving way neither to Men nor Horses,"[15] he was by no means mistaken.

As Fortune said, there were probably some dogs that did, indeed, have owners, but there was an incredibly large number of ownerless dogs in cities like Edo, Kanagawa, and Nagasaki. Now we can see why the dogs did not run away when Morse threw rocks at them. Even though the dogs did not have owners, they belonged to the townspeople who treated them as lower yet still equal members of the community. Thus, they had never experienced someone throwing rocks at them for no reason. Rickshaw drivers avoided dogs and cats in the streets the same way that they avoided children—a point that I mentioned in Chapter 10. In both cases, the adults cherished these small creatures and did not wish them harm.

Japanese dogs may have been defiant, but Japanese horses were notorious among the Westerners for their atrocious behavior. Raphael Pumpelly, for example, wrote about horses in Hokkaido and stated, "As they are always stallions, their worst qualities are generally the most apparent." The worst quality he was specifically referring to was their tendency to throw riders off their backs. Pumpelly even called these horses "vicious brutes."[16] The Eulenburg mission also had problems with the Japanese horses that they encountered. Albert Berg stated the following:[17]

> The horses are small and poorly built. They often run and gallop, but they seldom make any real headway, and when they do, it is often with great reluctance. They are extremely skilled at running up steep slopes and in places with stairs, however, which are everywhere. Only stallions are used for riding, and one must always be on his or her guard. This is because almost all of the horses have the habit of biting, and they also have the tendency to bite and kick one another.

Maclay wrote about his experiences with horses. When he arrived in Aomori by boat in 1873, he soon made preparations to leave for Hirosaki where he was set to work as an instructor at a local school. His retinue had originally planned to leave at 5 a.m. in the morning, but their departure time was delayed until 8 a.m. because it took so long to load their baggage onto the horses. Maclay even stated that "they were restless until they were satisfied with kicking and biting each other."[18]

George Smith, meanwhile, wrote about an incident involving horses in 1860. Britain, along with France, was seeking a final settlement to the Arrow Incident of 1856 and dispatched a military logistics official to Japan to buy 3,000 packhorses to be used in military operations in northern China. The bishop actually came across this procession of warhorses while he was in Nagasaki. He stated:[19]

> Some fifteen hundred horses were collected together awaiting transport to the vicinity of the Peiho. Some were shipped to Shanghae, but an

equestrian mutiny on board cost the French Government the loss of three-fourths of their first shipment. The high-spirited ponies broke loose, and struck, bit and tore at everything in their way. The European sailors suffered some severe wounds and refused to go among the infuriated animals. Out of three hundred scarcely sixty arrived after a week's voyage alive and safe at Shanghae.

A *mago* horse groom (illustration by Régamey, from Guimet, *Promenades Japonaises*)

Richard Jephson and Edward Elmhirst also had a negative impression of Japanese horses. After the British Ninth Regiment landed in Yokohama in 1866, the unit purchased some Japanese ponies. Jephson and Elmhirst stated that "most of these were untamed and savage brutes, about as well acquainted with the feeling of a saddle on their backs as a Bengal tiger." They described the eccentric nature of these animals and noted that there was even one which had "a disagreeable trick of determining for himself the moment when he fancies he has travelled far enough, and from that point refusing, in spite of all moral and physical persuasion, to move another step in advance."[20] What was most troubling was that Japanese horses were not accustomed to foreign visitors and tried to shake them off whenever they could. The horses found these strangers to be disagreeable. Ludovic de Beauvoir, for instance, mentioned the horses he passed by on the Tōkaidō Road and noted that "as soon as these beautiful untamed creatures see a European, they rear, back, break into houses, run over the passersby, [and] upset their loads."[21]

Horses were not commonly trained in Japan. This is because even the warriors, who were the only individuals who had the right to ride solo on a horse, usually just let a *mago*, or horse groom, pull their horse along with a rope it its mouth. Alcock remarked:[22]

He [a shogunate official] is perched on the top of a break-neck saddle, his bridle of silken folds is held one in each hand, and wide apart— by it, indeed, he seems to hold on—sawing at a small snaffle, to the destruction of his horse's mouth. A groom walks at his stirrup on each side, to defend him if attacked, or assist him to keep his seat if he should be in danger of falling, while two more lead the impetuous animal! More rarely some official sent on urgent business presses his steed into a sort of shambling gallop, to the peril of both man and beast, to all appearance, both being equally unaccustomed to such a pace. It is *vulgar* and *low* to ride fast in Japan.

Townshend Harris's observations were not that different. He stated the following, for example:"[23]

The Japanese are no horsemen; both hands are employed in holding the reins; they have no martingale, the horse therefore carries his head very high with his nose stuck out straight. They therefore have no command over him. Usually the groom leads the horse by a third rein put on for that purpose.

According to Harris, the Kanagawa magistrate was "very fearful for my safety" for this reason. He said, "they assured me that the Japanese horses were so vicious, that my life would be in danger if I attempted to ride in any different manner from their mode." As he heard it from the magistrate, "their horses all would bite and kick." However, Harris rode his horse in the Western fashion and rode "up and down" the steep streets of Shimoda, which were filled with steps in many places. He also wrote how "Mr. Heusken's performances on horseback, and my riding, have raised us to a pinnacle of glory among the Japanese."

Edouard Suenson also said there were very few adept riders among the Japanese, and the reason he gave for this was the same as Alcock's, namely that the higher one's status in society was, the slower and more dignified one had to be.[24] Thus, galloping and trotting were not considered dignified actions. However, there were some opposing views to this point, and conflicting records made by foreign observers can be troublesome. Reinhold von Werner, for instance, thought the Japanese were generally good at riding. He attributed this to an experience he had in which his party had some fun with the shogunate officials by showboating and galloping around on their horses in a bid to surprise their Japanese hosts. However, the officials were able to courageously keep up with him. At any rate, Werner stated that the equestrian skills of the warriors were impeccable.[25] Beauvoir also wrote, "Sometimes they [the officials] gallop playfully, two and two, side by side, holding hands as if in some merry fantasia."[26] This means that there were, indeed, some shogunate officials who were excellent riders. However, it probably was not by chance that Werner and Beauvoir encountered some talented Japanese riders, which, as Suenson mentioned above, were actually few and far between. There was a good reason for this. The shogunate would never had thought of dispatching poor riders to serve as guards for Westerners who were proficient riders. It would have made them look bad. The officials Werner and Beauvoir saw were likely selected by their superiors for this reason. The vast majority of shogunate officials simply "rode" around on horses led by grooms who pulled the animals with a rope. This was a widely accepted reality, so well-known, in fact, that we do not even need to detail examples such as the Osaka magistrate falling from his horse when his animal was startled by gunfire during the Ōshio Rebellion of 1837 to prove it.

The officials may not have been the best riders, but they certainly looked good while doing so. Aleksei Vysheslavtsov, for instance, wrote:[27]

> The mounted corps was led by two *yakunins* [officials], who stretched their backs and straddled their excitable steeds with the utmost grace and elegance. The wide sleeves of their magnificent, thick coats spread out like the wings of a butterfly, and their round straw hats with bow-like eaves were pleasant to look at.

Vysheslavtsov even said that the Japanese riders had a classy, almost flashy riding style, one that was refined and beautiful, courageous and impressive. In addition, he also said they possessed a softness which, along with their courageousness, gave them an almost feminine appearance. These feminine men who wore silk clothing and slicked their hair back truly looked impressive as they skillfully handled their wild horses. Alfred Roussin also stated that the warriors on their horses looked like something out of a painting, covered in silk clothes and donning lacquered hats with large brims that stretched down to their foreheads.[28]

Japanese saddles and stirrups were also quite beautiful, but many of the Westerners decried them for being impractical and dangerous. According to Berg, for example, long rides with such implements were tantamount to torture.[29] According to Humbert, meanwhile, when the Japanese cavalry switched to using European-style equipment with the advent of military reforms enacted by the Meiji government, he said that the equipment and, consequently, the riders lost much of their opulence. He attributed this to the fact that European leather, bridles, and saddles, as well as their attachments, looked extremely dull and mundane upon comparing them with cords made of silk and other materials, the tassels, the lacquered front rings of the saddles, and the stirrups that the Japanese warriors brandished as symbols of their pride.[30]

In other words, at the end of the Edo period, the Japanese considered riding to be a fashionable trend rather than a military skill. Naturally, this related to their need to express their social standing, but it actually followed the trends of beautification and artistic interests developing within the country at the time. Thus, Vysheslavtsov was correct in pointing out the softness and feminine beauty inherent in the hairstyles and clothes employed by the shogunate officials. The Edo period was one in which the psyche of the society as a whole had become extremely feminine.

A shogunate official on horseback (from Alcock, *Tycoon*)

Let us return to the main point, namely, the Japanese horses. These animals behaved so badly that even the Japanese themselves recognized and complained about the problem. However, the animals kicked and bit people and other horses for the simple reason that they had not undergone sufficient training. Ishikawa Eisuke (1933–), a Japanese writer who has done considerable research on the Edo period, stated the following:[31]

> When the average person rode a horse in those days, a driver simply led the animal by a rope in front. Therefore, horse trainers usually found it practical to just teach a young foal how to go in the direction it is pulled. In this way, there was no need to spend a great deal of time and effort on training the animals, nor was it necessary to subject them to beatings and other measures associated with breaking and domesticating them. The people had no desire to do so anyway. The horses probably also found this to be quite agreeable.

Based on evidence such as this, it is apparent the Japanese went easy on the horses and pampered them a great deal. Their bad behavior came about because they were used to doing whatever they wanted and were suddenly being forced to do tasks they were not trained for and, basically, did not want to do. Their wildness was still on display in the late 1880s and early 1890s. Alice Bacon, for instance, wrote, "Japanese ponies are rarely good-natured, and are always looking for a chance to kick, bite, or strike out with their forefeet."[32]

However, Isabella Bird probably provided the most detailed explanation about the nature of Japanese horses. This is because she spent almost the entire time on horseback while traveling across the Tohoku region on her way to Hokkaido. She said, for instance, that she had "ridden or rather sat upon seventy-six horses, all horrible" until she reached Kubota (present-day Akita City).[33] After she had completed her entire journey, she had probably ridden on close to 100 horses. As I mentioned earlier, she used Imperial Army station horses. She started using them from Nikko, and the horses that she rode on to Niigata Prefecture via Fukushima Prefecture were all extremely calm. This was because all of these horses were mares. Bird mentioned these mares all had saggy hair that drooped down over their eyes, making it hard for them to see. She also said each horse "blindly follows his leader, who trudges on six feet in front of him." Even if there were a bridle, she said, "you are quite helpless, for he doesn't understand a bridle." Riding was extremely uncomfortable, so Bird joked that she was actually "relieved when I found that I had slid over the horse's head into a mudhole." The horses were also made to wear straw shoes, which made their legs weak. Thus, they were not the best animals Bird had at her disposal, but they were calm and gentle.[34]

However, things changed for the worse after she left Komatsu in Yamagata Prefecture. She stated that "Two horridly fierce-looking creatures were at the door" to the inn that she was staying at in the town. This was where she "encountered for the first time the terrible Japanese packhorse." The horse that she rode on was startled by a crowd of roughly 1,500 people, who had gathered to see the rare sight of a Western woman, and broke free from its ropes, and "he proceeded down the street mainly on his hind feet, squealing, and striking savagely with his fore feet," causing the onlookers to scatter away. Bird went on to say that "looking round, I saw Ito's horse on his hind legs and Itō [Bird's interpreter] on the ground." Bird's horse jumped over ditches and attacked people with its teeth, and when she jumped off the horse and fell to the ground, it came after her as well.[35]

Bird certainly had some trouble with horses before this incident occurred, however. When she was in a hamlet, Katakado, in Fukushima Prefecture, for instance, she saw "one mob of pack-horses, biting, squealing, and kicking," and described how "one vicious creature struck at me violently." She went on to say that "My baggage horse showed great fury after he was unloaded. He attacked people right and left with his teeth, struck out savagely with his fore feet, lashed

A Japanese packhorse (1861)

out with his hind ones, and tried to pin his master up against a wall."[36] Even so, this incident, and the aforementioned mares that Bird used for the first leg of her journey, paled in comparison to the horses she encountered in Yamagata. Part of the problem was that they were stallions that had not been castrated. According to Bird, they were frightening animals. One day she mounted a particularly nasty horse that "never met man, woman, or child, without laying back his ears and running at them to bite them." She also said that as soon as she put her hands on the saddle, the beast swung his hindlegs around to kick her. The horse also hated flies and tried to kick them off his nose with his hindlegs, which caused everything stowed upon him to come crashing down. It put on quite a show, it seems.[37]

Harris thought that Japanese horses behaved the way they did because their owners branded their bellies every month.[38] He viewed Japan in a favorable light in his later years, but he wrote this passage in his journal when he made a point to highlight and, consequently, blow each and every bad quality of the Japanese out of proportion. It remains unclear where Harris got this suspicious information from, but Bird saw things completely differently. She stated the following:[39]

> I used to think horses were made vicious either by being teased or by violence in breaking; but this does not account for the malignity of the Japanese horses, for the people are so much afraid of them that they treat them with great respect; they are not beaten or kicked, are spoken to in soothing tones, and on the whole live better than their masters. Perhaps this is the secret of their villainy.

In short, Bird wanted to say that Japanese horses were spoiled and pretentious. She went on to say, "I have never seen any overloading or ill-treatment… [They are not] threatened in rough tones, and when they die they are decently buried, and have stones placed over their graves."[40] In other words, the horses were like members of their owners' families. Bird also noticed how the *mago* gave almost ceaseless words of encouragement to their horses while cajoling them up steep streets.

Quite a few Japanese writers also wrote about relationships between horses and people. Noda Shigesuke, for instance, detailed a particularly noteworthy example. During his pilgrimage around Japan, he entered the crater floor of Mount Aso, an area called "Nangodani," in the tenth month of 1812 and stayed the night at a farmhouse in Shimoichi Village. The family had a son who had just turned twenty, and he was caring for a horse and apparently spoke to it like a person.[41] Noda probably recorded this incident because he felt that the young man took his relationship with his horse a bit too seriously, but though this might have been an extreme case, it is a pretty typical example of how the Japanese of yesteryear treated their horses.

The Japanese also did not know the techniques required to castrate their stallions. Actually, I should probably say that they did not bother to learn these skills because they did not want to do this to their animals. A postal station system and a pasture system both existed in old Japan, so there was, indeed, a need to control large groups of horses. Therefore, there has to be a reason why castration and other methods of control were almost never used. This was, of course, probably due to the fact that the Japanese identified with their horses as friends and companions and, therefore, treated them as they would other people. In other words, they did not want to harm the animals for the sake of their own convenience. When Bird tried to bridle one of her horses, for example, she met with fierce resistance from those around her. The Japanese men told her, "'No horse ever opens his mouth except to bite and eat,'" and were convinced that it was impossible to put a bridle in the horse's mouth. Bird explained to them that "the creature would open her mouth voluntarily if the bit were pressed close to her teeth," and they finally seemed convinced after she showed them.[42] In other words, Japanese farmers who raised horses thought making their animals bite down on bits went against their true nature and, therefore, was something they could never force them to do. They also likely saw castration as too extreme and unnatural. The Japanese obviously wanted their horses to be useful, yet they did not think such measures were acceptable in achieving this goal. They also wanted their horses to be happy. For these reasons, the Westerners found the way that Japanese treated their horses, in which they tried to find a balance between their own benefits and the happiness of the animals, to be extremely backward and inconvenient. This is probably why Ishikawa Eisuke said that if he were a nineteenth-century horse, he would definitely have wanted to be born in Japan rather than Britain because carriage horses in nineteenth-century Britain were often made to work so hard that very few lived for four years or longer.[43]

However, Ishikawa's point seems unfair if we add the fact that the unrelenting abuse of horses took place in Hokkaido in 1878, something that Bird witnessed firsthand. From what she could see, the horses in Hokkaido had horrible wounds on their backs, some of which had "holes in their backs into which I could place my hand." She attributed this to the "rude, ungirthed pack-saddle and its heavy load." In addition, the animals were "beaten unmercifully over their eyes and ears with heavy sticks."[44] One time, she witnessed the sight of a Japanese horse being trained. It was the first time the horse had someone on its back, and it actually did not display any sign of wildness at first. Even so, the mounted man spurred the horse into riding at full speed and beat it mercilessly with a board whenever it tried to stop to catch its breath. Eventually, the horse began spitting up blood and collapsed. The rider dexterously dismounted and pulled the poor horse into a shed once it was able to stand again. Bird went on to say, "He was 'broken,' effectively spirit-broken, useless for the rest of his life."[45] It goes without saying that this sort of obedience training was a new custom in Japan and may have developed in tandem with new developments in the wild frontier of Hokkaido. Such abuse changed these horses. They would fight each other when they were brought together and would play all sorts of tricks on people, such as lying down in shallow water, drenching their riders on purpose. In addition, the horses longed to rejoin the herds of wild horses roaming the mountains and along the coasts from which many of them had originally been captured. Herbert Ponting, a photographer who visited Japan in the early 1900s, also said, "The Japanese horse is by no means the best treated equine in the world…and is…often the victim of ill-treatment and abuse."[46] A new era was certainly spreading across the entire county of Japan.

Harris, moreover, wrote a troubling story in his diary about how he almost had to kill a horse that had become injured and was, therefore, useless. Apparently, Henry Heusken, who was an avid horseback rider, had injured the horse that he had borrowed from Harris. According to Harris, "a difference in opinion arose between Mr. Heusken and the horse," and, as a result, the horse's shoulder slipped out of its socket. According to Heusken's own diary, the animal "slips and wrenches the muscles of his right shoulder"[47] while they were riding down a steep slope. Whatever the case, the horse was now completely lame. Harris continued by saying, "I ordered the poor brute killed, but no one would perform the butcher's part." He also did not have a pistol on hand and could not stomach the thought of slitting the horse's throat. As luck would have it, Harris "succeeded in giving him away." He went on to write:[48]

> Think of that! Ye Knackers of London and Masters of the Abattoir at Montmartre and manufacturers of "real bologna" sausages in Germany! What a country it is for you, where it is considered a favor to accept a horse as a gift with full privilege to "look in his mouth."

Naturally, the Japanese did not practice the custom of eating cattle and horses. Thus, they practically never slaughtered animals for food. In 1868, Prussian diplomat Max von Brandt acquired a pig in Osaka, but the priest of the temple at which Brandt's party was staying would not allow the animal to be killed on temple grounds. After making several offerings to the priests, Brandt finally received permission to kill the pig in the most-secluded corner of a vegetable garden that lay adjacent to the temple.[49] Christopher Hodgson, meanwhile, brought sixteen sheep with him on his transfer to Hakodate in 1859 that he had planned to eat. The priest and monks at the temple that the consulate had been established at quite vehemently opposed Hodgson's request to even accommodate the animals for some time, and once the sheep were killed in the central garden of the temple, it shocked the monks a great deal. Hodgson wrote the following:[50]

When the first poor creature was doomed to be slaughtered in the yard all the bonzes [priests] looked on with awe and trembling; whilst the Ōchāu [Oshō, or head priest] rushed into my office, and begged and entreated me to order that for the future the necessary sacrifice might be perpetrated within the wooden walls of the outhouse.

It goes without saying that Buddhist priests detested the slaughter of living creatures within the temple grounds. However, the average Japanese at the time were also against the killing of their livestock not just because of the Buddhist commandment against killing living things, but because the animals were like members of their family. In 1881, for example, Arthur Crow was staying at a Japanese inn in Kisofukushima Town (located in Nagano Prefecture) and obtained a chicken to eat. It was as hard as "leather," and its owner had apparently drowned the bird in a river so as to hide the fact that he had killed it. Crow went on to state:[51]

Partly owing to the Buddhist creed, which discountenances the shedding of blood, and partly to their kindly natures, the Japps (excluding those demoralized by contact with Europeans) will seldom part with their fowls, if to be killed, though they do not mind robbing them of their eggs. They are usually the family pets, and allowed to strut about the matted rooms at their own sweet will...Most of the fowls I have seen are of a fancy bantam breed, very handsome birds, kept spotlessly clean by one of the women of the house, who washes and smooths down their feathers, as carefully as though combing a pet lap-dog. We frequently see them being attended to in this respect.

Bird said the same thing when she mentioned that "though there are plenty of chickens in all the villages, the people won't be bribed to sell them for killing, though they would gladly part with them if they were to be kept to lay eggs."[52] This was something Bird encountered in Kubota (Akita City), but she had a similar experience in Muroran, Hokkaido. She wrote, "Ito bought a chicken for my supper, but when he was going to kill it an hour later, its owner in much grief returned the money, saying she had brought it up, and could not bear to see it killed."[53] This chicken was a member of the woman's family and had provided her with eggs for a long time.

Meanwhile, Richard Henry Brunton (1841–1901), a Scotsman invited to Japan by the Meiji government in 1868 to help with the construction of lighthouses, bought a black ox that had been used as a pack animal when he reached Kii Oshima Island in Wakayama Prefecture. He said a price was reached that satisfied both sides, but then the islanders eventually figured out that he had made the purchase for food, and "They then resolutely refused to close the bargain. They were willing to sell if the animal died a natural death, but refused if the intention was to kill it."[54] Brunton wrote that he bought the animal in the end by raising the price and using "a little harmless deceit" to procure it, but naturally, the islanders could not bear the thought of slaughtering the ox, which had until that time worked for them as a member of their family.

The Japanese also had proscriptions about milk. During part of her journey through Yamagata, for example, the local people actually gave Bird a beautiful cow to ride on instead of a horse. The thought of getting fresh milk from the animal also pleased her, but the Japanese laughed at her when she expressed her intentions to them. According to Itō's explanation, the people thought milk was only for calves to drink and considered human consumption to be the "most disgusting" behavior.[55] In other words, the Japanese believed that drinking milk was tantamount to stealing from the calves. In addition, a number of people probably even felt that drinking milk violated the taboo against sexual desire to a certain degree.

Immediately after Harris secured his lodgings in Shimoda, he requested the provision of milk from the magistrate's office. The magistrate dispatched his interpreter Moriyama Einosuke (also known as "Takichirō") with the following answer:[56]

The Japanese people never consume the milk of a cow, particularly the farmers, who only keep these animals to help them plow their fields or, as much of the land was fields and mountains, to transport their goods. The people do not breed cows on purpose, and in the rare event that a cow gives birth to a calf, all of its milk is provided to the young animal to help with its development. For this reason, I am afraid I must completely decline your request for the provision of milk .

The magistrate simply gave Harris an honest reason why it was hard to acquire milk from this particular area of Japan in his reply, but even so, it does seem like he chided the American a bit by telling him milk was only for calves. Based on Japanese sensibilities at the time, cows did more than their fair share of work, both in the fields and on the roads, and they were expected to work just as hard as every other member of the family. Therefore, the Japanese felt that it was a bit too inhumane to take away from cows the milk that was normally given to the cows' young offspring. It was asking too much of the animals. Thus, the idea of drinking milk had not yet taken root in Japan.

One day in Hakodate, Hodgson asked one of his British servants to milk the cows. The sight of the man squeezing the udders caught the attention of the Japanese, and soon a group of onlookers had gathered in such numbers that two shogunate officials had to be called in to hold them back. When the servant had obtained about a pint of milk, there was a huge commotion among the crowd. Hodgson even said, "some astonishment…was manifested at their not having discovered this useful necessary before."[57] He went on to say that eventually even the priest at the temple began to take milk in his tea. The people were probably not only surprised by the fact that this method of using their cows existed, but they also felt that the Westerners were going too far in their exploitation of the cows. They empathized with the animals. In the Edo period, the Japanese certainly had some practical uses for domesticated animals such as horses, cattle, and chickens, but they also respected their livestock, considered them to be indispensable companions, and thanked them for giving up their freedom in the wild to share in the daily struggles of life.

Another story from Hodgson leads back to the point that the people of old Japan treated animals as equals. In this case, Hodgson retold a story that he had heard from a friend of his. One day, Hodgson's friend looked outside his window and "saw a poor man, half tipsy, fall into a ditch near a temple." He also noticed a puppy had fallen into the same ditch just a few feet away from the man and was struggling to swim out. A low-level priest just happened to be passing by at that very moment, and Hodgson's friend thought that he would certainly help the man in trouble, but "the bonze quietly pulled the dog out of the ditch, patted him kindly, but never so much as looked on the unfortunate old man."[58] It goes without saying that Hodgson's friend was furious with the priest, as was Hodgson when he had heard the story, saying, "The priest could not rescue one of his countrymen; but to save the soul of a puppy he would soil his fingers in a filthy ditch!" At first glance, one might be tempted to agree with Hodgson and his friend, but they probably did not understand the whole situation. The priest likely knew the predicament that the "poor man" was in. He knew that he had been drinking since noon and had clumsily fallen into a ditch, but his life was certainly not in any danger. In time, he could easily crawl out on his own volition. However, it was different with the puppy. The creature would have drowned if left to its own devices.

In any case, Westerners such as Hodgson found scenes like this to be repulsive. In their minds, it was sacrilege to put an animal before a fellow human being, the race made in God's image. Such behavior disrupted the very root of their morals. This does not mean they did not care for animals. Quite the contrary, they were often quite vocal in their opposition to animal cruelty as seen in some of the examples mentioned in this chapter. However, they primarily viewed animals as servants and believed it was their noble moral duty to treat animals kindly. However, they considered it a blasphemy to confuse this kindness with the love shared among humans—the only beings that they believed had a soul.

Naturally, Edo-period Japanese also viewed their animals as beasts. At the same time, however, they thought that being a human being did not make them any better. They knew people were imperfect. They probably did feel some sense of superiority to animals, but they did not completely separate themselves from beasts from a qualitative standpoint as the Christian worldview did. As expressed in the Buddhist phrase *sōmoku kokudo shikkai jōbutsu*, which roughly translates as the "trees, plants, and the earthly realm all attain buddhahood," humans were on similar paths with the birds and the beasts, all of which were living beings. As a case in point, a Japanese man invited missionary Samuel Robbins Brown (1810–1880) to his home in 1863 to read the Sino-Japanese translation of the *Book of Genesis*. However, when they got to the section that stated that man was the greatest of all of God's creatures, the Japanese man cried out in disbelief at the proposition that people were above the trees, animals, and other living things on Earth.[59]

In other words, the Japanese did not see human beings as noble or worthy of respect. In other words, they had not yet discovered the concept of "humanism." This is why Alcock said, "If any one is in danger of forgetting how precious a bond of society this is, he has only to come to Japan, and live where it is wholly unknown."[60] He actually wrote this as an angry response to the pathological lying he encountered among the Japanese, but at the time, it is likely that no one in the country believed the bonds of society would come crashing down due to the constant lies they told in pursuit of the truth. They knew that they, as human beings, were irresponsible, and knowing this meant they understood their humanity. This humanity, in turn, is one of the bonds that gave birth to Edo society.

Other observers also noticed the apparent lack of humanism in Japan. For instance, French writer André Bellesort (1866–1942), who visited Japan in the 1890s, was saddened by the Hansen's disease patients that he saw thronging at Kumamoto's Honmyōji temple and concluded that although the Japanese were kind and courteous, such courtesy did not extend beyond the love they expressed for their families.[61] This was a truly reasonable judgment. Bellesort was saying that universal humanism did not exist in Japan. However, when he wrote that the suffering of others did very little to move the hearts of the Japanese, he was clearly mistaken. It is true that modern Japanese intellectuals have quoted Bellesort and repeatedly used his view that the Japanese only expressed sympathy and compassion for relatives, friends, neighbors, and former domain advisors to back up their own endless claims that communal isolation and universal solidarity among the Japanese are defective principles, but a number of other points contradict this assessment.

Obviously, the Japanese did not know about universal humanism. Moreover, they had never heard of Christian philanthropy, which believes that people receive their souls from God and, therefore, that each person's life is precious and that we cannot ignore individual tragedies. At the same time, however, this also means that the Japanese did not know of the truly unique humanist view that states that out of all the animals on Earth, only human beings were exalted by God. In the Japanese worldview, human beings were certainly worthy of respect, but in terms of existing in this world, their privileged status was not that far removed from the birds and the beasts. In other words, Edo-period Japanese did not think that being human was that much better than being a beast, nor did they believe that they reigned supreme.

In addition, they felt that the birds and beasts experienced happiness and tragedies just like human beings did. Existing in this world meant accepting happiness along with pain and misfortune. God did not play favorites with human beings and did not relieve them from pain. This was a far cry from humanism, an ideology which puts people on a pedestal. Humanism also did not contradict the concept of hunting a certain animal species to extinction, which, as we have seen in numerous examples, was unheard of in Japan.

Thus, if we go back to Bellesort's view that Edo-period Japanese treated sick and disabled people with indifference, we can see that many of them believed this was fate. They were resigned to the fact that bad luck and unhappiness were simply just a part of life. It was not a matter of ignoring the suffering of others. If someone experienced the same pain and suffering, they could deal with the issue with a sort of silent, empathetic perseverance. Modern humanism could never accept this, but the Japanese believed unhappiness was simply a fate one had to abide by. The Japanese, after all, were always ready to die. This did not just apply to the samurai, either. Average, everyday people held the same belief. Willem Kattendijke wrote about this in the following passage:[62]

The Japanese are truly unique in that they do not fear death. Of course, even the Japanese succumb to sadness when they lose a close family member, but they are quite calm about the journey we will all make from this world to the afterlife. In addition, they talk about the death of a family member like it were an everyday occurrence, and they often joke about earthquakes, fires, and other disasters as if they were no big deal…During one of my walks in an area just outside Nagasaki, I came across a funeral by chance. The procession, which even consisted of some extremely high-ranking officials, was hoisting the coffin in a way that would be deemed most improper in Europe. The people almost looked as if they were frolicking about in one of their festivals.

Werner also saw a funeral procession in Nagasaki and noted that the participants were fooling around and laughing.[63] He went on to say that the Japanese did not mourn death. It appeared to him that the Japanese thought death was unavoidable and, therefore, they were always ready for it. Some may wonder if Nagasaki was special in regard to the way people behaved at funerals, but Margaret Ballagh wrote about the local funeral customs that she witnessed in Kanagawa, where she lived. She stated the following:[64]

Their seeming incapacity for conceiving sorrow is one of the most characteristic features of this people. Perhaps this is due to the influences amidst which this free and happy people have the privilege of living. As some one has said, "Where nature is always bright and beautiful, the inhabitants, like the scenery, seem to expand under its influence, and to become bright and happy." Such is the case with these people, who while yielding almost unconsciously to these influences, deepen them by their eager pursuit of all things gay and handsome.

Morse, meanwhile, said, "Their [the Japanese] self-composure, or rather reticence, in grief reminds one of the North American Indian."[65] At first glance this may seem to contradict the cheerful, joking nature of the Japanese mentioned in the examples above, but we could say that they were dealing with death and other tragedies in life in the same basic way.

Morse also frequently touched on the way the Japanese viewed and dealt with fires, and these were clearly additional examples of "their self-composure in grief." On one occasion, Morse heard about the aftermath of a fire from his friend, "Mr. Scott," who was without a doubt Marion McCarrell Scott (1843–1922), an American who came to Japan in 1871 and taught at both the Daigaku Nankō (Southern College of the University, later the

University of Tokyo) and the Tokyo Normal School, in which "the people that have been burned out always look happy and smiling." Morse, himself, also witnessed such scenes. One night there was a great fire, and Professor Smith, most likely Robert Henry Smith (1852–1916), a Scotsman who came to Japan to teach at Kaisei Gakkō in 1874, asked him if he wanted to go see it in person. The two men hired a rickshaw and went to the site of the fire. Once there, they saw "groups of people gathered about their scant belongings" and men and women of all ages "with smiles on their faces as if a festival were going on." Morse went on to state, "During the whole night I never saw a tear or an impatient gesture or heard a cross word. Loud cries were heard at times when the standard-bearers stood in peril of their lives, but I did not see an expression of distress or concern."[66]

Suenson, meanwhile, described what he saw immediately after the Butaya Fire of 1866 in Yokohama. He said the Japanese were fatalists and wrote the following:[67]

> The Japanese continued to maintain their cheerful and carefree attitude. They did not waste time grieving over the fire, even if they had lost everything…The most remarkable aspect of the Japanese character is the courage and composure they display in the face of misfortune and ruin.

Edwin Arnold also witnessed two conflagrations during his stay in Tokyo between the years 1889 and 1890. He wrote the following:[68]

> The self-possession of the residents is remarkable, and due, no doubt, to the fact that few or none of them own the dwellings which they inhabit. As soon as they have removed their few belongings, they seem rather to enjoy the spectacle of the scarlet tongues licking up a large portion of their city, and the black smoke making great strange clouds in the sky.

Arnold also mentioned that mothers and grandmothers with babies in tow were placed in charge of the wardrobes pushed out to the side of the road and commented that one of them "calmly smokes her pipe, lighted from some convenient burning fragment of a neighbour's abode."

Clara Whitney (1860–1936) also witnessed a fire in Japan. Whitney was an American girl around fourteen years old who came to Japan in 1875 with her father, who had been invited to teach at Shōhō Kōshujo (Commercial Training College, the predecessor of Hitotsubashi University). A fire broke out in Tokyo's Ginza area in November 1876, and Whitney quickly went to see the site the next morning and wrote:[69]

It was really charming to see the lightheartedness of these people-laughing, talking, and joking, smoking, eating or drinking, and helping each other. They seemed like one large family turned out of house and home, yet bent on making merry over it and helping one another. I did not see anyone in tears.

Whitney also added, "Already the debris was being cleared away by busy workmen, who to our amazement were already erecting frames for new buildings here and there- the progress they made was astonishing."

Erwin Bälz (1849–1913), a German who came to Japan in June 1876 to teach at Tokyo Medical School (renamed the "Faculty of Medicine" of the University of Tokyo in 1877) also described this great fire, which was said to have burned 10,000 houses stretching over an area from Nihonbashi to Kyōbashi. He wrote:[70]

They are a wonderful people, these Japanese! This afternoon, barely thirty-six hours after the conflagration, houses have already sprung up (mere booths, of course) as if they had grown out of the ground...In groups of from three to six, women, men, and children squat round a little fire, sucking at their pipes and chattering. Not a sign of melancholy on their faces. I saw many of them joking and laughing as if they had never a care in the world. Not a woman among them weeping or wringing her hands, not a child clamouring for his bed, not a man making a parade of his misfortune.

Whitney and Bälz may have written eerily similar accounts in their diaries, but they had never met. Nevertheless, it is interesting to note that Bälz was acquainted with the Whitney family because Clara's older brother was a student of his.

The people of Edo were used to fires, so it became almost a tradition for them to quickly rebuild their homes in the aftermath of such disasters. Eliza Scidmore also noted that "The amazing quickness with which Japanese houses rise from their ashes defies comparison. In twelve hours after a conflagration the little shopkeepers will resume business at the old stand."[71] Mary Fraser, meanwhile, said, "The ground is hardly cold before the carpenters are at work."[72] Jephson and Elmhirst also stated:[73]

The way in which the Japanese run up new houses on the sites of old ones which have been burnt down is astounding. While the remains of the latter are still smouldering, the former are seen to rise Phoenix-like from their ashes; and in a few hours after the fire has passed, a whole street will be very nearly rebuilt. At the great fire at Yokohama, in November, 1866, nearly an entire street had been rebuilt in this manner, when the wind suddenly shifting, the fire retraced its course, and utterly consumed the newly-built dwellings.

The Japanese of this era calmly accepted and sometimes even joked about death and disaster, which is something most people living in the modern era consider outrageous. Whether it was the way people reacted to fires or the indifference that Bellesort saw in the way people dealt with Hansen's disease patients, the Japanese were simply accepting their own misfortune as fate. They had not yet contemplated what it meant to be human in the modern sense of the term. They saw themselves as being nothing more than one part of nature.

However, it bears mentioning that the Japanese did not just limit their compassion to the scope of their family and friends, even in disasters such as the fires stated above. Mary Fraser, for instance, stated that "in general, great kindness is shown to the sufferers, and a whole quarter will open its houses to shelter the people who have been deprived of their homes."[74] Ludwig Riess (1861–1928), a German historian who came to Japan in 1887, taught history at Tokyo Imperial University for fifteen years, and built the foundation of Japanese modern history, also touched on the kindness and assistance people gave to their neighbors and stated that it was actually quite similar to what occurred in small cities in his homeland.[75] He questioned, therefore, whether Tokyo could be called a "big city," even though it did have a population that reached 1.5 million people. In other words, according to Riess, the residents of Tokyo were not big city residents who were indifferent to the fate of their neighbors, but rather active members of a community bound together by a sense of solidarity within the local society.

Naturally, the people also showed compassion for others in instances other than fires. Sometimes, this was even directed at complete strangers. For example, when Vasily Mikhailovich Golovnin (1776–1831), captain of the Russian naval frigate, *Diana*, was captured by the Japanese at Kunashir Island in 1811 and taken to Hakodate and then again when he was recaptured after escaping from his prison cell in Matsumae, the people standing along the road wept for the poor prisoner they saw and even gave him food.

However, Bellesort and many other observers were not wrong in thinking that the Japanese appeared to have no understanding of universal humanism. Their compassion for animals equaled or surpassed the aforementioned examples in many cases. Morse, for example, was moved by seeing the Japanese suspend large straw mats over the heads of cattle pulling a cart to shade them from the sun.[76] In addition, he was impressed by the boldness of the crows he saw in Japan. On one occasion, he saw a woman cleaning fish over the side of a boat while a crow sat next to her and silently watched her work.[77] On another occasion, he was putting on his overcoat next to a rickshaw when a crow swooped down, tore open a hole in the paper lantern set up on the vehicle, and proceeded to devour the candle inside.[78] The inseparable harmony between humans and beasts that Morse wrote about was a characteristic of this world in which the people were just as concerned about animals as they were with themselves. It predated the establishment of universal humanism.

Beauvoir also saw instances of the Japanese compassion for animals. While he was staying at a famous teahouse, called "Myōgaya," in Hakone's Hatajuku area, he witnessed the strange behavior of the servant girls. Around the time that the misty haze of dusk had begun to set in, the girls made a ring around a nearby pond, clapped their hands, and began chasing after fish in the water. He went on to write the following:[79]

> They [the girls] explained to us that every night they made the fish go down to the bottom of a grotto, cut in artificial rock, where they remained all night, safe from the pursuit of hawks and other birds. Oh! how very eccentric this nation of children is, putting the fish to bed!

Four years later, Joseph Hübner stayed at the same teahouse and, naturally, he also wrote about this rather peculiar event. Thus, the Japanese also considered fish to be their friends and companions, and the same was true for turtles. After the Meiji Restoration, the Katsuragawa clan, Imaizumi Mine's family, had to move out of their Tsukiji estate. Imaizumi wrote the following about saying farewell to the turtles that lived there:[80]

> Turtles and their babies lived in this pond for a long time, and I always enjoyed their company, but now it was truly time to say goodbye to them. When I said, "I wish I could take you all with me, but I have to leave you here as there is no pond where we are going. Never leave this pond and keep playing together while I'm gone," everyone around me started sniffling and then fought back the tears while saying their goodbyes. It seems like only yesterday that I saw Chiyo, who was now an old woman, standing there motionless, overcome with grief at having to part company with her friends.

The Katsuragawa estate was also frequented by tanukis, or Japanese racoon dogs. Like many Japanese at the time, the family considered these animals to have magical powers and treated them with respect. Whenever Imaizumi's grandfather, Katsuragawa Hoken, checked on things late at night, for example, he would often hear a thumping sound coming from the door. Then he would say, "Oh, it's you, tanuki. Please come in," and the door would swing open. To Hoken, it often seemed like the tanuki took on the tone of the shogun himself and said, "What are you doing at this hour?" This would stun the calm, cool, and collected Hoken, who would beg the tanuki to stop. Then, he always gave the animal some deep-fried bean curd to eat.[81] The Katsuragawa family was known for its leadership in Dutch studies over the course of several generations. If a member of this upstanding family interacted with a wild animal that had found its way inside his home in such a way, then it is not at all strange to think that foxes, racoon dogs, and other species were welcomed into the homes of other warrior families as well.

Yamakawa Kikue also told a similar story about foxes that lived in the hills behind the residence of the Ogasawara clan, the family responsible for training members of the Mito domain in both archery and firearms. It was actually a story that Yamakawa's mother, Chiyo, often heard her own mother tell when she was young, and she believed all of it. According to the tale, the Ogasawara family had a stipend of one hundred *koku* per year, yet was extremely poor, and their home had fallen into disrepair. It was so bad that the grandfather would always sit on the worst-looking straw mat whenever a guest came calling. His wife was an old woman who always laughed at his feeble attempts to hide their poverty, and she was actually the same woman I mentioned in an earlier chapter who had the bad experience at the bathhouse in Edo in her younger days. Foxes that lived on the estate often stole clogs and sandals from the family home. The old woman would leave plates of red rice and deep-fried bean curd by the foxholes as offerings to secure the return of her children's and grandchildren's footwear. Surprisingly, the foxes always returned what they stole, and she would find all of it lying on the veranda the next morning. She believed the foxes took the footwear to give to their own children to play with. The foxes were also thought to be doppelgangers who shapeshifted into young girls and came to the house to ask the old couple if they wanted to play games together. However, according to the old woman, she could always tell it was a fox right away because although they could speak like human beings, they would start their sentences quite articulately, but then proceed to mumble their words so badly that no one could understand what they were saying. The foxes were quite courteous and sometimes even left a pheasant on the porch for the old couple to eat.[82]

The Japanese from this era all seemed to consider foxes to be rather conscientious creatures. According to Negishi Shizumori (1737–1815), one day a wealthy guest appeared in the entry way to the home of Kobori Kazuma, the Kyoto magistrate, with a formal entourage that looked suited for someone worth three thousand *koku* and greeted the magistrate by thanking him for his kindness over the years, along with informing him that he had received a generous promotion and was moving to a different province in the country. Thus, he had come to say farewell. Kobori had no recollection of meeting this guest and let the strange incident pass, but one night, a white fox, which was the guardian of the home, appeared in his dream, and he realized that the fox had impersonated the guest and came to say goodbye in human form.[83]

Tadano Makuzu (1763–1825), meanwhile, was the eldest daughter of Kudō Heisuke (1734–1800), an author known for writing *Aka Ezo fūsetsukō* [A Look at the Russians]. In her own book, titled *Mukashibanashi* [Tales from Long Ago], many supernatural beings, including shapeshifting foxes and tanukis, appear. Naturally, she believed that these creatures existed. In addition, she claimed that foxes and tanukis were not the only animals that could change into human form. Cats also had this supernatural ability. When the Sendai domain set up the domain residence in Edo's Sodegasaki district, for example, she wrote that a number of supernatural events took place, such as rocks flying into the main house and mosquito net hangers falling down without warning. Later, people found a large ugly cat sleeping under the eaves of the main house, and someone shot and killed it. Tadano wrote that after the miserable creature was disposed of, the strange events suddenly stopped.[84]

However, Tadano insisted that some of these shapeshifting cats were quite lovable creatures. In Kariya Castle, the residence of the Doi family, which governed Yamashiro Province (located in present-day southern Kyoto Prefecture), a cat about the size of a small dog lived there without anyone noticing it. On one particularly fine and quiet spring day in which the flowers all seemed more beautiful than usual, the samurai guards on duty decided to have lunch on the lawn of the outer courtyard while viewing the flowers. Out of nowhere an indescribably cute kitten with lovely spotted hair and a red collar appeared and started pawing wildly at a butterfly. It was so cute that all of the guards noticed it immediately, but then they realized that it was someone's pet because it had a collar. One of the guards said that it was strange that someone's pet kitten had managed to find its way into the castle and then threw a grilled rice ball at the animal. Suddenly, the cute kitten showed its true form and turned into a large cat and ate the food. The animal may have been embarrassed about showing its true form for it never showed itself again.[85] Tadano believed everything in these strange stories, but she was by no means an unenlightened woman from the working class.

She was a scholar whose exceptional knowledge was even recognized by Takizawa Bakin (1767–1848), also known as "Kyokutei Bakin," a famous author from the Edo period who wrote *Nansō Satomi Hakkenden* [Legend of the Eight Dog Warriors].

Speaking of cats, Yamakawa Kikue's mother Chiyo had also heard a tale like this. This was also something that the old woman from the Ogasawara family had told her. One day, the old woman saw a cat sitting next to her, and she complained to the animal that her *obi*, or kimono belt, was so old that the insides were coming out and that she wanted a new one. A few days later, the cat showed up with a new sash in its mouth. This was similar to another popular story at the time in which a cat brought someone a succulent fish to eat. At any rate, the point of the story was to avoid complaining to cats, for they were wily creatures.

Chiyo probably had a look a disbelief on her face when she heard this tale because it sounded all too familiar, but the sequel to the old woman's story convinced Chiyo that it was all true. A few days after the kimono incident, a tofu peddler was passing by the Ogasawara residence when the old woman asked Matsu, the servant girl, to call the merchant. However, the girl may not have heard the call, because there was no reply. Then, a cat suddenly stood up and opened the paper-covered sliding door and said, "Miss Matsu, tofu!" Matsu just happened to be in the kitchen at the time and cried out "Oh! A talking cat!" The cat then jumped out of the house and never showed itself again.[86] Yamakawa reasoned that the old woman from the Ogasawara family enjoyed making up stories like these, but it was hard for her to tell if the woman was joking or if she truly believed cats had such powers. Most likely, however, people around the old woman believed the stories. Otherwise, she would never had told such stories in the first place.

Talking cats also appear in Negishi's *Mimibukuro* [Essays]. One story starts off by saying that the home of a low-ranking samurai had been completely decimated by mice because his family did not have a cat. The tale then flashes back two generations, a time in which the lord of the house had an adorable cat. One day, the cat apparently jumped at a sparrow perched on the edge of the veranda, but it missed its mark and cried out, "Oops!" The lord was shocked that one of his animals could talk and wanted to send the devilish beast back to hell by burning it alive over a fire, but then the cat uttered, "I never said anything" and disappeared forever. From that point on, the family never let cats back into their home, making it fair game for generations of mice damage.[87]

In another similar story, a Buddhist priest at a temple caught sight of a cat getting ready to pounce on a dove. The priest shouted and scared the bird away, to which the cat said, "Oh no!"[88] A number of other strange tales about foxes and other animals appeared in *Mimibukuro*, but the author, Negishi Shizumori, was an exceptional official who had served as a comptroller of finance and a town magistrate during his career. Like Tadano, he was a well-respected intellectual who, nevertheless, believed in the magical abilities of animals.

Tadano and Negishi both lived in the eighteenth to the nineteenth centuries and, therefore, did not live to see the end of the Edo period. However, even in the early Meiji period, a great many people still believed that cats had supernatural powers. One could even say that even though Japan increasingly found itself on the world stage at the beginning of the twentieth century, modern Japanese people still interacted with the world around them based on their acceptance of the mysteries of nature, such as cats and foxes. If this were not the case, then Natsume Soseki's masterpiece *Wagahai wa Neko dearu* [I Am a Cat] might never have been written. This work was by no means influenced by Ludwig Tieck (1773–1853) and E.T.A. Hoffmann (1776–1822), German writers who added animals, including cats, to several of their stories. It was, rather, a novel filled with the imagination of the Edo period in which people spoke with and confided in cats about their problems.

For the most part, people living in the civilization of old Japan, which has long since disappeared, did not keep cats, dogs, and birds as pets. Rather, the people considered these animals to be friends, companions they shared both the pleasures and struggles of life with. Yamakawa gave another example of this in the following passage:[89]

> Every house was surrounded by large groves of trees so there were a great many owls. However, there were also beautiful azure-winged magpies that lived in the trees. They were small, adorable tricksters with long, deep azure tail feathers and soft, white chest feathers, and it looked like they wore black velvet hats on their heads. These birds enjoyed the company of humans and made excellent playmates for children, so many neighborhoods believed an azure-winged magpie in the home could even babysit a young girl. Some of these birds even made a nest in the big paulownia tree near Chiyo's house, and every summer the mama and papa birds would bring several of their adorable little chicks to play in the garden as if to say with pride, "Look at our beautiful babies!"

Sometimes people took their relationships with animals too seriously. According to Imaizumi, for example, this was the case with one particular member of the Katsuragawa family, a man who likely lived in the early

1800s because Jippensha Ikku mentioned that he often met and consulted with him. For generations, the greatest scholar of this family was usually the younger brother of the head of the family. The man in question here was apparently so into his studies that he lived at his older brother's home his entire life and hardly ever left his desk to bathe. In time, he developed a lice problem, and people even began calling him the "Lord of Lice." Strangely, however, he formed a bond with these tiny creatures. Apparently, it got to the point where he could not calm down and concentrate on his studies without lice hopping around on his back, so whenever he was forced to take a bath and change all of his clothes, including his underwear, he would start crying and then put his hands together in prayer and implore the rest of the family to keep at least one of the lice alive.[90] As strange as it may seem to consider lice to be friends, this man's mindset was quite in tune with the civilization of this era.

Morse, Bird, and other foreign observers thought the way that the Japanese related to other living things was strange and described this in their writings, but this Japanese mindset was actually built on the foundation of a collective psyche in which people and other living things existed and interacted with one another on equal terms. Naturally, this was not a uniquely Japanese cultural phenomenon. A similar collective psyche used to exist in Western Europe at one time, although it differed slightly. However, this psyche completely vanished from Western Europe long before the modern era. Therefore, Westerners living in the nineteenth century considered such behavior to be a unique characteristic of old Japan.

I already made this clear in the opening of the book, but I am not concerned with theories on Japan and the Japanese, let alone the Japanese identity or other related topics. I am concerned with what the old Japanese civilization looked like before the modern era destroyed it, as well as its individual character. It is important to separate these viewpoints. In addition, I am interested in this unique civilization and its individual aspects because it existed prior to the modern era that I belong to. However, after considering the fact that people living in this era believed that tanukis acted like the shogun and cats brought kimono belts and fish to people's homes, I wonder if it is even worth calling it a civilization. It is embarrassing if you think about it. Ask any Japanese person who was born after the Meiji period and who has been illuminated by the reason of modern Western civilization whether he or she is embarrassed by this undeveloped civilization and the unequivocal answer will probably be "Yes." I would argue that every Japanese person from the Meiji period onward probably thinks this way.

Japanese intellectuals in the Meiji period were particularly ashamed of their past, and, as we heard from Chamberlain, the Japanese generally held unfavorable views of their old civilization. Bälz also encountered the same situation soon after he arrived in Japan in 1876. He wrote the following in a letter to his homeland:[91]

Modern Japanese have their eyes fixed exclusively on the future, and are impatient when a word is said of their past. The cultured among them are actually ashamed of it. "That was in the days of barbarism," said one of them in my hearing. Another, when I asked him about Japanese history, bluntly rejoined: "We have no history. Our history begins today." Others have smiled in an embarrassed way when I have asked them such questions, and did not thaw until they at length came to realize that I had a genuine interest in the matter.

Bälz went on to say that these new Japanese people were always far more concerned with being praised for their new but apparently unreasonable systems than their old but truly reasonable culture.

We should sympathize with the founding fathers of the early Meiji period as depicted here. As I mentioned in an earlier chapter, when Edwin Arnold praised Japan as a beautiful fairyland, the Meiji officials derided his speech as a sneer against what the efforts of their modernization had accomplished in the twenty years that had passed since the advent of the new era. We should share their feelings. Believing in supernatural foxes and tanukis was definitely "barbarism." If Japan had not separated itself from this mindset and followed the path of modernization, it would never have survived on the international stage in the late nineteenth century. It was better to forget the past and focus on the future.

Today, however, modern Japan must read into the context of this past "barbarism" in a completely different light now that the country has reached the level of an "advanced nation." We can see that the people were a bit unenlightened in believing that foxes could bewitch people and cats could talk. However, this collective psyche in which people interacted and exchanged courtesies with other living beings was neither barbaric nor unenlightened. It was a separate and unique world that valued life. Bälz touched on this and could not help feeling that the Japanese were a happy people with a happy character.[92] This was not a theory he made about the Japanese. This was simply how they behaved in his eyes, and even with the wave of the cultural revolution (Bälz's words) that had come crashing into Japan, they continued to act like this. Bälz's words painted a brilliant afterglow of the long-lost civilization of old Japan.

Notes:

1 Hodgson, *Residence*, 114–7.

2 Ballagh, *Glimpses*, 58, 57, 72.

3 Humbert, *Japan and the Japanese*, 43.

4 Lühdorf, *Acht Monate*, 262.

5 Oliphant, *Narrative*, 388.

6 Lühdorf, *Acht Monate*, 66, 69.

7 Fortune, *Yedo and Peking*, 96–8.

8 Smith, *Ten Weeks*, 306–7. It goes without saying that the reality that Kaempfer stated in his travel logs and his book *History of Japan* was due to Shogun Tokugawa Tsunayoshi's *Shorui awaremi no rei*, an edict enacted to promote the humane treatment of all living things. As for the question about plagiarism on the part of Fortune, meanwhile, plagiarism seemed to be perfectly acceptable in his time, as copyright laws were not nearly as strictly enforced as they are today. Even the word "plagiarism" had a different nuance. In fact, there were quite a few cases of authors borrowing the quotes of others without permission and passing them off as their own words. Likely, they did this to make their own work more solid. For these reasons, it is necessary to differentiate between whether a given quote is based on the author's own experiences or has been pulled from previous literary sources, particularly in descriptions that take on a generally accepted view. However, even in the event that an author used someone else's words, in many cases it was also backed up by his or her own experiences. In the case of Fortune, for example, it is obvious that he borrowed quite a bit from Smith in his descriptions of dogs, but he probably also saw examples of the abuse of these animals firsthand.

9 Alcock, *Tycoon*, Vol. 1, 128.

10 Yamakawa, *Bakumatsu*, 214.

11 Takaya, *Hebon*, 64.

12 Ballagh, *Glimpses*, 46.

13 Maclay, *A Budget*, 178.

14 Morse, *Day by Day*, Vol. 1, 33, 193.

15 Kaempfer, *History of Japan*, Vol. 2, 89.

16 Pumpelly, *Across America*, 145.

17 Berg, *Eulenburg Expedition*, Vol. 1, 117.

18 Maclay, *Budget*, 44.

19 Smith, *Ten Weeks*, 176–7.

20 Jephson and Elmhirst, *Our Life*, 56, 38.

21 Beauvoir, *Pekin, Jeddo, and San Francisco*, 146–7.

22 Alcock, *Tycoon*, Vol. 1, 136.

23 Harris, *Complete Journal*, 398–9.

24 Suenson, *Skitser*, 81.

25 Werner, *Die Preussiche Expedition*, 119–20.

26 Beauvoir, *Pekin, Jeddo, and San Francisco*, 156.

27 Vysheslavtsov, *Ocherki perom*, 138–9.

28 Roussin, *Une Campagne*, 68.

29 Berg, *Eulenburg Expedition*, Vol. 1, 117.

30 Humbert, *Japan and the Japanese*, Vol. 2, 91 (translated from the Japanese version).

31 Ishikawa Eisuke, *Ōedo Tekunorojii Jijō* [Technology of Edo] (Kodansha Bunko, 1995), 220.

32 Bacon, *Japanese Interior*, 124. Japanese horses were veritable ponies to Westerners.

33 Bird, *Unbeaten Tracks*, Vol. 1, 322.

34 Bird, *Unbeaten Tracks*, Vol. 1, 124, 155, 162.

35 Bird, *Unbeaten Tracks*, Vol. 1, 265–6.

36 Bird, *Unbeaten Tracks*, Vol. 1, 186.

37 Bird, *Unbeaten Tracks*, Vol. 1, 294.

38 Harris, *Complete Journal*, 399.

39 Bird, *Unbeaten Tracks*, Vol. 1, 294–5.

40 Bird, *Unbeaten Tracks*, Vol. 1, 322.

41 Noda, *Shūgyō Nikki*, 15.

42 Bird, *Unbeaten Tracks*, Vol. 1, 153–4.

43 Ishikawa, *Ōedo*, 233.

44 Bird, *Unbeaten Tracks*, Vol. 2, 126, 139.

45 Bird, *Unbeaten Tracks*, Vol. 2, 124.

46 Ponting, *Lotus-land*, 178.

47 Heusken, *Japan Journal*, 106.

48 Harris, *Complete Journal*, 383.

49 Brandt, *Dreiunddreissig*, 128.

50 Hodgson, *Residence*, 150.

51 Crow, *Highways and Byeways*, 114–5.

52 Bird, *Unbeaten Tracks*, Vol. 1, 321–2.

53 Bird, *Unbeaten Tracks*, Vol. 2, 128.

54 Richard Henry Brunton, *Building Japan 1868-1876* (New York: Routledge, 2013), 69.

55 Bird, *Unbeaten Tracks*, Vol. 1, 258.

56 Harris, *Complete Journal*. This letter only appears in the Japanese translation of Harris's journal. This is a direct translation of the Japanese into English.

57 Hodgson, *Residence*, 151.

58 Hodgson, *Residence*, 147–8.

59 Takaya, *S. R. Buraun*, 141.

60 Alcock, *Tycoon*, Vol. 1, 363.

61 André Bellesort, *Les Journées etles Nuit Japonaises*, 1900 (Paris, 1906). No English translation of Bellesort's work exists, so passages that appear in this book have been translated from the Japanese version. See Berusōru [Bellesort], *Meiji taizai nikki* [Record of a Stay in Meiji Japan] (Shinjinbutsu Oraisha, 1989), 150–1. Subsequent citations will appear as Bellesort, *Les Journées*, and will list page numbers from the Japanese text.

62 Kattendijke, *Uittreksel*, 130.

63 Werner, *Die Preussiche Expedition*, 176–7.

64 Ballagh, *Glimpses*, 62.

65 Morse, *Day by Day*, Vol. 1, 229.

66 Morse, *Day by Day*, Vol. 1, 355–6.

67 Suenson, *Skitser*, 104.

68 Arnold, *Seas and Lands*, 393–5.

69 Clara Whitney, *Clara's Diary: An American Girl in Meiji Japan* (Tokyo: Kodansha, 1979), 110–11.

70 Bälz, *Awakening Japan*, 27–8.

71 Scidmore, *Jinrikisha*, 61.

72 Fraser, *Diplomatist's Wife*, 283.

73 Jephson and Elmhirst, *Our Life*, 331–2.

74 Fraser, *Diplomatist's Wife*, 282.

75 Ludwig Riess, *Allerei aus Japan*, 1905 (Rüsch, 1927). No English translation of Riess's work exists, so passages that appear in this book have been translated from the Japanese version. See Rīsu [Riess], *Doitsu rekishisha no tennō kokkakan* [A German Historian's View of the Japanese Imperial State] (Shinjinbutsu Oraisha, 1988), 169. Subsequent citations will appear as Riess, *Allerei*, and will list page numbers from the Japanese text.

76 Morse, *Day by Day*, Vol. 1, 152.

77 Morse, *Day by Day*, Vol. 2, 82.

78 Morse, *Day by Day*, Vol. 2, 80.

79 Beauvoir, *Pekin, Jeddo, and San Francisco*, 214.

80 Imaizumi, *Nagori*, 162.

81 Imaizumi, *Nagori*, 64.

82 Yamakawa, *Buke*, 110–2.

83 Negishi, *Mimibukuro*, Vol. 1, 106–7.

84 Tadano Makuzu, *Mukashibanashi* [Tales of Long Ago] (Heibonsha Toyo Bunko, 1984), 18–20.

85 Tadano, *Mukashibanashi*, 155.

86 Yamakawa, *Bakumatsu*, 192–3.

87 Negishi, *Mimibukuro*, Vol. 2, 50.

88 Negishi, *Mimibukuro*, Vol. 1, 243.

89 Yamakawa, *Buke*, 105.

90 Imaizumi, *Nagori*, 109–10.

91 Bälz, *Awakening Japan*, 17.

92 Bälz, *Awakening Japan*.

Chapter 13

Religious Beliefs and Festivals

In the eyes of foreign observers, the Japanese of the late Edo and early Meiji periods did not come across as a devoutly religious people at all. Aleksei Vysheslavtsov, for example, said the following when he visited Edo in 1859:[1]

The Japanese celebrate holidays on a grand scale, almost as if it were a pastime of theirs, but they are completely unconcerned with religion itself. One could even go so far as to say that it has absolutely no influence on satisfying their spiritual desires. Superstition, on the other hand, is quite widespread, and one often sees the people attach lucky charms and other such symbols to their homes and other possessions. They believe, for example, that they can stave off disease by nailing crabs to the doors of their homes. They also consider certain days to bring good fortune, while others are portents of bad luck, and even the cardinal directions have some meaning for them in this regard, as they never think of leaving the harbor without checking their almanacs to see which directions are safe to steer their boats in. Only old women and children go to the temples and shrines, but while the old women are praying and reciting the *nenbutsu* (invocation to Amida), the children scream and frolic about the holy sites as if they were at a playground.

The foreign observers soon discovered that only working-class Japanese men and women of all classes went to temples and shrines to pray. Henry Tilley, for instance, observed a temple in Hakodate in 1859 and said, "Seldom an officer, or a man of rank was seen; the poor and the women seemed the only worshippers."[2] According to Henry Heusken, it was the same situation in Shimoda in 1857. He stated, "It is noteworthy indeed that one always sees women at their devotions and so seldom men."[3] Christopher Hodgson, who served as the British consul in Hakodate from 1859 to 1860, wrote:[4]

I have lived near a temple for sixteen months, and have always remarked that the larger proportion of the visitors consisted of women of all classes, children, and beggars. The men who attended the ceremonies were chiefly merchants (who are despised in Japan, and not even allowed to ride a horse), and shopkeepers, and the rabble, and these in no great numbers. It was very rare to see a two-sworded individual, even of the lowest rank, attend at any time, unless at the burial of a friend, or at the celebration of some rite to the memory of a departed hero or sovereign.

This reality did not change even in the 1890s. Austrian art collector Adolf Fischer (1856–1914), for example, said that all over Japan, the only people who worshipped at the temples were farmers and the desperately poor.[5] According to Albert Berg, the "cultured" Japanese, or, in this case, the warrior class, actually looked down on the Buddhist religion and its priests. Berg said that the warriors felt this way because they believed that the priests had succeeded in deceiving the commoners with their sermons and were trying to do the same thing to them. They also believed that being deceived would effectively lower their prestige as warriors, something they greatly resented.[6] Townshend Harris, meanwhile, wrote the following in his diary in May 1857:[7]

> I do not see any special religious attendance. I must say that I never was in a country so abounding with priests, temples, *mias*, statues, etc., etc., where there was so great indifference on religious subjects as there is in Japan. I believe all the higher classes are in reality *atheists*.

One day, Vysheslavtsov actually asked a shogunate official why no one went to the temples. The man replied that if he went to a temple, the priests and monks would not have any work to do. He explained to Vysheslavtsov that it was the clergy's job to pray for everyone.[8] German missionary Carl Munzinger (1864–1937), who stayed in Japan in the 1890s, also judged that the upper classes were atheists. In contrast to this, the masses, particularly the common people, craftsmen, farmers, laborers, and women, were all quite religious and had been so for some time.[9] As a matter of fact, Vasily Golovnin was well aware of the reality that the warriors did not concern themselves with religion and looked down on priests as early as the 1810s. He stated, "There are Free-thinkers among the Japanese, as among us, and perhaps they are as numerous…there are Atheists and Sceptics." He went on to say that, "We knew several Japanese who made it a boast that they never visited a temple, and who ridiculed the religious customs."[10] Naturally, the only Japanese people that Golovnin came into contact with were primarily warriors since he was a prisoner being held by the shogunate in the Hokkaido cities of Hakodate and Matsumae.

A number of theories have been postulated as to why the upper-class Japanese separated themselves from religion. One of these states that the Japanese intelligentsia moved away from the country's traditional religions of Buddhism and Shinto as a result of modernization and secularism in the

Meiji period and beyond and, consequently, cut themselves off from the common people who continued to preserve these old beliefs. Surprisingly, however, this trend developed much earlier during the Edo period. It simply amplified over time.

As a case in point, Joseph Hübner, who traveled to Japan in 1871, visited Ikegami Honmonji temple (located in present-day Ōta Ward, Tokyo) where he was moved by the beauty of its architecture. However, the government officials who had accompanied him, "with pipes in their mouths, had gone into the sanctuary laughing and chattering, [and] ...openly mocked both at the priest and his god." Hübner also wrote:[11]

> Religion is at a low ebb. None but women and old men go out of their houses morning and evening, at sunrise and sunset, to adore the beneficent luminary...They have a whole heap of superstitious ceremonies; but among the upper classes and intellectual circles there is an entire absence of faith or religion...I have many times questioned the notables of the country on the subject of their belief. They all answered, laughing, that it was all folly.

During her journey across Tohoku in 1878, meanwhile, Isabella Bird stopped to tour a teachers' college in Kubota (present-day Akita City). When she asked the principal and vice-principal if they taught the students religion, both of them "laughed with undisguised contempt." Then, she wrote that the vice-principal said, "We have no religion...and all your learned men know that religion is false." Bird went on to write:[12]

> An imperial throne founded on an exploded religious fiction, a State religion receiving an outward homage from those who ridicule it, scepticism rampant among the educated classes, and an ignorant priesthood lording it over the lower classes; an Empire with a splendid despotism for its apex, and naked coolies for its base, a bald materialism its highest creed and material good its goal, reforming, destroying, constructing, appropriating the fruits of Christian civilisation, but rejecting the tree from which they spring—such are among the contrasts and incongruities everywhere!

As I stated earlier, however, the lack of any religious beliefs among Japanese intellectuals was not a unique characteristic of the new Meiji period. We should view the disrespectful attitude of the government officials that Hübner saw and the anti-religious answer that Bird received from the teacher as being rooted in the mentality of the intelligentsia that developed during the *ancien régime* of the Edo period. Naturally, this was based on the Confucian rationalism and widespread secularism that existed at the time.

Visitors to Japan at the end of the Edo period gave some testament to this. Rudolf Lindau, for example, said that the Japanese were the most-unreligious people he had ever come across. He noted that this was the case even though there were so many temples and shrines scattered across the country. He went on to say that no one respected the Buddhist priests and actually viewed them as being foolish and lazy. Many of the people even believed that the clergy did not understand the meaning of the doctrines that they were preaching. There were also ambiguous distinctions between Buddhism and Shinto, and the people would pray at any temple or shrine they came across, regardless of its sect. However, Lindau stated that the people stopped to pray at these places simply to pay their respects to the holy sites rather than through any adherence to religious beliefs.[13] His views were based on his experiences in the early 1860s (the Bunkyū era). Edouard Suenson, meanwhile, stated the following based on his observations during the mid-1860s (the Keio era):[14]

> Although the Japanese show signs of respect for priests and other clergy, they are almost wholly lukewarm in their religious beliefs. I asked several Japanese about their beliefs, and none of them could give me a satisfactory answer. Usually they just danced around the question or said something that made absolutely no sense. Others, meanwhile, uttered such nonsense as claiming that their religions and priests were frauds or that they only went to a temple in order to preserve their honor and dignity...I found that many people from the upper echelons of society, particularly the intellectuals, were quite neutral on the subjects of Shinto and Buddhism. They avoid outward religious expression and strictly adhere to doctrines that build on and amend the teachings of Confucius...Such devotees generally come across as atheists.

Basil Chamberlain also asked people about their beliefs, and he thought it was interesting that "On more than one occasion we have heard a Japanese asked by a European traveler what his religion was, whether Buddhist or Shinto, and been amused at his look of blank perplexity."[15] Again, this was by no means a Meiji-period phenomenon.

Suenson said there was a surprising level of tolerance between the various religious sects, and this likely became a fairly commonplace opinion after Jesuit missionaries came to Japan and established their religion there. Willem Kattendijke also felt that no other people were as tolerant as the Japanese. He went on to say that if the Japanese had never learned about the nature of Christian believers throughout history, he believed that they would have had no qualms about erecting statues of Christ next to their own gods.[16] Meanwhile, when George Smith was in Nagasaki, he stayed at Sōfukuji temple. When he asked the priest of the temple if he could have a bigger room, the clergyman quickly cleared the Buddhist statues out of a "small chapel" that lay adjacent to the main temple so that Smith could use it.[17] I wonder whether Christian missionaries would have accommodated a Buddhist priest staying at an English church in the same manner by moving statues of Christ out of a small chapel. James Hepburn and Samuel Brown both lived at Jōbutsuji temple in Kanagawa (Hepburn stayed in the main hall while Brown stayed in the head priest's quarters), and Hepburn was also able to move all of the Buddhist statues out of the main hall to worship on the day of the Sabbath.[18] Brown, meanwhile, wrote the following in a letter about his experience at the temple in the late 1850s (the Ansei era):[19]

It is quite strange that these people make no qualms about letting foreigners use their temples for prayer. Many of the idols and other Buddhist implements in this temple, for instance, were pushed into the dark corners of the altar in the main hall and shut behind wooden doors…The priest went elsewhere. Now this old man, who may very well be over ninety years old, lives in the house next to the temple.

This temple was quite poor and the kitchen was damaged quite a bit, and the priest seemed to be satisfied with the rent that Hepburn and Brown paid, but even so, Brown reminisced that he was surprised that the priest agreed to move the Buddhist altar and statues out of the hall. The speed with which he accomplished this was also surprising.

Unquestionably, however, the Western observers did not just focus their attention on the tolerance of the Japanese. Rather, they truly wondered what kind of religion would allow its clergy to relinquish its own holy spaces to a god of a different religion without any remorse or suspicion. Some of them even questioned whether this could be called religion. They soon viewed Japanese religious tolerance as a byproduct of the lack of spiritual beliefs among the people, or at least beliefs that were important enough for them to stake their lives on.

The Western observers at the time were clearly preoccupied with such suspicions. During his post at the Tokyo School of Foreign Languages, for example, Léon Metchnikoff (1838–1888) received a request from a student to transfer to the Russian school at Nikolai-dō in Tokyo. He told the student that he would have to be baptized and convert to the Russian Orthodox Church if he went there. The student replied with an anxious, yet innocent look on his face that he had seen the rite of baptism performed before and that if it were summer, he could handle being subject to the cold water used in the ritual, but since it was winter, he decided against it. Metchnikoff, who was a Narodnik in exile, said that the boy was clearly afraid of having cold water sprinkled on his head. From a religious standpoint, however, the boy was obviously unconcerned with the doctrines of the Russian Orthodox Church and this allowed him to change his mind so easily.[20] Metchnikoff reasoned that the same was true for all the Japanese. Metchnikoff, who was himself a non-believer, praised this boy, but others, particularly Victorian British and Puritan Americans who felt that religious beliefs formed the base of not only one's individual life but society as a whole, would likely have seen his story as unshakable proof that the Japanese did not make religion a prime consideration and simply viewed it as a convenient societal custom.

More than anything, however, the Western observers were quite vocal in their criticism that religion in Japan appeared to be nothing more than entertainment. They saw this relationship the Japanese had with the enormously large number of temples and shrines found in every nook and cranny of the country, especially when they witnessed festivals and other ceremonies taking place. Rutherford Alcock, for instance, stated the following about the scene he saw in Asakusa:[21]

Religion, in any form, does not enter very largely into the life of the people, and…the higher and educated classes are all more or less skeptical and indifferent. The strange mode in which their religious ceremonies and temples are made to amalgamate with and subserve their popular amusements is one of the evidences on which my convictions rest. Plays are performed in their temple gardens, which also contain shooting-galleries, bazars, tea-houses, flower-shows, menageries of wild beasts, and exhibitors of models like those of Madame Tussaud in Baker Street. Such a medley can scarcely consist with any reverential feeling or serious religious convictions.

Isabella Bird had a more-concise view of the situation when she said, "The Japanese are the most irreligious people that I have ever seen—their pilgrimages are picnics, and their religious festivals fairs."[22] She went on to say that, "A pious spirit must have existed once at Tōkiyō, for an immense quantity of ground is taken up" by the temples. However, with the advent of the Edo period, pilgrimages became pleasure trips and religious festivals became bazaars.

Alcock also said:[23]

If "to give and preserve what is vital in religion—religion as Christians know it—and with this to stimulate the highest aspirations of the heart and the noblest conceptions of the intellect; not only to abate superstition and inculcate tolerance, but to introduce in the place of the first a living faith and true motive to action, the highest of which humanity is susceptible"—if this be civilization, the Japanese have it not.

Obviously Alcock was not denying that civilizations outside of Christendom existed when he said this. However, it is quite apparent that he believed that Christian civilization and its ethos were the pinnacle of humanity. Therefore, since he prescribed that religion should follow the tenets of Christianity, what he saw in Japan looked like nothing more than a mixture of superstitious rituals and entertainment, a point that even made him question whether religion existed in Japan.

Alcock was not the only one who felt this way, either. The vast majority of Western observers at the time viewed religion as a way to bring about high moral standards and spiritual refinement through both individual and societal interactions with the deity. In other words, their religious beliefs helped shape a nineteenth-century philosophy that sought to perfect humanity and facilitate moral advancement. When these observers compared this philosophy to what they saw in Japan, it was only natural for them to think that the Japanese at the end of the Edo period and the beginning of the Meiji period were irreligious non-believers.

Despite such critique, however, some of the observers noticed that the Japanese did, in fact, have a unique system of religious beliefs that they strictly followed, although in many cases they completely differed from the religious ideals of the West. When Chamberlain wrote that the Japanese were "undevotional" in the chapter titled "Religion" in his book *Things Japanese*,[24] for example, this actually angered Lafcadio Hearn quite a bit. It is well known that Hearn conducted his own investigation into the religious beliefs of the Japanese people, but I will refrain from going into the specifics of his unique ideas here. Other observers, however, offered equally solid evidence that refuted Chamberlain's claim.

W. G. Dickson, for example, witnessed pious behavior among the Japanese when he climbed Mount Fuji during his second visit to Japan in 1883. He spent the night at the eighth station of the mountain, and the next morning he saw some pilgrims, including an elderly woman, prostrating themselves in prayer to the rising sun. Dickson also said that they bowed down in prayer and did not move for three minutes.[25] Such behavior certainly shows that the pilgrims were not climbing Mount Fuji to have a picnic.

Later on, in the 1890s, Herbert Ponting also climbed Mount Fuji and came across a woman over seventy years old walking around the crater rim by herself. It apparently took her seven days to reach the summit and she had long since fallen behind her fellow pilgrims. Ponting wrote, "Truly that wrinkled body was but the earthly covering of a noble, indomitable soul." He also wondered how many British women, "with but half the old woman's measure of years, would embark on such a task for such an object."[26]

Georges Bousquet, meanwhile, visited Lake Chūzenji (located in Nikko, Tochigi Prefecture) in 1875 and met a group of pilgrims. They arrived and soaked themselves in the lake water, which was as cold as ice, and then brought their hands together to pray. Bousquet wrote that this was the only truly moving act of prayer he witnessed in Japan.[27] Even Alcock, who spoke of the irreligiousness on the part of the Japanese, was quick to agree "That the Japanese should, nevertheless, be very much addicted to pilgrimages with professedly religious objects, may be taken, on the other hand, as an evidence that, among the lower orders at least, there is a religious sentiment of some vitality."[28]

The foreign observers witnessed such religious fervor not only on pilgrimages but on other occasions as well. When Dickson was in Kyoto, he saw some Japanese attempting to rebuild Higashi Honganji temple to its former glory. He discovered that such construction was made possible by voluntary donations from worshippers, which, apparently, reached a total of twenty million yen. Then, he went on to describe the ground work at the main gates of the temple. The workers were using two weights to drive stones into the earth, one with machinery and the other with a group of around thirty men with ropes. Dickson focused on the latter because worshippers were taking the opportunity to help pull the ropes. He also said that there were two large coiled ropes "three inches in diameter, …four feet in height, and six in diameter" lying next to the main gate, and these were made with black hair donated by female worshippers to the temple. Dickson also stated:[29]

It is a mistake to think that there is no personal religious feeling in Japan. Both men and women are to be seen constantly praying at the temples; and even in the mornings, about sunrise, individuals of the household or of the hotel may be seen turning towards the sun and offering a silent prayer. My native friend told me that one of the attendants at Miyanoshta [Miyanoshita] asked him what the foreign gentlemen were doing when she and her companions had sometimes touched the paper-screen with their tongues, and pushing their finger through, had seen the young men on their knees, their faces buried in their beds. "Oh," he said, "that was their way of worshipping God." "Do foreigners ever worship?" she said; "we thought they never did."

Robert Fortune described his own interactions with some Japanese religious believers. He stated that the small temple adjacent to the lodging that he was staying at in Kanagawa was overflowing with worshippers from the end of the sixth month to the beginning of the seventh month in 1861. Nine-tenths of these temple-goers were women and included everyone from cheerful farmers' wives, who had brought their red-faced daughters with them, to courtesans from the teahouses clad in their gorgeous outfits and white-powdered faces. They were all seated on cushions with a small bell in front of them. When the priest began chanting a sutra, the entire congregation began ringing the bells and chanting "Nam, nam," which Fortune did not understand. The service continued for an hour or so, with the women taking breaks to imbibe generous amounts of sake.

Fortune again heard the bells and chanting of "Nam, nam, nam" on the second day of the seventh month, so he went to see the ceremony. After watching the proceedings for a few minutes, he decided to return to his quarters. Suddenly, he noticed that the congregation had followed him out of the temple, and he figured that they were returning the courtesy of his visit with one of their own. Among the group were some old men who could just barely walk, but the majority were women and children. The women began inspecting Fortune's clothing, books, and specimens. He even said that his butterflies, beetles, and land snails were the target of their fascination and suspicion. They did all of this to see what kind of person he was and what he did for a living. He said that the wiser ones among them thought that he was going to "make medicine." Then, they asked him his age and if he were married. Fortune said, "Many a goodhumoured joke was, no doubt, passed round amongst them at my expense." Some of the women even approached him and one by one asked his opinion of them and whether they would make a good wife. Then, someone reminded the congregation that they had to return to the temple service, so the women bowed politely and left. Shortly thereafter, Fortune heard the bells and chanting once again. He went on to write:[30]

All at once the sounds ceased, and I concluded that the services of the day were over. In this, however, I was mistaken; for shortly afterwards I heard sounds of merriment, very different from those devotional ones which had preceded them. I was therefore induced to visit the congregation a second time, in order to satisfy my curiosity. When I reached the court in front of the temple a curious scene presented itself to my eyes. There was the same congregation in the same room in which they had been so devout a short time before, now engaged drinking saki, and already—judging from the loud laugh which was going round, and the boisterous merriment—somewhat under its influence. When I was perceived in front of the door the intelligence was quickly passed round the room, and I was received by the assembly with a scream of delight. The hospitality of these people, in so far as saki was concerned, was boundless; and many invitations were given me to join the various groups...At an appointed time the priests appeared in their robes of office, the saki which remained unconsumed was put away, the countenances of the congregation changed from gay to grave— some of them, it is true, were a little more ruddy than before—and the religious services again commenced.

Fortune's description paints an excellent picture of what religious ceremonies actually looked like at temples belonging to the Jōdō Shinshū (True Pure Land) sect of Buddhism, which, along with the Nichiren sect, was the most highly organized sect in the Edo period. Such ceremonies likely had a bright, enjoyable atmosphere. This enabled villagers to pray at a temple, which, according to Rennyo (1415–1499), the great restorer of the Jōdō Shinshū sect, was the most-important thing people could do to save themselves in their next life. However, it was also an event in which the people could relax and jovially interact with others.

The Bishop of Victoria (Hong Kong), George Smith, was obviously critical of the state of Japanese religion, which he saw as a blend of superstition, spiritual benefits, and entertainment, but even he noticed the formal yet relaxed nature of Japanese holy sites, namely the temples and shrines, during his stay in Nagasaki in 1860. The grounds of shrines were veritable playgrounds for children. Smith observed one particular group of children and said:[31]

Close to the very shrine they danced, leaped, wrestled, threw somersets in the air, and shook the roof with their merry laughter, as they tripped each other up by the heels and exulted in any one of their number coming down with a more than commonly heavy fall on the ground.

Smith also said the children could not help playing with the bells in front of the shrine and that they tried racing each other to the ceiling of the bell tower by clambering up the ropes that the bells were suspended from. Even though adults were watching, not one of them scolded the children in any way. The bishop had heard that shrines were not as strict as Buddhist temples, so he thought this might be the reason why the children behaved as they did. However, he witnessed a similar scene of noisy children when he visited a temple. He concluded that both temples and shrines were enjoyable places for children and adults alike. On another occasion, the bishop saw about fifty young girls between the ages of ten and twenty gather at a neighboring temple. They proclaimed to Smith and his comrade Mr. Williams that they had "come to enjoy a Zondag." They wore beautiful silk kimonos with wide kimono belts tied in the back in large bows, had put on copious amounts of makeup, and "shook the roof of the sacred edifice with their merry peals of laughter."[32] The temple was also a place of entertainment for the girls.

Smith felt that Buddhism was a gloomier and more austere religion than Shinto, for the following reason:

> [Buddhism] professes to regard sorrow as inseparable from existence...The adherents of Sintoism [Shinto] on the other hand appear to make happiness in the enjoyment of the present world the great object of aim, taking a more cheerful view of human life, and preferring to contemplate the brighter side of mundane affairs.

Smith also mentioned that Shinto turned its religious holidays into festivals. However, the same was true for Buddhism. In terms of doctrine, it was certainly more austere, as Smith said, but the Japanese people were consciously aware that temples were the same as shrines in that they provided their worldly lives with happiness and good fortune. When Émile Guimet visited Yokohama's Asama Shrine in 1876, he felt that everything about the place was agreeable and full of life. He added that people did not go there out of fear of the gods, but to become more familiar with them.[33] However, Guimet also felt that the nature of Buddhism was pleasant and agreeable when he visited Tokyo's Sensōji temple and saw how the religion related to all of the sights and sounds that he experienced. He stated that Buddhism was enjoyable and pleasing to the soul and even compared it to the religion of the ancient Greeks.[34]

Smith critiqued the Japanese approach to Buddhism in the following passage:[35]

> On ordinary occasions the religious zeal of the Japanese is at a low ebb, and the temples are wellnigh deserted. Daily services are seldom attended by the laity, and commonly intermitted by the priesthood. The recurrence of special holidays revives all the superstitious devotion of the multitude; and these annual festivities bring immense crowds to the temple rites. Feastings and rejoicing form no small part of their religion.

Edwin Arnold, on the other hand, did not think that this style of religion was dubious or debased in any way.[36] Arnold was not particularly fond of rigoristic Protestantism, so he saw Buddhism as the ideal religion. He echoed Smith's observations by saying "They blend every *Ennichi* or *Matsuri*, that is to say, their 'Saints' days,' with a fair or festival" and that "Religion and pleasure go hand in hand in Japan," but unlike the bishop, he praised rather than criticized these points. We can see this in his depictions of festivals detailing how full of joy and happiness these events were. It is also important to note that he said that the Japanese "are an extremely undevotional people, without being on that account irreligious." In other words, he did not like impassioned believers who sacrificed themselves to God. His idea of a desirable religion, conversely, was similar to Guimet's. Namely, it was a pleasant and agreeable religion that blended with the happiness of life. Arnold believed this existed among the Japanese.

In addition to this, the Japanese also interacted with the gods and buddhas outside the shrines and temples. Fortune, for example, described the simple form of worship that people engaged in before the small Buddhist statues that dotted the countryside. He wrote the following based on his experiences in 1861:[37]

There are little roadside altars in many of the fields near Kanagawa, on which the natives burn incense, and offer salt, cash, and other things to a deity rudely carved in stone. On one occasion I came up with three women, rather respectably dressed, and looking like they belonged to the higher classes of Japan. They were accompanied by a man-servant, who carried in his hands a bundle of joss-sticks and paper as an offering to the god. They looked pleased to see a foreigner, were very polite, and asked me where I was going to, whence I came, and to what nation I belonged. On my returning the compliment by asking them the same questions, they informed me they had come from Kanagawa, and were about to offer incense at a little altar situated in a field some hundred yards ahead of us. Being anxious to witness the ceremony, I walked with them to the altar. When we reached the little stone god, one of the ladies, apparently the highest in rank, took the incense out of the hand of the servant, lighted it, and placed it in a stone basin in front of the image. She then bent low before the altar, all the time rubbing a string of beads which she held in her hands and muttering some prayers. The second in rank stood behind her in a devout attitude, while behind the second stood the third, who made short work with her devotions, and laughed and talked to me while the others were engaged with their prayers. At the conclusion of the ceremony, which lasted only about two minutes, the three ladies pulled short tobacco-pipes out of their pockets, filled them with tobacco from their pouches, and begged me to give them a light from my cigar. I willingly complied with the request, and, after having a comfortable little smoke together, we parted the best of friends.

Most likely, the stone Buddhist statue that the women were visiting was Jizō, a deity known for working miracles, so it is quite possible they had come to pray and have their wishes granted. In other words, the women were engaging in the "superstitious" behavior that both Vysheslavtsov and Smith denounced as having nothing to do with religion. However, if we set aside the question of why the Westerners considered making wishes to a stone Buddha on the roadside to be superstition while praying to the one God in Heaven was, in their minds, a perfectly acceptable religious practice, we cannot deny the fact that these women were communicating with the all-encompassing spiritual world that includes this world. This was true even if they were, in fact, asking Jizō to grant their wishes with prayers and offers of incense.

Max von Brandt had an experience similar to Fortune. Brandt accompanied the physicians Leopold Mueller (1822–1893) and Theodor Hoffman (1837–1894), both of whom were professors at Tokyo Medical School, to see the graves of the famous lover Hirai Gonpachi and his wife, Komurasaki. When they arrived, they saw an old woman earnestly rubbing the foot of a bronze statue of a *tengu*, which were known to have healing powers. When they asked her what she was doing, she replied that her grandson had hurt his foot and that she had come here to pray to the *tengu* and ask it to heal his affliction. The child was actually waiting in the teahouse below where they were, so Brandt quickly dispatched the two doctors to examine the child. Luckily, they were able to transport the boy to the college hospital, where he underwent an operation. Thanks to Brandt and the doctors, the boy completely recovered. However, when the old woman came to thank them in person, Brandt asked her whether it would have better if she had sought medical attention immediately rather than go to the *tengu* statue. She replied that might be true, but if she had not gone there to pray, she would never have met Brandt and his col-

Roadside shrine (from Alcock, *Tycoon*)

leagues. In other words, it was fate. Brandt wrote that after this episode, he gave up trying to play down superstition.[38] In other words, this woman inspired him to believe in the complex chain of mysteries that shape this world.

Fortune and Brandt were beginning to understand the religious consciousness of the Japanese. Ludwig Riess, however, analyzed this from his perspective as a historian. Giv-

Stone statues on Mount Atago, Kyoto (Humbert, *Japan and the Japanese*)

ing the gods Fudō (Sanskrit: Acala), Jizō (Sanskrit: Ksitigarbha), Enma (Sanskrit: Yama), Kannon (Sanskrit; Avalokitesvara), and Binzuru (Sanskrit: Pindola Bharadvaja) as examples, he wrote:[39]

> Among the Japanese, almost everyone from the lower classes, the women, and children believe in the five gods. If there were a Japanese person who had a free spirit, he would say he had been set free from this religious mindset, a world of fairy tales that his nanny had told him in his youth.

In other words, Riess believed that even though the religious world of the lower classes, women, and children had some spiritual use, it was little more than "superstition" that the people had to break free from. Riess was close to understanding the religious consciousness of the Japanese people, but he threw it out and began debating the "political religion" of the Japanese, or, namely, ancestor worship—a belief system that the Japanese have followed since ancient times and that they continue to follow in the present day. Riess, who was a direct disciple of German historian Leopold von Ranke, probably lacked any real sensitivity to the people's beliefs even before he came to Japan, a far cry from what compatriot Heinrich Heine spoke of in his essay, *Gods in Exile*.

In the end, Alice Bacon was the one who came closest to understanding the deep meaning of religious beliefs among Japanese commoners. During her second visit to Japan (1900 to 1902), she spent a few weeks at a spa in the mountains. There, she befriended an old married couple who ran a small teahouse outside the village. The husband was a craftsman who carved *tengu* and other mysterious creatures out of the roots of trees, and the cheerful old woman was always in the mountains looking for such roots to give to her husband. Whenever Bacon and her party visited their teahouse, the old woman always struggled to retrieve some cold spring water that flowed out of the rocks nearby, make tea, and set out some *yōkan* or other sweets for them to enjoy, and then she entertained Bacon and her party with gossip and local folk tales. In one of these stories, the old woman said a *tengu* built the top of the rock that overlooked the village, and one day she actually led Bacon's party to the *tengu*'s cave. She also said that the *tengu* had long since left the forest. She knew this because she checked the area every night after she closed her teahouse and never found any trace of the creature. She went on to say that monkeys living in the forest had decreased in number as well. Bacon also heard her tell the tale of how one could make medicine by catching a viper in the forest and soaking it in sake. In fact, Bacon and her companions remembered seeing jars filled with coiled snakes on the shelves of the village grocer, and now they knew why. One day, the old woman called for Bacon and her party and said that they should have come sooner. Apparently, a big black snake, a messenger for the god of the mountain, had just slithered past the teahouse. She went on to say that she had seen the snake before and that it was not that rare, but she thought for sure that Bacon and her friends would be interested in seeing it. Bacon also said:[40]

> Poor little old lady, with her kindly face and pleasant ways, and her friendly cracked voice. Her firm belief in all the uncanny and supernatural things that wiser people have outgrown brought us face to face with the childhood of our race, and drew us into sympathy with a phase of culture in which all nature is wrapped in inscrutable mystery.

It was a waste of energy to ask about anything pertaining to the Japanese religious mind, namely, Buddhist and Shinto doctrines, or any of the activities and ceremonies associated with these religious organizations. Moreover, the priests had high social status, but people looked down on them. Reinhold von Werner said it was surprising to see how the Buddhist and Shinto priests looked at people with pallid and idiotic looks on their faces. According to him, the Buddhist priests were much worse in this regard.[41] However, even a new generation of priests who tried to reform the lethargic nature of the Buddhist world had almost no effect on the fundamental religious feelings of the Japanese. When Bird visited Nishi Honganji temple in Kyoto, for example, she met Akamatsu Renjō (1841–1919), a reformist Jōdō Shinshū priest who actually went to Britain to study in 1872, and sought his opinion on the current state of Japanese religion.[42] Bird enticed him by saying, "In spite of certain superstitious observances, I could not but regard the Japanese as a most irreligious people." Akamatsu answered:

The Confucian philosophy spread rapidly long ago among the higher classes, and educated and thinking men denied immortality, and became what you would call materialists. Gradually their unbelief sank downwards through the *heimin* [commoners], and there is little real belief in Japan, though much superstition still exists.

Bird also asked him, "what he considered the most prevalent 'unrighteousnesses' among his countrymen," and he answered "'truthlessness and licentiousness.'" It is interesting to note that his answer shows that Akamatsu shared the same standards of judgment concerning religion that many of the Westerners did. He countered Bird by saying, "'Buddhism may yet revive; it teaches men purity, it shows that the end of righteousness is rest; purity is the plain road to rest; the moral teachings of Buddha are higher than those of Christ.'" Such language shows his religious philosophy followed the Christian model and, at the same time, exposed the fact that he had very little understanding of the religious world of the Japanese commoners and even looked down on it.

Thus, the Westerners and reformists such as Akamatsu did not consider the true essence of religious feelings among the Japanese of yesteryear to be religion in the strict sense of the word, as they believed that religion in Japan was nothing more than superstition or entertainment. However, we have to consider this point from a different perspective. Shinoda Kōzō (1871–1965) recorded the tale an old woman who told him about the fun she had on her pilgrimage of the eighty-eight temples in Shikoku and included it in his book, *Bakumatsu-Meiji onna hyakuwa* (A Hundred Tales of Women from the Bakumatsu-Meiji Era).[43] This old woman embarked on the pilgrimage with her son and daughter-in-law, and soon they joined a large group of men and women. She heard romantic tales and jokes, and she always cleared her mind and felt at peace when she prayed at one of the temples, but I wonder what this "worship" actually entailed. The true enjoyment she found on the trip was likely hiking forty-eight kilometers every day, listening to romantic stories and jokes from her fellow pilgrims, and communicating with people at each one of her destinations. When she was in Nerima, for instance, she said that the villagers greeted them with thick slices of pickled radish and boiled vegetables. In return, she opened her boxed lunch and shared her food with them. She actually knew ahead of time that the villagers expected this, so she prepared some sushi rolls and mixed sushi rice and, much to the villagers' delight, set these succulent dishes on a tray that the villagers used to collect the food they exchanged with the pilgrims.

This was not just a pleasure trip. The villagers showed the woman's group hospitality because they were on a religious journey, and her party answered their warmhearted nature with gifts of their own. There was probably no specific reason why the woman went to worship at the temples. She was likely just happy to have lived long enough to see her son get married and, moreover, wanted to pray for good fortune and her family's future. However, she sensed something extraordinarily sacred and grand, and this is why her heart and mind were so radiant. Here, as medieval historian Katsumata Shizuo stated, the tradition of seeing pilgrims, which had existed since the Middle Ages, made people recognize connections with the gods and buddhas, helping to break off various ties with the secular realm.[44] This situation was still very much on the minds of the people. Communication between the pilgrims and the villagers created this extraordinary dimension.

There were other views of Japanese religious beliefs. Nikolai, the bishop of the Japanese Russian Orthodox Church, differed from the Protestant missionaries of the West in that he found the religious mindset of the Japanese commoners wanting to get close to Jizō and Inari to be the true religious mind that resembled the essence of Christianity.[45] Whenever he visited the countryside, for example, he always came across women and children who were praying to decorated statues of Jizō or Inari. He considered such behavior to be the result of active religious emotions. At a temple that was celebrating the birth of Buddha, meanwhile, he identified with the people pouring sweet tea on the Buddhist statues. He did not think that this action was superstitious, and he wanted other foreign visitors to know that the Japanese people were sophisticated and did not engage in simple acts of pleasure at the expense of a deity. As he put it, God had granted them new and lively souls. He added that Christians in Russia were the same.

According to scholar Nakamura Kennosuke, Russian Orthodox Christianity did not follow the religious reforms of the Renaissance nor was it swept away by the secularism of Western Europe. Rather, it preserved the essence of Christian beliefs that existed in premodern times. This was the real religion that Nikolai hoped to bring to Japan. He thought Protestantism just preached about rational righteousness and practical morality and did not possess the true religious mindset. In addition, he felt there was a dark side to Protestantism that lured the Japanese to follow its beliefs by seducing them with the charms of Western civilization. In Nikolai's eyes, the Japanese intellectuals who were attracted to this mindset became Protestants and this, in turn, was no different from atheism. Nikolai's hopes focused on the Japanese lower classes because they openly and honestly recognized that religion was something that satisfied the inerasable desires of their souls. Nakamura summed it up best when he said that the Russian Orthodox Church was a Christian sect, but it was also a religious belief system that could blend with the so-called premodern religious mind and religious feelings among the Meiji-period Japanese. He also said that Nikolai believed in this idea.

The reason Nikolai considered the religious beliefs of the Japanese commoners to be the manifestation of the true religious mind that had nothing to do with the Protestant view of religion was likely because he was quite familiar with the reality of Christian beliefs in his homeland. It is well known, for example, that Russian author Fyodor Dostoevsky found the true mental spirit of Christianity among the innocent serfs of Russia and in their worship of the saints and pilgrimages. Nikolai was on the same spiritual roadmap as Dostoevsky.

This religious spirit was not just limited to Russia. If we go back in time to the Middle Ages, for example, we can see that religious beliefs among the common people all over Europe were actually similar to the religious world of the Japanese commoners. By the nineteenth century, however, this had all but ceased to exist in the Western consciousness. Some of the observers did, in fact, notice that the atmosphere of Japanese Buddhist temples was very similar to that of Catholic cathedrals, and they gave countless examples of such similarities. Alcock described one of these examples in the following passage:[46]

> I never entered one of these Buddhist temples without a mental conviction of identity, and the reflection that either the Buddhists of a later day have borrowed from the Roman church, or the Roman church of an early date borrowed from them…The uproar created by the rushing in and out of the populace following our footsteps, with small reverence for the house of worship, only seemed to add another feature of resemblance; for in St. Peter's at Rome I have seen dogs and children on high holidays mingling in a crowd which passed in and out, and with quite as little outward show of reverence either for the temple or the Deity.

However, as we can see in Alcock's statement above, despite the similarities, the observers did not get any hints about the nature of the common people's religious beliefs.

Moreover, the observers also thought that members of the warrior class had no religious beliefs. This observation was probably accurate to a certain degree. This is because it is an established theory that, during the Edo period, Confucian rationalism had thoroughly spread throughout the warrior class and solidified their moral secularism. However, if we read various essays and travel accounts written by warriors of this age, it is hard to believe that they were completely insensitive to the spiritual world of the gods and buddhas as a result of their persistent rationalism. They were likely just simply looking down on existing religions, which had become mere façades.

If we look at Sugimoto Etsuko's recollection of Bon festival events at the residence of the Inagaki family, the head of which used to be an advisor to the Nagaoka domain,[47] we can see that, although the warriors were considered to be atheists, the reality was quite different. Sugimoto's recollections may even be the best guidance we have in truly understanding Bon festival events, which, for the Japanese of yesteryear, were solemn rituals that were full of life. She experienced these events when she was around seven or eight years old, which means the year was 1879 or 1880.

Sugimoto Etsuko, also known as "Etsu Inagaki Sugimoto"

Preparations for the festival started days before it actually began, and everyone from Sugimoto's mother to the family servants took part. This included cutting and trimming the trees and hedges in the garden, washing off the stones, and sweeping the ground, even under the house. They also took out the tatami mats and cleaned them, and then they wiped down all of the woodwork, including the ceiling boards, the crossbeams, the columns, and the transom windows, with hot rags. Sugimoto said that "the entire house, from thatch to the under-floor ice-box, was as fresh and clean as rain-water falling from the sky."

When the festival finally arrived, the family altar was the center of the events. On that day, a male servant that Sugimoto called "Jiya" went down to the lotus pond to collect flowers before the sun had come up, "for it is only with the first rays of sunrise that the 'puff' comes, which opens the pale green buds into snowy beauty." After this, members of the family made cow and horse figures out of eggplants and cucumbers and placed them on the altar as offerings. Other vegetables were also piled on top of lotus leaves. Then, Ishi, the maid, "hung the white Bon lantern high above everything." When she lit it, the braided paper began to whirl around and it "looked like a flock of tiny birds." Sugimoto then went on to say, "Like all the children I had always looked forward with pleasure to the visit of the ancestors, but after Father's death, I felt a deep personal interest, and my heart was beating with excitement, as the family met at the shrine." She said, "O Shorai Sama [the spirits of all ancestors] came riding on a snow-white steed from 'the land of darkness, the shores of the unknown, the place of the dead.'"

At dusk, the entire family gathered in two lines and waited for the spirits at the big gate. Everyone, even the servants, was wearing new clothes and dresses, and they all bowed their heads. Sugimoto went on to describe the scenes that followed:

All the town was silent and dusky except for hundreds of tiny fires, for one was blazing at every gateway. As I bowed, my longing heart seemed to pull my father to me. Through the distance I could hear the sound of soft, galloping feet, and I knew the snow-white steed was approaching. The moment's blaze of the hemp-stem fire was dying…Slowly we rose with bowed heads and walked back…When we reached the shrine Mother struck the gong and we all bowed with the dignified cheerfulness of our usual greeting to a welcome guest… The next two days the town was full of lanterns…Our home was filled with an atmosphere of pleasant thoughts, unselfish acts, and happy laughter; for we felt that our kind guests enjoyed our simple pleasures of new clothes, company courtesies, and our daily feasts with them of the shrine food consisting of fruits, vegetables, and rice dumplings.

Sugimoto mentioned that the past few days had been happy ones, but the final day of the Bon festival had come, and it was time for the spirits of their ancestors to leave. She said, "I think we all felt sad." After that, her mother made a canoe for their ancestors to float away on and every member of the family went to the river before sunrise to see the small boat set sail. She went on to say the following:

The silence was unbroken except for the loud cries of the birds, then a sudden ray of sunlight shot across a distant mountain and hundreds of figures stooped and launched the little canoes…We waited until the sunlight broke into brilliance; then, as the light came racing down the mountain-side, a soft, deep murmur rose from the bowing figures all along the shores. "Farewell, O Shorai Sama," we all gently called. "Come again next year. We will be waiting to welcome you!" The crowd scattered, and with satisfied faces, made their way homeward. Mother and I walked happily along.

Was Sugimoto's experience really just ancestor worship, which many have decried as a primitive state of religion? Her family obviously worshipped their ancestors, but what is presented here, rather, is likely their conviction that the soul is eternal. More than anything, however, we can clearly see the existence of a realm of souls that goes beyond this world yet also permeates it. Connecting with this realm once a year brings the salvation that we could call the core belief of religion.

Sugimoto went on to write, "The anxious look that Mother's face had lost during the last few days did not come back, and I felt that Father had really been with us bringing comfort and help to us all; and now he had gone, leaving behind him, not loneliness, but peace." However, this kind of salvation for the soul came about, as we saw earlier, through strict ceremonial rituals. In other words, Sugimoto's family exhibited a religious consciousness that was the extreme opposite of modern Protestantism, which rejects ceremony and which values direct exchanges with God on a personal level. On the contrary, it completely aligned with the religious philosophy of Nikolai, who said that union with God only came about through established rituals and ceremonies. In addition, we also cannot overlook the fact that members of the Inagaki family, who belonged to the warrior class, become one with their servants, who were commoners, and took part in these religious events together as equals.

Funerals were another event in which the Japanese displayed their religious beliefs. In the previous chapter, I stated that foreign observers were in awe at seeing the cheerfulness among Japanese funeral processions. Bacon also mentioned this in the following passage:[48]

A funeral procession is an imposing spectacle, and, to the uninstructed foreigner, a cheerful one; for there is nothing sad or somber in the white, or bright-colored, robes of the priests, the white, tinsel-decorated bier, the red and white flags borne aloft, the enormous bunch of gay-colored flowers;- the very mourners in white silk, and with faces apparently unmoved by grief, bring no thought of the object of the procession to the Western mind. It seems more like a bridal than a burial.

After Bacon sated this, however, she added that, if one went to the cemetery, he or she would definitely feel the sadness of the people placing sacred sakaki leaves and incense on the coffin of the deceased. She reasoned that one would thereafter find such funerals to be sad and mournful sights.

Upon viewing the cemeteries, many other observers also realized that the Japanese embraced devout feelings in cherishing the dead. Rutherford Alcock, for instance, stated, "In describing their temples, I ought not to omit some notice of their cemeteries, by far the most remarkable and pleasant part of their religion, and the one which is most in harmony with our own feelings of the sanctity due to a place of rest for the dead."[49] Alcock was referring to the cemetery at Tōzenji temple, the grounds of which lay adjacent to the British Legation. Raphael Pumpelly, meanwhile, stated, "In all that relates to their dead, the Japanese exhibit a refinement one does not expect to find out of Christian countries."[50] British naval officer J. M. Tronson saw the cemeteries in Nagasaki in 1854 and felt that they "evinced a regard for the homes of the dead as generous and warm as is shown by the most civilised nation of the West."[51] Many foreign visitors echoed Tronson's praise for the beauty of the cemeteries in Nagasaki. Richard Brunton, meanwhile, wrote about the burial proceedings on the shore of Hiroshima for a British military officer cadet who had died on a ship conducting a survey for the installation of a lighthouse. After the funeral, which was conducted by all of the crew members and the Japanese officials, "a very pretty sight was presented by quite a number of aged men and women approaching with shrubs and twigs, which they reverently laid on the grave." Brunton, who often grew angry with the Japanese, wrote that this incident showed "a most pleasing and praiseworthy phase of Japanese character."[52]

As explained earlier, religious festivals at temples and shrines looked like nothing more than simple forms of entertainment and pastimes that lacked the seriousness of religion, in the eyes of observers. It was a reality that the Japanese were the most playful people in the world and that they also applied this playfulness to their religion. Margaret Ballagh, for instance, was astonished to see "On great matsuri, or religious holidays the throng of gaily dressed humanity of all ages." She witnessed the festival at Bugenji temple in Kanagawa and mentioned that both sides of the road leading to the temple were filled "many little booths, having for sale abundance of toys, dolls, and everything to delight the eye of children." She also said, "The farmer who brings his daughter, turns from prayer with a smile on his face to purchase pomatum or a mirror for her." When she entered the main part of the temple, she saw "the great building which is 'neither consecrated nor clean,'" and continued by saying, "No feeling of reverence came over our spirits or that of those assembled there." She even saw people throwing "spitballs" at the Buddhist statue. Apparently, if the spitballs stuck, it was a good omen. There was a screen set up in front to prevent the idol from being completely covered in white wads of paper.[53] We can see, therefore, that the people had fun at religious festivals, but did their behavior not contradict the solemnness of religion in interacting with the spiritual world?

Perhaps we can answer this question with Bird's experiences. During her Kansai journey, for example, she came across a festival in Ōtsu. After finishing her dinner at an inn, she mixed in with the crowd and saw the town undergo a complete transformation. She stated that "the long, mean streets were glorified by light and colour, the shop fronts were gone, and arches and festoons of coloured lanterns turned the whole into fairyland." Lanterns three feet long hung from the eaves of every house with the name of the god on the front with the *tomoe*, a swirl design, on the back. The shops had all turned into large spaces upon removing the screen doors, "with backs and sides of splendid folding screens with peonies, lotuses, and irises painted on a dead gold ground." Some of the houses even looked like something out of a fairytale, and a few of them even displayed decorated portable shrines, some of which had "mythological scenes in very ancient needlework, so exquisitely fine, that for some time I supposed them to be paintings." Vases of beautiful chrysanthemums were placed on the floors. Bird said that people were clearly competing for the most beautiful decorations. She also mentioned, "An orderly crowd of many thousands quietly promenaded the narrow streets, admiring and comparing, the *tableaux vivants* in the house fronts nowise moved by all." At the street intersections, strings of lanterns were suspended to a height of twenty-five feet. Naturally, there were also stalls along the streets, and the people were quite boisterous and noisy. In a word, the town was filled with an otherworldly feel.[54] With this, I believe that the question of the previous paragraph has been answered.

Notes:

1 Vysheslavtsov, *Ocherki perom*, 76–7.

2 Tilley, *Japan, the Amoor*, 116.

3 Heusken, *Japan Journal*, 112.

4 Hodgson, *Residence*, 19.

5 Fischer, *Bilder*, 44.

6 Berg, *Eulenburg Expedition*, Vol. 1, 183.

7 Harris, *Complete Journal*, 366.

8 Vysheslavtsov, *Ocherki perom*, 77.

9 Munzinger, *Japaner*, 151, 155.

10 Vasily Mikhailovich Golovnin, *Japan and the Japanese: Comprising the Narrative of my Captivity in Japan, 1811-1813* (London: Colburn and Co., 1852), Vol. 2, 108–10.

11 Hübner, *Ramble*, 298–9.

12 Bird, *Unbeaten Tracks*, Vol. 1, 314.

13 Lindau, *Un Voyage Autour*, 44–7.

14 Suenson, *Skitser*, 158–9.

15 Chamberlain, *Things Japanese*, 409.

16 Kattendijke, *Uittreksel*, 161.

17 Smith, *Ten Weeks*, 13–4.

18 Takaya, *Hebon*, 19.

19 Takaya, *S. R. Buraun*, 17, 46.

20 Metchnikoff, *Bōmei*, 109–10.

21 Alcock, *Tycoon*, Vol. 2, 265–6.

22 Bird, *Unbeaten Tracks*, Vol. 2, 181.

23 Alcock, *Tycoon*, Vol. 2, 229.

24 Chamberlain, *Things Japanese*, 408.

25 Dickson, *Gleanings*, 58.

26 Ponting, *Lotus-land*, 198–9.

27 Bousquet, *Le Japon*, Vol. 2, 622.

28 Alcock, *Tycoon*, Vol. 2, 266.

29 Dickson, *Gleanings*, 290–2.

30 Fortune, *Yedo and Peking*, 215–20.

31 Smith, *Ten Weeks*, 50–1.

32 Smith, *Ten Weeks*, 124.

33 Guimet, *Promenades-Kanagawa*, 42.

34 Guimet, *Promenades-Tokyo-Nikko*, 59.

35 Smith, *Ten Weeks*, 216.

36 Arnold, *Japonica*, 15, 68.

37 Fortune, *Yedo and Peking*, 206–7.

38 Brandt, *Dreiunddreissig*, 242. Based on the length of time that Brandt, Mueller, and Hoffman stayed in Japan, this incident took place sometime between 1872 and 1875.

39 Riess, *Allerei*, 137–40.

40 Bacon, *Japanese Girls*, 465–8.

41 Werner, *Die Preussiche Expedition*, 69.

42 Bird, *Unbeaten Tracks*, Vol. 2, 250–2.

43 Shinoda, *Onna hyakuwa*, 51–4.

44 Katsumatsu Shizuo, *Sengoku jidairon* [Theories on the Warring States Period] (Iwanami Shoten, 1996), 227.

45 Nakamura Kennosuke, *Senbokushi Nikolai to Meiji Nihon* [The Missionary Nikolai and Meiji Japan] (Iwanami Shoten, 1996). See Chapter 5. Excerpts from Nikolai's diary, which Nakamura introduces in his book, appear here along with the author's own opinions.

46 Alcock, *Tycoon*, Vol. 2, 271–2.

47 Sugimoto, *Daughter*, 73–81.

48 Bacon, *Japanese Girls*, 347–8.

49 Alcock, *Tycoon*, Vol. 2, 285.

50 Pumpelly, *Across America*, 140.

51 Tronson, *Personal Narrative*, 405.

52 Brunton, *Building Japan*, 71.

53 Ballagh, *Glimpses*, 78–80.

54 Bird, *Unbeaten Tracks*, Vol. 2, 296–8.

Chapter

14

Barriers of the Mind

One of the biggest differences between Western observers and the Japanese at the time had to do with how they viewed themselves and those around them, as well as their relationships with others. The Japanese of the Edo period had relatively low mental barriers, which seemed to connect to their peaceful, easygoing nature. The Western observers, on the other hand, had embraced modern humanism and placed considerable importance on the individual. Thus, their mental barriers were much higher. To explore this point, let us embark on a journey.

A good place to start the journey is with Rudolf Lindau. Lindau first visited Edo in 1859 with Henry Heusken, an interpreter for the American Legation, as his guide. The two men met in Kawasaki and departed for Edo on a rural road that led to the city. When they arrived, Lindau noted that everything was peaceful and calm. He said the same thing about the villages and wide fields filled with crops that they passed along the way, as well as the farmers who were busy working in those fields. He went on to say that everything he saw induced feelings of peace and relaxation: the sailboats gliding across the azure sea, the rice paddies that looked like green gardens, the temples surrounded by trees that were hundreds of years old, the breeze that was filled with the scent of flowers, and the all-pervasive solitude. Lindau had never felt the level of happiness that people living in this natural environment enjoyed.[1] However, the peace he spoke of had nothing to do with the lack of crime in the country. As stated earlier, Japanese homes were never burglarized even though the people often left their doors unlocked. However, Lindau was actually referring to an overwhelming sense of happiness that seemed to prevail across the land in addition to the glorious scenery and friendly people that he encountered along the way. He was ecstatic with what he found.

Meanwhile, George Smith went on a journey to the Ōmura domain (located in present-day Ōmura City, Nagasaki Prefecture) during his stay in Nagasaki in 1860. On the way, he stopped and rested at a teahouse for four hours in order to escape the daytime heat. The teahouse was filled with vacationers and travelers, and he noticed a group of priests who seemed to be on their way home from a long journey. In their group, there was a girl who was around ten years old, and she was entertaining the other guests by dancing and singing in exchange for some treats. The one-room establishment was primarily occupied by a two-sworded samurai and five or six of his retainers. Smith saw them leave before long and noticed that

Teahouse by the side of a road

they were making their journey on foot. There were also a number of travelers mounted on horses who had stopped at this teahouse to change the
straw sandals on their horses. All of this was playing out in beautiful natural
surroundings. For instance, there was a beautiful wisteria trellis in front of
the teahouse that stretched over the road, and its lovely bough of flowers
cast a cool shadow on the ground. Smith thought that this scene of travelers relaxing at this clean teahouse with some refreshments was one of the
most pleasant experiences he had in Japan. Some of the other guests at the
teahouse picked some flowers and gave them to him and tried to engage him
in conversation by teaching him the names of various things in their mother
tongue. They also found that Smith sitting on the tatami mats was interesting because he was obviously not used to doing so, and it appeared as if he
were having some trouble eating and drinking without a table and chair.[2]

Richard Jephson and Edward Elmhirst, officers of the British Ninth
Regiment, stayed in Japan in the mid-1860s. During their visit to the Great
Buddha of Kamakura, they met a party of traveling entertainers on their
way to Yokohama. They quickly convinced them to perform their entire
repertoire for a few silver pieces. The officers tied up their horses and sat
down on the grass in the shade of a tree along the side of the road. The view
was beautiful, and the sun was bright. The entertainers were performing in
front of foreign visitors for the first time, so they often peeked at the officers

and snickered even as they were lowering their props to the ground to set up for their show. The performance featured top-spinning, magic tricks, butterfly tricks, and other performances well-known to most Japanese at the time. The top-spinning performance was spectacular. The butterfly art was beautiful. Everything was perfect. After the performers announced that the show was over and the two groups parted to set off again on their respective journeys, Jephson and Elmhirst noted that their new Japanese friends kept turning around and crying "Sayonara" ["Farewell"] over and over. When Jephson and his party reached a bend in the road, the performers stopped them again with cries and gestures of concern. When the British officers turned around, they saw that four of the performers had started playing a farewell march with taiko drums and flutes while everyone else was waving goodbye. Jephson's party answered them by taking off their hats to salute them. Until that time, the officers of the Ninth Regiment had seen tricks and feats of magic in gorgeous theaters and drawing rooms the world over, but none of those shows compared to what they had just seen. Jephson and Elmhirst commented:[3]

> Never have we enjoyed anything of the sort as much as we did that half-hour with these top-spinners, in that shady, quiet little glade, with its soft, grassy bank whereon to recline and smoke the fragrant cheroot, and its clear limpid stream, at which to slake our thirst.

Kite-flying, which was itself almost a performance art in Japan, was a dizzying sight to behold. In the spring of 1861, Robert Fortune, who had come to Japan the previous year and who was now on his second visit to the country, saw a number of kites soaring in the sky above both the city of Nagasaki and its suburbs. At first, he mistook the kites for a flock of seagulls. The kites were diamond-shaped and painted in vivid hues of red, white, and blue. Fortune said, "In every street, on the house-tops, on the hill-sides, and in the fields, there were numbers of both sexes and of all ages thus amusing themselves, and all seemed gay, contented, and happy."[4] Reinhold von Werner also saw a kite-flying event that was part of a ceremony on Nagasaki's Mount Konpira in April of the same year. Werner's party hiked the 1.6-kilometer road that led to the top of the mountain and soon encountered a line of people that looked like beads on a bracelet. They climbed for two and a half exhausting hours and finally reached the top, which, they discovered, was a round plateau. There they saw that several thousand kites were already whizzing around the sky about thirty meters above the ground. At least 10,000 people had gathered. The plateau was surrounded by luxuriant, green forest, and families had found places to rest and spread out their

A scene on New Year's Day (illustrated by Wirgman, 1865)

picnic lunches. Werner and his party sat down in a grassy area that seemed to extend everywhere. Some of the Japanese in attendance offered his party some sake, tea, food, and tobacco. In other words, they treated the men with hospitality in the hope that they would enjoy themselves. The experience moved Werner, and he even stated that the ceremony was like a poem. It was as if comedic lyrics, pastoral poems, and romanticism—everything that people wanted—had come together in perfect harmony. Scenes of peace, extreme happiness, and refreshing contentment were on display right before his eyes.[5]

Thus, a world of peace and repose appeared in front of the foreign observers who visited Japan at the end of the Edo period, and they did much to praise it in their writings. As mentioned in an earlier chapter, some people criticized such views for being nothing more than a focus on the positive aspects of Japan that developed in relation to their high hopes for what they would find in the country. However, we should let the critics find the dark aspects. They have actively tried to pick out elements of chaos, deviance, strife, abnormalities, and disorder from the underbelly of society at the end of the Edo period and the beginning of the Meiji period, all of which have become popular explanations that the structure of the modern era itself gives birth to. It is not my intention to support or refute such views in this book. All I want to do is repeat what the foreign observers saw without worrying about whether they considered their discoveries to be good or bad. If we come across an image that appears to be overly positive, we should turn our attention to any evidence to support this claim. After all, every civilization has a dark side. In addition, it is likely the existence of a dark side that actually makes a civilization rich. My primary goal is to remember that the civilization that existed in Japan at the end of the Edo period displayed some physiognomic aspects of happiness and repose, even if this was just one characteristic of the civilization. I hope to do this because that civilization has long since vanished.

This world of repose and affinity even allowed the mentally ill to be active members. Fortune, for instance, visited Kamakura with Walter Dickson and some other colleagues, and they saw a woman sitting in the middle of the road take off her kimono, strip naked, and then start smoking her tobacco pipe. It was quite apparent that she was mad. The woman appeared again while Fortune's party was resting at a teahouse, and she gave their horses some straw and water and then brought her hands together and muttered a kind of prayer for the animals. Despite her mental condition, she seemed harmless, and children were apparently not afraid of her. Later, Fortune's party visited the Great Buddha of Kamakura, and, on the way back, they stopped at the teahouse again to take a nap. When Fortune woke up and peeked into the neighboring room, he saw the same woman sitting by a sleeping member of his party, fanning him with an *uchiwa*, a type of Japanese fan. She stopped every so often to put her hands together and utter a prayer. Later, she brought four cups of tea and a handful of rice and laid them down as an offering to the party. Fortune went on to say, "As soon as she saw us awake and noticing her movements, she rose quietly and walked out of the room without paying the slightest attention to any of us."[6] The woman was free to come and go at the teahouse, and no one reproached her for her actions. The civilization at the time did not actually do much to protect the rights of the mentally disabled, but as long as such individuals did not harm anyone, they were accepted by the people and were even able to mix in and live among them.

As we can see from all of the examples thus far, barriers of the mind, which people use to separate themselves from others, were extremely low in Japan. The people were cheerful and warmhearted and did not hold grudges against others. Edward Morse also stated:[7]

Among the lower classes it is amazing to see their excessive good nature. A jinrikisha man, for example, will smile and laugh in the heartiest way while demanding a few more pennies than you have paid him and which he has reasons for believing are not enough. You repel him harshly, but that makes no difference; he smiles and retires with a kindly grin.

Vasily Golovnin had already realized this reality while he was being held in an Ezo (Hokkaido) prison cell in 1810. He stated:[8]

The Japanese are always good-humoured and cheerful. I never saw those with whom we were acquainted melancholy. They are fond of lively conversation, and jesting; they always sing when at work, and if the work is of such a kind, that it can be performed to the measure of a tune, such as rowing or carrying burthens, they sing.

In February 1905, Erwin von Bälz strolled through Sugita, a village in the outskirts of Yokohama that was famous for plum blossoms. It was still winter, so the blossoms had not yet bloomed, and a piercing cold wind was blowing. Bälz came across a group of women carrying some baskets and buckets that were so heavy that they were practically dragging them along the ground. They were returning home with shellfish that they had collected from the shallows of the nearby sea (present-day Tokyo Bay). Even though a cold, unforgiving headwind was lashing them, "they were chattering like magpies and laughing merrily as they went along." Bälz also wrote, "What a happy nature these people have."[9] In March of the same year, Bälz went to the imperial villa in Shizuura (located in present-day Numazu City, Shizuoka Prefecture) to give the Crown Prince (who would later become Emperor Taishō, also known as "Yoshihito" in the West) a physical examination. As soon as Bälz reached Numazu Station, he noticed that a train carrying Russian prisoners had also just arrived, and he said, "The onlookers made no hostile demonstration, and indeed for the most part seemed sympathetic towards the poor devils." After Bälz finished examining the prince, he returned to Tokyo by train. When he boarded the steam locomotive, he saw that crowds of people were waiting along the railroad tracks so as to get a view of the prisoners passing by. When the train that Bälz was on approached them, he said they all stretched their necks and stood on their tiptoes to get a peek inside. However, when they realized that the passengers were just ordinary Japanese people, they looked disappointed at first, but then almost immediately broke down laughing at being fooled by the passing train. Bälz remarked that Westerners would probably have cursed in anger in a similar situation, but the Japanese just laughed cheerfully and waited patiently for the next train to come. He could not help thinking that they were a happy people with happy tendencies.[10]

This carefree nature of the Japanese connected to their sense of humor.

Bälz also attested to this point. The German doctor greatly extolled the medicinal properties of Kusatsu Hot Springs. One night when he was in the area, all of the landowners in Kusatsu invited him to a teahouse. The gathering took a merry turn, and soon these prominent members of the town were doing strange dances and singing funny songs. Bälz, at seeing all of this, could not help being moved by "how amazingly humorous are the Japanese, and what a talent for caricature they possess." He also said, "they were as merry as children." This is a curious notion because how, exactly, were they able to relax and frolic like children if so many of them were in debt and living on hard times? Bälz also could not believe that these were the same people who had done all they could to protect their homeland from the dangers of the Russo-Japanese War (1904–1905).[11]

We can see another example if we turn back the clock to Willem Kattendijke's time of the late 1850s. The Dutch captain wrote that he would never forget the sights that he saw at the Nagasaki *shoro-nagashi*, or spirit boat procession, which took place during the Bon festival. At the same time, however, he saw funny pictures that the Japanese haphazardly drew on the banners, and he could not help remarking that even on solemn occasions, it was in the Japanese nature to somehow satisfy their playful hearts.[12] Rutherford Alcock echoed this sentiment, for when he saw a top-spinning performance similar to the one that Jephson and Elmhirst had described, he was impressed by the performers' skill, and thought that "there is evidently a great amount of humor and *vis comica* in the Japanese character, which tends to make all these exhibitions doubly amusing."[13]

However, the people were not just being merry and childlike. They often viewed themselves objectively and could not help laughing at themselves if they found their actions and appearance to be ridiculous and comical. The people that Bälz saw along the railroad tracks, for example, had succumbed to this kind of laughter. Basil Chamberlain also unquestionably saw aspects of this reality when he said, "It [Japanese humor] is more like what we may picture to ourselves in the noisy revelling of the Roman saturnalia, the broad jest, the outrageous pun, the practical joke, [and] the loud guffaw." However, he was completely wrong when he said that Japanese humor "lacks alike the hidden tear and the self-criticism of humour: it has no irony, no side-lights."[14] Chamberlain was an intellectual and quite sentimental about what he witnessed, but he could not free himself from the framework of Western thought and was a little insensitive to things. Thus, he failed to see that Japanese humor could also be bitter. According to Russian author Ivan Goncharov (1812–1891), for example, when the Russian party in Nagasaki showed some Japanese officials a map of the world, "they good-naturedly started to laugh" at how small Japan was.[15] Albert Berg wrote about the same kind of reaction in his report. When members of the Eulenburg expedition used a globe to show the shogunate magistrates of foreign affairs the course that they had taken to get to Japan, the officials roared with laughter at seeing that the islands of Japan were so small that they were almost invisible.[16] This likely demonstrates the witty sense of humor on the part of the shogunate officials that the people of Edo were known for. They did not feel belittled by the fact that their homeland was as small as a millet grain on the world map, but they also could not take pride in this distinction. The reality of the situation was simply amusing to them. Obviously, this humor, which the Japanese based on their own objective reality, may have been a sign of the times and appeared to be cheerful on the surface, but we should also admit that there was a deeper bitterness to it that was hard for them to swallow.

Vasily Golovnin often wrote about Japanese humor in his diary during his captivity. When the Matsumae magistrate interrogated him, a laborer who professed to know the Russian language was used as an interpreter. At first the magistrate said something to the man who then turned to Golovnin and said, "'Thou art a man- I am a man- such another is a man- say what sort of man?'" It was clear that the man did not understand Russian well enough to be an interpreter. Later, the magistrate found out that the man did not even know the Russian word for "father," but he and the other officials simply dismissed him with gut-wrenching laughter.[17] What kind of humor was this? It was probably true that the ridiculousness of the man butting in to serve as an interpreter even though he could hardly understand the Russian language made everyone laugh, but from a more-fundamental perspective, they may have found humor in the reality that people and languages were different and that fellow human beings displayed various kinds of foolishness. Even if this were the case, it was a tolerant and generous humor. Golovnin was deeply grateful to the kindness shown to him, especially by Matsumae Magistrate Arao Shigeaki, who held the post when Golovnin was first taken to Matsumae (Arao also held the position of governor of Tajima Province). When Arao was succeeded by the new magistrate, Ogasawara Osayuki (1746–1812), Golovnin drafted a thank-you letter to his benefactor. The seventy-four-year-old Ogasawara, who also held the position of governor of Ise Province, read this letter and laughed. Golovnin wrote, "that fate, in ordaining we should become the prisoners of the Japanese, had, to our good fortune, singled out the period when Arrao-Madsimano-Kami [Matsumae Magistrate Arao] was invested with the government of Matsmai [Matsumae]," but Ogasawara jokingly asked, "whether we supposed any other Japanese nobleman, in the like situation, would not have treated us with equal kindness."[18] This was an intelligent, good-natured sense of humor.

These cheerful people filled with humor were also calm in the face of hardship. In July 1879, Bälz met with a violent thunderstorm while having lunch at his friend's house. He wrote:[19]

> At sea, in front of us, about two hundred yards away, we saw a yellowish-brown cloud of smoke appear and vanish. It came from a junk. The mast had been struck by lightning. Taking a bottle of brandy with us, we jumped into a little boat and rowed off to the scene of the disaster. What we found on arrival seemed barely credible. Round the mast, split by the discharge, so that fragments were lying all over the place, sat the crew of the junk, quietly smoking as if nothing happened. They were obviously surprised that we foreigners had taken the trouble to pay them a visit, but when asked whether any one had been hurt replied cheerfully, "No, but we were startled!" That was all.

In 1865, French naval officer Maurice DuBard (1845–?) boarded a ship in Osaka bound for Fushimi. The small steamboat apparently had engine trouble, and an awful noise reverberated throughout the ship, almost as if the vessel would split in half at any second. Finally, there was a loud boom, and the ship shook horribly, but apparently the jolt fixed whatever was wrong and the boat continued on its journey without any problems. Dubard wrote:[20]

> During this commotion, I observed the people who were on the boat with me, particularly the women and young girls, but none of them even moved so much as an eyebrow. French women in a similar circumstance would have screamed in unpleasant, shrill voices at even the slightest sense of danger, be it real or imagined, yet these Japanese women did not utter a peep from their tiny mouths.

In addition, Dubard also related the following tale. A high-ranking Japanese government official invited Dubard to his home, where he spent the night. He stayed in a room next to the official's wife, and all through the night he heard people talking and going in and out of her room. The next morning, the official apologized to Dubard for how noisy it must have been the night before. Apparently, the man's wife had given birth to a baby boy. Dubard replied that he had heard footsteps and people talking in low voices, but he was shocked that he did not hear any cries of pain. Later, Dubard went to meet the man's wife and praised her for her courage. She promptly replied that only foolish women raised their voices while giving birth. We should obviously remember that women who raise their voices during childbirth are by no means fools. However, the self-control and calm nature exuded by this woman obviously touched Dubard's heart.

Such episodes show that the foreign observers were witnessing a unique civilization that had attained perfection in the late Edo period. They could not help praising the peace and contentment on the people's faces, the joy and resignation they selflessly enjoyed in a life granted by the gods, and the process by which they made the natural environment and the movements of the sun and moon yearly events that shaped their lives. However, it was a civilization that was doomed to vanish. Society in the late Edo period would soon meet with destruction in the areas of politics and economics due to the systematic inconsistencies of the so-called shogunate-domain system. More than anything, however, capitalism had set its sights on the untapped, blank spaces on the map, which Japan was a part of, so it was necessary for the old civilization to end its life. Lindau, for instance, stated that civilization is an irresistible force that acts without mercy or compassion. He added that oftentimes it induces violent change and that throughout the pages of history, countless episodes are written in words of blood and fire.[21] Naturally, Lindau was referring to modern industrial civilization. Alcock, meanwhile, stated something that Karl Marx might have said. He said, "Commerce, proceeding from the West to the East, is an agent of revolutionary character, however little the merchant may wish to make it so, or however much governments desire to prevent it."[22]

I do not intend to argue about the forces at work in the world and Japan at the time, or the necessity they brought about, but I do have a question. Setting aside any political or economic motives, why did the Japanese themselves have to inform the rest of the world about their gradual separation from this perfect and beautiful civilization through what is known as the Meiji period? I wish to focus on this point from the perspective of the mental qualities that build up and form the base of a civilization.

Western observers commonly gave the Japanese high marks for their moral standards. Albert Berg, the author of the *Eulenburg Expedition*, for example, stated that those who saw the cheerful and harmonious lives in Japanese homes, consideration and respect for the elderly and children, and courtesy that was more than suitable for social interactions among the people could not refute the claim that the Japanese were at a high stage in terms of moral education despite having several faults.[23] Meanwhile, Edward Morse, who was the greatest defender of the Japanese of yesteryear, continuously praised their virtues. On the other hand, however, many other foreign observers could not help having serious doubts about the moral qualities of the Japanese.

The first thing that troubled them was the compulsive lying of the Japanese, which, since the arrival of the Jesuits in the sixteenth and seventeenth centuries, had already become legendary. They considered the trickery used by Japanese merchants to be outrageous, but they may have overlooked many of these examples since the merchants were just being merchants. After all, similar practices also existed in Europe. What Alcock and Harris could not forgive, however, was the pathological lying on the part of the shogunate officials. Harris, if you remember, angrily stated, "They are the greatest liars on earth," and Alcock lamented that the greatest vice among the Japanese was their propensity to lie. However, this problem was primarily related in the process of diplomatic negotiations, a point I shall consider in my next book.

Alcock recognized that the Japanese "are a well-to-do, flourishing, and advancing people, and for generations and centuries have maintained a respectable level of intellectual cultivation and social virtues," but, nevertheless, he also could not help feeling "essentially a sordid, sensual life, 'irradiated by no sublime principles, no romantic visions, no active self-renouncing faith.'"[24] Regarding material civilization, meanwhile, Alcock believed that the Japanese could hold their own with the countries of Europe save, of course, for their rudimentary machinery and general lack of the applied sciences,[25] but he also judged that "Their intellectual and moral pretensions, on the other hand, compared to what has been achieved in the more civilized nations of the West during the last three centuries, must be placed very low."[26]

In other words, Alcock wanted to say that the praiseworthy virtues of the Japanese mainly fell into the dimension of social life rather than mental and spiritual orientations of a higher order. Georges Bousquet was more candid about this point. According to him, Japanese society lacked the spiritualism found in the superior elements of the Christian faith, internalized superhuman ideals, and lacked the private impulses that yearn for Heaven, absolute beauty, and eternal happiness. He also said their arts lacked inspiration, sublime aspirations, and an excitement for the absolute.[27] In addition, Bousquet also said that the Japanese language was closely related to this since it was essentially naturalistic and entirely problematic in terms of its abstract words and oftentimes metaphysical ideas.[28]

Percival Lowell, meanwhile, emphasized that the old Japanese civilization was one that had only developed halfway and that it was impersonal and lacked any imagination.[29] Carl Munzinger also added that the Japanese were only interested in reality and concrete ideas, and, therefore, he deplored the fact that they did not show any interest in metaphysical or abstract issues.[30] In short, many foreign observers, such as Alcock and Bousquet, wanted to say that the Japanese buried themselves in reality and did not concern themselves with a higher spiritualism. Faced with intrusions from the West, several Japanese intellectuals at the end of the Edo period dreamed of a synthesis between Eastern spiritual morals and Western material technology. However, Westerners at the time thought that the Japanese were characterized by their material lifestyles while the West, conversely, was characterized by its spiritual dynamics.

The observers discovered a number of praiseworthy traits among the Japanese commoners. At the same time, however, they detected something vulgar and almost asinine in their indifferent expressions. As Aimé Humbert put it, popular arts in Japan contained the true freshness of a culture that had just become civilized, but he also could not abide by the childishness he felt.[31] From the standpoint of Alcock's Victorian sensibilities, meanwhile, it looked like Japanese art was "over a wide area of the least cultivated in pandering to the lower desires, and often to grossness and obscenity."[32]

In addition to these issues, with the coming of the Meiji period, foreign observers began staying at inns and were shocked by the fact that the Japanese did not consider the needs of fellow guests staying in neighboring rooms. In many cases, they called in geisha and other entertainers and noisily cavorted until the sun came up. Even if they did not request a geisha or other entertainment, they would still find ways to frolic with their friends all night long. Even people who were on holy pilgrimages took part in the festivities. Some foreign observers complained, in their diaries, about noisy Japanese guests and not being able to sleep. However, there is ample evidence that this was the case and that such was a tradition that carried over from the Edo period. Noda Shigesuke, the mountain ascetic who traveled across Japan in the early 1800s, wrote about the experience he had when he stayed at a merchant inn in Yanagawa, Kyushu. He stated that the people drinking, singing, and gambling all through the night were outrageous and that he and his party could not sleep due to the ruckus. In his words, the whole town had let loose.[33] In addition, Noda also wrote that, at an inn in Minamata, Kyushu, six or seven guests were gambling all night and just ignored the innkeeper when he told them to stop.[34] Meanwhile, Kawai Tsuginosuke (1827–1868), who would go on to become a senior advisor to the Nagaoka domain (located in present-day Niigata Prefecture), traveled to Nagasaki from 1859 to 1860. When he stayed the night at an inn at the end of the Sanjō Ōhashi Bridge in Kyoto, about thirty palanquin-bearers began gambling and were so noisy that, in the end, Kawai could not get to sleep.[35] Such people were quite literally shameless while they were traveling.

Speaking of the shame of traveling, most Japanese people probably recall Jippensha Ikku's shameless and comical story, *Tōkaidōchū Hizakurige* (Travels on the Tōkaidō Road). The beginning of this tale is particularly strange and raunchy. Yajirobē, one of the main characters in the story and who Japanese readers often lovingly refer to as "Yaji-san," was a merchant in Fuchū, Suruga Province (located in present-day Shizuoka City, Shizuoka Prefecture). He had inherited his business from his father and was quite successful, but he gives himself to debauchery and ends up with a male prostitute named Hananosuke. The two of them burn through Yajirobē's money and then leave together for Edo. Hananosuke's real name is Kitahachi, who is often referred to as "Kita-san," and he begins working for a merchant family while Yajirobē makes a living painting pictures on inkstone cases and tiered boxes at a tenement house in Hatchōbori (located in present-day Chūō Ward, Tokyo). Yajirobē also works at a manor where he meets a woman whom he takes as his wife. They idle away for the next ten years. However, one night, a samurai with a woman, who we discover is the samurai's younger sister, appears and demands that Yajirobē marry her. Yajirobē actually remembers her from his time in Suruga, so due to the circumstances, he takes her as his wife in order to honor the samurai. Yajirobē's current wife, meanwhile, recalls some good times she had over the past ten years, but she also understands the situation and agrees to leave and let Yajirobē marry the new woman. She probably sees it as a good time to do so.

In reality, however, the entire episode that transpired was a ruse designed by Yajirobē, and the samurai and the girl were his partners in crime. They were actually a retired *hatamoto* while she was a female servant whom he had impregnated, and the *hatamoto* was offering fifteen *ryo* to anyone who would take the blame for her pregnancy. Apparently, Yajirobē planned to claim the money, so in order to do so, they decided to get rid of Yajirobē's troublesome wife. He actually wanted the fifteen *ryo* because Kitahachi had embezzled the same amount from the store he worked at and they needed to cover the books. The owner of that store marries a beautiful woman, but his health begins to decline to the point where he could die at any time. If he does die, Kitahachi is poised to take the young heiress as his own and take over the business. Therefore, in order to cover the money that he owes, he implores Yajirobē to help him with the aforementioned scheme. Anyway, the woman delivers the fifteen *ryo*, and Yajirobē seems eager to gloat in the success of his plan, but it is here that Kitahachi's true intentions appear. We learn that the woman is actually a female servant who works at the same store as Kitahachi. The two of them become intimate, and he, not the retired *hatamoto*, is the one who gets her pregnant. Kitahachi, who would have been in big trouble with the heiress if she had discovered his misdeed, gives the servant girl fifteen *ryo*, makes her look like the retired samurai's sister, and pushes her off on Yajirobē. Therefore, embezzling from the store is a bald-faced lie.

This fifteen *ryo* and the journey it makes is quite strange. Yajirobē receives it from the female servant of the retired *hatamoto* and plans to pass it on to Kitahachi. However, in Kitahachi's mind, the fifteen *ryo* that the woman brings him was supposed to have been money that Yajirobē raised. The mysterious paradox in this tale that plays out like a snake eating its own tail shows more of an indifferent irresponsibility on the part of the characters than any foolishness. In short, this is a story in which everything is just short of being suitable. If things go well, there is a good outcome, and even if things were never meant to go well, no one seems to mind in the end. Everything that the characters do results from their constant indifference and their spirit of irresponsibility.

The opening chapter of the tale does not end there. After Kitahachi's lie is discovered and a scuffle ensues, the servant woman starts going into labor and shockingly dies soon thereafter. The reader knows that she is dead, but the two men seem completely unconcerned with the situation. Instead, they buy some food and sake and have a big party, getting so drunk that they decide to put the girl in a basket and take her to a Buddhist temple. One of them asks where the temple is, and the other scolds him for being so foolish as to believe that there is a temple in his house. After this, they take everything they see with them, and then, in rather poor taste, joke that someone might pay for her funeral if they march around the town shouting, with her in tow. In time, a man claiming to be the father of the girl answers their call and appears, but after staring into their basket, he says nonsensically that she is not his daughter because "she does not have a neck and has hair growing on her chest." Apparently, Yajirobē and Kitahachi had clumsily placed her corpse in the basket upside down, so the man, who was obviously looking at the woman's legs and nether regions, seemed to exhibit a sense of bad taste in coming to this conclusion so quickly.

While all of this is going on, the owner of the store that Kitahachi works at dies that very night, and the young heiress decides to fire Kitahachi because she does not like the licentious way in which he had been looking at her. Quite annoyed with the situation, Yajirobē and Kitahachi make up and set off on a pilgrimage to Ise Shrine—the main part of their story in which they have many adventures or, rather, misadventures together.[36]

Naturally, the tale of Yajirobē and Kitahachi is quite ridiculous, and the main characters come across as excessive and scatterbrained individuals. However, we have to consider that the same sort of sordidness and anarchy was also quite common in Western European tales from the Middle Ages to the beginning of the modern era. Even so, we have to question what exactly created the mindset behind Yajirobē casting aside his wife as if she were nothing or Kitahachi having a huge party after the woman he got pregnant dies. This is by no means a misogynistic story. Yajirobē's wife probably left him because she was sick of him, and if the roles had been reversed and Yajirobē and Kitahachi were the ones who had died, neither the wife nor the pregnant servant girl would have shed a tear. Moreover, Yajirobē and Kitahachi do not just look down on the lives of the women—they also look down on their own lives. The key point to the story that comes to the surface here is that no one accepts responsibility for anything. In other words, the theme that persists throughout this story is likely the mindset that people who take this world too seriously are fools. This world and its people mean very little, and if this is the case, it is better to avoid getting preoccupied with anything. Life is too short, so one should live it with ease while poking fun at the world. This is the feeling that passes through the main characters and controls them, and it combines with a certain sense of nihilism. Yet it is a cheerful nihilism. Wanting to blow out the existence of being human like a candle is, conversely, a tolerance for humanity. Yajirobē and Kitahachi were once very close friends, but they easily betray one another for their own purposes even though their ties of friendship are supposed to be strong. However, even though they betray one another, their relationship continues as if nothing happened. This is because they knew the nature of humanity. In other words, they reasoned that they would have done the same thing if they had been in their friend's shoes. In addition, knowing this forced them to embrace humor—not a dark nihilism—when contemplating the selfishness of human existence, along with embracing a tolerance for their own humorous mutual existence. Therefore, the road ahead has many vulgar and obscene episodes in store for them, but this is also a series of extremely innocent and silly stories. The characters argue over their selfish desires, but this never creates any serious problems, and, in time, a peaceful and mutually compassionate world develops. It is almost as if the trip were another traveling companion and the world was the compassion.

Naturally, most of the commoners of the Edo period were not wild and easygoing souls like Yajirobē and Kitahachi, and it goes without saying that most of them made efforts to live honest and serious lives. Yajirobē and Kitahachi were idlers, as we can clearly see from their exploits. However, their story was overwhelmingly welcomed by those of the lower class. In other words, the mindset of said class was connected to Yajirobē and Kitahachi on a fundamental level. For the modern reader, this tale, particularly the opening section, features a number of developments that completely go against the grain of our moral sensibilities, but when it first came out, it is quite likely that no one criticized the main characters for being lewd because, after all, if they did, they would be looked upon as hopeless fools.

However, we find the humor in this story to be strange and even nauseating to a certain extent today. This is because we seek definite proof of the individual in our own existence as well as in the existence of others. In other words, we have been baptized by the humanism of Western European modernism. Naturally, modern humanism remains in the crossfire of the debate about its importance as a value system that has brought stability to the world. Even so, we cannot return to a time before humanism in terms of our sense of being alive. We can never live like Yajirobē or Kitahachi did, nor would we want to.

Feeling a definite sense of the individual in our existence meant that the barriers of the mind had to be built higher. Let us return to Noda's tale at the inn, for example. If we follow the idea that someone could sympathize with the other guests who started getting rowdy and believe that they would probably do the same thing if they had come with their own friends, then they probably would not have any trouble sleeping through the night. It also makes sense that he or she might open the screen door separating their rooms and comment on how much fun they seemed to be having. In this case, the partiers would have welcomed him or her to join in the festivities. Only the high barrier of the self-awareness of the individual would have made this person unable to take part or decide not to do so.

People like Edwin Arnold, who fell head over heels in love with the peace and easygoing nature of the Japanese lower classes, were those who had grown weary of the high Western European barriers of the mind. However, the barriers did more than this. The fact that the barriers were high meant that the limits of human ability to think, feel, and express through individualism had expanded exponentially. Alcock and Bousquet felt that this country lacked the spiritual development to make this world of the individual possible.

It was also the case with Sugimoto Etsuko. Her husband passed away while she was living in the United States, so she decided to return to Japan with her two daughters, Hanano and Chiyo. However, after a while they had to go back to America because Sugimoto was struck by the change that appeared in her older daughter, Hanano. Sugimoto wrote:[37]

> I wondered if Hanano was ever really happy any more. She never seemed sorrowful, but she had changed. Her eyes were soft, not bright; her mouth drooped slightly and her bright, cheery way of speaking had slowed and softened. Gentle and graceful? Yes. But where was her quick readiness to spring up at my first word? Where her joyous eagerness to see, to learn, to do? My little American girl, so full of vivid interest in life, was gone.

This was not just a case of cultural differences in disciplining the girl. It was also not just the case of Sugimoto's family demanding that the girl follow the traditional virtues of women as espoused by an elite warrior family. The world of the individual that had been bred into Hanano's soul had likely been suffocated under the change to her environment. Sugimoto herself expressed her astonishment at how the foreign teachers during her days at Aoyama Gakuin (present-day Aoyama Gakuin University) "were all young, lively, [and] most interesting," for she could not recall seeing people from her childhood showing their true feelings.[38] Morse also said, "One notices in the Japanese face no strongly marked expression."[39] Today we can question whether showing strong emotions makes us happy or if embracing a fixed sense of the individual self is really that great of a quality to have. The episode with Hanano, for instance, could invite an almost endless debate about this point. However, necessity has always been a part of human history. The old and wonderful civilization of Japan had to end its life in this way.

Notes:

1 Lindau, *Un Voyage Autour*, 152–3.

2 Smith, *Ten Weeks*, 185–8.

3 Jephson and Elmhirst, *Our Life*, 81–3.

4 Fortune, *Yedo and Peking*, 171–2.

5 Werner, *Die Preussiche Expedition*, 162–4.

6 Fortune, *Yedo and Peking*, 228–9, 233–4. Dickson related another story about this woman a few days later. According to this account, she recovered at the hospital, married a Chinese man, and had a son by him. However, her husband took the boy with him back to China, and she once again fell into madness. When Dickson returned to Japan in 1883, she was in a much-worse condition than she was before. See Dickson, *Gleanings*, 136.

7 Morse, *Day by Day*, Vol. 1, 44.

8 Golovnin, *Captivity*, Vol. 2, 149.

9 Bälz, *Awakening Japan*, 345.

10 Bälz, *Awakening Japan*, 359–64.

11 Bälz, *Awakening Japan*, 305.

12 Kattendijke, *Uittreksel*, 189.

13 Alcock, *Tycoon*, Vol. 2, 281.

14 Chamberlain, *Things Japanese*, 195.

15 Goncharov, *Pallada*, 277.

16 Berg, *Eulenburg Expedition*, Vol. 1, 220.

17 Vasily Golovnin, *Memoirs of a Captivity in Japan, during the Years 1811, 1812, and 1813* (London, 1824), Vol. 1, 199–200.

18 Golovnin, *Memoirs*, Vol. 2, 81.

19 Bälz, *Awakening Japan*, 48.

20 Dubard, *Pittoresque*, 144–7.

21 Lindau, *Un Voyage Autour*, 16.

22 Alcock, *Tycoon*, Vol. 2, 313.

23 Berg, *Eulenburg Expedition*, Vol. 1, 195–6.

24 Alcock, *Tycoon*, Vol. 1, 322–3.

25 Alcock, *Tycoon*, Vol. 2, 225–6.

26 Alcock, *Tycoon*, Vol. 2, 264.

27 Bousquet, *Le Japon*, Vol. 2, 563, 733.

28 Bousquet, *Le Japon*, Vol. 2, 375.

29 Lowell, *Soul*. See Chapter 1 and Chapter 8.

30 Munzinger, *Japaner*, 69.

31 Humbert, *Japan and the Japanese*, Vol. 2, 145 (translated from the Japanese version).

32 Alcock, *Tycoon*, Vol. 2, 223.

33 Noda, *Shūgyō nikki*, 39.

34 Noda, *Shūgyō nikki*, 12.

35 Kawai Tsuginosuke, "Jinko" ["Dustpail"], in *Nihon Shomin Seikatsu Shiryō Shūsei* [Lives of the Japanese People] (Sanichi Shobō, 1969), Vol. 2, 404.

36 Jippensha Ikku, *Tōkaidōchū Hizakurige* [Travels on the Tōkaidō Road] (Iwanami Bunko, 1973). This synopsis comes from the opening chapter of the book. An English translation by Thomas Satchell, titled *Shank's Mare*, also exists.

37 Sugimoto, *Daughter*, 271.

38 Sugimoto, *Daughter*, 120.

39 Morse, *Day by Day*, Vol. 1, 124.

Afterword

I do not really remember when, exactly, I got it in my head to take on the ridiculous task of writing an epic tale about modern Japan. I think that the lectures I gave on modern Japanese history at a temple called Shinshūji twice a month definitely helped get the ball rolling, however. I started giving these talks in October 1980, and we met 110 times before completing the series in May 1985. During this time, I believe the late Hisamoto Santa, then president of Ashi Shobō Publishing, wanted to compile all of the topics of my lectures into a book.

Naturally, I did not want to put the contents of my lectures, which were primarily for young people who came to the temple, into book form. What I really wanted to write about was the Shōwa period of Japan (1926–1989), particularly the time before World War II, as, to me, the Shōwa period ended in 1945. For better or worse, I was a child of these times. By the time I turned 50 in 1980, a burning desire to analyze the structure of this time period in order to understand the meaning of my own life had been welling up inside me. I actually started writing a serial called "Shōwa no Gyakusetsu" ("The Shōwa Paradox") for the magazine *Kurago*, but due to certain circumstances, the series ended prematurely.

Meanwhile, it was clear to everyone at the time that the modern era, one particular period in human history, was coming to an end. Japan in the 1980s was dominated by postmodern discourse, but the moniker of "post" only made the theories floating around sound like fashionable, ultramodern mannerisms that could not explain how the modern era actually came to an end. Even though the conditions were ripe to objectively view and understand the process of Japanese modernism, there was, conversely, a rampant spread of ultramodern values that hampered this to some degree.

Starting in 1982, I taught an outrageous course called "Theories on Japanese Culture and Western Culture" as a part-time lecturer at Kumamoto Junior College (now known as Kumamoto Gakuen University Junior College). For the first time ever, this gave me the chance to read through several articles written by foreign observers who visited Japan during the end of the Edo period/beginning of the Meiji period. I was amazed by the true sense of freshness in their portrayals of old Japan, and this made me seriously contemplate what Japan's modern era entailed. In order to ask questions about the meaning of the Shōwa period, we have to ask questions about the meaning of the opening of Japan and, in turn, the state of its civilization before the country opened itself to the rest of the world in the mid-to-late 1800s. Ishiwara Kanji is famous for stating that Commodore Perry should have been resurrected and put on trial at the International Military Tribunal for the Far East, as Ishiwara claimed that it was Perry's American imperialism that Japan emulated and eventually led the country down the path of war. After reading all of the records I had come across, I felt it was truly time to search out the meaning to Ishiwara's words in a different light.

Mr. Hisamoto, who knew of my intent to write a very long tale with modern Japan as the main character, told me that he would be more than happy to personally publish this work. Now that the first volume of this book is finally being published by Ashi Shobō, I think I have fulfilled the promise we made before he died. However, I also have to mention the efforts made by a friend of thirty years, Mr. Sudō Nobuhiro, in making my wish a reality. The first draft of this manuscript was published in serial form in *Shūkan Ekonomisuto* [The Weekly Economist], a magazine published by the *Mainichi Shimbun* newspaper. Mr. Sudō was the editor-in-chief of this magazine, which ran my articles from 1995 until the following year. If it had not been for Mr. Sudō's kindness and encouragement, I would probably still be buried in a mountain of lingering resources, trying to get the work done at my typical snail's pace.

After running what would become the prologue and the first chapter of this book in the *Economist*, the serial ended halfway through the second chapter, tentatively titled "The Peace of the Tokugawa Age." Even though we had initially agreed to run the serial for only a year, it stretched on for another four months or so before ending. I went into the project thinking that I could at least get the first part of my tale published in the magazine, but after the serial ended, I realized I had not even told a third of the story.

In touching on the entire book here, I realize it is going to be much longer than I expected, and I can only guess at how many volumes it will come to. Even though I want to continue telling my story until 1945, I admit that this will be impossible considering my age. I also never had the intention to write a general history. I therefore named the book *Nihon Kindai Sobyō* [A Rough Sketch of Modern Japan], but in order to write about the end of the Edo period, I have to go through the entire Tokugawa era, and in order to do this, I have to go all the way back to the Muromachi period (1392–1573). This would unquestionably make the book even longer, and the task seems to grow more impossible with each passing day. It also did not help that I started working on the project at least ten years too late. Time is running out, and there is still too much work to do. Even though the first few volumes are finished, I am resigned to the fact that it may be impossible.

I combined the aforementioned prologue and first chapter that ran in the *Economist* into this volume, but due to some additional writing and editing, the amount of material almost doubled in size over what appeared in the magazine. As I said earlier, I had no intention of writing a general, overarching history of Japan, so please think of this volume as an independent work. Based on the big picture, I also designed my book *A Rough Sketch of Modern Japan* to be more of a collection of independent volumes rather than one continuous work.

This volume uses a substantial number of works by British and American authors that have not been translated into Japanese. I would like to express my thanks to the university interlibrary loan service for allowing me to access so many of these tomes and a very special thank you to all of the wonderful staff in the Kumamoto University Library Information Service Department for their efforts. I would also like to express my profound thanks to each university library that loaned me these books—books that have become so rare in the present day—as well as all the staff and others involved, who are too numerous to name here. In addition, I also wish to thank Ms. Kitahara Kanako for her insight on Maclay and Mr. Kitazawa Sakae for sending me the articles by Lafarge and Arnold that originally ran in magazines. I am also deeply grateful to President Mihara Hiroyoshi and everyone at Ashi Shobō Publishing for putting up with my obstinacy and for doing so much tedious work on my behalf. I also wish to thank Mr. Yamada Masahiko and his lovely wife Risa from the bottom of my heart. This work would have truly been impossible without their devotion and cooperation.

Finally, I would like to say a word about the state of the translations of the diaries and other records made by foreign visitors to Japan that appear in this book. Even though many trivial and relatively unimportant works have been translated and met with great fanfare over the years, I have noticed that many standard works have not been translated into Japanese. Records made by such authors as Sherard Osborn, George Smith, J.M. Tronson, and Henry Tilley just after Japan opened its doors to the world contain a number of valuable observations and evidence, and Jephson and Elmhirst's book makes for an interesting read. I also find it surprising that Edwin Arnold's diary about his stay in Japan has never been translated. Alice Bacon's major works have also never been translated, and Isabella Bird's massive work does not have a complete translation. It would also be nice to have an amended translation of Robert Fortune's book. I wonder if it would be arrogant of me to consider this book the catalyst we need to improve this situation.

Watanabe Kyoji
June 1998

A Postscript to the Heibonsha Library Edition

It comes as a great joy and relief to see *Remnants of Days Past* get republished by Heibonsha Library. Since the original publisher stopped printing this book, it became a rarity of sorts that no one could find at any used bookstore. Because of this, numerous readers have contacted me about this issue and implored me to do something. As a result, I had to give away all but one of the few copies I had left. I think that the addition of the Heibonsha Library edition will make everyone happy. Therefore, I would like to offer my deepest thanks to Heibonsha editor-in-chief, Mr. Ninomiya Yoshihiro, for taking an interest in this book and seeing its second publication to fruition.

I am an author who does not sell many books, but I am fine with that. Sometimes my books find their way into various anthologies or become mass-market paperbacks and sell in the neighborhood of several tens of thousands of copies, but I think the first edition of any book that is really important has usually been limited to 3,000 copies and never received a reprint. However, this book did sell well, and perhaps one of the reasons for this was that a number of people have lauded it, even though they would never benefit from such praise. At any rate, I am sorry this book did not become a bestseller while Mr. Hisamoto Santa, the late president of Ashi Shobō Publishing who published a number of my books that did not sell, was still alive. In addition, I also want to repay a debt of gratitude to Mr. Mihara Hiroyoshi, who was president at the time of publication, for being a partner who put up with me for over thirty years.

It is, of course, a pleasure to know that so many people have bought and enjoyed my book, but at the risk of saying something that may come back to haunt me, there was also quite a bit that made me feel a little uneasy. There were a lot of book reviews and critiques, for example, that were hard to deal with. This is because, sure enough, there were some people in Japan who thought, or wanted to think, that I was boasting that Japan used to be this great country even though I never stated this outright.

I certainly introduced remarks made by foreign observers that stated that old Japan was so beautiful that it was like something out of a dream. I also stated the case that we should not let the now-sloppy design of Orientalism and other paradigms haphazardly overshadow this assessment. However, I never had any intention of boasting about my homeland. I just wanted to use this book to present a frame of reference in order to relativize the present day. Old Japan is one such frame of reference and nothing more. Compared to my previous books, some readers may have felt a sudden change in direction, but as my central theme has always been my own uncomfortable feelings about the unique state of modern human society, I can assure you that this is not the case. However, I do not wish to write about these overly exhausted points any longer. The questions that this book has evoked and my answers to such have already been stated in my short essay *Yukishi yo to Gendai* [Days Past and the Modern Age], which appears in *Watanabe Kyoji Hyōron Shūsei III: Kōya ni Tatsu Niji* [Collection of Essays by Watanabe Kyoji III: Rainbows in the Wilderness] (Ashi Shobō Publishing, 1999).

In talking about the concept of "Japan," I am fed up with having to make "Japan" an issue each and every time. I do not want to talk about "Japan" any longer. The only world I know is the one that I possess, and even though I realize that we need to be responsible and respond to the reality that is, of course, made up of the various phenomena of politics, economics, and culture that form the basic divisions of a nation-state, I think this is just one aspect. The reality that I live in is unquestionably Japan as an integral of history, but regarding whether this is good or bad, all I can do is participate in the world possessed by humankind as someone molded and shaped as such.

When speaking of tradition these days, the current trend is to call it a fictional social phenomenon that was created only in the latter part of the modern era. Naturally, this could very well be the case. However, my very existence cannot be a brand new one that has no connection with the past. Therefore, aside from whether we could call it tradition, there is a dual existence of the self: one built on integrals of the past and one that tracks one's own decisions in the present and future. In that sense, I am a Japanese person. However, this differs from limiting myself to being a member of the nation-state of Japan. I am aware of the fate of being formed within the land, climate, and history of Japan and having to participate in the experience of being human.

Fate is evocative yet troublesome. I grew up in the Chinese cities of Beijing and Dalian. For me, Japan was a pure and untainted country famous for its cherry blossoms. They also bloom in Dalian, but this Chinese city is more famous for the bluish-white apricot blossoms that are more numerous and that come out long before the cherry trees start to bloom. They resemble cherry blossoms, and I actually prefer them because they are more beautiful and delicate. In the heart of spring, meanwhile, the lilacs bloom and one can smell the scent of the black locust trees in the air. In summer, the sky is a deep ultramarine color in the truest sense of the word. We can also tell when autumn has come because the wind changes direction and starts blowing in from the harbor. In winter, thick snow clouds hang low across the land, and the world has the strange luster of a gloomy work by Johannes Brahms. Kiyooka Takayuki, a famous Japanese poet who graduated from the same junior high school eight years before I did, was not the only one to call Dalian home. It was also my hometown.

As fate would have it, however, Dalian was a foreign land, and I was not destined to live there. Eventually, I returned to my "homeland" of the cherry blossoms, an experience that had both positive and negative aspects. Since then, I have always felt like a pseudo-foreigner in this country. Even so, I did not rebel against Japan, which seems to be a trend these days. Those who profess to and find joy in rebelling against Japan only expose their own ignorance. The problem I had with Japan was that I simply could not get used to the country. Above all, I could not get used to interacting with Japanese intellectuals. That is all I will say on this matter here, but I can assure you that I also felt uneasy about Japan's natural environment.

I entered a tuberculosis sanatorium when I was eighteen and stayed there for four and a half years. The facility was located about ten kilometers or so northeast of Kumamoto City and was surrounded by a gorgeous plateau of fields and forests known as "Miyoshino." It was here that I first felt the natural beauty of this country. The beauty I encountered was more like author Miyazawa Kenji's "Ihatov" and probably differed a great deal from the more-general natural areas in Japan. However, the paleness of the cobalt blue skies still could not compare with the ones I experienced in China. That pale blue sky was still beautiful in early spring, but in midsummer it felt a bit underwhelming. From that moment on, I did notice the various aspects of natural beauty that the foreign observers in this book praised, but even so, there was still too much in the way of making me think that I truly belonged to the natural scenery of this country.

For one thing, I did not care for the dampness in Japan. When Japanese people visit famous Shinto shrines and Buddhist temples, they often become engrossed in the beautiful moss that grows in such areas, but I cannot abide the dampness of these green carpets. Even when I walk through fantastic gorges in the mountains, the tops of the trees always strike me with their beauty, but I cannot stand the dampness of the leaves piled up on the forest floor that we walk on. Even if I get drawn in by mist forming in the fields, fog springing from the valleys, and other elements of silent splendor that look like something out of a *sansui* landscape painting, the natural scenery of Japan still looks so lonely. I often feel chills running up and down my entire spine at the thought of dying in a place like this.

You could say, therefore, that in writing this book, I did so as a cohort to all of the foreign observers introduced within its pages when they visited Japan. In other words, I was writing about a foreign country. Moreover, I saw Japan directly through their eyes rather than examining how they saw it. Like them, I was charmed by the unique and separate foreign culture of old Japan.

Old Japan as I refer to here is the civilization that reached its zenith during the Edo period in the middle part of the eighteenth century. I wrote another book after this one about the unique atmosphere of the time, titled *Edo to iu Genkei* [Edo the Illusion] (Gen Shobō, 2004). Naturally, there was quite a bit of criticism about focusing on the peaceful nature of the Edo period. Some of my critics stated this was just one aspect of the era, and, as several authors have also attested to, there was certainly a dark side. The only response I had for them was "And?" I even emphasized the fact that no society exists without a dark side in this book. My point was that the peace of the Edo civilization is, with all the dark elements that certainly existed, worth our interest in the present meaning of things. The problem was: where did the mentality behind this impudent criticism come from? This is one of the points that I often refer to when discussing with Japanese intellectuals.

I do have the temptation to one day thoroughly discuss the structure and characteristics of Edo society when it was fully developed. However, I wonder if I will have the time and energy to do this. I will say the following, though. When I was a boy, I considered myself luckier to be born in the Shōwa period than the Edo period. Now, however, I honestly believe that my life as a person may have been better if I had been born in the Edo period and lived in a second-floor room above a *nagauta* music master or spent my entire life as a *terakoya* private school teacher in a village somewhere.

One of the nice things about releasing this book is that more people, or, rather, a greater range of readers than ever before, are reading my books. Prior to this, I only thought about a small group of readers. There were just a few hundred avid readers of my books, but again that was just fine with me. Now, my books are reaching a wider range of readers, and that truly makes me happy.

Finally, I would like to express my regrets about something. The first edition that was published by Ashi Shobō Publishing included the subtitle, "Nihon Kindai Sobyō 1" ["A Rough Sketch of Modern Japan 1"], but this was, by nature, removed from the paperback edition. I realized this subtitle was actually a big mistake on my part. I guess you could say it was the result of my delusions of grandeur. Naturally, I had planned to write a series of books to follow this one, but all my time was taken up in writing two other books that were a byproduct of this one: one was the aforementioned *Edo the Illusion*, and the other was titled *Nihon Kinsei no Kigen* [Origins of Modern Japan] (Yudachisha, 2004). This left me exhausted. I felt I was done with dealing with modern Japan—especially the ideas of Japanese intellectuals. In the future, I might feel like writing about this again, and I admit that I have the responsibility to complete successive volumes because I said I would, but at any rate, I regret using this now-pointless subtitle. Even so, I wonder just how many years I have left.

Moreover, in the afterword to the first edition, I wrote about how disappointed I was that the Japanese translations of Bird, Smith, Osborn, and Arnold's works did not exist (in the case of Bird, a complete translation did not exist). However, each of these works now has a translation, thanks to the efforts of Yushodo Publishing and an anthology they released, titled *Shin Ikoku Sōsho Dai Sanshū* [New Collection of Foreign Writings, Vol. 3]. This is a welcome development.

Watanabe Kyoji
July 2005

Commentary
Sympathy is the Best Method for Understanding

By Hirakawa Sukehiro

Professor Emeritus at The University of Tokyo
Critic and Researcher of Comparative Culture and Comparative Literature

Remnants of Days Past is a book with an emotionally stirring title that seeks to discover and understand the civilization that existed before the end of the Meiji period. Namely, this was the civilization crushed by the Westernization and modernization of Japan. The author, Watanabe Kyoji, has laid out this epic tale in a huge book by closely examining an incredible number of records written by foreign observers who visited the country during the end of the Edo period and into the Meiji period. Watanabe, who feels a fresh sense of surprise in seeing old Japan as reflected in the eyes of these Westerners, does not succumb to ideology or prejudice and responds candidly to their descriptions. This, along with the author's eloquent prose, makes this book worth reading. It is a true testament to how sympathy, on an equal level with criticism, is the best way to understand things and other people. However, this book is not just an encyclopedic trip down memory lane. It also includes issues the author is known for tackling time and time again. What, exactly, is the pathos that Watanabe uses to make this book so lively and fill its paragraphs with such vigor?

Watanabe was born in 1930 and currently lives in Kyushu. He is a historian of ideas and has never belonged to any public academic circles, and this book was first published in 1998 by Ashi Shobō, a distinguished publisher in Fukuoka. Watanabe has not adhered to the strict paths often followed in the academic world either, and despite that, he is a great author who has gained strength little by little with every step forward, and now readers can hear him stomping like a thunderous giant. Watanabe has long held the view and even states in this book that "In order to ask questions about the meaning of the Shōwa period, we have to ask questions about the meaning of the opening of Japan and, in turn, the state of its civilization before the country opened itself to the rest of the world in the mid-to-late 1800s." (See the Afterword to the first edition.) In this case, Watanabe defines civilization as that which "embodies the historical characteristics of the lifestyle of a people as a whole" and that "individual social structures, customs, and lifestyles, and these aspects stretch into how people relate to nature and other living things." (See Chapter 1.) In other words, Watanabe believes culture does not vanish—it simply transforms, whereas a civilization, as displayed in the lifestyles of the people and other aspects mentioned above, actually can vanish. He also recognizes that the history of modern Japan was built on top of the corpse of the civilization of the previous era. In other words, his view is that "a one-time civilization with its own organic individuality completely vanished." (See Chapter 1.) Therefore, the author is attempting to reconstruct the past in seeking this lost civilization. Moreover, he exhibits considerable passion for his quest because he believes this old civilization is worthy of our interest and respect. The question, therefore, is whether the world of the past civilization that has been recreated is simply an illusion created by the author or if it is the remnant of something real and truly beautiful.

Watanabe states that, in order to envision what the old Japanese civilization looked like, we must rely on the testimony of foreign observers. This is because the Japanese were playing out these scenes in their daily lives and could not view them from the standpoint of someone on the outside looking in. In other words, they were accustomed to everything around them and were not aware of any unique characteristics. Watanabe also divides and details these characteristics that only the Westerners paid attention to into more than ten fascinating chapters, focusing on such topics as "Cheerful People," "Simplicity and Wealth," and "Friendliness and Courtesy." The book, which could even be called a sociographic record of Japan at the time when it opened itself to the rest of the world, also includes topics such as the "A Children's Paradise," "Religious Beliefs and Festivals," "The Status of Women," "The Naked Body and Sex," and other areas related to the strange civilization of Japan that the Westerners wrote about with surprise. Watanabe has put everything into good order, offered detailed explanations, and made use of clear and concise sentences. He leaves the reader with the same affable impression he or she may get from viewing the remarkable sketches by Félix Régamey, Charles Wirgman, and other artists that are scattered throughout this text. Illustrations such as Régamey's "Teahouse girl in Enoshima," which appears in Chapter 6, are as beautiful as paintings of Mother Mary from the Italian Renaissance.

Incidentally, Japanese critic Katō Shūichi and other individuals used this angle of "Japan seen through the eyes of foreign observers" immediately after the end of World War II. However, Watanabe makes the following point in the first chapter, imparting unique values to this book:

> One of these issues is that intellectuals focusing on Japan tend to dismiss such records as nothing more than glorified illusions based on the argument that impulses and strong emotions move and determine recorded history. It is also true that we cannot even take one step forward without examining the Japanese quality of self-denial.

Well then, what, exactly, caused these impulses of denial to develop? For one thing, many intelligent professors and journalists from national and private universities felt that old Japan was something that needed to be discarded in order to pursue the latest trends of Western thinking. They had no confidence and pride in being Japanese and insisted that their country's past had no value. This is probably what led to them to jump to and adopt new ideas so easily. Immediately after the war, for example, some of these intellectuals hailed the French Resistance writers, trumpeted Sartre's existentialism, and praised the ideas of Paris Mode. Eventually, they became big-name critics and essayists for major Tokyo newspapers and still continue to reign high in critical spheres today. Such individuals have only made this movement possible by denying Japan's past as being nothing more than fanciful illusion. However, some of these people are frauds. These "New Left" intellectuals simply were taken in by novelties—one could even call this a chronic affliction. Even so, these critics are the ones who occupy most of the critical spheres of Japan. All they do is praise new knowledge and thinking while ignoring or even discarding old knowledge. However, Watanabe is different. He has calmly yet sternly called out this superficial movement as the "emperor with no clothes" situation that it is.

Remnants of Days Past does not aim at enumerating and trumpeting foreign interest in the exoticism of Japan. However, the author does not deny the descriptions made by the Westerners as beautified illusions. Critics of French literature who have occupied critical spheres in postwar Japan have wholly denied pre-modern Japan with a priori conception, and, ironically, those who have opposed such an attitude probably agree with Watanabe. This may also be the reason why Japanese author and former Governor of Tokyo Ishihara Shintarō, who seems to have run out of patience with intellectuals who look down on Japan and its past, rated this book so highly.

Watanabe is true to his own sensibilities. Therefore, he does not necessarily deny foreign interest in the exoticism of Japan, which has actually soured of late. He also turns the criticism around on Said's disdain for orientalism from time to time. The author values the principle that "The exotic turns the eye to the detailed aspects of life that people are not used to seeing, and, consequently, this can recreate the feel of a certain civilization" (See Chapter 1.) He certainly made this statement based on his own feeling. The style of life in Meiji Japan was multifaceted. Still, many foreign observers unanimously focused on some particular points without realizing it. The remnants of the old civilization lie here. The past has not completely vanished from our minds. The remnants of days past are evocative because they continue to murmur ever so slightly in our hearts.

References
Important People of Note

Rutherford Alcock (1809–1897), British Consul-General

Vittorio F. Arminjon (1830–1897), Italian navy commander and Italian admiral, explorer, writer

Edwin Arnold (1832–1904), English poet and journalist

Alice Mabel Bacon (1858–1918), instructor at a school for noble girls

Margaret T.K. Ballagh (1840–1909), wife of an American missionary

Erwin Bälz (1849–1913), German physician

Albert Bauduin (1829–1890), Dutch Consul at Nagasaki

Ludovic Marquis de Beauvoir (1846–1929), author and 19th-century voyager

André Bellesort (1866–1942), French writer

Albert Berg (1825–1884), member of the Eulenburg expedition and author of the expedition's official reports

William Sturgis Bigelow (1850–1926), American collector of Japanese art

Isabella Lucy Bird (1831–1904), British explorer, writer, photographer, and naturalist

John Reddie Black (1826–1880), Scottish publisher, journalist, writer, photographer, and singer

Georges Hillaire Bousquet (1846–1937), Frenchman who stayed in Japan from 1872 to 1876 as an advisor to the Ministry of Justice, French legal scholar

Max von Brandt (1835–1890), German diplomat, East Asia expert, and publicist, member of the Eulenburg expedition

Admiral Cyprian Arthur George Bridge (1839–1924), British Royal Navy officer

Samuel Robbins Brown (1810–1880), American missionary

Richard Henry Brunton (1841–1901), industrial designer

E. Cavaglion (dates unknown), French tourist

Basil Hall Chamberlain (1850–1935), professor of Japanese at Tokyo Imperial University

Edward Warren Clark (1849–1907), American educator

Joseph F. Cook (1838–1901), clergyman from Boston

Edmond Cotteau (1833–1896), French travel writer

Francisco Diaz Covarrubias (1833–1889), Mexican astronomer

Arthur H. Crow (1840–1915), author

Jan Hendrik Donker Curtius (1813–1879), Dutch Commissioner in Japan

Walter G. Dickson (dates unknown), author

William Gray Dixon (1854–1928), Scottish Presbyterian minister

L.F. Maurice Dubard (1845–?), French naval officer

Edward Pennell Elmhirst (1845–1916), captain in the British military, author

Count Friedrich Albert Graf zu Eulenburg (1815–1881), Prussian diplomat and politician

Henry Faulds (1843–1930), British doctor and missionary, Scottish doctor, missionary and scientist, related to Tsukiji Hospital, known for fingerprinting

Adolf Fischer (1856–1914), Austrian art researcher

Edward B. de Fonblanque (1821–1895), British military logistics officer who came to Japan in 1860

Robert Fortune (1813–1880), English botanist

Mary Fraser (1851–1922), wife of British Envoy to Japan Hugh Fraser (1837–1894)

Luís Fróis (1532–1597), Portuguese missionary

Philip Kemball Fyson (1846–1929), British missionary

Vasily Mikhailovich Golovnin (1776–1831), captain of the Russian naval frigate, the *Diana*

Ivan Alexandrovitch Goncharov (1812–1891), member of Russian Admiral Yevfimiy Putyatin's diplomatic mission

Koenraad Wolter Gratama (1831–1888), Kaiseijo Institute chemistry instructor

William Elliot Griffis (1843–1928), an instructor at the Fukui domain school and at Daigaku Nankō

Émile E. Guimet (1836–1918), French industrialist, traveler and connoisseur

Townsend Harris (1804–1878), New York City merchant and minor politician

Lafcadio Hearn (1850–1904), writer

Peter B.W. Heine (1827–1885), German-American painter, traveler, and writer; also active as a United States soldier and diplomat

James Curtis Hepburn (1815–1911), missionary

Henry Heusken (1832–1861), Dutch-American interpreter

Christopher Pemberton Hodgson (1821–1865), English colonial pastoralist, traveler, and writer

Theodor Hoffman (1837–1894), German physician

Henry Holmes (dates unknown), captain of a British trading ship, came to Nagasaki in 1859

Count Josef Alexander von Hübner (1811–1892), senior Austrian diplomat

Aimé Humbert (1819–1900), came to Japan in 1863 as the leader of the Swiss delegation

Imaizumi Mine (1855–1937), daughter of Katsuragawa Hoshū, a physician to the family of a shogun and a scholar of Dutch learning

Ishikawa Eisuke (1933–), writer

Leroy Lansing Janes (1838–1909), instructor who travelled to Kumamoto to teach English

Richard Mounteney Jephson (1842–1906), writer

Engelbert Kaempfer (1651–1716), German naturalist, physician, and explorer writer

Kaibara Ekiken (1630–1714), Japanese Confucianist and herbalist

Katsu Kaishū (1823–1899), Japanese statesman and naval engineer

Willem Huyssen van Kattendijke (1816–1866), career officer of the Royal Dutch Navy and a politician

Kawai Koume (1804–1889), Japanese writer

Kawai Baisho (dates unknown), Kishū-domain Confucian scholar

Kawazoe Noboru (1926–2015), Japanese architect, architectural critic

Raphael von Koeber (1848–1923), lecturer of philosophy at Tokyo Imperial University

Gustav Kreitner (1847–1893), lieutenant in the Austrian army, came to Japan as a member of Count Béla Széchenyi's expedition in 1878

Kudō Heisuke (1734–1800), physician

John La Farge (1835–1910), American painter

Rudolf Lindau (1829–1910), German diplomat and author

Pierre Loti (1850–1923), French naval officer and novelist

Percival Lowell (1855–1916), American businessman, author, mathematician, and astronomer

Friedrich August Lühdorf (1834–1891), German trader

Arthur Collins Maclay (1853–1930), instructor at Tōō Gijuku School in Hirosaki

Daniel J. Macgowan (1814–1893), American missionary

Matsura Seizan (1760–1841), Hirado-domain lord

Pompe van Meerdervoort (1829–1908), physician attached to the same naval training center led by Willem Huyssen van Kattendijke

Germain Felix Meijlan (1785–1831), headed the Dutch trading house in Nagasaki from 1827 to 1830

Lev Ilich Metchnikov (1838–1888), also known as "Léon Metchnikoff," taught Russian at the Tokyo School of Foreign Languages from 1874 to 1875

Algernon Freeman-Mitford (1837–1916), British diplomat, collector, and writer

Wenceslau de Moraes (1854–1929), Portuguese writer

Edward Sylvester Morse (1838–1925), American zoologist and Orientalist

Leopold Mueller (1822–1893), German physician

Carl Munzinger (1864–1937), German missionary

Nicolay Muravyov-Amursky (1809–1881), Russian general, statesman, and diplomat

Frederick Gerhard Myburgh (1838–1868), British consul at Hyōgo (later Kobe)

Nakao Sasuke (1916–1993), botanist

Negishi Shizumori (1737–1815), Japanese essayist

Curt Adolph Netto (1847–1909), German metallurgist and educator

Laurence Oliphant (1829–1888), South African-born British author, traveler, diplomat, and Christian mystic

Sherard Osborn (1822–1875), Royal Navy admiral and Arctic explorer; in 1857, he commanded the HMS *Furious* and escorted a fleet of gunboats to China, where Britain was again at war. When peace had been concluded, he was active in the development of European trade with China and Japan.

J.F. van Overmeer Fischer (1800–1848), agent of the VOC Opperhoofden from 1820 to 1829

Henry Spencer Palmer (1838–1893) journalist, associated with *The Times*

Matthew C. Perry (1794–1858), commodore of the United States Navy, commanded ships in several wars, and played a leading role in the opening of Japan to the West with the Convention of Kanagawa in 1854

Dirk de Graeff van Polsbroek (1833–1916), Dutch diplomat

Herbert George Ponting (1870–1935), British photographer

Raphael Pumpelly (1837–1923), mining technician

Félix Régamey (1844–1907), French painter and cartoonist

Ludwig Riess (1861–1928), German historian

Léon Roches (1809–1901), French envoy

Alfred Roussin (1839–1919), French naval officer

Katherine Sansom (1883–1981), wife of British diplomat and historian George Bailey Sansom, author on Japanese topics

John Saris (1579–1643), associated with East India Company

Ernest Mason Satow (1843–1929), British scholar, diplomat, and Japanologist

Heinrich Schliemann (1822–1890), German businessman and a pioneer in the field of archaeology

Eliza Ruhamah Scidmore (1856–1928), correspondent in Japan

Marion McCarrell Scott (1843–1922), American educator and government advisor in Meiji-period Japan

Shiba Kōkan (1747–1818), Japanese painter and printmaker during the Edo period

Shinoda Kōzō (1871–1965), Taisho-period reporter

Philipp Franz von Siebold (1796–1866), German physician, botanist, and traveler

Alexander von Siebold (1846–1911), German translator and interpreter

George Smith (1815–1871), bishop of the Anglican Church in Hong Kong

Richard Gordon Smith (1858–1918), British traveler, sportsman, and naturalist

Robert Henry Smith (1852–1916), Scotsman who came to Japan to teach at Kaisei Gakkō in 1874

Gustav Spiess (dates unknown), delegate with the Saxony Commerce Association

Edouard Suenson (1842–1921), Dane who traveled to Japan as a member of the French navy

Sugimoto Etsuko (1873–1950), Japanese autobiographer and novelist

Tadano Makuzu (1763–1825), writer of commentaries on Japan's social and political problems

Takizawa Bakin (1767–1848), Edo-period *gesaku* author

Carl Peter Thunberg (1743–1828), Swedish doctor who worked at the Dutch trading house in Nagasaki

Henry Arthur Tilley (dates unknown), author

J.M. Tronson (dates unknown), member of the fleet commanded by Admiral James Stirling

Ujiie Mikito (1954–), author

Utsunomiya Saburō (1834–1903), chemist

Aleksei Vysheslavtsov (dates unknown), doctor who accompanied the Siberian Military Flotilla of the Russian Pacific Fleet, which was commanded by General Nikolay Muravyov-Amursky, to Edo in 1859

Gottfried Wagener (1831–1892), German scientist and technician

Reinhold Werner (1825–1909), commander of the transport ship, the *Elbe*, on the Eulenburg expedition

Walter Weston (1861–1940), pioneer in modern mountaineering

Clara Whitney (1860–1936), author

Channing Moore Williams (1829–1910), Episcopal Church missionary, later a bishop

Samuel Wells Williams (1812–1884), accompanied Commodore Matthew C. Perry on his journeys and served as his Chinese interpreter

William Willis (1837–1894), medical officer at the British Legation

Olof Eriksson Willman (1823–1873), Swede who accompanied the Dutch mission to Edo in 1652

Charles Wirgman (1832–1891), English painter

Yamakawa Kikue (1890–1980), essayist, activist, and socialist feminist

John Russell Young (1840–1899), accompanied U.S. General Ulysses S. Grant on his visit to Japan in 1879

Bibliography

(Limited to records made by foreign observers and to related research)

Abe, Toshiharu. *Afurikajin no Seikatsu to Dentō* [The Lives and Traditions of African Peoples]. Sanseido, 1982.

Alcock, Rutherford. *The Capital of the Tycoon: A Narrative of a Three Years' Residence in Japan, 2 vols.* New York: The Bradley Co., 1863.

Anethan, Eleanor Mary. *Fourteen Years of Diplomatic Life; Leaves from the Diary of Baroness Albert d'Anethan*. London: Stanley Paul and Co., 1912.

Aoki, Tamotsu. *Bunka no Honyaku* [Cultural Translation]. Tokyo University Press, 1978.

Ariès, Philippe. *Centuries of Childhood: A Social History of Family Life*. Translated by Robert Baldrick. New York: Vintage, 1965.

Arminjon, Vittorio F. *Il Giappone e il Viaggio della Corvetta Magenta nel 1866*. Genova, 1869.

———— [Aruminyon]. *Itaria Shisetsu no Bakumatsu Kenbunki* [Record of the Italian Expedition to Japan at the End of the Edo Period]. Shinjinbutsu Oraisha, 1987.

Armstrong, William Nevins. *Around the World with a King*. New York: Frederick A. Stokes Co., 1904.

Arnold, Edwin. *Japonica*. New York: Charles Scribner's Sons, 1891.

————. *Seas and Lands*. London: Longmans, Green, and Co., 1892.

Bacon, Alice Mabel. *A Japanese Interior*. Boston and New York: Houghton Mifflin Co., 1894.

————. *Japanese Girls and Women, Revised and Enlarged Edition*. Boston and New York: Houghton Mifflin Co., 1902.

Ballagh, Margaret T.K. *Glimpses of Old Japan 1861-1866*. Tokyo, 1908.

Bälz, Erwin von. *Awakening Japan: The Diary of a German Doctor: Erwin Baelz*. Indiana University Press, 1932.

Beauchamp, Edward R. *An American Teacher in Early Meiji Japan*. Hawaii: University of Hawaii Press, 1976.

Beauvoir, Ludovic marquis de. *Pekin, Jeddo, San Francisco: The Conclusion of a Voyage Round the World*. Translated by Agnes and Helen Stephenson. London: John Murray, 1872.

Bellesort, André. *Les Journées etles Nuit Japonaises, 1900*. Paris, 1906.

———— [Berusōru]. *Meiji Taizai Nikki* [Record of a Stay in Meiji Japan]. Shinjinbutsu Oraisha, 1989.

Berg, Albert. *Die Preussiche Expedition nach Ost-Asien nach amtlichen Quellen*. Berlin, 1864.

———— [Beruku]. *Oirenburuku Nihon Enseiki* [Record of the Eulenburg Expedition to Japan]. Yushodo Shuppan, 1969.

Bessatsu, Taiyō. *Bigō ga Mita Seikimatsu Nippon* [Late Nineteenth Century Japan Seen through the Eyes of Georges Ferdinand Bigot]. Heibonsha, 1996.

Bird, Isabella Lucy. *Unbeaten Tracks in Japan: An Account of Travels on Horseback in the Interior, 2 vols.* New York: G. P. Putnam's Sons, 1880.

Bitō, Masahide. *Edo Jidai towa Nani ka* [What Is the Edo Period?]. Iwanami Shoten, 1992.

Black, John Reddie. *Young Japan: Yokohama and Yedo*. London: Trubner and Co., 1880.

Bodart-Bailey, Beatrice M. [Bodaruto-Beirī]. *Kenpuru to Tokugawa Tsunayoshi* [Engelbert Kaempfer and Tokugawa Tsunayoshi]. Translated by Nakamura Naoichi. Chuko Shinsho, 1994.

Bauduin, Albert [Bōdovan]. *Oranda Ryōji no Bakumatsu Ishin: Nagasaki Dejima kara no Tegami* [Letters from the Dutch Consulate at Dejima from the Late Edo to Early Meiji Periods]. Heibonsha Toyo Bunko, 1981.

Bousquet, Georges H. *Le Japon de nos jours et les échelles de l'extrême Orient*. Paris, 1877.

———— [Busuke]. *Nihon Kenbunki* [Experiences in Japan]. Misuzu Shobo, 1977.

Brandt, Max von [Buranto]. *Doitsu Kōshi no Mita Meiji Ishin* [The Meiji Restoration Seen through the Eyes of a German Diplomat]. Shinjinbutsu Oraisha, 1987.

————. *Dreiunddreissig Jahre in Ost-Asien: Erinnerungen eines Deutschen Diplomaten* [Thirty-three Years in East Asia: Memories of a German Diplomat]. Leipzig, 1901.

Brunton, Richard Henry. *Building Japan 1868-1876*. New York: Routledge, 2013.

Cain, P.J., and A.G. Hopkins. *British Imperialism*. Routledge, 2016.

Cavaglion, E. *254 Jours Autour du Monde*. Paris, 1894.

———— [Kavariyon]. "Meiji Japan- 1891." In Monburan (Montblanc), et al. *Monburan no Nihon Kenbunki* [Record of Count Charles du Montblanc's Visit to Japan and Other Records]. Translated by Morimoto Hideo. Shinjinbutsu Oraisha, 1987.

Chamberlain, Basil Hall. *Things Japanese*. London: John Murray, 1905.

————. *Things Japanese, Complete Edition*. Tokyo: Meicho Fukyukai, 1985.

Chamberlain, Basil Hall, and W.B. Mason. *A Handbook for Travellers in Japan*. London: John Murray, 1901.

Checkland, Olive. *Britain's Encounter with Meiji Japan, 1868-1912*. Palgrave Macmillan, 1989.

————. *Isabella Bird and a Woman's Right: To Do What She Can Do Well*. Aberdeen: Scottish Cultural Press, 1996.

Clark, Edward W. *Life and Adventure in Japan*. New York: American Tract Society, 1878.

Claudel, Paul [Kurōderu]. *Asahi no naka no Kuroi Shima* [The Black Island in the Rising Sun]. Kodansha Gakujutsu Bunko, 1988.

Cortazzi, Hugh. *Dr. Willis in Japan, 1862-1877*. London: Bloomsbury, 2013.

————. *Victorians in Japan: In and around the Treaty Ports*. London: Bloomsbury, 2012.

Cortazzi, Hugh ed. *Mitford's Japan*. London: Routledge, 2013.

Cotteau, Edmond [Kotō]. *Bon Jūru Japon* [Bon Jour, Japan]. Shinhyoron, 1992.

————. *Un Touriste dans l'Extrême Orient*. Paris, 1884.

Crow, Arthur H. *Highways and Byeways in Japan*. London: Sampson Low, Marston, Searle, and Rivington, 1883.

Diaz Covarrubias, Francisco [Diasu Kobarubiasu]. *Nihon Ryokōki* [A Record of a Trip to Japan]. Yushodo Shuppan, 1983.

————. *Viaje de la Comission Astronomica Mexicana al Japon*. Mexico, 1876.

Dickson, W.G. *Gleanings from Japan*. Edinburgh and London: Willian Blackwood and Sons, 1889.

Dixon, William Gray. *The Land of the Morning: An Account of Japan and Its People, Based on a Four Years' Residence in that Country*. Edinburgh, 1882.

Doeff, Hendrik. *Recollections of Japan*. Translated by Annick M. Doeff. Victoria: Trafford, 2003.

Donker Curtius, Jan Hendrik [Donkeru Kuruchiusu]. *Bakumatsu Dejima Mikōkai Bunsho* [Unreleased Writings about Dejima at the End of the Edo Period]. Shinjinbutsu Oraisha, 1992.

Dubard, L.F. Maurice. *Le Japon Pittoresque* [Picturesque Japan]. Paris, 1879.

———— [Dubāru]. *Ohanasan no Koi* [A Love for Flowers]. Yurindo, 1991.

Engels, Friedrich. *The Condition of the Working Class in England in 1844.* Translated by Florence Kelley Wischnewetzky. New York: John W. Lovell Co., 1887.

Eulenburg, Friedrich [Oirenburuku]. *Dai Ikkai Doitsu Kennichi Shisetsu Nihon Taizaiki* [Record of the First German Expedition to Japan]. Toko Shoin, 1940.

————. *Ost-Asien 1860-1862 in Briefen des Grafen zu Eulenburg.* Berlin, 1900.

Faulds, Henry. *Nine Years in Nipon: Sketches of Japanese Life and Manners.* Boston: Cupples and Hurd, 1888.

Fischer, Adolf. *Bilder aus Japan* [Images of Japan]. Berlin, 1897.

———— [Fisshā]. *100 Nenmae no Nihon Bunka* [Japanese Culture 100 Years Ago]. Chuo Korinsha, 1994.

Fischer, J.F. van Overmeer. *Bijdrage Tot de Kennis van Het Japanische Rijk* [Contributions to the Knowledge of the Japanese Realm]. Amsterdam, 1833.

———— [Fisseru]. *Nihon Fūzoku Bikō* [Notes on Japanese Customs]. Heibonsha Toyo Bunko, 1978.

Fonblanque, Edward B. de. *Niphon and Pe-che-li* (London: Saunders, Otley, and Co., 1862).

Fortune, Robert. *Yedo and Peking: A Narrative of a Journey to the Capitals of Japan and China.* London: John Murray, 1863.

Foss, Miyako. *Bakumatsu Dejima Mikōkai Bunsho: Donkeru Kuruchiusu Oboegaki* [Unreleased Writings about Dejima at the End of the Edo Period: Notes on Jan Hendrik Donker Curtius]. Shinjinbutsu Oraisha, 1992.

Fraser, Mary. *A Diplomatist's Wife in Japan: Letters from Home to Home.* London: Hutchinson and Co., 1899.

Fróis, Luís. *Kulturgegensätze Europa-Japan.* Tokyo: Sophia Universität, 1955.

———— [Huroisu]. "Nichiō Bunka Hikaku" ["A Cultural Comparison of Japan and Europe"]. In *Daikōkai Sōsho Dai-11-kan* [Great Voyages Series, Vol. 11]. Iwanami Shoten, 1965.

Fujiki, Hisashi. *Toyotomi Heiwarei to Sengoku Shakai* [Toyotomi Hideyoshi's Peace Ordinances and Warring States Society]. Tokyo Daigaku Shuppankai, 1985.

Geerts, Antonius Johannes Cornelius [Hērutsu]. *Nihon Nenpō* [Annual Reports on Japan]. Yushodo Shuppan, 1983.

Gildemeister, Martin Hermann [Girudemaisutā]. *Girudemaisutā no Tegami* [The Letters of Martin Hermann Gildemeister]. Yurindo, 1991.

Girón, Bernardino Avila [Hiron]. "Nihon Ōkokuki" ["Record of the Kingdom of Japan"]. In *Dai Kōkai Sōsho Dai Jūikkan* [Great Voyages Series Vol. 11]. Iwanami Shoten, 1965.

————. *Relación del Reyno del Nippon que Llamaron Corumptamente Jappon.* Spain, 1615.

Golovnin, Vasily Mikhailovich. *Japan and the Japanese: Comprising the Narrative of my Captivity in Japan, 1811-1813.* London: Colburn and Co., 1852.

————. *Memoirs of a Captivity in Japan, during the Years 1811, 1812, and 1813.* London, 1824.

Goncharov, Ivan A. *The Frigate Pallada.* Translated by Klaus Goetze. New York: St. Martin's Press, 1987.

Gordon Smith, Richard. *Travels in the Land of the Gods, 1898-1907: The Japan Diaries of Richard Gordon Smith.* London, 1986.

Gratama, Koenraad Wouter. *Leraar onder de Japanners: Briven van Dr. K. W. Gratama Betreffende Zijn Verblijf in Japan, 1866-1871*. Amsterdam, 1987.

———— [Haratama]. *Orandajin no Mita Bakumatsu-Meiji no Nihon: Kagakusha Haratama Shokanshū* [Bakumatsu and Meiji-period Japan Seen through the Eyes of a Dutchman: The Letters of Koenraad Wolter Gratama, Chemist]. Saikon Shuppan, 1993.

Griffis, William E. *The Mikado's Empire*. New York: Harper and Brothers, 1876.

Guimet, Émile [Gime]. *1876: Bon Jūru Kanagawa* [1876: Bon Jour, Kanagawa]. Yurindo, 1977.

————. *Promenades Japonaises*. Paris, 1878, 1880.

———— [Gime]. *Tōkyō Nikkō Sansaku* [A Ramble through Tokyo and Nikko]. Yushodo Shuppan, 1983.

Harris, Townsend, *The Complete Journal of Townsend Harris*, edited by M.E. Cosenza. New York: Doubleday, Doran and Co., Inc., 1930.

Hawks, Francis, ed. *Narrative of the Expedition of an American Squadron to the China Seas and Japan, Performed in the Years 1852, 1853, and 1854 under the Command of Commodore M. C. Perry, United States Navy*. Washington, 1856.

Hayami, Akira. "Kinsei no Keizai Hatten to 'Industrious Revolution' ["Modern Economic Development and the Industrious Revolution"]. In the Saitō and Sugiyama eds., *Tokugawa Shakai kara no Tenbō* [Views from Tokugawa Society]. Dobunkan, 1989.

Hearn, Lafcadio. *Japan: An Attempt at Interpretation*. London: Macmillan and Co., 1904.

————. *Stories by Pierre Loti*. Tokyo: Hokuseido Press, 1933.

Heine, Wilhelm. *Reise um die Erde nach Japan*. Leipzig, 1856.

———— [Haine]. *Sekai Shūkō Nihon he no Tabi* [A Cruise around the World: Traveling to Japan]. Yushodo Shuppan, 1983.

Heusken, Henry. *Japan Journal, 1855-1861*. Translated by Jeannette C. van de Corput and Robert Arden Wilson. Rutgers University Press, 1964.

Hirakawa, Sukehiro, and Tsuruta Kinya, eds. *Uchinaru Kabe: Gaikokujin no Nihonjinzō, Nihonjin no Gaikokujinzō* [Inner Walls: Foreign Images of the Japanese, Japanese Images of Foreigners]. TBS-Britannica, 1990.

Hiramitsu, Yoshirō. *Edo no Tsumi to Batsu* [Edo Crime and Punishment]. Heibonsha, 1988.

Hisano, Akiko. *Rokumeikan no Kifujin: Ōyama Sutematsu* [A Noble Lady of the Rokumeikan: Ōyama Sutematsu]. Chuko Bunko, 1993.

Hodgson, Christopher P. *A Residence at Nagasaki and Hakodate in 1859-1860*. London, 1861.

Holmes, Henry. *My Adventures in Japan: Before the Treaty Came into Force, February, 1859*. London: R.E. King and Co., Ltd., 1904.

Hübner, Alexander F.V. *A Ramble round the World*. Translated by Lady Herbert. London: MacMillan, 1878.

Humbert, Aimé [Anbēru]. *Bakumatsu Nippon Zue* [Illustrations of Japan at the End of the Edo Period]. Yushodo Shuppan, 1969.

————. *Japan and the Japanese Illustrated*. Translated by Cashel Hoey. London: Richard Bentley and Son, 1874.

Imaizumi, Mine. *Nagori no Yume* [Remains of a Dream]. Heibonsha Toyo Bunko, 1963.

Iseki, Takako. *Iseki Takako Nikki* [Diary of Iseki Takako]. Buneisha, 1978.

Ishikawa, Eisuke. *Ōedo Tekunorojī Jijō* [Technology of Edo]. Kodansha Bunko, 1995.

Isono, Naohide. *Mōsu Sono Hi Sono Hi* [Edward Sylvester Morse, Day by Day]. Yurindo, 1987.

Iwao, Seiichi, ed. *Gaikokujin no Mita Nihon Dai Ikkan: Nanban Torai Igo* [Japan in the Eyes of Foreigners Volume 1: After the Arrival of the Barbarians]. Chikumashobo, 1962.

Janes, Leroy Lansing. *Kumamoto, An Episode in Japan's Break from Feudalism*. University of California Press, 1970.

———— [Jēnzu]. *Kumamoto Kaisō* [Memories of Kumamoto]. Kumamotonichinichi Shimbun, 1978.

Jephson, R. Mounteney, and Edward Pennell Elmhirst. *Our Life in Japan*. London: Chapman and Hall, 1869.

Jippensha, Ikku. *Tōkaidōchū Hizakurige* [Travels on the Tōkaidō Road]. Iwanami Bunko, 1973.

Kaempfer, Engelbert. *The History of Japan*. New York: Macmillan Co., 1906.

Kasatkin, Nicholas. *Dnevmiki Sviatogo Nikolaia Iaponskogo* [Diary of Nikolai]. St. Petersburg, 2004.

———— [Nikorai]. *Nikorai no Mita Bakumatsu Nihon* [Japan at the End of the Edo Period Seen through the Eyes of St. Nikolai]. Kodansha Gakujutsu Bunko, 1979.

Kasaya, Kazuhiko. *Kinsei Buke Shakai no Seiji Kōzō* [The Political Structure of Warrior Society in Modern Times]. Yoshikawa Kobunkan, 1993.

Kasaya, Kazuhiko. *Shukun: "Oshikomi" no Kōzō* [Lords: The Structure of "Force"]. Heibonsha, 1988.

Katsumatsu, Shizuo. *Sengoku Jidairon* [Theories on the Warring States Period]. Iwanami Shoten, 1996.

Kattendijke, Willem Hyussen van [Kattendīke]. *Nagasaki Kaigun Denshūsho no Hibi* [Daily Life at the Nagasaki Naval Training Center]. Heibonsha Toyo Bunko, 1964.

————. *Uittreksel uit het dagboek van W. J. C. Ridder Huyssen van Kattendijke: gedurende zijn verblijf in Japan in 1857, 1858 en 1859*. Van Stockum, 1860.

Kawai, Koume. *Koume Nikki* [Diary of Koume]. Heibonsha Toyo Bunko, 1964.

Kawai, Tsuginosuke. "Jinko" ["Dustpail"]. In *Nihon Shomin Seikatsu Shiryō Shūsei* [Lives of the Japanese People]. Sanichi Shobō Publishing, 1969.

Kawakita, Minoru. *Igirisu: Hanei no Atosaki* [Britain: The Reversal of Prosperity]. Daiyamondosha, 1995.

————. "Igirisu Kindaishi no Uchi to Soto" [The Ins and Outs of Modern British History"]. In Chizuka, Tatami, and Kondō Kazuhiko, eds. *Sugisarō to Shinai Kindai* [The Modern Age Lingers on]. Yamakawa Shuppansha, 1993.

————. *Kōgyōka no Rekishiteki Zentei* [The Historical Premise of Industrialization]. Iwanami Shoten, 1983.

Kawasaki, Seirō. *Bakumatsu Chūnichi Gaikōkan, Ryōjikan* [Diplomats and Consuls Stationed in Japan at the End of the Edo Period]. Yushodo Shuppan, 1988.

Kawazoe, Noboru. *Tōkyō no Genfūkei* [Scenic Spots in Historic Tokyo]. NHK Books, 1979.

Kiyokawa, Hachirō. *Saiyūsō* [Trip to the West]. Iwanami Bunko, 1993.

Kobori, Keiichirō. *Sakoku no Shisō* [Thoughts on the National Isolation of Japan]. Chuo Shinsho, 1974.

Koeber, Raphael von [Kēberu], *Kēburu Hakase Zuihitsushū* [A Collection of Essays by Dr. Raphael von Koeber]. Translated by Tsutomu Kubo. Iwanami Bunko, 1957.

————. *Kleine Schriften: Philosophische Phantasien, Erinnerungen, Keitzerein, Paradoxien, 1918-1925.* Iwanami Bunko, 1928.

Kreiner, Josef [Kurainā], ed. *Kenperu no Mita Tokugawa Japan* [Tokugawa Japan seen through the Eyes of Engelbert Kaempfer]. Rokko Shuppan, 1992.

Kreitner, Gustav von. *Im fernen Osten*. Vienna, 1881.

———— [Kuraitonā]. *Tōyō Kikō* [An Account of a Voyage to the Far East] Heibonsha Toyo Bunko, 1992.

Kusuya, Shigetoshi. *Nezumi ha Mada Ikiteiru: Chenbaren no Denki* [The Rat is Still Alive: A Biography of Basil Hall Chamberlain]. Yushodo Shuppan, 1986.

La Farge, John. *An Artist's Letters from Japan*. New York: The Century Co., 1897.

Lin, Yutang. "How to Understand the Chinese." In *The Little Critic, Second Series: 1933-1935.* The Commercial Press, 1935.

Lindau, Rudolf [Rindau]. *Suisu Ryōji no Mita Bakumatsu Nihon* [Japan at the End of the Edo Period Seen through the Eyes of a Swiss Consul]. Shinjinbutsu Oraisha, 1986.

————. *Un Voyage Autour du Japon*. Paris, 1864.

Linden [Rinden]. "Nihon Inshōki" ["Impressions of Japan"]. In *Nagasaki Dansō* [Series of Talks on Nagasaki].

Loti, Pierre [Roti]. *Aki no Nihon* [Japan of Autumn]. Kadokawa Bunko, 1953.

————. *Japoneries D'Automne*. Paris, 1889.

———— [Roti]. "Nihon no Fujintachi" ["Japanese Ladies"]. In *Rochi no Nippon Nikki* [Pierre Loti's Journal of Japan]. Yurindo, 1979.

———— [Roti]. *Okikusan* [Madame Chrysanthème]. Iwanami Bunko, 1929.

———— [Roti]. *Rochi no Nippon Nikki* [Pierre Loti's Journal of Japan]. Yurindo, 1979.

————. *Madame Chrysanthème*. Translated by Laura Ensor. London: George Routledge and Sons, Ltd., 1897.

Lowell, Percival. *The Soul of the Far East*. Boston and New York: Houghton, Mifflin, and Co., 1888.

Lühdorf, Friedrich August. *Acht Monate in Japan nach Abschluß des Vertrages von Kanagawa*. Bremen, 1857.

———— [Ryūdoruhu]. *Guretagō Nihon Tsūshōki* [Records of Trade with Japan Aboard the Greta]. Yushodo Shuppan, 1984.

Luo, Sen. "Journal of the Second Visit of Commodore Perry to Japan." In Hawks, ed. *Narrative of the Expedition of an American Squadron to the China Seas and Japan, Performed in the Years 1852, 1853, and 1854 under the Command of Commodore M. C. Perry, United States Navy*. Translated by Samuel Wells Williams. Washington, 1856.

MacDonald, Ranald. *The Narrative of His Life, 1824-1894*, edited by William S. Lewis and Murakami Naojirō. Portland: Oregon Historical Society Press, 1990.

Maclay, Arthur Collins. *A Budget of Letters from Japan: Reminiscences of Work and Travel in Japan*. New York: A.C. Armstrong and Son, 1886.

Matsura, Seizan. *Kasshi Yawa* [Kasshi Night Stories]. Heibonsha Toyo Bunko, 1977.

Metchnikoff, Léon. *L'empire Japonais: Pays, Peuple, Histoire*. Geneva, 1881.

Metchnikov, Lev Ilich [Mēchinikohu]. *Bōmei Roshiajin no Mita Meiji Ishin* [The Meiji Restoration Seen through the Eyes of a Russian Exile]. Translated by Watanabe Masashi. Kodansha Gakujutsu Bunko, 1987.

———— [Mēchinikohu]. *Kaisō no Meiji Ishin* [Memories of the Meiji Restoration]. Translated by Watanabe Masashi. Iwanami Bunko, 1987.

Mitford, Algernon Bertram. *Memories*. London: Hutchinson and Co., 1915.

————. *Tales of Old Japan*. London: Macmillan and Co., 1883.

Miyazaki, Masaaki. *Shirarezaru Japanojisuto: Rōeru no Shōgai* [The Unknown Japanologist: The Life of Percival Lowell]. Maruzen Library, 1995.

Mizutani, Mitsuhiro. *Eikoku Kizoku to Kidai* [British Nobility and the Modern Age]. Tokyo Daigaku Shuppankai, 1987.

Moeshart, Herman J. *Journaal van Dirk de Graeff van Polsbroek 1857-1870*. Netherlands, 1987.

Moraes, Wenceslau de [Moraesu]. "Nihon no Tsuibo" ["Memories of Japan"]. In *Meiji Bungaku Zenshū, Dai 49-kan* [Complete Works of Meiji Literature, Vol. 49]. Chikumashobo, 1968.

———— [Moraesu]. "Nihon Seishin" ["Japanese Spirit"]. In *Meiji Bungaku Zenshū, Dai 49-kan* [Complete Works of Meiji Literature, Vol. 49]. Chikumashobo, 1968.

————. *Tracos do Extremo-Oriente*. Lisbon, 1895.

Morse, Edward Sylvester. *Japan Day by Day*. Boston: Houghton Mifflin, 1917.

————. *Japanese Homes and Their Surroundings*. Boston: Ticknor and Company, 1886.

Munzinger, Carl [Muntsigā]. *Doitsu Senkyōshi no Mita Meiji Shakai* [Meiji Japanese Society Seen through the Eyes of a German Missionary]. Shinjinbutsu Oraisha, 1987.

————. *Japan und die Japaner*. Berlin, 1898.

Mūsuharuto [Moeshart]. *Porusuburukku Nihon Hōkoku 1857-1860*. [*Dirk de Graeff van Polsbroek's Record of Japan 1857-1860*]. Yushodo Shuppan, 1995.

Nakamura, Kennosuke. *Senbokushi Nikolai to Meiji Nihon* [The Missionary Nikolai and Meiji Japan]. Iwanami Shoten, 1996.

Nakanishi, Akira. *Nagasaki no Oranda Itachi* [Dutch Doctors of Nagasaki]. Iwanami Shoten, 1975.

Nakao, Sasuke. *Hana to Ki no Bunkashi* [The Cultural History of Flowers and Trees]. Iwanami Shinsho, 1986.

Negishi, Shizumori. *Mimibukuro* [Essays]. Heibonsha Toyo Bunko, 1972.

Netto, Curt Adolph, and Gottfried Wagener. *Japanischer Humor* [Japanese Humor]. Berlin, 1901.

———— [Nettō and Wāgunā]. *Nihon no Yūmoa* [Japanese Humor]. Toko Shoin, 1971.

Noda, Shigesuke. "Nihon Kyūhō Shūgyō Nikki" ["Diary of a Pilgrimage to the Nine Peaks of Japan"]. In Suzuki, Tōzō, ed. *Nihon Shomin Seikatsu Shiryō Shūsei* [Lives of the Japanese People]. Sanichi Shobō, 1969.

Notehelfer, F.G. *American Samurai: Captain L. L. Janes and Japan*. Princeton University Press, 1985.

Oliphant, Laurence [Orifanto]. *Eruginkyō Kennichi Shisetsuroku* [Narrative of the Earl of Elgin's Mission to Japan]. Yushodo Shuppan, 1968.

————. *Narrative of the Earl of Elgin's Mission to China and Japan in the Years 1857, '58, '59, 2 Vols.* Edinburgh and London: William Blackwood and Sons, 1859.

Oliphant, Laurence and William Willis [Orifanto and Wirisu]. *Eikoku Kōshikanin no Ishin Sensō Kenbunki* [Accounts of Wars during the Meiji Restoration as Recorded by Members of the British Legation]. Azekura Shobō, 1974.

Osborn, Sherard. *A Cruise in Japanese Waters*. Edinburgh and London: William Blackwood and Sons, 1859.

Ōta, Yūzō. *B. H. Chenbaren* [B. H. Chamberlain]. Libro Port, 1990.

———. *E. S. Morse* [E. S. Morse]. Libro Port, 1988.

———. *Rahukadio Hān* [Lafcadio Hearn]. Iwanami Shinsho, 1994.

Palmer, Henry Spencer. *Letters from the Land of the Rising Sun*. Yokohama: Japan Mail, 1894.

Perry, Matthew C. *The Japan Expedition 1852-854: The Personal Journal of Commodore Matthew C. Perry*, edited by Roger Pineau. Washington: Smithsonian Institution Press, 1968.

Ponting, Herbert George. *In Lotus-land Japan*. London: Macmillan and Co., 1910.

Pompe van Meerdevoort, Johannes L.C. [Ponpe], *Nihon Taizai Kenbunki* [Records of My Stay in Japan]. Yushodo Shuppan, 1968.

———. *Vijf Jaren in Japan, 2dls, Leiden, 1867-1868*. Firma Van Den Heuvell and Van Santen, 1868.

Pumpelly, Raphael. *Across America and Asia*. New York: Leypoldt and Holt, 1870.

Régamey, Félix. *Japon*. Paris, 1903.

——— [Regame]. *Nihon Sobyō Ryokō* [Sketches of a Journey to Japan]. Yushodo Shuppan, 1983.

Riess, Ludwig. *Allerei aus Japan, 1905*. Rüsch, 1927.

——— [Rīsu]. *Doitsu Rekishisha no Tennō Kokkakan* [A German Historian's View of the Japanese Imperial State]. Shinjinbutsu Oraisha, 1988.

Roussin, Alfred [Rusan]. *Huransu Shikan no Shimonoseki Kaisenki* [A French Officer's Record of the Battle of Shimonoseki]. Shinjinbutsu Oraisha, 1987.

———. *Une Campagne Sur le Côtes du Japon*. Paris, 1866.

Saeki, Shōichi, and Haga Tōru, eds. *Gaikokujin ni yoru Nihonron no Meicho* [Famous Works on Theories of Japan by Foreign Authors]. Chuo Shinsho, 1987.

Said, Edward W. *Orientalism*. India: Penguin Books, 2006.

———. "Orientalism Reconsidered." In *Cultural Critique*, No. 1 (autumn 1985).

Sansom, Katherine Sansom. *Living in Tokyo*. London: Harcourt, Brace and Co., 1937.

Satō, Tsuneo. *Binnō Shikan wo Minaosu* [Reviewing Historical Views of Poor Farmers]. Kodansha Gendaishinsho, 1995.

Satow, Ernest Mason. *The Diaries and Letters of Sir Ernest Mason Satow, 1843-1929: A Scholar in East Asia*. Edwin Mellen Press, 1998.

———. *A Diplomat in Japan*. London: Seeley, Service, and Co., Ltd., 1921.

———. "Travels in the Interior: Yedo to Nikko and Back." In *Collected Works of Ernest Mason Satow Part 2: Collected Papers*. Tokyo, 2001.

———. *The Voyage of Captain John Saris to Japan, 1613*. London, 1900.

Schliemann, Heinrich. *La Chine et Le Japon au Temps Présent*. Paris, 1867.

——— [Shurīman]. *Nihon Chūgoku Ryokōki* [A Record of a Voyage to Japan and China]. Yushodo Shuppan, 1982.

Schwantes, Robert S. *Japanese and Americans: A Century of Cultural Relations*. New York: Harper and Brothers, 1955.

Schwartz, Henry B. *In Togo's Country: Some Studies in Satsuma and Other Little Known Parts of Japan*. Cincinnati: Jennings and Graham; New York: Eaton and Mains, 1908.

Scidmore, Eliza Ruhamah. *Jinrikisha Days in Japan*. New York: Harper and Brothers, 1891.

Shiba, Kōkan. "Kōkan Saiyū Nisshi" ["Shiba Kōkan's Diary of a Journey to the West"]. In *Nihon Shomin Seikatsu Shiryō Shūsei* [Lives of the Japanese People]. Sanichi Shobō, 1969.

Shinoda, Kōzō. *Bakumatsu-Meiji Onna Hyakuwa* [A Hundred Tales of Women from the Bakumatsu-Meiji Era]. Iwanami Bunko, 1997.

Shirohata, Yōzaburō. *Puranto Hantā* [Plant Hunter]. Kodansha, 1994.

Siebold, Alexander. *Fr. Von Siebold's Letzte Reise nach Japan*. Berlin, 1903.

——— [A. Jīboruto]. *Jīboruto Saigo no Nihon Ryokō* [Philipp Franz von Siebold's Last Trip to Japan]. Heibonsha Toyo Bunko, 1981), 130–31.

Siebold, Heinrich von [Shīboruto]. *Shō Shīboruto Ezo Kenbunki* [The Younger Siebold's Record of Hokkaido]. Heibonsha Toyo Bunko, 1996.

Siebold, Philipp Franz von [Jīboruto]. *Edo Sanpu Ryokō* [Travels to Edo]. Heibonsha Toyo Bunko, 1967.

———. *Nippon: Archiv zur Beschreibung von Japan*. Wurzburg and Leipzig, 1897.

Smith, George. *Ten Weeks in Japan*. London: Longman, Green, Longman, and Roberts, 1861.

Smith, Thomas C. *Native Sources of Japanese Industrialization, 1750-1920*. University of California Press, 1988.

Snow, Henry James. *Notes on the Kuril Islands*. London: John Murray, 1897.

Spiess, Gustav. *Die Preussiche Expedition nach Ost Asien während der Jahre 1860-1862*. Leipzig, 1864.

——— [Supīsu]. *Supīsu no Puroshia Nihon Enseiki* [Gustav Spiess's Record of the Prussian Expedition to Japan]. Okugawa Shobō, 1934.

Suenson, Edouard [Suenson], *Edo Bakuhu Taizaiki* [A Record of a Visit to Japan at the End of the Edo Period]. Shinjinbutsu Oraisha, 1989.

———. *Skitser fra Japan*. Copenhagen, 1869–1870.

Sugimoto, Etsu Inagaki. *A Daughter of the Samurai*. New York: Doubleday, Page and Co., 1926.

Tadano, Makuzu. *Mukashibanashi* [Tales of Long Ago]. Heibonsha Toyo Bunko, 1984.

Takaya, Michio, ed. *Hebon Shokanshū* [The Letters of Dr. J.C. Hepburn]. Toshin Shobō, 1955.

———. *S. R. Buraun Shokanshū* [The Letters of S.R. Brown] United Church of Christ – Japan Publishing Section, 1965.

Takeuchi, Hiroshi, ed. *Rainichi Seiyōjinmei Jiten* [Encyclopedia of Foreign Visitors to Japan]. Nichigai Associates, 1995.

Thunberg, Carl Peter. *Travels in Europe, Africa, and Asia Performed between the Years 1770 and 1779*. London, 1795.

Thouars, Abel-Nicolas Bergasse Dupetit [Tuāru]. *Huransu Senchō no Mita Sakai Jiken* [The Sakai Incident Seen through the Eyes of a French Naval Commander]. Shinjinbutsu Oraisha, 1993.

Tilley, Henry Arthur. *Japan, the Amoor, and the Pacific: With Notices of Other Places, Comprised in a Voyage of Circumnavigation in the Imperial Russian Corvette "Rynda" in 1858-1860*. London: Smith, Elder, and Co., 1861.

Titsingh, Isaac [Tichingu]. *Nihon Fūzoku Zushi* [Illustrations of Japanese Customs]. Yushodo Shuppan, 1970.

Tōda, Masahiro. *Daieiteikoku no Ajia Imēji* [Images of Asia in the Eyes of the British Empire]. Minerva Shobo, 1996.

Tomita, Hitoshi. *Jiten: Gaikokujin no Mita Nihon* [Encyclopedia: Japan Seen through the Eyes of Foreign Observers]. Nichigai Associates, 1992.

Tronson, J.M. *Personal Narrative of a Voyage of Japan, Kamtschatka, Siberia, Tartary, and Various Parts of Coast of China; in H. M. S. Barracouta*. London: Smith, Elder, and Co., 1859.

Tsunoyama, Sakae and Kawakita Minoru, eds. *Rojiura no Daiei Teikoku* [Backstreets of the British Empire]. Heibonsha, 1982.

Ujiie, Mikito. *Edo no Shōnen* [The Youth of Edo]. Heibonsha Library, 1994.

Vysheslavtsov, Aleksei Vladimirovich. *Ocherki perom i karandashem iz krugosvietnago plavaniıa v 1857, 1858, 1859 i 1860* [Sketches in Pen and Pencil from a Trip Around the World in the Years 1857, 1858, 1859, and 1860]. Saint Petersburg: M.O. Wolf, 1867.

———— [Vishesurahutsohu]. *Roshia Kantai Bakumatsu Raihōki* [Record of the Russian Fleet Visit to Japan]. Shinjinbutsu Oraisha, 1990.

Watarai, Yoshiichi. *Vikutoriachō no Sei to Kekkon* [Sex and Marriage in Victorian Britain]. Chuko Shinsho, 1997.

Werner, Reinhold. *Die Preussiche Expedition nach China, Japan und Siam*. Leipzig, 1863.

———— [Verunā]. *Erubagō Kanchō Bakumatsuki* [Japan at the End of the Edo Period as Recorded by the Captain of the Elbe]. Shinjinbutsu Oraisha, 1990.

Weston, Walter. *Mountaineering and Exploration in the Japanese Alps*. London, 1896.

————. *A Wayfarer in Unfamiliar Japan*. London: Houghton Mifflin, 1925.

———— [Wesuton], *Wesuton no Meiji Kenbunki* [Walter Weston's Travels in Meiji Japan]. Shinjinbutsu Oraisha, 1987.

Whitney, Clara. *Clara's Diary: An American Girl in Meiji Japan*. Tokyo: Kodansha, 1979.

Will, John Baxter. *Trading under Sail off Japan, 1860-1899; the Recollections of Captain John Baxter Will, Sailing-master and Pilot*, edited by George Alexander Lensen. Tokyo: Sophia University Press, 1968.

Williams, Samuel Wells. *A Journal of the Perry Expedition to Japan 1853-1854*. Kelly and Walsh, 1910.

Willman, Olof Eriksson. *The Journal of Olof E. Willman: From His Voyage to the Dutch East Indies and Japan, 1648-1654*. Translated by Catharina Blomberg. Global Oriental, 2013.

———— [Viruman]. *Nihon Taizaiki* [Record of a Stay in Japan]. Yushodo Shuppan, 1970.

Wirgman, Charles. *A Sketchbook of Japan*. Yokohama, 1884.

Yamakawa, Kikue. *Buke no Josei* [Samurai Women]. Iwanami Bunko, 1983.

————. *Oboegaki: Bakumatsu no Mito Han* [Memoir: The Mito Domain at the End of the Edo Period]. Iwanami Shoten, 1974.

Yanagita, Kunio, ed. *Meiji Bunka 13: Fūzoku* [Meiji Culture Vol. 13: Manners and Customs]. Hara Shobo, 1979.

Yokoyama, Toshio. *Japan in the Victorian Mind: A Study of Stereotyped Images of a Nation 1850-80*. London: Palgrave Macmillan UK, 1987.

Young, John Russell. *Around the World with General Grant*. New York, 1879.

Index

About the author

Watanabe Kyoji, a historian of modern Japan, was born in Kyoto in 1930. He has worked as a book review editor and is currently a chief researcher at Kawai Institute for Culture and Education in Fukuoka. He lives in Kumamoto City. Watanabe has published numerous books, including: *Kita Ikki* [Kita Ikki] (Chikuma Shobo), *Nihon Komyun Shugi no Keifu* [The School of Japanese Communism] (Ashi Shobo), *Hyoden Miyazaki Toten* [Biography of Miyazaki Toten] (Daiwa Shobo), *Watanabe Kyoji Hyōron Shūsei* 1–4 [Collected Works of Watanabe Kyoji, Volumes 1–4] (Ashi Shobo), *Nihon Kinsei no Kigen* [The Birth of Modern Japan] (Yosensha), *Edo to iu Genkei* [Fantastic Views of Edo] (Gen Shobo), and *Genpatsu to Janguru* [Nuclear Power Plants and the Jungle of Man] (Shobunsha).

© 2016 Ishiuchi Miyako

About the translator

Joseph Litsch was born in 1976. He graduated with a degree in geography from the University of Missouri in 1998 and received his Master's degree in Japanese studies from the University of Sheffield in 2010. He currently owns and operates a private language school in northern Japan. He has also been active as a translator for several years and has translated books such as *Learning the Key to Successful Reforms from Hokoku Yamada* (Meitoku Publishing).

Although Mr. Litsch is busy with his teaching and translation duties, his passion is Japanese history. He is especially interested in how the Japanese have dealt with natural disasters, famines, and other crisis situations over the centuries. His other interests include traveling, swimming, and spending time with his wife and two sons.

（英文版）逝きし世の面影
Remnants of Days Past: A Journey through Old Japan

2020年3月27日　第1刷発行

著　者　　渡辺京二
訳　者　　ジョセフ・リッチ
発行所　　一般財団法人出版文化産業振興財団
　　　　　〒101-0051　東京都千代田区神田神保町2-2-30
　　　　　電話　03-5211-7283
　　　　　ホームページ　https://www.jpic.or.jp/

印刷・製本所　　大日本印刷株式会社

© 2005 Watanabe Kyoji
Printed in Japan
ISBN 978-4-86658-140-8